Ray's wReckingyard Roster

by Ray & Ruth Harvey

Printed in the United States of America

Published by: Ray's Rosters
Impact Information Services
1042 Stallion Dr
Cheyenne, WY 82009

ISBN 0-9675389-0-4
Library of Congress: number pending

Front cover photos:
    Hudsons: Cheyenne, WY
    VW Bugs: Speedway Auto Wreckers, Erie, CO
    Yard: Balcaen's Auto Parts, Cheyenne, WY
Title page: Balcaen's Auto Parts, Cheyenne, WY
Back cover: '47 Pontiac, Hauf Auto Salvage, Stillwater, OK
    Military Truck, Blackburn Equipment, Douglas, WY
    '53 Packard, Cheyenne, WY

Dedicated to:

Larry Lessard & Elmer Balcaen

and the family and friends who miss them.

With acknowledgement and *thanks* to all whose co-operation and encouragement enabled us to compile this book particularly:

Bill Albright
Elmer Balcaen
Dan Greer
Mary Guthrie
Michael Riversong
Al Saffrahn
"Mom"
All the thousands of people at the salvage yards across the USA
       who took the time to give the information in this book

We would like to mention a few others who gave special inspiration in the past for this project.
Waldie Gravenstien
Jay Nell
Members of the Piston Ring, Republic of South Africa
Members of the Hudson, Essex, Terraplane Club
Members of the Oak Spokes, Cheyenne, WY

Heard from an operator in the Pacific Northwest:

FORWARD

As I was making research calls for this book, one yard operator told me: "I'm going to be 62 years old next year. I'm going to crush all these cars and sell this yard and retire. I've been doing this for over 30 years and there's no money in it." This was from a wrecking yard operator in the upper mid-west near a small town. Most of our friends in our car clubs have similar tales and we all keep hearing of recently closed yards where all the cars were crushed and this valuable resource was lost forever. Our goal in creating this book is to provide a means to bring the persons in need of salvage, vintage parts together with the owners of the yards who have these parts no matter where in the United States they are located.

How many times have you or your friends set out to drive to an auction in Phoenix, a car club meet in Wichita, a car show in Cheyenne or a swap meet at Hershey or Turlock and wished you had a ready reference to the salvage yards along your route? Sure, some existing publications occasionally publish a list of wrecking yards, but these lists rarely include more than 100 salvage yards and often times are much shorter. Frequently these lists repeat the same large yards located in only a few more populous areas. Many small wrecking yards in out of the way places are known to a few local people only. So if you have not heard of a yard through someone in your club or some other casual source, you are reduced to stopping occasionally and looking up yards in the phone book or inquiring of local club members.

My first licensed vehicle was a 1947 Crosley pick up truck, an extremely rare vehicle that used more oil than it did gasoline. When a lady in a DeSoto trying to beat a red light abruptly destroyed it in an accident, I took my insurance money and purchased a '51 Ford 2-door sedan. Shortly after I changed the oil for the first time, the rods started to knock and I was forced to replace the engine. At the tender age of 17, I was not yet aware of what happens when you change the oil in a car when the previous owner had never changed it and had only added it as needed. Though that old Ford vapor locked and/or over heated regularly, I dated many young ladies in it and it became our "second car" after Ruth and I were married. (Our "first" car was a '56 Lincoln Premier hard top.) As time went on we traded the Lincoln for a brand new '66 Mustang. Eventually I parked the '51 Ford in storage and our family moved on through various cars and pick-ups. I still have the '51 Ford. But memories of my parents Terraplane, '46 Hudson Super 6, and my grandfather's fine, black 49 Hudson Commodore Coupe have made me a Hudson collector for life.

In the past 40 years as an "old car nut," I have experienced most of the problems related to owning, maintaining, and getting parts for these rolling bits of history. I have often wished for a reference book such as this. *Ray's wReckingyard Roster* is our legacy to all the friends we have made over the years who also enjoy these time machines. Ruth & I hope that this will encourage you and help you maintain your old car hobby.

Ray & Ruth Harvey

Wheels & Tires
Martin Supply & Salvage
Windsor, CO

INTRODUCTION

We called each of the yards listed in this book. Our emphasis has been on complete and accurate data. We represented ourselves as a customer and asked the same questions that any car collector or restorer would ask. Changes could occur, yards could be sold, policies may be altered since the time of the call. We plan to pursue this cause so we are continuing to collect data about wrecking yards. We have provided post cards in the back of the book with our address in the hopes that you, our valued reader, can provide up to date information from your personal experience about yards we may have missed. We also encourage the yard operators to check their listing and let us know about changes required to make the data as accurate as possible.

We have three categories of yards - Vintage, Late Vintage and Late Model. The general definitions of these are:

Vintage - yard contains older vehicles up to the late 60s

Late Vintage - Late 60s to Late 80s

Late Model - 90s to present day cars

We asked for the types of vehicles in the yard. This includes cars, pickups, bigger trucks, military, construction equipment and farm equipment. We wanted to know about domestic and foreign, and then the specific makes. We noted any makes mentioned but this could mean only one vehicle or many. The number of each make would change in the due course of their business therefore it seemed imprudent to ask exact numbers of each in the yard. We did not list hours as these often change. We asked for toll free, FAX and e-mail numbers in addition to their regular business number.

Other items covered include whether they take credit cards, are open Saturdays, do they ship parts and can the customer remove the part. There are four basic approaches to getting the parts. Most yards prefer to remove the parts themselves. If there is no reference, this is assumed. When the customer may pick the part and remove it himself, we termed this UR. If the customer may look through the yard to find his part but a staff member must remove it, we called it Browsing (Br). Browsing may be escorted or unescorted depending on local conditions. Finally, there is the warehouse approach where it is already removed and you order the part at the counter (Wr).

We have tried to provide information on the size of the yard in acres and/or number of cars in the yard. We have also included a few places that specialize in engines and body parts. These are not true wrecking yards but we felt they would be useful to the restorers. We must regretfully reserve the right to refuse to list a wrecking yard or related business.

We have provided maps of each state. These are for reference only – not navigation. Only the cities which have yards listed in our book are on the maps. The approximate location can then be deciphered and used for trip planning.

At the back of the book is a cross-reference by make that has the unusual vehicles mentioned to us by the yard operators. We have provided post cards for you to use to update info on yards already listed as well as comments on this book. Also, please use these cards to tell us about yards we missed. This information will be included in future editions.

Ray's wReckingyard Roster
1042 Stallion Dr
Cheyenne, WY 82009

Key to Entries

Example of an Entry:

1.   **2.**
[*Cheyenne;*]   Balcaen's Auto Parts, 3001 S Greeley Hwy, 82007;]

                        3.   **4.**   **5.**
[307-634-5859, FAX 307-634-4413, 800-288-5859;]   [CC, Sp, Br;]   [20ac, 3300;]

            6.   **7.**
[30+; D, F, PU, 4x4, Trk;]   [B3, AMC, Jp, IH, Hd, Ns, St, Pk, Ks, Fr, Wy, VW;]

            8.
[Jpa, few Eur; Spc: 4x4]

1.   Name of city in which yard is located;
2.   Name & address of wrecking yard;
3.   Phone numbers: Business, FAX, 800, Web Site or E-mail;
4.   Business practices, i.e. business accepts Credit Cards (CC),
                    open on Saturdays (Sa),
                    if parts are Shipped (Sp),
                    You can Browse (Br; usually escorted),
                    You Remove (UR) parts with permission or
                    Staff removal of parts only (no symbol),
                    Warehouse (Wr) parts;
5.   Size of yard in acres (ac) and/or # of vehicles in yard;
6.   Years of cars in yard in either a range of years or + indicating that year to present. General info about whether they have Domestic (D), Foreign (F), Pick-ups (PU), 4x4s, Trucks (Trk), Farm (Fm), Industrial (In) or Construction (Cn) equipment in yard;
7.   Makes of cars in yard as of yard contact date;
8.   Any other comments including specialties of the yard.

Abbreviations

#4

CC..Accepts Credit Cards
Sa ....Open on Saturdays
Sp.. Will ship parts
UR ....You may remove parts
Br ....Browsing Allowed in Yard but Parts removed by staff
Wr ....Parts already removed and stored in warehouse
PL ....Parts Locator Service

#5

ac ....Acres

#6

D .... Domestic Makes of Cars
F... Foreign Makes of Cars
PU ....Pickup
4x4 ....Four Wheel Drive
Trk ....Trucks larger than 1 ton
Mil ....Military
In ....Industrial
Cn .... Construction
Fm .... Farm

#7

B3 .... Big 3 = Ford, GM & Chrysler
GM...General Motors
Fd.. Ford
Chr .... Chrysler
Eur .... European Makes
Jpa..Japanese/Asian Makes
AMC... American Motors Co
Jp ....Jeep
IH.. International Harvester
Hd .... Hudson
St... Studebaker
Pk...Packard
Ns...Nash
Wy .... Willys
Ks.. Kaiser
Fr ....Frasier
Cr... Crosley
VW ....Volkswagon

#8

Spc: .... Specializes in...

Ray's wReckingyard Rules
(as heard from yard operators)

All parts have value to the salvage business. Avoid damaging any part while removing another.

Ask the price prior to removal. This avoids any missunderstanding after the work is done.

Shipping parts is an area of concern for both the seller and buyer. Get a detailed description of the part before placing the order to avoid unpleasant surprises.

Never climb on vehicles to get a "better view". Fenders, hoods and other body parts can be damaged. Worse yet, you could fall.

Policies differ. Some yards only allow removal of small parts. Find out ahead of time what is permitted.

Take care to keep track of children and friends. You will be held responsible for their behavior. Make sure that you and those who accompany you behave as "guests".

Watch your step! The typical yard has many obsticles to navigate around to reach the desired vehicle.

If you are unsure of the proper name of the part you want, either research prior to your visit or let the operator know. It wastes everyone's time and energy to go for the wrong part.

Be sure the part you want is the part you need. Yards do not want to take back parts where you mis-diagnose the problem. One sign we saw read: "If you bought the wrong part, you now have a spare."

Try to find your part prior to closing. Many yard owners complained about having to send out search parties at closing.

Safety first! The greatest risk to you and to the operator lies with liability and insurance. A few states have stopped self removal of parts altogether due to the risk of injury.

1927 Chevrolet, Martin Supply & Salvage
Windsor, CO

1920 Paige Glenbrook
Fresno, CA

ALABAMA

Please mention you saw'em in Ray's wReckingyard Roster when contacting these yards

Athens; Burnett Used Auto Parts, 15650 Hastings Rd, 35613; 256-232-1297; CC, Sa, Sp; 2000; **40+; D, PU, 4x4; B**3**, AMC, Jp, IH**

Attalla; Gibbs Junk Yard, 205 Willis Dr, 35954; 256-538-8326; Sa, Sp, Br; 75ac; **50-95; D, PU, Fm; B**3**, Jp, St; few 50s Lincolns**

Bessemer; Sam's Auto Salvage, 2900 12th Av N, 35020; 205-428-0811; Sa, Sp; 1000; **50+; D, F, PU, 4x4; B**3

Birmingham; U-Pull-It Auto Parts, 822 15th St N, 35203; 205-328-9768; CC, Sa, UR; 150+; **60+; D, F, PU, 4x4; B**3

Cullman; Auto Salvage, 11259 US Hwy 278 W, 35057; 256-747-4006, FAX 256-747-8775, 800-291-7801; Sp; 700; **55-95; D, F, PU, 4x4; B**3**, Jp**

Hendrix Used Parts, 9350 US Hwy 278 E, 35055; 256-796-6121; Sa; 500+; **60+; D, F, PU, 4x4; B**3**; some 50s**

Yearwood's Used Auto Parts, 115 County Rd 709, 35055; 256-739-0684; Sa, Sp, Br; 15ac; **48+; D, F, PU, 4x4; B**3**; mostly 80+**

Daleville; Baird's Auto & Truck Salvage, Rt 1 Box 146A, 36322; 334-598-8849; Sa; 17ac, 1000+; **50s-92; D, F, PU, 4x4; B**3**, Jp, Ks; does restorations**

Rodgers Used Parts, 10 W Main St, 36322; 334-598-4973; CC, Sa; 1500+; **40+; D, PU; B**3**, St**

Dothan; City Used Parts Co, 2875 E Cottonwood Rd, 36301; 334-667-3280, 800-844-9180; Sp; 600; **80s, few 50-70s; D, F, PU; B**3**, Hd, Chevelle**

Vickers & Sons Auto Salvage, 321 Horseshoe Loop, 36301; 334-671-3637; Sa, Sp, UR, PL; 150; **40-85; D, F; B**3

Eight Mile: ABC Auto Salvage, 5745 Hwy 45, 36613; 334-679-0097; Sa; 2000; **60-90, few 50's; D, F, PU, 4x4; B**3**, AMC, IH, VW**

Florence; Butler's Used Parts, 706 Thompson St, 35630; 256-767-6645; Sa; **50-89; D, F, PU, 4x4; B**3

Fultondale; Best Auto Parts & Salvage, 3010 Stouts Rd, 35068; 205-631-7110 or 849-7110, FAX 205-849-7111; Sp; UR; 6ac; 3**6-92; D, F, PU; B**3**, AMC, Jp, IH, St, Pk, Wy**

Hartford; Hartford Auto Salvage, Rt 3 Box 709 Hwy 167 S, 36344; 334-588-2218; Sa, Sp, UR; 300+; **50-90; D, F, PU; B**3

Harvest; Alabama A-Z Used Auto Parts, 1928 Nick Davis Rd, 35749; 256-837-6700, 888-369-0678; Sp, UR; 500+; **49+; D, F; B**3

Huntsville; Auto Salvage, 2505 Holmes Av NW, 35805; 256-539-5701; CC, Sa; 4ac; **50s-90s; D, F, PU; B**3**, VW**

Mobile; A & A Auto Salvage, 2965 Bear Fork Rd, 36613; 334-452-2100; Sa, UR; **50-89; D; B**3

A-1 Auto Salvage, 3944 Moffett Rd, 36618; 334-343-8300, FAX 334-343-0634, 800-231-6524; CC, Sp; 800; **60+; D, F, PU, 4x4; B**3**, Jp, VW**

Moulton; Larry's Mustang Supply, 18141 Co Rd 460, 35650; 256-974-9580; Sa, Sp, UR; 2ac; **70+; D, F, PU; B**3**; new & used parts for Mustang**

New Market; North Alabama Used Auto Parts, 1630 Joe Quick Rd, 35750; 256-828-1918, www.alabamausedautoparts.rnrws.com; CC, Sa, Sp; 1800; **60+; D, F, PU, 4x4; B**3**, Volvo, BMW**

Piedmont; Dave's 278 Salvage, 1470 US Hwy 278 W, 36272; 256-447-8415; Sa; 50; **60+; D, F, PU, 4x4; B**3

Prattville; 82 Auto Parts & Wrecker Svc, 1450 Hwy 82 W, 36067; 334-361-5315; CC, Sa; 400+; **60+; D, F, PU; B**3

Remlap; Herren's Auto Salvage, 1406 State Hwy 75, 35173; 205-681-7704, 800-392-2269; Sa, Sp; 750; **30+; D, F, PU, 4x4; B**3

Midway Used Auto & Truck Parts, 19924 State Hwy 75, 35133; 205-681-1914; Sa, UR; 4ac, 400+; **50+; D, F, PU, 4x4; B**3

Salem; Johnson Auto Salvage, 984 Lee Rd 203, 36874; 334-298-6993; Sa, UR; 500; **60-94; D, F, PU, 4x4; B**3

Talladega; Jackson & Son Jeep Parts, 67655 Al Hwy 77, 35160; 256-362-7772, FAX 256-362-7738, 800-445-7835; CC, Sp, Wr; **50+; 4x4; Jp; Jeeps only**

Theodore; B & L Auto Salvage, 9550 Old Pascagoula Rd, 36582; 334-653-9167; Sa, UR; 300; **49+; D, F, PU; B3; mostly Pickups in older years**

Webb; Conner's Auto Salvage, 5766 E State Hwy 52, 36375; 334-792-3611, 800-525-7946; Sp, UR, PL; 3500; **60+; D, F, PU, 4x4; B3, Jp, VW**

LATE VINTAGE

Albertville; Billy's Used Parts, Hwy 75 S, 35950; 256-878-0700; Sa, Br; 600; **80-93; D, PU; B3; Spc: Camaro**

Alexander; City McGuire Used Parts, 6021 Cowpens Rd, 35010; 256-329-1797; Sp; 800; **70-95; D, F, PU, 4x4; B3**

Andalusia; Lester's Auto Salvage, 1309 Brooklyn Rd, 36420; 334-222-3540, FAX 334-222-4562, 800-334-3614; Sa, Sp; 1000+; **70+; D, PU; B3, AMC, Jp**

 Morris Auto Salvage, see Vintage

Anniston; Joyce's Salvage, 1620 Bynum Leatherwood Rd, 36201; 256-237-2115; Sa, Sp, UR; 2000+; **60-95; D, F, PU, Trk; B3**

Arley; Hearn's Salvage Co, Rt 2 Box 143, Arley Rd, 35541; 205-387-7281, FAX 205-387-7281, 800-231-2768; Sa, Sp; 1000; **79+; D, F, PU, 4x4; B3, Jp, IH, VW**

Athens; Burnett Used Auto Parts, see Vintage

Attalla; Gibbs Junk Yard, see Vintage

Bessemer; Sam's Auto Salvage, see Vintage

 St John's Auto & Truck Salvage, 1329 Eastern Valley Rd, 35020; 205-428-6633; Sa, Sp; 100; **77-90; D, F, PU, 4x4; B3, AMC**

Birmingham; Cherry Av Towing Inc, 2905 Cherry Av, 35214; 205-674-1864, FAX 205-674-9474, 800-982-8736; CC, Sa, Sp, Br; 6000+; **78-95; few D, F, PU, 4x4; B3**

 U-Pull-It Auto Parts, see Vintage

Boaz; Ace Auto, 70 Red Apple Cutoff Rd, 35957; 256-593-3515; Sa, Sp; 600; **60-90, few 50's & 60's; D, F; B3**

Calera; Shorty's Used Auto Parts, 8350 Hwy 25, 35040; 205-668-4708; Sa, UR; 800; **73-95 D, F, PU; B3, VW**

Centre; 411 Used Parts, 5705 US Hwy 411 N, 35960; 256-927-3774, 888-927-3774; Sa, Sp; 1000; **67-85; D, F, PU, 4x4; B3**

Citronelle; Midway Wrecking, 3575 Coy Smith Hwy, 36522; 334-866-2383; Sa, Sp, UR; 1000; **75-89; D, F, PU, 4x4; B3, AMC, Jp; open Sunday**

Cullman; Auto Salvage, see Vintage

 Hendrix Used Parts, see Vintage

 Yearwood's Used Auto Parts, see Vintage

Dothan; City Used Parts Co, see Vintage

Daleville; Baird's Auto & Truck Salvage, see Vintage

 Rodgers Used Parts, see Vintage

 Ron's Auto Wrecking, 696 Lynwood Rd, 36322; 334-598-6158; Sa, Sp, UR; 5.5ac; **70+; D, F, PU; B3**

 City Used Parts Co, 2875 E Cottonwood Rd, 36301; 334-794-5835, 800-844-9180; Sp; 600; **50-90; D, F, PU; B3, Hd, Chevelle; mostly 80-90**

 Vickers & Sons Auto Salvage, see Vintage

Eight Mile; AAA Jim Revette Used Auto, 2942 Bear Fork Rd, 36613; 334-456-7700; Sa; 250; **75+; D, F, PU; B3, AMC, VW**

Eight Mile: ABC Auto Salvage, see Vintage

 Automotive Recyclers, 4370 Lott Rd, 36613; 334-645-1488, FAX 334-645-1422, 888-646-1488, www.arinissan.com; CC, Sa, Sp; 130; **79+; F; Nissan only**

Fairhope; S & W Wrecking Co, 15655 Greeno Rd, 36532; 334-928-9634; **70-89; D; B3**

Flomaton; Marvin's You Pull It, 590 Welka Rd, 36441; 334-296-4111, 888-299-8243, 800-221-4467; Sa, Sp, UR; 2000+; **80-95; D, F, PU, 4x4; B3, AMC; 2 yards**

Florence; Butler's Used Parts, see Vintage

 Horne Salvage, 1625 State St, 35630; 256-764-5538, 800-982-7124; Sa, Sp, PL; 400; **70-95; D, F; B3; full towing services**

Fort Payne; Northside Auto Salvage, 893 Co Rd 97, 35968; 256-845-5913; Sp; 250+; **84-94; D; B3**

Fultondale; Best Auto Parts & Salvage, see Vintage

Gadsden; JBL Used Auto Parts, 3002 Hickory St, 35904; 256-547-0054, FAX 256-546-7786; Sa, Wr; 200; **78-87; D, F, PU; B3**

Hartford; Hartford Auto Salvage, see Vintage

Harvest; Alabama A-Z Used Auto Parts, see Vintage

Hazel Green; Hazel Green Auto Salvage, 119 Bledsoe Rd, 35750; 256-828-1366; Sa; 250; **70-90; D, F; B3**

Huntsville; Auto Salvage, see Vintage

   Jordan Lane Auto & Truck Salvage, 3350 Hwy 53, 35806; 256-859-3300; Sa, Sp, UR; 500; **75-95; D, PU; B3**

Killen; Bill Creasy's Used Parts, RR 2 Box 442D, 35645; 256-757-1817, FAX 256-757-1808; Sa, Sp; 500; **70-90s; D, F, PU; B3**

Laceys Spring; Dean's Wrecker Svc & Auto Parts, Hwy 231 S, 35801; 256-881-0539; Sa, Br; 3ac; **70-86; D, F, PU, 4x4; B3**

Luverne; Baker's Garage & Salvage, RR 1 Box 8, 36049; 334-335-5192; Sp; **80-92; D, F, PU; B3**

Mobile; A & A Auto Salvage, see Vintage

   A-1 Auto Salvage, see Vintage

   Alabama Auto Dismantlers, 7480 Moffat Rd, 36618; 334-649-4795; CC, Sa, Sp, UR; 400; **70-80's; D, F; B3**

   American & Import Auto Salvage, 7985 Tanner Wiliams Rd, 36608; 334-633-3909, FAX 334-633-5838, 800-333-3909; CC, Sp; 2500; **70+ German; 80+ Jpa; F, PU, 4x4**

   Atlas Auto Sales, 610 Hwy 43, 36611; 334-457-7516, FAX 334-457-0956; Sa, UR; 200; **70+; D, F; B3**

   Camaro Heaven, 7620 Harding Blvd, 33608; 334-633-7899, 800-501-7844; CC, Sa, Sp; 700; **60+, PU 70+; D, PU; Camaro, Firebird, Mustang, Corvette**

   Mobile U-Pull-It Auto Parts, 7960 Tanner Williams Rd, 36608; 334-639-0046; Sa, UR; 1100; **75-95; D, F, PU; B3**

   Reid's Auto Slvg, 6700 Hwy 45, 36613; 334-679-9560; Sa; 25-3000; **70+; D, F, PU; B3**

Montgomery; Auto Recycling of Montgomery, 2320 Lower Wetumpka Rd, 36110; 334-832-9229; Sa; 700; **80s-90s; D, PU; B3; Spc: S-10 & Blazer**

   Norman Bridge Rd Used Auto, 4444 Norman Bridge Rd, 36105; 334-288-9408; Sa, UR; 3500+; **75-95; D, F, PU, 4x4; B3, AMC, VW**

Moulton; Larry's Mustang Supply, see Vintage

Mulga; 269 Auto Parts & Used Cars, 6332 Birmingport Rd, 35118; 205-491-3127; Sa, Sp, UR; 100; **70-80s; D, F; B3**

New Market; North Alabama Used Auto Parts, see Vintage

Oxford; Rite Way Auto Salvage, 2344 US Hwy 21 S, 36203; 256-831-6760, 800-365-8036; CC, Sa, Sp; 500; **80+; D, F, PU, 4x4**

Piedmont; Dave's 278 Salvage, see Vintage

Pinson; Rusty's Used Cars & Parts, 4940 Pinson Valley Pkwy, 35215; 205-680-8900; Sa, Wr; **D, F, PU, 4x4; B3; mostly engine & transmission**

Prattville; 82 Auto Parts & Wrecker Svc, see Vintage

Remlap; Herren's Auto Salvage, see Vintage

   Midway Used Auto & Truck Parts, see Vintage

Repton; Lenox Auto & Truck Salvage, HC 60 Box 16, 36475; 334-248-2923, FAX 334-248-2620, lenox@frontiernet.net; Sa, UR; 15ac, 500; **85-92; D, F, PU, 4x4; B3**

Salem; Johnson Auto Salvage, see Vintage

Seale; Walton's Auto Slvg, 160 Padgett Rd, 36875; 334-291-5000; UR; 200+; **75+; D, F, PU; B3**

Selma; B & S Used Auto Parts, 904 Kings Bend Rd, 36701; 334-874-6629, FAX 334-874-9604, 800-526-8876; CC, Sa; 10000; **79+; D; B3**

   Central Alabama Truck Parts, 101 Sands St, 36701; 334-874-1328, 888-874-1328; CC, Sa; 3000; **79+; D, F, PU, 4x4; B3**

Semmes; D & M Used Auto Parts, 9091 Spice Pond Rd Ext, 36575; 334-649-8762; Sa, Sp; 200+; **70+; D, F, PU, 4x4, Trk; B3**

5

Somerville; 67 Auto Salvage, 2236 Hwy 67 S, 35670; 256-355-9092, 351-9140; Sa, Sp; 7ac; **75-90s; D; B3**

Talladega; Hindman Used Parts, 221 Costner St, 35160; 256-362-2779, FAX 256-362-0013; CC, Sa; **70-90; D, F, PU; B3**

    Jackson & Son Jeep Parts, see Vintage

Theodore; B & L Auto Salvage, see Vintage

    Pete's Auto Salvage & Repair, 5423 Carol Plantation Rd, 36582; 334-653-6666; Sa; **70-90; D, PU; B3**

Thomasville; Larrimore's Salvage, PO Box 133, 36784; 334-636-4018; Sa, Sp, UR; 40; **80+; D, F, PU; B3, few Volvo; part-time in afternoons**

Trafford; Blount Auto Salvage, 24559 State Hwy 79, 35172; 205-680-1750; Sa; 500; **70-85; D, F, PU; B3**

Webb; Conner's Auto Salvage, see Vintage

LATE MODEL

Andalusia; Lester's Auto Salvage, see Late Vintage

Arley; Hearn's Salvage Co, see Late Vintage

Athens; Athens Auto Recycling, 15770 York Ln, 35611; 256-232-6199, FAX 256-232-6051; CC, Sp; 1000; **F, PU; Japanese only**

    Burnett Used Auto Parts, see Vintage

Atmore; Atmore Auto Salvage, 5642 Hwy 31, 36502; 334-368-1686, 800-368-1686 AL only; Sp; 300; **D, F, PU, 4x4**

Bessemer; Astro Auto Dismantlers, 5205 Bessemer Super Hwy, 35020; 205-425-2447, 800-999-2448; CC, Sp; 200; **D, PU, 4x4; Ford only**

    Ken's Auto Salvage, 5600 5th St N, 35020; 205-428-5111; Sp; 300; **D, F, PU, 4x4; B3**

Birmingham; B & D Auto Recyclers, 3055 35th Av. N, 35207; 205-841-8733, FAX 205-841-8973, 800-321-3209; CC, Sp; 1500; **D, F, PU, 4x4; B3**

    Fultondale Auto Salvage, 2506 Northwood St, 35217; 205-608-0320, FAX 205-608-0359, 800-827-8938 AL only; Sp; 3ac, 300+; **D, F, PU, 4x4; B3, Jp; Spc: Pickup**

    Import Salvage Inc, 2500 Alton Rd, 35203; 205-833-2253; CC, Sa, Sp; 300; **F, PU, 4x4**

    U-Pull-It Auto Parts, see Vintage

Brownsboro; Big Cove Salvage, 5649 Hwy 431 S, 35741; 256-518-9500; Sa, Sp, UR; 100+; **D, F, PU; B3; other yard: 852-1088**

Calera; Billy's Toyota Parts, 964 Hwy 202, 35040; 205-668-0105, FAX 205-668-1164; CC, Sp; 3000+; **F; Toyota cars only**

    Graham's Camaro & Firebird, 970 Hwy 202, 35040; 205-668-1169, FAX 800-289-1607, 800-824-3897, www.scott.net/~bgraham; CC, Sa, Sp, Wr; 200; **D; Camaro & Firebird only**

Citronelle; Thompson's Auto Salvage, 17260 Hwy 45, 36522; 334-866-7022, FAX 334-675-0695, 888-725-8244; Sp; 250; **D, F, PU, 4x4; B3**

Cullman; Hendrix Used Parts, see Vintage

    Willingham Salvage Co, 1645 4th St, 35055; 256-737-9070, FAX 256-734-3944; Sa, UR; 4ac; **D, F; B3**

    Yearwood's Used Auto Parts, see Vintage

Daleville; Rodgers Used Parts, see Vintage

    Ron's Auto Wrecking, see Late Vintage

Dothan; Tallent's Used Auto Parts, 174 Tallent Ct, 36301; 334-792-7420, FAX 334-677-0051, 800-844-8500; CC, Sp; 1500; **D, F, PU**

Eight Mile; AAA Jim Revette Used Auto, see Late Vintage

    Automotive Recyclers, see Late Vintage

Falkville; Butler Used Auto Parts, 213 Co Rd 1393, 35622; 256-775-6825; Sa; 200; **D, F, PU, 4x4, Trk**

Florence; Steve Bevis Used Parts, 350 Cty Rd 357, 35633; 256-766-2149, FAX 256-766-2149, 800-851-1176; CC, Sp; 4000; **D, F, PU; B3**

Grand Bay; P & D Auto Parts, 2300 Hwy 90 E, 36541; 334-865-6696; 1000; **D, PU**

Greenville; Boutwell Auto Salvage & Garage, 140 Luverne Rd, 36037; 334-382-8552, 800-726-1629; CC, Sa, Sp; 2000+; **D, F, PU, 4x4, Trk; Spc: 4x4 & Ford**

Harvest; Alabama A-Z Used Auto Parts, see Vintage

6

Huntsville; A-1 Used Auto Parts, 6106 Stringfield Rd NW, 35806; 256-859-6480, 800-999-6480; Sp; 300+; **D**

A-72 East Auto Salvage, 117 Holder Rd, 35811; 256-852-1088, 800-638-9738; CC, Sa, Sp; 500; **D, F, PU**

Afco Auto Parts, 6942 Stringfield Rd NW, 35806; 256-859-1377; CC, Sa, Sp; 200+; **D, F**

Northside Auto Salvage, 3006 Meridian St N, 35811; 256-536-7892; Sa; 300; **D, F, PU**

Irondale; Clint's Chrysler Used Parts, 1879 Ruffner Rd, 35210; 205-956-5235, 800-888-6983, www.mypartshop.com; CC, Sp, PL; 500; **D; Chrysler only**

Jacksons Gap; Midway Auto Salvage & Sales, 10634 W Hwy 280, 36861; 256-825-9830, 800-643-9297; CC, Sp, PL; 800; **D, F, PU, 4x4**

Leeds; Jerry's Used Auto Parts, 2305 Hwy 78, 35094; 205-699-5100; Sa; 200+; **D, F, PU**

Leighton; Hanback's Used Parts, RR2 Box 464C, 35674; 256-381-1708; CC, Sa; 100; **D, PU**

Mobile; A-1 Auto Salvage, see Late *V*intage

All American Automotive, 5900 Hwy 45, 36613; 334-675-6460, FAX 334-679-8811, 800-447-1683; CC, Sp; 700; **D, F, PU, 4x4**

American & Import Auto Salvage, see Late *V*intage

Atlas Auto Sales, see Late *V*intage

Express Auto Salvage, 7491 Theodore Av, 36685; 334-653-9800; Sa; 20; **F, PU**

Joe Pounds Used Auto Parts, 2230 Boykin Blvd, 36605; 334-473-4896, 800-852-5173; CC, Sp, PL; 800; **D, PU; Spc: Chrysler**

Pete Bates Auto Parts, 3019 St. Stephens Rd, 36612; 334-456-6551, FAX 334-456-5309, 800-457-6551; CC, Sp; 1000; **D, F, PU, 4x4**

Reid's Auto Salvage, see Late *V*intage

Montgomery; Foreign Auto Salvage, 5185 Lower Wetumpka, 36110; 334-263-0241, 800-392-8087; CC, Sp, Br; 1000+; **F, PU, 4x4**

Moulton; Larry's Mustang Supply, see *V*intage

Nauvoo; Scott's Auto Salvage, 58351 Hwy 13, 35578; 205-924-9606, FAX 205-924-9106, 800-874-8609; CC, Sp; 3000; **D, F, PU, 4x4; Jp**

New Market ; North Alabama Used Auto Parts, see Late *V*intage

Oxford; Rite Way Auto Salvage, , see Late *V*intage

Piedmont; Dave's 278 Salvage, see Late *V*intage

Prattville; 82 Auto Parts & Wrecker Svc, see Late *V*intage

Remlap; Herren's Auto Salvage, see *V*intage

Midway Used Auto & Truck Parts, see *V*intage

Scottsboro; Jackson County Salvage, 18905 Al Hwy 35, 35768; 256-259-1319, 800-239-1319; CC, Sa, Sp; 300+; **D, F, PU**

Seale; Walton's Auto Salvage, see Late *V*intage

Selma; B & S Used Auto Parts, see Late *V*intage

Central Alabama Truck Parts, see Late *V*intage

Semmes; D & P Auto Wreckers, 3267 Schillinger Rd N, 36575; 334-649-5862, FAX 334-649-5865, 800-552-0284; CC, Sp; 1000; **D, F, PU, 4x4**

Spanish Fork; Spanish Fork Auto Dismantlers, 10880 Hwy 31 N, 36527; 334-626-2611, FAX 334-626-2736, 800-432-2611; CC, Sp; 1000; **D, F, PU, 4x4**

Spanish Fort Wrecker Svc, Hwy 31 N, 36527; 334-626-2611, FAX 334-626-2736, 800-432-2611; CC, Sa, Sp; **D, F, PU, 4x4, Trk, In; forklifts**

Talladega ; Jackson & Son Jeep Parts, see *V*intage

Theodore; Mobile Import Salvage, 7471 Theodore Dawes Rd #B, 36582; 334-653-4050, FAX 334-653-0679, 800-223-9093; CC, Sp; 500+; **F**

Tuscaloosa; A-1 Auto Repair & Salvage, 5860 Old Montgomery Hwy, 35405; 205-758-8602; 700; **D, PU, 4x4; Spc: Chevy Pickup & front wheel drive**

Auto Recks, 2007 Culver Rd, 35401; 205-345-2886; Sp; 500; **F, PU, 4x4**

Webb; Conner's Auto Salvage, see Late *V*intage

Woodstock; Woodstock Auto Salvage, 25498 Hwy 5, 35188; 205-938-9988; Sp; 1000+; **F, PU; Jpa only**

Alaska

Please use the cards in the back to let us know about yards we may have missed, or any other comments or information for future editions of Ray's wReckingyard Roster

ALASKA

VINTAGE

Palmer; Boot Hill Auto Salvage, P.O. Box 3110, Mile 13 Palmer Alt, 99645; 907-745-1027; Sa, UR; 2ac, 50; **40-75; D; B3, IH, St, Ks, DeSoto; Builds street trikes**

Wasilla; Durgeloh's Truck Salvage, 2200 Wasilla Fishhok Rd, 99645; 907-376-3958, Fax 907-357-3958; Sa, Sp; 1000; **40+; D, PU, B3, Jp, IH, Wy; Trucks & Vans Only**

   Knik Towing & Wrecking, HC 30 Box 12885, Mile 2 Hollywood Rd, 99654; 907-376-2584, FAX 907-373-2584; Sa, Sp, Br; 20ac, 1700+; **60+; D, F, PU, 4x4; B3, AMC, Jp, IH, Wy**

   Wasilla Auto Salvage, Mile 4.l5 Schrock Rd, 99654; 907-376-2039; CC, Sa, Sp; 20ac, 1500+; **55+; D, F, PU, 4x4, Trk; B3, Jp, IH, VW, Subaru**

LATE VINTAGE

Anchorage; Dean's Auto Salvage, 720 Whitney Rd, 99501; 907-258-6832; CC, Sa, Sp; 300; **PU 73+, Car 89+; D, F, PU, 4x4; B3**

   Engine & Core Supply, 1341 E. 70th Av, 99518; 907-349-5225, FAX 907-522-2302; CC, Sa; **70-90+; D, F, PU, 4x4, Mil; B3, Jp, IH**

   O'Malley Auto Parts, 12751 Old Seward Hwy, 99515; 907-345-5072; CC, Sa, Sp; **70-94; D, F, PU, 4x4; B3**

Fairbanks; Action Auto Parts & Glass, 3225 Leasure St, 99701; 907-456-1818, FAX 907-456-8094, CC, Sa, Sp, UR; 200+; **67+; D, F, PU, 4x4; B3, AMC, Jp, VW**

   Interior Towing & Salvage, 3230 Van Horn Rd, 99709; 907-479-4266, FAX 907-479-9703; CC, Sa, Sp; 13ac, 600; **cars 78+ trk 67+; D, F, PU, 4x4; B3, AMC, Jp, Subaru**

   Miller Salvage Inc, 1485 30th Av, 99701; 907-451-7278, FAX 907-451-3659, 800-451-7279; CC, Sa, Sp, Wr, PL; 10ac, 500; **cars 90+, Trk 70+; D, F, PU, 4x4, Trk; B3, AMC, Jp, IH, Wy, Subaru**

Palmer; Boot Hill Auto Salvage, *see Vintage*

Wasilla; Durgeloh's Truck Salvage, *see Vintage*

   Knik Towing & Wrecking, *see Vintage*

   Little Cache Auto Recycling, 2 Church Rd, 99654; 907-376-2190; Sa; 700+; **65-89; D, F, PU, 4x4; B3, AMC, Jp, VW**

   Wasilla Auto Salvage, *see Vintage*

LATE MODEL

Anchorage; Alaska Towing & Wrecking, 401 W. Chipperfield Dr, 99501; 907-276-6417, FAX 907-277-3721, 800-276-6417 AK ONLY; CC, Sa, Sp, UR; 400; **D, F, PU, 4x4**

   Dean's Auto Salvage, *see Late Vintage*

   Engine & Core Supply , *see Late Vintage*

   Northwest Auto Parts, 5700 Camelot Dr, 99504; 907-333-6531, FAX 907-333-7035, 800-770-6531 AK only, nwautoparts@gci.net; CC, Sa, Sp, UR, PL; 200; **D, F, PU, 4x4; Subaru; Mostly SUVs, Connection with 5 yards on mainland**

Chugiak; Hilltop Sales & Svc, 16849 Old Glenn Hwy, 99567; 907-696-2246, FAX 907-696-0704; CC, Sa, Sp, Br; 1000; **Mostly PU & 4x4; Subaru**

Fairbanks; Action Auto Parts & Glass, *see Late Vintage*

   Interior Towing & Salvage, *see Late Vintage*

   Miller Salvage Inc, *see Late Vintage*

Wasilla; Knik Towing & Wrecking, *see Vintage*

   Wasilla Auto Salvage, *see Vintage*

<hr/>

Sturdy Cars Get to Alaska

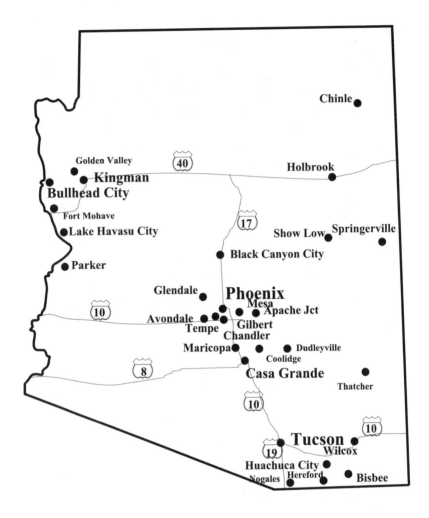

Arizona

Remember not to copy, reproduce or
distribute this list in any way without the
written permission of
Ray's wReckingyard Roster

Arizona

VINTAGE

Apache Junction; A-1 Truck & Van Wrecking, 1708 S Tomahawk Rd, 85219; 602-983-0511; Sa, Wr; **65+; D, F, PU, 4x4; B3, Jp**

Apache Auto Wrecking, 1861 E 12th Av, 85219; 602-982-3600, FAX 602-982-9263, 800-297-9494; CC, Sa, Sp; 8.5ac, 1200+; **60+; D, F, PU, 4x4; B3**

Franks Auto & Truck Salvage, 3701 S Meridian Rd, 85220; 602-983-3135 or 983-8087, FAX 602-671-0671, 800-863-3135; CC, Sa, Sp, UR; 8ac, 1200+; **50+; D, PU, 4x4; B3, AMC, Jp, IH, St, VW; Spc: Ford**

Avondale; Jurys Auto Wrecking, 12451 W Buckeye Rd, 85323; 602-932-3190; Sa, Sp; 7ac, 500+; **57- 80s; D, PU; B3, AMC, VW**

Casa Grande; La Palma Auto & Truck Salvage, 145 S Hwy 87, 85222; 520-723-9683; CC, UR; 5ac, 200+; **42+; D, PU, 4x4; GM; Spc: Chevrolet**

Southwest Salvage, N Sunland, Gin Rd, 85222; 520-836-9269, FAX 520-836-5819; CC, Sa; 14ac, 1000+; **60+; D, F, PU, 4x4, Trk; B3, AMC, Jp, VW**

Wisemans Auto Salvage, 900 W Cottonwood Ln, 85222; 520-836-9269, FAX 520-836-5819; CC, Sa; 20ac, 1000+; **20-80s; D, F, PU, 4x4, Trk, Fm; B3, AMC, Jp, Hd, St, Pk, Ns, Wy, Ks, Fr, Cr, VW**

Chinle; Arrowhead Auto Salvage, 86503; 520-674-5745; Sa, UR; 200+; **60-80s; D, F, PU, few Trk, few Fm; B3, AMC**

Coolidge; Cantrells Used Auto Parts, 1122 E Martin Rd, 85228; 520-723-5783; UR; 5ac, 300+; **50+; D, F, PU, few 4x4; B3, AMC; Spc: Chevy**

Dudleyville; Desert Air Salvage, 3569 San Pedro Rd, 85292; 520-357-6027, 800-650-6027; Sa, Sp, UR; 3.5ac; **20s-70s; D, PU, 4x4, Trk; B3, Pk**

Glendale; All Star Import, 5233 W Lamar Rd, 85301; 602-931-5000, FAX 602-931-3800, 888-820-0308; CC, Sa; 5ac, 200+; **60+; F, PU, 4x4; New, used & rebuilt parts**

J & J Salvage Co, 6424 W Orangewood Av, 85301; 602-939-5932, FAX 602-439-7421, 888-820-0308; CC, Sa; 5ac, 450+; **50-92; D, PU, 4x4; B3, AMC, IH, few St; Camaro & Firebird**

Golden Valley; A 1 Auto & Wrecking, HC 37 Box 927, 86413; 520-767-3360, FAX 520-767-4990, a1aitp@ctaz.com; Sa, Sp; 5ac, 300+; **30-70s; D, PU, 4x4; B3, AMC, St; Mail Order Only**

Dans Auto Salvage, 2666 S Hwy 66, 86413; 520-753-3993, 800-945-1075; Sa, Sp, UR; 900+; **50-80s; D, F, PU, 4x4; B3, few AMC, few Jp, Pk, VW**

Holbrook; Kachina Auto Salvage, 704 S Apache Dr, 86025; 520-524-3534, FAX 520-524-6884; Sa, Sp; 15ac; **50-97; D, F, PU, 4x4, Fm; B3, AMC, Jp, IH, St, Pk, Cr, VW**

Huachuca City; Fort Auto Parts & Wrecker Service, 152 Huachuca Blvd, 85616; 520-456-9082; Sa, Sp; 5ac, 700+; **30-70s; D, PU; B3, AMC, Jp, IH, Hd, St, Pk, Ns, Wy, Ks, Fr, Cr; Nash Metropolitan, Terraplane & Graham; Spc: Chevy**

Ralphs Auto Wrecking, 2186 N Bowers Rd, 85616; 520-456-9127; Sa, UR; 25ac, 1000+; **60-70s; D, few F, PU, 4x4; B3, IH, VW**

Kingman; Freds Auto & Truck Salvage, 2112 Railroad St, 86401; 520-753-3005, 800-678-3810; Sa, Sp, UR; 5ac, 250+; **40+; D, few F, PU, 4x4, few Trk, Cn; B3, AMC, Jp, IH; Checker, Bordward; Spc: Pickup**

Salvage 1, 19415 N Hwy 93, 86401; 520-767-3638, FAX 520-767-3638; Sa, UR; 10ac, 700+; **50-80s, few 40s; D, F, PU, Trk; B3, AMC, Jp, IH**

Lake Havasu City; B & R Auto Salvage, 1555 Dover Av, 86404; 520-855-9885, www. brsalvage@interworldnet.net; Sa; 5ac, 300+; **60s-90; D, F, PU, 4x4; B3, few Jp, few IH**

Maricopa; Al's Hudson Cars & Parts, 32425 W Nam Vo Rd, 85239; 520-568-2911, FAX 520-568-2105; Hr, Sp; **10-50s; D; Hd; few Prewar; Spc: Hudson; Repairs all classics**

Alley Towing & Recycling, 53501 W Jersey Dr, 85239; 602-252-0304; Sa, Sp; 10ac, 1800+; **60-80s; D, 4x4; B3, AMC, VW, Yugo, Hyundai; few 50s**

Hidden Valley Auto Parts, 21046 N Rio Bravo Rd, 85239; 520-568-2945, FAX 520-258-0951, 602-252-2212; CC, Sa, Sp, UR; 80ac, 8000+; **20-80s, Mostly 50s-60s; D, F, PU, 4x4, Trk; B3, AMC, Jp, Hd, St, Pk, Ns, Wy, Ks, Fr, Cr, VW, Checker, Sunbeam, Hilman, Jag, Mercedes, Fiat, Simca, Peugeot & More**

11

Parker; Deb's Garage, 912 S Hopi Av, 85344; 520-669-2743; **50-80s; D, F, PU, 4x4; B3, Jp, IH, St**

Phoenix; A & C Wrecking, 4050 S 19th Av, 85041; 602-276-1040; CC, Sa, Sp; 3.5ac, 900+; **50-80s; D, F, PU; B3**

A-A National Auto Parts, 3410 W Washington St, 85009; 602-272-5331, FAX 602-233-2079, 800-653-5865; CC, Sa, Sp, Br; 500+; **61-88; D, few F; GM, Chr; Spc: Cadillac & Chryslers**

A-AA 20th St Auto Parts Inc, 2000 E Jefferson St, 85034; 602-258-2020, FAX 258-2216, 800-999-4911; CC, Sa, Sp, UR; 200+; **60+; D, F, PU, 4x4; B3, Porsche, Corvette; installation**

AAA Broadway Auto Parts, 2000 W Broadway Rd, 85041; 602-276-1200, FAX 602-276-9130; CC, Sa, Sp, Br; 8ac, 700+; **60+; D, PU, 4x4; B3; Spc: Ford, Mustang, Bronco**

AAA United Auto & Truck Parts, 6047 N 57th, 85012; 602-931-3919; Sa, Sp; 2ac; **50+; D, PU, 4x4; GM, 55 & 57 Chevy**

Adobe Auto & Truck LLC, 22444 N 23rd Av, 85027; 602-582-9300, FAX 602-582-0275; CC, Sa, Sp; 6ac, 900+; **60+; D, F, PU, 4x4; B3, AMC, few Jp, few IH; restorable vehicles**

All Auto & Truck, 3245 W Broadway Rd, 85041; 602-268-0271, 800-954-0271; Sa, Sp, Br; 1ac, 400+; **40-90; D, F, PU, 4x4, Trk; B3, AMC, Jp, Hd, St**

All European Models, 3405 S 40th St, 85040; 602-470-1922, FAX 602-470-8061, 800-937-1473; CC, Sa, Sp, UR; 2ac; **60+; F; Jag, Porsche, Lexus, Mercedes, Saab**

Angel Auto, 2450 S 35th Av, 85009; 602-269-7295, FAX 602-269-3644; Sa, Sp, Br; 6ac, 800+; **50-90s; F, PU, 4x4; Eur, Jpa; Fiat, Alfa Romero, Audi, Mercedes, AMW, VW, Spitfire, Midget**

Arizona Mustang Mart, 429 S 35th Av, 85009; 602-233-0616; Sa, Sp; 400+; **65-73; D; Mustang only**

Art Coffer Auto Dismantlers, 3127 W Broadway Rd, 85041; 602-276-7377; CC, Sa, Sp, Br; 200+; **60+; D; Chrysler only**

Askren Auto Parts, 3309 W Broadway Rd, 85041; 602-276-2555; Sa, Sp, UR; 500+; **31-80s; D, F, PU, 4x4; B3, AMC, Jp, St, Ns, Hr; Spc: Chevy**

Benrich Auto Wrecking, 9206 N 10th Dr, 85021; 602-997-9451; Sp, Wr; 2ac; **40+; D, F; B3, AMC, Jp, VW, Saab, Porsche, Mercedes; Spc: 64 & older Chrysler**

Big Daddys Auto Salvage, 612 W Broadway Rd, 85041; 602-268-0266; Sa, Sp, Br; 3ac, 400+; **39+; D, F, PU, few 4x4, few Trk; B3, AMC, Jp, few VW; Spc: 65-72 Muscle Cars**

Bills Truck Parts, 3402 S 40th St, 85040; 602-437-1300, FAX 602-899-2870, 888-528-0876; Sa, Sp, Wr; **46+; Not a yard, Spc: rebuilt auto/light trk engines gas & diesel**

Blair & Sons Auto Parts, 3140 W Broadway Rd, 85041; 602-243-1238; Sp; 3ac, 300+; **40-79; F, PU; VW; Spc: Beetles, Bugs & Karmann Ghia**

Boatwrights Wrecking Yard, 3121 S 51st Av, 85043; 602-278-9721; Sa, Sp, UR; 1200+; **40s-70s; D, F, PU; B3, AMC, St, VW**

Boneyard Stan, 218 N 69 Av, 85043; 602-936-8045; Sp, Br, PL; 2ac, 200; **50-80s; D, PU, few Trk; GM; Spc: Pontiac**

Broadway Auto Wreckers, 2000 W Broadway, 85041; 602-276-1200; CC, Sa, Sp; 3+ac, 1000+; **Prewar+; D, Fd; Spc: Model A, Mustangs**

Certi-Fit Body Parts, 216 N 47th Av, 85043; 602-278-4700, FAX 602-278-7523, 800-548-5091; CC, Sp; **60+; D, F, PU; New Body Parts only; 13 Stores**

Chi Town Auto Wrecking, 2935 W Broadway Rd, 85041; 602-268-2400, FAX 602-268-8527; CC, Sa, Sp, Br; 3.5ac; **65+; D, F, PU; B3, AMC; has 3 yards**

Desert Valley Auto Parts, 2227 W Happy Valley Rd, 85027; FAX 602-582-9141, 800-905-8024, www.dvap.com; CC, Sa, Sp; 40ac, 5000+; **40-80; D, PU; B3, AMC, Jp, IH, Hd, St, Pk, Ns, Wy Ks, Fr; Few Prewar, Spc: Pre 80 Domestic**

Eagle Auto & Truck, 3605 W Lower Buckeye Rd, 85009; 602-269-6359, FAX 602-269-1326, 888-56-EAGLE; CC, Sa, Sp, Br; 6.5ac, 1000; **60-80; D, F, PU, 4x4; B3, Jpa, BMW, Mercedes; Spc: Datsen 240-280Z**

Falcon Auto Parts, 3443 N 31st Av, 85017; 602-253-9665, 800-525-4038; Sa, Sp; 50+; **60-70s; Ford Falcons only; Evenings & Saturdays only**

Arizona-Vintage

Family Auto Recyclers, 225 S 35th Av, 85009; 602-269-3969, FAX 602-269-9204, 888-269-3969; CC, Sa, Sp; 200+; **65-80s; D, F, PU, 4x4; Spc: Early Broncos & older 4x4**

G & G Auto Parts, 2544 W Broadway Rd, 85041; 602-243-2776, FAX 602-305-9293; Sa, Sp; 6ac, 800+; **42+; D, F, PU; B3**

G & S Auto Wrecking, 3215 W Broadway Rd, 85041; 602-268-2011; CC, Sa, Br; 3ac, 500+; **60+; D, F, PU, 4x4; B3, AMC**

J & L Auto Wreckers, 1640 W Broadway Rd, 85041; 602-243-6722; Sa, Br; 2ac, 400+; **50s-90; D, F, PU, 4x4, Trk; B3; Mostly Japanese, some European**

Jess & Sons Automotive, 4202 S 27th Av, 85041; 602-268-8871; Sa, Sp, Br; 3ac; **30+; D, F, few PU; B3, Jpa**

K & D Auto Wrecking, 2145 W Broadway Rd, 85041; 602-243-0675, FAX 602-494-1073; Sa, Sp, Br; 2ac, 200+; **60+; D, few F, few PU; B3, Jp, Jpa; Jaguar**

Mc Intyre Auto Parts, 3445 S 24th St, 85040; 602-268-1409; CC, Sa, Sp; 13ac; **60-80s; D, PU; B3, AMC, few Jp**

Reeves Auto Wrecking, 1322 W Magnolia St, 85007; 602-340-0633, FAX 602-268-6675, 800-441- 9936; Sa, Sp, Br; 4ac, 1000+; **60+; D, PU, 4x4; B3, Jp, Chevelle, Cutlass; some muscle cars**

Salvage City, 2940 W Lincoln St, 85009; 602-272-1008, FAX 602-272-2813, 800-489-2489; CC, Sa, Sp, UR; 2.5ac, 1000+; **50+; D, F, PU, 4x4; B3, Jpa, Eur; Spc: PU & Vans; few Eur**

Speedway Automotive, 2300 W Broadway Rd, 85041; 602-276-0090, FAX 602-276-1053, www.thebuickplace.com; CC, Sa, Sp; 800+; **61+; D, Buick only**

Show Low; Show Low Auto Sales & Wrecking, 3301 E Deuce of Clb, 85901; 520-537-2911, 888- 378-9700; CC, Sa, Sp, UR; 300+; **60-90s, few 40s & 50s; D, F, PU, 4x4, Trk; B3, AMC, Jp, Pk**

Springerville; Springerville Auto Wreckers, 403 US Hwy 180, 85938; 520-333-2230, FAX 520-333-4849; Sa, Sp, UR; 5ac, 1000+; **50+; D, F; B3; Most makes**

Tempe; Mercedes Pete, 1988 E 1/2W 1st St, 85281; 602-829-7826, FAX 602-968-6935; CC, Sp, Br; 5ac, 550+; **55+; F; Mercedes only**

Pick-A-Part of Tempe, 225 N McClintock Dr, 85281; 602-968-1111; Sa, Sp, UR; 5ac, 1400+; **50+; D, F; B3, AMC; Spc: Rambler; Open Sunday**

Tri Star Pete, 1988 W 1st St, 85281; 602-829-7257, FAX 602-968-6935; CC, Sp; 3ac, 500+; **58-89; F; Mercedes Only**

Thatcher; Valley Auto Wrecking, Inc, 3983 W Main St, 85552; 520-428-3645, FAX 520-428-4062, 800-824-1465; CC, Sp, Br; 32ac, 4000+; **38+; D, F, PU, 4x4, Trk, Mil; B3, AMC, Jp, Ns, Ks, Fr, VW**

Tucson; ACS Used Auto Parts, 4353 E Illinois St, 85714; 520-747-8965, FAX 520-747-4800, www.autopartsused.com; CC, Sa, Sp; 4ac, 1000+; **50+; D, F, PU, 4x4; B3, AMC; Spc: Impala**

Action Auto & Truck, 4301 E Illinois St, 85714; 520-790-3600, 800-432-5394; CC, Sa, Sp, Br; 2.5ac, 500+; **60+; D, F, PU, 4x4; B3, AMC, Jp, IH; Spc: GM cars & IH**

All Richt Auto, 5251 E Drexel, 85706; 520-574-0888; Sa; 2.5ac, 350+; **55-85; D, few PU; B3**

Arizona Auto Wrecking Inc, 5561 S Park Av, 85706; 520-889-0461, FAX 520-889-6272; CC, Sa, Sp; 3ac, 600+; **49+; D, PU; GM, Chr; Mopar, Lemans, Cadillac, Imperial**

Charlies Auto & Truck Salvage, 5411 S Rosemont Av, 85706; 520-574-9130; **50-80s; D, PU, GM; Buick, Cadillac, Spc: 62-82 Chevelle, PU 75+**

Classic Auto Parts, 4865 E Cindrich St, 85706; 520-574-0308; Sa, Sp, UR; 500+; **40-74; D, few PU; B3**

Millies Auto & Truck Salvage, 4260 E Illinois St, 85714; 520-748-1444; Sa; 2.5ac, 200+; **50s-85; D; Spc: AMC & Cadillac**

Parts R Us, 4302 E Illinois St, 85714; 520-571-7899; CC, Sp; **60-80s; D, F, PU, 4x4; B3**

Revolvstore Volvo Parts, 5275 Drexel, 85706; 602-574-1717, FAX 520-574-3629, 800-288-6586, www.revolvstore.com; CC, Sa, Sp; 200+; **50+; Volvo only; new & rebuilt parts**

Sanford & Sons Auto & Truck, 3721 S Country Club Rd, 85713; 520-792-1811; Sa; 300+; **50-80s; D, F, PU; B3; Spc: Mustang, Chevelle**

Star Auto Parts & Sales Inc, 2003 S 4th Av, 85713; 520-623-5755, 800-635-4819; Sa, Sp; 1ac; **32-58; D, Fd; Ford only; NOS, 28-31 engines, V-8 engines**

Wahl Brothers Truck Salvage, 3147 E Ajo Way, 85713; 520-792-2385, FAX 520-623-6215, 800-214-2385; CC, Sp; 5ac, 850+; **60+s; D, PU; B3; Spc: Chevy Pickup & Vans**

Wilcox; Wilcox Wrecking Yard, 85643; 520-384-2688, 800-491-2688; Sp; 15 ac, 400+; **40-90s; D, F, PU, 4x4, Trk; B3, AMC, IH, Ns, St, Ks, Fr, VW; few prewar**

LATE VINTAGE

Apache Junction; A-1 Truck & Van Wrecking, see Vintage

Apache Auto Wrecking, see Vintage

Franks Auto & Truck Salvage, see Vintage

Avondale; Jurys Auto Wrecking, see Vintage

Bisbee; Zips Auto, 2227 S Naco Hwy, 85603; 520-432-5926; Sa, Sp, UR; 4ac, 300+; **70+; D, F, PU, 4x4**

Bullhead City; Big Ds Towing & Salvage, 3526 Pass Canyon Rd, 86429; 520-754-4661; Sa, UR; 10ac, 400+; **73-88; D, PU; B3, AMC**

Casa Grande; La Palma Auto & Truck Salvage, see Vintage

Southwest Salvage, see Vintage

Wisemans Auto Salvage, see Vintage

Chinle; Arrowhead Auto Salvage, see Vintage

Coolidge; Cantrells Used Auto Parts, see Vintage

Dudleyville; Desert Air Salvage, see Vintage

Gilbert; Baseline Auto Recyclers, 117 E Baseline Rd, 85233; 602-892-0495, FAX 602-497-5040; CC, Sa, Sp; 1800+; **70+; D, F, PU, 4x4; Spc: Wheels**

Glendale; All Star Import, see Vintage

AMC Salvage, 6741 W Belmont Av, 85303; 602-937-5899, 800-882-5337; CC, Sa, Sp; **76+; D; Jeep parts only**

J & J Salvage Co, see Vintage

JBS Imports, 5239 W Lamar Rd, 85301; 602-939-2096, FAX 602-939-0774, 800-4MYSAAB; CC, Sa, Sp; 200+; **80-90s; F; Spc: Saab, Volvo**

Richard's Used Pickup Parts, 6851 W Belmont Av, 85303; 602-931-5200, FAX 602-939-7309, 800-945-1075, thunder1@doitnow.com; CC, Sp; 1.5ac, 150+; **70+; D, PU, 4x4; B3**

Golden Valley; A 1 Auto & Wrecking, see Vintage

Dans Auto Salvage, see Vintage

Hereford; M & R Auto Inc, 5131 E Hereford Rd, 85615; 520-378-2343, 800-362-0810; CC, Sp; 20ac, 2500+; **80s+; D, F, PU, 4x4**

Holbrook; Kachina Auto Salvage, see Vintage

Huachuca City; Fort Auto Parts & Wrecker Service, see Vintage

Ralphs Auto Wrecking, see Vintage

Kingman; Freds Auto & Truck Salvage, see Vintage

Kingman Car Co, 3890 E Andy Devine Av, 86401; 520-757-0444, FAX 520-757-0446; 10ac, 1200; **70s-80s; D, F, PU, 4x4; B3, Jp, IH**

Salvage 1, see Vintage

Lake Havasu City; B & R Auto Salvage, see Vintage

Maricopa; Alley Towing & Recycling, see Vintage

Hidden Valley Auto Parts, see Vintage

Mesa; BPI Used Engines, 416 E Baseline Rd, 85204; 602-497-8031, FAX 602-497-8369, 800-778-0302; CC, Sa, Sp, Wr; **84-97; F; Jpa Engines only**

F & L Auto Wrecking, 120 S Extension Rd, 85210; 602-834-4040, 800-352-8715; Sa, Sp; 10ac, 800+; **70-80s; D, F, PU, few 4x4; B3, Jp**

Nogales; Holler's Auto Salvage, 450 N Western Av, 85621; 520-287-4470, FAX 520-287-2407; Sa; 12ac, 1000; **70s-80s; D, F; B3**

Parker; Debs Garage, see Vintage

Phoenix; 20th St Auto Parts, 2000 E Jefferson St, 85034; 602-258-2020, FAX 602-258-2216, 800-999-4911; CC, Sa, Sp; 150; **80+; D, F, PU; B3; Corvette, Porsche, Audi**

A & C Wrecking, *see Vintage*

A & S Auto Wrecking, 2528 Broadway Rd, 85041; 602-243-9119; CC, Sa, Sp; 1ac; **73+; D, F, PU, 4x4; B3; Spc: Pickup**

A to Z Auto Recyclers, 2724 W Buckeye Rd, 85323; 602-272-1680, FAX 602-272-0854; CC, Sa, Sp; 2.5ac, 300; **67-85; D, F, PU, 4x4; B3, few Jp**

A-A National Auto Parts, *see Vintage*

A-AA 20th St Auto Parts Inc, *see Vintage*

A-Salvage City, 2930 W Lincoln St, 85009; 602-272-1008 or 272-6781, FAX 602-272-2813, 800-489-CITY; CC, Sa, Sp, Br; 1000; **78-86; D, F, PU, 4x4; B3, few AMC**

AAA Broadway Auto Parts, *see Vintage*

AAA United Auto & Truck Parts, *see Vintage*

Ace Auto Recycling, 2150 W Broadway Rd, 85041; 602-276-1217, FAX 602-268-6366; Sa, Br; 3ac, 600; **75-86; D, F, few PU, few 4x4; B3, few AMC, few Jp, few VW**

Adobe Auto & Truck LLC, *see Vintage*

Advantage Auto Recyclers, 2155 W Broadway Rd, 85041; 602-268-3306, FAX 602-304-9514; CC, Sa, Sp, UR; 3ac, 600+; **70+; D, F, PU, 4x4; B3, AMC, Jp**

All Auto & Truck, *see Vintage*

All European Models, *see Vintage*

All Imports, 5000 S 16th St, 85040; 602-268-4617, FAX 602-268-4617; Sa, Sp, Br; 4ac, 1200+; **80+; F, PU, 4x4, Trk**

All Mercedes Benz Parts, 2350 W Broadway Rd, 85041; 602-268-9109; Sa; 100+; **70-89; F; VW Rabbits, Mercedes, BMW**

All Models Foreign, 3024 S 40th St, 85040; 602-437-0185, FAX 602-437-5130; CC, Sa, Sp, UR; 2ac; **80+; F, PU, 4x4; mostly Jpa, some Eur**

All Models Ltd, 3002 S 40th St, 85040; 602-437-0194, FAX 602-437-5730; CC, Sa, Sp, UR; 2ac; **80+; F, PU, 4x4; mostly Jpa, some Eur**

American Truck Salvage, 4141 S 35th Av, 85041; 602-268-2546, FAX 602-268-0837, 800-242-0201, paulkz@aol.com; CC, Sa, Sp, Br; **80+; Trk; IH, Peterbilt, Hino, KW**

Angel Auto, *see Vintage*

Any Make Auto Parts, 3445 S 24th, 85040; 602-268-1409, 888-268-1409; CC, Sa, UR; 14ac, 3000; **69+; D, F, PU, 4x4; B3**

Arizona 4x4 Recyclers Inc, 3125 W Broadway Rd, 85041; 602-276-9606, FAX 602-276-0274, 800-829-5337; CC, Sp; 1.5 ac; **70+; D; Jp; Used & Rebuilt Jeep Parts**

Arizona Auto Parts, 2021 W Buckeye Rd, 85009; 602-640-1208, FAX 602-256-0597, 800-666-5265; CC, Sa, Sp, UR; 16 ac, 2000+; **67+; D, F, PU, 4x4; B3, AMC, Jp, VW, Jpa; Spc: Japanese**

Arizona Japanese Models, 3405 S 40th St, 85040; 602-437-0750, FAX 602-470-8061, 800-470-1922; CC, Sa, Sp, Br, PL; 3ac; **70-94; F; Jpa**

Arizona Mustang Mart, *see Vintage*

Arizona Wheelcovers, 4053 E Washington St, 85034; 602-275-9211, FAX 602-275-9600, 800-334-4496; CC, Sa, Sp; 17000 wheels; **75+; D, F; Few earlier, recond & chroming**

Art Coffer Auto Dismantlers, *see Vintage*

Askren Auto Parts, *see Vintage*

Benrich Auto Wrecking, *see Vintage*

Big Daddys Auto Salvage, *see Vintage*

Bills Truck Parts, *see Vintage*

Blair & Sons Auto Parts, *see Vintage*

Boatwrights Wrecking Yard, *see Vintage*

Boneyard Stan, *see Vintage*

Broadway Auto Wreckers, *see Vintage*

Certi-Fit Body Parts, *see Vintage*

Chi Town Auto Wrecking, *see Vintage*

Desert Valley Auto Parts, *see Vintage*

Don Hoctors Auto Wrecking, 3604 S 36th St, 85040; 602-437-0304, FAX 602-437-2218; CC, Sa, Sp, Br; 6ac, 1200+; **70s-90s; D, F, PU, 4x4; B3, AMC; Spc: GM**

Eagle Auto & Truck, *see Vintage*

Ecology Auto Wrecking, 320 S 27th Av, 85009; 602-233-2277, FAX 602-352-6160; CC, Sa, UR; 10ac, 3000; **70+; D, F, PU, 4x4; B3, AMC; Open Sunday**

Falcon Auto Parts, *see Vintage*

Family Auto Recyclers, *see Vintage*

Fred's Auto Wrecking, 22201 N 21st St, 85027; 602-869-9550; Sa, Sp; 1500+; **80+; D, few F, PU; B3**

G & G Auto Parts, *see Vintage*

G & S Auto Wrecking, *see Vintage*

German Auto Salvage, 2902 S 40th St, 85040; 602-437-3046, FAX 602-437-1629, salvage@inficad.com; CC, Sa, Sp; 200; **67+; F; VW bugs, Audi**

Grand Used Auto Parts Inc, 2501 W Buckeye Rd, 85009; 602-272-6785, FAX 602-233-3971; CC, Sa, Sp; 10ac, 1500; **77+; D, F, PU; cars Domestic only, Pickup Domestic & Foreign**

Hoctors Southwest Auto, 3220 W Broadway Rd, 85041; 602-268-0761, FAX 602-243-5179; CC, Sa, Sp, Br; 12ac, 800; **70+; D, F, few PU, few 4x4; B3, AMC, Jpa; scarce parts, plus rebuilt**

Honda Auto Salvage, 4039 E Winslow Av, 85040; 602-470-0789, www.hasport.com; CC, Sa, Sp, Br; 1.5ac, 300+; **70+; F; Honda & Acura only**

J & L Auto Wreckers, *see Vintage*

Jess & Sons Automotive, *see Vintage*

Joe & Son Auto & Truck Parts, 2720 W Broadway Rd, 85041; 602-276-6010; Sa, Sp; **70-90; D, F, PU; B3**

Just Truck & Van, 2801 S 35th Av, 85009; 602-243-6002, FAX 602-278-9590; CC, Sa, Sp, Br; 5ac, 400; **67+; D, F, PU, 4x4, Trk, Mil; B3; Spc: Pickup & Van**

K & D Auto Wrecking, *see Vintage*

Mc Intyre Auto Parts, *see Vintage*

North 19th Auto Wrecking, 2250 N 21st Av, 85027; 602-242-4226; Sa, Sp, Br; 4ac, 900+; **80+; D, PU, 4x4; B3, few AMC, few Jp**

Payless Auto Parts, 2121 W Broadway Rd, 85041; 602-243-1991, FAX 602-243-1674; CC, Sa, Sp, Br; 1ac, 300+; **80+; D, F, PU, 4x4; B3**

R & M Auto Salvage, 2454 S 35th Av, 85009; 602-278-8338, FAX 602-278-1802; CC, Sa, Sp, Br; 3ac, 600; **70+; D, F, PU, 4x4; B3, Jpa**

Ray & Bobs Truck Salvage, 101 S 35th Av, 85009; 602-278-7411, FAX 602-233-1158, 888-828-2172; Sa, Sp, Br; **70s-90s; D, F, PU, few 4x4, Trk; Volvo, Mercedes, Hino, Isuzu**

Reeves Auto Wrecking, *see Vintage*

Riteway Auto Parts, 2502 W Broadway Rd, 85041; 602-268-1482 or 268-1481, FAX 602-268-6989, 800-USE-USED, www.ritewayauto.com; CC, Sp; 7ac, 2000+; **70+; F; Jpa; Spc: Datsun 70-96 & Z cars**

Ron's Used Pickup Parts, 602 S 23rd Av, 85009; 602-252-2301; Sa, Sp, Wr; 200+; **73+; D, PU only, 4x4; Spc: Ford, Chevy**

S & D Auto Wrecking, 3201 W Broadway Rd, 85041; 602-268-2921; Sa, UR; 2ac; **70+; D, F, PU, 4x4; B3, AMC, Jp**

Salvage City, *see Vintage*

Speedway Automotive, *see Vintage*

Sports Car Recycling, 4034 E Superior Av, 85040; 602-470-1622; CC, Sa, Sp; 270; **69+; D, F; B3, BMW, Volvo**

U-Pull-It, 3250 W Broadway Rd, 85041; 602-243-3933; CC, Sa, Sp, UR; 20ac, 1000+; **60-80s; D, F, few PU, few 4x4; B3; Open Sunday**

Yank Your Part, 2104 W Broadway Rd, 85041; 602-268-4444, FAX 602-268-6299; CC, Sa, Sp, UR; 10ac, 2000+; **70+; D, F, PU, 4x4; B3, AMC; motorcycles & boats, Open Sunday**

Show Low; Arrow Metals & Auto Recycling, Hwy 77 N, 85901; 520-537-7132, 800-229-7132; Sa; 11.5ac; **70+; D, F, PU; B3**

Show Low Auto Sales & Wrecking, *see Vintage*

Springerville; Springerville Auto Wreckers, *see Vintage*

Tempe; Mercedes Pete, *see Vintage*

Pick-A-Part of Tempe, *see Vintage*

Reed's Auto Parts, 1851 E Pima St, 85281; 602-967-7807; Sa, Sp; 5ac, 500; **80s+; D, F, few PU, few 4x4; B3**

Tri Star Pete, *see Vintage*

Thatcher; Valley Auto Wrecking, Inc, *see Vintage*

Tucson; A A Pull Your Part, 4570 E Irvington Rd, 85714; 520-571-8050; CC, Sa, UR; 2ac; **70-85; D, F, few PU; B3**

ACS Used Auto Parts, *see Vintage*

Action Auto & Truck, *see Vintage*

Ajo Way Wrecking, 3615 e Ajo Way, 85713; 520-748-8558; Sa; 5ac, 800+; **73-90; D, few F, few 4x4; B3; Spc: Ford Van**

All Richt Auto, *see Vintage*

Arizona Auto Wrecking Inc, *see Vintage*

Arizona U-Pull & Save Auto Parts, 5602 N Camino de la Tierra, 85705; 520-293-2310; CC, Sa, UR; 7ac, 400; **70-82; D, F, few PU; B3**

Arizona Wrecksperts, 5280 N Hwy Dr, 85705; 520-888-8407; CC, Sa, Sp; **70+; F, PU, 4x4**

Auto & Truck Salvage Co, 3207 E Ajo Way, 85713; 520-792-9616; CC, Sp; 2ac; **84+; D, F, PU; Spc S10 Ranger Pickup mostly**

Beep Beep Foreign Parts, 5555 S Arcadia Av, 85706; 520-574-1234; Sa, Sp; 4.5ac, 600; **69+; F, PU, 4x4; Japanese only**

Big Southwest Import Salvage, 5130 E Canada St, 85706; 520-574-1465, FAX 520-574-1424, 800-456-6767; CC, Sp, Br; 4ac, 600; **80s+; F, PU, 4x4; Jpa, 70+ Mercedes**

Catalina Auto Recycling, 4811 E Cindrich St, 85706; 520-574-0555, FAX 520-574-5757; CC, Sa, Sp, UR; 10ac, 2000+; **80+; D, F, PU, 4x4**

Charlies Auto & Truck Salvage, *see Vintage*

Classic Auto Parts, *see Vintage*

Dixies Auto & GTruck Salvage, 5591 S Arcadia Av, 85706; 520-574-0044; Sa; 4ac; **70+; D, F, few PU, few 4x4; B3**

Drake & Son Used Auto & Truck Parts, 4220 E Illinois St, 85714; 520-748-8734, 800-839-8734; CC, Sa, Sp; 5ac; **70s-90s; D, few F, few PU, few 4x4; B3; Spc: Chrysler**

Jakes Auto Parts Co, 1809 S 4th Av, 85713; 520-623-5453, 800-654-0628; Sa; 1ac, 200; **80+; D, few F, PU, few 4x4; B3; Spc: Pickup**

Millies Auto & Truck Salvage, *see Vintage*

Mission Auto Parts, 5001 E Drexel Rd, 85706; 520-574-0360, 800-974-0393; CC, Sa, Sp; 2ac, 500+; **60s-96; D, 4x4; B3, Jp; Spc: Jeep**

Parts R Us, *see Vintage*

Obarr Auto & Truck Salvage, 1425 W Grant Rd, 85745; 520-623-9411; Sa, Sp, UR; 4+ac; **81+ cars, 67+ PU; D, PU, 4x4; B3, AMC, Jp**

Revolvstore Volvo Parts, *see Vintage*

Sanford & Sons Auto & Truck, *see Vintage*

Wahl Brothers Truck Salvage, *see Vintage*

Willcox; Ellis Wrecking Yard, Packing Plant Rd, 85643; 520-384-4773; Sa, Sp, UR; 400; **70s-85; D, few F; B3, few AMC**

Wilcox Wrecking Yard, *see Vintage*

LATE MODEL

Apache Junction; A-1 Truck & Van Wrecking, *see Vintage*

Apache Auto Wrecking, *see Vintage*

Franks Auto & Truck Salvage, *see Vintage*

Bisbee; Zips Auto, see *Late Vintage*

Casa Grande; La Palma Auto & Truck Salvage, *see Vintage*

R&G Auto Salvage Inc, 840 W Cottonwood Ln, 85222; 520-836-0552, FAX 520-421-3705, 888-742-8867; Sa, Sp; 30ac, 2700+; **D, PU, 4x4**

Southwest Salvage, *see Vintage*

Chandler; American Auto Recycling, 301 N 56th St, 85226; 602-961-1112, FAX 602-961-1975, 800-522-9122, www.americanautorecycling.com; CC, Sa, Sp; 6ac, 1000+; **D, few F, few PU, few 4x4; B3, Jp**

Coolidge; Cantrells Used Auto Parts, *see Vintage*

Fort Mohave; Ace Auto Wrecking, 1745 E Lipan Blvd, 86427; 520-768-1188, FAX 520-768-5711; Sp; 5ac, 500+; **D, F, PU, 4x4**

Gilbert; All Models East, 625 W Guadalupe Rd, 85233; 602-892-4300, FAX 602-892-6590, 800-700-7091; CC, Sp, UR; 10ac, 1200+; **D, F, PU, 4x4, Trk; Spc: Front wheel drive**

Baseline Auto Recyclers, see *Late Vintage*

Glendale; AAA United Auto Parts, 6047 N 57th Av, 85301; 602-931-3919; Sa, Sp; 1.5ac; **88+; D, F, PU, 4x4, Trk; B3; Jp, IH; Spc: Chevy & Dodge Pickup; Corvette, Camaro, Mustang, Cadillac**

All Star Import, *see Vintage*

AMC Salvage, *see Vintage*

Auto Paradise, 7639 N 67th Av, 85301; 602-939-9743; 5ac; **D, PU, 4x4; B3; Domestic only**

J & J Salvage Co, *see Vintage*

JBS Imports, *see Late Vintage*

Japanese Engines by Winter, 6825 N 54th Dr, 85301; 602-930-9112, FAX 602-930-9112; **F; Spc: Used Japanese Engines only**

Richard's Used Pickup Parts, *see Late Vintage*

Hereford; M & R Auto Inc, *see Late Vintage*

Holbrook; Kachina Auto Salvage, *see Vintage*

Kingman; Freds Auto & Truck Salvage, *see Vintage*

Laveen; Ivan's Auto Body Paint, 5620 S 67 Av, 85339; 602-237-2220; 2ac, 150; F; Jpa; Spc: auto body & paint

Mesa; Alma Imports, 236 S Alma School Rd, 85210; 602-898-0311, FAX 602-898-7230, 800-424-2562; CC, Sp; 2ac, 350+; **88+; F, PU, 4x4; Jpa**

BPI Used Engines, see *Late Vintage*

Phoenix; 20th St Auto Parts, see *Late Vintage*

A Select Auto Inc, 3627 W Grant St, 85009; 602-269-1770, FAX 602-415-9722, 800-743-4243; CC, Sa, Sp; 5ac, 800+; **F, PU; mostly Japanese**

A & S Auto Wrecking, *see Late Vintage*

A to Z Auto Recyclers, *see Late Vintage*

A-AA 20th St Auto Parts Inc, *see Late Vintage*

AAA Broadway Auto Parts, *see Vintage*

AAA Late Model Auto Parts, 2532 W Broadway Rd, 850141; 602-268-6809, FAX 602-304-1255; CC, Sa, Sp; 7ac, 900; **D, F, PU, 4x4; B3, Jp, VW**

AAA United Auto & Truck Parts, *see Vintage*

AAA Van & Truck Wrecking Inc, 110 S 32nd St, 85041; 602-267-8056, FAX 602-267-1858, 800-423-2493; CC, Sp; 2ac, 300; **D, PU, 4x4; B3; Pickup & van only; new & used parts**

Adobe Auto & Truck LLC, *see Vintage*

Advantage Auto Recyclers, *see Late Vintage*

All European Models, *see Vintage*

All Imports, see *Late Vintage*

All Japanese Auto & Truck Inc, 4234 E Elwood St, 85040; 602-437-4730, FAX 602-437-4893, 800-888-5277; CC, Sp; 3ac, 800+; **D, F, PU, 4x4; Jpa, vans, few Domestic Pickup & mini-vans**

All Models Foreign, *see Late Vintage*

All Models Ltd, *see Late Vintage*

All Mustang All Camaro, 3230 S 40th St, 85040; 602-437-2727, FAX 602-437-2477, 800-454-8387, www.allmustang.com; CC, Sa, Sp; **60+; D; Fd, Chevy; Mustang, Camaro, Firebird**

American Truck Salvage, *see Late Vintage*

Angel Auto, *see Vintage*

Any Make Auto Parts, *see Late Vintage*

Arizona 4x4 Recyclers Inc, *see Late Vintage*

Arizona Auto Imports, 2405 W Broadway Rd, 85041; 602-243-7447; Sa, Sp, Br; 6ac, 700+; **F; Eur, Jpa; Mostly Japanese**

Arizona Auto Parts, *see Late Vintage*

Arizona Japanese Models, *see Late Vintage*

Arizona Wheelcovers, *see Late Vintage*

Art Coffer Auto Dismantlers, *see Vintage*

Auto Salvage, 943 W Magnolia St, 85007; 602-252-4591; Sp; 3ac; **D; Chr, AMC; Spc: Chrysler, Eagle**

Benrich Auto Wrecking, *see Vintage*

Big Daddys Auto Salvage, *see Vintage*

Bills Truck Parts, *see Vintage*

Broadway Auto Wreckers, *see Vintage*

Certi-Fit Body Parts, *see Vintage*

Chi Town Auto Wrecking, *see Vintage*

Continental Auto & Used Parts, 816 S 19th Av, 85009; 602-253-9504, FAX 602-253-9916; Sa, Sp; 2ac; **D; Lincoln only**

Don Hoctors Auto Wrecking, *see Late Vintage*

Ecology Auto Wrecking, *see Late Vintage*

Freds Auto Wrecking, *see Late Vintage*

G & G Auto Parts, *see Vintage*

G & S Auto Wrecking, *see Vintage*

German Auto Salvage, *see Late Vintage*

Grand Used Auto Parts Inc, *see Late Vintage*

Hirsch Industries Inc, 3219 S 40th St, 85040; 602-437-4495; Wr; **F; Volvo only**

Hoctors Southwest Auto, *see Late Vintage*

Honda Auto Salvage, *see Late Vintage*

I-17 Import Auto Salvage, 22242 N 24th Av, 85027; 602-582-3536; Sa, Sp, Br; 2.5ac, 800; **F, PU, 4x4; Japanese only**

J & R Auto Salvage, 2240 S 35th Av, 85009; 602-272-6416, FAX 602-270-5441, 800-293-0100; Sa, Sp, Br; 8ac; **D, F, PU, 4x4; B3, few AMC, few Jp, Jpa; few British**

Jess & Sons Automotive, *see Vintage*

Just Truck & Van, *see Late Vintage*

K & D Auto Wrecking, *see Vintage*

North 19th Auto Wrecking, *see Late Vintage*

Parts Yard Inc, 9204 N 10th Av, 85021; 602-944-3001; CC, Sp, Br; 3ac, 400; **F, PU, 4x4**

Payless Auto Parts, *see Late Vintage*

Pennington Auto Parts Inc, 3010 W Broadway Rd, 85041; 602-276-5578, FAX 602-276-2463, 800-322-5578; CC, Sa, Sp; 1200; **D, PU, 4x4; B3, Jp, Hr; Spc: Cadillac**

Precision Auto Parts, 1024 E Broadway Rd, 85040; 602-268-8888, FAX 602-268-0317, 800-352-3751, www.precisionteam.com; CC, Sp; 3ac, 2000; **D, few F, PU, 4x4; B3, Camaro, Firebird; mini-vans; wheels**

R & M Auto Salvage, *see Late Vintage*

Ray & Bobs Truck Salvage, *see Late Vintage*

Reeves Auto Wrecking, *see Late Vintage*

Riteway Auto Parts, *see Late Vintage*

Rons Used Pickup Parts, *see Late Vintage*

S & D Auto Wrecking, *see Late Vintage*

Salvage City, *see Vintage*

Speedway Automotive, *see Late Vintage*

Sports Car Recycling, *see Late Vintage*

Yank Your Part, *see Late Vintage*

Show Low; Arrow Metals & Auto Recycling, *see Late Vintage*

Show Low Auto Sales & Wrecking, *see Vintage*

Springerville; Springerville Auto Wreckers, *see Vintage*

Tempe; Mercedes Pete, *see Vintage*

Pick-A-Part of Tempe, *see Vintage*

Arizona – Late Model

Reed's Auto Parts, *see Late Vintage*

Thatcher; Valley Auto Wrecking, Inc, *see Vintage*

Tucson; Ace Pickup Parts, 9110 S Eisenhower Rd, 85706; 520-889-9000, FAX 520-889-5000; CC, Sp, Wr; 3ac; **D, F, PU, 4x4; Pickup & 4x4 Only**

ACS Used Auto Parts, *see Vintage*

Action Auto & Truck, *see Vintage*

Arizona Auto Wrecking Inc, *see Vintage*

Arizona Best Auto & Wrecking, 5151 S Swan Rd, 85706; 520-747-1988, 800-944-2526; CC, Sa, Sp; 8ac; **D, F, PU; B3**

Arizona Wrecksperts Inc, *see Late Vintage*

Auto & Truck Salvage Co, *see Late Vintage*

Automobile Recyclers Inc, 709 W 29th St, 85713; 520-792-0076, FAX 520-792-9474, 800-362-4895; CC, Sp; 7ac, 600; **D, F, PU, 4x4**

Aviation Auto Salvage Inc, 5231 E Drexel Rd, 85706; 520-574-1700, FAX 520-574-2270, 800-227-9746; CC, Sp; 10ac; **F; also domestic mini vans**

Beep Beep Foreign Parts, *see Late Vintage*

Best Salvage Inc, 5550 S Arcadia Av, 85706; 520-574-2448, FAX 520-574-1181; CC, Sp; 6ac; **D, F, PU, 4x4; B3, Nissan**

Big Southwest Import Salvage, *see Late Vintage*

Catalina Auto Recycling, *see Late Vintage*

D Ps Auto Salvage Inc, 5600 S Arcadia Av, 85706; 520-574-9444, FAX 520-574-9180, 800-588-6666; CC, Sa; 4ac, 4000+; **D, F, few PU**

Dixies Auto & GTruck Salvage, *see Late Vintage*

Drake & Son Used Auto & Truck Parts, *see Late Vintage*

Jakes Auto Parts Co, *see Late Vintage*

Mission Auto Parts, *see Late Vintage*

New Way Auto Sales & Parts, 1621 S 4th Av, 85713; 520-622-7781, FAX 520-620-0226, 800-522-7781; CC, Sa, Sp; 3.5ac, 300; **D**

Obarr Auto & Truck Salvage, *see Late Vintage*

Revolvstore Volvo Parts, *see Vintage*

Wahl Brothers Truck Salvage, *see Vintage*

Wilcox; Wilcox Wrecking Yard, *see Vintage*

**Al's Hudson Cars, Parts & Restoration
Maricopa, AZ**

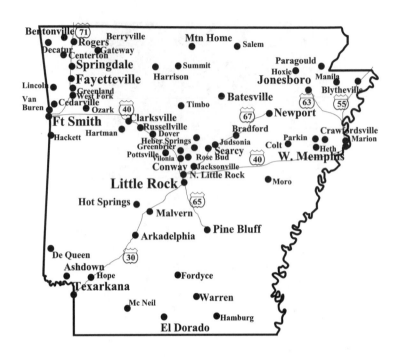

Arkansas

You may be a car nut if

You have more money invested in tools than in furniture

Ray's wReckingyard Roster makes a great gift for the "car nut" on your shopping list. To order, Call Toll Free: 877-4RAYS BOOKS

ARKANSAS

VINTAGE

Batesville; Chinquapin Salvage, 3555 N St Louis St, 72501; 870-698-2263; Sa; 500; 50+; **D, F, PU, 4x4; B**3

Bentonville; Economy Salvage, 513 SE Walton Blvd; 501-273-1049; Sa; 6ac; **40+; D, F, PU, 4x4; B**3**, AMC, VW**

    Gillis Used Cars & Auto Salvage, 2904 Edison Av, 72015; 501-778-3349, FAX 501-315-4446; Sa, Sp, Br; 300+; **50-89; D, F, PU; B**3**, DeSoto, Corvair, Mustang**

    LJC Auto Salvage, 10804 Old 88 Rd, 72015; 501-776-0294; Sa, Sp, UR; 3ac, 300+; **50-88; D, PU, 4x4; B**3**; Spc: Pickup & Vans**

Berryville; Berryville Auto Salvage, 417 Hwy 21 S, 72616; 870-423-6700, 877-277-6700, salvage2@yahoo.com; CC, Sp; 500+; **50+; D, F, PU, 4x4; B**3**, DeSoto; Vans**

Blytheville; Blytheville Auto Salvage, Mississippi Av Co Rd 647, 72315; 870-763-8962; Sa, Sp, UR; 2000; **60+; D, F, PU, 4x4; B**3**, VW**

    Oscars Auto Salvage, 3032 E Co Rd 378, 72315; 870-763-6527, 800-357-8329; Sa; 850; **60-90; D, F, PU, 4x4; B**3**, VW**

Bradford; Second Chance Auto Salvage, 241 Peacock Rd, 72020; 501-724-2038; Sa, Sp, UR; 20ac, 800+; **49-80 D, F, PU, 4x4; B**3**, AMC, Jp, IH**

    Vintage Auto Salvage, 7411 Hwy 367 N, 72020; 501-344-8370; Sa, Sp, UR; 6ac, 550; **26-78; D, PU, Trk; B**3**; Hd, St, Pk, Fr, VW, DeSoto**

Centerton; 102 Towing & Salvage, 13599 W Hwy 102, 72736; 501-795-2422; Sa, Sp; 600; **40-81; D, PU; B**3**; Hd, St, Ks**

Clarksville; Woodard's Auto Salvage, P.O. Box 1310 Hwy 64 E, 72830; 501-754-5533; CC, Sp; **60+; D, F, PU, 4x4, Trk; B**3

Decatur; Decatur Salvage, 8736 S Hwy 59, 72722; 501-752-3403; 3000; **50-95; D, F, PU, 4x4; B**3**, AMC, Jp, IH, VW**

Dover; Dover Auto Salvage, 344 Peaceful Valley Rd, 72837; 501-331-4866; Sa, Sp, UR; 250; **46+; D, F, PU, 4x4; Spc: GM**

El Dorado; Fallin's Wrecking Yard & Used Parts, 1705 S West Av, 71730; 870-862-6381; Sa, UR; 14ac; **46+; D, PU, 4x4, Fm; B**3**, IH; Spc: 70's Chevy Pickup**

    Rusty Acres Auto Salvage, 4687 Moro Bay Hwy, 71730; 870-862-7580, FAX 870-862-2011; Sa, Sp, Br; 7000+; **50+; D, F, PU, 4x4; B**3

Fordyce; Big Bens Used Cars & Salvage, Hwy 79 E, 71742; 870-352-7423, FAX 870-352-7424, 800-343-2367; Sp, UR; 2500; **60+; D, F, PU, Trk, Fm; B**3**, AMC, Jp, St; Spc: Chrysler, John Deere**

Fort Smith; Branson & Sons Salvage, 2615 N 17th St, 72904; 501-785-4273; Sa; 300+; **60-91; D, F, PU; B**3**, AMC; Spc: MGB & Corvair**

    Mayberry Auto Salvage, 1525 N 5th, 72901; 501-783-1500, 800-735-7300; CC, Sa, Sp; 400; **60+; D, F, PU, 4x4; B**3**, IH, VW; Spc: Corvette**

Hamburg; Levis Wrecking Yard, 954 Ashley Rd 12 W, 71646; 870-853-8184; Sa, Sp, Br; 1000; **70s-80s, few 50s & 60s; D, F, PU, 4x4; B**3

Heth; E & R Auto Sales & Salvage, 21458 Hwy 70 E; 870-657-2498; Sa, UR; 5ac; **55-83; D, PU; B**3

Hope; Wylie Glass & Salvage, 1501 Hwy 67 W, 71801; 870-777-2786, FAX 870-777-4213, 800-348-9894; CC, Sp; 500+; **50-90s; D, F, PU, 4x4, Trk; B**3

Hot Springs; Ed Jones Salvage Yard, 589 Fleetwood Dr, 71913; 501-767-1870; Sa; **60-89; D, F, PU; B**3**, AMC, VW**

Jacksonville; Daniel Salvage, 5715 Old Hwy 67, 72076; 501-982-7245; Sa; 1500; **30+; D, F, PU, 4x4; B**3**, AMC, Jp, IH**

Jonesboro; Gregg's Auto Salvage, 1715 Strawfloor Dr, 72404; 870-932-7006; 4000; **50s-91; D, F, PU, 4x4**

Little Rock; A-Auto Salvage, 6623 Asher Av, 72204; 501-562-8862; CC, Sa, UR; **50+; D, F, PU; B**3**; 50s mostly Ford & Chevy**

    Arch Street Auto Salvage & Sls, 10702 Arch St, 72206; 501-888-6623; CC, Br; 450+; **55-93; D, B**3

    N Little Rock Auto Salvage, 600 Dixie Ln N, 72002; 501-945-3364, 800-261-7602; CC, Sa, Sp, UR; **47+; D, F, PU, 4x4, Trk; B**3**, AMC, Jp**

U-Pull-It Auto Parts, 10312 Baseline Rd, 72209; 501-568-7771, FAX 501-568-2274, 800-310-7783 AR only; Sa, UR; 1400; **50+; D, F, PU, 4x4, Trk; B3, AMC, Jp, IH, VW**

Mc Neil; B & J Used Car & Truck Parts, 3475 Hwy 98, 71770; 870-695-3776; Sa, Sp, UR; 350; **41-87; D, F, PU, Trk; B3, St**

Mountain Hope; Buck or Two Auto Salvage, 21 Buck or Two Ln, 72653; 870-425-9035; Sa, Sp, UR; 500; **60-89; D, F, PU; B3**

Mountain Pine; Razorback Sales & Salvage, 403 Buckthorn Ln, 71956; 501-767-0577; Sa; 600; **60-85; D, F, PU, 4x4, Trk; B3, AMC**

Pine Bluff; Steve's Auto Salvage & Scrap, 135 Wally Dr, 71602; 870-247-2452; Sa, Sp, UR; 10ac; **60-90s; D, F, PU, 4x4, Trk, Fm, In, Cn; B3**

Rose Bud; Matthews Mustang Parts & Svc, 731 Hwy 5, 72137; 501-556-5617; CC, Sa, Sp, Wr; 200; **64+; D; Mustang only; also new parts**

Searcy; Searcy Auto Salvage, 3667 Hwy 367 S, 72143; 501-268-5824, FAX 501-268-3620, 800-444-2831; CC, Sp, UR; **13ac; 70+, few 50s & 60s; D, F, PU; B3**

Springdale; Horn's Auto Salvage, 2842 Habbeton Rd, 72764; 501-751-2612; Sa, Sp; 25ac, 2000; **50-94; D, PU; B3, St, Pk, Wy; Spc: 67-72 Pickup, Corvette, muscle cars**

Texarkana; A-1 Auto Salvage, 2815 East St, 71854; 870-773-6006, FAX 870-773-3315, 888-965-2715; CC, Sa; 4000; **60+; D, F, PU, 4x4; B3, AMC**

Timbo; Jennings Auto Salvage, HC 73 Box 616, 72680; 870-746-4647; Sa, Sp; 100; **70-93, few 34-69; D, F, PU, 4x4; B3, AMC, IH, VW**

Van Buren; Shibley's Salvage, 3522 Oliver Springs Rd, 72951; 501-474-9187; Sa, UR; 50; **60-90; D, PU, Trk, Fm; B3; Spc: Chevy Pickup 67-72, Vega**

Warren; Cowboy & Son Wrecking, 194 Bradley 95 Rd, 71671; 870-226-7276; Sa, UR; 600; **60-85; D, F, PU, 4x4; B3, VW**

West Memphis; Arkansas Bridgeport Rd Auto SL, 242 Worley Rd W, 38670; 870-735-3763; Sa, Br; 1200; **60-94; D, F, PU, 4x4; B3**

LATE VINTAGE

Arkadelphia; Gene's Auto Salvage, 3761 Old Hwy 67 S, 71923; 870-246-5294; Sa, UR; 200; **70-91; D, F; B3**

Batesville; Chinquapin Salvage, *see Vintage*

　Richardson Salvage, 349 Alan Chapel Rd, 72501; 870-251-2666; Sa; 100+; **80-92; D; B3**

Bentonville; Economy Salvage, *see Vintage*

　Gillis Used Cars & Auto Salvage, *see Vintage*

　LJC Auto Salvage, *see Vintage*

Berryville; Berryville Auto Salvage, *see Vintage*

Blytheville; Bills Auto Salvage, 2304 S Elm St, 72315; 870-763-1783, FAX 870-763-6788, 800-763-1787; CC, Sa, Sp, UR; 800+; **70-92; D, F, PU, 4x4; B3, AMC, IH, VW**

　Blytheville Auto Salvage, *see Vintage*

　Oscars Auto Salvage, *see Vintage*

　Steve Fulk's Auto Salvage, 536 Hillman St, 72315; 870-532-2270, 888-242-3078; Sa, Sp; 50; **70-90; D, F, PU, 4x4; B3**

Bradford; Second Chance Auto Salvage, *see Vintage*

　Vintage Auto Salvage, *see Vintage*

Cedarville; B & L Salvage, 10247 N Hwy 59, 72736; 501-474-6763; 250+; **80-94; D; Chr; Chrysler & Dodge only**

Centerton; 102 Towing & Salvage, *see Vintage*

Clarksville; Clarksville Salvage, Hudson Springs Rd S, 72830; 501-754-6125, 800-445-6125; CC, Sp; 17ac; **80s; D, Trk; B3; Spc: Truck**

　Woodard's Auto Salvage, *see Vintage*

Colt; Ben's Auto Salvage, 9680 Hwy 1 N, 72326; 870-630-1497; Sa, Sp; 475; **65+; D, F, PU; B3; Spc: Olds**

Decatur; Decatur Salvage, *see Vintage*

Dover; Dover Auto Salvage, *see Vintage*

El Dorado; Fallin's Wrecking Yard & Used Parts, *see Vintage*

　Rusty Acres Auto Salvage, *see Vintage*

Fayetteville; Sixty-Two Auto Salvage, 3595 W 6th St, 72701; 501-267-4433, FAX 501-443-2078, 800-632-0192; CC, Sp; 2200; **80+; D, F, PU, 4x4; B3, AMC, Jp**

Fordyce; Big Bens Used Cars & Salvage, *see Vintage*

Fort Smith; A-Jac's Auto Salvage, 410 N St, 72901; 501-783-5922; Sa; 100+; **80+; D, F, PU, 4x4; B3**

    Branson & Sons Salvage, *see Vintage*

    Mayberry Auto Salvage, *see Vintage*

    Sharps Auto Salvage, 13811 Hwy 45, 72916; 501-638-7005; **80-94; D, F**

Gateway; Gateway Auto Salvage, 19481 Hwy 62, 72733; 501-656-3211; 400; **70-89; D, F, PU, 4x4; B3, Jp; Spc: Pickup & vans**

Greenbrier; Watts Auto Salvage & Wrecker, 4 Oak Hill Ln, 72058; 501-679-5172; Sa, UR; 200+; **70-89; D, F, PU, 4x4; B3**

Greenland; Greenland Auto Salvage, 304 S Main St, 72737; 501-521-3137; Sp; 300; **70-93; D, PU, 4x4; B3**

Hamburg; Levis Wrecking Yard, *see Vintage*

Harrison; Terry Yeager Auto Salvage, PO Box 673; 6428 Hwy 65 N, 72601; 870-741-3500, FAX 870-741-3501, 800-632-2960; CC, Sp; 2000+; **70+; D, F, PU, 4x4; B3, AMC, Jp**

Heber Springs; Heber Truck Parts, 99 Spinks Rd, 72543; 501-362-8650; Sa, UR; 100; **70+; D, F, PU, 4x4, Trk; B3, Jp, IH; Pickup & Truck only**

    Jay's Auto Salvage, 1122 S 13th St, 72543; 501-362-2534, jaysmoto@arkansas.net; CC, Sa, Br; 300; **70-89; D, F, PU; B3**

Heth; E & R Auto Sales & Salvage, *see Vintage*

Hope; Wylie Glass & Salvage, *see Vintage*

Hot Springs; Ed Jones Salvage Yard, *see Vintage*

Jacksonville; Daniel Salvage, *see Vintage*

    Southbend Auto Salvage, 131 Christy Ln, 72076; 501-985-3361; Sa, Sp; 75+; **80-94; D, PU; B3**

Jonesboro; B & B Auto Salvage, 4606 Kellers Chapel Rd, 72404; 870-972-6650, FAX 870-268-0018; Sa, Sp, UR; 40ac, 300; **70+; D, F, PU, 4x4; B3, Jp, IH**

    Brown's Auto Salvage & Towing, 1510 Willett Rd, 72401; 870-932-5381, 800-530-7607; CC, Sp; 1500; **80-93; D, F, PU, 4x4; B3, AMC, VW**

    Gregg's Auto Salvage, *see Vintage*

    Sharp Industries, 300 Co Rd 764, 72401; 870-931-1955, FAX 870-935-2267, 800-824-6777; Sa, Sp, Br; 80+; **71+; F, PU, 4x4; VW; Spc: Japanese & German**

Judsonia; Y & Y Auto Salvage, 3438 Hwy 157, 72081; 501-729-3842; 3ac; **70+; D, PU; Ford & Chevy only; mostly rebuilds, sells spare parts**

Kenton; Bypass Auto Salvage, 814 Pete Hall Rd, 72802; 501-742-1602; Sp; 400; **70+; D, F, PU, 4x4; B3, AMC; Spc: Chrysler**

Little Rock; A-Auto Salvage, *see Vintage*

    Arch Street Auto Salvage & Sls, *see Vintage*

    Caples Auto Repair & Wrecking, 10702 Arch St, 72206; 501-888-2009; CC, Sa, Sp, Br; 40ac, 300; **70-85; D, F, PU, 4x4, Trk, Fm; B3, AMC, Jp, IH**

    Eureka Auto Salvage, 300 Bold Ln N, 72117; 501-945-3021; Sa, UR; 25+; **70-89; D, F, PU; B3**

    N Little Rock Auto Salvage, *see Vintage*

    Otter Creek Auto Salvage, 10616 Stagecoach Rd, 72209; 501-455-4431, FAX 501-455-1326, 800-446-8837; Sa, UR; 750; **80-94; D, F, PU, 4x4; B3, AMC, VW**

    Rose City Auto Salvage, 7205 Hwy 70 N, 72117; 501-945-9685, FAX 501-982-7452; CC, Sa, Sp; 250; **72+; D, F, PU, 4x4; B3; Spc: Chevy Pickup**

    Taylor's Auto Salvage, 7307 Hwy 70 N, 72117; 501-945-0406; Sa, UR, PL; 1000; **77-93; D, F, PU, 4x4; B3**

    U-Pull-It Auto Parts, *see Vintage*

Mc Neil; B & J Used Car & Truck Parts, *see Vintage*

Malvern; Williams & Son Wrecking Yard, Hwy 67 S, 72104; 501-332-6462; **75-89; D, PU; B3**

Manila; Tuckers Shop & Salvage, 2909 S State Hwy 77, 72442; 870-561-4801; **86-87; D; B3**

25

Marion; Airport Auto Salvage, 5848 US Hwy 70, 72364; 870-735-6000, FAX 870-735-4230, 800-704-2318; Sa, UR; 400+; **70-92; D, F, PU, 4x4; B3**

Moro; Lee County Auto Salvage, 5968 Hwy 79 W, 72368; 870-295-5652; Sa, Sp; 100; **85-90; D, F, PU; B3**

Mountain Hope; Buck or Two Auto Salvage, *see Vintage*

Mountain Pine; Razorback Sales & Salvage, *see Vintage*

Newport; Mc Clouds Auto Salvage, 6515 Hwy 67 N, 72473; 870-523-2950, 888-284-9076; Sa, Sp; 200; **80-90; D, PU; B3**

Ozark; Nichols Auto Salvage, RR2 Box 138 A, 72949; 501-667-4748, FAX 501-667-5650, 800-530-7576; Sa, UR; 450+; **80-90; D, F, PU; B3**

Paragould; Weaver Auto Sales & Salvage, 927 N 15th Av, 72450; 870-236-6895, 800-465-2737; Sp; 400; **70+; D, PU; B3**

Parkin; Alexander's Car Farm, 53 Cross 451, 72373; 870-755-9888; Sa, UR; 150+; **mid 70s-93; D, F, PU; B3**

Pine Bluff;

Pine Bluff; Smith Auto Salvage, 4001 W 9th Av, 71603; 870-534-7503; Sa; 1000+; **78-89; D, F, PU; B3**

Spurlock's Auto Salvage, 703 S Spruce St, 71603; 870-536-4955, FAX 870-536-3910, 800-950-4218; CC, Sp, Br; 6ac; **82-96; D, F, PU, 4x4; B3**

Steve's Auto Salvage & Scrap, *see Vintage*

Rose Bud; Matthews Mustang Parts & Svc, *see Vintage*

Russellville; Barefield's Auto Salvage, 3316 Bernice Av, 72802; 501-967-3263, FAX 501-968-5123, 800-748-8811; CC, Sa, Sp; 550+; **PU: 80+; Car: 90+; D, F, PU, 4x4; B3; Spc: Pickup & SUV**

Salem; Lynn's Auto Salvage & Sales, Box 131, Hwy 395 N, 72576; 870-895-2054, FAX 870-895-2322; CC, Sa; 500; **80-93; D, PU, 4x4, Trk; B3, IH; Spc: Pickup**

Searcy; Searcy Auto Salvage, *see Vintage*

Springdale; Horn's Auto Salvage, *see Vintage*

Meadors Truck & Van Salvage, 4003 Bus Hwy 71 S, 72764; 501-751-2349; Sa; 300; **80+, few 70s; D; B3; Spc: Pickup & Vans**

Summit; Mullins Salvage Yard, Hwy 202, 72677; 870-449-6941, FAX 870-449-5289, 800-494-8884; CC, Sp; 20ac, 500; **80+; D, F, PU, 4x4; B3**

Texarkana; A-1 Auto Salvage, *see Vintage*

Timbo; Jennings Auto Salvage, *see Vintage*

Van Buren; A-1 Auto Wrecking, 4306 Alma Hwy, 72956; 501-471-5220; Sa, UR; 250+; **65-89; D, PU; B3, AMC, IH**

Gene's Salvage, 3909 N Hwy 59, 72956; 501-474-2500; Sa; 400+; **80+, few earlier; D; Spc: Chrysler**

J & G Auto Sales & Salvage, 3409 Baggett Moses Dr, 72956; 501-474-5863; Sa, UR; 100; **70-89; D; Spc: Chevy; open weekends only**

Nichols Auto Salvage II, 4300 Alma Hwy, 72956; 501-474-5224, 800-462-8801; Sa, Sp, UR; 2ac, 300; **70+; F, PU, 4x4; Jpa, VW; Foreign only**

Shibley's Salvage, *see Vintage*

Vilonia; Volvos Only, 3 Charles Rd N; 851 Hwy 36, 72173; 501-849-2484, FAX 501-849-3119; CC, Sp; 300; **F; Volvo only; 240, 740, 960 series**

Warren; Cowboy & son Wrecking, *see Vintage*

W & A Auto Sales & Salvage, 519 Hwy 4 W, 71671; 870-226-5246, 800-581-4344; Sp; 700; **70+; D, F, PU, 4x4; B3; Spc: GM Pickup**

West Fork; J & L Auto Salvage, 6176 S Hwy 71, 72774; 501-839-3600; 200; **75-85; D, F, PU; B3**

West Memphis; Arkansas Bridgeport Rd Auto SL, *see Vintage*

<u>LATE MODEL</u>

Ashdown; Wheels Auto Salvage, 222 Hwy 71 S, 71822; 870-898-5174, FAX 870-898-2038; CC, Sa, Sp, PL; 1500; **D, F, PU, 4x4**

Batesville; Chinquapin Salvage, *see Vintage*

Bentonville; Economy Salvage, *see Vintage*

Berryville; Berryville Auto Salvage, *see Vintage*

Blytheville; Blytheville Auto Salvage, *see Vintage*

Cedarville; B & L Salvage, *see Late Vintage*

Clarksville; Woodard's Auto Salvage, *see Vintage*

Colt; Ben's Auto Salvage, *see Late Vintage*

Cochran Auto Salvage, 236 Jake Taylor Hill Rd, 72326; 870-633-8668; Sa; 500; **D, F, PU, 4x4**

Conway; Potter Salvage, 1310 E Oak St, 72032; 501-327-5170, FAX 501-327-6689, 877-870-4771; CC, Sa, Sp; 200+; **D, F, PU, 4x4; B3, Jp; Spc: 87-93 Mustang GT, Jeep Cherokee, Nissan 300ZX**

Worman's Auto Salvage, 650 Simon Rd, 72032; 501-327-0063, FAX 501-329-7339, 800-482-9338; CC, Sp; 900; **D, F, PU; Fd, GM**

Crawfordsville; Smith Auto Sales & Salvage, 7468 I-55, 72327; 870-732-5736, FAX 870-739-5605, 800-866-7920; Sp; 150; **D, PU, 4x4; Spc: Ford**

Decatur; Decatur Salvage, *see Vintage*

DeQueen; CCS Auto Salvage, 868 E Collin Raye Dr, 71832; 870-584-7615, FAX 870-642-7587, 800-426-9133; CC, Sp; 300; **D**

Dover; Dover Auto Salvage, *see Vintage*

El Dorado; Fallin's Wrecking Yard & Used Parts, *see Vintage*

Reed's Auto Salvage, 1709 N Quaker Av, 71730; 870-862-4291, 800-634-8338; CC, Sp; 500+; **D, F, PU, 4x4**

Rusty Acres Auto Salvage, *see Vintage*

Fayetteville; Highway 62 Auto Salvage, *see Late Vintage*

Mabry's Auto Salvage Inc, 185 E Mabry Ln, 72701; 501-521-1586, FAX 800-632-0026 x 227, 800-632-0026; CC, Sp, Br; 1000; **D, F, PU, 4x4**

Sixty-Two Auto Salvage, *see Late Vintage*

Fordyce; Big Bens Used Cars & Salvage, *see Vintage*

Fort Smith; A-Jac's Auto Salvage, *see Late Vintage*

Mayberry Auto Salvage, *see Vintage*

Sharps Auto Salvage, *see Late Vintage*

Greenland; Greenland Auto Salvage, *see Late Vintage*

Hackett; Smith Auto Salvage, 407 S Vine St, 72901; 501-638-8920; UR; 100+; **D**

Harrison; Harrison Auto Salvage, Hwy 62-65 S, 72601; 870-743-2308, FAX 870-743-5623, 800-432-9727, gfish@alltel.net; CC, Sp; 750+; **D, F, PU, 4x4**

Poor Boy's Auto Salvage, 1223 Hwy 7 N, 72601; 870-741-7283, 877-737-4022; CC, Sp; 300; **D, F, PU, 4x4, Fm; B3, Jp**

Terry Yeager Auto Salvage, *see Late Vintage*

Hartman; Arkansas Pik-A-Part Auto Salvage, Rt 1 Box 185; Hwy 352, 72840; 501-754-7652, FAX 501-754-6004, 800-267-7467; CC, Sa, Sp, PL; 1200; **D, PU, 4x4**

Heber Springs; Heber Truck Parts, *see Late Vintage*

Hope; Wylie Glass & Salvage, *see Vintage*

Hot Springs; Airway Auto Sales & Salvage, 119 Woodall Cir, 71913; 501-624-5166; Sp; 40+; **D, F, PU, 4x4; Spc: Pickup**

Dee's Auto Salvage, 511 Charming Heights Dr, ; 501-767-1400; **D, F, PU, 4x4**

Hoxie; Pratt's Auto Salvage, 170 Industrial Dr, 72433; 870-886-3205, FAX 870-886-1510, 800-348-6680; CC, Sp; 1000+; **D, F, PU, 4x4**

Jacksonville; Daniel Salvage, *see Vintage*

Jacksonville Auto Salvage, 2966 Arkansas Hwy 294, 72076; 501-982-6647, 800-355-6647; CC, Sp; 1200; **D, F, PU, 4x4; Spc: Cadillac**

Sonny's Auto Salvage, 3251 Arkansas Hwy 294, 72076; 501-982-7451, FAX 501-982-4876, 800-482-9985; CC, Sa, Sp; 350+; **D, F, PU, 4x4**

Southbend Auto Salvage, *see Late Vintage*

Jonesboro; A-State Auto Sales & Salvage, 2501 Greensboro Rd, 72401; 870-935-7400, FAX 870-935-3494, 800-632-1264; CC, Sp, PL; 800; **D, F, PU, 4x4; Spc: new headlights**

B & B Auto Salvage, *see Late Vintage*

Brown's Auto Salvage & Towing, *see Late Vintage*

Economy Auto Salvage, 327 Co Rd 311, 72401; 870-932-3789, FAX 870-932-7658, 800-543-5575; CC, Sp; 2000+; **D, F, PU, 4x4**

Sharp Industries, *see Late Vintage*

Judsonia; Y & Y Auto Salvage, *see Late Vintage*

Kenton; Bypass Auto Salvage, *see Late Vintage*

Lincoln; J & R Auto Salvage & Used Cars, 609 E North St, 72744; 501-824-5737; Sp; 8.5ac; **D, F, PU; B3**

Little Rock; A-Auto Salvage, *see Vintage*

All Late Model, 1700 Hwy 161 N, 72117; 501-945-9378, 888-945-8881, allcamaro@aol.com; CC, Sa, Sp, Wr; 1200; **D**

Arch Street Auto Salvage & Sls, *see Vintage*

Highway 5 Auto Salvage, 5721 Stagecoach Rd, 72204; 501-455-0024, FAX 501-455-8975, www.hwy5salv.aol.com; CC, Sa, Sp, UR; 450+; **D, F, PU, 4x4**

N Little Rock Auto Salvage, *see Vintage*

Otter Creek Auto Salvage, *see Late Vintage*

Rose City Auto Salvage, *see Late Vintage*

Taylor's Auto Salvage, *see Late Vintage*

U-Pull-It Auto Parts, *see Vintage*

Malvern; Clints Foreign Car Salvage, Hwy 270 N, 72104; 501-337-1453; Sp; **F**

Marion; Airport Auto Salvage, *see Late Vintage*

North Little Rock; Arkansas Foreign Car Parts Inc, 7005 Hwy 70, 72117; 501-945-2333, FAX 501-945-8057, 800-445-6730; CC, Sp; 700; **Foreign only**

J & J Foreign Auto Parts, 8226 MacArthur Dr, 72118; 501-771-2772, 800-433-6196; CC, Sa, Sp, Wr; **Foreign only**

Paragould; Weaver Auto Sales & Salvage, *see Late Vintage*

Parkin; Alexander's Car Farm, *see Late Vintage*

Pine Bluff; Spurlock's Auto Salvage, *see Late Vintage*

Steve's Auto Salvage & Scrap, *see Vintage*

Pottsville; 64/40 Auto Salvage & Glass, 5059 Hwy 64 E, 72858; 501-968-6440, FAX 501-968-8434, 800-748-8821; Sa, Sp, PL; 500; **D, F, PU**

Rogers; Junk Yard Dog, Inc, 2315 S 7 St, 72758; 501-636-8797, 800-422-6675; CC, Sa, Sp, UR; 10ac, 600; **D, F, PU, 4x4**

Payless Auto Salvage, 13385 Cloverdale Rd, 72756; 501-636-3225, FAX 501-636-4047; CC, Sa, Sp; 1000; **D, F, PU, 4x4**

Rose Bud; Matthews Mustang Parts & Svc, *see Vintage*

Russellville; Barefield's Auto Salvage, *see Late Vintage*

Salem; Lynn's Auto Salvage & Sales, *see Late Vintage*

Searcy; Searcy Auto Salvage, *see Vintage*

Springdale; Horn's Auto Salvage, *see Vintage*

M & M Slavage, 1574 Moody Ln, 72764; 501-756-3457; 1000; **D, F, PU, 4x4**

Meadors Truck & Van Salvage, *see Late Vintage*

Summit; Mullins Salvage Yard, *see Late Vintage*

Texarkana; A-1 Auto Salvage, *see Vintage*

Timbo; Jennings Auto Salvage, *see Vintage*

Van Buren; Gene's Salvage, *see Vintage*

Nichols Auto Salvage II, *see Late Vintage*

Russell Imports Auto Salvage, 2348 Old Uniontown Rd, 72956; 501-474-8559, 800-331-6388; CC, Sa, Sp; 400; **Foreign only**

West Memphis; A-1 Salvage, 1408 Thompson Av W, 72301; 870-735-3535, FAX 870-732-1010, 800-240-3795; CC, Sp, UR; **D, F, PU, 4x4**

Arkansas Bridgeport Rd Auto SL, *see Vintage*

Chevys
Speedway Auto Wreckers
Erie, CO

California – Central

Please use the cards in the back to let us know about yards we may have missed, or any other comments or information for future editions of Ray's wReckingyard Roster

CALIFORNIA – CENTRAL

VINTAGE

Adelanto; Ecology Auto Wrecking, 11200 Alden Rd, 92301; 760-246-8616, FAX 760-246-4027; CC, Sa, UR; 1700; **50+; D, F; B**3; **$1.00 admission**

Arroyo Grande; R & R Auto Wrecking, 738 Sheridan Rd, 93420; 805-343-6469; CC, Sa, Sp, UR; **50-89, few 90s; D, F, PU, Trk; B**3, **DeSoto**

Atascadero; Atascadero New-Used Auto Parts, 6501 Via Av, 93422; 805-466-0810; CC, Sa, Sp; 8ac, 200; **50+; D, F, PU, 4x4; B**3, **AMC, Jp, IH, VW**

Bakersfield; A & A Auto Wrecking, 2586 S Union Av, 93307; 805-832-2900; Sa, Br; 300; **53+; D, F; B**3; **65+ Mustang, 53+ Buick, 66-68 GTO**

Ace Auto Dismantler, 3209 Edison Hwy, 93307; 805-366-2040; CC, Sa; **60+; D, F; B**3

Ashmores Auto Wrecking, 2586 S Union Av, 93307; 805-832-2900; Sa, Sp; 300; **60+; D, F, PU, 4x4, Trk; B**3

C & L Auto Dismantlers, 3413 Edison Hwy, 93307; 805-366-7710, FAX 805-366-5670; CC, Sa, Sp; 4ac; **60+; D, F, PU; B**3; **Spc: Pickup**

J & J Auto Dismantling, 7780 S Union Av, 93307; 805-397-6020; Sa, Sp; 100; **55-83; D, F; B**3

Lamont Auto Wrecking, 7857 Berry Rd, 93307; 805-366-7112; Sa, Br; 300; **50-89; D, PU; B**3; **Mostly 70-89**

Pickup Salvage Co, 2143 S Union Av, 93307; 805-833-6100, FAX 805-833-2908, 800-323-1401, www.pickupsalvage.com; CC, Sa, Sp, Br; 2.5ac; **50+; D, F, PU, Trk; B**3; **Pickup & Truck only**

Pick Your Part Auto Wrecking, 2120 S Union Av, 93307; 805-833-0800, FAX 805-937-2193; CC, Sa, UR; 13ac; **50+; D, F; B**3; **$1 Admission**

Surgeners Auto Wrecking, 730 Angus Ln, 93308; 805-399-2331; Sp; 8ac; **50+; D, F, PU; B**3; **Mostly 70-89**

United Auto Dismantling, 2115 S Union Av, 93307; 805-832-8733, FAX 805-836-0290, 800-832-8733; CC, Sp; **60+; D, F, PU, 4x4; B**3; **Spc: Pickup**

Bishop; Mingo's Automotive, 640 S Main St, 93514; 760-873-4531; CC, Sp, UR; 300; **30+; D, F; B**3, **IH, St, Ks**

Bradley; Jardines Salvage & Auto, 2064 Jolon Rd, 93426; 805-472-2226; Sa, UR; 250; **60-79; D; B**3; **Mostly Chevy**

California City; Whites Auto Dismantling, 7731 Moss Av, 93505; 760-373-4205; CC, Sa, Sp, Br; 100; **50+; D, F, PU; B**3, **St**

Campbell; British Motorsports, 1143 Dell Av, 95008; 408-370-7174, FAX 408-370-0240; CC, Sa, Sp; .5ac; **50+; F; British only**

Dos Palos; Jones Wrecking Yard, 8869 Blossom Av, 93620; 209-392-3194; Sa, Sp, UR; 400; **50+; D, F; B**3; **Open Sunday**

Fresno; Continental Auto Dismantler, 3465 S Chestnut Av, 93725; 559-268-4623; Sa; 200; **65+; F; VW; All VW air cooled**

Dan's Auto Parts & Wrecking, 6130 W Shaw Av, 93722; 559-275-2799; Sa, Sp, Wr; 200; **60+; D, F, PU; B**3, **St; Open Sunday**

Fresno Auto Dismantling, 3515 Golden State Blvd, 93725; 559-485-3660, FAX 559-485-0513, 800-675-4880; Sa, Sp; 200+; **50+; D, F; B**3; **few 20+ wheels & parts**

Globe Antique Auto Parts, 2696 S Elm Av, 93706; 559-264-3295; Sp, Wr; **20s-53; D; B**3, **Hd, Ns, St, Pk; Other old parts**

Levan Auto Body Parts, 1828 G St, 93706; 559-264-0295, FAX 559-264-0298, 800-300-0295; CC, Sa, Wr; **65+; D; Ford Mustang after market exterior parts only**

Romo Auto Wrecking & Towing, 4625 N Golden State Blvd, 93722; 559-275-4823; Sa, Sp, Br; 12ac; **30-89; D, F, PU; B**3, **Hd, Ns, St, Pk**

Westside Self-Service Auto, 2640 W Whitesbridge Rd, 93706; 559-237-5591; Sa, UR; 11ac; **60-86; D, F, PU, 4x4; B**3

Gilroy; Gilroy Auto Wrecking, 6680 Monterey Hwy, 95020; 408-842-3598, FAX 408-847-6827; Sa, Wr; **55+; D, F, PU; B**3; **55-57 Chevy; Spc: 69+ Vans & Pickup**

Goleta; Goleta Auto Salvage, 5939 Placencia St, 93117; 805-964-6921; CC, Sa, Sp, Br; 300+; **50-90; D, F, PU, 4x4; B**3, **AMC, VW**

Santa Barbara Auto Salvage, 891 S Kellogg Av, 93117; 805-683-8557, FAX 805-683-2817; CC, Sa, Sp; 1000; **48+; D, F; B**3

Hanford; American Self Serve, 10644 8th Av, 93230; 559-587-9226; Sa, UR; 20ac, 2000; **60-91; D, F, PU; B**3, VW

Hanford Auto Dismantling, 12250 S 11th Av, 93230; 559-584-9274; Sa, Sp; 400+; **50+; D, F, PU; B**3

Hesperia; Atlas Truck & Auto Salvage, 10592 E Av, 92345; 760-244-9358, FAX 760-244-3001; CC, Sa, Sp (CA only); 10ac, 1000; **60+; D, F, PU, 4x4; B**3, VW

Chris Volkswagen Parts, 17011 Darwin Av, 92345; 760-244-3446, FAX 760-244-0669, vwprts4u@aol.com; CC, Sa, Sp; 350; **50-87; F; Eur; VW, Audi, Porsche; Spc: VW**

Cox Auto Salvage, 10801 E Av, 92345; 760-244-9333; Sa, Sp, Br; 10ac, 600; **30+; D, F, PU, 4x4; B**3, AMC, Jp, IH, Hd, Ns, St, Pk, Ks

King City; Sirak's Repair, 50381 Pine Canyon Rd, 93930; 831-385-4733; Sa, Sp, Br; 4000; **60+; D, F, PU, 4x4, Trk; B**3

Lamont; Weedpatch Auto Dismantling, 8209 Buena Vista Blvd, 93241; 661-845-9475; Sa, Sp; 150+; **60+; D, PU; B**3; Spc: Chevy PU, Camaro, Chevelle, Nova

Lancaster; West Coast VW Cores, 42559 6th St E, 93535; 805-726-9915; Sp, Wr; **50+; F; VW motors only**

Lemoore; Economy Auto Wrecking, 977 W Iona Av, 93245; 559-924-1045, FAX 559-924-1285; Sa, UR; 3000; **60+; D, F, PU, 4x4, Trk; B**3, AMC; Spanish

Hughes Auto Wrecking & Towing, 300 Hwy 41, 93245; 559-924-9521, 800-464-6263; CC, Sa, Sp, PL; 1500; **60+; D, F, PU, 4x4; B**3, VW

Littlerock; Jones Auto Dismantlers, 37855 90th St E, 93543; 805-944-1335; Sa, Sp, UR; 20ac; **60+; D, F; B**3; Spc: Rambler & Cadillac

Lompoc; Bedlo Inc, 3052 Harris Grade Rd, 93436; 805-733-2521; Sa; 1.5ac, 850; **60+; D, F; B**3, AMC

Los Banos; Romero's Towing, 1422 Ward Rd, 93635; 209-826-1605, FAX 209-826-9024; CC, Sa, Sp, UR, PL; 2000; **60-90; D, F, PU, 4x4, Trk; B**3

Madera; 3 Boys Auto Wrecking, 19480 Hwy 99, 93637; 559-674-7374, FAX 559-674-7494; CC, Sp; 500; **50+; D, F, PU, 4x4; B**3

Mariposa; Pearson's Auto Dismantling, 2343 Hwy 49S, 95338; 209-742-7442; Sa; 3000; **50+; D, PU; B**3, AMC, Ns, St; Open: Friday & Saturday only

Milpitas; Pick Your Part, 595 Trade Zone Blvd, 95035; 408-262-4500; CC, Sa, UR; 700; **60+; D, F, PU, 4x4; B**3, AMC, Jp, VW; Open Sunday

Modesto; Ace Auto Wreckers, 2736 W Hatch Rd, 95358; 209-537-4722; Sa; **60+; D, F, PU, 4x4; B**3

Auto Recyclers of Modesto, 432 S 9th St, 95351; 209-526-0181; CC, Sa, Sp; 200+; **50+; F, PU, 4x4**

Benson's Auto Dismantling, 573 Crows Landing Rd, 95351; 209-527-4000, FAX 209-527-3603; Sa, Sp; 300+; **60-89; D, PU, 4x4; B**3, IH; Spc: Lincoln & Mustang

Farriester Auto Wreckers, 547 Crows Landing Rd, 95351; 209-524-6730; Sa, Sp; 600; **46+; D; B**3, Pk

Holt Auto Wrecking, 707 Sutter Av, 95351; 209-524-7432; Sa, Sp; 300+; **60+; D, F, PU, 4x4; B**3, AMC, Jp, IH, St; Mostly Pickup & Vans

Holt Auto Wrecking, 2734 W Hatch Rd, 95358; 209-538-3803, FAX 209-538-8255; Sa; 200+; **50-89; D, PU, 4x4, Trk; B**3, IH, St, Cr; Spc: Chevy Trucks

Morgan Hill; California Salvage & Auto Parts, 18960 Monterey Rd, 95037; 408-779-9186, FAX 408-779-5827; CC, Sa, UR; 8ac, 800; **50-89; D, PU; B**3

Newhall; Giant Auto Wreckers, 23944 Pine St, 91321; 805-259-4678; CC, Sp, Br; 100; **50+; D, F, PU, 4x4, Trk; B**3, AMC, Jp

Oakdale; Oakdale Auto Wreckers & Towing, 10649 Sierra Rd, 95361; 209-847-2224, FAX 209-847-0316; CC, Sa, Sp; 3000; **50+; D, F, PU, 4x4; B**3, Jp, IH, VW

Orange Cove; Donaldson's Auto Dismantling, 143 Anchor Av, 93646; 209-626-4322; Sp; 10ac, 1000+; **23+; D, F; B**3; Dodge Bros, Ford Model A

Oxnard; Dynacorn International, 1050 S "A" St, 93030; 805-486-2611, FAX 805-486-7740, 800-766-5894, www.dynacorn.com; CC, Sa, Sp, Wr; **67+; D, F, PU, 4x4; B3, AMC, Jp, IH, VW; 67+ VW; Mostly 80+; Parts Only**

Fifth St Auto Salvage, 501 Pacific Av, 93030; 805-486-8429, FAX 805-487-8609; CC, Sa, Sp; 2ac; **60+; D, F, PU, 4x4, Trk; B3, AMC, VW**

Paso Robles; Paso Robles Auto Wrecking, 5755 Monterey Rd, 93446; 805-238-3738, FAX 805-238-5687, 800-549-3738; CC, Sa, Sp; 8ac, 1000; **30+; D, F, PU, 4x4; B3, AMC, Jp, IH, St, Pk; Tries to keep older cars; Builds up cars**

Plymouth; Foothill Garage & Wrecking, 9408 Pacific St, 95669; 209-245-3370, FAX 209-245-3370; CC, Sa, Sp, Br; 300; **50-93, few 40s; D, F, PU, 4x4, Trk; B3, AMC, Jp, IH**

Porterville; Cemo Motor Sales & Auto Wrecking, 1388 S Main St, 93257; 209-784-1389; Sa; 2ac; **50-90; D, F, PU, 4x4; B3, AMC, Jp, IH, Hd, Ns, St, Ks, Fr, VW**

Hoods Motors, 20990 Avenue 152, 93257; 209-784-1760; Sa, Br; 4ac; **50+; D, F, PU, 4x4, Trk; B3; Mostly 90+**

Tule Auto Dismantlers, 22045 Avenue 152, 93257; 209-781-0418; Sa, UR; **100+; 66+; D, F, PU; B3**

Ridgecrest; Sierra Auto Recycling, 401 W Inyokern Rd, 93555; 760-446-5559, FAX 760-446-3047, 800-346-8733; CC, Sp; 10ac, 2000+; **60+; D, F, PU; B3, IH**

Speedway Auto Dismantling, 1567 N Mahan St, 93555; 760-446-4592, FAX 760-446-0870; CC, Sa, Sp, UR; 5ac, 1000; **50-87; D, F, PU, 4x4; B3, AMC, Jp, IH, VW**

Rosamond; Hi Desert Auto & Truck Salvage, 2116 15th St W, 93560; 805-256-3469, FAX 805-256-3496; CC, Sa; 1500; **70-90, few 40-60s; D, F, PU, 4x4; B3, Jp, Fr; Spanish**

Salinas; Peninsula Auto Wreckers, 2590 El Camino Real N, 93907; 831-663-3842; Sa; 2ac, 400; **51-91; D, F; B3**

San Jose; General Truck & Land Cruiser, 1697 Pomona Av, 95110; 408-288-6684, 800-JEEP 501; CC, Sa; **60+; D, F, PU, 4x4; Jeep & Toyota Pickup only**

Levan International Auto Body, 210 E Alma Av, 95112; 408-293-1375, FAX 408-293-1381, 800-498-2496; CC, Sa, Wr; **65+; D, F, PU, 4x4; B3; After market new body parts only**

Navarra Truck-Van-Auto Wreckers, 1837 Monterey Hwy, 95112; 408-294-0202, 800-628-2772; CC, Sa, Sp; 3ac, 400; **48+; D, F, PU, 4x4; Up to 1 ton Pickup only**

Santa Clara; A & A Foreign Auto Wreckers, 800 Comstock St, 95054; 408-727-8722, FAX 408-727-8769, 800-79-PARTS, www.usedautopart.com; CC, Sa, Sp, Wr; **40+; 50+ Parts; 88+ Cars; F; Spc: Volvo; Rare European**

Cads Only, 750 Comstock St, 95054; 408-727-1121; CC, Sa, Sp; **63+; D; Cadillac only**

Carol's Automotive & Corvette, 1719 Grant St, 95050; 408-727-2316; CC, Sa, Sp; 20; **63+; D; Corvette only**

Mustang Fever, 611 Reed St, 95050; 408-748-1337, FAX 408-748-9221, fevertwo@aol.com; CC, Sa, Sp; **64-73; D; Ford Mustang only; Shop**

Santa Cruz; Ginos Santa Cruz Auto Wrecking, 3315 Portola Dr, 95062; 831-475-4113; Sa, Sp; 1000; **60+; D, F, PU, 4x4, Trk; B3**

Santa Maria; Black Road Auto, 1500 Black Rd, 93454; 805-346-2770, FAX 805-348-3291; CC, Sa, Sp, UR, PL; 2500; **60+; D, F, PU, 4x4; B3; open Sunday**

Mike's Auto Dismantling, 700 W Fesler St, 93454; 805-925-4561, FAX 805-922-4771; CC, Sa, Sp, PL; 150+; **50-early 90s; D, F, PU; B3**

Shafter; Dan's Auto Sales & Wrecking, 28905 W Lerdo Hwy, 93263; 661-746-2996; UR; 50; **28+; D, F; B3, few British 60s; Ford Model T**

Santa Fe Dismantling, 19461 Santa Fe Way, 93263; 661-588-8948; Sa, Sp, Br; 10ac; **50s-88; D, F, PU, 4x4, Trk, Cn; B3, AMC, Jp, IH, Hd, St**

Shandon; Cockrum Towing, 17795 Hwy 46, 93461; 805-238-0143, cockrum@tcsn.net; CC, Sp; **40-70; D, F, PU; B3, Fd, Chevy; By Appointment Only**

Simi Valley; Simi Valley Auto Wrecking, 900 W Los Angeles Av, 93065; 805-522-5865, FAX 805-522-7468, 800-660-6933; CC, Sa, Sp, Br; 5ac, 300+; **60+; D, F, PU, 4x4, Trk; B3, AMC, Jp, IH, VW**

Sonora; Sonora Auto & Truck Dismantlers, 10660 Hwy 49, 95370; 209-533-1476, FAX 209-533-1486, 888-442-4466; CC, Sa, Sp, UR; 400+; **40+; D, F, PU, 4x4, Trk; B3, IH, Subaru**

33

Stockton; Ben's Auto Dismantlers, 2041 Navy Dr, 95206; 209-464-1111, FAX 209-462-7091, 888-686-8700; CC, Sp; 300+; **60+; D, F, PU, 4x4; B3, Jp, BMW, VW; Spc: 60+ Volvo; Mostly 90+**

Charter Way Auto Recyclers, 930 E Charter Way, 95206; 209-466-2387, 800-672-5824, cwar@gotnet.com; CC, Sa, Sp; 600+; **60+; D, F, PU, 4x4; B3**

Debco Auto Wreckers, 2345 Navy Dr, 95206; 209-466-0161, FAX 209-463-2020, 800-451-8855, 72302.2375@compuserve.com; CC, Sa, Sp, PL; 800; **60+; D, F, PU, 4x4; B3, AMC, Jp, IH; Spc: Ford, Chevy**

Delta Auto Wreckers, 3151 Hwy 99, 95215; 209-948-6879; CC; **60+; D, F, PU, 4x4, Trk; B3; Spc: 60-89 Chevy & Ford Pickup**

Jaguar Heaven, 1433 Tillie Lewis Dr, 95206; 209-942-4524, FAX 209-942-4524, 800-969-4524; CC, Sp; 450; **50-94; F; Jaguar & Range Rover only**

Mathis Auto Wreckers & Parts, 3679 S El Dorado St, 95206; 209-982-3670; Sa, Sp; 2ac, 200+; **50+; D, F, PU; B3, AMC, St**

Mustangs Plus, 2353 N Wilson Way, 95205; 209-944-9977; CC, Wr; **65-73; D; Ford Mustang only; New parts**

Quinteros Auto Dismantling, 2966 Turnpike Rd, 95206; 209-466-4673; Sp; **50+; D, F, PU; B3, AMC; Spc: Ford; Spanish**

Red Wagon Recycling, 3532 E Miner Av, 95205; 209-462-5655, FAX 209-462-0589; CC, Sa, Sp; 1ac, 55+; **50-69; D, PU; B3, muscle cars**

Stockton Auto Dismantlers, 3239 S El Dorado St, 95206; 209-466-9531, FAX 209-466-2871, 800-235-8733; CC, Sp, 400+; **65+; F; Eur Only; Mercedes, Lexus, BMW, Range Rover & exotics**

Tulare; C & C Auto Dismantling, 3531 S K St, 93274; 559-686-8337, FAX 559-686-8339; CC, Sp, Wr; 5ac, 300; **50+; D, PU, 4x4; B3, Jp, IH; Spc: Pickup & Vans**

Tulare Auto Wrecking, 3748 S K St, 93274; 559-686-2871; Sa, Sp; 2000; **50+; D, F, PU, 4x4; B3, St**

Turlock; Golden State Auto Wrecking, 1565 S Paulson Rd, 95380; 209-634-9335, FAX 209-632-3076; CC, Sa, Sp; 400; **60+; D, F, PU, 4x4, Trk; B3, AMC, Jp, VW; Spanish**

Turlock Auto Wreckers, 1405 S Paulson Rd, 95380; 209-632-3176; Sp; 1000; **60+; D, F, PU, 4x4; B3, muscle cars**

Valley Auto Wrecker & Towing, 2136 S Daubenberger Rd, 95380; 209-632-6413, FAX 209-632-8174; CC, Sa, Sp, Br; 13ac; **50-89; D, F, PU, 4x4, Trk; B3**

Victorville; New & Used Auto Glass, 17229 Gasline Rd, 92394; 760-955-8276; **Glass - New & Used**

Visalia; Allied Auto Dismantling, 12769 Avenue 328, 93291; 559-734-4554; Sa, Sp, UR; 850; **50+; D, F, PU, 4x4, Trk, Mil; B3, Jp, IH**

Budget Auto Wrecking, 10430 Rasmussen Av, 93291; 559-651-2047; Sa, Sp; 2000; **32+; D, F, PU, 4x4; B3, AMC, Jp**

Watsonville; G & G Used Auto Parts, 600 Errington Rd #A, 95076; 831-728-2032, 800-840-8727; CC, Sa; 400+; **52-88; D; B3**

Salsipuedes Auto Wreckers, 213 Dias Ln, 95076; 831-728-1551, FAX 831-728-3587, 800-750-9732; CC, Sa, Sp; 250+; **40-90; D, F; B3**

Winton; Fisk Auto Wreckers, 5950 Princeton Rd, 95388; 209-358-5794; 100; **66+; D, F, PU, 4x4, Trk; B3; Pickup & Truck only**

Yermo; D & M Auto Truck & RV Repair, 38443 Athletic Field Rd, 92398; 760-254-4483, 888-652-7011; CC, Sa, Sp, Br; 25ac; **35+; D, few F, PU, 4x4; B3, St, Ks**

LATE VINTAGE

Adelanto; Ecology Auto Wrecking, *see Vintage*

Arroyo Grande; Jacob's Auto Wrecking, 2226 Gasoline Alley Pl, 93420; 805-343-2409; Sa, Sp; 1.5ac; **70-87; D, F, PU, 4x4; Pickup only**

R & R Auto Wrecking, *see Vintage*

Arvin; Carter's Automotive Svc, 941 S Derby St, 93203; 805-854-1949; 100; **80s; D; B3**

Atascadero; Atascadero New-Used Auto Parts, *see Vintage*

North CO, 6501 Via Av, 93422; 805-544-0810; CC, Sa, Sp; 6ac; **70+; D, F, PU, 4x4; B3**

Bakersfield; A & A Auto Wrecking, *see Vintage*

A-1 Auto Wrecking, 2005 S Union Av, 93307; 805-833-9369; Sa; 100+; **70+; D, PU, 4x4; B3; Spc: Chevy & Ford**

A-Auto Slvg, 1925 S Union Av, 93307; 805-831-7919; Sa; 10ac; **82+; D, F, PU, 4x4; B3**

Ace Auto Dismantler, *see Vintage*

American Auto Wrk, 2129 S Union Av, 93307; 805-831-8820; Sa, Br; **80+; D, F, PU, Trk**

Ashmores Auto Wrecking, *see Vintage*

C & L Auto Dismantlers, *see Vintage*

D C Auto Wrck, 1897 S Union Av #C, 93307; 805-835-7006; Sa; 300; **70+; D, F, PU; B3**

J & J Auto Dismantling, *see Vintage*

Lamont Auto Wrecking, *see Vintage*

Louie's Wrecking Yard, 1897 S Union Av, 93307; 805-831-8444, FAX 805-831-1201, 800-831-8444; CC, Sa, Sp; 400; **80+; D, F, PU; B3**

Pickup Salvage Co, *see Vintage*

Pick Your Part Auto Wrecking, *see Vintage*

Simpson's Towing, 5941 Panama Rd, 93307; 805-845-0256, FAX 805-845-1813; Sa, UR; **70-89; D, F; B3**

Surgeners Auto Wrecking, *see Vintage*

U-Pick U-Save Auto Dismantling, 1945 S Union Av, 93307; 805-831-1800, FAX 805-831-0124; CC, Sa, UR; 1300+; **65-89; D, F, PU; B3; Open Sunday**

United Auto Dismantling, *see Vintage*

Bishop; Mingo's Automotive, *see Vintage*

Bradley; Jardines Salvage & Auto, *see Vintage*

Burson; California Auto Recycling, 3365 W Hwy 12, 95225; 209-772-2900; Sa, Sp; Several yards; **70+; D, F, PU, 4x4; B3**

California City; Whites Auto Dismantling, *see Vintage*

Campbell; British Motorsports, *see Vintage*

Ceres; Ceres Auto Wreckers, 2701 E Service Rd, 95307; 209-537-4774, 800-533-1238; CC, Sa, Sp, PL; 500; **70+; D, F, PU, 4x4; B3, VW**

Clovis; Central Auto Dismantlers, 906 Hoblitt Av, 93612; 559-299-2531, FAX 559-299-8382, 800-444-2531, cad@qnis.net; CC, Sp, PL; 300; **75+; D, F, PU, 4x4, Trk; B3, Jp**

Clovis Foreign Car Wrecking, 1111 Hoblitt Av, 93612; 559-299-3129, FAX 559-299-8948; Sp; 500; **82+; F, PU, 4x4; Spc: Jpa**

Delano; Millikin & Sons Auto Wrecking, 10408 Mettler Av, 93215; 805-725-8995; Sa, UR; 300; **65-89; D, PU; B3; Spc: Chevy Pickup & Muscle Cars**

Dos Palos; Jones Wrecking Yard, *see Vintage*

Fillmore; Fillmore Auto Dismantling, 121 Santa Clara St, 93015; 805-524-2822, FAX 805-524-4650; Sa, UR; 1ac, 50; **75+; D, F, PU, 4x4; B3; Open Sunday**

Fresno; Continental Auto Dismantler, *see Vintage*

Dan's Auto Parts & Wrecking, *see Vintage*

Fresno Auto Dismantling, *see Vintage*

Fresno Truck Wrecking, 3536 S Maple Av, 93725; 559-441-0501, 800-464-0506; Sa, Sp; **65+; D, PU, 4x4; B3, Jp, 1H; Pickup only**

Gardens West Auto Dismantling, 2446 S West Av, 93706; 559-266-9200; Sa, Sp; 200 **84+; F, PU, 4x4; Jpa**

Levan Auto Body Parts, *see Vintage*

Pick-A-Part Auto Wrecking, 2274 E Muscat Av, 93725; 559-268-0216, www.pickapart.com; CC, Sa, UR; 12ac; **70+; D, F, PU, 4x4; B3; Chain store**

Robinson's Auto Dismantling, 4642 S Chestnut Av, 93725; 559-485-4640, FAX 559-485-3458, 800-499-4640; Sp, Br; 10ac; **80+; D, F, PU, 4x4, Trk; B3**

Romo Auto Wrecking & Towing, *see Vintage*

Westside Self-Service Auto, *see Vintage*

Gilroy; Gilroy Auto Wrecking, *see Vintage*

Goleta; Goleta Auto Salvage, *see Vintage*

Santa Barbara Auto Salvage, *see Vintage*

Gonzales; Kings Towing & Storage, 93926; 831-675-2112; Sa; 5ac; **70-89; D, F, PU; B3**

Hanford; American Self Serve, *see Vintage*

Central Auto Dismantling, 866 E 5th St, 93230; 559-582-3198; Sa, Sp; 200; **73-91; D, F, PU, 4x4, Trk; B**3 **VW**

Hanford Auto Dismantling, *see Vintage*

Hesperia; Atlas Truck & Auto Salvage, *see Vintage*

Chris Volkswagen Parts, *see Vintage*

Cox Auto Salvage, *see Vintage*

King City; Sirak's Repair, *see Vintage*

Lamont; Weedpatch Auto Dismantling, *see Vintage*

Lancaster; Pearson's Parts for Less, 361 E Avenue L12, 93535; 805-726-9493, FAX 805-948-4680; CC, Sa, Sp, UR; 7.5ac; **70-89; D, F, PU, 4x4; B**3

West Coast VW Cores, *see Vintage*

Lathrop; Highway 120 Auto Dismantlers, 3737 W Yosemite Av, 95330; 209-858-4216; CC, Sa, Sp; 6ac, 600; **80+; D, F, PU, 4x4; B**3, **IH**

Lemoore; Economy Auto Wrecking, *see Vintage*

Hughes Auto Wrecking & Towing, *see Vintage*

Lemoore Auto Wrecking & Salvage, 1069 W Iona Av, 93245; 559-924-3447; Sa; 3000; **70+; D, F, PU, 4x4; B**3, **Jpa**

Littlerock; Jones Auto Dismantlers, *see Vintage*

Lodi; Kalends Auto Wrecking, 530 Railroad Av, 95240; 209-334-4845; Sp; 120; **80-94; D, F, PU; Sp CA only; Spanish**

Lompoc; Bedlo Inc, *see Vintage*

Los Banos; Romero's Towing, *see Vintage*

Madera; 3 Boys Auto Wrecking, *see Vintage*

Pick-A-Part Auto Wrecking, 14494 Rd 22, 93637; 559-673-1281, FAX 559-673-5635; CC, Sa, UR; 3000; **70+; D, F, PU, 4x4; B**3, **AMC, VW; $1 admission**

Smith's Wrecking, 12389 Rd 29, 93638; 559-673-1158; Sa, UR; 4000+; **75-85; D, F, PU, 4x4; B**3, **VW; Spc: VW Bugs; Closed Thursday**

Whitakers 4x4 Heaven, 1500 N Gateway Dr, 93637; 559-661-5337, 800-253-2551; www.maderaonline.com, wrecker@madnet.net; CC, Sp; 800; **65+; D, PU, 4x4; B**3, **Jp, IH; 65+ Pickup; 80+ Car**

Mariposa; Pearson's Auto Dismantling, *see Vintage*

Mendota; Smitty's Towing & Auto, 643 Naples St, 93640; 559-655-3534, FAX 559-655-5211; CC, Sa, Sp, UR; 200+; **70+; D, F, PU, 4x4; B**3, **AMC, Jp, IH, VW; Spc: Ford & Chevy**

Merced; Freita's Auto Wreckers, 1308 E Childs Av, 95340; 209-722-7086; Sp; 800+; **70+; D, PU, 4x4; B**3 **Spc: Chevy & Ford Pickup**

Milpitas; Pick Your Part, *see Vintage*

Modesto; Ace Auto Wreckers, *see Vintage*

Auto Recyclers of Modesto, *see Vintage*

Benson's Auto Dismantling, *see Vintage*

Farriester Auto Wreckers, *see Vintage*

Holt Auto Wrecking, *see Vintage*

Holt Auto Wrecking, *see Vintage*

Mojave; Valpey's Auto & Truck Salvage, 426 E Hwy 58, 93501; 661-824-4506, FAX 661-824-4241; CC, Sa, Sp; 10ac, 1000; **70+; D, F, PU, 4x4; B**3

Morgan Hill; California Salvage & Auto Parts, *see Vintage*

Newhall; Giant Auto Wreckers, *see Vintage*

Nipomo; Almond Automotive, 2234 Oop Loop, 93444; 805-343-2550; Sa, Sp, Br; 100; **73-89; D, F, PU, 4x4, Trk, Cn; B**3, **AMC, VW**

Oakdale; Oakdale Auto Wreckers & Towing, *see Vintage*

Orange Cove; Donaldson's Auto Dismantling, *see Vintage*

Orosi; Gil's Auto Wrecking, 13205 Avenue 416, 93647; 559-528-2151; Br; 250; **75-85; D, F; B**3, **AMC**

Oxnard; Chuck's Auto Parts & Salvage, 3979 E Hueneme Rd, 93033; 805-488-4491, FAX 805-986-8112; CC, Sa, Sp, Br; 4ac; **73+; D, F, PU, 4x4; B**3, **AMC, VW**

Dynacorn International, *see Vintage*

Fifth St Auto Salvage, *see Vintage*

Pacific Auto Salvage, 655 Pacific Av, 93030; 805-486-7367; CC, Sa, Sp; 2ac, 350; **80-89; D, F, PU, 4x4; B3, Jp, VW**

Paso Robles; A-1 Metals & Auto Salvage, 5795 Stockdale Rd, 93446; 805-238-3545, FAX 805-238-0172; CC, Sa, Sp, UR; 12ac, 1000; **70+; D, F, PU, 4x4; B3, IH**

Paso Robles Auto Wrecking, *see Vintage*

Pixley; MC & Sons Auto Repair, 2289 N Cedar St, 93256; 559-757-3870, FAX 559-757-5403; CC, Sa, Sp; 1200+; **75-93; D, F, PU, 4x4; B3, VW**

Plymouth; Foothill Garage & Wrecking, *see Vintage*

Porterville; Cemo Motor Sales & Auto Wrecking, *see Vintage*

Hoods Motors, *see Vintage*

Mt View Auto Dismantlers, 111 W Gibbons Av, 93257; 209-781-3007, FAX 209-781-6184; CC, Sa, Sp; 700; **76+; D, F, PU, 4x4; B3**

Tule Auto Dismantlers, *see Vintage*

Ridgecrest; Sierra Auto Recycling, *see Vintage*

Speedway Auto Dismantling, *see Vintage*

Riverbank; Riverside Truck Wrecking, 3848 Hwy 108, 95367; 209-869-3611, FAX 209-869-3614, 888-890-7393; Sa, UR, Wr; 30; **70+; D, F, PU, 4x4; Minivan & Pickup only**

Rosamond; Hi Desert Auto & Truck Salvage, *see Vintage*

Salida; Late Model Auto Wreckers, 5123 Kiernan Av, 95368; 209-545-0455, FAX 209-545-8964; CC, Sa; 400; **70-89; D, F, PU; B3**

Salinas; Peninsula Auto Wreckers, *see Vintage*

San Jose; A-1 Auto Dismantlers, 200 Hillsdale Av, 95136; 408-225-5313, FAX 408-227-8735, 800-997-3254; CC, Sa, Sp, UR; 3ac, 300; **84+; F; VW**

AAAA Van Parts Inc, 477 Burke St, 95112; 408-286-9445, FAX 408-629-6430; CC, Sa, Sp, UR; **70+; D, F; Vans only; Van Accessories also**

European Specialty Auto Dismantling, 1731 Smith Av, 95112; 408-297-3434, FAX 408-297-3460, 800-286-1355; CC, Sa, Sp, UR; 2ac, 200; **80+; F; Eur; Audi, Porsche, BMW, Volvo, Saab, VW**

General Truck & Land Cruiser, *see Vintage*

GM Sports Salvage, 1964 Oakland Rd, 95131; 408-432-8498, FAX 408-432-8784, 800-427-9194, www.gmsports.com; CC, Sa, Sp; 2ac, 100; **64+; D; Corvette, Camaro, Firebird, Chevelle, El Camino**

Honda Heaven, 220 Hillcap Av, 95136; 408-227-8752, FAX 408-225-4802, 888-624-6632; CC, Sa, Sp, UR; 150; **F; Honda & Mazda including rotary engine; Spanish**

JT Truck Ctr, 855 Service St, 95112; 408-453-1950, FAX 408-453-2938, 800-543-7676; CC, Sa, Sp, Wr; **67+; D, PU; B3; Pickup & Van only**

Levan International Auto Body, *see Vintage*

Navarra Truck-Van-Auto Wreckers, *see Vintage*

Pick-N-Pull, 1675 Monterey Hwy, 95112; 408-452-1281, FAX 408-436-0317; Sa; Chain of yards; **70+; D, F, PU, 4x4; B3, VW**

Strictly Ford, 701 Kings Row, 95112; 408-271-9200, fordcom@pacbell.net; **79+; D; Ford**

Toyota Truck & 4x4 Dismantlers, 991 Berryessa Rd, 95133; 408-436-7890, FAX 408-436-9779; CC, Sa, Sp; **79+; F, PU, 4x4, Trk; Toyota Pickup & Truck only**

San Luis Obispo; Auto Parts Recyclers, 3045 Duncan Ln, 93401; 805-543-1215, 800-549-2019; CC, Sa, Sp; 4ac; **80+; D, F, PU, 4x4**

San Luis Auto Salvage, 281 Tank Farm Rd, 93401; 805-543-9509, 800-222-9509; CC, Sa, Sp; 14ac; **79+; D, F, PU, 4x4; B3**

San Martin; Ability Wreckers, 14240 Monterey Hwy, 95046; 408-779-9191; CC, Sa, Sp; 200+; **70+; D, F, PU, 4x4; B3, AMC, Jp**

Alf Auto Wreckers, 13075 Monterey Hwy, 95046; 408-683-2376, FAX 408-683-2923; Sa, Sp; 1000; **75+; D, F, PU, 4x4; B3, Jp**

Santa Clara; A & A Foreign Auto Wreckers, *see Vintage*

Cads Only, *see Vintage*

Carol's Automotive & Corvette, *see Vintage*

Drive Train Svc, 795 Comstock St, 95054; 408-727-2244, FAX 408-3847, santaclaratruck @hotmail.com; CC, Sa, Sp; 1ac; **73+; D, PU, 4x4; Chevy & Ford Pickup only**

European Wholesale Parts, 779 Parker St, 95050; 408-733-9573, 800-414-7541; Sp; **80+; F; Spc: Mercedes & BMW**

Hondas Only Auto Dismantlers, 790 Comstock St, 95054; 408-727-2400, 800-801-7278; Sa, UR; 1ac, 60+; **78+; F; Spc: Honda**

Mustang Fever, *see Vintage*

Santa Clara Wreckers, 795 Comstock St, 95054; 408-727-6595, FAX 408-727-3847; CC, Sa; 2ac, 300+; **73+; D, PU, 4x4; Spc: Ford & Chevy**

Santa Cruz; Bubba's Automotive Dismantling, 980 17th Av #D1, 95062; 831-462-0886; Sa; 2ac; **70-89; D, F, PU, 4x4; B**3

Ginos Santa Cruz Auto Wrecking, *see Vintage*

Santa Maria; Black Road Auto, *see Vintage*

Central Coast Auto Parts, 1400 Black Rd, 93454; 805-922-3513, 800-922-3513; CC, Sa, Sp, UR; 2ac, 350+; **70-93; D, F, PU; B**3

Mike's Auto Dismantling, *see Vintage*

Santa Paula; Pull Your Part, 936 Mission Rock Rd, 93060; 805-525-7414, www. pickapart.com; CC, Sa, UR; 800; **70-89; D, F, PU, 4x4; B**3**, AMC**

Selma; Don's Auto Wrecking, 11374 E Mountain View Av, 93662; 559-896-8234; Sa; **80+;D, F; Spanish**

Shafter; Dan's Auto Sales & Wrecking, *see Vintage*

Santa Fe Dismantling, *see Vintage*

Simi Valley; Simi Valley Auto Wrecking, *see Vintage*

Sonora; Sonora Auto & Truck Dismantlers, *see Vintage*

Stevinson; Valley Auto Wreckers, 1330 Lander Av, 95374; 209-667-0191; CC, Sa, Sp, UR; 400+; **70+; D, PU, 4x4; B**3

Stockton; Art's Auto Wrecking, 4223 Clark Dr, 95215; 209-466-2031; Sp; 2000; **70-90; F, PU, 4x4**

Ben's Auto Dismantlers, *see Vintage*

Charter Way Auto Recyclers, *see Vintage*

Debco Auto Wreckers, *see Vintage*

Delta Auto Wreckers, *see Vintage*

Jaguar Heaven, *see Vintage*

M & M Auto Dismantling, 1111 E Jefferson St, 95205; 209-943-6976, FAX 209-943-6906, 800-774-5865; Sa, Sp; 350+; **70-89; D, PU, 4x4; AMC & Jeep only**

Mathis Auto Wreckers & Parts, *see Vintage*

Mustangs Plus, *see Vintage*

Quinteros Auto Dismantling, *see Vintage*

Stockton Auto Dismantlers, *see Vintage*

Tulare; C & C Auto Dismantling, *see Vintage*

Tulare Auto Wrecking, *see Vintage*

Turlock; Golden State Auto Wrecking, *see Vintage*

Turlock Auto Wreckers, *see Vintage*

Valley Auto Wrecker & Towing, *see Vintage*

Witzel's Auto Wrck, 1204 S 1st St, 95380; 209-632-1329; Sa, Sp; 120; **75-85; D, PU; B**3

Victorville; New & Used Auto Glass, *see Vintage*

Visalia; Allied Auto Dismantling, *see Vintage*

Budget Auto Wrecking, *see Vintage*

Wasco; Wasco Auto Towing & Wrecking, 27178 Poso Av, 93280; 661-758-2761; CC, Sa; 200+; **70-90; D, F, PU; B**3

Watsonville; Coast Auto Dismant, 112 Lee Rd, 95076; 831-724-4892, FAX 831-722-6561, 800-852-8802, www.cacautosupply.com; CC, Sa, Sp; 500+; **80+; D, F, PU; B**3

G & G Used Auto Parts, *see Vintage*

Gerry's Foreign Auto Wreckers, 600 Errington Rd #B, 95076; 831-728-0121; Sa, UR; 400; **70+; F, PU; Eur & Jpa**

Lewis Road Auto Salvage, 848 Lewis Rd, 95076; 831-722-1113; Sa, UR; .5ac; **72-87; D, F, PU, 4x4, Trk; B**3

Salsipuedes Auto Wreckers, *see Vintage*

Winton; Fisk Auto Wreckers, *see Vintage*

Yermo; D & M Auto Truck & RV Repair, *see Vintage*

LATE MODEL

Adelanto; Ecology Auto Wrecking, *see Vintage*

Arroyo Grande; Sierra Auto Dismantling, 845 Sheridan Rd, 93420; 805-489-0745, FAX 805-343-7847, 800-281-0771; CC, Sa, Sp, PL; 300; **D, F, PU, Trk**

Atascadero New-Used Auto Parts, *see Vintage*

Cal West Truck Parts, 6915 Sycamore Rd, 93422; 805-466-2277, FAX 805-466-3316; Sp, Br; 25+; **D, PU; Chevy & GMC Pickup only**

North County, *see Late Vintage*

Bakersfield; A & A Auto Wrecking, *see Vintage*

A-1 Auto Wrecking, *see Late Vintage*

A-Auto Salvage, *see Late Vintage*

Abe's Auto Wrecking, 2119 S Union Av, 93307; 805-397-3350; Sa; 2ac; **D, F, PU**

Ace Auto Dismantler, *see Vintage*

American Auto Wrecking, *see Late Vintage*

Ashmores Auto Wrecking, *see Vintage*

Auto Mart Recycling, 7800 S Union Av, 93307; 805-397-2855, 877-397-2855; CC, Sa, Sp; 400; **F; Jpa**

C & L Auto Dismantlers, *see Vintage*

D C Auto Wrecking, *see Late Vintage*

Higgins Used Car & Auto Wrecking, 12825 S Union Av, 93307; 805-831-2411, FAX 805-397-5946, 800-652-2886; CC, Sa, Sp, Br; 10ac; **D, F, PU, 4x4, light Trk**

Louie's Wrecking Yard, *see Late Vintage*

Pickup Salvage Co, *see Vintage*

Pick Your Part Auto Wrck, 5311 S Union Av, 93307; 805-833-0800, FAX 805-837-4881; CC, Sa, UR

Pick Your Part Auto Wrecking, *see Vintage*

Pickup Tech, 1636 S Union Av, 93307; 805-833-6900; Wr, PL; **D, F, PU**

Surgeners Auto Wrecking, *see Vintage*

United Auto Dismantling, *see Vintage*

Bishop; Mingo's Automotive, *see Vintage*

Burson; California Auto Recycling, *see Late Vintage*

California City; Whites Auto Dismantling, *see Vintage*

Campbell; British Motorsports, *see Vintage*

Ceres; Ceres Auto Wreckers, *see Late Vintage*

Chowchilla; Robert's Auto Wrecking, 18409 Gordon St, 93610; 559-665-5730; Sa, Sp; 150; **D; Spc: GM Metro**

Clovis; Central Auto Dismantlers, *see Late Vintage*

Clovis Foreign Car Wrecking, *see Late Vintage*

Dos Palos; Jones Wrecking Yard, *see Vintage*

Fillmore; Fillmore Auto Dismantling, *see Late Vintage*

Fresno; Action Truck & Van Parts, 4688 S Chestnut Av, 93725; 559-268-5376, 800-321-9009, www.actiontruck.com; CC, Sp; 5ac; **D, PU, 4x4; Pickup only to 1 ton**

All 4x4 Dismantling, 628 W Whitesbridge Rd, 93706; 559-237-2263 , FAX 559-237-2265; Sa, Sp; 2.5ac; **D, F, PU, 4x4; Pickup & Van only**

Bauer's Auto Wrecking, 103 N Thorne Av, 93706; 559-233-9121, FAX 559-233-0513, 800-678-9046; CC, Br, PL; 3ac **D, F, PU**

Continental Auto Dismantler, *see Vintage*

Dan's Auto Parts & Wrecking, *see Vintage*

Dave's Auto Dismantling, 2446 S West Av, 93706; 559-266-9200; Sa, Sp; **F, PU, 4x4**

Fresno Auto Dismantling, *see Vintage*

Fresno Foreign Wrecking, 3525 S Golden State Blvd, 93725; 559-485-3666, FAX 559-485-0513, 800-541-4185; Sa, Sp; 300+; **D, F, PU, 4x4**

Fresno Truck Wrecking, *see Late Vintage*

Gardens West Auto Dismantling, *see Late Vintage*

Hub Caps Only, 505 N Fulton, 93728; 559-237-0553, FAX 559-237-0590; CC, Sp; **Hub Caps only**

Jamies Auto Dismantling, 2438 S West Av, 93706; 559-233-4674, 800-642-1110; Sp, PL; 8ac, 1000+; **D, F, PU**

Levan Auto Body Parts, *see Vintage*

Malaga Auto Wrecking, 3135 E Malaga Av, 93725; 559-233-3791; Sa; **F; Japanese only**

Ohnstads Foreign & American Auto & Mini, 4656 S Chestnut Av, 93725; 559-486-0280, FAX 559-486-1140, 800-541-2783 West Coast; CC, Sp, Br; 5ac; **D, F, PU, 4x4, Trk**

Pick-A-Part Auto Wrecking, *see Late Vintage*

Pick & Pull, 3230 E Jensen Av, 93706; 559-233-3881; UR; **D, F; Chain**

Robinson's Auto Dismantling, *see Late Vintage*

Gilroy; Gilroy Auto Wrecking, *see Vintage*

Goleta; Santa Barbara Auto Salvage, *see Vintage*

Hanford; Hanford Auto Dismantling, *see Vintage*

Hesperia; Atlas Truck & Auto Salvage, *see Vintage*

Cox Auto Salvage, *see Vintage*

Hollister; San Benito Auto Wrk, 2120 San Juan Rd, 95023; 831-637-5795; Sa, Sp; 200; **D, F**

King City; Sirak's Repair, *see Vintage*

Lamont; Weedpatch Auto Dismantling, *see Vintage*

Lancaster; Coast Auto Salvage, 46404 Division St, 93535; 805-942-3737; **D, F**

General Auto & Truck Salvage, 45339 Division St, 93535; 805-940-8747; **D, F**

Glendale Auto Pick & Pull, 43927 90th St E, 93535; 805-946-1076, FAX 805-946-7506; CC, Sa; 10ac, 1000; **D, F**

West Coast VW Cores, *see Vintage*

Lathrop; Highway 120 Auto Dismantlers, *see Late Vintage*

Lemoore; Economy Auto Wrecking, *see Late Vintage*

Hughes Auto Wrecking & Towing, *see Late Vintage*

Lemoore Auto Wrecking & Salvage, *see Late Vintage*

Littlerock; Jones Auto Dismantlers, *see Vintage*

Lodi; Kalends Auto Wrecking, *see Late Vintage*

Lompoc; Bedlo Inc, *see Vintage*

Lompoc; Perry's Auto Wrecking, 613 Avalon St, 93436; 805-736-6719; CC, Sa, Sp, Wr; 5+ac; **D, F**

Madera; 3 Boys Auto Wrecking, *see Vintage*

Shade Tree Auto Wreckers, 28745 Oregon Av, 93638; 559-661-1816; Sa, Sp, Br; **D, F, PU, 4x4; Spanish**

Pick-A-Part Auto Wrecking, *see Late Vintage*

Whitakers 4x4 Heaven, *see Late Vintage*

Mariposa; Pearson's Auto Dismantling, *see Vintage*

Mendota; Smitty's Towing & Auto, *see Late Vintage*

Merced; Freita's Auto Wreckers, *see Late Vintage*

Manuel's Auto Wrecking, 1839 E Gerard Av, 95340; 209-722-1316, FAX 209-722-1367, 800-653-5486; CC, Sa, Sp; 350+; **D, PU, 4x4; B3; Spc: Chevy & Ford Pickup**

Milpitas; Milpitas Auto Dismantlers, 225 Bothelo Av, 95035; 408-263-1846; Sa; **F; Jpa**

P & C Auto Recyclers, 573 Trade Zone Blvd, 95035; 408-262-5740, 800-807-2582; CC, Sp; 5ac, 500; **D, PU, 4x4; Spc: Ford & GM**

Pick Your Part, *see Vintage*

Quality Auto Dismantling, 625 Trade Zone Blvd, 95035; 408-262-5855, FAX 408-262-0488, 800-582-5489; CC, Sa, Sp, PL; 2.5ac, 400+; **D, F, PU, 4x4**

Modesto; Ace Auto Wreckers, *see Vintage*

Auto Recyclers of Modesto, *see Vintage*

Bonanza All Foreign Auto, 540 Crows Landing Rd, 95351; 209-527-2929, 800-292-0666; CC, Sa, Sp; 500; **F, PU, 4x4; Japanese only**

California Auto Parts, 618 S 9th St, 95351; 209-523-0751, 800-942-5885 CA only; CC, Sa; 5ac; **D, F, PU, 4x4**

D & W Auto Wreckers, 531 Crows Landing Rd, 95351; 209-524-7474; Sa, Sp, Br; 300+; **D, F, PU, 4x4; Spc: Late model engines; Closed Sunday & Tuesday**

Farriester Auto Wreckers, *see Vintage*

Holt Auto Wrecking, *see Vintage*

Modesto Auto Wreckers, 520 Crows Landing Rd, 95351; 209-523-8422, FAX 209-523-8074, 800-800-8421; Sa, Sp, PL; 300; **D, PU**

Wilson Auto Wreckers, 1917 W Hatch Rd, 95351; 209-529-5357

Mojave; Valpey's Auto & Truck Salvage, *see Late Vintage*

Moorpark; Coast Auto Salvage, 198 Lorraine Ln, 93021; 805-529-2122; Sa; **D, F, PU, 4x4**

Moss Landing; All Import Auto Wreckers, 516 Dolan Rd #F, 95039; 831-633-2188; CC, Sa; **D, F, PU, 4x4**

Moss Landing; Century Auto Dismantlers, 516 Dolan Rd, 95039; 831-633-5211; Sa; 300; **D, F, PU, 4x4; B3, AMC, Jp**

Pick n Pull, 516 Dolan Rd, 95039; 408-633-2955, 800-442-5865; Sa, UR; 1000+; **D, F**

Newhall; Giant Auto Wreckers, *see Vintage*

Oakdale; Oakdale Auto Wreckers & Towing, *see Vintage*

Orange Cove; Donaldson's Auto Dismantling, *see Vintage*

Oxnard; Chuck's Auto Parts & Salvage, *see Late Vintage*

Dynacorn International, *see Vintage*

Fifth St Auto Salvage, *see Vintage*

Gean's Auto Wrecker, 1515 Mountain View Av, 93030; 805-486-6000; Sa, Sp; **D, F; B3; Spc: Chevy PU**

Palmdale; Clark & Howard Auto Wrecking, 840 E Avenue R, 93550; 805-947-7112; Sa, Br; 300; **D, F, PU, 4x4, Trk; B3, VW**

Paso Robles; A-1 Metals & Auto Salvage, *see Late Vintage*

Paso Robles Auto Wrecking, *see Vintage*

Porterville; Hoods Motors, *see Vintage*

Mt View Auto Dismantlers, *see Late Vintage*

Tule Auto Dismantlers, *see Vintage*

Ridgecrest; Pearson's Auto Wrecking, 1317 W Inyokern Rd, 93555; 760-446-6583; CC, Sa

Sierra Auto Recycling, *see Vintage*

Riverbank; Riverside Truck Wrecking, *see Late Vintage*

Salinas; A-1 Self Svc Auto Wreckers, 20856 Spence Rd, 93908; 831-424-7333; Sa, UR; 5ac, 650

Peninsula Auto Wreckers, *see Vintage*

San Jose; 3 M Auto Wreckers, 1726 Smith Av, 95112; 408-998-8661, FAX 408-285-6749, 800-624-4454; CC, Sa, Sp; **D, F, PU, 4x4; Spc: Honda, Acura, Toyota**

A-1 Auto Dismantlers, *see Late Vintage*

A-1 Mini Truck & Mini Van, 200 Hillcap Av, 95136; 408-227-8730, FAX 408-227-8735, 800-825-0064; CC, Sa, Sp; 100; **D, F, PU, 4x4, Trk; Jpa; Mini PU & Mini Vans only**

A-German Auto Parts & Svc, 301 San Jose Av, 95125; 408-993-9711, FAX 408-993-9760, www.agerman.com; CC, Sa, Sp; **F; BMW, Audi, Mercedes, Volvo, Saab**

AAAA Van Parts Inc, *see Late Vintage*

Action Auto Wrecking, 242 Hillcap Av, 95136; 408-225-5553, FAX 408-225-4802, 800-606-9732, www.recar.com; CC, Sa, Sp, PL; 300; **D; B3; Spc: Ford, Lincoln, Mercury; some Cadillac & Grand Am**

All Japanese Auto Dismantlers, 1300 Old Bayshore Hwy, 95112; 408-291-5521, FAX 408-278-8588, 888-933-3030; CC, Sa, Sp; F, PU, 4x4; Jpa

American Import Auto Dsmntlr, 285 Leo Av, 95112; 408-275-9261, FAX 408-275-9030, 800-610-0070; CC, Sa, Sp; **F; Eur & Jpa; Spc: BMW, Audi, Porsche, Volvo, VW**

B2 Auto Dismantlers, 245 Leo Av, 95112; 408-971-1152; CC, Sa, UR; 100; **F**

41

Bay City Auto Wreckers, 1795 S 10th St, 95112; 408-293-4878; CC, Sa, Sp; **D, F; Eur; Spc: BMW, Audi, Porsche, Volvo**

Cash For Junk Cars, 1065 Commercial St, 95112; 800-442-5865; Sa, UR; **14 yrds in CA**

Dollar Auto Parts, 1699 S 10th St, 95112; 408-999-0909, FAX 408-999-0919; CC, Sa, UR; 1ac, 100; **D, F, PU**

European Specialty Auto Dismantling, *see Late Vintage*

General Truck & Land Cruiser, *see Vintage*

GM Sports Salvage, *see Late Vintage*

Greer Auto & Truck Wreckers, 1750 S 10th St, 95112; 408-288-5080, FAX 408-288-8528, 800-989-7278, greerauto@msn.com; CC, Sa, Sp; 150; **D, F, PU, 4x4**

Honda Heaven, *see Late Vintage*

J C Auto Wreckers, 1200 N 15th St, 95112; 408-287-5853, FAX 408-287-5859, 800-860-6606, www.jcauto.com/simplenet.com; CC, Sa, Sp; 60+; **F, PU**

JT Truck Ctr, *see Late Vintage*

Kings Auto Dismantlers, 650 Kings Row, 95112; 408-286-6864, FAX 408-286-6867, 800-898-6864; CC, Sa, Sp, UR; 2ac, 100; **D, F, PU; Spanish**

Levan International Auto Body, *see Vintage*

Mayfair Auto Wreckers, 18 N King Rd, 95116; 408-251-1727, FAX 408-251-7637; CC, Sa, Sp; 1ac, 60; **D, F, PU, 4x4**

Navarra Truck-Van-Auto Wreckers, *see Vintage*

Pacific Auto Parts, 1777 S 10th St, 95112; 408-293-6767, FAX 408-293-6579, 888-408-1777; CC, Sa, Sp; 300; **D; Spc: Minivans**

Pick-N-Pull, *see Late Vintage*

Saab & Volvo Auto Wreckers, 297 San Jose Av, 95125; 408-995-5678, FAX 408-993-9760; CC, Sa, Sp, UR; **F, PU; Saab, Volvo, VW, Eur; Spc: Saab & Volvo**

Strictly Ford, *see Late Vintage*

Toyota Truck & 4x4 Dismantlers, *see Late Vintage*

Vince's Foreign Auto Wrk, 1781 S 10th St, 95112; 408-293-9570, FAX 408-293-9614; CC, Sa, Sp, UR; 2ac, 300; **F; Mostly Japanese; Spanish**

San Luis Obispo; Auto Parts Recyclers, *see Late Vintage*

San Luis Auto Salvage, *see Late Vintage*

San Martin; Ability Wreckers, *see Late Vintage*

Alf Auto Wreckers, *see Late Vintage*

Santa Clara; A & A Foreign Auto Wreckers, *see Vintage*

A & T Pick & Pay, 735 Reed St, 95050; 408-986-1838; CC, Sa, Sp; 1000; **D, F, PU**

Atlas Auto Wreckers, 805 Comstock St, 95054; 408-727-8386, FAX 408-727-8590; Sa, Sp; 50+; **D**

Cads Only, *see Vintage*

Carol's Automotive & Corvette, *see Vintage*

Drive Train Svc, *see Late Vintage*

European Wholesale Parts, *see Late Vintage*

Hondas Only Auto Dismantlers, *see Late Vintage*

M C Auto Dismantlers, 780 Comstock St, 95054; 408-982-0812; CC, Sa, Sp; **F; Toyota & Nissan Only**

P & T Auto Wreckers & Prts, 1710 Grant St, 95050; 408-988-2452; CC, Sa; 500; **D, R, PU**

Santa Clara Wreckers, *see Late Vintage*

Volpar Inc, 941 Laurelwood Rd, 95054; 408-986-0848, 800-258-4545; CC, Sa, Sp. Wr; **F; Volvo only; back to B18B & P1800; Open Sunday**

Santa Cruz; Anthony's Auto Dismantling, 980 17th Av, 95062; 831-475-9657; CC, Sp

Ginos Santa Cruz Auto Wrecking, *see Vintage*

Specialized Auto Parts, 980 17th Av #C7, 95062; 831-462-3458, FAX 831-462-4573, www.volvoguy.com; CC, Sa, Sp, Wr; **F; Mostly Volvo; B18B & P1800; Also new parts**

Santa Maria; Black Road Auto, *see Vintage*

Selma; Don's Auto Wrecking, *see Late Vintage*

Shafter; Dan's Auto Sales & Wrecking, *see Vintage*

Simi Valley; Simi Valley Auto Wrecking, *see Vintage*

Sonora; Sonora Auto & Truck Dismantlers, *see Vintage*

Stevinson; Valley Auto Wreckers, *see Late Vintage*

Stockton; Ben's Auto Dismantlers, *see Vintage*

    Charter Way Auto Recyclers, *see Vintage*

    Debco Auto Wreckers, *see Vintage*

    Delta Auto Wreckers, *see Vintage*

    Jaguar Heaven, *see Vintage*

    Kalends Auto Wrecking, 8237 E Hwy 26, 95215; 209-931-0929, 800-957-9955 CA only; Sp; 600+; **D, F; Spc: Japanese**

    Kennedy Auto, 4421 Clark Dr, 95215; 209-466-4987, FAX 209-466-4982, 800-984-4410; CC, Sp; 400+; **D, PU**

    Mathis Auto Wreckers & Parts, *see Vintage*

    Mel's Auto Dismantlers, 2219 Navy Dr, 95206; 209-462-8394, 800-665-6198; CC, Sa, Sp; 400+; **D, PU, 4x4; B3**

    Quinteros Auto Dismantling, *see Vintage*

    Stockton Auto Dismantlers, *see Vintage*

Sunnyvale; A & H Auto Dismantling, 295 Commercial St, 94086; 408-735-8424; CC, Sa, Sp, UR; 1ac, 70; **F, PU, 4x4; Mostly Japanese**

Tracy; P & C Auto Wreckers, 2520 W Byron Rd, 95376; 209-833-0418, FAX 209-833-0462, 800-807-2582, www.pcautoparts.com; CC, Sp; 600+; D, F, PU, 4x4; Spc: Ford

Tulare; C & C Auto Dismantling, *see Vintage*

    Tulare Auto Wrecking, *see Vintage*

Turlock; Golden State Auto Wrecking, *see Vintage*

    Kelso's Auto Wrecking & Towing, 549 S Walnut Rd, 95380; 209-632-9961; Sp; **D, F**

    Turlock Auto Wreckers, *see Vintage*

Victorville; New & Used Auto Glass, *see Vintage*

Visalia; Aarons Auto Wrck, 1818 E Goshen Av, 93292; 559-625-1818, FAX 559-625-1819, 800-455-1818, autoparts@lightspeed.net; CC, Sa, Sp; 300; **D, F, PU, 4x4, Trk**

    Allied Auto Dismantling, *see Vintage*

    Budget Auto Wrecking, *see Vintage*

Waterford; Waterford Auto & Truck, 12616 Yosemite Blvd, 95386; 209-874-2315, FAX 209-874-1514, 800-544-3488; CC, Sa, Sp; 600+; **D, PU, 4x4; Spc: Minivan & Pickup**

Watsonville; Coast Auto Supply & Dismantling, *see Late Vintage*

    Gerry's Foreign Auto Wreckers, *see Late Vintage*

Winton; Fisk Auto Wreckers, *see Vintage*

Yermo; D & M Auto Truck & RV Repair, *see Vintage*

Always preserve the parts you don't want while getting the ones you do want

Yard Operators Tell us...

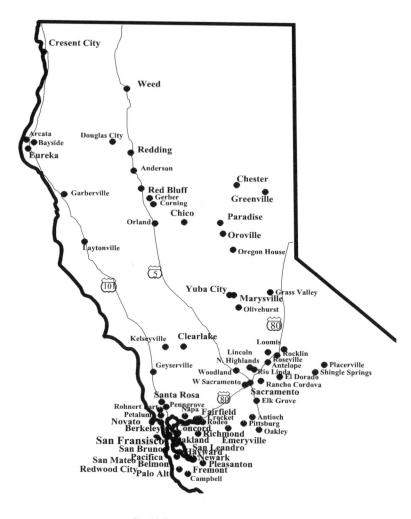

California - Northern

Please mention you saw'em in Ray's wReckingyard Roster when contacting these yards

CALIFORNIA – NORTHERN

VINTAGE

Anderson; All Car & Truck Recycling, 19555 Olinda Rd, 96007; 530-365-1119, FAX 530-365-4436, 800-959-2552; CC, Sp, UR; 600; **60+; D, F, PU, 4x4, Trk; B3**

Antelope; Antelope Foreign Dismantlers, 8634 Antelope North Rd, 95843; 916-723-3951, FAX 916-723-3304; CC, Sa, Sp; 120ac; **50+; F; Jag, MG, other British, more**

 J & W Auto Wreckers, 8626 Antelope North Rd, 95843; 916-723-3950, FAX 916-723-3953, www.jwjeep.com; CC, Sa, Sp, Br; 700; **50+; D; AMC, Jp; Spc: Jeep & AMC**

Belmont; Bibbs Auto Wreckers, 1695 Old County Rd, 94002; 650-593-9269; CC, Sa; 230; **49+; D, F; B3**

Campbell; Corvette Heaven, 892 Camden Av, 95008; 707-446-8595, FAX 707-446-8599, 800-557-8595; CC, Sa, Sp, Wr; **63-68; D; Corvette only; Also new & reproduction parts; Closed Monday**

Chester; Willis & Sons Auto Wrecking, 96020; 916-258-3478; CC, Sa, Sp, UR; 1000; **60+; D, F, PU, Trk; B3**

Chico; Fairview Auto Wrecking, 2437 Park Av, 95928; 530-343-1468; Sp; 100; **50-89; D; B3**

Clearlake; Middletown Towing Vehicle, 15970 Polk St, 95422; 707-995-2341; Sa; 10ac; **40+ Pickup, 50+ Car; D, F, PU; B3**

Concord; Rosal Auto Wreckers, 4030 Folsom Ct, 94520; 925-687-6621; Sa, Sp, UR; 400; **60+; D, F, PU, 4x4; B3; Spc: Honda Open Sunday**

Corning; All-Star Auto Wrecking, 22521 Capay Rd, 96021; 530-824-2880, FAX 530-824-4812; CC, Sa, UR; 1000+; **60+; D, F, PU, 4x4; B3; Spc: Mustang; Open Sunday**

Douglas City; Douglas City Garage, Hwy 3 & Marshall Ranch Rd, 96024; 530-623-4869; CC, UR; 1ac; **75+; 49-89; D, PU; B3; Upholstry repair, towing**

El Dorado; Kit Catterlin Truck & Auto, 4468 Forni Rd, 95623; 530-622-1721, FAX 530-622-9317, kitc@innersite.com; Sa, Sp, Br; 0.75ac; **60-89; D, F, PU, 4x4; Spc: 1/2-1 ton Pickup**

Elk Grove; Elk Grove Auto Dismantlers, 10250 Waterman Rd, 95624; 916-685-2583; Sa; 300+; **31-93; D, F, PU, 4x4; B3, Jp, IH, Pk; Closed Sunday & Monday**

Emeryville; European Auto Salvage Yard, 4060 Harlan St, 94608; 510-653-3279, FAX 510-653-3178; CC, Sa, Sp, Wr; **30; F; Porsche only, all series; New & used parts**

Eureka; John's Used Cars & Wreckers, 3008 Jacobs Av, 95501; 707-443-7065, FAX 707-443-2551, 800-400-7065; CC, Sa, Sp, UR; 3ac, 500; **53-93, mostly 70s & 80s; D, F, PU, 4x4; B3, AMC**

Fairfield; Fairvac Auto & Truck Wrecking, 5016 Peabody Rd, 94533; 707-437-5300, FAX 707-437-1460; Sa; 350+; **60+; D, F, PU; B3**

Gerber; Jim & Jerri's Auto Wreckers, 7980 State Hwy 99W, 96035; 530-385-1440; CC, Sa, Sp, Br; 7ac; **51+; D, F, PU, 4x4, Minivan, Trk, Fm; B3, Subaru; Spc: Foreign**

Geyserville; A-Auto Dismantlers, 19865 Geyserville Av, 95441; 707-433-9685, FAX 707-857-4455; Sa; 70; **60+; F; Mercedes**

Grass Valley; Kilroy's Auto Dismantling, 12077 State Hwy 49, 95949; 530-273-3495, FAX 530-273-6488; CC, Sa, UR; 3ac; **70s-89, few 40s-60s; D, F, PU, 4x4; B3, St**

Greenville; Carpenter's Auto Wrecking, 318 Ann St, 95947; 530-284-7221; Sp, Wr; **50-89; D, PU, 4x4; B3; Spc: Pickup & 4x4 70-89; Classic Section 50s-70s**

Hayward; Alfa Parts Exchange, 2000 National, 94545; 510-782-5800, FAX 510-782-4135, www.apedirect.com; CC, Sp, Wr; 2000; **50-95; F; Alfa Romeo, Land Rover only**

 Parts Heaven, 23694 Bernhardt St, 94545; 510-782-0354; CC, Sa, Sp, Wr; **F; Porsche only**

Kelseyville; Kelseyville Auto Salvage & Tow, 7666 Hwy 29, 95451; 707-279-2123; Sa, Sp, Br; 350; **50-90; D, F, PU, Trk; B3**

Lincoln; Euro Sport, 1825 Shamrock Ln, 95648; 916-645-9111, FAX 916-645-9119, eurosprtca@aol.com; CC, Sa, Sp; 60ac; **D, F; Porsche 911, English, Indy; Restoration, buys & sells exotics, will locate cars**

Marysville; Anderson Auto Wreckers, 4199 Feather River Rd, 95901; 530-743-6591; CC, Sa, UR; 250; **60+; D, F, PU, 4x4; B3, AMC, Jp, IH, VW; Open Sunday**

 Bill's Auto Wreckers, 5064 Feather River Blvd, 95901; 530-742-2423; Sa, UR; 3ac, 200; **60+; D, F, PU; B3**

Newark; Cash for Junk Cars, 7400 Mowry Av, 94560; FAX 916-639-6117, 800-442-5865; Sa, UR; 17ac; **60+; D, F, PU, 4x4, Trk; B3, AMC, Jp, IH, VW**

Novato; Turrinis Auto Salvage Inc, 8950 Redwood Hwy, 94945; 415-897-2090; CC, Sa; 7ac; 300; **60-89; D, F, PU, 4x4, Trk; B3, AMC, Jp, IH, VW**

Oakland; All Mercedes Dismantlers Inc, 1225 7th St, 94607; 510-763-8602, FAX 510-555-1235, 800-234-5594, www.allmercedes.com; Sa, Sp; **50-91; F; Mercedes only**

Cypress Salvage, 2717 Peralta St, 94607; 510-451-3034, FAX 510-451-5714, 800-573-7278; CC, Sp, Wr; 100; **60s & 88+; D, F, PU, 4x4; B3, Jp, VW; Spc: 60's Mustang, Cougar, Chevelle**

Dyno Automotives Inc, 9845 Bigge St, 94603; 510-632-9335, FAX 510-632-8539, 800-252-3966; CC, Sa, Sp, Wr; **60-90; F; Porsche only**

Oakley; A & A Auto Parts, 6240 Brentwood Blvd, 94561; 925-634-1188, 800-CADDY-51; CC, Sa, Sp, UR; 1000; **41-96; D; Cadillac only**

H & M Auto Dismantlers, 5740 Main St, 94561; 925-625-2100, FAX 925-625-2731, 800-973-2536; Sa, Sp, Br; 850+; **55-94; D, F, PU, 4x4, Trk; B3, IH**

Two Friends Auto Dismantlers, 6337 Brentwood Blvd, 94561; 925-634-2000; Sa, Sp, UR; 250; **58-93; D, F, PU, 4x4, Trk, Fm, In, Cn, Mil; B3, AMC, Jp, IH, VW**

Orland; Parts R Us Dismantlers, 3948 County Road 99W, 95963; 530-865-7160; Sp, Br; 2000; **60+; D, F, PU, 4x4, Trk; B3, AMC, VW**

Silveira Auto Wrecking, 3852 County Rd 99, 95963; 530-865-4196; Sp, Br; 5ac; **50-80s; D, PU, 4x4; B3, AMC**

Stoneycreek Auto Dismantlers, 4620 99 W, 95963; 530-865-3755, FAX 530-865-9603, 800-322-5458; CC, Sp; 8ac; **52+; D; B3, AMC**

Oroville; Nick's Automotive Svc, 4280 Lincoln Blvd, 95966; 530-533-1653, FAX 530-532-9113; Sa, Sp, Br; 2ac, 150; **30+; D, F, 4x4; B3, AMC, Jp**

Palo Alto; Infinity Auto Salvage, 2091 Bay Rd, 94303; 650-323-8588; Sa, Sp, Br; 2ac; **50+; D, F, PU, 4x4; B3**

Rogges Auto Wrecking, 150 Tara Rd, 94303; 650-324-0101; **60-80; D, F, PU, 4x4**

Pittsburg; M Fernandes Auto Dismantler, 650 W 10th St, 94565; 925-458-4400; CC, Sa, UR; 500+; **50+; D, F, PU, 4x4, Trk; B3, AMC, Jp, IH, VW; Open Sunday**

Placerville; Gillys Auto Wrckr, 2561 Blacks Ln, 95667; 530-622-4052, FAX 530-622-4074, 888-622-4052, ianjhunt@gillys.com, www.gillys.com; 600+; **50-72; D; B3**

Rancho Cordova; American Mustang Parts, 11315 Folsom Blvd, 95742; 916-635-7271, FAX 916-635-4647, 800-824-6026, www.american-mustang.com; CC, Sa, Sp, Wr; **65-73; D; Mustang only; New & used parts**

Rancho Cordova; Cadillac Auto Recycling, 3715 Recycle Rd, 95742; 916-638-5515, FAX 916-638-5699, 800-368-2223, www.cadauto.com; CC, Sa, Sp, Wr; **56+; D; Cadillac only**

Chevy Sports Recycling, 3750 Recycle Rd, 95742; 916-638-7039, FAX 916-638-0302; CC, Sa, Sp; 75+; **60-79; D; GM muscle cars; Steering column restoration, also new parts**

German Auto Recycling, 761 Recycle Rd, 95742; 916-631-7280, FAX 916-631-8708, 800-688-2834; CC, Sa, Sp, UR; 12ac, 2500; **50+; D, F, PU, 4x4, Trk, Fm; B3, AMC, Jp, IH**

Pull & Save Recycling, 11355 Dismantle Ct, 95742; 916-635-2000, FAX 916-635-3474; CC, Sa, Sp, UR; 14ac, 1600; **50+; D, F, PU, 4x4; B3; $1 admission**

Rancho Ford Truck Parts, 3731 Recycle Rd, 95742; 916-638-2222, FAX 916-638-1160, 800-434-2222, ; CC, Sa, Sp, Br; 1ac, 250+; **59+; D, PU, 4x4, Trk; Ford trucks only**

Rancho Jeep Recycling, 3551 Recycle Rd #2, 95742; 916-635-3800, 800-875-7570; CC, Sa, Sp; 150; **60+; D, 4x4; Jeep only**

Red Bluff; Truck World, 10095 State Hwy 99W, 96080; 530-529-1560; CC, Sp, UR; 12ac, 800; **60+; D, F, PU, 4x4, Vans; B3**

Redding; Clear Creek Auto Wreckers, 17091 Clear Creek Rd, 96001; 530-241-8808, FAX 530-241-8815, 800-409-9073; CC, Sa, Sp; **50+; D, F, PU, 4x4; B3, AMC, Jp, VW**

Cruzing Auto Wrecking, 10044 Old Oregon Trail, 96003; 530-223-3891; Sa; 500; **50-80; D, F; B3**

Gustafson's Auto Wrecking, 19748 Collyer Dr, 96003; 530-241-4246, 888-689-8668; Sp; 9ac, 1500; **30-90; D, F; B3, AMC, Jp, Ns, St, Pk, Ks, Fr, VW, Volvo, Saab**

Jeep Recycling, 10098 Limerick Ln, 96003; 530-221-8767, FAX 530-221-5956, 888-932-5337; CC, Sp, PL; 400; **50+; D, 4x4; Jeep only**

Steve's Auto Wrecking, 9972 Old Oregon Trail, 96003; 530-221-1747; 1ac; **60-89; D, PU, 4x4; B3; Spc: Pickup**

Redwood City; Greg's VW Svc Center, 2976 Middlefield Rd, 94063; 650-364-1406, 888-GREGSVW, www.gregsvw.com; CC, Sa, Wr; **48+; F; VW Restorations**

High Performance House, 2431 Spring St, 94063; 650-364-6234, FAX 650-364-6905, www.highperformancehouse.com, hphporsche@aol.com; CC, Sa, Sp, Wr; **D, F; Porsche & Viper only; 23 years experience, All Porsche series**

Richmond; Carlos Auto Wreckers, 51 Parr Blvd, 94801; 510-235-1226, FAX 510-235-3693; Sa, UR; 2ac, 150; **34-84; D, PU, 4x4; B3, AMC, Jp, Ks**

Deal Auto & Truck Wrecking, 400 W Gertrude Av, 94801; 510-232-0197, FAX 510-232-5224; CC, Sa, Sp, UR; 2000; **30+Domestic, 85+Foreign; D, F, PU, 4x4, Trk; B3**

Rio Linda; Capital Auto Parts & Towing, 6721 26th St, 95673; 916-991-3026; Sa, Sp; **60-72; D; mostly GM, Spc: Camaro, Monte Carlo**

Nelson's Auto & Truck Dismantler, 6801 W 6th St, 95673; 916-991-0083; Sa, UR; 2ac, 100; **60-80; D, F, PU, 4x4; B3**

Rocklin; Truck Rex Recyclers, 4080 Delmar Av, 95677; 916-624-0609, 800-300-1739; CC, Sa, Sp; 47-**81; D, PU; B3; Spc: Ford & Chevy Pickup**

Rodeo; Pinole-Rodeo Auto Wreckers, 700 Parker Av, 94572; 510-758-2095, FAX 510-758-4905, 800-750-2095; CC, Sa, Sp; 1ac; **60+; D, F, PU, 4x4, Minivans, Trk; B3**

Roseville; B W Auto Dismantlers, 2031 PFE Rd, 95747; 916-782-8469, FAX 916-782-2903, 800-327-0888; CC, Sa, Sp, Br, PL; 4ac, 500; **60+; F; VW & Audi only**

Chevy Truck Parts, 9280 Atkinson St, 95747; 916-786-9039, FAX 916-786-8919, 800-470-2438; CC, Sa, Sp; 0.5ac; **60+; D, PU, 4x4; Chevy Pickup only**

Sacramento; Buick Bonery, 6970 Stanyser Way, 95828; 916-381-5271; Sp; 175; **36-75; D; Buick only; By appointment only**

Chatfields Auto Dismantlers, 1101 Del Paso Blvd, 95815; 916-925-2736, FAX 916-925-4030, 800-700-2438; CC, Sa, Sp; 2ac, 175; **62-90; D; GM only**

Payless Auto Dismantlers, 7040 McComber St, 95828; 916-383-5853; Sp; 1ac, 75+; **60-89; D, PU; GM only; Spc: Chevette, Impala, Nova, Camaro**

Subway Truck Parts Inc, 903 Del Paso Blvd, 95815; 916-925-0458, FAX 916-925-2270, 800-782-9294; CC, Sp; **55+; D, PU, Trk; B3, IH; Trucks only**

Sweden Auto Warehouse, 8516 Fruitridge Rd #A, 95826; 916-387-6892, FAX 916-387-0187, 800-686-5868; CC, Sa, Sp, Wr; **60+; F; Volvo & Saab only; Some B18, 140 series, all other series**

San Francisco; A-All Auto Dismantlers, 1700 Evans Av, 94124; 415-826-0913, FAX 415-826-5005; Sa, UR; 350+; **60+; D, F, PU, 4x4; B3, Jp**

Air Cool Auto, 525 Phelps St, 94124; 415-826-0667, 888-4VWONLY, www.aircoolauto.com; CC, Sa, Sp, Wr; **46-79; F; VW only**

Bayside Auto & Truck Parts, 1900 Evans Av, 94124; 415-647-7505, FAX 415-647-0323; Sa, Sp, UR; 3ac, 300; **few 46-69, mostly 85+; D, F; B3, AMC, Jp**

Big J Used Auto Parts, 951 Hudson Av, 94124; 415-648-5571, FAX 415-648-2245; Sa, Sp, UR; 1ac, 30; **50-89; D, PU; B3, Jp; Transmission & engine repair**

Fender House Auto Wreckers, 3550 3rd St, 94124; 415-648-2100; CC, Sa, UR; 3ac, 1000; **60-79; D, F, PU, 4x4; B3**

San Leandro; Phelp's Auto Wreckers, 2640 Eden Rd, 94577; 510-569-4845; Sa; 2ac; **60s+; D, F, PU, 4x4; B3; Spc: Muscle cars**

Santa Rosa; All Trucks, 1516 Airport Blvd, 95403; 707-523-7589; CC, Sa, Sp, Br; 6ac; **59+; D, F, PU, 4x4, Trk; B3; Trucks only**

Shingle Springs; Bonanza Auto Dismantlers, 5200 Bonanza Auto Rd, 95682; 530-622-6184, FAX 530-677-4861, 800-559-0349 Local only; CC, Sa, Sp, UR; 2000; **57+; D, F, PU, 4x4, Trk; B3, AMC, Jp, IH, VW**

Weed; Black Butte Auto Dismantling, PO Box 65, 800 Hwy 97, 96094; 530-938-1110, FAX 530-938-4561; CC, Sa, Sp; 12ac; **60+; D, F, PU, 4x4, few Trk; B3**

Woodland; Metro Auto Dismantling, 19389 County Road 102, 95776; 530-662-9243, FAX 530-662-5966, 888-291-6871; CC, Sa, Sp, UR; 6ac; **40-85; D, F, PU, 4x4; B3**

Yuba City; A C Auto Dismantling, 800 Garden Hwy, 95991; 530-674-7721; Sa, Sp, Br, Wr; 3.5ac; **few 40-50, mostly 60+; D, F, PU; B3; Glass for older cars already removed**

B & B Auto Parts Inc, 1478 Garden Hwy, 95991; 530-673-4791; CC, Br; 5ac; **55+; D, F; B3, VW; Spc: Chevy, Corvette, Harley, VW Bug**

Dick's Auto Dismantling, 351 Samuel Dr, 95991; 530-673-8868; Br; 1ac; **60-89; D, F, PU, 4x4; B3**

Joe's GM Auto Parts, 236 Garden Hwy, 95991; 530-674-0640, FAX 530-674-1328, 800-336-0640; CC, Sp, Br; 1.5ac; **60-90; D, PU, 4x4; GM Pickup & 4x4 only**

LATE VINTAGE

Anderson; All Car & Truck Recycling, *see Vintage*

Antelope; Antelope Foreign Dismantlers, *see Vintage*

J & W Auto Wreckers, *see Vintage*

Antioch; A-1 Auto Dismantlers, 2707 Pittsburg Antioch Hwy #A, 94509; 925-777-1515; CC, Sa, Sp; 550+; **78-89; D, F, PU; B3**

Arcata; Arcata's S & H Auto Wreckers, 3028 Alliance Rd, 95521; 707-822-5914, FAX 707-822-7784, 800-400-5914; CC, Sa; 5ac; **70-89; D, F, PU; B3**

Bayside; Rogers Garage, 1622 Old Arcata Rd, 95524; 707-822-2931, FAX 707-822-5864, 835-7006; CC, Sp; 100; **70-89; D, F, PU; B3**

Belmont; Bibbs Auto Wreckers, *see Vintage*

Berkeley; Bay Motor Wrecking, 1017 Folger Av, 94710; 510-649-1112; CC, Sa, Sp, Wr; **66+; F; BMW**

European Auto Salvage, 1075 2nd St, 94710; 510-524-9022; CC; 35+; **76+; F; Mercedes only**

Wolfsport, 1453 4th St, 94710; 510-525-6000, FAX 510-525-4590, 800-342-8669, www.wolfsport.com; CC, Sa, Sp, Wr; 10; **80+; F; VW water cooled only, Audi, BMW Used & reproduction parts, mail order**

Chester; Willis & Sons Auto Wrecking, *see Vintage*

Chico; Fairview Auto Wrecking, *see Vintage*

Clearlake; Middletown Towing Vehicle, *see Vintage*

Concord; Bud's Bugs, 4055 Folsom Ct, 94520; 925-825-8338, www.budsbugs.com; CC, Sa, Sp, UR; 0.75ac, 100; **70+; F; VW only; Closed Monday**

Rosal Auto Wreckers, *see Vintage*

Corning; All-Star Auto Wrecking, *see Vintage*

Crescent City; A-1 Auto Wreckers, 1100 McNamara Rd, 95531; 707-464-7732; Sa; 4ac; 350+; **70-84; D, F, PU, 4x4; B3**

Douglas City; Douglas City Garage, *see Vintage*

El Dorado; Kit Catterlin Truck & Auto, *see Vintage*

Elk Grove; Elk Grove Auto Dismantlers, *see Vintage*

Emeryville; Easy Auto Salvage Yard, 4060 Harlan St, 94608; 510-653-5733, FAX 510-653-3178; CC, Sa, Sp, Wr; 50; **64-89; F; Mercedes, Porsche only; Used & reproduction parts**

European Auto Salvage Yard, *see Vintage*

Maz Auto, 3906 Adeline St, 94608; 510-428-3950; CC, Sa, Sp; 600; **70+; D, F, PU, 4x4; B3, AMC, Jp, IH, VW**

Eureka; John's Used Cars & Wreckers, *see Vintage*

Fairfield; Fairvac Auto & Truck Wrecking, *see Vintage*

Pick-N-Pull, 4659 Airbase Pky, 94533; 800-442-5865; Sa, UR; **D, F, PU, 4x4; B3, VW; Part of chain**

Fremont; Vintage Chevy Trucks, 3490 Fremont Blvd, 94538; 510-651-5874, FAX 510-651-7248, www.vintagechevytrucks.com; CC, Sa, Sp, Wr; **67-72; D; Chevy Pickup only**

Gerber; Jim & Jerri's Auto Wreckers, *see Vintage*

Geyserville; A-Auto Dismantlers, *see Vintage*

Grass Valley; Grass Valley Auto Dismantling, 647 E Main St, 95945; 530-273-5216; CC, Sa, UR; 1.5ac; **70-89; D, F, PU, 4x4; B3**

Kilroy's Auto Dismantling, *see Vintage*

Greenville; Carpenter's Auto Wrecking, *see Vintage*

Hayward; AAA Truck Wreckers, 3884 Depot Rd, 94545; 510-782-9433, FAX 510-782-2825; Sa, UR; **80+ D, 4x4; Be3, Jp, IH, St**

Alfa Parts Exchange, *see Vintage*

Double O2 Salvage Inc, 2034 American Av, 94545; 510-782-2002; Wr; **64+; D, F; Chevy, VW**

E & J Auto Wreckers, 2851 W Winton Av, 94545; 510-785-7244; Sa; 10ac; **80+; D, F, PU; B3**

East Bay Auto Dismantling, 3892 Depot Rd, 94545; 510-785-5850; CC; 2ac; **F; VW, Volvo**

Parts Heaven, *see Vintage*

Pick Your Part Auto Wrecking, 2557 W Winton Av, 94545; 510-785-3770; CC, Sa, UR; **D, F, PU, 4x4; B3**

Kelseyville; Kelseyville Auto Salvage & Tow, *see Vintage*

Laytonville; Laytonville Auto Wreckers, 201 Branscomb Rd, 95454; 707-984-6566; UR; 4ac; **65+; D, F; B3, AMC, VW**

Lincoln; Euro Sport, *see Vintage*

Loomis; Sierra Truck Div Loomis, 3363 Swetzer Rd, 95650; 916-652-5311; **72+; D, F, Trk**

Marysville; Anderson Auto Wreckers, *see Vintage*

Bill's Auto Wreckers, *see Vintage*

Marysville; United Truck Dismantlers, 2488 McGowan Pky, 95901; 530-742-8258, FAX 530-742-2605, 800-371-9555; CC, Sp; 5ac; 250+; **80+; D, PU, 4x4, SUV; B3**

Napa; Napa Auto Parts, 3117 California Blvd, 94558; 707-253-2886; CC, Sa, Sp; **80+; D, F; B3, AMC**

Newark; Ace Auto Wreckers, 7580 Mowry Av, 94560; 510-797-8922; Sa, UR; 10ac, 3000; **80-90, few older; D, F, PU, few 4x4, Trk; B3, AMC, VW**

Bay Area Bumper Svc, 7887 Enterprise Dr, 94560; 510-505-9010, FAX 510-505-9219, 800-285-2867; **80+; D, F; Spc: plastic bumpers**

Newark; Cash for Junk Cars, *see Vintage*

North Highlands; ABC Foreign Dismantlers, 6114 32nd St, 95660; 916-334-2226, 800-901-RECK; CC, Sa, Sp, Br; 2ac; **70+; F; Jpa**

Novato; Arnold's Auto Dismantler, 864 Vallejo Av, 94945; 415-892-3900, FAX 415-897-0511; **70+; D, F, PU, 4x4, Trk; B3, Jp, VW**

Turrinis Auto Salvage Inc, *see Vintage*

Oakland; All Mercedes Dismantlers Inc, *see Vintage*

Oakland; Cash for Junk Cars, 8451 San Leandro St, 94621; 510-729-7010, 800-442-5865; Sa, Sp, UR; **D, F; B3**

Dyno Automotives Inc, *see Vintage*

Mercedes Depot, 2904 Glascock St, 94601; 510-436-7888; Sa, Sp, UR; 60; **70+; F; Mercedes only**

Oakley; A & A Auto Parts, *see Vintage*

H & M Auto Dismantlers, *see Vintage*

Two Friends Auto Dismantlers, *see Vintage*

Orland; Parts R Us Dismantlers, *see Vintage*

Silveira Auto Wrecking, *see Vintage*

Stoneycreek Auto Dismantlers, *see Vintage*

Oroville; AGS Enterprises, 4248 Lincoln Blvd, 95966; 530-532-9648; CC, Sa; 500; **70+; D, F, PU, 4x4; B3, AMC, Jp, IH, VW**

B & E Auto Wrecking, 3301 Feather River Rd, 95965; 530-533-0717; CC, Sa, Sp; 5ac, 500+; **70-85; D, F, PU, 4x4; B3, AMC, Jp, IH, VW Rabbit**

Nick's Automotive Svc, *see Vintage*

Palo Alto; Infinity Auto Salvage, *see Vintage*

Rogges Auto Wrecking, *see Vintage*

Paradise; Skyway Auto Wreckers, 5628 Skyway, 95969; 530-877-7831; CC, Sa, Sp; 3ac; **69-95; D, F, PU, 4x4; B3, AMC, Jp, IH, VW**

Penngrove; Penngrove Auto Dismantlers, 6040 Old Redwood Hwy, 94951; 707-795-3674, 800-321-6981; CC, Sa, Br; 200; **68+; D, F, PU, 4x4; B3; Spc: Pickup**

Petaluma; C & W Auto Wreckers, 892 Lakeville St, 94952; 707-763-4057, FAX 707-792-0622; Sp; 0.5ac, 100; **70+; D, F, PU, 4x4; B3, VW**

California Crush, 92 Lakeville St, 94952; 707-763-9355; CC, Sp, Br; 2ac; **80-93; D, F, PU, 4x4; B3**

Pittsburg; M Fernandes Auto Dismantler, *see Vintage*

Placerville; Gills Auto Wreckers, *see Vintage*

Rancho Cordova; All Dodge Truck & Van, 11350 S Bridge St, 95670; 916-635-7602, 800-433-7667; CC, Sa, Sp, Wr; **72+; D, PU; Full size Dodge Pickup & Van**

All Japanese Auto Recyclers, 11301 Dismantle Ct, 95742; 916-635-2345, FAX 916-635-8100, 888-608-7278; CC, Sa, Sp, Br; 300; **80+; F; Jpa**

All Mini Truck & Van Inc, 3420 Sunrise Blvd, 95742; 916-852-0384, FAX 916-852-1405; CC, Sa, Sp; 2ac; **80+; D, F, PU; B3; Jpa; Mini Pickup & Van Only**

American Mustang Parts, *see Vintage*

American River Auto Wrecking, 3419 Sunrise Blvd, 95742; 916-635-2400, FAX 916-631-6814, 800-247-7477 N CA only; CC, Sa, Br; 10ac, 700; **82+; D, F, PU, 4x4; B3, Jp, Jpa; Spc: Chevy, Ford & minitrucks**

BOP Auto Recycling, 3469 Fitzgerald Rd, 95742; 916-638-4267, 800-576-6347, www.bopautorecycling.com; CC, Sa, Sp; 4ac, 400+; **80+; D; GM front wheel drive only**

Bavarian BMW Auto Recycling, 3688 Omec Circle, 95742; 916-635-4269, FAX 916-638-0469, 800-726-8145, www.bmrparts.com; CC, Sp, Wr; **68-95; F; BMW only**

Cadillac Auto Recycling, *see Vintage*

Cash for Junk Cars, 3445 Sunrise Blvd, 95742; 916-332-5573, 800-442-5865; Sa, UR; **D, F, PU, 4x4; B3**

Cats Auto Wrecking, 3400 Sunrise Blvd, 95742; 916-631-8004; Sa, Sp; 70+; **D, F, PU, 4x4, Trk; Chevy & Ford Trucks only**

Chevy Sports Recycling, *see Vintage*

German Auto Recycling, *see Vintage*

German Parts Warehouse, 3600 Recycle Rd, 95742; 916-635-6469, 800-464-5284, www.bugworld.com; CC, Sa, Sp; 300; **70+; F; VW only, mostly water-cooled**

Hap Recycling, 3450 Recycle Rd, 95742; 916-638-3311, FAX 916-638-8697, 800-999-9499, www.haprecyc.com; CC, Sa, Sp; 250; **80+; F; Honda & Acura only**

Mazda Auto Dismantlers, 3501 Recycle Rd, 95742; 916-638-2664, FAX 916-853-8577, 800-699-2664, www.mazda-dism.com; CC, Sa, Sp; 300; **79+; F; Mazda only, incl. RX-7**

Mazda Auto Recycling, 3636 Omec Cir, 95742; 916-635-5900, 888-926-5900, www.mazdarecycling.com; CC, Sa, Sp, Br, Wr; 300; **80+; F; Mazda only**

Pull & Save Recycling, *see Vintage*

Rancho Chevy Recycling, 3527 Recycle Rd, 95742; 916-635-5500, FAX 916-635-6410, 800-722-6015; CC, Sa, Sp; 450+; **73+; D, PU, Vans; Chevy, Camaro, Firebird, Corvette only**

Rancho Ford Truck Parts, *see Vintage*

Rancho Jeep Recycling, *see Vintage*

Silver Star Mercedes Benz & Porsche, 11315-A Dismantle Ct, 95742; 916-631-7300, FAX 916-852-5544, 800-783-4911; CC, Sa, Sp; 100; **65+; F; Mercedes, Porsche**

Sunrise Foreign Auto Dismantlers, 3370 Sunrise Blvd, 95742; 916-635-8600, 800-557-8674, www.sunfor.com; CC, Sa, Sp, PL; 300; **80+; F**

Sunrise Nissan, 3450 Sunrise Blvd, 95742; 916-631-8795, FAX 916-631-8849, 800-813-3345; CC, Sa, Sp; 150; **80+; F, PU; Nissan only**

Tap Recycling, 11337 Dismantle Ct, 95742; 916-631-7100, FAX 916-631-3528, 800-765-7100, www.taprecycl.com; CC, Sa, Sp; 400; **79+; F; Toyota & Lexus only**

Toyautomart, 310 Sunrise Blvd, 95742; 916-635-8900, FAX 916-635-8986, www.toy.com; CC, Sa, Sp; 200; **F, PU, 4x4; Toyota only**

Volvo & Saab Auto Dismantlers, 3539 Recycle Rd, 95742; 916-635-9970, FAX 916-635-0879, 800-700-VOLVO, www.volvosaabparts.com; CC, Sa, Sp, Wr; 200; **75+; F; Volvo & Saab only**

Red Bluff; Hess Brothers Auto Recyclers, 3650 Hess Rd, 96080; 530-527-0639; CC, Sa, Sp; 400; **70+; D, F, PU, 4x4; B3**

Truck World, *see Vintage*

Redding; Clear Creek Auto Wreckers, *see Vintage*

Cruzing Auto Wrecking, *see Vintage*

Gustafson's Auto Wrecking, *see Vintage*

Jeep Recycling, *see Vintage*

Steve's Auto Wrecking, *see Vintage*

Redding Auto Ctr, 2850 Viking Way, 96003; 530-222-1880, FAX 530-222-6377, 800-424-2002; CC, Sa, Sp; 22ac, 2000; **65+; D, F, PU, 4x4; B3**

Redding U-Pull-It Auto, 1393 Hartnell Av, 96002; 530-222-4998, 222-3729 to sell cars; Sa, UR; **D, F; $1 admission**

Viking Auto & Truck Wrecking, 19980 Viking Way, 96003; 530-223-3481, FAX 530-223-3281, 800-338-7474; CC, Sa, Sp; 22ac, 2500; **70+; D, PU, 4x4; B3, AMC, Jp, IH**

Redwood City; Greg's VW Svc Center, *see Vintage*

High Performance House, *see Vintage*

Van's Auto Wrecking, 1831 E Bayshore Rd, 94063; 650-367-8267; CC, Sa, Sp, PL; 3ac, 200; **65+; D, F, PU, 4x4; B3, IH, Jpa**

Richmond; Carlos Auto Wreckers, *see Vintage*

Deal Auto & Truck Wrecking, *see Vintage*

Rio Linda; Capital Auto Parts & Towing, *see Vintage*

Nelson's Auto & Truck Dismantler, *see Vintage*

Rocklin; Truck Rex Recyclers, *see Vintage*

Rodeo; Pinole-Rodeo Auto Wreckers, *see Vintage*

Rohnert Park; Camaroland, 640 Martin Av, 94928; 707-585-3272, FAX 707-568-7037; CC, Sa, Sp, Wr; 0.75ac, 200; **D; Camaro mostly**

Roseville; B W Auto Dismantlers, *see Vintage*

Chevy Truck Parts, *see Vintage*

Roseville Auto Dismantling, 1961 PFE Rd, 95747; 916-783-5216, FAX 916-783-8840, 800-833-9292, www.merkurgarage.com; CC, Sa, Sp, Br; 23ac, 1200; **75+; D, F; Fd, Lincoln, Mercury, Spc: Merkur**

Sacramento; A & M Auto Wreckers, 716 Bell Av, 95838; 916-922-8833, FAX 916-922-0843, 800-700-4426; CC, Sa, Sp; 2ac, 200; **65-73; D; GM, Ford only**

Ace Auto Wrecking, 523 1st Av, 95818; 916-443-8299, FAX 916-443-4023, 800-698-5060; Sa, Sp; 1ac, 30; **75+; F, PU; Honda, Toyota & Acura only**

All Ford Auto Recycling, 7050 McComber St, 95828; 916-383-8694; CC, Sa, Sp; **80+, few older; D; Ford only**

American Auto Wreckers, 6128 Stockton Blvd, 95824; 916-421-0840, FAX 916-421-0850; CC, Sa, Sp; 5ac, 750; **85-94; D, PU; B3; also 66-70 Pontiac**

Auto Gator Nissan Parts, 5325 Dry Creek Rd, 95838; 916-991-4191, 800-252-6662, www.autogator.com; CC, Sa, Sp, Wr; **70+; F; Nissan & Infiniti & 70+Zs**

Buick Bonery, *see Vintage*

Chatfields Auto Dismantlers, *see Vintage*

Cordova Truck Dismantlers, 4075 Happy Ln, 95827; 916-366-6892, FAX 916-366-7768, 800-273-4774; CC, Sp, Br; 6ac, 175; **80+; D, PU, 4x4; Fd, Chevy; Standard Transmission 366-6866 in same facility**

Florin Auto Wreckers, 7006 McComber St, 95828; 916-383-8200; Sa, Sp; 250; **75-90; D, F; B3**

Freeway Auto, 1961 Auburn Blvd, 95815; 916-927-2421, FAX 916-927-0287; CC, Sa, Sp, Br; 150; **80+; D; Ford only**

J B Otto Parts, 7946 Carlton Rd, 95826; 916-456-7130; CC, Wr; **85-89; F; Honda only**

Lucky's Auto Wreckers, 8560 Unsworth Av, 95828; 916-383-3003, FAX 916-383-3075; Sa; 5ac; **65+; D, F, PU; B3, AMC**

Payless Auto Dismantlers, *see Vintage*

Sacramento Towing By Chimas, 1933 Naomi Way, 95815; 916-332-4243, 800-959-8015; CC, Sa, Sp; 200; **80+; D, F, PU, 4x4; B3**

51

Subway Truck Parts Inc, *see Vintage*
Sweden Auto Warehouse, *see Vintage*
San Bruno; San Bruno Auto Dismantlers II, 1069 San Mateo Av, 94066; 650-873-2555, FAX 650-873-5829; Sa, Sp; 2ac, 75+; **80+; D, F, PU, 4x4; B3, Jp, VW**
San Francisco; A C Auto Wreckers, 220 Rankin St, 94124; 415-647-0389, 826-5454, FAX 415-642-2868; CC, Sa, Br; **65-90; D, F, PU, 4x4; B3**
San Francisco; A-All Auto Dismantlers, *see Vintage*
Ace Auto Dismantlers Inc, 2255 McKinnon Av, 94124; 415-282-1353, FAX 415-282-3237, www.jps.net/acescrap; CC, UR, Wr; 0.5ac; **69-92; D, F, PU, 4x4, Trk; B3, AMC, Jp, IH, VW; Spc: scrap metal**
Air Cool Auto, *see Vintage*
Big J Used Auto Parts, *see Vintage*
Fender House Auto Wreckers, *see Vintage*
Levan International Auto Body, 1201 Minnesota, 94107; 650-826-8441, FAX 650-826-0365, 800-809-9090; CC, Sa, Sp, Wr; 65+; **D, F, PU, 4x4, Trk; B3, AMC, Jp, IH, VW; Also reproduction parts**
San Leandro; Arrow Truck Parts, 2622 Eden Rd, 94577; 510-569-3663; CC, Sp; 200; **80+; D, F, PU, 4x4, Vans; B3; Vans & trucks only**
Phelp's Auto Wreckers, *see Vintage*
San Mateo; Tresser's Towing Svc, 120 S Amphlett Blvd, 94401; 650-343-6754, FAX 650-341-5653; CC, UR; 30; **70+; D, F, PU, 4x4; B3**
Santa Rosa; All Trucks, *see Vintage*
Bob Wescott's Auto Parts, 1569 Sebastopol Rd, 95407; 707-542-0311, 800-862-4670 local only; CC; **80-95; D, F, PU, 4x4; B3, AMC**
Faraudos Auto Dismantlers, 1061 N Dutton Av, 95401; 707-544-7550; CC, Sp; 120; **F; VW & Volvo only**
Van's VW, 412 Yolanda Av, 95404; 707-576-1216; CC, Sa, Sp; 100; **65+; F; VW only**
Shingle Springs; Bonanza Auto Dismantlers, *see Vintage*
Weed; Black Butte Auto Dismantling, *see Vintage*
W Sacramento; Carro Pacific Inc, 545 Jefferson Blvd, 95691; 916-372-7277, FAX 916-372-9384, 800-609-9918; CC, Sa, Sp, Wr; **70+; D, F, PU, 4x4, Trk; B3, AMC, Jp, VW**
Tom's Toys Import Connection, 2620 W Capitol Av, 95691; 916-371-7764, 800-221-8696 local only; CC, Sp, Br; 200; **80+; F**
Woodland; Metro Auto Dismantling, *see Vintage*
Yuba City; A C Auto Dismantling, *see Vintage*
B & B Auto Parts Inc, *see Vintage*
Dick's Auto Dismantling, *see Vintage*
Joe's GM Auto Parts, *see Vintage*
Town & Country Towing, 940 Von Geldern Way, 95991; 530-755-0480, 800-916-4973; CC, Sa, Sp; 1.5ac; **70+; D, F, PU; B3**
LATE MODEL
Anderson; All Car & Truck Recycling, *see Vintage*
Antelope; Antelope Foreign Dismantlers, *see Vintage*
J & W Auto Wreckers, *see Vintage*
James Auto Wreckers, 8650 Antelope North Rd, 95843; 916-725-2171, FAX 916-725-0782; CC, Sa, Sp; 12ac; **D, F, PU; B3**
Belmont; Bibbs Auto Wreckers, *see Vintage*
Berkeley; All Foreign Auto Salvage, 1507 2nd St, 94710; 510-525-5132; CC, Sa, Sp; 100; **F**
Attarco Inc, 707 Jones St, 94710; 510-525-3333; CC, Sa, Sp; **F, PU, 4x4; engines & transmissions only**
Bay Motor Wrecking, *see Late Vintage*
European Auto Salvage, *see Late Vintage*
Jetco Motors, 2370 4th St, 94710; 510-843-0400; **F: Jpa engines & transmissions only**
Wolfsport, *see Late Vintage*
Chester; Willis & Sons Auto Wrecking, *see Vintage*

Chico; Chico Auto & Truck Recovery, 2535 Fair St, 95928; 530-343-1468, FAX 530-343-1610; CC, Sa, Sp; 4ac; **D, Pickup mostly**

Rising Sun Engines, 2695 State Hwy 32, 95973; 530-895-0300, www.risingsunmotors.com; CC, Sa, Sp, Wr; **F; Japanese engines and transmissions only**

Steve's Auto Wrecking, 533 Orange St, 95928; 530-891-0211; Sa, Sp, UR, Wr; **D, F; B**3

Tach Engines, 900 Orange St, 95928; 530-893-8224; **F; engines only**

Clearlake; Middletown Towing Vehicle, *see Vintage*

Concord; B & D Auto Sales, 4000 Industrial Way, 94520; 925-689-1221, FAX 925-827-1221; CC, Sp, Wr; 20; **D, F, PU, 4x4; B**3

Bud's Bugs, *see Late Vintage*

Concord Auto Dismantlers, 2211 Arnold Industrial Wy, 94520; 925-685-7703; CC, Sp; 2ac, 350+; **D, F, PU, 4x4; B**3

McHugh's, 2297 Arnold Industrial Wy #D, 94520; 925-686-2343, FAX 925-676-5069; CC, Sa, UR; 2ac, 300; **D, F, PU, 4x4; B**3; **Open Sunday**

Rosal Auto Wreckers, *see Vintage*

Corning; All-Star Auto Wrecking, *see Vintage*

Crockett; Discount Auto Ctr, 24 Pomona Av, 94525; 510-237-4743, FAX 510-237-1492, 800-642-1582 ; CC, Sa, Sp, Wr; **D, F; GM, Jpa, Saturn**

Elk Grove; Elk Grove Auto Dismantlers, *see Vintage*

Emeryville; A Auto By Maz, 3800 San Pablo Av, 94608; 510-428-3958, FAX 510-601-8411; CC, Sa, Wr; **D, F; B**3; **Spc: Used Glass**

Alvin's Automotive Recycling, 3291 San Pablo Av, 94608; 510-658-3101, 888-833-9625; CC, Sa, Sp; **D, F, PU, 4x4; B**3

European Auto Salvage Yard, *see Vintage*

Foreign Auto Wreckers, 2847 Peralta St, 94608; 510-465-8812, FAX 510-465-5521; CC, Sa, Sp; 2.5ac, 300; **D, F, PU, 4x4; B**3, **VW, Jpa**

Maz Auto, *see Late Vintage*

Eureka; John's Used Cars & Wreckers, *see Vintage*

Fairfield; Fairvac Auto & Truck Wrecking, *see Vintage*

Pick-N-Pull, *see Late Vintage*

Travis Auto Recycling, 5155 Noonan Ln, 94533; 707-426-6600; CC, Sa, Sp; **D, F, PU, 4x4; B**3

Fremont; A C European, 4233 Peralta Blvd, 94536; 510-793-3131, FAX 510-793-2823; CC, Sa; **F; German-all years**

Garberville; Don's Auto Parts, 622 Locust St, 95542; 707-923-3961; CC, Sa, Wr; 40; **D, F, PU, 4x4; B**3

Gerber; Jim & Jerri's Auto Wreckers, *see Vintage*

Geyserville; A-Auto Dismantlers, *see Vintage*

Hayward; 4000 Auto Wreckers, 3810 Depot Rd, 94545; 510-785-8384, FAX 510-785-7482; CC, Sa, Sp; 400; **F; Jpa**

AAA Truck Wreckers, *see Late Vintage*

Alfa Parts Exchange, *see Vintage*

Ajax Auto Wreckers, 3764 Depot Rd, 94545; 510-782-7823; Wr;

Auto & Truck Bumpers, 23986 Foley St, 94545; 510-732-7832, FAX 510-732-7836; CC, Sa, Sp, Wr; **D, F, PU, Trk; B**3; **Mainly bumpers, will repair for older cars**

Dorris Auto Wrecking Inc, 3720 Depot Rd, 94545; 510-782-4392; CC, Sa; **D, F; B**3, **AMC**

Double O2 Salvage Inc, *see Late Vintage*

E & J Auto Wreckers, *see Late Vintage*

East Bay Auto Dismantling, *see Late Vintage*

Import Center, 3898 Depot Rd, 94545; 510-783-5322, FAX 510-266-5811; **F**

Shinwa International Inc, 670 Olympic Av, 94544; 510-538-5848; CC, Sa, Wr; **F**

Parts Heaven, *see Vintage*

Laytonville; Laytonville Auto Wreckers, *see Late Vintage*

Lincoln; Euro Sport, *see Vintage*

Loomis; Sierra Truck Div Loomis, *see Late Vintage*

Marysville; Anderson Auto Wreckers, *see Vintage*

53

Bill's Auto Wreckers, *see Vintage*

United Truck Dismantlers, *see Late Vintage*

Napa; Napa Auto Parts, *see Late Vintage*

Newark; Bay Area Bumper Svc, *see Late Vintage*

Cash for Junk Cars, *see Vintage*

EML Imports & Salvage, 7324 Wells Av, 94560; 510-795-8910; CC, Sa, Sp; **Foreign**

Little Al's Auto Wreckers, 7550 Mowry Av, 94560; 510-792-3353; CC, Sa, Br; 600+; **D, PU; GM, Fd**

North Highlands; ABC Foreign Dismantlers, *see Late Vintage*

Novato; Arnold's Auto Dismantler, *see Late Vintage*

Mac-Andy Used Auto Parts Inc, 310 Deer Island Ln, 94948; 415-892-0993, FAX 415-898-2706, 800-622-2639 Local only; CC, Sp; 250+; **D, F, PU, 4x4; B3, AMC, Jp, VW**

Oakland; Camco, 4401 Oakport St, 94601; 510-893-2865, FAX 510-532-1987, 800-893-2866; CC, Sa, Wr; **F; Japanese engines only**

Cash for Junk Cars, *see Late Vintage*

Cypress Salvage, *see Vintage*

Levan Group Inc, 1901 Poplar St, 94607; 510-451-2800; CC, Sa, Sp, Wr; **D, F, PU, 4x4; B3; Spc: Body parts & glass**

Mercedes Depot, *see Late Vintage*

Oakley; A & A Auto Parts, *see Vintage*

Contra Costa Auto Salvage, 1731 Main St, 94561; 925-757-4717, 800-345-7070; CC, Sp; **D; Chrysler & Jeep only**

Foreign Auto Dismantlers, 5290 Neroly Rd, 94561; 925-706-0500, FAX 925-706-0532; CC, Sa, Sp, Br; 200; **F; Hyundai, Acura, Mazda only**

H & M Auto Dismantlers, *see Vintage*

Two Friends Auto Dismantlers, *see Vintage*

Olivehurst; Keystone Automotive Dismantlers, 5066 Powerline Rd, 95961; 530-743-7439; Sa, Sp; 685; **D, F; B3**

Oregon House; Foothill Towing & Auto, 9351 Marysville Rd, 95962; 530-692-1639; CC, UR; 1ac; **D, F; B3**

Orland; Parts R Us Dismantlers, *see Vintage*

Stoneycreek Auto Dismantlers, *see Vintage*

Oroville; AGS Enterprises, *see Late Vintage*

Nick's Automotive Svc, *see Vintage*

Pacifica; Pacifica Auto Wrecking, 830 Palmetto Av, 94044; 650-355-4281; 1ac, 20; **D, F; B3**

Palo Alto; Infinity Auto Salvage, *see Vintage*

Paradise; Skyway Auto Wreckers, *see Late Vintage*

Penngrove; Penngrove Auto Dismantlers, *see Late Vintage*

Petaluma; C & W Auto Wreckers, *see Late Vintage*

California Crush, *see Late Vintage*

Pittsburg; Collins Auto Wrecking, 7 Industry Rd, 94565; 925-427-2122; Sa, Br; 75

M Fernandes Auto Dismantler, *see Vintage*

Pleasanton; R & R Auto Dismantlers, 3908 Old Santa Rita Rd, 94588; 925-224-9944, FAX 925-224-9973, 888-550-9944; CC, Sa, Sp, Br; 1.5ac, 200; **D, F, PU, 4x4; Mini-trucks & Suzuki motorcycles only**

Rancho Cordova; Accuracy Auto Recycling, 3392 Sunrise Blvd, 95742; 916-631-7788, FAX 916-635-8372, 888-554-7788; CC, Sa, Sp; 200; **F; Honda & Acura only**

Ads Dismantling & Sales, 3513 Recycle Rd, 95742; 916-853-2281; Sa; 20; **F**

All Dodge Truck & Van, *see Late Vintage*

All Foreign Auto Dismantlers, 11315 Dismantle Ct, 95742; 916-635-9550, FAX 916-635-9554, 888-541-9550 CA only; CC, Sa, Sp, Br; 250+; **F, PU, 4x4; Jpa, Eur**

All Japanese Auto Recyclers, *see Late Vintage*

All Mini Truck & Van Inc, *see Late Vintage*

American River Auto Wrecking, *see Late Vintage*

BOP Auto Recycling, *see Late Vintage*

Bavarian BMW Auto Recycling, *see Late Vintage*

54

Cadillac Auto Recycling, *see Vintage*

Cash for Junk Cars, *see Late Vintage*

Cats Auto Wrecking, *see Late Vintage*

CPD Auto, 3551 Recycle Rd #1, 95742; 916-638-1076, 800-638-7273; CC, Sa, Sp, PL; 130+; **D, PU, 4x4; Chr, Plymouth, Dodge only**

Dad's Auto Dismantling, 3606 Recycle Rd, 95742; 916-635-3622, FAX 916-852-9685, 800-321-3237, parts@dadsauto.com; CC, Sp; 130; **F; Audi, Saab only**

G M Auto Recycling Inc, 3486 Recycle Rd, 95742; 916-635-5001, 800-541-6189, www.gmauto.com, gmauto@pacbell.net; CC, Sa, Sp; 4ac, 700; **D, PU, 4x4; GM only**

Geo & Daihatsu, Hyundai & Isuzu Recycling, 11355 Dismantle Ct #2, 95742; 916-635-4129, 635-7558, FAX 916-635-2855, 800-863-7576, www.autorecycle.com; CC, Sa, Sp; 320; **F; Geo, Daihatsu, Hyundai, Isuzu only**

German Auto Recycling, *see Vintage*

German Parts Warehouse, *see Late Vintage*

Hap Recycling, *see Late Vintage*

M & S Body, 3565 Recycle Rd #1, 95742; 916-635-4700, FAX 916-635-1785, 800-695-4700, www.msrecycling.com; CC, Sa, Sp; 450+; **D, F, PU; Mitsubitshi, Saturn only**

Mazda Auto Dismantlers, *see Late Vintage*

Mazda Auto Recycling, *see Late Vintage*

Nissan Only Auto Recycling, 3561 Recycle Rd, 95742; 916-631-8333, FAX 916-631-7346, 800-649-9936, www.ninfiniti.com; CC, Sa, Sp; **F; Nissan only**

Pull & Save Recycling, *see Vintage*

Rancho Chevy Recycling, *see Late Vintage*

Rancho Ford Truck Parts, *see Vintage*

Rancho Jeep Recycling, *see Vintage*

Recycle Road Dismantling, 3723 Recycle Rd, 95742; 916-638-5400, FAX 916-638-4417, 800-884-6727; CC, Sa, Sp; 100; **D; GM front wheel drive only**

Silver Star Mercedes Benz & Porsche, *see Late Vintage*

Sunrise Foreign Auto Dismantlers, *see Late Vintage*

Sunrise Nissan, *see Late Vintage*

Tap Recycling, *see Late Vintage*

Toyautomart, *see Late Vintage*

Volvo & Saab Auto Dismantlers, *see Late Vintage*

We Got Cars Auto Recyclers, 3761 Recycle Rd, 95742; 916-635-2525, FAX 916-631-8708; CC, Sa, Sp, Br; 12ac; **89+; D, F, PU, 4x4; B3, AMC, Jp, IH, VW**

Red Bluff; Hess Brothers Auto Recyclers, *see Late Vintage*

Truck World, *see Vintage*

Redding; Clear Creek Auto Wreckers, *see Vintage*

Jeep Recycling, *see Vintage*

Redding Auto Ctr, *see Late Vintage*

Redding U-Pull-It Auto, *see Late Vintage*

Viking Auto & Truck Wrecking, *see Late Vintage*

Viking Import, 19895 Viking Way, 96003; 530-223-6911, FAX 530-223-6983, 800-252-5032 CA AZ OR NV only, www.vikingimport.com; CC, Sa, Sp; 4ac, 700; **F, PU, 4x4**

Redwood City; Greg's VW Svc Center, *see Vintage*

High Performance House, *see Vintage*

Van's Auto Wrecking, *see Late Vintage*

Richmond; Deal Auto & Truck Wrecking, *see Vintage*

Rodeo; Pinole-Rodeo Auto Wreckers, *see Vintage*

Roseville; B W Auto Dismantlers, *see Vintage*

Chevy Truck Parts, *see Vintage*

Roseville Auto Dismantling, *see Late Vintage*

Sacramento; Ace Auto Wrecking, *see Late Vintage*

All Ford Auto Recycling, *see Late Vintage*

American Auto Wreckers, *see Late Vintage*

California – Northern – Late Model

Attarco Inc, 1430 Auburn Blvd #A, 95815; 916-920-2522, FAX 916-920-9493, 800-475-3333 CA only; CC, Sa, Sp; **F, PU, 4x4; engines & transmissions only; Delivery within 75 miles**

Auto Gator Nissan Parts, *see Late Vintage*

Capitol Import Auto Wrecking, 4071 Happy Ln, 95827; 916-366-7470, FAX 916-366-0944, 800-259-5529; CC, Sa, Sp; 1ac, 75; **F, PU, 4x4; Toyota & Nissan only**

Cordova Truck Dismantlers, *see Late Vintage*

Freeway Auto, *see Late Vintage*

Lucky's Auto Wreckers, *see Late Vintage*

Mathers Auto Dismantlers, 4095 Happy Ln, 95827; 916-366-8211, FAX 916-362-6050, 800- 822-6110, www.mathersauto.com; CC, Sa, Sp; 7.5ac; **D; Chrysler, Dodge, Plymouth only**

Sacramento Towing By Chimas, *see Late Vintage*

Subway Truck Parts Inc, *see Vintage*

Sweden Auto Warehouse, *see Vintage*

San Bruno; San Bruno auto Dismantlers II, *see Late Vintage*

San Francisco; A-All Auto Dismantlers, *see Vintage*

ABC Auto Parts, 1650 Davidson Av, 94124; 415-826-8676, FAX 415-826-5386; CC, Sa, Sp; 500+; **D, F, PU; B3**

Bayside Auto & Truck Parts, *see Vintage*

Drive Shafts by Frank Wallace, 1830 Burrows St, 94134; 415-469-7722, 587-1650, FAX 415-469-7722; Sa, Sp, Wr; **D, F, PU; B3; Driveshafts only, machine work**

Levan International Auto Body, *see Late Vintage*

San Leandro; Arrow Truck Parts, *see Late Vintage*

Bert & Johnnies Auto Parts, 2550 Davis St, 94577; 510-568-6700; Sp; **D**

Phelp's Auto Wreckers, *see Vintage*

San Mateo; Tresser's Towing Svc, *see Late Vintage*

Santa Rosa; Acme Auto Wreckers Inc, 1885 Sebastopol Rd, 95407; 707-545-9075; CC, Sa, Sp, Br; 3ac, 300; **D, F, PU, 4x4; B3, AMC, Jp**

Acme Foreign Auto Wreckers, 305 Sebastopol Rd, 95407; 707-546-6816, 800-400-ACME; CC, Sa, Sp, Br; 250+; **F, PU, 4x4**

All Trucks, *see Vintage*

Bob Wescott's Auto Parts, *see Late Vintage*

Santa Rosa; Faraudos Auto Dismantlers, *see Late Vintage*

Rising Sun Eng, 1 Sebastopol Av, 95407; 707-546-8636, FAX 707-546-1060, 800-559-9367, www.risingsunmotors.com; CC, Sa, Sp, Wr; **F; Japanese engines & transmissions only**

Van's VW, *see Late Vintage*

Shingle Springs; Bonanza Auto Dismantlers, *see Vintage*

Weed; Black Butte Auto Dismantling, *see Vintage*

W Sacramento; BJ's Gear & Truck Sales, 501 Glide Av, 95691; 916-372-3518, FAX 916-372-3538; CC, Sa, Wr; **D, F; Trk; Repair & rebuild transmissions, rear ends, engines**

Carro Pacific Inc, *see Late Vintage*

Tom's Toys Import Connection, *see Late Vintage*

Tay Lih Transport Supplies Co, 1025 Triangle Ct, 95605; 916-372-9710; CC, Sa; **F; Japanese engines only**

Yuba City; A C Auto Dismantling, *see Vintage*

B & B Auto Parts Inc, *see Vintage*

Ray's Auto & Truck Recycling, 3988 Railroad Av, 95991; 530-673-7453; Sa, Sp; 6ac, 200; **D; Ford, Lincoln, Mercury only**

Town & Country Towing, *see Late Vintage*

1941 Hudson Station Wagon Super 6
Vintage Coach
Fontana, CA

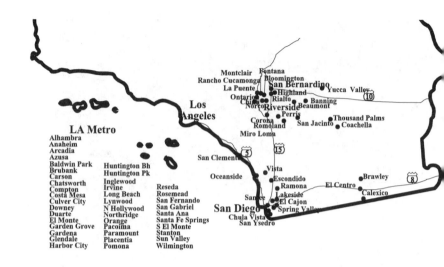

California – Southern

LA Metro

Alhambra		
Anaheim		
Arcadia		
Azusa		
Baldwin Park	Huntington Bh	
Brubank	Huntington Pk	
Carson	Inglewood	
Chatsworth	Irvine	Reseda
Compton	Long Beach	Rosemead
Costa Mesa	Lynwood	San Fernando
Culver City	N Hollywood	San Gabriel
Downey	Northridge	Santa Ana
Duarte	Orange	Santa Fe Springs
El Monte	Pacoima	S El Monte
Garden Grove	Paramount	Stanton
Gardena	Placentia	Sun Valley
Glendale	Pomona	Wilmington
Harbor City		

You may be a car nut if

You think a bonnet and a boot are parts of a car

CALIFORNIA – SOUTHERN

VINTAGE

Anaheim; AASE Bros Porsche Car, 701 E Cypress St, 92805; 714-956-2419, FAX 714-956-2635, 800-444-7444, www.aasebros.com, sales@aasebros.com; CC; 200+; **60+; F; Mercedes, BMW, Porsche only; Spanish**

All Ford, 6441 Jefferson St, 92807; 714-993-2110, FAX 714-993-6831; CC, Sp, Br; 400; **50s+; D, PU; Ford only**

Arcadia; Triangle Automotive, PO Box 2293, 91077; 626-357-2377; Sp; **64-77; D; Pontiac & Oldsmobile only**

Baldwin Park; Ted's Truck & Auto Used parts, 15028 Arrow Hwy, 91706; 626-813-1111, FAX 626-813-1604; Sa, Sp; **60+; D, F, PU, 4x4, Trk; B3**

Bloomington; AA Capital Auto Recycling, 2821 Industrial Dr, 92316; 909-877-2894; Sa; **80-90, few 60s-70s; F**

Brawley; Tucker Auto Dismantling, 615 US Hwy 111, 92227; 760-344-8293; CC, Sp, UR; 2ac; **60-90; D, F, PU, 4x4; B3**

Chatsworth; Star Truck, 21250 Nordhoff St, 91311; 818-882-1400, FAX 818-882-1589; CC, Sa, Sp; 200+; **50-95; D; Spc: Cadillac**

Chula Vista; American & Foreign Auto Wrecking, 775 Energy Way #B, 91911; 619-656-2590; Sp; 500; **50+; D, F, PU, 4x4; 60+ PU; 50+ Foreign; Eur: Triumph, Fiat**

Collision Parts Warehouse, 3740 Main St, 91911; 619-427-8127, FAX 619-585-8230; CC, Sa, Sp; **60+; D, F, PU, 4x4; B3; Body Parts only**

D & P Auto Dismantlers, 777 Energy Way, 91911; 619-421-6875, FAX 619-421-6672; CC, Sa; 60; **60+; F; VW only**

Onager Corp, 789 Energy Way, 91911; 619-421-3254, FAX 619-421-0357, www.onagermercedes.com; CC, Sp, Wr; **50-84; F; new & used parts; Mercedes only**

South Bay Auto Wreckers, 811 Energy Way, 91911; 619-421-5565; CC, Sa; 5ac, 700; **60+; D, F, PU, 4x4, Trk; B3**

Coachella; Abel's Dismantling & Auto Repair, 48150 Harrison St, 92236; 760-398-6277, FAX 760-398-6423; CC, Sa, Sp, UR; 300+; **80+, few 60s & 70s; D, F; B3; Mostly 80+**

Allkars, 84811 Av 48, 92236; 760-398-0770, 888-822-0770; CC, Sa, UR; 900+; **60-94; D, F, PU, 4x4; B3, AMC, Jp, IH, VW; Pickup section**

Desert Truck & Auto Parts, 48451 Harrison St, 92236; 760-398-0106, FAX 760-398-8737; CC, Sa, Sp, UR; 1500; **60+, few 50s; D, F, PU, 4x4, Trk; B3, Wy, VW**

Compton; Southeast Auto Salvage, 415 E Pine St, 90222; 310-638-8552, FAX 310-639-6176; CC, Sa, Sp; 4ac; **80+, few 50-79; D, F, PU, 4x4; B3**

Costa Mesa; Mesa West German Auto, 126-A E 16 St, 92627; 949-645-2374, FAX 949-645-0975; CC, Sp, Wr; **50-87; F; VW Spc: VW**

Duarte; Russ Recycling, 756 Alpha St, 91010; 626-303-4366; CC, Sa, Sp, Br; 4ac, 400; **61-92; F; VW, Auto, Porsche (914 & 924)**

Thomas Auto Wrecking, 712 Alpha St, 91010; 626-359-8148, FAX 626-359-0849; CC, Sa, Sp, Br; 1ac; **60+; D, PU; Chevy, Ford & Jeep only**

El Cajon; Autobahn Porscha Dismantling, 444 Vernon Way, 92020; 619-444-2290; CC, Sa; 1ac, 10+; **65+ Porsche, 69+ BMW; F**

Mustang Auto & Classic Cars, 727 El Cajon Blvd, 92020; 800-446-8782; CC, Sa, Sp; 15; **64-70; D; B3 classics Spc: Mustang**

Stan's Auto Body & Paint, 1880 Euclid Av, 92243; 760-352-4336; CC, Sp; 300; **62+; D, F, PU; B3**

El Monte; Collision Auto Salvage, 2440 Durfee Av, 91732; 626-444-1400 or 442-4414, FAX 626-444-4559; Sa, Sp; 1ac, 100; **60+; D, F; B3**

Escondido; Norman's Auto Parts, 2444 Barham Dr, 92029; 760-746-2655, FAX 760-746-2727; CC, Sa; 6ac; **D, F; Few old Fords the rest LM**

Fontana; A & A Fast Cash for Cars, 11175 Redwood Av, 92337; 909-355-4331, FAX 909-355-5246, 800-978-6422; CC, Sa, Sp, UR; 1500; **50+; D, F, PU, 4x4; B3; Call for info on Classic Car section**

A-A-A Jeep-4x4 & Pickup Salvage, 14349 Whittram Av, 92335; 909-829-2913; CC, Sa, Sp; 1000+; **42+; D, F, PU, 4x4; B3, Jp; Spc: Jeep**

Acey's Wreckers, 14659 Whittram Av, 92335; 909-355-1758; **60+; F; VW only**

California Truck Salvage, 15021 Whittram Av, 92335; 909-350-2946; Sa, Br; 500; **47+; D, F, PU, 4x4, Trk; B3, Jp, IH**

Inland Auto Wreckers, 14451 Whittram Av, 92335; 909-829-2041, FAX 909-822-9738, www.finsandflames.qpg.com; Sa, Sp, Br; 3ac; **50-69; D; B3, St**

J B Autowrecking, 14717 Whittram Av, 92335; 909-829-1199; Sa, Sp; 600+; **50+; D, F, PU, B3, St, VW**

Mustang Village, 14693 Whittram Av, 92335; 909-823-7915, FAX 909-823-5864, 800-310-7915 CA only; CC, Sa, Sp; 2ac, 200+; **64+; D; Ford only, Spc: Mustang; T Bird, Falcon, Ranger**

Vintage Coach-Twin H Ranch, 16593 Arrow Blvd, 92335; 909-823-9168; Sa, Sp, Hr, UR; 1ac, 75; **33-54; D, PU; Hd; Spc: Hudson; Pretty much anything for Hudson; Restoration shop; NOS parts; Restored cars for sale**

Gardena; A & B Auto Wrecking, 17120 S Figueroa St, 90248; 310-323-3231, FAX 310-323-6729; CC, Sa, Sp; **60+; F**

Auto Wreckers & Parts Co, 16619 S Main St, 90248; 310-329-0636; Sa; **60+; D; B3**

Big D Auto Wrecking, 16815 S Main St, 90248; 310-329-1034; Sa; **50+; D; B3**

Harbor City; Zacher's Auto Salvage, 25224 Vermont Av S, 90710; 310-326-7775, FAX 310-325-6989; Sa, Sp; 2 ac; **65+; D, F, PU, 4x4, Trk; B3, AMC; Rebuild Transmissions & Rear Ends**

Highland; Volvo Express Tom's Enterprises, 26892 Baseline St, 92346; 909-864-5649; CC, Sa, Sp; 500; **52+; F; Volvo Only**

Huntington Beach; Papke Enterprises, 17202 Gothard St, 92647; 714-843-6969; CC, Sa, Sp; 5+; **49-51; D; Ford & Mercury only**

Lakeside; Al's Auto Wrecking, 12650 Hwy 67, 92040; 935-443-3965; CC, Sa, Sp, Br; 600+; **57+; D, F; B3, AMC, VW**

Long Beach; Carson Auto, 22606 S Alameda St, 90810; 562-835-7291, FAX 562-952-0770; CC, Sa, Sp, Br; 3.5ac, 850; **60+; D; B3, AMC, Jp, IH**

Los Angeles; ABC Auto Dismantlers, 2145 Firestone Blvd, 90002; 323-583-3316; Sa, Wr; **60+; D, F; B3**

B & R Auto Wrecking, 12225 Avalon Blvd, 90061; 323-755-1161, FAX 323-755-0349; Sa, Sp, Br; 1 city block; **48+; D; Spc: Cadillac**

Dial A Hubcap, 8355 Lincoln Blvd, 90045; 310-216-3023, FAX 310-216-3024, 800-466-2544, www.airporthub.com; CC, Sa, Sp; **50+; D, F, PU; B3, AMC, Jp, IH; Hubcap only**

North Hollywood; Atlas Auto Parts & Salvage, 11801 Sherman Way, 91605; 818-765-6666, FAX 818-765-7853; CC, Sp, Br; 200; **63+; D; Spc: Chrysler**

Northridge; Le Mans Foreign, 18959 Parthenia St, 91324; 818-886-3672; CC, Sa, Sp, Br; 400+; **60-90; D, F, PU, 4x4, Trk; B3, AMC, Jp, IH, VW**

Orange; Mustang Salvage & Auto Parts, 711 W Collins Av, 92867; 714-997-2000; CC, Sa, Sp; .5ac; **64-73; D; Mustang only**

Pacoima; B W Parts, 9820 San Fernando Rd, 91331; 818-897-4324; Sa, Sp, Br; 700; **65-96; D, F, PU, 4x4, Trk; B3, AMC, Jp, VW**

Cad King, 9840 Fan Fernando Rd, 91331; 818-890-0621, FAX 818-890-3117; CC, Sa, Sp, Br; 5ac; **50+; D; Cadillac only**

Harry's Auto Wrecking, 9859 San Fernando Rd, 91331; 818-896-5025, FAX 818-899-2366; Sa, Sp, Br; 1ac, 200+; **60+; D, F, PU, 4x4, Trk; B3, AMC, Jp, IH, VW**

Paramount; Mustang Country, 14833 Lakewood Blvd, 90723; 562-633-2393, FAX 562-633-2397, 800-206-8782, www.mustangcountryintl.com; CC, Sa, Wr; **64+; D; Mustang only**

Perris; K & D Dismantling, 23900 State Hwy 74, 92570; 909-657-9072, FAX 909-940-4893; CC, Sa; 150; **50+; D, F, PU, 4x4; B3; Early years mainly Pickup**

Placentia; Atwood Auto Wrecking, 218 S Van Buren St, 92870; 714-528-7568, FAX 714-572-8804; Sa, Sp, Wr; >1ac, 30; **50s-70s, few 30s-40s; D, PU; B3, Ns, St, P**k

Pomona; A-Car Auto Wrecking, 10756 Kadota Av, 91766; 909-620-8198, FAX 909-620-9878; CC, Sa, Sp; 5ac, 500; **41+; D, F, PU, 4x4; B3, AMC, Jp, Hd, St, Pk, VW**

Tri-County 4x4s Gear Spec, 1143 W 2nd St, 91766; 909-623-3373, FAX 909-469-4685, www.tricountygear.com; CC, Sa, Sp; 30; **41+; D, PU, 4x4, Trk; B3, Jp; Jeep '41+**

West Coast Auto Wrecking, 4057 E Mission Blvd, 91766; 909-623-9757, FAX 909-629-5665; CC, Sa, Sp; 1ac; **60-92; D, F, PU, 4x4; B3; Open Sunday**

Reseda; Fiat Auto Svc, 18440 Hart St, 91335; 818-345-4458, FAX 818-345-6213, fiatsteve@aol.com; CC, Sa, Sp, Wr; **53-89; F; Fiat Only**

South El Monte; Southern California Import, 2328 Rosemead Blvd, 91733; 626-350-0200; Sa, Sp, Br; **50+; F; VW & Porsche Only**

San Bernardino; Downtown Auto Wrecking, 519 E Mill St, 92408; 909-889-8880, FAX 909-889-4373, sreich@autoclassicparts.com; Sa, Sp, Br; 400; **40-89; D, PU; B3, AMC, IH, St**

San Bernardino Pick a Part, 407 E 9 St, 92410; 909-884-5308, FAX 909-885-4420; CC, Sa, UR; 10ac, 900; **60+; D, F, PU, 4x4; B3, AMC, Jp, IH**

U & I Auto Wrecking, 1435 W Rialto Av, 92410; 909-888-6841, FAX 909-888-6845, joebprop@aol.com; Sp, UR, PL; 13ac, 2500; **40+; D; B3, St**

Waterman Auto Dismantlers, 701 N Waterman Av, 92410; 909-889-2731; Sp; **80+, few 60s & 70s; D, F, PU, 4x4; B3**

San Diego; A & B Truck Recycling, 2863 Commercial St, 92113; 619-234-5171, FAX 619-239-9625, 800-544-7657; CC, Sa, Sp, Wr, Br; **55+; D, F (Jpa), PU; B3; Pickup only**

San Diego Foreign Auto, , 92113; 619-239-8277, FAX 619-232-1156, sdfjunk@aol.com; Sa, Sp, Wr; **60+; F; Eur, Jpa**

San Fernando; American Auto & Truck, 12172 Truman St, 91340; 818-365-3908; Sa, Sp, Br, Wr; **55-89; D, PU, Trk; Spc: Chevy**

San Jacinto; Valley Auto Salvage, 1575 S State St, 92583; 909-925-0595; CC, Sa, Sp; **60+; D, F, PU, 4x4, Trk; B3**

San Ysidro; America Auto Wrecking, 920 Heritage Rd, 92173; 619-661-6141; CC, Sa, UR; 2ac; **60-90; D, F, PU, 4x4; B3 open Sunday**

Express Auto Wrecking, 1325 Otay Valley Rd, 92173; 619-661-7218; Sa, Sp; 1ac, 100; **60+; D, F, PU, 4x4; B3; Spanish**

Santa Ana; Chevy Truck Salvage, 3226 W 5 St, 92703; 714-554-1850, FAX 714-554-1794; Sa, Sp; 500+; **48+; D, F, PU; B3, Jp, IH**

Santa Fe Springs; Santa Fe Auto Wrecking, 12643 Imperial Hwy, 90670; 562-692-7516, FAX 562-929-4106, 800-800-7959, steinfarms@earthlink.net; Cc, Sa, Sp; 200; **60+; D, F, PU, 4x4**

Santee; Old Cars & Parts, 9945 Prospect Av, 92071; 619-449-0551, FAX 619-449-0552; CC, Sp; **9-48; D; Ford only**

Spring Valley; CRH Slvg; 4129 Bonita, 91977; 619-463-6495; UR; 2.75ac; **60-89; D; B3, Hr**

Sweetwater Auto Wrecking, 6301 Quarry Rd, 91977; 619-475-1005, FAX 619-475-4719, cudamark@aol.com; CC, Sa, Sp, Wr; **60-79; D, PU, 4x4, Trk; B3; Spc: Chrysler Mopar**

Stanton; Admore Auto Dismantling, 8188 Katella Av, 90680; 714-826-6000, FAX 714-898-9904; CC, Sa, Br; 6ac, 1000; **50-90; D, F, PU, 4x4, Trk; B3, AMC, Jp, IH, VW; open Sunday**

Best Deal, 8171 Monroe Av, 90680; 714-995-0081, FAX 714-995-5918, 800-354-9202, bestdeal@deltanet.com; CC, Sa, Sp; **54-89, few 90s; F; Porsche**

Sun Valley; A Truck Parts, 11675 Sheldon St, 91352; 818-768-1007, FAX 626-962-7749; CC, Sa, Sp, Br; **47+; D, F, PU, 4x4, Trk; B3, AMC, Jp, IH**

Aadlen Brothers Auto Wrecking, 11591 Tuxford St, 91352; 818-983-0862, FAX 818-767-4376, 800-422-3536; Sa, Sp, UR; 26ac; 3000+; **50+; D, F; All Makes & Models**

Bell's Auto Recycling, 12301 Branford, 91352; 818-767-7197, FAX 818-897-6520, 800-621-4484; CC, Sa, Sp; 1000; **60+; F; Spc: BMW & Mercedes**

Daytona Auto Wrecking, 12244 Branford St, 91352; 818-899-8891; CC, Sa, Sp, Br; 200; **60+; F; Eur**

Folkswagon, 11623 Sheldon St, 91352; 818-768-4555; CC, Sa, Sp, UR; **50+; 55+; F; VW**

Memory Lane Collector Car Dismantlers, 11311 Pendleton St, 91352; 818-504-3341, FAX 818-768-2613, 800-281-9273, www.oldautoparts.com; CC, Sa, Sp, Br; 6ac, 900+; **27-74; D, PU, 4x4, Trk; B3, AMC, Jp, IH, Hd, St, Pk, Ns, Wy, Ks; No Ramblers; Spc: American Classic & Muscle**

Miller's Auto Dismantling, 12055 Branford St, 91352; 818-983-1900, FAX 818-890-9900, 800-801-1400; Sa; **56-88; D; B3, St, Pk**

61

Pacific Truck Salvage, 11644 Sheldon St, 91352; 818-767-0203; CC, Sa; 2ac; **60-80; Pickup only**

Rollies Auto Wrecking, 9870 Glenoaks Blvd, 91352; 818-899-0209 or 767-1600; Sa, Sp; **1000+; 60+; D, F, PU, 4x4, Trk; B3,AMC**

Thousand Palms; Indio Auto Wrecking, , 92276; 760-398-9791; Sa, Sp; **60+; D, F, PU, 4x4**

Vista; Interstate VW Auto, 1303 Engineer St, 92083; 760-598-1376, FAX 760-598-7261; CC, Sa, Sp, Wr; 1ac; **60+; F; VW, Porsche, BMW, Audi, Mercedes; 95% VW**

Quality Truck Recycling, 1661 W Vista Way, 92083; 760-941-2894; CC, Sa; 5ac; **55-90; D, F, PU, 4x4; B3; Pickup only; few Foreign**

LATE VINTAGE

Anaheim; AASE Bros Porsche Car, *see Vintage*

All Ford, *see Vintage*

Import Auto Supply & Salvage, 101 N Manchester Av, 92802; 714-776-9900, FAX 714-776-2849; CC; 100; **80+; F**

Arcadia; Triangle Automotive, *see Vintage*

Azusa; Allied Auto Wrecking, 1042 W Gladstone St, 91702; 626-969-3413, FAX 626-815-0193; Br; 2ac; **80+; D, F**

Baldwin Park; Ted's Truck & Auto Used parts, *see Vintage*

Beaumont; M & M Auto Wrecking Yard, 249 Veile Av, 92223; 909-845-4315, FAX 909-769-0384; CC, Sa, Sp; 800; **75-85, few 90s; D, F, PU; B3**

Bloomington; AA Capital Auto Recycling, *see Vintage*

Ecology Auto Wrecking, 221 E Santa Ana Av, 92316; 909-877-6934; CC, Sa, UR; 1500; **70+; D, F, PU; B3; Chain of yards**

Three Brothers Auto Wrecking, 17565 Valley Blvd, 92316; 909-823-9000, FAX 909-823-4107, 888-457-1700; 500; **80+, few 70s; D, few F, PU, 4x4; B3**

Brawley; Tucker Auto Dismantling, *see Vintage*

Burbank; Mark's Off Road Enterprises, 437 N Moss St, 91502; 818-953-9230, FAX 818-953-7225; CC, Sa, Sp; 400; **70-79; F; Toyota Land Cruisers only**

Carson; Jags Services, 21023 Figueroa St, 90745; 310-533-4901, FAX 310-533-5924; CC, Sa, Sp, UR; **80+; F; Jaguar Only**

Carson; Scott's Auto Salvage, 21205 Main St, 90745; 310-835-3141; CC, Sa, Wr; **83+; D, F, PU, 4x4; B3**

Chatsworth; Star Truck, *see Vintage*

Chula Vista; A & E Auto Recycling, 775 Energy Way, 91911; 619-421-7911, 800-479-0220; Sa; 100; **70-89; D, F; B3, Jpa**

Action Auto Dismantlers, 151 Reed Ct, 91911; 619-426-0110; Sa; 3ac, 400; **85-early 90s; D, F, PU**

All Smash Auto Recycling, 791 Energy Way, 91911; 619-421-5397, FAX 619-421-6149, 800-266-4499; CC, Sa, Sp; 2ac, 150; **80-88; F; Open Sunday**

American & Foreign Auto Wrecking, *see Vintage*

Collision Parts Warehouse, *see Vintage*

D & P Auto Dismantlers, *see Vintage*

Fords Forever, 150 Reed Ct, 91911; 619-661-1133, FAX 619-425-6039; Sa, Sp; 2000; **82+; D, F, PU, 4x4; B3, Eur, Jaguar; Spc: Ford**

Leon Auto Wrecking, 1170 Otay Valley Rd, 91909; 619-661-1570; **70+; D, PU, 4x4; B3**

Lunas Auto Wrecking, 939 Heritage Rd, 91909; 619-661-9211; CC, Sa; 500; **80+; D, F, PU; B3**

Onager Corp, *see Vintage*

RC Import Auto Recycling, 777 Energy Way, 91911; 619-421-7151; Sa; 100; **78-90; F; Volvo**

South Bay Auto Wreckers, *see Vintage*

Standard Auto Recycling, 150 Reed Ct, 91911; 619-426-1166, FAX 619-425-6039; Sa, Sp, Br; 300; **80-90; D, F, PU, 4x4; Jpa, Domestic Pickup**

True Way Wrecking, 777 Energy Way, 91911; 619-421-7313; Sp; **70-89; F; BMW Subaru**

Universal Auto Recycling, 783 Energy Way #A, 91911; 619-482-7277, FAX 619-482-9151; CC, Sa; 1ac, 400; **79-89; D, F, PU, 4x4; B3**

Coachella; Abel's Dismantling & Auto Repair, *see Vintage*

Allkars, *see Vintage*

Ajax Auto Wrecking, 19315 Avenue 48, 92236; 760-398-0147, FAX 619-398-0596, 800-606-6043; CC, Sa, Sp; 2000; **70+; D, F, PU, 4x4; B3**

De Lara Auto Wrecking, 48050 Harrison St, 92236; 760-398-5410; **70-89; D, F; B3 Spanish**

Desert Pull-A-Part, 48451 Harrison St, 92236; 760-398-5575; Sa, UR; **70+; D, F; B3**

Desert Truck & Auto Parts, *see Vintage*

Compton; Southeast Auto Salvage, *see Vintage*

Corona; Indiana Truck Salvage, 1480 E 6 St, 91719; 909-737-7753; Sa, Sp; 750; **67+; D, F, PU, 4x4, Trk; Pickup & Truck only**

Costa Mesa; Action Auto Dismantlers, 2075 Placentia Av, 92627; 949-548-7013, FAX 949-548-0621; Sa, Sp; 2ac, 200+; **79+; D, F; B3**

Mesa West German Auto, *see Vintage*

Culver City; Studio City Auto Parts, 3434 Wesley St, 90232; 310-838-3661; Sa, UR; 1ac; **70+; D, F, PU, 4x4; B3**

Duarte; A-Abar Auto Wrecking, 863 Alpha St, 91010; 626-301-1050, FAX; Sa, Sp; 2ac, 500; **80+; D, F, PU, 4x4; B3**

Big J Auto Wrecking, 739 Alpha St, 91010; 626-305-7653; CC, Sa; <1ac, 100; **80s; D, PU; B3; Spanish**

LPD Auto Dismantling, 835 Alpha St, 91010; 626-359-8945, FAX 626-359-1542; CC, Sa; **80+; F**

Russ Recycling, *see Vintage*

Silver Star Auto Wrecking, 787 Alpha St, 91010; 626-357-4887, FAX 626-930-0395; CC, Sa; 5ac, 500+; **78+; F**

Thomas Auto Wrecking, *see Vintage*

Tru-Vu Auto Wrecking & Glass, 825 Alpha St, 91010; 626-357-9009, 888-WINDSHIELD; CC, Sa; 1ac, 30; **70-89; D, F, PU; B3; Spanish**

Super Auto Wrecking, 842 Alpha St, 91010; 626-303-5953, FAX 626-303-7626; UR; 1ac, 100; **80+; D, F, PU; B3; Spanish**

El Cajon; Autobahn Porscha Dismantling, *see Vintage*

El Centro; Pull Your Part, 2004 US Hwy 111, 92243; 760-337-8094, FAX 760-352-4993; Sa, Sp, UR; 500; **70-85; D, F, PU, 4x4, Trk; B3, AMC, Jp, IH, VW**

Stan's Auto Body & Paint, *see Vintage*

El Monte; A-Aero Truck Salvage, 12346 Valley Blvd, 91732; 626-444-1346; Sa, Sp; 30; **68+; D, F, PU, 4x4; B3**

Collision Auto Salvage, *see Vintage*

Escondido; Cardinal Auto Wrecking, 725 Rock Springs Rd, 92025; 760-726-5770; CC, Sa; **70+; D, F, Trk; B3, AMC**

Fontana; A & A Fast Cash for Cars, *see Vintage*

A-A-A Jeep-4x4 & Pickup Salvage, *see Vintage*

Acey's Wreckers, *see Vintage*

All Auto Parts, 15755 Arrow Blvd, 92335; 909-356-8686, FAX 909-428-1423, 800-797-4593, allautousedparts.com; CC, Sp; 8ac, 1500; **80+; D, F, PU, 4x4, Trk; B3, Jp**

California Truck Salvage, *see Vintage*

Epic Truck & Auto Dismantling, 15391 Arrow Blvd, 92335; 909-822-3715, FAX 909-822-4976, 800-527-2739, epicauto@worldnet.att.net; CC, Sa, Sp, PL; 1000; **78+; D, F, PU, 4x4; B3**

Fontana Auto Recyclers, 15228 Boyle Av, 92337; 909-356-1860, FAX 909-356-2094; Sa; 10ac, 1500; **80+; D, F; B3**

General Auto Dismantlers, 10625 Redwood Av, 92337; 909-356-0469; Sa, Wr; **82+; F**

J B Autowrecking, *see Vintage*

Jenny Auto Wrecking, 111000 Redwood Av, 92337; 909-823-8706, FAX 909-823-5869; Sa, Sp; 200; **86-90; D, F, PU; B3**

LTD Auto Dismantlers, 8750.5 Buck Av, 92335; 909-355-9591, FAX 909-355-9592; Sa; 150; **83+; F, PU; B3, AMC**

M & M Import Auto, 14643 Aniso Dr, 92337; 909-428-1111, FAX 909-428-6320, 800-429-9000; CC, Sa, Sp; **70+; F, PU, 4x4**

Mustang Village, *see Vintage*

National Auto Wrecking, 15115 Whittram Av, 92335; 909-357-3519; Sa; 2ac; **80+; F**

P & M Truck & Salvage Co, 14281 Whittram Av, 92335; 909-822-0811; Sp; **70+; D, Trk; Truck over 1 ton only**

Garden Grove; Honda Independent Auto, 13781 West St, 92843; 714-554-7657; CC, Sa; 1300; **77+; F; Honda only**

Gardena; A & B Auto Wrecking, *see Vintage*

A-1 Western Auto Salvage, 13424 S Western Av, 90249; 310-324-6306; Sa; **80+; D, F; B3**

Aaron Auto Parts, 16100 S Avalon Blvd, 90248; 310-329-6321, FAX 310-637-0532; CC, Sa, Sp; 1.5ac; **81+; D, F; B3; Spc: Saab, Volvo, Audi, GM, Chevy**

Acquisition Sales, 17800 S Vermont Av, 90248; 310-532-7630, FAX 310-532-0703; CC, Sa; 650; **80s; D; B3, AMC**

Auto Wreckers & Parts Co, *see Vintage*

Gardena; B & H Auto Wrecking, 16845 S Main St, 90248; 310-515-9501; Sa; **80+; D, F; B3**

Big D Auto Wrecking, *see Vintage*

Glendale; Collision Auto Salvage, 5500 San Fernando Rd, 91203; 213-245-2309; Sa, Sp; **70-89; D; B3**

Harbor City; Zacher's Auto Salvage, *see Vintage*

Highland; Volvo Express Tom's Enterprises, *see Vintage*

Lakeside; Al's Auto Wrecking, *see Vintage*

Long Beach; Carson Auto, *see Vintage*

City Wide Auto Wrecking, 6935 Cherry Av, 90810; 562-633-4433; **80+; D, F; B3**

Los Angeles; A-Best Auto Wrecking, 535 Gallardo St, 90033; 323-221-4706; Sa, Br; 100; **78-90; D, F, Trk; B3**

ABC Auto Dismantlers, *see Vintage*

B & R Auto Wrecking, *see Vintage*

Dearborn Auto Wrecking, 540 Gallardo St, 90033; 323-223-6013, FAX 323-223-1148; Sa, Sp, Br; 100; **70+; D, F, PU; B3**

Dial A Hubcap, *see Vintage*

E & U Auto Wrecking, 223 W Avenue 26, 90031; 213-223-6551; **80+; D; B3**

Ford Only Auto Parts, 7677 S Alameda St, 90001; 213-588-2296; **80+; D; Ford only**

Metro Auto Wrecking, 5534 Long Beach Ave, 90058; 323-581-2207; CC, Sa; .25ac; **77-85; D, F; B3**

Nayarit Auto Wrecking, 1850 E 41 St Pl, 90058; 323-231-1954; Sa, Sp, Wr; 20; **83+; D, F, PU, 4x4, Trk; B3, AMC**

T & H Auto Wrecking, 1809 Hancock St, 90031; 323-223-2964; Sa, Sp, UR; **82+; F**

T & J Foreign Auto Salvage, 505 N Mission Rd, 90033; 323-225-2372; CC, Sa, PL; **72-90; F; Jpa & Eur**

Tony's Auto Wrecking, 910 N San Fernando Rd, 90065; 323-227-4089, FAX 323-227-6178; Sa, Sp, UR; 1ac, 100+; **80+; D, F; B3**

Lynwood; Coco's Auto Dismantling, 11410 Alameda St, 90262; 310-763-8689; CC, Sa, Br; 200+; **82+; D, F, PU; B3, AMC**

Norco; Ingnorco Truck & Auto Parts, 2000 S Four Wheel Dr, 91760; 909-735-3353, FAX 909-735-4042, 800-734-1353 Cal only; CC, Sa, Sp, Br; 200+; 2ac; **80+; D, F, PU, 4x4, Trk; B3, AMC, Jp, VW**

North Hollywood; Atlas Auto Parts & Salvage, *see Vintage*

Foreign Auto Salvage, 12537 Sherman Way, 91605; 818-765-4247; CC, Sa, Sp; 200; **80-90; F; Japanese only**

IHS Motors Auto Dismantling, 7250 Coldwater Canyon Av, 91605; 818-765-5448, FAX 818-765-3314, 800-300-3242; Sa, Sp; **80+; D, Mostly F, PU, 4x4**

Northridge; Le Mans Foreign, *see Vintage*

64

Van Nuys Auto Wrecking, 18959 Parthenia St, 91324; 818-782-8604; CC, Sa, Sp, Br; 200; **80+; D, F, Trk; B3, AMC**

Oceanside; All Foreign Auto Dismantling, 1050 Airport Rd, 92054; 760-757-7101, FAX 760-759-1221; Sa, Sp, UR; 4ac, 300; **70-90; F, PU; VW**

Orange; Holmes Mini Truck Parts, 1002 N Parker St, 92867; 714-639-6346, FAX 714-744-3463; CC, Sa, Sp, Br; 100; **80+; D, F; Mini Trucks only**

Motor Sport Auto, 1139 W Collins Av, 92867; 714-639-2620, FAX 800-321-3777; CC, Sa, Sp; **70-96; F; Datsun Z Cars only**

Mustang Salvage & Auto Parts, *see Vintage*

Pacoima; B W Parts, *see Vintage*

Cad King, *see Vintage*

Harry's Auto Wrecking, *see Vintage*

Sam's Auto Wrecking, 9837 San Fernando Rd, 91331; 818-894-2820, FAX 818-686-3506; CC, Sa, Sp; 1000+; **80+; D, F, PU, 4x4; B3, AMC; Pickup & Minivans only**

Paramount; B K Auto Salvage, 14134 Garfield Av, 90723; 562-630-5223; Sa, Sp, UR; **mid 80s-90; Spanish**

Mustang Country, *see Vintage*

Perris; K & D Dismantling, *see Vintage*

Steve's Auto Dismantling, 152 Mountain Av, 92570; 909-657-9010, FAX 909-940-5809; CC, Sa, Sp, UR; 200; **80+; D, F, PU, 4x4; B3**

Placentia; Atwood Auto Wrecking, *see Vintage*

J J's Foreign Auto Wrecking, 455 S Van Buren St, 92870; 714-996-6100; CC, Sa, Sp; 170; **80+; F; Jpa**

Placentia Truck Van Wrecking, 461 S Van Buren St, 92870; 714-996-1620, FAX 714-996-1350; CC, Sa, Sp; 500; **77+; D, PU, 4x4; Pickup & Van only**

Pomona; A Auto Wrecking, 1420 E 1st St, 91766; 909-623-2888; Sa, Sp; 200; **84+; D, F, PU, 4x4; B3**

A-Car Auto Wrecking, *see Vintage*

Budget Auto Wrecking, 163 S Hamilton Blvd, 91766; 909-623-1206, FAX 909-629-5243, 800-720-5865; CC, Sa, Sp; 1ac, 100+; **80-89; D, F; Mostly Jpa**

California Mini Trucks, 4002 State St, 91766; 909-622-1381, FAX 909-623-3240; Sa, Sp; **69+; D, F, PU, 4x4, Trk; Pickup & Truck only**

Tri-County 4x4s Gear Spec, *see Vintage*

West Coast Auto Wrecking, *see Vintage*

Ramona; Ramona Auto Dismantling, 904 A St, 92065; 760-789-0331; CC, Sa; 3ac, 200+; **mid 80s-early 90s; D, F, PU, 4x4; B3**

Rancho Cucamonga; Alex Auto Dismantling, 13109 Whittram Ave #C, 91739; 909-899-8181; Sa, Br, Wr; 250; **80+; D, F; B3, AMC**

Reseda; Fiat Auto Svc, *see Vintage*

Rialto; ACA Auto Salvage 2, 2091 Stonehurst Dr, 92377; 909-356-8875, 800-698-3933; CC, Sa, Sp; 300; **70+; D, F, PU, 4x4; B3; Clips on shelf**

Riverside; Accord Auto Recycler, 3151 Kansas Av, 92507; 909-788-7788, FAX 909-788-1275; CC, Sa, Sp; 1ac, 40; **84+; F; Jpa; Honda & Accord only**

Hillside Auto Salvage, 3760 Pyrite St, 92509; 909-685-6744, FAX 909-685-8367; CC, Sa, Sp, UR; 3000; **70+; D, F, PU, 4x4; B3**

Honda & Foreign Parts, 2915 E La Cadena Dr, 92507; 909-686-8486; CC, Sa, Sp; 1ac, 25; **F; Honda & Volvo only**

K C Auto Dismantler, 3023 Kansas Av, 92507; 909-683-0181; Sp; **75-90 F; Mercedes & BMW only**

Romoland; Santa Fe Auto Salvage, 27687 Jackson Av, 92585; 909-928-3616, FAX 909-928-8088, 877-687-9273, 4autosalvage.com; 100+; **Cars=85+; PU=70+; D, F, PU, 4x4, Trk; B3, AMC**

San Bernardino; Chuck's Auto Wrecking, 1690 Walnut St, 92410; 909-888-4811; CC, Sa; 6ac, 500; **80+; D, F, PU; B3**

Downtown Auto Wrecking, *see Vintage*

Jimbo's Auto Wrecking, 527 E Mill St, 92408; 909-885-0748, FAX 909-885-4969; Sa, Sp; **80+; D, F, PU, 4x4; B3**

Merrell's Auto Dismantling, 827 N Waterman Av, 92410; 909-888-4768; CC, Sa, Sp; 5ac, 600; **75-89; D, F, PU, 4x4; B3, AMC, Jp**

Rambros Auto Parts, 211 S Mount Vernon Av, 92410; 909-884-0507, FAX 909-884-5681; Sa, Sp, Wr; **70+; D, F, PU, 4x4; B3, AMC, VW**

San Bernardino Pick a Part, *see Vintage*

Three Guys Auto Wreckers, 275 S Muscott St #B, 92410; 909-383-0852; Sa; 1ac, 110; **70+; D, F; B3**

U & I Auto Wrecking, *see Vintage*

Waterman Auto Dismantlers, *see Vintage*

San Diego; A & B Truck Recycling, *see Vintage*

American & Foreign Auto Wrecking, 2828 Market St, 92102; 619-239-2028; Sa, Sp; **80-87; D, F**

San Diego Foreign Auto, *see Vintage*

San Fernando; American Auto & Truck, *see Vintage*

San Jacinto; Valley Auto Salvage, *see Vintage*

San Ysidro; America Auto Wrecking, *see Vintage*

Brown Field Truck & Auto Dismantlers, 1342 Otay Valley Rd, 92173; 619-263-3898; **80+; D, F, PU, 4x4, Trk; B3**

Camino Auto Wrecking, 1001 Heritage Rd, 92173; 619-661-6308; Sa, UR; **80+; D; B3; Spanish**

Dave's Auto Wrecking, 970 Heritage Rd, 92173; 619-661-1181; Sa, Sp; 120; **80+; D, F, PU; B3; Spanish**

Ecology Auto Wrecking, 1180 Heritage Rd, 92173; 619-409-9200, FAX 619-426-3869; CC, Sa; 1000; **70+; D, F, PU, 4x4; Trk; B3, AMC, Jp, IH**

Express Auto Wrecking, *see Vintage*

Frontera Auto Wrecking, 6411 Datsun St, 92173; 619-661-1546; Sa; **80+; F; Mostly Japanese**

Rapido Truck & Auto Wrecking, 969 Heritage Rd, 92173; 619-661-6918; Sa, UR; 1ac; **80+; D, F, PU; B3, AMC, Jp, IH, VW**

Scorpio Auto Wrecking, 1218 Otay Valley Rd, 92173; 619-661-6060; Sp; **80+; D, F, PU, 4x4; B3; Spanish**

V & L Auto Sales & Dismantling, 1050 Heritage Rd, 92173; 619-661-0195, FAX 619-661-0385; CC, Sa, UR; 120; **70-89; D, F; B3**

Santa Ana; Affordable Truck & Auto, 518 Poinsettia St, 92701; 714-953-9533, FAX 714-953-9020; CC, Sa, Sp, Wr; **70-89; D, F, PU, 4x4; B3**

Certified Auto Salvage, 904 E 2 St, 92701; 714-835-4137; Sa, Sp; 200; **70-90; F; Eur; Spc: Volvo; 140, 122**

Chevy Truck Salvage, *see Vintage*

Ferman's Mini Trucks, 3409 W 5 St, 92703; 714-554-1391, FAX 714-554-1418; CC, Sa, Sp; **70+; F, PU**

Rice Auto Parts, 905 E 2 St, 92701; 714-542-4421; Sa, UR; 400; **75-85; D, F, PU; B3**

South El Monte; Illinois Auto Wrecking, 2014 Rosemead Blvd, 91733; 626-448-5319, FAX 626-579-5938; CC, Sa, Br; **82-94; D, F, PU, 4x4; B3**

Phil's Auto Salvage, 2405 Chico Av, 91733; 626-448-5987; Sa; **80+; D, F**

Southern California Import, *see Vintage*

Santa Fe Springs; Santa Fe Auto Wrecking, *see Vintage*

Spring Valley; CRH Slvg, *see Vintage*

Sweetwater Auto Wrecking, *see Vintage*

Stanton; Admore Auto Dismantling, *see Vintage*

Best Deal, *see Vintage*

Sun Valley; 2002 AD, 11066 Tuxford, 91352; 818-768-2697, 800-420-0223, bmwsales@2002ad; CC, Sa, Sp, Br; 400; **70-88 F; BMW only**

A & R Auto Dismantlers, 12143 Branford St, 91352; 818-897-2361, FAX 818-890-8005; Sa, Sp; 500; **78+; D, F; B3, Jpa**

A Truck Parts, *see Vintage*

Aadlen Brothers Auto Wrecking, *see Vintage*

Aaron's Auto Parts & Salvage, 9403 Glenoaks Blvd, 91352; 323-875-1760, FAX 818-768-8666; Sa, Sp; 2ac; **80+; D, F, PU, 4x4, Trk; B3, AMC, Jp, IH, VW**

Akron Auto Salvage, 9030 Norris Av, 91352; 818-768-0725, FAX 818-768-0695, akronsun@aol.com; Sa, Sp, Br; 1ac, 350+; **70+; D, F, PU, 4x4, Trk; B3, AMC, Jp, IH, VW**

All Truck Parts, 11549 Sheldon St, 91352; 818-983-1325, FAX 818-983-2126; CC, Sa, Br; 200; **80-90; D, F, PU, 4x4; Vans & Pickup only**

Arroyo Auto Dismantling, 9101 Glenoaks Blvd, 91352; 818-768-9322; Sa; 50; **80-92; D, F, PU, 4x4; B3, AMC; Vans**

Bells Auto Recycling, *see Vintage*

Best Auto Parts & Salvage, 12301 Branford St, 91352; 818-896-2622, 800-621-4484; CC, Sa, Sp; 3ac; **60+; F; BMW & Mercedes only**

Curt's Auto Wrecking, 8270 Tujunga Av, 91352; 818-768-3350; Sa, Br; 75; **69-89; D, F, PU, 4x4; B3**

Daytona Auto Wrecking, *see Vintage*

Discount Salvage Parts, 12246 Branford St, 91352; 213-875-1831, FAX 213-897-1416; Sa, Sp; 2ac; **80+; D, F; B3, AMC**

Folkswagon, *see Vintage*

Elite Auto Parts, 9944 Glenoaks Blvd, 91352; 818-767-0445, FAX 818-767-6179; Sa, Sp; 100; **84-92; F**

George & Sons Foreign Auto, 11058 Tuxford St, 91352; 818-767-6455, FAX 818-767-7499; CC, Sa, Sp; 100; **72+; F, PU, 4x4; Jpa, VW**

Glenoaks Auto Parts, 9350 Glenoaks Blvd, 91352; 818-768-8004, FAX 818-767-1135; CC, Sa, Sp, Wr; **68+; D, F, PU, 4x4; B3**

Honda Only Auto Dismantlers, 11611 Sheldon St, 91352; 818-768-6608, FAX 818-768-0640, 800-310-6608; Sa, Sp; 1ac, 250; **78+; F; Honda only**

Junior's Auto Parts & Salvage, 11171 Pendleton St, 91352; 818-767-1175; Sa; 100; **80+; D, F, PU, 4x4, Trk; B3, AMC, Jp, VW**

K & M Auto Dismantling, 8307 Tujunga Av, 91352; 818-768-3509; Sa; 10; **85-88; D, B3**

LA Nissan, 9343 Glenoaks Blvd, 91352; 818-767-3779, 800-767-3772; Sa; Sp; 500+; **80+; F; Nissan only**

Memory Lane Collector Car Dismantlers, *see Vintage*

Mike's Auto Wrecking, 12207 Branford St, 91352; 818-899-0011; Sa; 5ac; **70-85; D, F, PU, 4x4; B3**

Miller's Auto Dismantling, *see Vintage*

Nissan & Toyota Used Parts, 11223 Tuxford St, 91352; 818-768-7711, FAX 818-768-7722; 600+; **80-93; F; Nissan & Toyota only**

L A Toyota, 11115 Tuxford St, 91352; 818-768-4142; 5ac; **84-92; F; Toyota only**

Pacific Truck Salvage, *see Vintage*

Pit Stop Auto Wrecking, 12341 Branford St, 91352; 213-460-2098, FAX 818-897-3280; Sa, Sp; 300+; **80+; D, F; B3**

Pacoima Auto Recyclers, 12345 Branford St, 91352; 818-899-8333; CC, Sa, Sp, Wr; **80+; F; Jaguar only**

Q A Auto Dsmtlg, 12307 Branford St, 91352; 818-899-8181; Sa; 200+; **86-90; D, F, PU, 4x4**

Rollies Auto Wrecking, *see Vintage*

Sako's Auto Wrecking, 9048 Bradley Av, 91352; 818-768-0153; Sa; 500+; **78+; D, PU, 4x4; B3**

Thousand Palms; Indio Auto Wrecking, *see Vintage*

Vista; Interstate VW Auto, *see Vintage*

Quality Truck Recycling, *see Vintage*

Yucca Valley; Brust Auto Parts, 4181 Old Woman Springs Rd, 92284; 760-365-9119; UR; 2.5ac; **70+; D, F, PU, 4x4; B3**

LATE MODEL

Alhambra; Christian Bros Auto Wrecking, 3117 W Mission Rd, 91803; 323-283-2256, FAX 323-289-3614; CC, Sa, Sp; 250; **D, F, PU, 4x4, Trk; B3, AMC, Jp, IH**

One Way Auto Salvage, 3117 W Mission Rd, 91803; 213-283-2256, FAX 213-289-3614; CC, Sa, Sp; 2ac; **D, F, PU, Trk**

Anaheim; A-Professional Benz & Beemer, 1354 S Anaheim Blvd, 92805; 714-776-1152, FAX 714-776-9315; CC, Sa, Sp; **F; BMW & Mercedes only**

AASE Bros Porsche Car, *see Vintage*

All Ford, *see Vintage*

Import Auto Supply & Salvage, *see Late Vintage*

Pick Your Part Auto Recycler, 1235 S Beach Blvd, 92804; 714-385-1301; CC, Sa, UR; **D, F, PU; $1.00 admission**

Pull Your Part, 3200 E Frontera St, 92806; 714-632-7200, FAX 714-630-8931; Sa, UR; **D, F**

Azusa; Allied Auto Wrecking, *see Late Vintage*

M & G Auto Salvage-Foreign, 470 S Mira Loma Dr, 91702; 626-334-0311, FAX 626-334-2393; CC, Sa, Sp; 300; **D, F, PU, 4x4, Trk**

Baldwin Park; Discount Auto Wreckers, 5154 Bleeker St, 91706; 626-960-6366; CC, Sa, Sp; **D, F**

PV Dismantling, 775 Alpha, 91706; 626-301-9555; Sa; 1ac; **F**

Ted's Truck & Auto Used parts, *see Vintage*

Banning; Prices Auto Recycling, 275 E Lincoln St, 92220; 909-849-5488, FAX 909-794-5277; Sa, Sp; 100; **D, F, PU, 4x4**

Beaumont; M & M Auto Wrecking Yard, *see Late Vintage*

Bloomington; Ecology Auto Wrecking, *see Late Vintage*

Three Brothers Auto Wrecking, *see Late Vintage*

Calexico; A & A Auto Dismantlers, 30 W US Hwy 98, 92231; 760-357-0244, FAX; **Spanish**

Carson; Jags Services, *see Late Vintage*

Scott's Auto Salvage, *see Late Vintage*

Chatsworth; Star Truck, *see Vintage*

Chino; Chino Auto Salvage, 5154 G St, 91710; 909-628-0417, FAX 909-591-7497; CC, Sa, Sp; 150; **D, F**

Chula Vista; A Asian Auto Recycling, 150 Reed Ct, 91911; 619-661-6666, FAX 619-425-6039; Sa, Sp; 1500; **D, F, PU, 4x4; 2 locations**

Action Auto Dismantlers, *see Late Vintage*

All Trucs Wrecking, 793 Energy Way #D, 91911; 619-421-0711; Sa; <1ac, 40; **D, F; B3, Jpa**

American & Foreign Auto Wrecking, *see Vintage*

Calumet Auto Wrecking, 891 Energy Way, 91911; 619-421-1350, 800-443-6092; Sp; 200; **D, F, few PU**

Collision Parts Warehouse, *see Vintage*

D & P Auto Dismantlers, *see Vintage*

Ecology Auto Wrecking, 800 Energy Way, 91911; 619-409-9200; CC, Sa, UR; 1000; **D, F, PU; B3**

Fares Auto Recycling, 777 Energy Way, 91911; 619-421-6699, FAX 619-421-6672; CC, Sa; 50; **F; Honda**

Fords Forever, *see Late Vintage*

Honda Parts, 895 Energy Way, 91911; 619-482-8200, FAX 619-482-8281; CC, Sa, Sp; 500; **F; Honda**

Kit's Auto Recycling, 783 Energy Way #B, 91911; 619-421-9252; CC, Sa; <1ac, 30+; **F; Jpa**

Leon Auto Wrecking, *see Late Vintage*

Lunas Auto Wrecking, *see Late Vintage*

Quality Plus Automotive Parts, 611 Marsat Ct, 91911; 619-424-9991; Sa, Sp, Wr; **D, F, PU, 4x4**

South Bay Auto Wreckers, *see Vintage*

West Auto Wreckers, 2365 Main St, 91911; 619-423-1100, FAX 619-423-5149, 800-479-2001; Sp; 3ac, 250; **D, F, PU, 4x4, Cn, Fm; B3, Jpa, Eur**

Coachella; Abel's Dismantling & Auto Repair, *see Vintage*

Ajax Auto Wrecking, *see Late Vintage*

Allkars, *see Vintage*

Compact Truck & Auto Parts, 19457 Avenue 48, 92236; 760-398-3399; CC, Sa, Sp; 20; **F, PU; Jpa; Spc: Imports**

Desert Pull-A-Part, *see Late Vintage*

Desert Truck & Auto Parts, *see Vintage*

Compton; B-J Used Auto Parts, 7327 Rosecrans Av, 90221; 562-633-8810, FAX 562-633-5767; CC, Sa, Sp, Br; 1.5ac; **D, F, PU, 4x4**

Southeast Auto Salvage, *see Vintage*

Corona; Indiana Truck Salvage, *see Late Vintage*

Costa Mesa; Action Auto Dismantlers, *see Late Vintage*

Downey; B-J Used Auto Parts, 7000 Firestone Blvd, 90241; 562-927-8621, FAX 562-928-4137; CC, Sp; 2 locations; **D**

Duarte; A-Abar Auto Wrecking, *see Late Vintage*

Arrow Auto Salvage, 797 Alpha St, 91010; 626-359-8327, FAX 626-357-4792; Sa, Sp; 200+; **F; Jpa**

Cars, 872 Alpha St, 91010; 626-358-0265, FAX 626-389-9617; Sa, Sp, Br; 200; **D, F, PU; B3 AMC**

Cars Auto Wrecking, 872 Alpha St, 91010; 626-359-9866, FAX 626-359-9617; Sa; 1ac; 300; **D, F**

Fast Foreign Auto Salvage, 767 Alpha St, 91010; 626-357-3361, FAX 626-358-6618; CC, Sa, Sp; 1ac, 200; **F**

Jay's Auto Wrecking, 828 Alpha St, 91010; 626-303-3693, FAX 626-359-7263; CC, Sa; 1ac, 300+; **F, PU**

Lakeside Auto Dismantlers, 744 Alpha St, 91010; 626-301-0498; Sa, Sp; 1ac, 150; **D, F**

LPD Auto Dismantling, *see Late Vintage*

Silver Star Auto Wrecking, *see Late Vintage*

Singulyan Avetis, 711 Alpha St, 91010; 626-359-4475, FAX 626-359-6277; Sa, UR, PL; 1ac, 200; **D, F, PU, 4x4, Trk**

Slim & Ken's Auto Salvage, 864 Alpha St, 91010; 626-357-0028, FAX 626-359-4308; CC, Sa, Sp; 1ac, 150; **90% D, few F, PU**

Super Auto Wrecking, *see Late Vintage*

Thomas Auto Wrecking, *see Late Vintage*

El Cajon; Autobahn Porscha Dismantling, *see Vintage*

Autotech, 910 El Cajon Blvd, 92020; 619-588-5742, FAX 619-588-0022; CC, Sa, Wr; **F; Volvo**

El Centro; Stan's Auto Body & Paint, *see Vintage*

El Monte; A-Aero Truck Salvage, *see Late Vintage*

A-Auto Salvage, 12350 Valley Blvd, 91732; 626-442-4801; Sa, Sp; 100+; **D, F, PU**

Action Mini Truck Dismantling, 2247 Durfee Av, 91732; 626-448-6257, FAX 626-448-4225; CC, Sa, Sp, UR; **D, F, PU, 4x4, Trk; Pickup only**

Collision Auto Salvage, *see Vintage*

Five-Points Auto Salvage, 11847 Valley Blvd, 91732; 626-443-3044; Sa, UR; 100; **D**

S & P Auto Wrecking, 2749 Durfee Av, 91732; 626-444-9948, FAX 626-444-2802; Sa; 100+; **F; Spc: Japanese**

Escondido; Escondido Auto Wrecking, 895 Rock Springs Rd, 92025; 760-745-6761; **D, F**

Norman's Auto Parts, *see Vintage*

Fontana; A & A Fast Cash for Cars, *see Vintage*

A-A-A Jeep-4x4 & Pickup Salvage, *see Vintage*

Acey's Wreckers, *see Vintage*

All Auto Parts, *see Late Vintage*

Bill's Auto Wrecking, 13107 Whittram Av, 92335; 909-823-1290, FAX 909-899-7025, 800-403-3300; CC, Sa, Sp; 3ac; **F; European only & few older Mercedes**

California Truck Salvage, *see Vintage*

Dan's Auto Dismantling, 14985 Whittram Av, 92335; 909-350-2444, FAX 909-350-1047; CC, Sa, Sp; 2.5ac, 500; **F, PU, 4x4**

Epic Truck & Auto Dismantling, *see Late Vintage*

Express Auto Dismantling, 14597 Aliso Dr, 92337; 909-356-5050, FAX 909-355-9799, 800-95EXPRESS; Sa, Sp; 3ac; **F, PU, 4x4**

Express Import Auto Dismantling, 15750 Arrow Blvd, 92335; 909-350-3399; Sa, Sp; **F; Jpa**

Fontana Auto Recyclers, *see Late Vintage*

General Auto Dismantlers, *see Late Vintage*

Golden City Auto, 8750 Beech Av, 92335; 909-428-8550, FAX 909-428-8556, goldencityautowrecking@world.net.att.net; CC, Sa, Sp, PL; 50+; **D, F, PU**

Hi-Way Auto Wrecking, 14315 Whittram Av, 92335; 909-428-0404, FAX 909-428-6499, 800-898-8634 CA only, hi-way@sprynet.com; CC, Sa, Sp, PL; 50+; **D, F, PU**

J B Autowrecking, *see Vintage*

K & P Auto Wrecking, 14339 Whittram Av, 92335; 909-428-6898, FAX 909-428-4139, 800-909-6898; CC, Sa, Sp; 500; **F; Jpa**

Liberty Auto, 14639 Whittram Av, 92335; 909-356-5717, FAX 909-350-7302, 888-826-6006; Sa, Sp; 300+; **F; Jpa & German**

LTD Auto Dismantlers, *see Late Vintage*

M & M #1 Parts Center, 11080 Redwood Av, 92337; 909-428-2000, FAX 909-428-1345, 800-429-PART, www.mmparts.com; Sa, Sp, PL; 6ac, 500; **D, F, PU, 4x4; B3, Mercedes, BMW, Jaguar, Rolls, Land Rover**

M & M Import Auto, *see Late Vintage*

M & P Auto Dismantlers, 15666 Arrow Blvd, 92335; 909-357-0263 or 351-1977, FAX 909-357-2730, 800-352-9763; Sa; 5ac; **F; VW**

Mustang Village, *see Vintage*

National Auto Wrecking, *see Late Vintage*

P & M Truck & Salvage Co, *see Late Vintage*

Rite-Way Auto Dismantlers, 15765 Arrow Blvd, 92335; 909-350-2576, FAX 909-350-3497, 800-852-8733; CC, Sp; 400+; **D, F, PU, 4x4**

T & Y Truck Dismantling, 15303 Arrow Blvd, 92335; 909-823-3461, FAX 909-350-4416, 800-640-3461; CC, Sa, Sp; 200; **D, F, PU, 4x4**

VIP Auto Wrecking, 15395 Arrow Blvd, 92335; 909-355-2411, FAX 909-355-2636, 888-448-4VIP; Sa; 400; **D, F; Spc: Front Wheel Drive**

Garden Grove; Honda Independent Auto, *see Late Vintage*

Gardena; A & B Auto Wrecking, *see Vintage*

A-1 Western Auto Salvage, *see Late Vintage*

Aaron Auto Parts, *see Late Vintage*

Any Kar Auto Wrecking, 150 Lennon St, 90248; 213-321-0956, FAX 310-538-3503; CC, Sa; 100; **D, F; Spc: seats for Mini Vans**

Auto Wreckers & Parts Co, *see Late Vintage*

B & H Auto Wrecking, *see Late Vintage*

Big D Auto Wrecking, *see Vintage*

Capital Auto Salvage, 15326 S Figueroa St, 90248; 310-323-4242; CC, Sa, Sp; **D, F; Spc: Wheels**

Ideal Auto Parts & Salvage, 17505 S Main St, 90248; 310-532-5550; Sa, Sp; **D, F**

MDH Auto Wrecking, 15503 S Main St, 90248; 310-217-0302, FAX 310-217-1851; Sa; **F; Spc: Sports car**

Schulberg Auto Wreckers, 16100 S Avalon Blvd, 90248; 310-329-6322; **F; Eur**

Thomas Auto Salvage, 440 E Redondo Beach Blvd, 90248; 310-327-2950; CC, Sa; **F; Volvo only**

United Auto Dismantling, 17011 S Main St, 90248; 310-324-4728; Sa, Sp; **D, F**

Westway Auto Dismantling, 15414 S Figueroa St, 90248; 310-719-9520, FAX 310-516-6531; CC, Sa, Sp; 3ac; **D, F**

Glendale; Valley Auto Dismantlers, 5228 San Fernando Rd, 91203; 818-545-8232, FAX 818-240-8306; CC, Sp; 90+; **F**

Harbor City; Zacher's Auto Salvage, *see Vintage*

Highland; Volvo Express Tom's Enterprises, *see Vintage*

Huntington Park; B-J Used Auto Parts, 2461 E Slauson Av, 90255; 213-588-3241; CC, Sa; **D, F, PU**

Wheel & Deal Auto Wrecking, 8122 S Alameda St, 90002; 323-567-2283; CC, Sa, Sp, Wr; **D, F, PU, 4x4; B3; Spc: Pickup & Van**

Inglewood; Colorado Auto Salvage, 11308 Hawthorne Blvd, 90304; 323-678-5747, FAX 310-671-8973, 800-634-7407; Sp; 8.5ac; D, F, PU

Irvine; Volvo Express, 16372 Construction Cir E, 92606; 949-552-5255; **F; Volvo only**

La Puente; Ace Auto Parts & Salvage, 13025 Valley Blvd, 91746; 626-442-7589, FAX 626-330-5637, 800-924-0852, www.aceautopart.com; CC, Sa, Sp; **D, F, PU, 4x4**

Bassett Auto, 13166 Valley Blvd, 91746; 626-336-4521; Sa, Sp; **D, F, PU, 4x4**

Lakeside; Al's Auto Wrecking, *see Vintage*

Long Beach; Allco Auto Wrecking, 22632 S Alameda St, 90810; 562-424-8268, FAX 310-830-2062; CC, Sa, Sp, Br; 5ac; **D, F, PU, 4x4; Spc: Domestic**

Carson Auto, *see Vintage*

City Wide Auto Wrecking, *see Late Vintage*

Harbor Auto Parts, 1421 W Anaheim St, 90813; 562-437-6568; **D, F**

Maxfield's, 1320 E Hill St, 90806; 562-427-9949, FAX 562-492-9809; CC, Sa; **D, F; Spc: Manifold**

Super Towing, 1516 Hayes Av, 90813; 562-436-6386, FAX 562-436-7607; CC, Sa; **D, F; B3**

Los Angeles; A & A Auto Wrecking & Repair, 1806 Sichel St, 90031; 334-223-9481; **D, F**

A B Auto Dismantling, 1030 N San Fernando Rd, 90065; 213-225-8076, FAX 323-752-0433; **D, F Spanish**

A-Best Auto Wrecking, *see Late Vintage*

ABC Auto Dismantlers, *see Vintage*

ACA Auto Salvage, 538 N Mission Rd, 90033; 323-225-5997; **D, F**

ASI Auto Wreckers, 814 N Mission Rd, 90033; 323-221-2883; **D, F**

Aacon Auto Parts, 7721 S Alameda St, 90001; 323-589-5048; **D, F**

Ace Auto Wrecking, 1785 N Main St, 90031; 323-222-1313; CC, Sa, Sp, UR; 200; **F**

Advance & Boston Auto Salvage, 550 N Mission Rd, 90033; 323-223-4375; **D, F**

Advanced Auto Wrecking, 1757 N Main St, 90031; 323-222-9996; Sa; **F, PU, 4x4**

Alpine Auto, 337 W Av 26, 90031; 323-221-3126; Sa; **D, F**

B & R Auto Wrecking, *see Vintage*

B-1 Van Truck Wrecking, 9651 S Alameda St, 90002; 213-567-1388; **D, F**

Benson's Auto Dismantling, 7711 S Alameda St, 90001; 213-583-8941; **D, F**

Bob & Sons Auto Wrecking, 1720 Workman St, 90031; 213-223-2421; Sa; **D, PU, 4x4, Trk**

Dearborn Auto Wrecking, *see Late Vintage*

Dial A Hubcap, *see Vintage*

E & U Auto Wrecking, *see Late Vintage*

El Ahorro Used Auto Parts, 8833 S Alameda St, 90002; 213-277-2770; PL; **D, F**

Express Auto, 5180 Alhambra Av, 90032; 213-222-6499; **D, F**

Ford Only Auto Parts, *see Late Vintage*

Frank's Auto Parts & Salvage, 9501 S Alameda St, 90002; 213-566-3137; **F, D**

Friendly Neighbors Auto, 4525 Staunton Av, 90058; 213-234-7110; Sa; 2 lots

GTO Auto Glass, 995 N Mission Rd, 90033; 310-464-2565; **D, F**

General Auto Parts, 7673 S Alameda St, 90001; 213-588-6108; **D, F**

Grand Central Station, 1916 Darwin Av, 90031; 213-223-1886; Sa

Horizon Auto Dismantling, 2346 N San Fernando Rd, 90065; 213-222-1400; **D, F**

J & H Auto Wrecking, 5712 Morgan Av, 90011; 213-589-2774; **D, F**

J & J Auto Wrecking, 1026 E Cesar Chavez Av, 90033; 213-222-8548; **D, F**

Jalisco Auto Wrecking, 539 N Mission Rd, 90033; 213-222-9464; CC, Sa, UR; **D, F**

Japanese Auto Dismantler, 5534 Duarte St, 90058; 213-589-3219; **F; Jpa; Japanese only**

L A Auto Wrecking, 1718 Albion St, 90031; 323-223-0162, FAX 323-223-2554; Sa, Sp; 60; **D, F, PU, 4x4; Trk; B3, AMC, IH, Jp**

Mission Road Auto Wrecking, 126 S Mission Rd, 90033; 323-262-1935, FAX 323-262-4317; CC, Sa, Sp, UR; 100; **D, F, PU, 4x4; B3, AMC**

Nayarit Auto Wrecking, *see Late Vintage*

S CA Auto & Truck Wrecking, 8229 S Alameda St, 90001; 323-587-3144, FAX 323-587-3881; CC, Sa, Sp, UR; 3ac; **D, PU; Pickup only**

T & H Auto Wrecking, *see Late Vintage*

Tony's Auto Wrecking, *see Late Vintage*

U-Pick Parts, 8103 S Alameda St, 90001; 323-583-1094; Sa, UR; 500+; **D, F, PU, 4x4; open Sundays**

Lynwood; Coco's Auto Dismantling, *see Late Vintage*

Lynwood Auto Dismantling, 11400 Alameda St, 90262; 310-763-0509; CC, Sa, Sp; 800+

Miro Loma; Crossroads Classic Mustang, 12421 Riverside Dr, 91752; 909-685-7421, 800-443-3987; CC, Sa, Sp; 400; **D; Mustang only**

Montclair; GM Only Auto Parts, 4067 Holt Blvd, 91763; 909-621-5864, FAX 909-625-7392; CC, Sa, Sp, Wr; **D; Spc: GM**

Norco; Ingnorco Truck & Auto Parts, *see Late Vintage*

North Hollywood; Atlas Auto Parts & Salvage, *see Vintage*

B & H Auto Dismantling, 7337 Coldwater Canyon Av, 91605; 818-983-1694; Sa, Sp; **D, F, PU, 4x4, Trk; B3, AMC, VW**

IHS Motors Auto Dismantling, *see Late Vintage*

MIke's Foreign Auto Wrecking, 7330 Coldwater Canyon Av, 91605; 818-764-4336; Sa, Sp, UR; **F**

Sport Imports, 7054 Laurel Canyon Blvd, 91605; 818-765-3333; **D, F; Sports Cars**

Z Best Auto Dismantling, 10861 Vanowen St, 91605; 818-985-0790; Sa, Sp; 100+; **F, PU, 4x4**

Northridge; Van Nuys Auto Wrecking, *see Late Vintage*

Oceanside; A-1 Auto Dismantling, 1045 Airport Rd #A, 92054; 760-757-1400; CC, Sa, Sp; 3ac; **D, F, PU; B3, AMC, VW**

Cassan's Auto Wrecking, 1030 Airport Rd, 92054; 760-757-6111; CC, Sa, Sp; 200; **D, F, PU, 4x4, Trk; B3, VW**

Ecology Auto Wrecking, 2315 Carpenter Rd, 92054; 760-757-7770; CC, Sa, UR; 800+; **D, F; 3 additional yards in Chula Vista**

San Luis Rey Auto Salvage, 471 N El Camino Real, 92068; 760-757-4433, sanluisrey@aol.com; CC, Sa

Ontario; Can-Am Auto & Truck Parts, 1101 E California St, 91761; 909-983-9695, FAX 909-986-8328, 800-600-9695; CC, Sa, Sp, Br; 2ac; **D, F, PU, 4x4, Trk; B3, AMC, VW**

Eastern Auto, 802 Ontario Blvd, 91761; 909-391-2298; Sa, Sp; **F**

Kar King Auto Wrecking, 2151 E Philadelphia St, 91761; 909-947-3969, kormex@earthlink.net; CC, Sa, Sp; 800; **D, F, PU, 4x4; B3, AMC**

Milliken Truck Van 4x4, 2175 S Milliken Av, 91761; 909-390-4800, FAX 909-390-4805; CC, Sa, Sp; 300; **D, F, PU, 4x4, Trk; No cars**

Pick-A-Part Auto Dismantling, 2025 S Milliken Av #A, 91761; 909-390-5270, FAX 909-390-5276; CC, Sa, UR; 2000+; **D, F**

Orange; A-1 Auto Recycling, 815 N Batabia, 92868; 714-996-7070; **D, PU; Domestic Pickup only**

Holmes Mini Truck Parts, *see Late Vintage*

Motor Sport Auto, *see Late Vintage*

Pacoima; B W Parts, *see Vintage*

Cad King, *see Vintage*

Eagle Auto Dismantling, 12201 Montague St, 91331; 818-897-5106; Sa; **D, F, PU, 4x4; Spc: Ford & Chrysler**

Harry's Auto Wrecking, *see Vintage*

M G M, 9821 San Fernando Rd, 91331; 818-834-8880, FAX 818-896-8623; Sa, Sp; 1ac; 300; **D, F; B3, Asian, Eur**

Sam's Auto Wrecking, *see Late Vintage*

Paramount; Lynwood Auto Parts, 14116 Garfield Av, 90723; 562-633-2961; Sa; 200; **D, F, PU, 4x4, Trk**; **B**3

Mustang Country, *see Vintage*

Perris; K & D Dismantling, *see Vintage*

Steve's Auto Dismantling, *see Late Vintage*

Placentia; J J's Foreign Auto Wrecking, *see Late Vintage*

Placentia Truck Van Wrecking, *see Late Vintage*

Pomona; A Auto Wrecking, *see Late Vintage*

A-Car Auto Wrecking, *see Vintage*

All Car Auto Supply, 1327 W Holt Av, 91768; 909-623-3909; CC, Sa, Wr; **D, F, PU**; **Spc: Rebuilt Parts**

California Mini Trucks, *see Late Vintage*

R S Truck Parts, 10802 Kadota Av Unit A, 91766; 909-629-4111, FAX 909-629-4112; CC, Sa; 500; **D, F, PU, Vans, 4x4**

Tri-County 4x4s Gear Spec, *see Vintage*

U Pick-U Save Self-Serv Auto, 1560 E Mission Blvd, 91766; 909-623-6108; CC, Sa, UR; 1200; **D, F, PU, 4x4, Trk**; **open Sunday**

V & P Auto Dismantling, 4015 State St, 91766; 909-620-6770; CC, Sa; **D, F**

West Coast Auto Wrecking, *see Vintage*

Ramona; Ramona Auto Dismantling, *see Late Vintage*

Rancho Cucamonga; Alex Auto Dismantling, see Late Vintage

Kings Auto Wrecking, 13293 Whittram Av, 91739; 909-987-9800; Sa, Sp, PL; 200+; **D, PU, 4x4**

Rialto; A-1 Auto & Truck Wrecking, 2015 Stonehurst Dr, 92377; 909-822-6288, FAX 909-822-5342; CC, Sa, Sp, Br; 2.5ac, 250; **D, F, PU, 4x4, Trk**; **Spc: Pickup & Van**; **some RVs**

ACA Auto Salvage 2, *see Late Vintage*

Riverside; Accord Auto Recycler, *see Late Vintage*

Riverside All Foreign Parts, 3011 Vine St #A, 92507; 909-276-9679; Sa, Sp; **F**; **Eur & Jpa**; **BMW, Jaguar**

Hillside Auto Salvage, *see Late Vintage*

Honda & Foreign Parts, *see Late Vintage*

Romoland; Santa Fe Auto Salvage, *see Late Vintage*

Rosemead; AA Auto, 8500 Garvey Av, 91770; 626-288-8500, FAX 323-888-0001; CC, Sa, Sp, UR; **F**; **Lexus, Honda only**

San Bernardino; All GM Auto Parts, 330 E 6 St, 92410; 909-889-0206 or 884-0826, FAX 909-885-2531, 800-404-2531 S Cal only; CC, Sp; 2ac, 100; **D**; **B**3; **Spc: GM**

All You Need, 831 N Waterman Av, 92410; 909-888-0042, FAX 909-383-5413; Sa, Sp; 1ac, 125; **D, F**

American Auto Wrecking, 755 N Waterman Av, 92410; 909-884-5211, FAX 909-381-5708, 800-872-5211; CC, Sp; 1ac, 200; **D, F**

American Import Dismantlers, 1941 W 4 St, 92411; 909-888-0992, FAX 909-873-0920; CC, Sa, Sp, Br; 200; **F**; **Jpa**

Chuck's Auto Wrecking, *see Late Vintage*

Jimbo's Auto Wrecking, *see Late Vintage*

Rambros Auto Parts, *see Late Vintage*

San Bernardino Pick a Part, *see Vintage*

San Bernardino Truck Dismantlers, 1455 E San Bernardino Av, 92408; 909-796-5211, FAX 909-478-5533, 888-796-5211; CC, Sa, Sp; 500+; **D, F, PU, 4x4, Trk**; **Pickup, Truck & Van only**

Three Guys Auto Wreckers, *see Late Vintage*

U & I Auto Wrecking, *see Vintage*

Waterman Auto Dismantlers, *see Vintage*

San Clemente; Sam Clemente Auto Wrecking, 1520 N Avenida De La Estrella, 92672; 949-492-6121; CC, Sa, Sp; 1.5ac; **D, F, PU, 4x4**

San Diego; A & B Truck Recycling, *see Vintage*

A to Z Auto Wrecking, 3200 Main St, 92113; 619-234-6691, FAX 619-234-2476; CC, Sa, Br; 2.5ac; **D, F, PU, 4x4, Trk**

Able Auto Wrecking, 2704 Main St, 92113; 619-233-7276; CC, Sa; **F; Japanese only**

American & Foreign Auto Wrecking, 1615 Logan Av, 92113; 619-234-2049; Sa; **D, F**

British Foreign Auto Salvage, 2720 Main St, 92113; 619-544-0999, FAX 619-544-1067; CC, Sa, Sp, Wr; **F; British**

F & D Foreign, 1684 Logan Av, 92113; 619-239-9119; **F; Porsche**

Mini Trucks & Cars, 1700 Newton Av, 92113; 619-233-3884, FAX 619-233-8666, 800-827-1970; CC, Sa, Sp, UR; 200+; **F, PU, 4x4; Jpa**

National Auto Wrecking, 1643 National Av, 92113; 619-234-3134; CC, Sa, Wr; **D, R, PU, 4x4, Trk**

Pacific Internat. Auto, 1118 Garnet Av, 92109; 619-274-1920; Sa; Sp, UR; **F; British**

San Diego Foreign Auto, *see Vintage*

Shirinco Auto Parts, 2710 Garnet Av #110, 92109; 619-581-1800; **D, F**

Trolley Auto Parts, 2966 Commercial St, 92113; 619-232-9996; **D, F, PU, 4x4; Toyota only**

San Gabriel; Walker Four Hundred Auto, 400 W Valley Blvd, 91776; 626-576-1645, FAX 626-308-0287; CC, Sa, Sp, Wr; 10; **D, F, PU, 4x4**

San Jacinto; Valley Auto Salvage, *see Vintage*

San Ysidro; A-1 Auto Wrecking, 971 Heritage Rd, 92173; 619-661-6524; Sa, Sp, UR; 100+; **D, F; Spanish**

Baja Truck & Auto Dismantling, 1252 Otay Valley Rd, 92173; 619-661-6054; **D, F, PU, 4x4**

Bebos Auto Wrecking, 6401 Datsun St, 92173; 619-661-5595

Best Way Auto Wrecking, 935 Heritage Rd, 92173; 619-661-9171; CC, Sa, Sp, Wr; **D, F, PU, 4x4, Trk**

Brown Field Truck & Auto Dismantlers, *see Late Vintage*

Camino Auto Wrecking, *see Late Vintage*

Central Auto Parts, 1304 Otay Valley Rd, 92173; 619-661-9215, FAX 619-661-9128; Sa, Sp, UR; **D, F**

Dave's Auto Wrecking, *see Late Vintage*

Ecology Auto Wrecking, 981 Heritage Rd, 92173; 619-661-4545, FAX 619-426-3869; CC, Sa, Sp, UR; 1000+; **D, F; Open every day of the year; Chain of yards**

Ecology Auto Wrecking, *see Late Vintage*

El Cowboy Auto Wrecking, 6551 Datsun St, 92173; 619-661-6516; Sa, Sp, UR; 200; **D, F; Spanish**

Express Auto Wrecking, *see Vintage*

First Auto Wrecking, 6571 Datsun St, 92173; 619-661-2525; Sa, Sp, UR; **D, F, PU, 4x4; Spanish**

Fonsecas Auto Wrecking, 1080 Heritage Rd, 92173; 619-661-6430

Fords & Foreign Auto Wrecking, 950 Heritage Rd, 92173; 619-661-8085; **D, F**

Frontera Auto Wrecking, *see Late Vintage*

Goodyear Auto Wreckers, 1102 Heritage Rd, 92173; 619-661-6870, FAX 619-661-6864; Sa, UR; 250; **D, F, PU; Spanish; Open Sunday**

Guzman Auto Wrecking, 980 Heritage Rd, 92173; 619-661-6540; **D, F**

Hilltop Auto Wreckers, 1060 Heritage Rd, 92173; 619-661-6881; **D, F, PU; B3, Jp, IH**

International Auto Wreckers, 1284 Otay Valley Rd, 92173; 619-661-1190, FAX 619-661-1138; CC, Sa; 200; **D, F; Spanish**

Libra Auto Dismantling, 979 Heritage Rd, 92173; 619-661-6655, FAX 619-661-9059; Sa; **D, F, PU, 4x4, Trk**

MCM Auto Recycling, 6421 Datsun St, 92173; 619-661-9186, FAX 619-661-2192; CC, Sa, Sp; **D, F, PU, 4x4**

Middle East Auto Dismantling, 1318 Otay Valley Rd, 92173; 619-661-1131, FAX 619-661-1970; Sa; 1ac; **D; Spc: Cadillac**

Montoya's Auto Wrecking, 1320 Otay Valley Rd, 92173; 619-661-6503; CC, Sa, UR; 1.5ac, 300+; **D, F, PU, 4x4**

Padre Auto Dismantling, 6550 Datsun St, 92173; 619-661-5344, FAX 619-671-5842, 800-800-7759; CC, Sa; **D, F, PU, 4x4 Spanish**

Rabago Auto Wrecking, 6411 Datsun St, 92173; 619-661-8031; Sa, Sp, UR; 200; **D, F, PU, 4x4; Spanish**

Rapido Truck & Auto Wrecking, *see Late Vintage*

Scorpio Auto Wrecking, *see Late Vintage*

Silver Auto Wrecking, 1232 Otay Valley Rd, 92173; 619-661-6262; Sa; 7ac; **PU, 4x4, Trk**

Street & Sons Auto Wrecking, 1328 Heritage Rd, 92173; 619-661-6106, 800-727-8494; Sp, PL; **D, F, PU, 4x4**

Tapatio Auto Wrecking, 6507 Datsun St, 92173; 619-661-1528, FAX 619-661-1868; CC, Sa; **F, PU**

Tokyo II, 1040 Heritage Rd, 92173; 619-661-1141; CC, Sa; 100; **D, F, PU, 4x4, Trk**

Tokyo Auto Wrecking, 1120 Heritage Rd, 92173; 619-661-6636; Sa, Sp; 100; **D, F, PU; Spanish**

Tony's Auto Wrecking, 963 Heritage Rd, 92173; 619-661-6424; Sa, Sp, UR; 100; **D, F, PU, 4x4, Trk**

Union Auto Wrck, 1186 Otay Valley Rd, 92173; 619-661-6207; Sa; 600; **D, F, PU, 4x4, Trk**

Uruapan Auto Wreckage, 990 Otay Valley Rd, 92173; 619-661-9430, FAX 619-661-1494; CC, Sa; 1.5ac, 100+; **F; Eur & Jpa**

Western Auto Dismantlers, 1022 Otay Valley Rd, 92173; 619-661-6747; Sa; **F; Japanese only**

Santa Ana; A Freeway Auto Parts, 1041 E 6 St, 92701; 714-835-0505, FAX 714-835-8973, 800-959-8761; CC, Sa, Sp; 2.5ac, 250+; **D, F, PU, 4x4; Spanish**

ARS-Roccos Truck Van Wrecking, 3125 W 5 St, 92703; 714-554-9800, FAX 714-554-1794; CC, Sa, Wr; **D, PU, 4x4; B3; To 2 Ton Pickup & Van only**

All Cars Auto Parts, 2002 & 2006 W 5 St, 92703; 714-972-8382; CC, Sa, Sp; 3ac, 500; **D, F, PU, 4x4; B3, Jp; Glass & Transmissions; Open Sunday**

California Import & American, 1045 E 6 St, 92701; 714-542-2700; Sa; 250; **F**

Chevy Truck Salvage, *see Vintage*

Ferman's Mini Trucks, *see Late Vintage*

H Truck Dismantling, 936 E 3rd St, 92701; 714-835-8350, FAX 714-835-5206, 800-238-9308; CC, Sa, Sp, UR; **F, PU; Medium duty Pickup only**

Joe's Auto Wrecking, 3117 W 5 St, 92703; 714-554-9300; Sa, UR; 100+; **D, F**

Santa Ana Auto Salvage, 826 E Washington Av, 92701; 714-834-1300; Sa, Sp; 100; **D, F**

Wrecks West, 1804 W 5 St, 92703; 714-547-6245, FAX 714-547-9395, www.wreckswest.com; CC, Sa, Sp; 350+; **F, PU, 4x4; Eur, Jpa**

Santa Fe Springs; Auto Parts by Lakenor, 10950 S Norwalk Blvd, 90670; 562-944-6422, FAX 562-903-8502, 800-LAKENOR; CC, Sp; **D, F, PU, 4x4**

Santa Fe Auto Wrecking, *see Vintage*

South El Monte; El Monte Auto Wrecking, 10316 Rush St, 91733; 626-579-0366; Sa, Sp; 80+; **D, F, PU; B3, AMC, IH**

Illinois Auto Wrecking, *see Late Vintage*

Phil's Auto Salvage, *see Late Vintage*

South El Monte Auto Salvage, 11203 Rush St, 91733; 626-444-9521, FAX 626-444-1481; CC, Sa, Sp; **F, PU, 4x4, Trk**

Southern California Import, *see Vintage*

Stanton; Best Deal, *see Vintage*

Sun Valley; A A Alex Auto Dismantler, 8873 Norris Av, 91352; 818-768-9981, FAX 818-768-9982; Sa, Sp; **D; Chevy only**

A & R Auto Dismantlers, *see Late Vintage*

A to Z Auto Enterprises, 8751 Bradley Av, 91352; 818-504-4340; CC, Sa, Sp, Br; 300+; **D, F; B3, Jpa; Spc: Japanese**

A Truck Parts, *see Vintage*

A-1 Auto Wrecking, 11676 Sheldon St, 91352; 818-768-1568; Sa, PL; 300; **D, F**

A-King, 12105 Branford St, 91352; 323-466-3824, FAX 323-897-0999; Sa

75

AAA Foreign Auto Parts, 8981 San Fernanado Rd, 91352; 818-504-3939, FAX 818-768-8108; Sp; **D, F; Motors & Transmissions-Any car/Any year**

Aadlen Brothers Auto Wrecking, *see Vintage*

Aaron's Auto Parts & Salvage, *see Late Vintage*

Akron Auto Salvage, *see Late Vintage*

Arrow Truck Salvage, 8783 San Fernando Rd, 91352; 818-768-7786; CC, Sa, Sp; 1ac, 75+; **D, PU; Saturn & Pickup**

Arts Auto Salvage, 11163 Tuxford St, 91352; 818-767-4770, FAX 818-767-5492; Sa, Sp, Br; **F, PU; Jpa, Mazda**

Bells Auto Recycling, *see Vintage*

Best Auto Parts & Salvage, *see Late Vintage*

Blue Motors, 11146 Tuxford St, 91352; 818-768-3246, FAX 818-768-3968; **F; Hyundai, Acura**

Boat People Auto Dismantlers, 11209 Tuxford St, 91352; 818-767-7254; CC, Sa, Sp; **F, PU; Japanese Mini Truck only**

Brand Auto Dismantling, 8426 San Fernando Rd, 91352; 818-768-6665, FAX 818-768-7660; Sa, UR; **F; Jpa**

Branford Auto Wreckers, 12276 Branford St, 91352; 818-896-3737, 800-Part-411; CC, Sa, Sp, Br; 2ac; **D, F; B3**

Century Auto Wrecking, 11365 Pendleton St, 91352; 818-767-1975, FAX 818-767-5644; Sa, Sp; 200; **D, F, PU, 4x4; B3**

Daytona Auto Wrecking, *see Vintage*

Discount Salvage Parts, *see Late Vintage*

Dollar Wise Auto Wrecking, 12129 Branford St, 91352; 818-896-3516; Sa, Sp; .5ac; **D, PU, 4x4; B3, AMC**

E Z Auto Sales & Parts, 9415 Glenoaks Blvd, 91352; 818-767-5651, FAX 818-767-3510; Sa, Sp; 800; **D, F, PU; B3**

Elite Auto Wrecking, 9787 Glenoacks Blvd, 91352; 818-768-1350; Sa; 600; **F**

Folkswagon, *see Vintage*

Frontier Auto & Truck Salvage, 8787 San Fernando Rd, 91352; 323-875-1888, FAX 818-768-6839; **D, F, PU; Pickup only**

Galaxy Used Auto Parts, 12355 Branford St, 91352; 818-899-8333; CC, Sa, Sp, UR; **F; Jaguar only**

George & Sons Foreign Auto, *see Late Vintage*

Glenoaks Auto Parts, *see Late Vintage*

Grand Prix Auto Parts, 12071 Branford St, 91352; 818-834-1464, FAX 818-834-1466; CC, Br; 300; **D, F, PU, 4x4; B3**

H & R Auto Dismantling, 11184 Penrose St, 91352; 818-504-2822, FAX 818-504-6017; Sa, Sp, UR; 200; **D, F, PU; B3, Jp, IH**

Harry Grig Auto, 11210 Tuxford St, 91352; 818-504-0717, FAX 818-504-1720; Sa, Br; 300; **F**

Honda Only Auto Dismantlers, *see Late Vintage*

International Auto Wrecking, 12135 Branford St, 91352; 818-896-5241; Sa; 500+; **D, F, PU, 4x4, Trk; B3, Jp, IH**

Junior's Auto Parts & Salvage, *see Late Vintage*

K C Auto, 9597 Glenoaks Blvd, 91352; 818-768-9715, FAX 818-768-0004; Sa, Sp; 100+; **F; Nissan only**

K D Auto Dmtl, 12319 Branford St, 91352; 818-771-0101, FAX 818-899-4083; Sa; 100; **F**

Kaos Auto Dismantling, 9797 Glenoaks Blvd, 91352; 818-768-0000, FAX 818-768-1723; Sa, Sp, UR; 2ac; **F**

L A Japanese, 9928 Glenoaks Blvd, 91352; 818-771-0000, FAX 818-768-6666, 800-704-1212; CC, Sa, Sp; 1200; **F; Jpa**

L A Nissan, *see Late Vintage*

M-Mercedes Dismantlers, 11203 Tuxford St, 91352; 818-768-0704; CC, Sp; 2ac; **F; Mercedes only**

76

Marv's Auto Dismantling, 11021 Tuxford St, 91352; 818-767-6615, FAX 818-504-6313; CC, Sp; 2500; **D; B3, Jp; Spc: Ford, Chrysler, Jeep**

Nissan & Toyota Used Parts, *see Late Vintage*

Pacoima Auto Recyclers, *see Late Vintage*

Pit Stop Auto Wrecking, *see Late Vintage*

Prime Auto Parts & Salvage, 11153 Tuxford St, 91352; 213-462-5100; Sa; **D, F, PU, 4x4**

Prince Auto Dismantling, 11217 Tuxford St, 91352; 818-768-6060; Sa, Sp; 500+; D; **B3; SUV only**

Rainbow Auto Dismantling, 8917 Norris Av, 91352; 818-767-0316; Sa, Sp, Br; 100+; **F**

Rollies Auto Wrecking, *see Vintage*

Sako's Auto Wrecking, *see Late Vintage*

Statewide Auto Wrecking, 12039 Branford St, 91352; 818-897-1009, FAX 818-897-2401; CC, Sa; 400+; **F; Jpa, Eur; Spc: Mercedes, Lexus, Volvo**

Thousand Palms; Indio Auto Wrecking, *see Vintage*

Vista; Interstate VW Auto, *see Vintage*

Wilington; Japanese Truck Dismantling, 940 Alameda St N, 90744; 310-835-3100, FAX 310-835-7965; Cc, Sa, Sp; **F; Japanese only**

GTL Auto Dismantling, 1006 Vreeland Av, 90744; 310-513-1128; Sa, Sp; **F, PU; Spc: Toyota**

Yucca Valley; Brust Auto Parts, *see Late Vintage*

1967 Kaiser Jeepster Convertible
Ruth Harvey
Cheyenne, WY

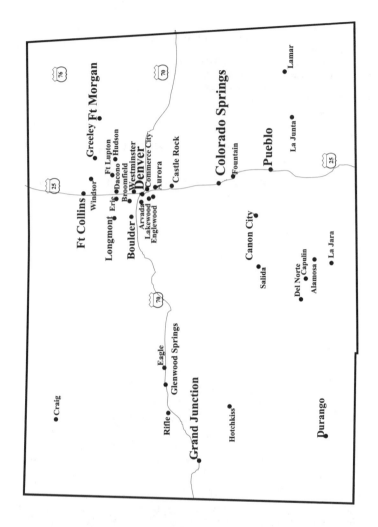

COLORADO

Alamosa; L & M Auto, 8425 County Rd 8 S, 81101; 719-589-9205, FAX 719-589-1620; CC, Sa, Sp, UR; 1500**; 40+; D, F, PU, 4x4, Trk; B3, AMC, Jp, IH, St, Pk, VW; few other independents**

Aurora; Aurora Auto Wrecking, 18350 E Colfax Av, 80011; 303-343-3395; CC, Sa, Sp, UR; 3ac, 150; **D, R, PU, 4x4; B3, AMC, Jp; engines 50+, body parts 67+**

Colorado Mustang Specialists, 19900 E Colfax, 80011; 303-343-7024, FAX 303-343-6582; 877-687-8864; CC, Sa, Sp; 10ac; **65-87; D; Mustang only**

Remember not to copy, reproduce or distribute this list in any way without the written permission of Ray's wReckingyard Roster

Canon City; Fremont Auto Sales Salvage, 12868 County Rd 3, 81212; 719-275-2504; Sa, Sp, Br; 65ac, 2000+; **60+; D, F, PU, 4x4; B3, Jp, IH, VW**

Capulin; Ernest's Auto Wrecking, PO Box 6, 81124; 719-274-5224, FAX 719-274-5235; Sa, Sp, Br; 25ac; **01-94; D F; B3, Ns, St; Spc: older MG**

Colorado Springs; A-1 Auto Recyclers, 3745 S US Hwy 85-87, 80906; 719-392-5900, 800-437-0964; 300+; **50+; D, F, PU, 4x4; B3, a few others**

ABC Used Auto Parts, 1143 S Royer St, 80903; 719-632-0846, 800-456-6517; CC, Sa, UR; 1000+; **60+; D, F, PU; B3**

Anything Automotive Inc, 701 E Las Vegas St, 80903; 719-471-7337, 800-828-8970; CC, Sp; 800+; **63+; D, F, PU, 4x4; B3**

Rodriguez Auto Salvage, 1006 S Institute St, 80903; 719-635-2733; Sa; 3000+; **60-90; D, F, PU, 4x4**

Craig; Ikes Automatic Transmission, 30966 E Hwy 40, 81625; 970-824-6475, 800-883-6475; CC, Sa, Sp, Br; 37ac, 4500; **30+; D, F, PU, 4x4; B3, AMC, Jp, IH, Hd, Ns, St, Pk**

Dacono; Elliotts Auto Parts, 5543 County Rd 13, 80514; 303-833-3501; Sa, Sp, UR; 5ac; **40+; D, F PU, 4x4; B3, AMC, Jp, Hd, Ns, St, Pk, Ks, Fr**

Denver; A Du-Well Auto, 5135 Emerson St, 80216; 303-293-2328, FAX 303-296-2922, http://www.aduwell.com; Sa, Sp, UR; 120; **65+; D, F, PU, Trk; AMC, IH, VW**

A-K Truck Parts, 5390 Adams St, 80216; 303-296-2966; Sp; 2ac, 125; **61-86; PU, 4x4, Trk; B3; Pickup, Truck & Van only**

AA Auto Parts Inc, 2180 W 60th Av, 80221; 303-425-1459, 800-784-1459; CC, Sa, Sp, Wr; **50+; D, PU, 4x4; B3, Jp, IH, Wy**

American Graffiti, 5351 W 6th Av, 80214; 303-275-9099; CC, Sa, Sp; 150+; **60-85; D; Chevelle, El Camino, Camaro, Monte Carlo, Nova; service**

Bevsons Import Parts & Svc, 5353 E 46th Av, 80216; 303-355-1604, 800-355-1604; CC, Sa, Sp; 30; **57+; F; VW only**

H & R Auto Salvage, 5340 Cook St, 80216; 303-296-0324, 800-757-7234; CC, Sa, Sp; 6ac; **60-85; D, PU, 4x4, Trk; B3, Jp**

Sidewinder, 4949 Washington St, 80216; 303-293-8610; Sa, UR; 900; **60+; D, F, PU, 4x4; AMC, Jp, IH, VW**

Tommy's Auto Repair & Salvage, 2860 W 60th Av, 80221; 303-433-0252; CC, Sa; 10ac; 1300; **50+; D, F, PU, 4x4; B3, AMC, Jp, IH**

Volvoparts Inc, 1801 W Evans Av, 80223; 303-937-1801, FAX 303-934-2099, 800-541-8686, 800-541-1801 CO only; CC, Sa, Sp, Wr; 1ac; **60+; F; Volvo only**

Durango; Basin Towing & Repair, 25823 Hwy 160, 81301; 970-247-9819, FAX 970-247-5290; CC, Sa, Sp, UR; 8ac; **40-89; D, F, PU, 4x4; B3**

Lon's Automotive Inc, 714 Saw Mill Rd, 81301; 970-253-4434, FAX 970-259-3919, 800-452-4542; CC, Sp, Br, Wr; 4ac, 2000; **50+; D, PU, 4x4; B3, AMC, Jp, IH, St, Wy, VW**

Eagle; Eagle Salvage & Towing, 16435 US Hwy 6 #C, 81631; 970-328-7769, FAX 970-328-1291, 800-331-9558; CC, Sp, Br; 8ac; **46+; D, F, PU, 4x4; B3**

Englewood; Arapahoe Auto Salvage, 2101 W Quincy Av, 80110; 303-781-0875, FAX 303-781-2238, 800-229-0875; Sa, Sp, UR; 2ac, 450; **53+; D; Cadillac only**

Fair Auto & Truck Wrecking, 2400 S Tejon St, 80110; 303-934-9326, FAX 303-934-5515, 800-748-2505; CC, Sp, PL; **60+; D, PU; Camaro, Firebird, Chevelle, Nova restor. Parts**

Svigel's Auto Parts, 4393 S Santa Fe Dr, 80110; 303-781-7859, FAX 303-781-0615; CC, Sa, Sp, Wr; 7ac, 300+; **30s-70s; D; B3, Hd, St, Pk, Ks, Fr, Cr, Wy**

Truckford Parts, 3300 W Hampden Av, 80110; 303-781-7865; CC, Sa, Sp, Wr; **59-96; D, PU, 4x4; Ford trucks only**

Erie; Erie Auto Wreckers, 4878 I 25 Frontage Rd, 80516; 303-833-5820, 303-571-5375 Denver area; CC, Sa, Br; 10+ac; **40-89; D, F, PU, 4x4, Trk, In; B3, Pk, Ks; cranes**

Jeeps Unlimited, 4245 Weld Co Rd 6, 80516; 303-666-9020; WR, PL; 100+; **40s+; D, PU; Jeep Only; Spc: Cherokee, Grand Cherokee, Comanche, Wrangler, Wagoneer, J Series & CJ**

Speedway Auto Wrecking, 4394 County Rd 12, 80516; 303-833-0332; Sa, UR; 1000+; **30-90; D, PU, 4x4, Trk, Farm; B3, AMC, Jp, IH, Hd, Ns, St, Pk**

79

Ft. Collins; Willox Wrecking Yard, 938 W Willox Ln, 80524; 970-484-3574, FAX 970-484-2162; CC, Sp, UR; 350+; **60+; D, F, PU, 4x4; B3**

Ft. Lupton; M B Auto Salvage & Sales, 2732 County Rd 27, 80621; 303-654-1882; Sa, Sp, Br; 18ac+; **60-90s; D, PU, 4x4; few 50s**

Fountain; Santa Fe Automotive, 12225 Millbrose Rd, 80817; 719-382-7070; Sa, UR; 10ac; **40-80s; D, F, PU, 4x4; B3, AMC, Jp, IH, Ns, St, Wy**

Ft. Morgan; West Side Auto Parts, 15859 US Hwy 34, 80701; 970-867-2486, 800-307-2487; CC, Sa, Sp; 800; **48-93; D, F, PU, 4x4, Trk; B3; Spc: 72-89**

Grand Junction; American Auto Salvage, 2773 D Rd, 81501; 970-242-5600, FAX 970-241-2696; CC, Sa, Sp, Br; 8ac, 550; **23-94; D, F, PU, 4x4, Mil; B3, AMC, Jp, IH, Hd, St, Pk, Wy, VW; Whole Cars available**

Greeley; A & S Salvage & Towing, 1100 Fern Av, 80631; 970-356-0408; Sa, UR; **35+; D, F, PU, 4x4; B3, AMC, IH, St, VW; few prewar**

A to Z Auto Salvage, 2589 49th St, 80634; 970-339-3275; CC, Sa, Sp; 4000+; **39-94; D, F, PU, 4x4, Trk; B3, AMC, Jp, IH, St**

Riverside Truck & Auto, 3696 1st Av, 80631; 970-339-5338, FAX 970-339-3390, 800-423-4862; CC, Sa, Sp; 60ac; **60+; D, F, PU, 4x4, Trk; B3; Pickups & Trucks only**

Hotchkiss; Phil's Auto Salvage, 1246 3700 Rd, 81419; 970-527-5656; Sp, UR; 800; **60-89; D, F, PU, 4x4; B3**

Hudson; Active Truck Sales & Parts Inc, 19640 Country Rd 28, 80642; 303-534-5102, 800-783-5102; CC, Sp; 7ac; **60+; D, PU, 4x4, Trk; B3, AMC; few Japanese**

La Junta; Roberson Wrecking, 3021 San Juan Av, 81050; 719-384-8036; Sa, UR; **60+**

Lamar; Woller Auto Parts, 8227 Rd 33, 81052; 719-336-2108, FAX 719-336-7157, 800-825-0210; CC, Sa, Sp, Br; 60ac, 5000; **55-95; D, PU 4x4, Trk; B3, AMC, Jp, IH; "Beautiful Wrecks & Glamorous Bodies"; GM, Mustangs & GTO**

Longmont; Auto Truck Salvage, 202 Martin St, 80501; 303-651-6127; Sa, UR; 7ac; **50-91; D, F, PU, 4x4, few Trk, Farm; B3, AMC, Jp, IH**

Pueblo; Bonnie's Car Crushers, 544 Kennie Rd, 81001; 719-372-6617, FAX 719-372-7667, 800-610-8074, CC, Sa, Sp; 500+; **40-90s; D, F, PU; B3, St, Pk, Ks, Fr**

Morgan Auto Parts, 722 Kennie Rd, 81001; 719-545-1702, FAX 719-546-2834, 800-333-3140; CC, Sa, Sp, Wr; 4ac; **50-95; D, PU, 4x4; B3**

West 29th Auto Inc, 3200 W 29th St, 81003; 719-543-4247 or 543-4249, FAX 719-543-1655, CC, Sa; 8000; **50+; D, F; B3, Hd, Ns, St; Old Stock Glass**

Rifle; Spangler's Auto Salvage, 27925 Hwy 6, 81650; 970-625-1477, FAX 970-625-3450; Sa, Sp; 1700+; **40+; D, F, PU; B3, Jp, IH, St, Pk, Wy**

Salida; South Side Salvage, 5550 E US Hwy 50, 81201; 719-539-6284, 800-759-0337; CC, Sa, Sp; 500+; **40+; D, F, PU; B3, Jp, IH, Hd, St, Pk, VW**

Windsor; Martin Supply & Salvage Yard, 8405 US Hwy 34, 80550; 970-686-2460; CC, Sa, Sp, UR; 17+ac; **30s-80s; D, PU, 4x4, Trk, Fm; B3, St, Pk, Ks, Cr & a few other independents; some prewar & Model A Ford; lots of older Wheels, Tractor parts**

<u>*LATE VINTAGE*</u>

Alamosa; L & M Auto; *see Vintage*

Aurora; A & A Auto Wrecking, 18640 E Colfax Ave, 80011; 303-364-4221; CC, Sa, Sp; 5+ac; **80s+; D; B3**

Action Auto Wrecking, 18000 E 14th Av, 80011; 303-364-7002; Sa, Sp, UR; 20ac, 1000; **70+; D, F, PU, 4x4, Trk; B3, AMC, IH, VW**

Aurora Auto Wrecking, *see Vintage*

Colorado Mustang Specialists, *see Vintage*

Boulder; D-C Auto Sales & Parts, 6095 Valmont Rd, 80301; 303-447-8872; Sa, Wr; **70+; D, F, PU, 4x4; B3; warehouse only**

Broomfield; Foothills Auto Salvage, Dillon Rd, 80020; 303-466-1989; CC, Sa, Sp, UR; 4ac; 65; **73-94; D, PU, 4x4; B3; Pickup only**

Canon City; Fremont Auto Sales Salvage, *see Vintage*

Indian Springs Auto Salvage, 1533 Temple Canyon Rd, 81212; 719-275-4974, FAX 719-269-7459; Sa, Sp, UR; 250; **70+; D, F, PU, 4x4; B3, AMC**

Capulin; Ernest's Auto Wrecking; *see Vintage*

Castle Rock; Audi Salvage, 2629 N Liggett Rd, 80104; 303-688-4644, FAX 303-660-4067, 800-444-2834; CC, Sa, Sp, UR; 3ac, 150; **70-91; F; Audi only**

Colorado Springs; A & A Truck Parts, 221 S Chestnut St, 80905; 719-634-1322; CC, Sa, Br; 2ac; **70+; D, F, PU; B3**

    A-1 Auto Recyclers; *see Vintage*

    ABC Used Auto Parts, *see Vintage*

    Anything Automotive Inc, *see Vintage*

    Best Foreign Used Parts, 400 S 16th St, 80904; 719-633-5658, 800-624-7364; CC, Sp, UR; 250+; **79-89; F**

    Best Foreign Used Truck Parts, 302 S 11th St, 80904; 719-578-9262, 800-892-3512; UR; 700+; **70+; F, PU**

    Bob's Foreign Used Car Parts, 1210 S El Paso St, 80903; 719-635-2635; 1ac; **83-95; F, PU**

    One Stop Used Parts, 1145 S Royer St, 80903; 719-578-1240; CC, Sp, UR; 3ac; **75-95; D, F, PU**

    P & L Scrap Iron & Metals, 617 Gillette St, 80903; 719-471-9876; CC, Sa, UR; 300; **80-92; D, F, PU; B3**

    Rodriguez Auto Salvage, *see Vintage*

Craig; Ikes Automatic Transmission; 5135 Emerson St, 80216; 303-293-2328, FAX 303-296-2922, http://www.aduwell.com; Sa, Sp, UR; 120; **65+; D, F, PU, Trk; AMC, IH, VW**

Dacono; Elliotts Auto Parts; *see Vintage*

Del Norte; Northside Salvage, 19198 Country Rd 15, 81132; 719-657-2593; Sa, Br; **80+; D, F, PU, 4x4, Trk; B3, VW**

Denver; A Du-Well Auto, *see Vintage*

    A-K Truck Parts *see Vintage*

    AA Auto Parts Inc; *see Vintage*

    ABC Imports 301, Kalamath St, 80223; 303-629-5111, FAX 303-629-9728, 800-472-9337; CC, Sa, Sp, UR; 1/2ac, 250; **73-97; F, PU, 4x4; Spanish**

    American Graffiti, *see Vintage*

    Badwrench Automotive, 1120 Depew Ct, 80214; 303-233-5865; Sa, UR; 2ac, 300; **80-93; D, PU, 4x4; B3**

    Bevsons Import Parts & Svc, *see Vintage*

    Billy's Auto Wrecking, 4235 Columbine St, 80216; 303-295-2152; Sa; 100; **78-91; D, PU, 4x4**

    Crusher Auto & Truck Salvage, 4980 Brighton Blvd, 80216; 303-297-0962, FAX 303-295-2209, 800-789-6521; CC, Sa, Sp, Wr; 3ac; **65+; D, F, PU, 4x4, Trk; B3**

    Foreign Used Auto Parts, 2424 E 40th Av, 80205; 303-296-2224, FAX 303-296-7480, CC, Sa, Sp; 4ac, 600; **F, mostly Japanese/Asian, few BMW; Spanish**

    H & R Auto Salvage, *see Vintage*

    Mile Hi Body Shop, 519 Lipan, 80204; 303-595-4646, FAX 303-595-0124, 800-757-7222, http://www.milehibodyshop.com; CC, Sp, UR; 1ac, 100; **70+; F; Saab only**

    Sidewinder, *see Vintage*

    Tams #1 Imports, 1937 S Bannock St, 80223; 303-744-0414; Sa, Sp, Wr; 2ac; **70+; F; mostly Jpa & German, Volvo, Saab**

    Tommy's Auto Repair & Salvage; *see Vintage*

    Volvoparts Inc, *see Vintage*

    Western Auto Recycling, 6100 Federal Blvd, 80221; 303-427-8185, FAX 303-427-1957; CC, Sa, UR; 5ac, 400; **70-89; D, F, PU, 4x4; B3, AMC, Jp**

Durango; AA American, 28753 Hwy 160, 81301; 970-247-4651, FAX 970-259-9188; CC, Sa; **70-89; D, F, PU, 4x4; B3**

    Basin Towing & Repair; *see Vintage*

    Lon's Automotive Inc; *see Vintage*

Mac's Foreign Auto Parts, 20091 Hwy 160, 81301; 970-259-1001, 800-748-2630; Sp; 3ac; **80+; F, PU, 4x4; Spc: Japanese, SUV; few European**

Eagle; Eagle Salvage & Towing; *see Vintage*

Englewood; A & A Toyota Parts, 1841 W Harvard Av, 80110; 303-934-3729, FAX 303-936-8077; CC, Sa, Sp, UR; 3ac, 300; **70-89; F, PU, 4x4; Toyota only**

ABZ Truck Parts Only, 1922 W Warren Av, 80110; 303-936-7359; CC, Sp, Wr; 1ac; **73+; D, PU, 4x4; B3; Trucks & vans only**

Arapahoe Auto Salvage; *see Vintage*

Colorado Auto & Parts, 2151 W Radcliff Av, 80110; 303-761-0112, FAX 303-762-8986, 800-222-0743; CC, Sa, Sp, UR; 10ac, 1000+; **70+; D, F, PU, 4x4; B3; Spanish**

D & L Auto Parts, 4040 S Clay St, 80110; 303-789-2586, 888-575-8559; CC, Sa, Wr, UR; 1ac; **75+; D, PU, 4x4; B3, AMC, Jp; mostly engines**

Eur-Asian Foreign Auto Parts, 2330 S Raritan St, 80110; 303-922-8396, FAX 303-922-0724, 800-944-3215; CC, Sa, Sp, UR; 3ac, 500; **75+; F; VW, Jaguar, European**

Fair Auto & Truck Wrecking, *see Vintage*

Svigel's Auto Parts; *see Vintage*

Truckford Parts; *see Vintage*

Erie; All American Pickup & SUV Parts, 4245 WCR 6, 80516; 303-666-9410; PL; 100; **80+; D, PU; B3; Jp; Spc: Domestic Pickup & SUV new & used parts**

Blake's Small Car Salvage, 2559 County Rd 5, 80516; 303-665-4312, FAX 303-828-2452, 800-665-4326; CC, Sa, Sp, Br; 13ac, 1200; **75+; F; VW; Spc: British; 2 mi W of I-25**

Erie Auto Wreckers; *see Vintage*

Jeeps Unlimited, *see Vintage*

Speedway Auto Wrecking; *see Vintage*

Fountain; Santa Fe Automotive; *see Vintage*

Ft. Collins; Willox Wrecking Yard, *see Vintage*

Ft. Lupton; M B Auto Salvage & Sales, *see Vintage*

Ft. Morgan; West Side Auto Parts; *see Vintage*

Glenwood Springs; Junk Yard Ranch, 484 County Rd 113, 81601; 970-945-7892; Sa, UR; 1000+; **70+; D, F, PU, 4x4, Trk; B3**

Grand Junction; American Auto Salvage; *see Vintage*

Greeley; A & S Salvage & Towing; *see Vintage*

A to Z Auto Salvage; *see Vintage*

Riverside Truck & Auto, *see Vintage*

Hotchkiss; Phil's Auto Salvage, *see Vintage*

Hudson; Active Truck Sales & Parts Inc, *see Vintage*

La Jara; De Herrera Towing & Repair Svc, 21343 US Hwy 285, 81140; 719-274-5965, FAX 719-274-5032, 800-748-1928; CC, Sa, Sp; 500+; **70+; D, F, PU, 4x4; B3**

La Junta; Adams Wrecking II, 30586 E US Hwy 50, 81050; 719-384-2071, 800-748-2332; CC, Sa, Sp; 1500+; **80-89; D, F; B3**

Roberson Wrecking, *see Vintage*

Lamar; Woller Auto Parts; *see Vintage*

Longmont; A-1 Auto Salvage, 40 Gay St, 80501; 303-772-1520; CC, Sa; 2ac; **70s-90s; D, F, PU, 4x4; B3**

Auto Truck Salvage; *see Vintage*

Pueblo; Bonnie's Car Crushers; *see Vintage*

Morgan Auto Parts; *see Vintage*

West 29th Auto Inc; *see Vintage*

Rifle; Spangler's Auto Salvage; *see Vintage*

Salida; Salida Auto Salvage, 7710 County Rd 150, 81201; 719-539-6816, 800-288-0677; CC, Sa, Sp; 300+; **70-94; D, F, PU, 4x4; B3, Jp, IH**

South Side Salvage; *see Vintage*

Windsor; Martin Supply & Salvage Yard; *see Vintage*

LATE MODEL

Alamosa; L & M Auto; *see Vintage*

Arvada; Arvada Auto Wrecking, 5700 W 56th Av, 80002; 303-423-0248, 800-268-4733; CC, Sa, Sp, UR; 1.5ac, 200; **D, F, PU, 4x4**

Aurora; Action Auto Wrecking; *see Late Vintage*

Aurora Auto Wrecking; *see Vintage*

Boulder; D-C Auto Sales & Parts; *see Late Vintage*

Canon City; Fremont Auto Sales Salvage; *see Vintage*

Indian Springs Auto Salvage; *see Late Vintage*

Capulin; Ernest's Auto Wrecking; *see Vintage*

Colorado Springs; A & A Truck Parts; *see Late Vintage*

A-1 Auto Recyclers; *see Vintage*

ABC Used Auto Parts; *see Vintage*

AJ Salvage, 526 Hugo St, 80903; 719-578-1876; CC, UR; 500+; **F; Japanese only**

Anything Automotive Inc, *see Vintage*

Barnes Truck Parts Inc, 2735 E Las Vegas St, 80906; 719-392-3424; Sa; 200; **Pickup only**

Best Foreign Used Truck Parts; *see Late Vintage*

Bob's Foreign Used Car Parts; *see Late Vintage*

Ken's Foreign Used Parts, 1121 S El Paso St, 80903; 719-632-8225, 800-777-3855; CC, Sa, Sp, UR; 2ac; **F**

One Stop Used Parts; *see Late Vintage*

P & L Scrap Iron & Metals Inc; *see Late Vintage*

Commerce City; Commerce City Auto Salvage, 7481 Kearney St, 80022; 303-287-9716, 888-287-6264; CC, Sa, Sp; 5ac; **PU; Pickup & Van only**

Craig; Ikes Automatic Transmission; *see Vintage*

Dacono; Elliotts Auto Parts; *see Vintage*

Denver; A Du-Well Auto; *see Vintage*

AA Auto Parts Inc; *see Vintage*

ABC Imports; *see Late Vintage*

Adopt-A-Part Co, 5030 York St #C, 80216; 303-296-2211, 800-508-2211; CC, Sa, Sp, UR; 2ac, 500; **F, PU, 4x4; Russian**

All Imports, 300 Kalamath St, 80216; 303-571-1500; CC, Sa, Sp; 3ac, 500; **F, PU, 4x4; vans; Spanish, Arabic**

Badwrench Automotive; *see Late Vintage*

Bennett Auto Salvage, 2927 Larimer St, 80205; 303-294-0453; Sa, UR; 2ac; **D**

Bevsons Import Parts & Svc; *see Vintage*

Bone Yard, 5301 Monroe St, 80216; 303-295-3534; Sa, Sp; 2ac, 100; **D, PU, 4x4**

Boot Hill Auto & Truck Salvage, 5385 Jackson St, 80126; 303-294-0466, 800-762-7042; CC, Sa, Sp; **D, PU, 4x4**

Central Foreign Auto Parts, 3403 Brighton Blvd, 80216; 303-295-2277, FAX 303-296-6202, 800-869-9025; CC, Sa, Sp; 5ac, 400; **F, PU, 4x4**

Crusher Auto & Truck Salvage; *see Late Vintage*

Denver Ford Parts Ltd, 3400 E 52nd Av, 80216; 303-295-2668, FAX 303-295-0018, 800-400-6012, denverford@aol.com; CC, Sa, Sp; 3ac, 250; **D; Ford only**

Denver Used Pickup Parts, 3789 Walnut, 80205; 303-297-2272, FAX 303-297-1654, 800-888-2272, denverusedpickup@msn.com; CC, Sa, Sp; 2ac; **D, PU, 4x4; Pickups only**

EDA Import & Auto Wrecking, 2815 W 8th Av, 80204; 303-446-2552; CC, Sa, UR; 1ac, 80; **F, PU, 4x4; Japanese only**

Foreign Used Auto Parts; *see Late Vintage*

Japa Import Auto Wrecking Inc, 451 S Federal Blvd, 80219; 303-922-4459; Sa; 1ac; **F, PU; mostly Japanese**

Kevin's Import Salvage Inc, 1372 W Maple Av, 80223; 303-733-6306, FAX 303-733-6329; Sa, UR; 2ac, 100+; **F, 4x4; Japanese only**

Lakewood Foreign Auto Salvage, 5575 W 11th Av, 80214; 303-237-6906, FAX 303-237-0636; Sa; 3ac; **F; VW; Mostly Jpa, some Golf & Jetta**

Mile Hi Body Shop Inc; *see Late Vintage*

Mr. Mazda Inc, 5690 Logan St, 80216; 303-297-0100; CC; 1ac; **F; Mazda only, few RX-7**

National Differential, 850 E 73rd Av, 80229; 303-286-0338, 800-893-0338; Sp; 6ac; **PU, 4x4, Trk; PU & Trk only, new & used parts, transfer cases & transmissions**

Rocky Mountain Imports, 4200 Morrison Rd, 80219; 303-936-3421, CC, Sa; 2ac; **F; Japanese & German only**

S K & J Truck Axle Specialist, 3576 E 52nd Av, 80216; 303-292-3137, 800-292-3137; CC, Sa, Sp, Br; 1ac; **D, PU, 4x4, Trk; Jp, IH; a few older trucks**

Sidewinder; *see Vintage*

Stadium Auto & Truck Parts Inc, 2323 W Mulberry Pl, 80204; 303-825-1049, FAX 303-534-8130, 800-825-8733, www.stadiumautoparts.com; CC, Sa, Sp, Wr; 2ac; **D, F, PU, 4x4**

Tams #1 Imports; *see Late Vintage*

Tommy's Auto Repair & Salvage; *see Vintage*

Volvoparts Inc; *see Vintage*

Durango; Lon's Automotive Inc; *see Vintage*

Mac's Foreign Auto Parts; *see Late Vintage*

Eagle; Eagle Salvage & Towing; *see Vintage*

Englewood; ABZ Truck Parts Only; *see Late Vintage*

Accurate Import Parts, 2350 S Raritan St, 80110; 303-934-6041; CC, Sp; 1ac, 100+; **F; VW; mostly German**

Adams Imports & Wrecking, 2060 W Radcliff Av, 80110; 303-761-4995; Sa; 400; **F; German & Japanese only**

Arapahoe Auto Salvage; *see Vintage*

Auto Recyclers, 2200 W Radcliff Av, 80110; 303-761-0552, FAX 303-806-9900, 888-837-5036; CC, Sa, Sp, PL; 11ac, 1000+; **D, F, PU, 4x4, Trk**

Big D Auto Salvage, 2480 S Raritan St, 80110; 303-936-8077, bigdparts@aol.com; CC, Sa; 10ac, 450; **D, PU, 4x4**

Colorado Auto & Parts; *see Late Vintage*

D & L Auto Parts; *see Late Vintage*

Eur-Asian Foreign Auto Parts; *see Late Vintage*

Fair Auto & Truck Wrecking, *see Vintage*

Truckford Parts; *see Vintage*

Universal Auto Wrecking, 1741 W Harvard Av, 80110; 303-936-5865, FAX 303-936-2455

Erie; All American Pickup & SUV Parts, *see Late Vintage*

Blake's Small Car Salvage; *see Late Vintage*

Jeeps Unlimited, *see Vintage*

Ft. Collins; Aragon Iron & Metal Inc, 516 N US Hwy 287, 80524; 970-484-2577, FAX 970-484-9759, 800-424-2577; CC, Sp; 13ac; **D, F, PU, 4x4, Trk; mostly Japanese, few BMW**

Scotts Auto Recyclers Inc, 2140 La Porte Av, 80521; 970-498-0662; CC, Sp; 150; **F; Honda, Acura**

Willox Wrecking Yard; *see Vintage*

Ft. Lupton; M B Auto Salvage & Sales, *see Vintage*

Glenwood Springs; Junk Yard Ranch; *see Late Vintage*

Grand Junction; American Auto Salvage; *see Vintage*

Greeley; Ninth Av Auto Wrecking, 500 N 9th Av, 80631; 970-353-4127; CC, Sp; 12ac; **D, F, PU, 4x4**

Riverside Truck & Auto; *see Vintage*

Hudson; Active Truck Sales & Parts Inc; *see Vintage*

La Jara; De Herrera Towing & Repair Svc; *see Late Vintage*

La Junta; Roberson Wrecking; *see Vintage*

Lakewood; Metro Import Salvage, 1405 Quail St, 80215; 303-232-1446, FAX 303-232-2476; Sa, Sp; 3ac, 425; **D, F, PU, 4x4**

Lamar; Woller Auto Parts; *see Vintage*

Longmont; Bradley Auto Salvage, 7 S Sunset St, 80501; 303-776-5465, FAX 303-772-2911, 800-345-7290 US, 800-523-1058 in CO; CC, Sa, Sp, UR; **5ac; D, F, PU, 4x4; Pickup, Van, SUV only**

Pueblo; Bonnie's Car Crushers; *see Vintage*

Rifle; Spangler's Auto Salvage; *see Vintage*

Salida; South Side Salvage; *see Vintage*

Westminster; Honda Stuff, 7110 Lowell Blvd, 80030; 303-426-1144, FAX 303-426-1109, 888-383-1565; CC, Sa, Sp, Wr; 75; **F, Honda only**

Westminster Foreign Auto, 7071 Lowell Blvd, 80030; 303-428-0495, FAX 303-428-5224, 800-930-8733; CC, Sp; 5ac, 900; **F, PU, 4x4; Asian only**

Jeeps Unlimited
Erie, CO

85

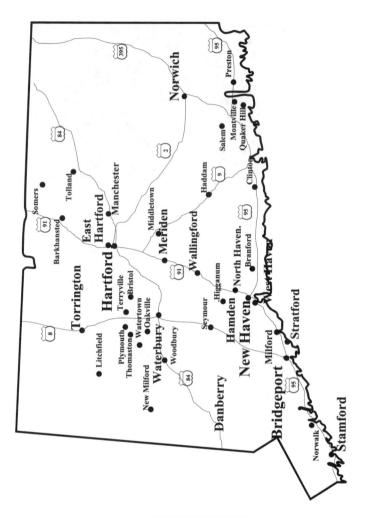

CONNECTICUT

Bridgeport; Connecticut Mustangs, 14 River St, 06604; 203-384-05025, FAX 203-384-0524; CC, Sa, Sp; 200; **64+; D; Fd; Spc: Mustangs**

East Coast Auto Parts, 14 River St, 06604; 203-335-5407, FAX 203-384-0524; CC, Sa, Sp; 100+; **60s; D; Fd; Spc: Mustangs**

Kochis Auto Wrecking, 125 Island Brook Ave, 06606; 203-335-0795, FAX 203-384-0524; CC, Sa, Sp; 1.5ac, 250+; **64+; D; Fd; Spc: Mustangs**

Clinton; Nichols Used Truck Parts, 46 Meadow Rd, 06413; 860-669-2808, 800-962-0008; CC; 150; **60-80s; D, F, PU, 4x4, Trk; B3, IH**

Haddam; Michael's Auto Salvage, 539 Plains Rd, 06438; 860-345-4574, FAX 860-345-7417, 800-622-0050; CC, Sp; 1000; **60+; D, F, PU, 4x4; B3**

Hamden; Mostly Mustangs, 55 Alling St, 06517; 203-562-8804, FAX 203-562-4891; Sa, Sp, Wr; **40+; 60+; D; Fd; Spc: Mustangs; other classic Ford parts; Restoration work**

North Haven; Chuck & Eddie Used Auto Parts, 349 Sackett Point Rd, 06473; 203-281-3951, 800-423-8353; CC, Sa, Sp; 30ac; 2500+; 60+; **D, F, PU, 4x4; B3**

Plymouth; Mt Tobe Auto Parts, Mount Tobe Rd, 06782; 203-753-0332; CC, Sa, Sp; 1500+; **20-80s; D, F; B3, Hd, Ns, St, Pk, Vw, VW; ONLY OPEN SA. Call first-Leave Message**

Preston; Kleemann's Auto Parts, 49 Long Society Rd, 06365; 860-889-0680; Sa, Sp; 1400+; **60+; D, F, PU; Limited 60s & 70s**

Salem; Leo Winakor & Sons, 470 Forsyth Rd, 06415; 860-859-0471; Sa, Sp, Br; 1500+; **20-80s; B3; Open Sat & Sun only, Closed Winter, Call first**

Terryville; Terryville Auto Parts, 33 Fall Mountain Rd, 06786; 860-589-0942, FAX 860-584-4601; CC, Sa, Sp; 500+; **60-80s; D; Chr; Spc: Chrysler only**

Thomaston; Johnny's Auto Parts, 695 Fenn Rd, 06787; 860-283-5470; Sa, Sp, UR; 500+; **60+; D, F, PU, 4x4, Trk; B3; State Dump Trk, 60s Dart & Valient**

Wallingford; Chick's Used Auto Parts, 403 N Cherry St Ext, 06492; 203-269-5836; CC, Sa, Sp; **30-70s; D; B3; Edsel; Has tried to keep all he could since '35**

Watertown; Peter B Cura & Sons, 1460 Echo Lake Rd, 06795; 860-274-2566; Sa, Sp; 400; **60+ D, F, PU; B3, 60s Buicks**

LATE VINTAGE

Barkhansted; Stewart's Used Auto Parts; *see Vintage*

Bridgeport; A-1 Auto Wrecking, 440 Central Ave, 06607; 203-333-1470; Sa; 40; **80+; D, F, PU; B3; limited parts sales**

Bens Auto Slvg, 453 Asylum St, 06610; 203-576-0364; Sa, Sp; 100+; **80+, few 70s; D; B3**

Connecticut Mustangs; *see Vintage*

D & T Auto Salvage, 1 Island Brook Ave, 06606; 203-336-1100; Sa; 50; **79+; D, F; B3**

Kochis Auto Wrecking; *see Vintage*

Clinton; Nichols Used Truck Parts; *see Vintage*

East Hartford; A & B Auto Salvage, 54 Wrobel Pl, 06108; 860-528-2124, FAX 860-528-8859, 800-346-6318; CC, Sa, Sp; **70+; D, F, PU; B3**

Haddam; Michael's Auto Salvage; *see Vintage*

Hamden; Mostly Mustangs; *see Vintage*

Hartford; De Milo & Co, 26 Liebert Rd, 06120; 860-525-8915; Sa; 1.25ac; **70-88; D, F, PU; B3**

Higganum; East Coast Auto Salvage, 733 Killingworth Rd, 06441; 860-345-4591, FAX 860-345-9191, 800-231-9121; CC, Sa, Sp; 6ac; **70+; D, F, PU, 4x4; B3; A few older than 70**

Milford; Milford Auto Recycling, 70 S Washington Ave, 06460; 203-878-0645, FAX 203-878-0000, www.jetracing.com/milfordauto; Sa, Sp; 200; **70-92; D, F, PU, 4x4; B3**

New Haven; A & A Used Auto Parts, 190 Middletown Ave, 06513; 203-562-7195, FAX 203-752-9791 Sa; 900; **80+; D, F, PU, 4x4; B3; S-10 Blazer, Corvettes**

Chet's Auto Parts, 87 Welton St, 06511; 203-787-2532, 800-848-3347; CC, Sa, Sp; 500+; **70+; D, F, PU, 4x4, Trk; B3**

Elm City Auto Wrecking, 46 Middletown Ave, 06513; 203-865-4995, FAX 203-867-4082; Sa; 1ac; 400+; **80+ D, F, PU, 4x4, Trk; B3**

Petrillos Auto Parts, 150 Middletown Ave, 06513; 203-865-1749, FAX 203-624-7473, 800-648-6457; Sa, Sp; 15ac; **70+; D, F, PU, 4x4, Trk; B3**

New Milford; New Milford Auto Wrecking, 407 Kent Rd, 06776; 860-354-8083, Sa; 300+; 83+; **D, F, PU, 4x4, Trk; B3**
North Haven; Camerota Truck Parts, 166 Universal Dr, 06473; 203-782-0360, FAX 203-787-9440, 800-446-3056; CC, Sp; **70+; D, F, PU, 4x4, Trk, Mil; Jp, IH; Spc: PU & Trk; B3**
  Chuck & Eddie Used Auto Parts; *see Vintage*
Norwalk; Lajoie Auto & Scrap Recycling, 40 Meadow St, 06854; 203-866-6650, FAX 203-866-6154, 800-448-1399; CC, Sa, Sp; 500+; **60+, mostly 90s; D, F, PU; B3; trying to keep 60s & 70s**
Norwich; Boyd's Used Auto Parts, 133 Corning Rd, 06360; 860-887-3153, 800-573-3153; CC, Sa, Sp; 3000+; 80+ **D, F, PU, 4x4, Trk; B3**
Plymouth; Mt Tobe Auto Parts; *see Vintage*
Quaker Hill; Dean's Auto Recycling, 42 Bloomingdale Rd, 06375; 860-443-4219, 800-853-3267; Sa; 300; 80+; **D, F, PU, 4x4; B3**
Salem; Leo Winakor & Sons; *see Vintage*
  Marvin's Used Auto Parts, 532 New London Rd, 06415; 860-537-2701, FAX 860-537-3672; 40+; **80s; D; B3**
  Sid's Used Auto Parts & Sales, 243 Forsyth Rd, 06420; 860-859-0000, 800-962-0712; CC, Sa, Sp; 1200; 80+; **D, F, PU, 4x4; B3**
Somers; Leveilles Auto Recycling, 96 Egypt Rd, 06071; 860-749-3705; CC, Sa, Br; 15ac; **80+; D, F, PU, 4x4, Trk; B3**
Stamford; County Auto Wrecking & Sales, 124 Magee Ave, 06902; 203-325-1305; Sa; **80s; D, F, PU; B3; Few F & PU**
Stratford; Bob's Auto Removal, 1870 Barnum Ave, 06497; 203-377-4795; CC, Sa, Sp; **70-80s; D; Fd; Mustangs only**
  Kramer's Used Auto Parts, 11 Old South Ave, 06497; 203-378-7400, FAX 203-381-1332, 800-828-7579; CC, Sa, Sp, Br; 1.5ac; 80+; **D, F, PU, 4x4, Trk; B3**
Terryville; Terryville Auto Parts; *see Vintage*
Thomaston; Johnny's Auto Parts; *see Vintage*
Tolland; Bill's Auto Parts Tolland, 844 Tolland Stage Rd, 06084; 860-875-6231, FAX 860-875-6171, 800-552-4557; CC, Sa, Sp; 800+; **82-92; D, F, PU; B3**
Wallingford; Chick's Used Auto Parts; *see Vintage*
  Underpass Used Auto Parts, 1125 S Broad St, 06492; 203-235-7283, FAX 203-949-9016; Sa; 300; 80+; **D, F, PU, 4x4; B3; Few 60s & 70s**
  Wallingford Used Prts Recyc, 1120 S Broad St, 06492; 203-284-8562; Sa; **80s; D, F, PU; B3**
Waterbury; Conn Used Parts & Auto Wrecking, 36 Brewery St, 06708; 203-575-9642, FAX 203-575-0303, 800-458-0437; CC, Sp; 400; **80s+; D, F, PU; B3**
  DeCapua Auto Slvg, 77 Denver Pl, 06708; 203-754-3811; Sa; 200; 80+; **D, F, PU, 4x4; B3**
  Reidville Used Auto Parts, 260 Mulloy Rd, 06705; 203-754-8100; Sa; 2ac; **70+; D, F; B3; Few 60s & 90s**
Watertown; Peter B Cura & Sons; *see Vintage*
West Haven; Classic Used Auto Parts, 9 spring St, 06516; 203-933-7277, 800-782-4965; CC, Sa, Sp; 200; 80+; **D, F, PU; B3**
Woodbury; Woodbury Auto Salvage, 970 Park Rd, 06798; 203-263-5927; Sa, Sp; 100; 80+ **D, F, PU; B3**
LATE MODEL
Barkhansted; Stewart's Used Auto Parts, *see Vintage*
Branford; S & R Auto Wrecking, *see Vintage*
Bridgeport; A-1 Auto Wrecking, *see Late Vintage*
  Bens Auto Salvage, *see Late Vintage*
  Connecticut Mustangs, see *Vintage*
  D & T Auto Salvage, *see Late Vintage*
  Kochis Auto Wrecking , *see Vintage*
Bristol; Ross Auto Parts, 470 Terryville Rd, 06010; 860-589-6660; Sa; 100+; **D, F, PU; Few PU & Trk**

Tom's Used Auto Parts, 578 Terryville Rd, 06010; 860-582-7056, 800-255-6656; CC, Sa, Sp; 600; **D**

Danbury; Dells Auto Wrecking ,Plumtrees Rd, 06810; 203-743-6779

East Hartford; A & B Auto Salvage, *see Late Vintage*

Haddam; Michael's Auto Salvage, *see Vintage*

Hamden; Mostly Mustangs, *see Vintage*

Higganum; East Coast Auto Salvage, *see Late Vintage*

Litchfield; Ding's Auto Sales & Salvage, 99 Little Pitch Rd, 06759; 860-567-5539; Sa, Sp; 3000; **D, F, PU, 4x4**

Manchester; Parker Street Used Auto Parts, 775 Parker St, 06040; 860-649-3391, FAX 860-647-8880, 800-247-6761; CC, Sp; 300; **D, F**

Meriden; North End Auto Parts, 963 N Colony Rd, 06450; 203-237-2619, 800-274-1302; Sa; 300+; **D, F**

Middletown; Bills Auto Parts, 1462 Saybrook Rd, 06457; 860-347-4484, FAX 860-347-6236, 800-331-3170; CC, Br; 2500+; **D, F, PU, Trk**

Milford; Milford Auto Recycling, *see Late Vintage*

Montville; Yale & Three Mad Men Auto, 06353; 860-848-9245, FAX 860-848-2383, 800-243-0874; CC, Sa, Sp; 1000+; **D, F, PU, 4x4, Trk**

New Haven; A & A Used Auto Parts, *see Late Vintage*

   Atlas Auto Recycling, 159 Middletown Ave, 06513; 203-624-7985; CC, Sa, Sp; 40+; **D, F, PU, Trk; Spc: Pickup**

   Chet's Auto Parts, *see Late Vintage*

   Elm City Auto Wrecking, *see Late Vintage*

   Petrillos Auto Parts, *see Late Vintage*

New Milford; New Milford Auto Wrecking, *see Late Vintage*

North Haven; Camerota Truck Parts, *see Late Vintage*

   Chuck & Eddie Used Auto Parts, *see Vintage*

Norwalk; Lajoie Auto & Scrap Recycling, *see Late Vintage*

   Le Blanc's Auto Parts, 34 Meadow St, 06854; 203-866-9248; FAX 203-866-7940. 800-882-6354; CC, Sa, Sp, PL; 300+; **D, F, PU**

Norwich; Boyd's Used Auto Parts, *see Late Vintage*

Oakville; Fuscos Inc, Ledge Rd, 06779; 860-274-6338, 800-562-9639; CC, Sa, Sp; 1500+; **D, F, PU**

Preston; Kleemann's Auto Parts, *see Vintage*

Quaker Hill; Dean's Auto Recycling, *see Late Vintage*

Salem; Sid's Used Auto Parts & Sales, *see Late Vintage*

Seymour; Larry's Auto Parts, 130 Silvermine Rd, 06483; 203-888-2533; **D, F**

Somers; Leveilles Auto Recycling, *see Late Vintage*

Stratford; East Coast Towing Svc, 25 Taff Ave, 06902; 203-358-8311, FAX 203-969-1938; CC, Sp, UR; 50+; **D, F**

   Kramer's Used Auto Parts, *see Late Vintage*

Terryville; Webster's Used Auto Parts, 488 Main St, 06786, 860-589-3010, 800-692-1231; CC, Sa, Sp; 2000; **D, F, PU, 4x4**

Thomaston; Bill's Used Auto Parts, 422 Railroad St, 06787; 860-283-0760, 800-560-0760; CC, Sp; 300; **D, F, PU, 4x4**

   Johnny's Auto Parts, *see Vintage*

Torrington; Rick's Auto Parts, 16 Riccordone Ave, 06790; 860-489-4173, FAX 860-496-8576, 800-404-4197; CC, Sa, Sp, Br; 100+; **D, F, PU**

   Town Line Used Wrecking, 1165 S Main St, 06790; 860-482-6978

Wallingford; Underpass Used Auto Parts, *see Late Vintage*

Waterbury; Conn Used Parts & Auto Wrckn , *see Late Vintage*

   Peter B Cura & Sons, *see Vintage*

   Reidville Used Auto Parts, *see Late Vintage*

West Haven; Classic Used Auto Parts, *see Late Vintage*

Woodbury ;Woodbury Auto Salvage, *see Late Vintage*

DELAWARE

VINTAGE

Greenwood; Greenwood Auto Salvage, RD2 Box 14A, 19950; 302-349-9121, FAX 302-349-9806, 800-349-9121; CC, Sa, Sp; 1000; **65+; D, F, PU; B3; Spc: mid 60's Ford**

Laurel; Mitchell's Auto & Truck Salvage, 64 Whitesville Rd, 19956; 302-875-7129; Sa, Br; 2000; **60+; D, F, PU; B3**

Milford; Lindale's Used Autos & Parts, 3494 Williamsville Rd, 19954; 302-422-5613; Sa, Sp, UR; 500; **50+; D, F, PU, 4x4, Trk; B3; 50's Pickup**

LATE VINTAGE

Dover; White Oak Salvage, White Oak Rd, 19901; 302-674-1785; CC, Sa, Br; 8ac; **68-89; D, F, PU, 4x4; B3**

Ellendale; J H Auto Salvage, Route 16, 19941; 302-422-3199; Sa, UR; 300; **80's; D, F; B3**

Greenwood; Greenwood Auto Salvage, *see Vintage*

Laurel; Mitchell's Auto & Truck Salvage, *see Vintage*

Milford; Lindale's Used Autos & Parts, *see Vintage*

New Castle; Breitenbach Towing & Auto Salvage, 409 Old Airport Rd, 19720; 302-328-0980; Sa; 4ac; **67-89; D, PU; B3; Camaro, Firebird, Nova; mostly GM**

Necastro Auto Salvage, 495 Old Airport Dr, 19720; 302-322-1616; Sa; 1500; **78+; D, F, PU, 4x4, Trk; B3, AMC, Jp, IH**

Wilmington; A M Domino Jr Salvage Co, 810 S Walnut St, 19801; 302-654-3284; CC; 6+ac; **78-85; D; B3**

LATE MODEL

Greenwood; Greenwood Auto Salvage, *see Vintage*

Laurel; Mitchell's Auto & Truck Salvage, *see Vintage*

Milford; Lindale's Used Autos & Parts, *see Vintage*

New Castle; Delaware Auto Salvage, 445 Old Airport Rd, 19720; 302-322-2328, FAX 302-322-2813, 800-452-2328; CC, Sa, Sp, UR; 400+; **D, F**

Experienced Auto Parts, 461 Old Airport Rd, 19720; 302-322-3344, FAX 302-322-3345, 800-326-9093; CC, Sp; 200+; **D, F; Spc: Suburban, Chrysler, Probe**

Necastro Auto Salvage, *see Late Vintage*

Wilmington; Shuster's Auto Salvage, 520 S Market St, 19801; 302-652-3431; 6+ac; **D, F; B3**

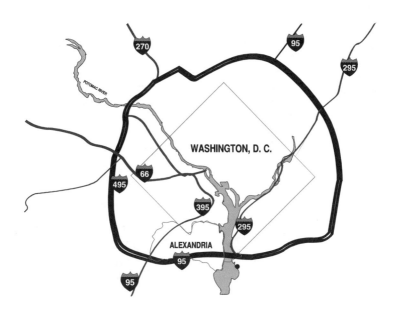

DISTRICT OF COLUMBIA

LATE VINTAGE
Washington; A Northwest Auto Body & Auto Parts, 1325 Naylor Ct NW, 20001; 202-234-7393; CC, Sa; **80s; D, F; B3**
LATE MODEL
Washington; A & R Auto Parts Inc, 1824 Bladensburg Rd NE, 20002; 202-526-4447, FAX 202-526-7312, 800-838-8333; CC, Sa, Sp; 500; **D, F, PU**
  Discount Used Auto Parts, 2607 Reed St NE, 20018; 202-529-7000, FAX 202-529-5954; CC, Sa, Sp; 150+; **D, F, PU, 4x4; mostly Foreign**

You may be a car nut if

Your garage is bigger than your house

Please mention you saw'em in Ray's wReckingyard Roster when contacting these yards

Florida

Please use the cards in the back to let
us know about yards we may have
missed, or any other comments or
information for future editions of
Ray's wReckingyard Roster

FLORIDA

VINTAGE

Apopka; A-1 Auto Salvage, 2324 Vulcan Rd, 32703; 407-299-4060, FAX 407-299-0307, 800-486-4061; CC, Sa; 38ac; **62+; D, F, PU, 4x4; B**3**, Jp**

Big Mikes Auto Salvage, 2450 Vulcan Rd, 32703; 407-291-9300; CC, Sa, Sp; 7.5ac; **50+; D, F, PU, 4x4; B**3

End of the Road Auto Recycling, 3024 Apopka Blvd, 32702; 407-290-1833, FAX 407-297-4124, 888-221-8645; CC, Sa, Sp, UR; 200+; **60-89; D, F, PU; B**3**, VW; Spc: Riviera**

Avon Park; Mac's Auto Salvage, 105 N Hart Av, 33825; 941-452-2268, 800-330-2268; CC, Sa, Sp; 1000+; **42+; D, F; B**3**, Hd**

Bunnell; A-1 Auto Parts & Salvage, US Hwy 1, 32110; 904-437-3438; Sa, PL; 100; **30-89; D, F, PU, 4x4, Trk, Fm, In, Cn; B**3**, AMC, Jp**

Johns Auto Parts, US Hwy 1 S, 32110; 904-437-2163, 800-833-4358; Sa, Sp, Br; 5000+; **30+; D, F, PU, 4x4; B**3

Clearwater; Big 3 Truck Salvage, 3595 118th Av N, 33762; 727-572-6300, FAX 727-572-7615, 800-735-9940, big3truck@gte.net; CC, Sa, Sp; 20ac; **50+; D, F, PU, 4x4, Trk, vans; B**3**; truck & van only**

Doc & Bill's Auto Salvage, 1711 N Betty Ln, 33755; 727-442-7853; Sa, Sp; 300+; **60-89; D, PU, 4x4; B**3**; vans, muscle cars: GTO, Firebird, Camaro**

Cocoa; Quarno's Auto Salvage, 550 Quarno Rd, 32927; 321-632-7541, FAX 321-631-3766*2, 800-952-1561; CC, Sp; 2500; **50+; D, F, PU, 4x4; B**3**, AMC, Jp, IH, VW**

Crawfordville; Economy Used Auto Parts, 572 Woodville Hwy, 32327; 850-421-2277, FAX 850-421-2084, 800-435-8040, jnkman@earthlink.net; CC, Sa, Sp, UR, Wr; 10ac; 500+; **48+; D, F, PU, 4x4, Trk; B**3**, AMC, Jp, VW**

Crescent City; Triple D's Auto Salvage, Co Rd 308, 32112; 904-698-4410; CC, Sa; 250+; **60+; D, F, PU; B**3**, AMC**

Dade City; Sunshine Corvettes, 17951 US 301, 33526; 352-567-4458, FAX 352-567-4460, 877-325-8388; CC, Sa, Sp; 350+; **53+; D; Corvette only**

Ft Lauderdale; All Auto Parts Inc, 1157 NW 31st Av, 33311; 954-584-8550; Sa, Sp; 4ac; **50+; D, F, PU, 4x4; B**3

Ft Myers; Burkett's Auto Parts & Salvage, 10361 Orange River Blvd, 33905; 941-694-0161, FAX 941-694-8251, 800-282-4896; CC, Sa, Sp, UR, PL; 20ac; **50+; D, F, PU, 4x4 Trk; B**3**, Jp, IH, VW; Spc: GM**

Hollywood; Pre 73 Pontiac Sales, 5641 Dawson St, 33023; 954-966-0591, FAX 954-966-0311, 800-598-8870; Sa, Sp; 20; **64-73 D; GTO, Tempest, LeMans, Bonneville**

Homosassa; A & J Auto Salvage, 1612 S Suncoast Blvd, 34448; 352-795-5865, www. btropical.com; CC, Sa, UR; **50+; 50-88; D, F; MG, Triumph, Mercedes, Datsun Z-cars**

Hudson; Hudson Salvage, 17039 Ridgeline Trl, 34667; 727-869-5919; Sa, UR; 300+; **50-95; D, F, PU, 4x4; B**3**, AMC, Jp**

Immohalee; Alley Auto Parts, Rt 2 Box 551, 33934; 941-657-3541, 800-282-7728; Sa, Sp, Br; 300; **80s, few 60s & 70s; D, PU, 4x4, Trk; B**3

Jacksonville; Main Street Auto Parts, 14355 N Main St, 32218; 904-757-0811, FAX 904-757-9742, 888-757-0811; CC, Sa, Sp; 3-4000; **50+; D, F, PU, 4x4; B**3

Lady Lake; Lady Lake Auto Salvage, 552 S US Hwy 441, 32159; 352-753-3011, FAX 352-753-9825, 800-537-6191; CC, Sa, Sp; 10ac+; **85+, few 65-84; D, F, PU, 4x4; B**3

Lake City; Lake City Auto Recyclers, Hwy 47 S, 32025; 904-758-9577; Sp; **30-67; D; Chevy sub-frames only; builds street rods; body shop**

Sunrise Auto Sales & Slvg, Rt 3 Box 6, 32055; 904-755-1810, FAX 904-755-1855, www. sunriseauto.qpg.com; CC, Sa, Sp, Br, Wr; 10ac; 750; **30-76; D, PU; B**3**, AMC, Hd, St, Pk**

Lake Wales; Nations Auto Salvage, 4600 Lake Buffum Rd, 33853; 941-537-1219, FAX 941-537-1299; Sa, Sp; 1400; **50-90; D, F, PU, 4x4; B**3**, AMC, Jp**

MacClenny; Deerfield Auto Salvage, 32063; 904-259-6917; Sa; 150+; **50s-80s; D, PU, 4x4; B**3**, Jp; Pickup & vans only; open Sunday, out in the woods**

Mims; Mims East Coast Auto Salvage, 2555 Hammock Rd, 32754; 407-267-1170, FAX 407-267-1407, 800-432-2869; Sa, Sp, Br; 1500; **65+; D, F, PU; B**3**, AMC; Spc: Camaro & Chevelle**

Ocala; Gator Hook Salvage, 7100 NW 44th Av, 34482; 352-351-4830; Sa; 150; **65-80; D; B3**

West 326 Auto Salvage, 5801 W Hwy 326, 34475; 352-622-7763; Sa, Sp; 300; **60+; D, F, PU; B3**

Okeechobee; Action Auto Salvage, 2266 NW 42nd Av, 34972; 941-763-2141, FAX 941-763-5995; CC, Sa, Sp; 800; **62+; D, F, PU, 4x4, Fm; B3, AMC, Jp, School Buses; Spc:** 4x4

Old Town; Old Gold Cars & Parts, HC04 Box 630, 32680; 352-542-8085, FAX 352-542-8978, 800-736-0262, www.oldgoldcars.com, oldgold@inetw.net; CC, Sp; 5000; **46-79; D, PU; B3, AMC**

Orlando; Airport Salvage, 7245 Narcoossee Rd, 32822; 407-275-8821; Sa, UR; 15ac, 1000+; **60+; D, F; B3**

Oxford; Brooks Truck Salvage, 10865 N US Hwy 310, 34484; 352-748-2681, www. rpmworld.com/Brooks; Sa, UR; 1000; **30+; D, F, PU, 4x4, Trk; B3, AMC, Jp, IH, VW**

Palm City; Florida Mustang, 5727 SW Moore St, 34990; 561-288-4068, FAX 561-288-4068*51; CC, Sa, Sp, Wr; **64-73; D; Fd Mustang only; used & new parts**

Panama City; Budget Auto Salvage, 2306 Transmitter Rd, 32405; 850-785-5590; Sa, Sp, UR; 10ac, 800; **60+; D, F, PU, 4x4, Trk, Fm, In; B3, AMC, IH, VW**

Max's Auto Parts, 1139 N Tyndall Pkwy, 32405; 850-747-9060, FAX 850-763-4878, 888-763-7613, www.mypartsshop.com; CC, Sp; 500; **60+; D, F, PU, 4x4; B3, Jp, VW, Jpa, Chevy Pickup**

Pensacola; Baker's Auto Salvage, 824 W Michigan Av, 32505; 850-435-7377; Sa, Sp, Br; 500; **57+; D, F, PU; B3, AMC, Jp, VW, vans, motor homes, RV, buses**

Pompano Beach; Dixie Auto Parts, 1621 S Dixie Hwy, 33060; 954-783-1933; CC, Sa, Sp, UR; 6ac, 1500; **60+; D, F, PU, 4x4; B3**

Reddick; Buie's Auto Salvage, 17800 NW 100th Av, 32686; 352-591-1988; Sa, Sp, UR; 200; **30-95; D, F, PU, 4x4; B3, AMC, VW**

Rockledge; Lucky's Auto Salvage, 7050 Korbin Av, 32955; 407-636-5555; Sa, UR; 2ac, 300; **60-89; D, F, PU; B3, Chevelle, Trans Am, Camaro, muscle cars**

Sarasota; Collector's Choice Automo Auto, Box 7605, 34278; 941-923-4514, choiceparts @home.com; CC, Sp; 100ac; **40s-80s; D, PU; B3, Ns, St, Pk; a few back to 20's, MAIL ORDER ONLY**

St Cloud; Hixon Trucks & Salvage, 3874 Hixon Av, 34772; 407-892-4494, FAX 407-892-8133, 800-511-1831; Sa, Sp, Br; 15ac, 250+; **61+; D, F, PU, 4x4, Trk; B3, Jp, IH; import/export license**

Starke; Ward Auto Salvage, N Hwy 501, 32091; 904-964-7345; Sp; UR; 10ac; **80-91, 80+, few 60-70s; D, F, PU, 4x4; B3**

Summerfield; Highway 42 Salvage, 5686 SE Hwy 42, 34491; 352-347-5588; Sa, Sp, Br; 200; **60+; D, F, PU, 4x4, Trk, Cn; B3, AMC; Spc: Ford**

Tallahassee; Seminole Pick-N-Pull, 3900 Woodville Hwy, 32311; 850-878-6773; Sa, UR; 1000; **60-90; D, F, PU, 4x4, Trk; B3, AMC, Jp, IH, VW**

Tarpon Springs; D & D Salvage, 784 Anclote Rd, 34689; 727-934-8387; Sa, Sp, UR, PL; 300+; **60-89; D, F, PU, 4x4; B3; Open Sunday**

Umatilla; Umatilla Auto Salvage, 19714 Saltsdale Rd, 32784; 352-669-6363; Sa, Sp, Br; 1000+; **50-89; D, F, PU, 4x4; B3, AMC, St**

Vero Beach; Cars, 4845 45th St, 32967; 561-562-0778; Sa; 7ac, 2000; **60-93; D, F, PU; B3, VW**

Wildwood; B & S Salvage, 3637 S Hwy 301, 34785; 352-748-1150, 800-474-1150; Sa, Sp, PL; 10ac, 2500; **64+; D, F, PU, 4x4, Trk; B3, AMC, Jp, VW; also mobile homes, trailers**

Zephyrhills; Deal Auto Salvage, 39850 Co Rd 54, 33540; 813-782-4805; Sa, UR; 800+; **60-89; D, F, PU; B3, AMC**

LATE VINTAGE

Apopka; A-1 Auto Salvage, *see Vintage*

AAAA Trucks & Vans Salvage, 2773 Apopka Blvd, 32703; 407-297-0226; CC, Sa, UR; 200+; **67+; D, F, PU, 4x4; B3 PU & Vans only**

Big Mikes Auto Salvage, *see Vintage*

Cheap Dave's Auto Salvage, 3070 Apopka Blvd, 32703; 407-293-1313, FAX 407-290-1844; CC, Sa, Sp; 300+; **84-95; D, F, PU, 4x4; B3, AMC, Jp, VW, Jpa, Peugeot**

End of the Road Auto Recycling, *see Vintage*

Orlando Auto Recyclers, 3116 Overland Rd, 32703; 407-290-3440, FAX 407-290-3477, 800-229-3116; CC, Sa, Sp, UR; 1100; **85-95; F; Jpa**

Auburndale; Auburndale Auto Salvage, 501 W Bridgers Av, 33823; 941-965-0083; **D, F, PU, 4x4**

Avon Park; Mac's Auto Salvage, *see Vintage*

Baker; C & J Auto Salvage, 5655 Buck Ward Rd, 32531; 850-537-9501, 800-990-8890; CC, Sa, Sp, UR, PL; **70+; D, F, PU, 4x4, Trk; B3, AMC, Jp, IH, VW, Jaguar, Mercedes, BMW, Audi**

Belleview; 484 Auto Salvage, 13174 SE 39th Ct, 34420; 352-347-8500; Sa, Sp, UR; 200; **70+; D, F, PU, 4x4; B3, AMC**

Belleview Auto Salvage, 8635 SE Co Hwy 25, 34420; 352-245-7373; Sa; 1200; **80-89; D, F, PU, 4x4; B3, AMC, VW**

Big Pine Key; B & B Used Auto Parts, 75 Industrial Rd, 33043; 305-745-3517 or 872-9761, FAX 305-872-5781; CC, Sa, Sp, Br; 1200+; **70-90; D, F, PU; B3, AMC, VW**

Boca Raton; Programma Tools, 301 W Camino Gardens Blvd, 33432; 561-750-4511, FAX 561-338-8447, 800-668-8843; CC, Sp; **80+; F; Eur, BMW, Porsche, Mercedes, Volvo, Saab; Spc: Remanufactured electronic control units**

Bradenton; West Coast Slvg, 1855 63rd Av E, 34203; 941-758-8080; CC; 300; **70-90; D; B3**

Bunnell; A-1 Auto Parts & Salvage, *see Vintage*

Johns Auto Parts, *see Vintage*

Chiefland; Art's Auto Salvage, 2008 SW 4th Pl, 32626; 352-493-7969; UR; **70-89; D, F, PU; B3**

Clearwater; Affordable Auto Salvage, 3999 118th Av N, 33762; 727-573-2133; CC, Sa, Sp, PL; 600+; **70+; D, F, PU, 4x4; B3**

Big 3 Truck Salvage, *see Vintage*

Doc & Bill's Auto Salvage, *see Vintage*

Cocoa; Quarno's Auto Salvage, *see Vintage*

Crawfordville; Economy Used Auto Parts, *see Vintage*

Crescent City; Triple D's Auto Salvage, *see Vintage*

Crestview; Gulf Coast Salvage, 3138 E Chestnut Ave, 32536; 850-682-5877, FAX 850-682-7328; CC, Sa; 5ac; **70-89; D, F, PU, few 4x4, few Trk; B3**

Dade City; Sunshine Corvettes, *see Vintage*

Davie; M & L Auto Wrck & Truck, 4126 SW 47th Av, 33314; 954-792-1935, FAX 954-792-3880, 800-716-5575; Sa, Sp, UR, PL; 2500; **80+; D, F, PU; B3, AMC, VW; open Sun**

De Land; De Land Auto Salvage, 210 N Ridgewood Av, 32720; 904-734-3335, www.delandautosalvage/apg.com; CC, Sa, Sp; 900; **68+; D, F, PU, 4x4; B3, Jp, IH, VW; Spc: Pickup**

Delray Beach; Tri-County Auto Salvage, 101 NW 18 Av, 33444; 561-276-7558, 800-535-0249; Sa, Sp; 800+; **80+; D, F, PU, 4x4; B3**

Frostproof; Frostproof Auto Recycling, 560 N Scenic Hwy, 33843; 941-635-3818; Sa, Sp, UR; 200; **D, F, PU, 4x4, Trk; B3, Jp;**

Ft Lauderdale; All Auto Parts Inc, *see Vintage*

Bailey's Camaros & Firebirds, 745 NW 7th Av, 33311; 954-463-7770; CC, Sa, Wr; 100; **67-92; D; Camaro, Firebird, Z-28, TransAm**

Jeff's Eldorados, 2337 NW 30th Ct, 33311; 954-733-4216; Sa, Sp, Wr; **71-78; D; Cadillac Eldorado only; many parts compatible with other GM models**

Ft Myers; Burkett's Auto Parts & Salvage, *see Vintage*

Ft Pierce; Auto Busters, 4190 Selvitz Rd, 34981; 561-466-5122, FAX 561-466-5884, 800-330-2886; CC, Sa, Sp, Br; 6ac, 400; **80+; D, F, PU, 4x4; B3, Jp**

Ft Walton Beach; Wright Auto Salvage, 911 Dee St, 32548; 850-864-1581; Sa, UR; 200; **80s; D, F; B3**

Gibsonton; Ralph's Auto Salvage, 8516 Nundy Av, 33534; 813-677-7254; UR; 200; **70-89; D, F, PU, 4x4, Trk; B3, AMC**

Gulf Breeze; A & A Auto Salvage, 6124 Gulf Breeze Prky, 32561; 850-934-1647; Sa, Sp; 400; **80-89; D, F, PU; B3, AMC, VW**

Hollywood; Pre 73 Pontiac Sales, *see Vintage*

Homosassa; A & J Auto Salvage, *see Vintage*

  Dale's Auto Parts & Salvage, 6643 W Linden Dr, 34446; 352-628-4144, FAX 352-628-5866, 800-584-5639; Sa, Sp; 900+; **70-85; D, F, PU, 4x4; B3, Jp, IH**

Hudson; Hudson Salvage, *see Vintage*

  Pasco Auto Salvage, 9910 Houston Av, 34667; 727-868-9583, FAX 727-863-3945, 800-548-4418; CC, Sa, Sp, UR; 1000+; **80+; D, F, PU, 4x4; B3**

Immokalee; Alley Auto Parts, *see Vintage*

  Robert's Auto Salvage & Rpr, 106 Dixie Av E, 34142; 941-657-5220; Sa, Sp; 300; **77+; D, F, PU, 4x4; B3; open Sunday**

Jacksonville; Main Street Auto Parts, *see Vintage*

  Moose Junk Yard, 10440 Sandler Rd, 32222; 904-771-1517; Sa; 1000; **70-90; D, F, PU, 4x4; B3, AMC, Jp, VW**

Jasper; Macs Auto Repair, Rt 2 Box 242-B, 32052; 904-792-1485; CC, Sa, UR; 200; **67+; D, F, PU, 4x4; B3**

Kissimmee; Campbell City Auto Salvage, 4691 S Orange Blossom Trl, 34746; 407-847-0083, 800-771-0083; CC, Sa, Sp, UR; 1500; **75+; D, F, PU, 4x4; B3, AMC, Jp, IH, VW**

Lady Lake; Lady Lake Auto Salvage, *see Vintage*

Lake City; Halls Salvage City, E Hwy 100A, 32055; 904-755-0666; Sa; 200; **80s-90s, few earlier; D, F, PU, 4x4; B3**

  Sunrise Auto Sales & Salvage, *see Vintage*

Lake Wales; Nations Auto Salvage, *see Vintage*

Lakeland; All County Auto Salvage, 4145 US Hwy 92 E, 33801; 941-665-7278, FAX 941-667-0813; CC, Sa, UR; 300; **68+; D, F, PU, 4x4; B3, AMC, Jp, IH, VW; open Sunday**

  Mid Way Salvage & Used Auto, 4410 Maine Hwy 542, 33801; 941-665-9031; Sa; 100; **70s; D, PU, 4x4; B3, AMC**

Loxahatchee; J & B Towing, 3940 B Rd, 33470; 561-640-0709; Sa, Sp; **68+; D, PU, 4x4, Trk; B3 mostly towing & locksmith, limited parts sales**

MacClenny; Deerfield Auto Salvage, *see Vintage*

Marathon; Southern Salvage, 1255 107th St Gulf, 33050; 305-289-0100; Sa; .5ac; **70-89; D, F, PU; B3**

Melbourne; Auto Salvage Unlimited, 7629 Coral Dr, 32904; 407-768-2286; Sa, Sp, UR; 120; **60s-90s; D, F, PU, 4x4; B3**

Merritt Island; A-1 Auto, 475 W Merritt Island Cswy, 35952; 407-453-2277 ans serv, or 453-0400; Sa, Sp; 2ac; **80s; D, F, PU; B3**

  A-1 Island Auto Salvage, 1800 Worley Av, 32952; 321-453-0400; Sa, Sp, Br; 200; **80s; D, F, PU; B3, AMC**

Miami; Bobs U Pick Auto Parts, 9800 NW South River Dr, 33166; 305-884-8574, FAX 305-884-0584; Sa, UR; 1000; **79-85; D, F, PU; B3, AMC**

  Perrine Auto Salvage, 9800 SW 168th Ter, 33157; 305-235-7651, FAX 305-235-0848; Sa, Sp; 150; **80+; D, F; B3**

Milton; Slim's Auto Salvage, 5837 Myrtle Rd, 32572; 850-626-6730; Sa, Sp, Br; 100+; **70-85; D, F, PU, 4x4; B3; Spc: Pickup**

Mims; Mims East Coast Auto Salvage, *see Vintage*

New Smyrna Beach; Airport Auto Salvage, 1295 Kennard St, 32168; 904-428-5000, FAX 904-426-0895, 800-548-9118; Sa, Sp; 900; **80+; D, F, PU; B3**

Ocala; Beavers Auto Svc & Salvage, 4803 NW 61st Ln, 34482; 352-369-1990; Sa, UR; 100+; **70-89; D, F, PU; B3**

  Belleview U-Pull-It, 4395 SE 95th St, 34480; 352-307-1071; Sa, UR; 300; **78-90; D, PU; B3**

  Gator Hook Salvage, *see Vintage*

  Markel Automotive Dismantlers, 7405 Crill Av, 32177; 904-325-6464, 800-232-7454; Sa, Sp; 400; **77-89; D, F; B3**

  West 326 Auto Salvage, *see Vintage*

Okeechobee; Action Auto Salvage, *see Vintage*

Old Town; Old Gold Cars & Parts, *see Vintage*

Ona; Triangle Auto Salvage, 4320 Stevens & Carlton, 33865; 941-735-1700; Sa, Sp, UR; 600; **70-89; D, F, PU; B3; open Sunday**

Opa Locka; Ferny's Auto Salvage, 12770 Cairo Ln, 33054; 305-681-9073; CC, Sa; 700; **80+; D, F; B3**

Toyota Kings, 13105 Cairo Ln, 33054; 305-688-6200, FAX 305-688-5014, 877-688-6200; CC, Sa, UR; 400; **70+; F, PU, 4x4; Toyota only**

Orlando; Airport Salvage, *see Vintage*

Disney Auto Dismantlers, 104 Seminole Trl, 32833; 407-568-0118; Sa, Wr; 400; **80+; D, F, PU, 4x4; B3**

Osteen; Newton & Sons Salvage, 145 Buckskin Ln, 32764; 407-322-5990; UR; 200+; **70-89; D, F, PU; B3**

Oxford; Brooks Truck Salvage, *see Vintage*

Palm City; Florida Mustang, *see Vintage*

Palmetto; B & F Auto Parts Inc, 5112 US Hwy 41 N, 34221; 941-722-6279, 800-288-3177; CC, Sa, Sp, Br; 900; **78+; D, F, PU, 4x4; B3, AMC, Jp, VW**

Panama City; Budget Auto Salvage, *see Vintage*

Max's Auto Parts, *see Vintage*

Van Horn's Auto Salvage, 2137 Sherman Av, 32401; 850-763-4000; CC; **70-93; D, F; B3**

Pensacola; Al-T's Auto Salvage, 7065 Mobile Hwy, 32526; 850-944-5006, FAX 850-944-1288; CC, Sa; 600; **78-91; D, F, PU; B3, AMC, VW**

B & C Auto Salvage, 3906 W Navy Blvd, 32507; 850-457-4141; Sa, Sp; 300+; **70+; D, F, PU, 4x4, Trk; B3, AMC**

Baker's Auto Salvage, *see Vintage*

D & J Auto Wrecking, 2975 E Johnson Av, 32514; 850-476-4758, 800-315-4758, dturner@ksinc.net; CC, Sa, Sp; 400+; **64+; D, F, PU; B3**

Expert Auto Parts & Salvage, 6845 Pine Forest Rd, 32526; 850-944-8802, FAX 850-944-0895, 888-735-1713, jsmith@ksinc.net; Sa, UR, PL; 300+; **80+, few 70s; D, F, PU, 4x4; B3, Mercedes**

Pompano Beach; Dixie Auto Parts, *see Vintage*

Sams Recycling & Junk Cars, 1610 N Powerline Rd, 33069; 954-972-1111, FAX 954-972-2824; Sa, Sp, UR; 5ac, 300; **70-89; D, F; B3, AMC; open Sunday**

Reddick; Buie's Auto Salvage, *see Vintage*

Chuck's Used Parts, 18455 NW US Hwy 441, 32681; 352-591-5020, FAX 352-591-3260; Sa, Sp; 20+; **75+; D, F, Trk; Isuzu, Volvo, Peterbuilt, Ford, Kenworth; Truck only**

Rockledge; Lucky's Auto Salvage, *see Vintage*

Sanford; M & M Auto Parts & Salvage, 3301 W 1st St, 32771; 407-322-0303, FAX 407-327-7598; Sa, UR; 7ac; **70-92; D, F, PU, 4x4; B3, VW**

Marc's Import Auto Salvage, 1661 Sipes Av, 32771; 407-322-8961; Sa, Sp; 342; **78-91; F; Mazda RX7, Datsun Z cars**

Sarasota; Collector's Choice Antique Auto, *see Vintage*

Sorrento; Sorrento Salvage, 31703 Church St, 32776; 352-735-1234; Sa, UR; 100+; **68-92; D, F; B3**

St Augustine; Florida Auto & Salvage, 1875 State Rd 207, 32086; 904-824-3144; CC; 50; **70+; D, F, PU, 4x4; B3**

St Cloud; Hixon Trucks & Salvage, *see Vintage*

St Cloud Auto Salvage, 5285 E Irlo Bronson Meml Hwy, 34769; 407-892-3569; CC, Sa, Sp, Br; 1000+; **68+; D, F, PU; B3, AMC, Jp, VW**

St Petersburg; ABC Auto Salvage & Recycling, 2221 5th Av S, 33712; 727-327-8893; CC, Sa, Sp, PL; 150; **68+; D, F; B3**

Lester's Auto Salvage, 2550 30th Av N, 33713; 727-321-6601, FAX 727-327-6321, 800-365-6601; CC, Sa, Sp; 900; **80+; D, F, PU; B3**

Starke; Thornton Salvage, N Hwy 301, 32091; 904-964-6243; UR, Wr; 15+; **70+; D, F, PU; B3**

Ward Auto Salvage, *see Vintage*

Summerfield; Highway 42 Salvage, *see Vintage*

97

Tallahassee; Seminole Pick-N-Pull, *see Vintage*

Tarpon Springs; D & D Salvage, *see Vintage*

Titusville; All Auto Salvage, 4755 Cheney Hwy, 32780; 407-269-5800; CC, Sa, Sp; 12ac; **75-90; D, F, PU, 4x4, Trk; B3**

Umatilla; Bronco Don's A-1 Auto Wrecking, 19646 Saltsdale Rd, 32787; 352-669-2344; CC, Sp, Br; 80+ **D, F, PU; B3**

    Umatilla Auto Salvage, *see Vintage*

Vernon; Parrish Auto Salvage, 2776 River Rd, 32762; 850-535-2000; Sa; 500; **75-85; D, F, PU; B3**

Vero Beach; AAA Auto Slvg, 4506 45th St, 32967; 561-567-6000; Sa; 200; **70-90; D, F; B3**

    Cars, *see Vintage*

West Palm Beach; P & L Salvage, 4537 45th St, 33407; 561-689-4144, FAX 561-689-0638; CC, Sa; 2ac, 400; **80s; D, F, PU, 4x4, Trk; B3**

Wildwood; B & S Salvage, *see Vintage*

Winter Haven; Bolin's Auto Salvage, 205 Bomber Rd, 33880; 941-293-4470, FAX 941-293-1942; Sa, UR; 900; **73-89; D, F, PU, 4x4; Thursday-Saturday only**

Youngstown; Jakes Auto Salvage, 3906 E Hwy 388, 32466; 850-722-4825; **70-89; D, F**

Zephyrhills; Deal Auto Salvage, *see Vintage*

Zolfo Springs; Reeds Auto Salvage Inc, 730 7th Av, 33890; 941-735-0838, FAX 941-735-2715, 800-768-1833; CC, Sa, Sp; 500; **80+; D, PU, 4x4, Trk; B3**

LATE MODEL

Apopka; A-1 Auto Salvage, *see Vintage*

    AAAA Trucks & Vans Salvage, *see Late Vintage*

    Big Mikes Auto Salvage, *see Vintage*

    Cheap Dave's Auto Salvage, *see Late Vintage*

    Papi's Auto Recycling, 2662 Overland Rd #A, 32703; 407-521-1988; CC; 500; **F, PU; Spanish**

Avon Park; Mac's Auto Salvage, *see Vintage*

Baker; C & J Auto Salvage, *see Late Vintage*

Belleview; 484 Auto Salvage, *see Late Vintage*

Boca Raton; Programma Tools, *see Late Vintage*

Bonifay; Landress Auto Wrecking, Hwy 90 W, 32425; 850-547-3671, 800-888-3671; CC, Sp; **D, F, PU**

Boynton Beach; Astro Auto Salvage, 12608 S Military Tr, 33436; 561-499-5600, 800-499-5666; CC, Sa Sp; 7ac; **D, F, PU, 4x4; B3**

Bradenton; Royal Auto Recycling, 2000 63rd Av E, 34203; 941-758-1833, FAX 941-739-1862, 800-839-6151; CC, Sp, Br; 10ac; **D, F, PU, 4x4; B3**

Brooksville; J's Used Auto Salvage, 1490 Ponce De Leon Blvd, 34601; 352-796-9890, 800-237-6559; CC, Sa, Sp; 500; **D, F, PU, 4x4; B3**

Bunnell; Johns Auto Parts, *see Vintage*

Cantonment; Neese Auto Salvage, 3332 Hwy 29 N, 32533; 850-587-2138, 888-500-2354; CC, Sp, UR; 300; **D, PU; B3**

Clearwater; Affordable Auto Salvage, *see Late Vintage*

    Big 3 Truck Salvage, *see Vintage*

Cocoa; Quarno's Auto Salvage, *see Vintage*

Crawfordville; Economy Used Auto Parts, *see Vintage*

Crescent City; Triple D's Auto Salvage, *see Vintage*

Dade City; Sunshine Corvettes, *see Vintage*

Davie; M & L Auto Wrecking & Truck, *see Late Vintage*

Daytona Beach; Franks Auto Parts, 1339 Center Av, 32117; 904-253-6625; CC, Sa, Sp, Br; 400; **D, F, PU, 4x4; B3**

Daytona Beach; Mike Moore's Auto Salvage, 330 14th St, 32117; 904-677-3500, 800-676-3356; CC, Sa, Sp, Br; 0.5ac; **D, F, PU; Jpa**

De Land; De Land Auto Salvage, *see Late Vintage*

Delray Beach; Tri-County Auto Salvage, *see Late Vintage*

Ft Lauderdale; All Auto Parts Inc, *see Vintage*

All Auto Recycling Inc, 840 NW 7th Ter, 33311; 954-767-0847, FAX 954-761-3301; Sa, Sp; 300; **D, F, PU, 4x4, Trk; Spc: Honda, Toyota, Nissan**

Davie Auto Salvage, 4221 SW 57th Ter, 33314; 954-587-0854, FAX 954-587-2960; Sa, Sp, UR; 2ac, 200; **D, F, PU, 4x4, Trk**

Foreign Parts Ltd Inc, 4 NW 7th St, 33311; 954-763-5677, FAX 954-764-6077, 800-535-1977; CC, Sa, Sp; 10ac, 1000; **F, PU, 4x4; incl foreign exotics**

Ft Myers; Burkett's Auto Parts & Salvage, *see Vintage*

Hialeah; Rastro 10 Court, 5141 E 10th Ct, 33013; 305-688-8919; Sa, Sp; **F; Spanish**

Hudson; Hudson Salvage, *see Vintage*

Pasco Auto Salvage, *see Late Vintage*

Immokalee; Robert's Auto Salvage & Rpr, *see Late Vintage*

Jacksonville; Arlington Slvg, 1754 E 7th St, 32206; 904-353-6709; Sa; 1800+; **D, F, PU; B3**

Main Street Auto Parts, *see Vintage*

Jasper; Macs Auto Repair, *see Late Vintage*

Kissimmee; Campbell City Auto Salvage, *see Late Vintage*

Lady Lake; Lady Lake Auto Salvage, *see Vintage*

Lake City; Columbia Auto Salvage, Rt 12 Box 746, Hwy 252, 32025; 904-752-1611, FAX 904-752-1620, 800-445-4879; CC, Sa, Sp; 800; **D, F, PU, 4x4; B3, Jp**

Halls Salvage City, *see Late Vintage*

Lakeland; All County Auto Salvage, *see Late Vintage*

Salvage City, 3610 Deeson Rd, 33810; 941-859-0606, FAX 941-859-0407, 877-727-8669; CC, Sa, Sp, PL; 2000; **D, F, PU, 4x4; B3**

Loxahatchee; J & B Towing, *see Late Vintage*

Melbourne; Auto Salvage Unlimited, *see Late Vintage*

Classic Auto Salvage, 2259 Avocado Av, 32935; 407-259-3000, FAX 407-259-1406; Sa, UR; 700; **D, F, PU, 4x4; B3**

P & E Automotive, 2821 Electronics Dr, 32935; 407-254-9717; Sa, Sp; 300; **D, F, PU; B3; Spc: Chrysler**

Miami; Perrine Auto Salvage, *see Late Vintage*

Mims; Mims East Coast Auto Salvage, *see Vintage*

New Smyrna Beach; Airport Auto Salvage, *see Late Vintage*

Ocala; West 326 Auto Salvage, *see Vintage*

Okeechobee; Action Auto Salvage, *see Vintage*

Old Town; Davis Auto Salvage, HC 3 Box 542, 32680; 352-498-7000, FAX 352-498-0102, 800-226-7077; CC, Sa, Sp, PL, 40ac; **D, F, PU, 4x4; B3**

Opa Locka; Ferny's Auto Salvage, *see Late Vintage*

Toyota Kings, *see Late Vintage*

Orlando; Action Auto Salvage & Parts, 11215 S Orange Av, 32824; 407-851-0931; CC, Sa, Br; 300; **D, F, PU, Trk; B3; 25 years in business**

Airport Salvage, *see Vintage*

B & T Auto Parts, 5604 Old Winter Garden Rd, 32811; 407-293-2534, 800-548-9116; Sa, Sp; 5.5ac, 800; **D, F, PU, 4x4; B3**

Discount Used Auto Salvage, 332 N Co Rd 13, 32833; 407-568-3633

Disney Auto Dismantlers, *see Late Vintage*

Fosters Auto Crushing, 312 N Ortman Dr, 32805; 407-299-5262; Sa, UR; 3ac, 450; **D, F, PU, 4x4; B3**

Lents Auto Parts, 9205 E Colonial Dr, 32817; 407-273-0600, FAX 407-275-6836, 800-405-7188; Sp; 10+ac, 1000+; **D, F, PU; B3**

Oxford; Brooks Truck Salvage, *see Vintage*

Palm Bay; Diamond Used Auto Parts, 3052 Dixie Hwy NE, 32905; 407-724-1277, FAX 407-724-1278; Sa, Sp; 6ac, 800; **D, F, PU, 4x4; B3**

Palmetto; B & F Auto Parts Inc, *see Late Vintage*

Panama City; Budget Auto Salvage, *see Vintage*

Hawkins Auto Wrecking, 510 E 23rd St, 32405; 850-785-4667, 800-585-7785; Sp, UR; 2000+; **D, F, PU; B3**

Max's Auto Parts, *see Vintage*

Van Horn's Auto Salvage, *see Late Vintage*

Pensacola; B & C Auto Salvage, *see Late Vintage*

Baker's Auto Salvage, *see Vintage*

D & J Auto Wrecking, *see Late Vintage*

Expert Auto Parts & Salvage, *see Late Vintage*

Pompano Beach; Brocks Auto Salvage, 1750 N Powerline Rd, 33069; 954-977-9922, FAX 954-977-6477, 888-870-7080; Sa, Sp; 700+; **D, F, PU, 4x4; B3, Jp, VW**

Dixie Auto Parts, *see Vintage*

Reddick; Buie's Auto Salvage, *see Vintage*

Chuck's Used Parts, *see Late Vintage*

Riverview; American Auto Salvage, 12020 US Hwy 301 S, 33602; 813-677-9164, FAX 813-671-3034, 800-282-5674; CC, Sa, Br; 37ac; **D, F, PU, 4x4; B3**

Rockledge; A & D Auto Salvage, 5105 Korbin Ave, 32955; 407-632-8050; CC, Sa, Sp, UR; · 500; **D, F, PU; B3; Spc: Ford Crown Victoria police package**

St Augustine; Florida Auto & Salvage, *see Late Vintage*

St Cloud; St Cloud Auto Salvage, *see Late Vintage*

St Petersburg; ABC Auto Salvage & Recycling, *see Late Vintage*

Lester's Auto Salvage, *see Late Vintage*

St Cloud; Hixon Trucks & Salvage, *see Vintage*

San Antonio; Dons Towing & Auto Salvage, 11607 Ossie Murphy Rd, 33576; 352-588-3828, FAX 352-588-3847, 877-588-3828; CC, Sa, Sp; 2ac, 200; **D, F; B3**

Sanford; M & M Auto Parts & Salvage, *see Late Vintage*

Sebring; Jim's Auto Salvage, 3900 Cemetery Rd, 33870; 941-385-6196, FAX 941-382-1504, 800-282-4620, jimsauto@strato.net; CC, Sa, Sp; 2000; **D; B3**

Starke; Thornton Salvage, *see Late Vintage*

Summerfield; Highway 42 Salvage, *see Vintage*

Tallahassee; Garry's Auto Salvage, 3900 Woodville Hwy, 32311; 850-878-2877, FAX 850-878-0842, 800-440-2877; CC, Sp, PL; 200; **D, F, PU; B3; 4 locations in FL**

Tampa; Copher Bro Auto Salvage, 5015 S 22n St, 33619; 813-247-3171, 800-282-4283; CC, Sa, Sp; 2000; **D, F; Spc: Ford**

Rex Davis Auto Parts, 8802 N 12th St, 33604; 813-935-4687; Sa, Sp; **D, F; B3**

Titusville; North Brevard Auto Salvage, 2600 S Hopkins Av, 32780; 407-267-1357, FAX 407-383-0001, 800-851-4703; CC, Sp; 2000; **D, F, PU, 4x4; B3**

Umatilla; Bronco Don's A-1 Auto Wrecking, *see Late Vintage*

Venus; Ole South Auto Salvage, 480 US Hwy 27 N, 33852; 941-465-5810, FAX 941-465-3255, 800-393-1134; Sp; 3500+; **D, F, PU, 4x4, Trk; B3**

Vero Beach; Cars, *see Vintage*

Indian River Auto Salvage, 4600 45th St, 32967; 561-567-2742; 300; **D, PU, 4x4; Chevy Pickup only**

Three D Auto Salvage, 5075 45th St, 32967; 561-567-6575, FAX 561-567-6583, 800-826-0307 FL only; Sa, Sp; 2ac, 200; **D, F, PU, 4x4; B3**

Wauchula; Carl's Auto Salvage, 2000 Old Airport Rd, 33873; 941-773-4300; Sa, UR; 1000; **D, F, PU, 4x4; B3**

West Palm Beach; Barney's Junkyard, 6840 Haverhill Rd N, 33407; 561-842-6909; Sa, Sp; 3ac; **D, F, PU, 4x4**

Wildwood; B & S Salvage, *see Vintage*

Winter Gardens; Budget Auto Parts, 881 9th St, 34787; 407-656-4707, 888-656-4707; CC, Sa; 600; **D, F, PU, 4x4**

Zephyrhills; Rigsby's Auto Salvage, 40147 Lynbrook Dr, 33540; 813-782-5541, 800-231-2013; CC, Sa, Sp; **D, F, PU, 4x4**

Zolfo Springs; Reeds Auto Salvage Inc, *see Late Vintage*

Blackburn used Farm
and Construction Equipment
Douglas, WY

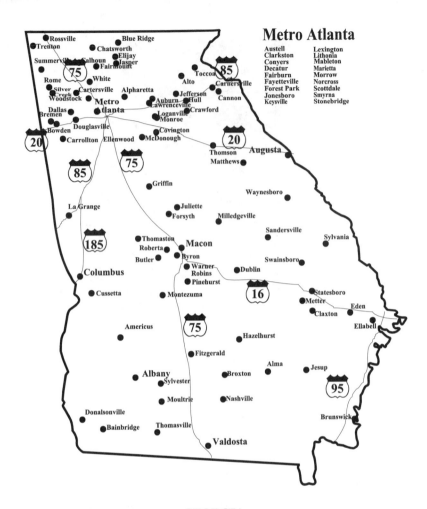

Metro Atlanta

Austell	Lexington
Clarkston	Lithonia
Conyers	Mableton
Decatur	Marietta
Fairburn	Morrow
Fayetteville	Norcross
Forest Park	Scottdale
Jonesboro	Smyrna
Keysville	Stonebridge

GEORGIA

Craven's Auto & Truck Salvage, 2535 Mike Padgett Hwy, 30906; 706-790-6365, 800-626-3645; Sa, Sp; 2000; **60+; D, F; B3**

Austell; R & M Auto Salvage, 101 White Rd, 30036; 770-739-0124, FAX 770-944-0121; Sa, Sp, UR; 400; **50+; D, F, PU, 4x4; Fd, Chevy, Jp**

Blue Ridge; Fannin Salvage & Wrecker Svc, 134 Salvage Ln, 30513; 706-632-2814; Sa; 1000; **60-91; D, F; B3, VW**

Brunswick; Davis Auto Salvage, 355 New Sterling Rd, 31525; 912-264-1605; Sa, Br; 300+; **60-93; D, F, PU, 4x4, Trk; B3, AMC, Jp, IH; few older cars**

Byron; Bob's Auto Salvage, 7611 Houston Rd, 31008; 912-788-4918, 800-222-4918; CC; 2500; **65+; D, F, PU, 4x4; B3, AMC, Jp, VW; major parts only**

Mustang Central, 975 Lakeview Rd, 31008; 912-956-3871, FAX 912-956-5078, www.mustangcentral.com; CC, Sa, Sp, Wr, UR; 300+; **64+; D; Mustang only; builds trans, differentials, race engines, conversions; body**

Calhoun; South Forty-One Auto Salvage, 3212 Hwy 41 South SE, 30701; 706-602-0400; Sa, Sp, PL; 600; **55+; D, F, PU, 4x4, Trk, Fm; B3, AMC, Jp, IH, VW**

Carrollton; Collins Junk Cars, 301 Cross Plains Hulett Rd, 30117; 770-834-2520; Sa, UR; 10ac; **50+; D, F, PU; B3**

Griffin's Used Auto Parts, 2656 Whooping Creek Rd, 30116; 770-854-5222; Sa; 2000+; **60+; D, F, PU, 4x4, Trk; B3, VW**

Cartersville; Brook's Auto Salvage, 833 Hwy 293 SE, 30120; 770-974-6699; Sp, PL; **60+; D, F, PU, 4x4; B3**

Clarkston; Prestige Mustangs, 1092 Vaughan St, 30021; 404-294-4869; CC, Sa, Sp, Wr; 150; **64+; D; Mustang only**

Crawford; Johnson's Auto Salvage, Hwy 78, 30648; 706-743-3329; Sa; **60-89; D, F, PU; B3**

Cussetta; Cusseta Auto Salvage, Hwy 26, 31805; 706-989-3458; Sa, UR; 500; **64-88; D, F, PU; B3; Spc: Ford Pickup, Mustang 74-86**

Decatur; Pro Adjustments Svc, 3864 Redan Rd, 30032; 404-792-9944; Sa; 10ac, 400+; **80+, few 50-70s; D, F, PU, 4x4, Trk; B3; 50s=Ford**

Donalsonville; Bill's Used Auto Parts, Rt 1 Box 101, GA Hwy 91 N, 31745; 912-524-8857; Sa, Sp, UR; 800+; **50-79; D, F, PU; B3, AMC; Spc: Ford; some 80's**

Ellabell; Price's Junkyard, PO Box 360, 31308; 912-858-3142; Sa, Sp, UR; 200; **00-89; D, F, PU, 4x4; B3, AMC, Jp, IH**

Ellenwood; David K Crane Used Auto Parts, 761 Clark Rd, 30294; 770-474-4417; Sa, Sp; 1000; **30+; D, F, PU, 4x4; B3, AMC, Jp, IH; open Sunday**

Fairmount; Townsend Wrecker Svc, 300 Townsend Dr SE, 30139; 706-337-2497; Sa, Br; 1ac, 200; **50+; D, PU; B3**

Fayetteville; Graves Auto Slvg, 205 Eastin Rd, 30214; 770-461-7953; Sa; **60+, few 50s; D, F, PU; B3**

Fitzgerald; W L's Used Auto Parts, 249 Camp Brooklyn Rd, 31750; 912-423-5614, FAX 912-423-4887, 800-559-5614; Sa, Sp; 650+; **60-85; D, F, PU, 4x4; B3, Jp, IH, VW**

Griffin; Bob's Auto Salvage Parts, 112 Patton Rd, 30224; 770-228-4079; Sa, UR; 3ac; **60+; D, F, PU, 4x4; B3**

Johnson Auto Salvage, 1029 Country Line Rd, 30224; 770-227-4244, FAX 770-229-4248, www.autosalvage.org; CC, Sa, Sp, UR; 2000+; **50-90; D, F, PU; B3, AMC, VW**

Hull; Bo Alewine Auto Salvage, 8221 Hwy 29 S, 30646; 706-543-1350, FAX 706-208-1188, 800-545-5302; CC, Sp; 30ac, 1500; **60+; D, F, PU, 4x4; B3**

Jonesboro; Jonesboro Salvage & Recycle, 222 Turner Rd, 30236; 770-477-6663; Sa, Sp; 500; **50+; D, F, PU, 4x4, Trk; B3, Ks**

Juliette; J & W Auto Salvage, 1086 Pea Ridge Rd, 31046; 912-994-0530; CC, Sa, UR; 450+; **60+; D, F, PU; B3; Mostly 80+; Spc: Nissan-Z**

La Grange; Ray's Auto Salvage, 827 Smokey Rd, 30241; 706-882-0459; Sa, Sp; **50-80s; D; B3; mostly GM**

Lawrenceville; Brownlee's Old Time Auto Parts, 281 W Pike St, 30045; 770-963-7315; CC, Sa, Sp; **32-72; D; Ford, Mercury, Chevy only; reproduction parts only**

Loganville; Gary Dean Auto Salvage, 6089 Hwy 20, 30052; 770-466-8644, 800-667-5518; Sa, Sp, PL; 3000+; **50+; D, F, PU, 4x4, Trk; B3**

103

Georgia –Vintage

Marietta; Fiat Lancia World, 1111 Via Bayless, 30066; 770-928-1446, FAX 770-928-1342, 800-241-1446, www.baylessfiat.com; CC, Sp, Wr; **52-89; F; Fiat, Lancia Beta only; CALL IN ADVANCE - no walk-ins**

Marietta Auto Salvage, 317 Freys Gin Rd #B, 30067; 770-423-0198, FAX 770-422-8059, 800-287-3620, www.mypartshop.com; CC, Sp, Br; 1000; 47+; **D, F, PU, 4x4; B3; Mostly 85+; Spc: 47+ Chevy Pickup**

Matthews; B & C Auto Sales & Salvage, 20999 Hwy 1 N, 30818; 706-547-0881, 800-554-0881; Sa, Sp, UR; 500+; **60+; D, F, PU, 4x4; B3, VW**

Milledgeville; Baldwin Auto Salvage, 2925 Irwinton Rd, 31061; 912-452-6491; Br; 2800; **63+; D, F, PU, 4x4, Fm; B3, IH**

Monroe; Hodges Salvage Yard & Wrecker, 1435 Bradley Gin Rd NW, 30656; 770-267-3461; Sa, UR; 15ac; **40-89; D, PU, 4x4, Trk; B3, St**

Montezuma; Martin's Auto Salvage, McKenzie Rd, 31063; 912-472-2632, 800-649-8903; Sa; 300; **40+; D, F, PU, 4x4, Trk, Fm; B3, St, VW**

Nashville; Sky Wrecking, RR 2, 31639; 912-686-2284; Sa, Sp, UR; 2ac; **50+; D, F, PU; B3**

Sandersville; Avant Salvage Co, 219 Waco Dr, 31082; 912-552-1901, FAX 912-552-6179, 800-553-8192, jbavant@worldnet.att.net; CC, Sp; 1000; **60+; D, F, PU, 4x4; B3, Jp, IH, VW; Spc: GM 6.2 & 6.5 diesel engines**

Silver Creek; Advance Used Auto Parts, 364 Pleasant Valley Rd SE, 30173; 706-235-9528, 800-238-6480; Sa, Sp; 3000; **30+; D, PU, 4x4, Boat; B3, Jp**

Smyrna; Embee Parts, Inc., 4000 Lee Rd, 30080; 770-434-5686; Sa, Sp, Br; 600+; **34-88; F; Mercedes**

Statesboro; Edward's Wrecking Yard, 3180 Westside Rd, 30458; 912-865-2295, FAX 912-865-2265, 800-822-3346; CC, Sa, Sp, Br; 450+; **60+; D, F, PU, 4x4; B3**

Sylvania; Buddy's Used Parts & Salvage, 975 Buttermilk Rd, 30467; 912-564-7654; UR; 200+; **40-89; D, F, PU; B3**

Thomaston; S & S Auto Salvage, 2207 Hwy 19 S, 30286; 706-647-4974; Sa, Sp; 300+; **60+; D, F, PU, 4x4; B3**

Thomaston; W & W Used Auto Parts, 1430 Atwater Rd, 30286; 706-648-4318; Sa, Sp, UR; 150; **40+; D, F, PU, 4x4; B3, AMC; Spc: Jaguar, Mercedes, Corvair; open Sunday**

Valdosta; Valdosta Wrecking, 1303 S Patterson St, 31601; 912-242-5166, FAX 912-242-8756, 800-552-7271; CC, Sp; 800; **few 60s & 85+; D, F, PU; B3, VW**

Warner Robins; R & R Auto & Truck Salvage, 101 Booth Rd #A, 31088; 912-922-3289, FAX 912-922-8899, www.autotruckworld.com; CC, Sa, Sp, UR; 600; **80+, few 50-70s; D, F, PU, 4x4; B3**

Waynesboro; Dixon Wrecking Co, 349 Hwy 24, 30830; 706-554-2814; CC, Br; 500+; **60+; D, F, PU, Trk; B3, AMC, VW**

White; Old Car City USA, 3098 Hwy 411 NE, 30184; 770-382-6141, FAX 770-387-2122; Sa, Sp; 4000+; **18-72; D, PU; B3, Hd, Ns, St, Pk, Ks**

LATE VINTAGE

Alma; Larry's Auto Salvage, RR 1 Box 41B, 31510; 912-632-6132; Sa, UR; **70+; D, F, PU, 4x4, Trk; B3**

Americus; Americus Auto Salvage, 889 Hwy 30 W, 31709; 912-924-4024; Sa, UR; 125; **70-89; D, F, PU, 4x4; B3, AMC, Jp**

Atlanta; Benin Used Auto Parts, *see Vintage*

Eagle Auto Parts & Salvage, *see Vintage*

Auburn; Collins Auto Salvage, *see Vintage*

Augusta; Cochise Auto Wrecking & Parts, *see Vintage*

Craven's Auto & Truck Salvage, *see Vintage*

Jones Old Cars & Parts, 2027 Tobacco Rd, 30906; 706-771-9820, aoj7711@aol.com; Sp, PL; 100+; **76+; D, F; B3**

Austell; R & M Auto Salvage, *see Vintage*

Bainbridge; Sammy's Truck Sales & Salvage, 112 Long Rd, 31717; 912-246-5775; Sa, UR; 500+; **D, F, PU, 4x4; B3; Spc: GM PU; Pickup only**

Blue Ridge; Fannin Salvage & Wrecker Svc, *see Vintage*

Bremen; Wood Salvage Auto Parts, 8060 US Hwy 78, 30110; 770-537-1350; CC, Sa, Sp; 400; 65-91; **D, F, PU, 4x4; B3; some hot rods**

Broxton; Kenny's Auto & Truck Slvg, 5898 Douglas Broxton Hwy, 31519; 912-359-2222, FAX 912-359-3940, 877-389-7229; Sa, Sp; 700+; **70+; D, F, PU, 4x4, Trk, Fm; B3, Jp, IH, VW**

Brunswick; A & A Auto Wrecking, 7024 New Jesup Hwy, 31523; 912-265-9181; Sa, Br; 10ac, 100; **86-88; D, F, PU, Trk; B3**

    Davis Auto Salvage, *see Vintage*

Byron; Bob's Auto Salvage, *see Vintage*

    Mustang Central, *see Vintage*

Calhoun; South Forty-One Auto Salvage, *see Vintage*

Canon; Segars Used Cars & Parts, 154 Old Royston Rd, 30520; 706-245-8819; Sa; 30ac; **67+; D, F, PU, 4x4; B3; mostly sells whole cars**

Carnersville; Auto-Cycle Salvage, 19 Goolsby Rd, 30521; 706-384-2000, FAX 706-384-2007, 888-809-3708; Sa, Sp, PL; 1000; **78+; D, F, PU, 4x4; B3**

Carrollton; Collins Junk Cars, *see Vintage*

    Griffin's Used Auto Parts, *see Vintage*

Cartersville; Brook's Auto Salvage, *see Vintage*

Clarkston; Prestige Mustangs, *see Vintage*

Claxton; Claxton Auto Salvage, Hwy 301 N, 30417; 912-739-4917, FAX 912-739-8309, 800-943-5865; Sp; 750+; **80+; D, F, PU, 4x4; B3**

Columbus; Discount Auto Salvage, 3123 Victory Dr, 31906; 706-682-2525; CC, Sa; **80-90; D, F; B3**

Crawford; Johnson's Auto Salvage, *see Vintage*

Cussetta; Cusseta Auto Salvage, *see Vintage*

Decatur; Budget Auto Salvage, 2929 S Rainbow Dr, 30034; 404-243-0793; Sa; 900; **80+; D, F, PU, 4x4; B3**

    Pro Adjustments Svc, *see Vintage*

Donalsonville; Bill's Used Auto Parts, *see Vintage*

Dublin; Ben Maddox Used Parts, 1347 Buckeye Rd, 31027; 912-272-1420, FAX 912-272-0143, 800-342-1951; CC, Sa, Sp, PL; 3500; **80+; D, F, PU, 4x4, Trk, Mil; B3**

Elijay; Cartecay Used Cars & Parts, Hwy 52E, 30540; 706-273-3848; Sa; 150+; **80+; D, F, PU; B3**

Ellabell; Price's Junkyard, *see Vintage*

Ellenwood; David K Crane Used Auto Parts, *see Vintage*

Fairburn; Coleman Auto Salvage, 6737 Roosevelt Hwy, 30213; 770-943-8402, FAX 770-969-7541, 800-317-3582; CC, Sp, Br, PL; 8000; **75+; D, F, PU, 4x4; B3, VW**

Fairmount; Townsend Wrecker Svc, *see Vintage*

Fayetteville; Graves Auto Salvage, *see Vintage*

    Quality U-Pull-It, 205 Roberts Rd, 30214; 770-716-7879; Sa, UR; 500+; **65-91; D, F, PU, vans; B3; open Sunday**

Fitzgerald; W L's Used Auto Parts, *see Vintage*

Forest Park; US Auto Parts & Salvage, 4020 Jonesboro Rd, 30050; 404-366-2441, FAX 404-366-2049; Sa, UR; **80+; D, F, PU; B3; open Sunday**

Forsyth; Peach State Auto Salvage, 129 Town Creek Rd, 31029; 912-994-5345, FAX 912-994-6988, 800-222-4573; CC, Sa, Sp; 700; **75+; D, F, PU, 4x4; B3, Jp, VW**

Griffin; A & B Auto Salvage, 1523 High Falls Rd, 30223; 770-229-9122, FAX 770-412-0986, 800-726-1570; CC, Sa, Sp; 5ac; **70+; D, F, PU, 4x4; B3; Spc: Corvette, Ford Pickup**

    Bob's Auto Salvage Parts, *see Vintage*

    Johnson Auto Salvage, *see Vintage*

Hazelhurst; R & D Auto & Truck Salvage, 565 Baxley Hwy, 31539; 912-379-0388, 888-257-2633; CC, Sp, PL; 400; **70+; D, F, PU; B3**

Hull; Bo Alewine Auto Salvage, *see Vintage*

    Diamond Rock Auto Salvage, 149 Joe Graham Dr, 30646; 706-548-5815; CC, Sa, Sp; 750+; **80+; D, F, PU, 4x4; B3**

105

Palmers Auto Salvage, Hwy 29 N, 30646; 706-549-1377, 800-332-2528; CC, Sp; 33ac; **77+; D, F, PU; B3; part of chain**

Jasper; Jasper Auto Salvage, 1874 E Church St, 30143; 706-692-2113; Sp; **70+; D, F, PU, 4x4; B3, AMC, Jp, VW**

Jefferson; Jones Autoparts & Recycling, 2932 Hwy 124W, 30549; 706-367-8632; Sa, UR; **6000; 70-89; D, F, PU, 4x4, Trk, Fm; B3, AMC, IH, VW, Mercedes, BMW**

Jonesboro; Jonesboro Salvage & Recycle, *see Vintage*

Juliette; J & W Auto Salvage, *see Vintage*

Keysville; Anderson Jones Auto Repair, Hwy 80, 30816; 706-554-3178; Sa, Br; **70-84; D, F, PU, 4x4; B3, Jpa**

La Grange; Capital Auto Salvage, 1207 New Franklin Rd, 30241; 706-884-5340; Sa, Sp; **550+; 70-89; D, F, PU, 4x4; B3**

Ray's Auto Salvage, *see Vintage*

Lawrenceville; Brownlee's Old Time Auto Parts, *see Vintage*

Lithonia; DeKalb Auto Salvage, 7043 Covington Hwy, 30058; 770-981-1200, FAX 770-981-3860, 800-943-9344; CC, Sa, Sp, UR; **600; 70+; D, F, PU, 4x4; B3, VW**

Nicholson's Used Auto Parts, 1969 Rogers Lake Rd, 30058; 770-482-2138; 2ac; **70+; D, F, PU, 4x4; B3**

Southeast Auto Salvage, 7666 Old Covington Hwy, 30058; 770-482-6864, FAX 770-482-4010; Cc, Sa, Sp; **350+; 75+; D, F, PU; B3, Jp; Spc: Toyota**

Loganville; Gary Dean Auto Salvage, *see Vintage*

McDaniel Used Auto Parts, 2278 Piney Grove Rd, 30052; 770-466-4378; Sa, Sp; **70+; D, F, PU, 4x4; B3**

Macon; Bibb Auto Salvage & Recycling, 1849 Emery Hwy, 31217; 912-743-8682; CC, Sa, Sp; **300; 70-89; D, PU; B3**

Doodles Auto Slvg, 31211; 912-745-4868; Sa, Br; **200+; 75+; D, F, PU; B3, VW, Jpa**

Peacock Auto Salvage, Hwy 49, 31211; 912-743-2484, FAX 912-743-6549, 800-743-6930; CC, Sp; **10000+; 80+; D, F, PU, 4x4, Trk; B3, Jp, VW, Jpa**

Marietta; Fiat Lancia World, *see Vintage*

Marietta Foreign Auto Parts, 44 S Fairground St NE, 30060; 770-422-4043, FAX 770-422-4568; CC, Sa, Sp, Wr; **80+; F; VW, Mercedes, BMW, Audi**

Matthews; B & C Auto Sales & Salvage, *see Vintage*

Milledgeville; 49 Auto Salvage & Repair, 357 GA Hwy 49 W, 31061; 912-453-0466; CC, Sa; **700+; 71-89; D, F, PU, 4x4; B3, VW**

Baldwin Auto Salvage, *see Vintage*

Monroe; Hodges Salvage Yard & Wrecker, *see Vintage*

Montezuma; Martin's Auto Salvage, *see Vintage*

Moultrie; A & K Auto Salvage, 1551 Sylvester Hwy, 31768; 912-985-9215; CC, Sa, Br; **600+; 70-85; D, F, PU; B3**

Nashville; Nashville Auto Wrecking, 1285 Ray City Hwy, 31639; 912-686-3421, FAX 912-686-3248, ruger@surfsouth.com; Sa, Sp; **80-89; D, F, PU, 4x4, Trk; B3, AMC**

Sky Wrecking, *see Vintage*

Tyler Wrecking, RR 1, 31639; 912-686-7090; Sa; **650; 75-90; D, F PU; B3**

Norcross; Pull-A-Part, 4416 Buford Hwy, 30071; 770-242-8844; Sa, UR; **2000+; 2 locations, other at 1540 Henrico Rd, Atlanta; open Sunday; Spanish**

Sandersville; Avant Salvage Co, *see Vintage*

Silver Creek; Advance Used Auto Parts, *see Vintage*

Smyrna; Embee Parts, Inc., *see Vintage*

Statesboro; Edward's Wrecking Yard, *see Vintage*

Stonebridge; A-1 Used Auto Parts, 5801 Hwy 42, 30281; 770-474-7721, FAX 770-474-2921, 888-474-7921; CC, Sa, Sp, Br; **1000+; 80+; D, F, PU, 4x4; B3**

Summerville; Gills Auto Salvage, Spring Creek Rd, 30747; 706-857-3467; Sa, Sp, UR; **500+; 70-90; D, F; B3, AMC**

Swainsboro; Spence Wrecking, 526 Fairground Rd, 30401; 912-237-6059, FAX 912-237-6950; Sp, UR; **100+; 75+; D, F, PU, 4x4; B3**

Sylvania; Buddy's Used Parts & Salvage, *see Vintage*

Sylvester; Ivey's Used Auto Parts, 107 Johnny Aultman Rd, 31791; 912-776-3938; Sa, UR; 70-**90; D; B3**

Thomasville; Moultrie Road Auto Salvage, 13142 US Hwy 319 N, 31792; 912-228-0057; 350; 70-**93; D, F, PU; B3**

Thomaston; S & S Auto Salvage, *see Vintage*
   W & W Used Auto Parts, *see Vintage*

Thomson; McTier Used Auto Parts, 1738 Augusta Rd, 30824; 706-595-4344; Sa, Br; 1000; 70-**89; D, PU; B3**

Toccoa; Pritchett Auto Salvage & Sales, 895 Burnette Rd, 30577; 706-779-3283; Sa, Br; 10ac, 500; **73+; D, F, PU, 4x4, Trk; B3, AMC, Jp**

Trenton; McBryar Auto Salvage, 234 Porter Rd, 30752; 706-657-7531, FAX 706-657-8037, 800-352-4837; CC, Sp; 3000; **80+; D, F, PU, 4x4; B3, AMC, Jp; Spc 4x4**

Warner Robins; R & R Auto & Truck Salvage, *see Vintage*

Woodstock; Call's Used Auto Parts, 10140 Main St, 30188; 770-926-6409, FAX 770-926-6400; 300+; 70+; **D, F, PU, 4x4; B3; Spc: Late Model Pickup**
   T C Auto Parts & Glass, 8011 Hwy 92, 30189; 770-926-4646, FAX 770-924-1800; CC, Sa, Br; 16ac, 2000+; **80+; D, F, PU, 4x4, Trk; B3**

Waynesboro; Dixon Wrecking Co, *see Vintage*

White; Old Car City USA, *see Vintage*

LATE MODEL

Albany; Albany Auto Salvage, 1805 Westtown Rd, 31707; 912-431-1018; **D, F**

Alma; Larry's Auto Salvage, *see Late Vintage*

Alpharetta; Grimes Auto Salvage, 6730 Hwy 9 N, 31510; 770-475-3777; Sa, Sp, UR; 200; **D, F, PU, 4x4; B3, Mercedes**
   Hyundai Heaven Used Parts, 1320 Union Hill Rd, 30004; 770-475-5181, FAX 770-569-8292, 800-762-8464; CC, Sa, Sp; 100; **F; Hyundai only**

Alto; 365 Auto Salvage, 482 Crane Mill Rd, 30501; 706-778-1919, FAX 706-778-8007, 800-243-0365; CC, Sp; 900; **D, F, PU, 4x4; B3**

Atlanta; Benin Used Auto Parts, *see Vintage*
   Best & Reliable Used Auto Parts, 2559 Jonesboro Rd SE, 30315; 404-622-5600, FAX 404-622-1179, 877-238-5600; Sa, Sp; 1200; **D, F; B3, Spc: Mercedes BMW**
   C & L Used Auto Parts, 570 Glenn St SW, 30312; 404-755-3595, FAX 404-755-5003, 800-453-7640, www.atlantaautonet.com/c/used; CC, Sa, Sp, Wr; 1200; **D, F, PU, 4x4; B3**
   Eagle Auto Parts & Salvage, *see Vintage*
   Gray & White Used Auto Parts, 1184 Capitol Av SE, 30301; 404-525-7727, FAX 404-525-7996, 888-374-PART, www.atlantaautonet.com/gawauto.html; CC, Sa, Sp, UR; 4ac; **D, F, PU, 4x4; B3**

Augusta; Craven's Auto & Truck Salvage, *see Vintage*
   Fenders Auto Wrck, 2218 Martin L King Jr Blvd, 30904; 706-733-0564, FAX 706-737-6336, 800-533-3633; CC, Sa, Sp, Br; 13ac, 2500+; **D, F, PU, 4x4, Trk; Spc: Pickup**
   Gibbs Auto Wrecking Co, 329 Sandbar Ferry Rd, 30901; 706-722-6848, 800-831-4354; CC, Sa, Sp, Br; 35ac, 3000; **D, PU; B3**
   Jones Old Cars & Parts, *see Late Vintage*

Austell; R & M Auto Salvage, *see Vintage*
   Richards Auto Salvage, 4792 Old Westside Rd, 30106; 770-948-1555, FAX 770-948-4166, 800-826-2414; CC, Sp; 1300+; **D, F, PU, 4x4; B3**

Bainbridge; Dollars Used Cars & Salvage, 172 Green Shade Rd, 31717; 912-246-5875; Sa; 3ac; **D, F, PU, 4x4; B3**
   Sammy's Truck Sales & Salvage, *see Late Vintage*

Bowdon; V & W Motors & Used Auto Parts, 1519 S Hwy 100, 30108; 770-258-2597; Sa, Sp; 550+; **D; B3**

Bremen; Greg's Used Cars & Parts, 40 Windy Lake Rd, 30110; 770-537-9903; **F**

Broxton; Kenny's Auto & Truck Salvage, *see Late Vintage*

Butler; Tab's Auto Salvage, Hwy 19 N, 31006; 912-862-3002; Sp; 200; **D, PU; B3**

Byron; Bob's Auto Salvage, *see Vintage*
   Mustang Central, *see Vintage*

Calhoun; South Forty-One Auto Salvage, *see Vintage*

Canon; Segars Used Cars & Parts, *see Late Vintage*

Carnersville; Auto-Cycle Salvage, *see Late Vintage*

Carrollton; Collins Junk Cars, *see Vintage*
   Griffin's Used Auto Parts, *see Vintage*

Cartersville; Brook's Auto Salvage, *see Vintage*

Chatsworth; Mountain View Motors & Salvage, 1819 Brown Bridge Rd, 30705; 706-695-2022; Sa; **PU, 4x4, vans**

Clarkston; Prestige Mustangs, *see Vintage*

Claxton; Claxton Auto Salvage, *see Late Vintage*

Conyers; Mitchell's Used Auto Parts Inc, 2701 Flat Shoals Rd SE, 30013; 770-483-4716, FAX 404-292-1035, 800-682-9257; Sa, Sp; 1000+; **D, F, PU, 4x4; B3; main yard in Scottdale**

Covington; Newton Auto Salvage, 635 Rocky Plains Rd, 30016; 770-787-1431, FAX 770-787-1562, 800-552-2659; CC, Sp, PL; 400; **D, F; B3**

Dallas; Auto Parts Recycled, 3434 Atlanta Hwy, 30132; 770-445-6053, 800-444-1756; CC, Sa, Sp; 2000; **F**

Decatur; Pro Adjustments Svc, *see Vintage*

Douglasville; Austin Used Truck Parts, 2545 Cochran Industrial Blvd, 30134; 770-942-5245; CC, Sa; **D, PU, 4x4, Trk; Spc: Ford**

Dublin; Ben Maddox Used Parts, *see Late Vintage*

Eden; East of Eden Auto Salvage, 1652 Hwy 80, 31306; 912-748-9777; Sa, Sp, UR; 2000; **D, F, PU; B3**

Elijay; Cartecay Used Cars & Parts, *see Late Vintage*
   Gilmer Used Parts & Wrecker, 2143 S Main St, 30540; 706-635-5105; CC, Sa; 600; **D, F, PU, 4x4, Trk; B3**
   Southside Salvage & Sales, 2197 S. Main, 30540; 706-276-1917, FAX 706-276-1918; Sa; 10+; **D, F, PU, 4x4; B3**

Ellenwood; David K Crane Used Auto Parts, *see Vintage*

Fairburn; Coleman Auto Salvage, *see Late Vintage*

Fairmount; Townsend Wrecker Svc, *see Vintage*

Fayetteville; Graves Auto Salvage, *see Vintage*

Forest Park; US Auto Parts & Salvage, *see Late Vintage*

Forsyth; Peach State Auto Salvage, *see Late Vintage*

Griffin; A & B Auto Salvage, *see Late Vintage*
   Bob's Auto Salvage Parts, *see Vintage*
   Palmers Auto Salvage-Griffin, 2343 N Expressway, 30223; 770-227-5313, FAX 770-227-5388, 800-583-5105; CC, Sp; 300; **D, F, PU; B3; part of chain**

Hazelhurst; R & D Auto & Truck Salvage, *see Late Vintage*

Hull; Bo Alewine Auto Salvage, *see Vintage*
   Diamond Rock Auto Salvage, *see Late Vintage*
   Palmers Auto Salvage, *see Late Vintage*

Jasper; Jasper Auto Salvage, *see Late Vintage*

Jesup; Dixie Auto Salvage, 2291 Savannah Hwy, 31545; 912-427-7788; Sa, Sp; 3000+; **D, F, PU, 4x4; B3**

Juliette; J & W Auto Salvage, *see Vintage*

Lawrenceville; Garnett Lance Used Auto Parts, 375 Maltbie St, 30243; 770-963-0555; Cc, Sa, Sp; 3000; **D, F, PU, 4x4; B3**

Lexington; Bud Alewine Auto Salvage, Hwy 78 E, 30648; 706-743-5444, FAX 706-743-3637, 800-242-6047; CC, Sa, Sp; 3000; **D, F, PU; B3, Jp**

Lithonia; DeKalb Auto Salvage, *see Late Vintage*
   L Three R Used Auto Parts, 1906 Rogers Lake Rd, 30058; 770-482-8753, 800-601-8753; CC, Sa, Sp, PL; **D, F, PU, Trk; B3**
   Nicholson's Used Auto Parts, *see Late Vintage*
   Southeast Auto Salvage, *see Late Vintage*

Loganville; Gary Dean Auto Salvage, *see Vintage*

108

McDaniel Used Auto Parts, *see Late Vintage*

Mableton; Action Used Auto Parts, 700 Bankhead Hwy SW, 30126; 770-739-7815; CC, Sa, Sp; 300; **D, F, PU, 4x4; B3**

Macon; Doodles Auto Salvage, *see Late Vintage*

Peacock Auto Salvage, *see Late Vintage*

McDonough; McDonough Used Auto Parts, 942 Hwy 42 N, 30253; 770-957-9808, FAX 770-898-4800, 888-426-4840; CC, Sa, Sp; 60ac; **D, F, PU, 4x4; B3, VW**

Marietta; Marietta Auto Salvage, *see Vintage*

Marietta Foreign Auto Parts, *see Late Vintage*

Matthews; B & C Auto Sales & Salvage, *see Vintage*

Metter; B & W Salvage, Rt 3 Box 431, Hwy 46, 30439; 912-685-2250, 800-284-6626; Sa, Sp, Br; 600; **D, F, PU, 4x4; B3**

Milledgeville; Baldwin Auto Salvage, *see Vintage*

Milledgeville Auto Salvage, 117 Fox Hill Cir SW, 31061; 912-452-2635, 888-497-9385 GA only; Sa, Sp; 1000+; **D, F, PU; B3**

Monroe; Palmer's Auto Salvage, 682 Hwy 78 NW, 30655; 770-267-5965, FAX 770-267-0456, 800-942-7278, pas@atl.com.net; CC, Sp, Br; 6ac; **D, F, PU, 4x4; B3**

Montezuma; Martin's Auto Salvage, *see Vintage*

Walters' Auto Recycling, Hwy 26 E, 31063; 912-472-6458, FAX 912-472-9850

Morrow; Southern Auto Salvage, 1751 Forest Pkwy, 30260; 404-362-0671, FAX 404-362-9445, 888-285-0799; CC, Sp, Br; 500+; **D, F, PU, 4x4; B3**

Nashville; Sky Wrecking, *see Vintage*

Pinehurst; Dupree Auto-Truck Slvg, State Hwy 41 N, 31070; 912-645-3600; 20; **D, PU; B3**

Roberta; Childres Auto Salvage, Rt 1 Hwy 128, 31078; 912-836-4744; Sa; 300+; **D, F, PU, 4x4; B3**

Rome; J & J Used Auto Parts, 1282 Turkey Mtn Rd NE, 30165; 706-232-0459; **D, F, PU**

Rossville; Allstate Auto Salvage, 1029 Wilson Rd, 30741; 706-861-9363; Sp; 2000; **D, F; B3**

Cargon Used Auto Parts, 1000 Wilson Rd, 37415; 706-861-5338, 800-895-5338; CC, Sp; 1000; **D, F, PU, 4x4; B3**

Sandersville; Avant Salvage Co, *see Vintage*

Scottdale; Mitchell's Used Auto Parts, 632 Woodland Av, 30079; 404-292-1161, FAX 404-292-1035; CC, Sp; **D, F, PU, 4x4, Trk; B3**

Silver Creek; Advance Used Auto Parts, *see Vintage*

Statesboro; Edward's Wrecking Yard, *see Vintage*

Whitaker Motors Used Auto Parts, 9013 US Hwy 301 S, 30458; 912-681-2428, 800-356-6470; CC, Sp; 1500+; **D, F, PU, 4x4; B3**

Stonebridge; A-1 Used Auto Parts, *see Late Vintage*

Rockdale Auto Slvg, 3465 Hwy 138 SW, 30281; 770-922-6166; Sa, Sp, UR; 400; **D, F**

Swainsboro; Spence Wrecking, *see Late Vintage*

Thomaston; S & S Auto Salvage, *see Vintage*

Stallings Used Auto Parts, 1072 N Church St, 30286; 706-648-6798, 800-682-1550; Sa, Sp; 450+; **D, F, PU, 4x4; B3, AMC, Jp; Spc: Corvette, Mustang**

Thomaston; W & W Used Auto Parts, *see Vintage*

Thomasville; Moultrie Road Auto Salvage, *see Late Vintage*

Toccoa; Pritchett Auto Salvage & Sales, *see Late Vintage*

Trenton; McBryar Auto Salvage, *see Late Vintage*

Valdosta; Valdosta Wrecking, *see Vintage*

Warner Robins; Central Georgia Auto Salvage, 11128 Hwy 247 N, 31093; 912-328-2960, 800-328-2960; CC, Sp; 1000; **D, F**

R & R Auto & Truck Salvage, *see Vintage*

Waynesboro; Dixon Wrecking Co, *see Vintage*

Woodstock; Call's Used Auto Parts, *see Late Vintage*

T C Auto Parts & Glass, *see Late Vintage*

Wahiawa
Waianae Kahalui
Pearl City
Honolulu

Kealakekua Hilo
Captain Cook

HAWAII

LATE VINTAGE

Captain Cook; Mike's Auto Wrecking, P.O. Box 812, 96704; 808-323-2590; Sa, U-Pk; 100+; **80's; D, F; B3**

Haiku; Herman's Repair Auto Wrecking, 1550 Kapukalua, 96708; 808-572-8445; CC, Sp; 500; **80+; D, F, PU, 4x4; B3**

Hilo; Hilo Auto & Truck Svc, 191 Waianuenue Av, 96720; 808-935-8868, FAX 808-935-6911; CC, Sa, Sp; 400+; **70s+; D, F, PU, 4x4; B3**

Honolulu; Drive Line Components, 2831 Kaihikapu St, 96819; 808-839-9771, FAX 808-833-3386; Sa, Sp, Wr, PL; 1ac; **70+; D, F, PU, 4x4; B3; shipping to other islands, largest used parts inventory in HI**

Kealakekua; Big Island Towing Svc, 1037 Keopuka Rd, 96750; 808-323-3338; Sa, Sp; 1ac, 200; **70+; D, F, PU, 4x4; B3, AMC, Jp, VW**

Pearl City; Abes Auto Recyclers Inc, 96-1268 Waihona St, 96782; 808-455-4200, FAX 808-456-1681, 800-556-8534 HI only, abes@poi.net; CC, Sa, Sp, U-Pk; 2000; **85-95; D, F, PU, 4x4, Fm; B3; open Sunday**

Waianae; BFD Auto Wrecking, 85-574 Plantation Rd #A, 96792; 808-697-0233; Sa, Wr, U-Pk; 30; **80+; D, F, PU, 4x4; B3**

LATE MODEL

Haiku; Herman's Repair Auto Wrecking, *see Late Vintage*

Hilo; Hilo Auto & Truck Svc, *see Late Vintage*

Honolulu; Auto Recycling, 1045 Makepono St, 96819; 808-841-7872, FAX 808-848-4832; Sa, Sp, Wr; **D, F, PU, 4x4**

    Drive Line Components, *see Late Vintage*

    Golder Tire Shop, 2008 Republican St, 96819; 808-841-6121, FAX 808-848-2903; CC, Sp; **D, F, PU, 4x4; mostly mini trucks, ship to other islands**

Kahului; Maui Auto Wrecking, Mokulele Hwy, 96732; 808-871-9400, FAX 808-871-9401; Sp; 200; **D, F, PU, 4x4; inter-island shipping only**

Kealakekua; Big Island Towing Svc, *see Late Vintage*

Pearl City; Abes Auto Recyclers Inc, *see Late Vintage*

Wahiawa; Country Locksmith & Towing, 823 Olive Av, 96786; 808-621-1432, FAX 808-621-8114; CC, Sa, U-Pk; 20; **D, F, PU, 4x4**

Waianae; BFD Auto Wrecking, *see Late Vintage*

Please mention you saw'em in Ray's wReckingyard Roster when contacting these yards

Blackburn Farm &
Construction Equipment
Douglas, WY

You may be a car nut if

You think that
hot August nights
is a car meet

Idaho

IDAHO

VINTAGE

Boise; All Makes Auto Salvage, 4026 Banner, 83709; 208-362-7111; Sa, Sp, UR; 350+; **51-90; D, F, PU, 4x4; B**3

Early Bronco Specialties, 3550 Moore, 83703; 208-338-1449; Sp; **66-77; D, 4x4; Fd; Spc: Ford Bronco only**

Caldwell; B & T Auto Salvage, 22483 US Hwy 30N, 83605; 208-459-0866; CC, Sa, UR; 15ac; **40+; D, F, PU, 4x4, Trk; B**3**, AMC, Jp, IH, St, Wy, VW**

Hopkins Antique Autos & Parts, 24833 Hwy 30, 83605; 208-459-2877; Sa, Sp, UR; 700; **20+; D, F, Trk; B**3**, AMC, He, Ns, St, Pk, Ks, Fr**

Parts & Pieces, 4113 E Ustick, 83605; 208-455-2697; CC, Sa, Sp, UR; Wr; **60-85; D, F, PU, 4x4; B**3

Grangeville; Dale Rescue Towing, , 83530; 208-983-0671, 888-829-9109; CC, Sa, Br; 40ac; **40-79; D, F, PU; B**3**, AMC, Ns, St, VW**

Hayden; Garwood Wrecking, Hwy 95, 83835; 208-772-3993; Sa, UR; 10ac; **70-89, few 50-60s; D, PU, 4x4; B**3**, IH; Spc: Pickup & 4x4**

Pegasus Auto Wrecking, 18100 N Hwy 95, 83835; 208-772-3791; UR; 350; **40-69; D, F, PU; B**3**, AMC, Hd, St, Pk**

Hayden Lake; Classic Auto Parts, 18090 Hwy 95, 83835; 208-762-8080; CC, Sp; 300+; **32-75; D; B**3**, AMC, Pk; Mostly 50s & 60s**

Heyburn; Kelley Truck & Auto Salvage, 1130 J, 83336; 208-678-9086, 800-331-3978; CC, Sa, Sp; 16ac; **50+PU, 60+cars; D, F, PU, 4x4, Trk; B**3**, Jp, IH, St**

Idaho Falls; A-P Salvage, 1294 E Iona Rd, 83401; 208-525-8026; Sa, UR; 3000; **60+; D, PU, 4x4, Trk; B**3**, Jp, IH**

Charlie's Auto Recycling, 1488 E Iona Rd, 83401; 208-523-6248; Sa, Sp; 1500; **50+; D, F, PU, 4x4; B**3**, Hd, St**

Valley Salvage, 277 N 4200 E, 83401; 208-745-8463; Sa; 1500; **60+; D, F, PU, 4x4; B**3**, AMC, Jp, IH**

Valley Salvage, 3836 E 100 N, 83442; 208-745-8600, 888-745-8601; CC, Sa, Sp, UR; 4200; **60+; D, PU, 4x4; B**3**, AMC, IH**

Indian Valley; Morris Antique & Classic Cars & Parts, 83632; 208-256-4313, lbmorris@cyberhighway.net; Sp; 400+; **11-75; D, F; B**3**, Hd, Ns, St, Ks, Fr, Wy; Jewel, Rio, Essex, Edsel; By Appointment Only**

Kamiah; Jackson's Wrecking, Airport Rd, 83536; 208-935-2572, FAX 208-935-2295, 800-882-1412; CC, Sa, Sp, UR; 15ac; **50+; D, F, PU, 4x4, Fm; B**3**, AMC, Jp, IH**

Kuma; Mustang Idaho, 11855 W Hubbard Rd, 83634; 208-362-4821; CC, UR; 8ac, 500+; **60+; D, F, PU, 4x4, Trk; B**3**, AMC, IH, St, VW; Mustang all years; Ford Model T**

Lewiston; Central Crade Auto Parts, 500 Central Grade Rd, 83501; 208-743-9505; DD, Sp; 18ac; **50+; C, F, PU, 4x4; B**3**, AMC, Jp, IH, Pk, VW**

Central Crade Auto Parts, 500 Central Crade Rd, 83501; 208-743-9505; CC, Sp; 3000; **60+; D, F. PU, 4x4; B**3**, AMC, Jp, IH, Wy, VW**

Forest Auto & Truck Parts, 566 Mill Rd, 83501; 208-743-3546, FAX 208-743-6430; CC, Sa, Sp; 800+; **50+; D, F, PU 4x4, Trk; B**3**, AMC, Jp, IH**

Montpelier; Henning's Auto Salvage, W of Montpelier, 83254; 208-847-2195; Sa, UR; 500+; **20+; D, F, PU, B**3**, St, VW**

Mountain Home; Hwy 30 Auto Salvage, 960 Sunset Strip, 83647; 208-587-4429, FAX 208-587-5556, 800-540-4073; Sp; 250; **30-83; D, F, PU, 4x4; B**3**, Jp**

Nampa; All Hours Auto Salvage, 3100 Caldwell Blvd, 83651; 208-466-9848, 800-223-7794; CC, Sa, Sp; 35ac, 4000; **50+; D, F, PU, 4x4; B**3**, AMC, Jp, IH, St; Buses**

Buy-Rite Auto Salvage, 272 Caldwell Blvd, 83651; 208-466-5301; Sa, UR; 1ac, 400; **50-89, few 90s; D, F, PU, 4x4; B**3

Jalopy Jungle, 3931 Garrity Blvd, 83687; 208-466-8468, FAX 208-466-9393, 800-360-5865; CC, Sa, UR; 1200; **60-85; D, F, Trk; B**3**, Jp, IH, VW**

New Meadows; Bernie Green Auto Salvage, 5607 Pines Rd, 83654; 208-628-3429; 7ac, 500; **60-89; D, PU, 4x4; B**3

Payette; Country Boy Auto Salvage & Sales, 10800 Hwy 95, 83661; 208-642-4367, FAX 208-642-1955, 800-331-9630; CC, Sp; 25ac; **60+; D, F, PU, 4x4; B**3**, Jp, IH**

Pinehurst; Pine Creek Wrecking & Repair, 3280 Pine Creek Rd, 83850; 208-682-2709; Sa, Sp, UR; 5ac, 200; **50-89; D, PU, 4x4; B3, Wy**

Pocatello; Vintage Jeep Parts, 3888 N Gateway Dr, 83204; 208-233-3219, FAX 208-233-3139, 800-690-3219; CC, Sa, Sp; **40+; D; Jp; Jeep only**

Potlatch; Potlatch Auto Sales, 4006 Hwy 6, 83855; 208-875-1451; Sa, Sp; 20ac, 500; **60-85; D, F, PU, 4x4, Fm, In, Cn; B3, AMC, IH**

Preston; Idaho Salvage & Metals, 540 W Oneida St, 83263; 208-852-1386, FAX 208-852-0158; CC, Sa, Sp, UR; 5ac, 450; **40+; D, PU, 4x4, Trk, Fm, In, Cn, Mil; B3, AMC, Jp, IH, Hd**

Sandpoint; Dad's Auto & Truck Wrecking, 31594 Hwy 200, 83864; 208-263-7531; CC, Sa, Sp; 5ac, 500; **65+; D, F, PU, 4x4, Trk; B3, AMC, Jp, IH**

Twin Falls; Idaho Equipment & Salvage, 1750 Osterloh Av, 83301; 208-734-5350; CC, Sa, Sp, PL; 800+; **49+; D, F, PU, 4x4, Trk; Spc: Pickup**

Weiser; Myers Auto Salvage, 532 Hwy 95, 83672; 208-549-1076; Sa, Sp; 5ac, 500; **47-89; D, PU, 4x4, Trk, Fm, In, Cn; B3, AMC, Jp, IH, Hd, St, VW; Fords**

Wendell; L & L Classic Auto, 2742 State Hwy 46, 83355; 208-536-6606, FAX 208-536-2009; CC, Sp; 7000; **20+; D, F, PU, 4x4, Trk; B3, Jp, IH, Hd, Ns, St, Pk, Ks**

LATE VINTAGE

Boise; All Makes Auto Salvage, *see Vintage*

Barger Mattson Auto Salvage, 5501 W State St, 83703; 208-853-2002, FAX 208-853-2004, 800-846-2774; CC, Sa, Sp; 1500; **80+; D, F, PU, 4x4; B3, AMC, Jp, IH, VW; Three yards**

Early Bronco Specialties, *see Vintage*

Used VW Parts, 1619 N Phillippi St, 83706; 208-377-8733; CC, Sa, Sp; 4700 sq ft; **70+; F; VW; Spc: VW air cooled**

Caldwell; All Parts Brokers, 3515 Cleveland Blvd, 83605; 208-454-0713, FAX 208-454-0714, 800-678-7474; CC, Sp, Br; 7ac; **70+; D, F, PU; B3, IH; Pickup only**

B & T Auto Salvage, *see Vintage*

Hopkins Antique Autos & Parts, *see Vintage*

Parts & Pieces, *see Vintage*

Red Line, 5517 Cleveland Blvd, 83605; 208-454-8665, 800-436-3868; Sp; 10ac; **70+; D, F, PU, 4x4; B3**

Coeur d'Alene; Foreign Engines, 417 Northwest Blvd, 83814; 208-664-1559, 800-552-1595; CC, Sa; **80+, few 70s; F; Japanese engines only**

Spalding Auto Parts, 83814; 208-765-9848, FAX 208-928-2454, 800-366-2070; CC, Sa, Sp; **80+; D, F, PU, 4x4, Trk; B3**

Emmett; Gem County Auto & Truck, 603 S Johns Av, 83617; 208-365-7773; 10ac, 500; **80+; D, F, PU, 4x4, Trk; B3**

Fruitland; Leo's Auto Repair & Sales, 1795 SW 2nd Av, 83619; 208-452-3637; Sp, UR; 500; **70-89, few 60s; D, F, PU; B3, Jp, IH**

Grangeville; C & B Towing & Auto, 1100 N B St, 83530; 208-983-2378, FAX 208-983-2810, 800-289-4869; CC, Sa, Sp, Br; 5.5ac, 350; **70-89, few 60s; D, F, PU, 4x4; B3**

Dale Rescue Towing, *see Vintage*

Hayden; Garwood Wrecking, *see Vintage*

Heyburn; Kelley Truck & Auto Salvage, *see Vintage*

Snake River Towing & Salvage, I-84, 1840 Hwy 30, 83336; 208-678-9038, 800-660-9038; CC, Sa, Sp; 400+; **70+; D, F, PU, 4x4; B3, Jp, IH, VW**

Idaho Falls; A-P Salvage, *see Vintage*

All Star, 2715 N 15 E St Leon Rd, 83401; 208-523-4187, FAX 208-523-3432, 800-444-9707; CC, Sa, Sp, UR; 1200; **70+; D, F, PU, 4x4; B3, AMC, Jp, IH, VW**

Bonneville Auto Wrecking, 2997 N 15 E, 83401; 208-524-4452, FAX 208-535-2976, 800-888-4079; CC, Sa, Sp; 1900; **70+; D, F, PU, 4x4; B3 AMC, Jp, IH, VW**

Charlie's Auto Recycling, *see Vintage*

Valley Salvage, *see Vintage*

Valley Salvage, *see Vintage*

Indian Valley; Morris Antique & Classic Cars & Parts, *see Vintage*

114

Kamiah; Jackson's Wrecking, *see Vintage*

Kuma; Mustang Idaho, *see Vintage*

Lewiston; Central Crade Auto Parts, *see Vintage*

Central Crade Auto Parts, *see Vintage*

Forest Auto & Truck Parts, *see Vintage*

McCall; MTA Salvage, 125 Mission St, 83628; 208-634-5342; CC, Sp; 200; **75-85; D, F, PU, 4x4, B3, Jp, IH**

Meridian; AMT Parts Recyclers, 1515 E Fairview Av, 83642; 208-888-1978, FAX 208-888-7874, 800-887-1978; CC, Sa, Sp; 5ac; **70+; D, F, PU, 4x4; B3**

Ro-Ho Truck & Auto Salvage, 245 W Overland Rd, 83642; 208-888-1665; Sa, UR; **60+ PU, 70+cars; D, F, PU; B3**

Montpelier; Henning's Auto Salvage, *see Vintage*

Mountain Home; Hwy 30 Auto Salvage, *see Vintage*

Nampa; All Hours Auto Salvage, *see Vintage*

Buy-Rite Auto Salvage, *see Vintage*

Idaho Z, 2913 Garrity Blvd, 83687; 208-466-0004, www.zthespy.com; CC, Sa, Sp; **F; Z cars only**

Jalopy Jungle, *see Vintage*

New Meadows; Bernie Green Auto Salvage, *see Vintage*

Payette; Country Boy Auto Salvage & Sales, *see Vintage*

Goff's Auto Recyclers, 475 6th Av S, 83661; 208-642-9336, FAX 208-642-2009; Sa, Sp, UR; 40ac, 6400; **70-89; D, F, PU, 4x4, Trk; B3, AMC, Jp, IH, VW**

Pinehurst; Pine Creek Wrecking & Repair, *see Vintage*

Pocatello; Bailey Truck & Auto Supply, 5200 S 5 Av, 83204; 208-232-6918, 800-597-6665; CC, Sa, Sp; 6ac, 600; **80+; D, F, PU, 4x4; B3**

Vintage Jeep Parts, *see Vintage*

Potlatch; Potlatch Auto Sales, *see Vintage*

Preston; Idaho Salvage & Metals, *see Vintage*

Rigby; Intermountain Auto Recycling, 198 N Yellowstone Hwy, 83442; 208-745-8766, FAX 208-745-8798, 800-742-8766, booneh@ida.net; CC, Sa, Sp; 700+; **65+PU, 78-90 cars; D, F, PU, 4x4; B3, AMC, Jp, IH**

Sandpoint; Dad's Auto & Truck Wrecking, *see Vintage*

Twin Falls; Budget Auto Salvage, 1154 Addison Ave W, 83301; 208-733-6363, FAX 208-734-7821, 800-632-0836, www.bargermattson.com; bargerm@rmli.net; CC, Sa, Sp, UR; 20ac, 2000; **75+; D, F, PU, 4x4; B3, VW**

Idaho Equipment & Salvage, *see Vintage*

Weiser; Myers Auto Salvage, *see Vintage*

Wendell; L & L Classic Auto, *see Vintage*

Worley; Meredith's Repair & Towing, Hwy 95, 83876; 208-686-1312; CC, Sa, UR; 2 ac, **50+; 70-89; D, F, PU, 4x4; B3**

LATE MODEL

Boise; Barger Mattson Auto Salvage, *see Late Vintage*

Dillon Auto Parts, 520 E 47th St, 83714; 208-375-9461, FAX 208-375-9467, 800-888-8733; CC, Sp; 6ac; **D, F, PU, 4x4**

TNT Auto Salvage, 4010 W Gowen Rd, 83709; 208-362-4211, FAX 208-362-9632, 800-636-0114; CC, Sa, Sp; 5ac; **D, F, PU, 4x4**

Used VW Parts, *see Late Vintage*

Caldwell; All Parts Brokers, *see Late Vintage*

B & T Auto Salvage, *see Vintage*

Dillon Auto Salvage, 6515 Cleveland Blvd, 83605; 208-459-1591, FAX 208-459-1603, 800-777-0482; CC, Sp, Br; 6ac; **D, F, PU, 4x4**

Hopkins Antique Autos & Parts, *see Vintage*

Red Line, *see Late Vintage*

Coeur d'Alene; Coeur d'Alene Auto Wrecking, 2755 E Thomas Ln, 83814; 208-664-4383; CC, Sa; 5ac; **D, F**

Foreign Engines, *see Late Vintage*

115

Spalding Auto Parts, *see Late Vintage*
Emmett; Gem County Auto & Truck, *see Late Vintage*
Fort Hall; Ed's Auto Wrecking, Cattles Trl Rd, 83203; 208-237-2205; Sp, UR; **D, F, PU**
Fruitland; Leo's Auto Repair & Sales, *see Late Vintage*
Heyburn; Kelley Truck & Auto Salvage, *see Vintage*
    Snake River Towing & Salvage, *see Late Vintage*
Idaho Falls; A-P Salvage, *see Vintage*
    All Star, *see Late Vintage*
    Charlie's Auto Recycling, *see Vintage*
    Idaho Falls; Bonneville Auto Wrecking, *see Late Vintage*
    Valley Salvage, *see Vintage*
    Valley Salvage, *see Vintage*
Kamiah; Jackson's Wrecking, *see Vintage*
Kuma; Mustang Idaho, *see Vintage*
Lewiston; Central Crade Auto Parts, *see Vintage*
    Forest Auto & Truck Parts, *see Vintage*
Meridian; AMT Parts Recyclers, *see Late Vintage*
    Ro-Ho Truck & Auto Salvage, *see Late Vintage*
Montpelier; Henning's Auto Salvage, *see Vintage*
Mountain Home; Hwy 30 Auto Wrecking, *see Late Vintage*
Nampa; All Hours Auto Salvage, *see Vintage*
    Barger-Mattson Auto Salvage, 3326 Garrity Blvd, 83687; 208-466-7817, FAX 208-466-7830, 800-999-9076; CC, Sp, UR; 600; **D, F, PU, 4x4; B3, IH**
Payette; Country Boy Auto Salvage & Sales, *see Vintage*
Pocatello; Bailey Truck & Auto Supply, *see Late Vintage*
    Shaw Auto Parts, 1445 N 1st & Gould, 83201; 208-232-5952, FAX 208-233-0904, 800-479-7429, www.shawautoparts.com , SHAW@shawautoparts.com; CC, Sp; 6ac, 800; **D, F, PU, 4x4**
    Stan's Auto Wreckage Co, 270 E Day St, 83201; 208-232-1941, FAX 208-232-1942, 800-235-1941; CC, Sp; 200; **D, F, PU, 4x4**
    Vintage Jeep Parts, *see Vintage*
    Wayne's Salvage Parts, 3655 Hwy 30 W, 83201; 208-232-6311; Sa, Sp; 3ac, 200; **D, F, PU, 4x4**
Preston; Idaho Salvage & Metals, *see Vintage*
Priest River; Priest River Towing & Wrecking, 414 High St, 83856; 208-448-1523, 800-TOW-TRUCK; CC, Sa, Sp, Br; 80; **D, F, PU, 4x4, Trk**
Sandpoint; Dad's Auto & Truck Wrecking, *see Vintage*
Twin Falls; Budget Auto Salvage, *see Late Vintage*
    Idaho Equipment & Salvage, *see Vintage*
Wendell; L & L Classic Auto, *see Vintage*

You may be a car nut if
You bought
this
Book

Rare General Tractor
Martin Supply & Salvage Yard
Windsor, CO

Tractors
Martin Supply & Salvage Yard
Windsor, CO

117

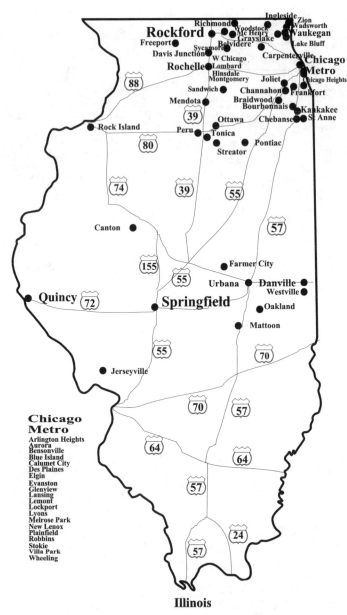

Illinois

Please mention you saw'em in Ray's wReckingyard Roster when contacting these yards

ILLINOIS

Arlington Heights; A-1 Rust Free Auto Parts, 2211 E Oakton St, 60005; 847-640-8288, www.rustfreeautoparts.com; CC, Sa, Sp, Wr; **60-89; D, PU, 4x4; Spc GM, Fd; Parts shipped in from California**

Aurora; Naperville Auto Recycling, 3570 E New York St #A, 60504; 630-851-9481, FAX 630-851-2007, 888-581-7393, naperville@prodigy.com; CC, Sa, Sp, Wr; 4.5ac; **65-89; D, F, PU, 4x4; B3**

   TAD Auto Parts, 512 N Broadway, 60505; 630-896-8563; CC, Sa, UR; 1000+; **60+; D, F, PU, 4x4; B3, Vans**

Bensenville; Victory Auto Wreckers Inc, 710 E Green St, 60106; 630-860-2000, FAX 630-860-2170; Sa, UR; 1000; **60+; D, F; B3**

Blue Island; ABC Auto Parts, 13741 Ashland Av, 60406; 708-389-1456, FAX 708-389-5126; CC, Sa, Sp, UR; 15ac, 1500; **mostly 80+; D, F, PU, 4x4; B3; UR back to 56**

   Broadway Auto Wrck, 13545 Sacramento Av, 60406; 708-371-9300, FAX 708-371-9304; Sa, Sp; 9ac, 1000; **60+; D, F, PU, 4x4, Trk; B3, AMC, Jp, IH, VW; RTA Buses, Corvair**

Braidwood; Hilemans Motor Mart, 298 S Division St, 60408; 815-458-6212; Sa, Sp, Br; **40-69; D, F, PU, 4x4, Trk; B3, AMC, Jp, IH, St, Pk, VW; some antiques**

Chebanse; Thompson Auto Wreckers, 5049 S 1400W Rd, 60922; 815-697-2223; Sa, Sp; 1800; **30-89; D, F, PU, 4x4 Fm; B3, AMC, Jp, IH, St; Hubcaps**

Chicago; Bargain Auto Pt, 521 E 71st St, 60619; 773-874-9797; CC, Sp; 3000; **50+; D, F; B3**

Chicago Heights; Speedway Auto Parts & Recycler, 551 E Lincoln Hwy, 60411; 708-758-0002, FAX 708-758-2839; CC, Sa, Sp, UR; 11ac, 1400; **60-96; D, F, PU, 4x4; B3**

Des Plaines; Schimka Auto Wreckers, 1132 E Thacker St, 60016; 847-699-3078; CC, Sa; **40-94; D; B3**

Elgin; Elgin Super Auto Prt, 225 Willard Av, 60120; 847-695-4000, 800-232-5564, elgin super@aol.com; CC, Sa, Sp, Wr; 25ac; **60+; D, F, PU, 4x4; B3, Jp; Spc: Toyota & Lexus**

Farmer City; Isaacs Salvage, 1010 N Plum St, 61842; 309-928-2466; Sa, UR; 8ac, 350; **53-91; D, F, PU, 4x4, Trk; B3, IH**

Frankfort; Hilemans Motor Mart, 60423; 815-458-6212; Sa, Sp, UR; 5ac; **50-85; D, F, few PU, few 4x4, few Trk; B3; Spc: Mercury**

Hinsdale; Hub Auto Parts & Wreckers, 9900 State Rt 83, 60521; 630-323-5865; Sa, UR; 23ac, 5000; **58-93; D, F, PU, 4x4; B3, AMC, IH, VW; Spanish**

Jerseyville; Ehlers Auto Salvage & Towing, Rt 2 Box 18, 62052; 618-498-2923; Sa, UR; 5ac, 600; **40-91; D, PU, Trk; B3, AMC, IH, DeSoto; 40s Pickup**

Joliet; A-Affordable Auto Parts, 328 Patterson Rd, 60436; 815-722-9072, FAX 815-722-2169, 800-750-3408; CC, Sa, Sp, UR, PL; 4ac, 900; **63+; D, F, PU, 4x4, B3, AMC, Jp, IH**

   Low Cost Auto Parts, 2221 Maple Rd, 60432; 815-727-4699; Sa; 300; **55-94; D, F, PU, 4x4, Trk, Fm; B3, Jp**

Kankakee; Acme Auto Parts Inc, 2016 E 1000N Rd, 60901; 815-939-3030, FAX 815-939-2020, 800-666-5538; CC, Sa, Sp, UR; 350; **60+; CC, Sa, Sp, UR; 32ac, 3000; full service, body shop, glass, engine install**

Lake Bluff; Certified Auto Parts, 13833 Leola Dr, 60044; 847-367-0441, FAX 847-367-7881, 800-452-8128; CC, Sa, Sp, UR; 500; **51-97; D, F, PU, 4x4; B3, Jp, VW**

Lemont; Cal-Sag Auto Parts, 60439; 630-257-7234, FAX 630-257-2211; CC, Sa; 40ac; **60+; D, F, PU, 4x4, Trk, Cn**

   Jerrys Valley Auto Parts, 10685 Archer Av, 60439; 630-257-6401; Sa, UR, PL; 22ac, 4000+; **60+; D, F, PU, 4x4; B3, AMC, Jp, VW**

   Valley Auto Wreckers & Towing, 10685 Archer Av, 60439; 630-257-6401; Sa, Sp, UR, PL; 22ac; **60+; D, F, PU, 4x4; B3**

Lockport; Canal Auto Salvage & Sales, 2601 Canal Rd, 60441; 815-838-3098; Sa, Br; 8ac; **40-93; D, F, PU, 4x4, Trk; B3**

   Southwest Auto Salvage, 3451 S State St, 60441; 815-723-6878, FAX 815-723-3470; CC, Sa, Sp, UR; 7ac; **50+; D, F, PU, 4x4; B3, AMC, Jp, IH, Hd, Ns, St, Pk, VW**

Mendota; Sprowls Body Sp & Auto, 4538 E 2nd Rd, 61342; 815-539-5846, FAX 815-539-6907; Sa, Sp, Br; 2000; **37-97; D, F, PU, 4x4, Trk, Fm, Cn, In, Mil; B3, AMC, Jp, IH, VW; Edsel**

Illinois - Vintage

Pontiac; Childers Auto Salvage & Wrecker, 701 W Lincoln Av, 61764; 815-844-5640; Sa, UR; 1000+; **60-92; D, F, PU, 4x4, Trk; B3**

Rockford; All Auto Parts Recycling, 2235 Kishwaukee St, 61104; 815-965-3545, FAX 815-965-2912; CC, Sa, UR; 6ac, 850; **60+; D, F, PU, 4x4, Trk; B3**

Tonica; Ace Auto Salvage, 127 Hwy 51, 61370; 815-442-8224, FAX 815-442-3325; Sa, UR; 2000; **46-90; D, F, PU, 4x4, Trk, Fm, Mil; B3, AMC, Jp, IH, VW; older Ford, bumpers**

Westville; Bryant's Auto Parts, RR 1, 61883; 217-267-2124, 800-252-5087; CC, Sa, Sp, Br; 5000; **39+; D, F, PU, 4x4; B3, AMC, Jp, IH, VW**

LATE VINTAGE

Arlington Heights; A-1 Rust Free Auto Parts, *see Vintage*

Aurora; City Auto Wreckers, 690 McClure Rd, 60504; 630-898-2900, FAX 630-898-4004, 800-898-CITY; CC, Sa, Sp, UR; 10ac; **80+; D, few F, PU; B3,**

Naperville Auto Recycling Co, *see Vintage*

TAD Auto Parts, *see Vintage*

Valley Auto Wreckers, 610 Hill Av, 60506; 630-898-6829; Sa, Br; 4ac; 70+; **D, F, PU, 4x4; B3**

Belvidere; Berman Auto Parts, 8727 Townhall Rd, 61008; 815-544-3811; Sa, Sp, Br; 7ac; **80+; D, F, PU, 4x4; B3**

Bensenville; Victory Auto Wreckers Inc, *see Vintage*

Blue Island; ABC Auto Parts, *see Vintage*

Broadway Auto Wreckers Ltd, *see Vintage*

Calumet City; Economy Auto Parts, 630 State St, 60403; 708-868-6390, FAX 708-868-8925; Sa, Sp, UR; 1000; **65-92; D, F, PU; B3, AMC, VW**

Canton; Flynns Auto Parts & Salvage, 390 E Alder Rd, 61520; 309-647-7011; Sa; 400; **80-92; D, F, PU, 4x4, Trk; B3**

Carpentersville; Chets Auto & Towing, 232 Park Av, 60110; 847-426-8424; Sa; 80; **80-95; D, F, PU, 4x4**

Channahon; Als Garage & Salvage, 24804 W Eames St, 60410; 815-467-5289; Sa, UR; 1.5ac; **75-85; D, F, PU, 4x4; B3**

I-55 Auto Salvage, 22661 S Frontage Rd, 60410; 815-467-2938; CC, Sa, Sp, Br; 10ac, 2500+; **84-93; D, F, PU, 4x4, Trk; B3**

Chebanse; Thompson Auto Wreckers, *see Vintage*

Chicago; A & B Auto Wrck, 8415 S Halsted St, 60620; 773-846-1933; Sa; 60; **75-88; D; B3**

Advance Auto Wreckers & Towing, 356 S Kolmar Av, 60624; 773-261-9317; CC, Sa; 40+; **79-82; D, F, PU, 4x4; B3**

Bargain Auto Parts, *see Vintage*

Cats Auto Parts, 7370 S Chicago Av, 60619; 773-947-0500; CC, Sa, Sp; 400; **85-95; D, F, PU, 4x4; B3, Jp**

El Paso Used Auto Parts, 3245 S Kostner Av, 60623; 773-927-7979; Sa, Wr; **80+; D; GM, Fd; Spanish**

Englewood Towing, 620 W 59th St, 60621; 773-651-0400; CC, Sa; 400; **80+; D, F, PU, 4x4; B3**

Fernandez Used Auto Parts, 2358 S Blue Island Av, 60608; 773-247-4470, FAX 773-247-4531; CC, Sa; 400+; **70+; D; B3; Spanish**

Harrison Flournoy Auto Wrecker, 2609 W Harrison St, 60612; 773-638-2282; Sa, Sp; **50+; 80+; D, F, PU, 4x4; B3**

J & S Automotive Wreckers, 4219 S Cicero Av, 60632; 773-582-6111; Sa; 5ac, 450; **80-95; D, F, PU; B3, VW**

Jacks Towing, 2535 Oakton, 60202; 773-561-8697; Sa, Sp, UR, PL; 200; **80+; D, F; B3**

Johnnys Auto Wrck, 2559 W Lake St, 60612; 312-421-3124; CC, Sa; **D, F, PU, 4x4; B3**

Juans Auto Parts, 9351 S Baltimore Av, 60617; 773-978-4600, FAX 773-978-6113; CC, Sa, Sp, PL; 300; **80+; D, F, PU, 4x4; B3; Spanish**

Mobleys Auto Wrecking, 2511 W Lake St, 60612; 312-243-6306; Sa; 40; **80-90; D; B3**

North Grand Auto Wreckers, 4545 W Grand Av, 60639; 773-235-2717; Sa, UR; 4ac, 700; **80-93; D, F, PU, 4x4; B3; also glass shop**

120

Pats Used Auto Parts, 4219 S Cicero Av, 60632; 773-582-5947, FAX 773-582-8010; Sa, UR; 450; **80+; D, F, PU, 4x4, Trk; B3**

Robbins Auto Salvage Inc, 5845 S Seeley Av, 60636; 773-925-6100, FAX 773-925-6939; CC, Sa, Sp; 3ac, 900; **80+; D, F, PU, 4x4; B3**

S & G Auto Parts, 7500 S Ashland Av, 60620; 773-846-1343, FAX 773-723-9273; Sa; **80+; D, PU, 4x4; B3**

Sarabia Used Auto Parts, 3899 S Iron St, 60609; 773-927-6262; Sa, Wr; **70+; D, F, PU; B3**

Universal Auto Parts Inc, 2703 S Loomis St, 60608; 312-949-1711; Sa, Sp, Wr; **85+; D, F, PU, 4x4; B3**

Windsor Auto Slvg, 13610 S Av D, 60633; 773-646-2700; Sa, Sp; 125; **73+; D, F, PU; B3**

Chicago Heights; Pagoria Auto & Truck Prt, 89 E Sauk Trl, 60411; 708-754-0060, Fax 708-754-0275, 888-462-0056, pagparts@aol.com; CC, Sa, Sp; 350; **83+; D, F, PU, 4x4; B3, VW**

Speedway Auto Parts & Recycler, *see Vintage*

Danville; Bill Smith Auto Parts, 400 Ash St, 61832; 217-442-0156, FAX 217-442-8976, 800-252-3005, bsap@soltec.com; CC, Sa, Sp; 23ac, 1800; **80s+; D, F, PU, 4x4, Trk; B3**

Davis Junction; 3-B Used Parts, 14035 E Hwy 72, 61020; 815-874-2380, 800-974-2380; Sa, Sp, UR, PL; 25ac, 500; **78-93; D, F, PU, 4x4; B3, AMC; has 3 other yards**

Decatur; Decatur Auto Parts Inc, 2500 N Woodford St, 62526; 217-877-4371, 800-728-8733; CC, Sp; 9ac, 1200; **80+; D, F, PU, 4x4; B3; Spc: sheet metal**

Des Plaines; Kevin Des Plaines Auto Slvg, 1331 E Golf Rd, 60016; 847-297-7810, FAX 847-297-8342; CC, Sa, Sp; 4ac; **85-91; D, F, PU, 4x4; B3**

Schimka Auto Wreckers, *see Vintage*

Elgin; Auto Parts Express/Midwestern, 1201 Bluff City Blvd, 60120; 847-888-9500, FAX 847-888-5454; Sa, Sp, UR; 100+; **68-90s; D, PU, 4x4; B3, Jp; Spanish**

Elgin Super Auto Parts, *see Vintage*

Evanston; North Shore Towing, 2527 Oakton St, 60202; 847-864-2828, FAX 847-864-0980; CC, Sa, UR; 100+; **77+; D, F, PU, 4x4; B3, AMC, Jp, VW**

Farmer City; Isaacs Salvage, *see Vintage*

Frankfort; Hilemans Motor Mart, *see Vintage*

Glenview; Reds Auto Body Shop, 1904 Lehigh Av, 60025; 847-724-7920, FAX 847-724-8084; CC, Sa, Sp, UR; 2ac, 100; **75-85; D; B3**

Hinsdale; Hub Auto Parts & Wreckers, *see Vintage*

Ingleside; Royale Truck & Auto Salvage, 36250 N Wilson Rd, 60041; 847-587-9522, FAX 847-587-9526, 800-681-5999; CC, Sa, Sp; 2ac, 100; **80s; D, PU, Trk only, 1/2 ton+**

Jerseyville; Ehlers Auto Salvage & Towing, *see Vintage*

Joliet; A-Affordable Auto Parts, *see Vintage*

All Will County Auto Wreckers, 1014 E Washington St, 60433; 815-723-3011, FAX 815-723-5575, 800-834-7133; Sa; 26ac, 1500; **78-92; D, F, PU, 4x4; B3, AMC, Jp**

Low Cost Auto Parts, *see Vintage*

Kankakee; Acme Auto Parts Inc, *see Vintage*

Lake Bluff; Certified Auto Parts, *see Vintage*

Lansing; Witvoet Auto Parts, 18210 Dorchester Av, 60438; 708-474-1981; Sa; **80+; D, F, PU, 4x4; B3**

Lemont; Cal-Sag Auto Parts, *see Vintage*

Jerrys Valley Auto Parts, *see Vintage*

Valley Auto Wreckers & Towing, *see Vintage*

Lockport; Canal Auto Salvage & Sales, *see Vintage*

Southwest Auto Salvage, *see Vintage*

T & S Auto Recycling Inc, 3519 S State St, 60441; 815-722-5138; CC, Sa, Sp, UR; 6ac; **78+; D, F, PU, 4x4; B3**

Lyons; Public Iron & Metal Co, 7735 47th St, 60534; 708-447-4710; Sa, UR; 300+; **72+; D, F, PU, 4x4, Trk; B3**

Mattoon; Mattoon Auto Salvage, Box #E RR Box 12, 61938; 217-234-8873; Sa; 300; **77-89, few 90s; D, PU, 4x4; B3, AMC**

Mc Henry; Nelson Auto, 3420 N Richmond Rd, 60050; 815-344-0950, FAX 815-344-8044, 800-762-7257; Sa; **D, F, PU, 4x4, Trk; B3, AMC, Jp, IH, VW**

121

Melrose Park; West Melrose Auto Wreckers, 4613 W Lake St, 60160; 708-343-4140, FAX 708-343-4049; Sa, Sp, UR; 1000; **80-89; D, F, PU, 4x4, Trk, Fm, Cn, In; B3, AMC, Jp, IH, VW**

Mendota; Sprowls Body Shop & Auto, *see Vintage*

Montgomery; Dels Towing & Auto Repair, 1341 S Spencer St, 60538; 630-978-7324; Sp, Wr; 10; **70-80; D, PU, 4x4; B3, AMC**

New Lenox; Spencer Auto Salvage, 1010 Spencer Rd, 60451; 815-485-6306; Sa, UR; 1ac **70-89; D; B3**

Oakland; Coles County Auto Slvg, 23255 E County Rd 1470 N, 61943; 217-346-2254, FAX 217-346-3294, 800-233-5426; Sa, Sp; 23ac; **78+; D, F, PU, 4x4; B3, AMC, Jp, IH, VW**

Ottawa; R & R Sales & Salvage, 301 W Marquette St, 61350; 815-433-4303; Sa, Sp, UR; 200; **70-89, few 60s; D, F, PU, 4x4; B3, AMC, Jp; mostly Chevy**

Peru; Auto Salvage Co, Route 6, 61354; 815-223-3993, FAX 815-224-9022, 800-300-9173; Sa, Sp; 1500; **75+; D, F, PU, 4x4, Trk; B3, Jp**

Pontiac; Childers Auto Salvage & Wrecker, *see Vintage*

Quincy; C & M Auto & Truck Salvage, 62301; 217-224-3600, 800-689-6091; CC, Sa, Sp, Br; **D, F, PU, 4x4; B3, AMC, Jp, IH, VW**

Richmond; Route 12 Auto Parts Inc, 4202 US Hwy 12, 60071; 815-675-6661; CC, Sa, Sp, Wr; 6ac, 600; **80-95; D, F, PU, 4x4, Trk; B3, AMC, Jp, IH, VW; some 70s parts**

Robbins; Thompson & Sons Towing, 13744 S Sacramento Av, 60472; 708-388-4160; **70+; D, F, PU, 4x4; B3**

Rochelle; Juans Salvage Inc, 10508 E Titus Rd, 61068; 815-562-7212; Sa, UR; 5ac; **72-89; D, F, PU, 4x4, Trk; B3, AMC, VW**

    Lunardon Auto Wrecking Co, Rt 38 W of Rochelle, 61068; 815-562-7530; Sa, Sp; 5ac, 600; **80-90; D, F, PU, 4x4, Trk; B3, AMC, Jp, IH,VW**

Rock Island; E & J Used Auto & Truck Prt, PO Box 6007; 315-31st Av, 61204; 309-788-7686, FAX 309-788-7695, 800-728-7686; CC, Sa, Sp, Br; 2000; **70+; D, F, PU, 4x4; B3**

Rockford; Abe's Towing, 601 Harrison Av, 61104; 815-226-0984; CC, Sa, Sp; 25ac, 1000; **75-90; D, F, PU, 4x4, Trk; B3, AMC, VW**

    All Auto Parts Recycling, *see Vintage*

    Rock River Auto Recycler, 2703 Falund St, 61109; 815-229-8665; Sa, UR; 2ac; **80s; D, F, PU, 4x4; Trk; B3, AMC**

Saint Anne; Tom Hodge & Son Auto Parts, 4252 S 16000E Rd, 60964; 815-944-6006; Sa, Br; 400; **73+; D, F, PU, 4x4, Trk; B3, AMC, Jp, IH, VW**

Sandwich; Yingling Salvage Inc, 1110 E Church St, 60548; 815-786-2359, 800-892-2576 N IL only; Sa, Sp, UR; 8ac, 1500; **70-90; D, PU, 4x4, Trk; B3, AMC, Jp, IH, VW**

Skokie; Century Auto Parts, 7720 Austin Av, 60077; 847-966-6040; CC, Sa; **80-90; D, F, 4x4; B3, AMC, Jp**

Springfield; Wrecked Cars of Springfield, 3701 N Dirksen Pky, 62707; 217-525-1028, 800-252-1079; CC, Sa, Sp; 4700; **80+; D, F, PU, 4x4, Trk; B3**

Tonica; Ace Auto Salvage, *see Vintage*

Villa Park; North Avenue Auto Parts, 17W737 North Av, 60181; 630-832-1936, FAX 630-832-1947; CC, Sa, Sp; 6ac, 300; **81+; D, F, PU, 4x4, Trk; B3, AMC, VW; open Sunday**

Waukegan; Auto Parts City Inc, 3570 Washington St, 60085; 847-244-7171, FAX 847-244-7279; Sa, UR; 7ac; **D, F, PU, 4x4; B3, AMC, Jp, IH**

Westville; Bryant's Auto Parts, *see Vintage*

Wheeling; A & G Auto Parts Inc, 727 S Milwaukee Av, 60090; 847-537-1424, FAX 847-395-1077; CC, Sa, Wr; 1ac; **83+; D, F, PU, 4x4; B3, AMC, VW**

Zion; BC Automotive Inc, 2809 Damascus Av, 60099; 847-746-8056, FAX 847-746-7701; CC, Sa, Sp, Br; 7ac; **82+; D, few F, PU, 4x4, Trk; B3, AMC, Jp, VW**

LATE MODEL

Aurora; City Auto Wreckers, *see Late Vintage*

    TAD Auto Parts, *see Vintage*

    Valley Auto Wreckers Inc, *see Late Vintage*

Belvidere; Berman Auto Parts, *see Late Vintage*

Bensenville; Victory Auto Wreckers Inc, *see Vintage*

122

Blue Island; A-Reliable Auto Parts & Wreckers, 2247 139th St, 60406; 708-385-5595; Sa, Sp; **D, F, PU; B**3

ABC Auto Parts, *see Vintage*

Broadway Auto Wreckers Ltd, *see Vintage*

W & W Foreign Auto Parts Inc, 12301 Vincennes Rd, 60406; 708-385-4000, FAX 708-385-6445, www.foreignIBM.net; CC, Sa, Sp, Br; 4.5ac; **F, PU, 4x4**

Bourbonnais; Kankakee Auto Recyclers Inc, 1764 N State Rt 50, 60914; 815-939-7597, FAX 815-936-4355, 800-532-8862; CC, Sa, Sp, UR; 5ac, 600; **D, F, PU, 4x4; B**3**, AMC**

Calumet City; City Auto Prt, 2305 E 142nd St, 60409; 708-862-2700, 800-362-0576; CC, Sa

Carpentersville; Chets Auto & Towing, *see Late Vintage*

Channahon; I-55 Auto Salvage, *see Late Vintage*

Chicago; A-Bumpers, 4501 W Grand Av, 60639; 773-252-8883; CC, Sa, Sp, Wr; **D, F; bumpers, head & tail lights, tires**

Bargain Auto Parts, *see Vintage*

Bionic Auto Parts & Sales Inc, 4655 W North Av, 60639; 773-489-6020, FAX 773-489-4722, 800-626-9618, abionic@aol.com; CC, Sp, PL; 500+; **D, F, PU, 4x4; B**3

C & J Auto Parts, 3200 Archer Av, 60608; 773-523-8121, 800-783-8121; CC, Sa, Sp; 400; **D, F, PU, 4x4**

Cats Auto Parts, *see Late Vintage*

Dons Auto Parts, 9503 S Torrence Av, 60617; 773-721-2800, FAX 773-721-6997; CC, Sa, Sp; 300; **D, PU, 4x4**

El Paso Used Auto Parts, *see Late Vintage*

Englewood Towing, *see Late Vintage*

Fernandez Used Auto Parts, *see Late Vintage*

Gonzalez Auto & Truck Parts, 3405 S Lawndale Av, 60623; 773-523-0992; Sa, Sp; 200+; **D, F; B**3**; Spanish**

Harrison Flournoy Auto Wrecker, *see Late Vintage*

J & S Automotive Wreckers, *see Late Vintage*

Jacks Towing, *see Late Vintage*

Juans Auto Parts, *see Late Vintage*

Mc Coy Auto Parts Inc, 2301 S Pulaski Rd, 60623; 773-277-0111; Sa, Sp; 100; **D, F; B**3**; Spanish**

Milwaukee Avenue Auto Parts Co, 1780 N Milwaukee Av, 60647; 773-384-5200, FAX 773-384-3395, 800-662-7797; Sa, Sp; 100+; **D, F, PU, 4x4, B**3

Pats Used Auto Parts, *see Late Vintage*

Robbins Auto Salvage Inc, *see Late Vintage*

S & G Auto Parts, *see Late Vintage*

Sarabia Used Auto Parts, *see Late Vintage*

Three Qs Auto Parts Inc, 1465 E 130th St, 60633; 773-646-1600, 888-646-6799; PL; **F**

Universal Auto Parts Inc, *see Late Vintage*

Windsor Auto Salvage Inc, *see Late Vintage*

Chicago Heights; Pagoria Auto & Truck Parts Inc, *see Late Vintage*

Speedway Auto Parts & Recycler, *see Vintage*

Danville; Bill Smith Auto Parts, *see Late Vintage*

Davis Junction; 3-B Used Parts, *see Late Vintage*

Decatur; Decatur Auto Parts Inc, *see Late Vintage*

Des Plaines; Schimka Auto Wreckers, *see Vintage*

Elgin; Elgin Super Auto Parts, *see Vintage*

H & H Used Auto-Truck Parts, 1175 Bluff City Rd, 60120; 847-695-4843; CC, Sa, Sp, UR; 6ac, 550; **D, F, PU, 4x4; B**3

Evanston; North Shore Towing, *see Late Vintage*

Freeport; Freeport Auto Parts, 530 N Henderson Rd, 61032; 815-233-5863, FAX 815-235-1050; Sa, Sp, UR; 15ac, 60+; **D, PU, 4x4; B**3

Grayslake; Toms Auto Wreckers, 216 W Belvidere Rd, 60030; 847-546-5422, FAX 847-546-5483, 800-798-5321; CC, Sa, Sp; 3ac; **D, F, PU, 4x4, Trk; B**3

Joliet; A-Affordable Auto Parts, *see Vintage*

Berlinsky Scrap, 212 Page Av, 60432; 815-726-4334, 726-3279; Sa, UR; **D, PU; 2 yds**
Low Cost Auto Parts, *see Vintage*
Speedway Auto Parts Ltd, 700 Railroad St, 60436; 815-726-0666, FAX 815-726-9427, 800-437-8733, www.speedil.com; CC, Sp; 350; **D, F, PU; B3**
Kankakee; Acme Auto Parts Inc, *see Vintage*
Kankakee Auto Parts, W Jeffery St, 60901; 815-939-3534; Sa, Sp, Br; 10ac, 3500; **D, F, PU, 4x4, Trk; B3**
Thompson Auto Wreckers, 7764 W State Route 17, 60901; 815-939-7300; Sa, UR; 5ac, 800; **D, PU, 4x4, Trk; B3**
Lake Bluff; Certified Auto Parts, *see Vintage*
Lansing; Witvoet Auto Parts, *see Late Vintage*
Lemont; Cal-Sag Auto Parts, *see Vintage*
Jerrys Valley Auto Parts, *see Vintage*
Valley Auto Wreckers & Towing, *see Vintage*
Lockport; Canal Auto Salvage & Sales, *see Vintage*
Southwest Auto Salvage, *see Vintage*
T & S Auto Recycling Inc, *see Late Vintage*
Lombard; Lombard Auto Wreckers, 640 E Saint Charles Rd, 60148; 630-495-3132, 800-433-8728; CC, Sp, Wr; 2ac; **D, F, PU, 4x4; B3**
Lyons; Public Iron & Metal Co, *see Late Vintage*
Mendota; Sprowls Body Shop & Auto, *see Vintage*
Montgomery; Staffords Auto Parts, 900 N Main St, 60538; 630-896-1342, FAX 630-892-4234, 800-437-1770; CC, Sa, Sp; 15ac, 1000; **D, F, PU, 4x4; B3, AMC, Jp, IH, VW**
Oakland; Coles County Auto Salvage, *see Late Vintage*
Peru; Auto Salvage Co, *see Late Vintage*
Plainfield; Speicher & Gaylord Auto Wreckers, 1021 E 143rd St, 60544; 815-436-6050, FAX 815-436-3652; CC, Sa, Sp; 500+; **D, F, PU, 4x4, Trk, Fm, Mil; B3, AMC, Jp, IH, VW**
Richmond; Route 12 Auto Parts Inc, *see Late Vintagev*
Robbins; Thompson & Sons Towing, *see Late Vintage*
Rock Island; E & J Used Auto & Truck Parts, *see Late Vintage*
Rockford; Abe's Towing, *see Late Vintage*
All Auto Parts Recycling, *see Vintage*
Rockford Auto Parts, 923 Seminary St, 61104; 815-964-3396, FAX 815-964-0993, 800-392-5595; Sa, Sp; 9ac, 700; **D, PU, 4x4, Trk; B3, Jp**
Saint Anne; Tom Hodge & Son Auto Parts, *see Late Vintage*
Springfield; Wrecked Cars of Springsfield, *see Late Vintage*
Streator; Jim Berninger Auto Wrecking, 31968 N Ooeast Rd, 61364; 815-673-1754; Sa
Sycamore; B-O Used Auto Parts, 800 Brickville Rd, 60178; 815-895-6744; Sa, Sp UR; 10ac, 1500; **D, F, PU, 4x4, Trk, Fm, Cn, In; B3, AMC, Jp, IH, VW**
Urbana; Bill Smith Auto Parts, 3405 N Countryview Rd, 61802; 217-367-5090, FAX 217-367-5099, 800-252-7698; CC, Sa, Sp, Br; **D, F; B3, AMC**
Mack's Auto Recycling Inc, 1309 E Kerr Av, 61802; 217-367-6219, FAX 217-367-9001, 800-252-9148; CC, Sa, Sp; 10ac; **D, F, PU, 4x4, Trk; B3, AMC, Jp, IH, VW**
Villa Park; North Avenue Auto Parts Co, *see Late Vintage*
Wadsworth; Hy-Way Auto Parts Inc, 60083; 847-395-7600, FAX 847-395-1077, 800-DIALHWY; CC; 20ac; **main office at Auto Parts City, Waukegan**
Waukegan; A & M Automotive Prt, 3145 Grand Av, 60085; 847-244-1015; Sa, Sp, PL; **D, F**
West Chicago; West Chicago Auto Wreckers, 641 W Washington St, 60185; 630-231-6322; Sa; 300; **D, F, PU, 4x4; B3, AMC, VW**
Westville; Bryant's Auto Parts, *see Vintage*
Wheeling; A & G Auto Parts Inc, *see Late Vintage*
Woodstock; Route 14 Auto Parts, 14020 Washington St, 60098; 815-338-2800, FAX 815-338-2803; CC, Sa, Sp, UR; 2300; **D, F, PU, 4x4, Trk; B3, AMC, Jp, IH, VW; open Sunday**
Zion; BC Automotive Inc, *see Late Vintage*

Checker Cab
Lincoln Valley
Auto Wreckers
Cheyenne, WY

INDIANA

Gary; I-80 Auto Parts, 3349 Burr St, 46406; 219-838-4388; Sa, Sp, PL; **30+; D, F, PU; B3**

Western Scrap Corp, 6901 Chicago Av, 46406; 219-944-9749; Sa; **50-69; D, F, PU; B3**

Greenfield; Fields Auto Parts Inc, 5388 E 600 N, 46140; 317-326-2271, 800-252-6291; Sa, UR; 6500; **50+; D, F, PU; B3, VW**

Jack & Son's Auto Salvage, 318 E South St, 46140; 317-462-7667; Sa; 900; **65-93; D, F, PU, 4x4; B3, AMC, Jp, IH, VW; Spc: Monte Carlo, Mustang**

Huntington; Webb's Classic Auto Parts, 5084 W State Rd 114, 46750; 219-344-1714, FAX 219-344-1754, user.huntington.in.us/jwebb/; CC, Sp, Wr; 100; **D; AMC, Rambler only**

Lagrange; Curtis Wrecking Yard, 700 N Detroit St, 46761; 219-463-3432, FAX 219-463-3135, 877-439-5489; Sa, Sp; **40-69; D, F; B3**

New Waverly; Canfield Motors, Main St, 46961; 219-722-3230; Sa, Sp; 1000; **30-69; D, F, PU, 4x4, Trk; B3, AMC, Jp, IH, Hd, Ns, St, Pk, Ks, VW**

Noblesville; Bill Shank Auto Parts, 14648 Promise Rd, 46060; 317-776-0080; Sa, Sp, UR; 1000+; **60+; D, F, PU, 4x4, Trk, Fm, In, Cn; B3, AMC, Jp, IH, VW; Mercedes, House trailers, Schoolbuses, buses**

North Salem; Joe Goode Excavating, 7901 N Country Road 775 W, 46165; 765-676-5555; Sp; **25-65; D; B3, Ks, Fr**

Peru; Wright's Auto & Truck Salvage, Rt 4 Box 17-A, 46970; 765-472-3032; Sa, Sp; 34ac; **35-90; D, F, PU, 4x4, Trk; B3, AMC, Jp, IH, St, Pk**

Petersburg; Pike County Auto Recycling, 1513 S State Rd 57, 47567; 812-354-9221; Sa, Sp; 40ac; **40+; D, F, PU; B3**

Richmond; Junction Auto, 3275 Hillcrest Rd, 47374; 765-935-5812; Sa, Sp; 10ac, 1000; **40-96; D, F, PU, 4x4; B3, AMC, Jp, IH, St, Pk, VW**

Salem; Gilstrap Auto Salvage, W Joseph St, 47167; 812-883-5201; Sa, UR; 3ac; **70-85, few 50-60s; D, F, PU; B3**

Valpraiso; Metro Auto Parts, 2155 Lincolnway, 46383; 219-462-3753, FAX 219-462-6929, 800-686-3753; CC, Sa, Sp, UR; 1000; **50+; D, F, PU; B3; Mustang, Cadillac**

Washington; Highway 57 Auto Parts, State Hwy 57 S, 47501; 812-254-6241; Sa, Sp; 2000+; **50+; D, F, PU, 4x4; B3, AMC, Jp, IH**

Winchester; Fritt's Wrecking Yard, 600 S West St, 47394; 765-584-4313; Sa, Sp, UR; 2ac; **60-89; D, PU, 4x4; B3; Spc: Chrysler**

LATE VINTAGE

Bloomington; Auto Heaven, *see Vintage*

Buffalo; Liberty Auto Salvage, State Rd 16 E, 47925; 219-278-7103; 50; **70-89; D; B3**

Demotte; R Town Automotive Inc, 901 Orchid St SE, 46310; 219-987-4444, FAX 219-987-4435; Sa, Sp, UR; 800; **80+; D, PU, 4x4; B3**

Dunkirk; Millikan Auto Salvage, County Rd 825 E, 47336; 765-768-6814; Sa, UR; 10ac; **70-93; D, F, PU; B3**

Fort Wayne; Jerry Doran Auto Parts, 2901 Brooklyn Av, 46809; 219-747-1516; CC, Sa, Sp, UR; 4000; **70+; D, F, PU, 4x4; B3**

Gary; B & B Used Auto Parts, 3875 Georgia St, 46409; 219-884-1011; **70-89; D; B3**

Central Auto Wrecking, 1008 Virginia St, 46402; 219-882-5865; Sa, UR; 3000; **80+; D, F, PU; B3**

Chase Street Auto Wrecking, 2800 Chase St, 46404; 219-944-9200; CC, Sa; 2000; **75+; D, F, PU, 4x4; B3**

Cousins Auto Wrecking, 4470 Whitcomb St, 46408; 219-980-1166, FAX 219-980-1167; Sa, Sp, PL; 250; **80+; D; GM, Chr**

Gary; I-80 Auto Parts Co, *see Vintage*

O K Auto Sales, 2197 Colfax St, 46406; 219-845-0569; Sa; 50; **80+; D, F; B3**

Paul's Auto Yard, 7100 W 15th Av, 46406; 219-944-3233; Sa, Sp, UR, PL; 400; **70+; D, F, PU; B3**

Raw Auto & Metal, 3313 Liverpool Rd, 46405; 219-962-1485; Sa; 200; **80-93, few 70s; D; B3**

Republic Frame & Axle, 7500 Melton Rd, 46403; 219-938-7040, FAX 219-938-7329; CC, Sa, Sp; 5ac; **80+; D, F, PU, 4x4; B3; Body, frame, axle, paint shop**

Greenfield; Fields Auto Parts Inc, *see Vintage*

127

Jack & Son's Auto Salvage, *see Vintage*

Griffith; Griffith Auto Wrecking, 1405 E Main St, 46319; 219-924-5222; Sa, UR; 400; **80+; D, F, PU, 4x4, Trk; B3**

Hammond; Calumet Auto Recycling & Sales, 6205 Indianapolis Blvd, 46320; 219-844-6600, FAX 219-844-2715, 800-331-0334, www.calumetauto.com; CC, Sa, Sp; 10ac, 1500; **80+; D, F, PU, 4x4; B3**

Midwest Auto Recycling, 19 Marble St, 46327; 219-937-9381; Sa; **70-89; D, PU; B3**

Paul's Auto Yd, 2015 Summer St, 46320; 219-845-2676; Sa, Sp, UR; **80s+; D, F, PU; B3**

T & T Auto Wreckers, 2164 Summer St, 46320; 219-844-8300; Sa; 200; **70-89; D, PU; B3**

Harlan; Garmater's Auto Salvage Inc, 14007 Bull Rapids Rd, 46743; 219-657-5129; Sa, Sp, UR; 1500; **65+; D, F, PU; B3, IH; Scout**

Hobart; American Auto Parts, 3513 Michigan St, 46342; 219-962-1126; CC, Sa, Br, Wr, PL; **70-95; D, F, PU, 4x4; B3**

Huntington; Clark's Auto Parts, 100 Hitzfield St, 46750; 219-356-8314, FAX 219-356-2475; Sa, UR; 500; **70-90; D, F, PU; B3**

Webb's Classic Auto Parts, *see Vintage*

Indianapolis; A & L Salvage, 401 S Tibbs Av, 46241; 317-247-7725, FAX 317-247-7780; CC, Sa; 300; **80+; D, PU, 4x4; B3; "We will buy what people ask for."**

A-1 Auto Salvage, 1425 W Ray St, 46221; 317-632-3511; Sa; 250; **80-92; D, PU, 4x4; B3**

Imperial Auto Parts Inc, 1130 E 25th St, 46205; 317-926-5459; CC, Sa, Sp, UR; 500; **70-89; D, F, PU; B3**

Prospect Auto Parts, 2925 Prospect St, 46203; 317-639-3506, FAX 317-639-0098; Sa, Sp, UR; 1000; **80+; D, F, PU; B3**

Skiles Country Auto Parts, 3013 Stanley Av, 46227; 317-787-7555, FAX 317-787-7752; Sa, Sp, UR; 3ac; **70-89, few 90s; D, F, PU; B3**

Trucks Plus Auto Salvage Inc, 1501 W McCarty St, 46221; 317-632-9066, FAX 317-632-0779; CC, Sa; 300; **70-89; D, PU, 4x4; B3; Spc: Pickup**

Kokomo; Beetle Shop, 1936 N Washington St, 46901; 765-452-3581; Sa, UR; 200; **70-89; D, F, PU, 4x4; B3, VW; Spc: Chevy & Ford Pickup**

Merrillville; Nummies Used Auto Parts, 6530 Broadway, 46410; 219-769-2441, 800-669-2890; Sa, Sp; 500+; **80s, few 70s; D, F, PU; B3**

Michigan City; Brinckman's Auto Salvage, 2806 E Michigan Blvd, 46360; 219-872-7744; CC, Sa; 700; **80+; D, F, PU; B3**

Mishawaka; Scottland Yard Inc, 55780 Filbert Rd, 46544; 219-259-8707; Sa; 200; **80-92; D, F, PU; B3**

Noblesville; Bill Shank Auto Parts, *see Vintage*

Peru; Wright's Auto & Truck Salvage, *see Vintage*

Petersburg; Pike County Auto Recycling, *see Vintage*

Portland; Adams Auto Wrck, Fort Recovery Rd, 47371; 219-335-2321; Sa, Sp; **70+, few earlier parts; D; B3**

Richmond; Junction Auto, *see Vintage*

Saint John; Stan's Auto Salvage, 7967 Wicker Av, 46373; 219-365-8558; CC; 700+; **80+; D, F; B3**

Salem; Gilstrap Auto Salvage, *see Vintage*

South Bend; K Auto Salvage, 56670 Sonora Av, 46619; 219-287-4593; Sa; 100; **80-90; D, PU; B3**

Terre Haute; Mike's Auto Wrecking, 3030 4th Av, 47803; 812-232-3508, FAX 812-234-7028; Sa; 1800; **70+; D, F, PU; B3**

Southwest Auto Co, 1901 Prairieton Rd, 47802; 812-232-0455, 800-466-5441; CC, Sa, Sp; 2000; **80+; D, F, PU; B3**

Thorntown; Barrett & Belcher Auto Salvage, 302 W Church St, 46071; 765-436-7962, FAX 765-436-7011; Sa; 300; **70-89; D, F, PU; B3**

Valpraiso; Metro Auto Parts, *see Vintage*

Washington; Highway 57 Auto Parts, *see Vintage*

Winchester; Fritt's Wrecking Yard, *see Vintage*

LATE MODEL

Bloomington; Auto Heaven, *see Vintage*
Demotte; R Town Automotive Inc, *see Late Vintage*
Dunkirk; Millikan Auto Salvage, *see Late Vintage*
Fort Wayne; Allied Economy Auto Parts Corp, 5114 Old Maumee Rd, 46803; 219-749-8313;
   Jerry Doran Auto Parts, *see Late Vintage*
   Smitty's Auto Parts, 3917 Meyer Rd, 46806; 219-447-1173; Sa, Sp; **D, F, PU; B3**
Gary; Central Auto Wrecking, *see Late Vintage*
   Chase Street Auto Wrecking, *see Late Vintage*
   Cousins Auto Wrecking, *see Late Vintage*
   I-80 Auto Parts Co, *see Vintage*
   I-94 Auto Recyclers Inc, 2932 Burr St, 46406; 219-845-4030; Sa, Sp; 4ac, 600; **D, PU, 4x4; B3**
   O K Auto Sales, *see Late Vintage*
   Paul's Auto Yard, *see Late Vintage*
   Raw Auto & Metal, *see Late Vintage*
   Republic Frame & Axle, *see Late Vintage*
Greenfield; Fields Auto Parts Inc, *see Vintage*
   Jack & Son's Auto Salvage, *see Vintage*
Griffith; Griffith Auto Wrecking, *see Late Vintage*
Hammond; Calumet Auto Recycling & Sales, *see Late Vintage*
   Northlake Auto Recyclers Inc, 105 Industrial Rd, 46320; 219-937-3960, FAX 219-937-3963; Sp; 2200; **D, F, PU, 4x4; B3**
   Paul's Auto Yard, *see Late Vintage*
Harlan; Garmater's Auto Salvage Inc, *see Late Vintage*
Hobart; American Auto Parts, *see Late Vintage*
Indianapolis; A & L Salvage, *see Late Vintage*
   A-1 Auto Salvage, *see Late Vintage*
   Hix Auto Parts Inc, 3200 Bluff Rd, 46217; 317-782-3000; **D**
   Prospect Auto Parts, *see Late Vintage*
   Skiles Country Auto Parts, *see Late Vintage*
Kokomo; Warren's Auto Salvage, 1105 Home Av, 46902; 765-452-2775, FAX 765-459-0658, 800-648-7174; CC, Sa, Sp; 3000; **D, PU; B3**
Merrillville; Wild Bill's Auto Parts, 4431 W Lincoln Hwy, 46410; 219-769-5121; **D**
Michigan City; Brinckman's Auto Salvage, *see Late Vintage*
Mishawaka; Scotland Yard Inc, *see Late Vintage*
Monticello; Macowan Cars & Parts, 69 S 300 E, 47960; 219-583-4500, FAX 219-583-7782, 800-289-6975; CC, Sa, Sp, UR; 2000; **D, F, PU; B3**
Noblesville; Bill Shank Auto Parts, *see Vintage*
Osceola; G & N Used Auto Parts, 214 N Chestnut St, 46561; 219-674-8805, FAX 219-674-5730; CC, Sa, Sp, PL; 500; **D, F, PU, 4x4; B3, Jp**
Petersburg; Pike County Auto Recycling, *see Vintage*
Portland; Adams Auto Wrecking, *see Late Vintage*
   Williams Auto Parts, 127 S Detroit Av, 47371; 219-726-8001, FAX 219-726-8015, 800-669-5762; Sa, Sp; 1500; **D, PU; B3**
Richmond; Junction Auto, *see Vintage*
Saint John; Stan's Auto Salvage, *see Late Vintage*
Terre Haute; Mike's Auto Wrecking, *see Late Vintage*
   Southwest Auto Co, *see Late Vintage*
Valpraiso; Archie's Used Auto Parts, 818 N County Rd 360 W, 46383; 219-762-6581, FAX 219-763-0451; Sp; 1000; **D, F, PU, 4x4; B3**
   Metro Auto Parts, *see Vintage*
Washington; Highway 57 Auto Parts, *see Vintage*
West Terre Haute; AAA Auto Parts, 3001 W US Hwy 40, 47885; 812-533-2800; Sa, Br; 300; **D, F, PU; B3**
Whitestown; Wrecks Inc, 7060 S Indianapolis Rd, 46075; 317-769-6111, FAX 317-769-5557, 800-553-1122; CC, Sa, Sp; 60ac; **D, F, PU, 4x4; B3**

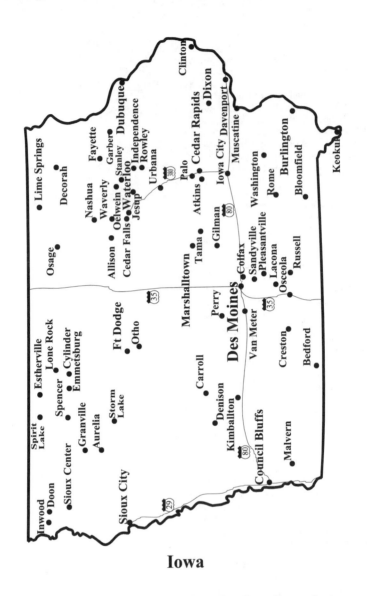

Iowa

Please use the cards in the back to let us
know about yards we may have missed, or
any other comments or information for
future editions of
Ray's wReckingyard Roster

IOWA

VINTAGE

Allison; Ron's Auto Salvage, RR2 Box 54, 50602; 319-267-2871; Sa, Sp, Br; 2000+; **40-90; D, F; B3, AMC, Jp, IH, Ns, Pk, Ks Fr, Wy, VW**

Atkins; Becker's Auto Salvage, Hwy 30 West, 52206; 319-446-7141; CC, Sa, Sp, Br; 10ac; **40+; D, F, PU, 4x4; B3, AMC**

Aurelia; County Line Auto Salvage, 2498 Hwy 7, 51005; 712-434-5923, clauto@webtv.net; Sa, Br; 20ac; **50+; D, F, PU, 4x4, Trk, Fm, In; B3; Spc: Chevy Pickup**

Burlington; Plank Road Salvage, Plank Rd, 52601; 319-752-6504; Sa, Sp; 23ac; **70-89 few 30s-50s; D, PU, 4x4; B3, Jp, Hd, Ns**

Cylinder; Alderson Salvage, 3684 530th Av, 50528; 712-424-3750; Sa, Sp, UR, PL; 200; **40-90; D, F; B3, AMC**

Decorah; Borsheim & Son Auto Salvage, 2612 River Rd, 52101; 319-382-2052; Sa, UR; 250; **47-93; D, F, PU, Fm; B3**

Des Moines; Yaw's Auto Salvage, 919 SE 21, 50317; 515-266-2046, 800-728-2046; Sp; 900; **30+; D, F, PU, 4x4; B3, Jp, St, Pk**

Dubuque; Roger's Auto Sales & Salvage, 3270 Dodge St, 52003; 319-583-9204, FAX 319-583-1468, 800-376-6980; CC, Sa, Sp, Br; 400; **60-96; D, F, PU, 4x4, Cn; B3, AMC, Jp**

Estherville; Dean's Auto Salvage & Repair, 3920 190 St, 51334; 712-362-2116; Sa, UR; 7ac; **20+; D, F, PU, 4x4; B3, IH, Hd; Spc: Model T & Model A Ford**

Fayette; Lau Auto Repair & Salvage, 8979 Kornhill Rd, 52142; 319-425-4546; Sa, UR; 250; **50-89; D, PU, 4x4; B3, Pk, DeSoto**

Fort Dodge; Frank's Auto & Truck Salvage, 3304 Vincent Dr, 50501; 515-955-4477, FAX 515-955-5865; Sa, Sp, UR; 60ac; **30+; D, F, PU, 4x4, Trk; B3, Hd, Ns, St, Pk, Ks, Fr**

    Netlands Auto-Truck Salvage, 1900 Kountry Lane, 50501; 515-576-0441; Sa, Sp; 70ac; **30-60; D, F, PU, 4x4, Trk; B3, AMC, Hd, Ns, St, Pk, VW**

Garber; Sear's Auto Salvage, 35402 Iowa Av, 52048; 319-255-2570; Sa; 1500; **50-90; D, PU, 4x4; B3, St**

Iowa City; Boot Hill Auto Recycling, Hwy 65 N, 50126; 515-648-5432; CC, Sa, Sp, Br; 9ac; **40-88; D, F, PU, 4x4; B3, St**

Keokuk; E & E Auto & Truck Salvage, 2420 Johnson St Rd, 52632; 319-524-3862; Sa, UR; 6ac; **37-92; D, F, PU, 4x4, Trk, Fm; B3, Pk**

Kimballton; D & L Salvage, 2424 1000th St, 51543; 712-773-4462, 800-942-5350; Sa, Sp; 450; **50+, few earlier; D, PU, 4x4, Fm; B3**

Lacona; Jacob's Boneyard, 133 Reagon Dr, 50139; 515-947-2600, 888-293-6533; Sa, Sp, UR; 400+; **40-89; D, PU, 4x4, Trk, Cn; B3, Jp, IH, Buses, Ambulances**

Lone Rock; Monson Salvage, 809 290 St, 50559; 515-925-3587; Sa, Sp, UR; 5ac; 600+; **60-89; D, PU, 4x4; B3**

Osage; Osage Auto Slvg, 121 N 1st, 50461; 515-732-3603; Sa, Sp; 1000; **60-88; D; B3, AMC**

Oto; Lyle's Auto Salvage, 235 1 Av, 51044; 712-827-4556; Sa, Sp, UR; 1100; **60+; D, F, PU, 4x4; B3, AMC, Jp, IH**

Palo; Hayes Slvg, RR 1, 52324; 319-396-5818; Sa, UR; 600; **80+, few 50-70s; D, F, PU, 4x4; B3, Pk**

Pleasantville; Mid State Truck & Auto Salvage, 503 N Hwy 5, 50225; 515-848-3183, FAX 515-848-3432, 800-876-1216; Sa, Sp; 4000+; **90+, few 40-80s; D, PU, 4x4, Trk, Fm; B3, Jp, Hd**

Russell; Pollard Salvage, E Shaw St, 50238; 515-535-6242; Sa, UR; 2000; **60+; D, F, PU, 4x4, Trk; B3, AMC, IH, St, VW**

Spencer; VanderHaag's Inc, 3809 4th Av W, 51301; 712-262-7000, FAX 712-262-7421, 800-831-5164, www.vanderhaags.com; CC, Sa, Sp; 500+; **40-96; D, PU, 4x4, Trk; no cars, trucks only**

Spirit Lake; Hawn's Salvage Co, 24760 165 St, 51360; 712-336-4364; Sa, Sp; 200+; **45-95; D, F, PU, 4x4, Trk; B3, AMC, St**

Stanley; Berry's Salvage Yard, 13038 10th St, 50671; 319-634-3714; Sa, Br; 10ac; **29-89; D, F, PU, 4x4, few Trk, Fm; B3, AMC**

131

Storm Lake; Beckman Salvage, 6458 Hwy 71, 50588; 712-732-3368; Sa; 700; **60-88; D, F, PU; B**3

Urbana; Mid-State Slvg, I-380 Ex 41, 52213; 319-443-2391, FAX 319-443-2391, 800-242-0666; CC, Sa, Sp, Br, PL; 600; **63+; D, F, PU, 4x4, Trk, Fm; B**3**, AMC, Jp, IH, VW**

Washington; Piper Auto Salvage, 2324 Hwy 1 & 92, 52353; 319-653-4312, FAX 319-653-4909, 877-247-9135; CC, Sa, Sp, Br, PL; 500; **60+; D, F, PU, 4x4; B**3

LATE VINTAGE

Allison; Ron's Auto Salvage, *see Vintage*

Atkins; Becker's Auto Salvage, *see Vintage*

Aurelia; County Line Auto Salvage, *see Vintage*

Bedford; Southwest Salvage, 2201 257th St, 50833; 712-523-2729; Sa, UR; 17ac; **70-89; D, F, PU, 4x4; B**3**; Spc: 70-85 Pickup & 4x4**

Burlington; Plank Road Salvage, *see Vintage*

Carroll; Carroll Auto Salvage, 810 E Hwy 30, 51401; 712-792-4136, 800-524-4136; Sa, Sp, Br; 3ac; **70+; D, F, PU, 4x4; B**3

    Quandt Auto Salvage Inc, Hwy 30 W, 51401; 712-792-9204, FAX 712-792-3433, 800-522-1903; CC, Sa, Sp, Br; 52ac; **77+; D, F, PU, 4x4, Trk; B**3**, AMC, Jp, IH, VW**

Cedar Rapids; Denny's Wrecker Svc, 1318 3rd St SE, 52401; 319-364-0365, FAX 319-364-0088; Sa, UR; 35+; **80-89; D, PU; B**3**, AMC**

Clinton; A to Z Auto Salvage, 563 17 Av S, 52732; 319-242-3941; Sa, Sp, Br; 400; **75-96; D, F, PU, 4x4; B**3

Colfax; Batt's Camaro, 808 W State St, 50054; 515-674-4201, FAX 515-674-4355, 800-853-4201; CC, Sa, Sp, Wr; **67-89; D; Camaro only; New and used parts**

Creston; Charlie Brown Used Auto Parts, 1455 Hwy 34, 50801; 515-782-6561, FAX 515-782-7812; Sa, Sp; 7ac, 600; **73+PU, 85+cars; D, PU, 4x4; B**3**, AMC, Jp, IH**

    Hulett & Son Auto Salvage, 103 S Osage St, 50801; 515-782-4807; Sa, Sp, UR; 20ac, 1500; **80-89; D, F, PU, 4x4; B**3**, AMC**

Cylinder; Alderson Salvage, *see Vintage*

Davenport; B & C Auto Wrckr, 2118 W 49th St, 52806; 319-391-2501, FAX 319-391-5152; CC, Sa, UR; 3ac, 350+; **70-91; D, F, PU, 4x4; B**3**, AMC**

    Midwest Auto & Truck Salvage, 5831 S Concord St, 52802; 319-322-3885, 800-666-6621; CC, Sa, Sp, UR; **68+; D, PU; B**3**; Spc: Chevelle**

Decorah; Borsheim & Son Auto Salvage, *see Vintage*

Denison; Rath Salvage, 2574 Hwy 59, 51442; 712-263-6220, tooter@pionet.net; Sp; 450; **78+; D, PU, 4x4; GM, Ford only**

Des Moines; Carroll Auto Wrecking, 1610 Scott Av, 50317; 515-288-2244, FAX 515-288-1409, 800-532-1233; CC, Sa, Sp, PL; 60ac; **80+; D, F, PU, 4x4; B**3

    Dean's Trails End Auto Salvage, 1600 NE 44th Av, 50313; 515-265-5696, 800-717-6505; Sa, Sp, UR; 1600; **79-89; D, F, PU, 4x4, Trk; B**3**, AMC, Jp, IH, VW**

    Sunset Beach Auto Salvage, 1111 SE 30th St, 50317; 515-266-5201, 800-383-5201; CC, Sa, Sp; 2000; **80-95; D, F, PU, 4x4, Trk; B**3**, AMC, VW**

    Swift Auto Parts, 1720 E Washington Av, 50316; 515-262-8860, 800-627-8788; CC, Sa, Sp; 1000; **80+; D, F, PU, 4x4, Trk; B**3**, AMC, Jp, IH**

    Yaw's Auto Salvage, *see Vintage*

Dixon; Koester's Wrck, 7990 Buena Vista Rd, 52745; 319-843-2373; **70-89; D, F, PU; B**3

Dubuque; North End Wrecking Inc, 55 West 32nd St, 52001; 319-556-0044, FAX 319-556-5097, 888-545-8885; CC, Sp, Br; 1200+; **80+, few 70s PU; D, F, PU, 4x4; B**3

    Roger's Auto Sales & Salvage, *see Vintage*

Emmetsburg; Wickman Auto Salvage, Airport Rd, 50536; 712-852-2392; Sa, Sp, UR; 400; **69-96; D, PU, 4x4, Trk; B**3**, AMC**

Estherville; Dean's Auto Salvage & Repair, *see Vintage*

Fayette; Lau Auto Repair & Salvage, *see Vintage*

Fort Dodge; Frank's Auto & Truck Salvage, *see Vintage*

Garber; Sear's Auto Salvage, *see Vintage*

Gilman; Barker Enterprises, 121 S Mill, 50106; 515-498-2184; CC, Sa, Sp; 250; **70-90; D, F, PU, 4x4; B**3**, AMC, Jp, IH**

Granville; Terry's Auto Parts, Box 105, 51022; 712-727-3273; Sa, Sp, Br; 350+; **65+; D, PU, 4x4; B**3**, AMC**

Independence; West Edge Auto Salvage, Hwy 20 W, 50644; 319-334-2048, FAX 319-334-6768, 888-484-9344; CC, Sa, Sp, PL; 12ac; **70+; D, F, PU, 4x4; B**3**; Spc: Pickup**

Inwood; G & T Auto Salvage, 1446 US 18 St, 51240; 712-753-4841; Sa; 400+; **70-90, few 50-60s; D; B**3

Iowa City; Boot Hill Auto Recycling, *see Vintage*

Jesup; Clayton Auto Salvage, 1270 Clayton Blvd, 50648; 319-827-6155; Sa, Br; 250; **80+; D, F, PU, 4x4; B**3

Keokuk; E & E Auto & Truck Salvage, *see Vintage*

 Rairden's Auto Salvage, 3944 S 7, 52632; 319-524-3721, FAX 319-524-3764; CC, Sa; 750+; **70-95; D, F, PU, 4x4; B**3**, AMC**

Kimballton; D & L Salvage, *see Vintage*

Lacona; Jacob's Boneyard, *see Vintage*

Lime Springs; Quam Auto Svc & Salvage, 17375 Hwy 9, 52155; 319-547-5318, FAX 319-547-6981; CC, Sa, Sp, Br; 400; **70-89; D, PU, 4x4, Trk; B**3

Lone Rock; Monson Salvage, *see Vintage*

Marshalltown; Barry's Auto Parts & Salvage, 2001 E Church, 50158; 515-752-4344, 800-383-2716; CC, Sa, Sp; 1500+; **75-85; D, F, PU; B**3

Muscatine; Island Auto Salvage, 2385 57th St, 52761; 319-264-3899, FAX 319-262-3795; CC, Sa, Sp, Br; 20ac, 1000; **80-95; D, F, PU, 4x4; B**3**, AMC, Jp, IH, VW**

Nashua; Wilken Auto Wrecking, 1157 275th St, 50658; 515-435-4077, FAX 515-435-2515, 888-435-8222; Sa, Sp; 23ac, 3000; **70+; D, F, PU, 4x4, Fm; B**3**, AMC, Jp**

Oelwein; Key's Motor Company Salvage, 1440 S Frederick Av, 50662; 319-283-3500, 800-543-JUNK IA, MN, WI, IL only; CC, Sa, Sp; 250; **80+; D, PU; B**3

Osage; Osage Auto Salvage, *see Vintage*

Oto; Lyle's Auto Salvage, *see Vintage*

Palo; Hayes Salvage, *see Vintage*

Perry; Billy's Sales & Salvage, 1425-1/2 W 9 St, 50220; 515-465-2573; Sa, Sp, Br; 5ac; **70+; D, F, PU, 4x4; B**3

Pleasantville; Mid State Truck & Auto Salvage, *see Vintage*

Rome; Pulse Auto Salvage, RR 3, 52641; 319-986-6323, 800-292-0095; Sp; **80+; D, PU, 4x4; B**3**, AMC, Jp**

Rowley; Olsen's Auto Salvage, 2730 Coots Blvd, 52329; 319-938-2292, FAX 319-938-2626; swordehoff@sbtek.net; Sa, Sp; 600; **80-89; D, PU, 4x4; B**3

Russell; Pollard Salvage, *see Vintage*

Sandyville; Phillips Jim Auto Salvage, 6634 Union St, 50001; 515-961-3871; Sa; 1ac; **70+; D, F, PU, 4x4; B**3

Sioux Center; B & B Salvage, 298 7 St NW, 51250; 712-722-1731, FAX 712-722-1733, 800-395-9219; CC, Sa, Sp; 8.5ac; **80+; D, PU, 4x4; B**3

Sioux City; Meiers Auto Salvage, 5400 N US Hwy 75, 51108; 712-239-1344, FAX 712-239-5141, 800-944-1344; CC, Sa, Sp, Br; 1000; **70-90, few earlier; D, F, PU, 4x4, Trk; B**3**, AMC, Jp, IH, VW**

Spencer; VanderHaag's Inc, *see Vintage*

Spirit Lake; Hawn's Salvage Co, *see Vintage*

Stanley; Berry's Salvage Yard, *see Vintage*

Storm Lake; Beckman Salvage, *see Vintage*

Tama; Bennett's Salvage, 2369 360th St, 52339; 515-484-3613; Sa, UR; 100; **70-89; D, F, PU, 4x4; B**3

 Sand Hill Auto Salvage, 1981 Hwy E64, 52339; 515-484-2057, FAX 515-484-5555, 800-542-7880; Sa, Sp; 2000; **70+; D, F, PU, 4x4; B**3**, Jp, IH, VW**

Urbana; Mid-State Salvage, *see Vintage*

Van Meter; Hawkeye Auto Salvage, 3638 N Av, 50261; 515-834-2436, 800-362-1654; CC, Sa, Sp; 35ac, 300+; **70+; D, F, PU, 4x4; B**3

Washington; Piper Auto Salvage, *see Vintage*

Waterloo; Northside Auto Salvage, 821 Dearborn Av, 50703; 319-234-1595; 100; **80+; D; B**3
  Quail's Auto Salvage, 202 Glendale St, 50703; 319-234-7715; Sa, UR, Wr; 1ac, 50; **70-89; D; B**3
  Waterloo Auto Parts Inc, 1501 Grandview Av, 50703; 319-234-5207; CC, Sa, Sp, Br; 3000; **82+; D, F, PU, 4x4; B3, AMC, Jp, VW**
  Wilber Auto Salvage, 2220-1/2 Easton Av, 50702; 319-232-1747, 800-747-7048; Sa, Sp; 900+; **80+; D; B**3

LATE MODEL

Atkins; Becker's Auto Salvage, *see Vintage*
Aurelia; County Line Auto Salvage, *see Vintage*
Bloomfield; Pipers Auto Svc, Route 1, 52537; 515-664-1840; CC, Sa, Sp; 25ac, 7000; **D, PU, 4x4, Trk; GM only**
  Piper Auto Salvage, PO Box 37, 52537; 515-664-1820, FAX 515-664-1822, 800-247-9135; CC, Sa, Sp, Br; 5ac; **D, F, PU, 4x4; B**3
Carroll; Carroll Auto Salvage, *see Late Vintage*
  Quandt Auto Salvage Inc, *see Late Vintage*
Cedar Falls; Aikey Auto Salvage, 1524 Independence Av, 50613; 319-266-4763, FAX 319-266-8578, 800-722-4763; CC, Sa, Sp, UR; 11ac; **D, F, PU, 4x4; B**3
Clinton; A to Z Auto Salvage, *see Late Vintage*
Council Bluffs; Action Truck Parts, 1021 S 17th St, 51501; 712-322-4029; Sa, Sp; 100; **D, PU; B3; Pickup only**
  Hi-Way 92 Salvage, 3629 Richland Dr, 51501; 712-366-2281, 800-286-3281 W IA & E NE only; Sa, Sp; 300; **D; GM only**
  Vehicular Resource Recovery, 1304 S 16th St, 51501; 712-328-9475; Sa, Sp; 800; **F; VW**
Creston; Charlie Brown Used Auto Parts, *see Late Vintage*
Davenport; Hickory Grove Auto Parts, 3300 Hickory Grove Rd, 52806; 319-386-3311; CC, Sa, UR; 1000; **D, F, PU, 4x4**
  Midwest Auto & Truck Salvage, *see Late Vintage*
Denison; Rath Salvage, *see Late Vintage*
Des Moines; Carroll Auto Wrecking, *see Late Vintage*
  Don's Auto & Truck Slvg, 1500 SE 30 St, 50317; 515-262-8283, FAX 515-262-8283, 800-372-6000, www.donsautotruck.com; CC, Sa, Sp; 33ac; **D, F, PU, 4x4, Trk, Fm, In, Cn; B**3
  R & R Auto Crushing, 2208 Maury, 50317; 515-265-5903; Sa; 200; **D, F**
Sam's Riverside Auto Salvage, 3900 Vandalia Rd, 50317; 515-265-8792, FAX 515-265-3927, 800-383-2163; CC, Sa, Sp; 40ac; **D, F, PU, 4x4, Trk; B3; Sales Sunday** 1-5
  Sunset Beach Auto Salvage, *see Late Vintage*
  Swift Auto Parts, *see Late Vintage*
  Yaw's Auto Salvage, *see Vintage*
Doon; Lem's Auto Recyclers, 402 Gere Av, 51235; 712-726-3202, 800-257-9634, www.lemsauto.com; CC, Sa, Sp, UR; 2000; **D, F, PU, 4x4; B**3
Dubuque; North End Wrecking Inc, *see Late Vintage*
  Roger's Auto Sales & Salvage, *see Vintage*
Emmetsburg; Wickman Auto Salvage, *see Late Vintage*
Estherville; Dean's Auto Salvage & Repair, *see Vintage*
Fort Dodge; Frank's Auto & Truck Salvage, *see Vintage*
  Ron's Auto Parts, 1803 19th Ave S, 50501; 515-573-5904, FAX 515-576-3308; Sa; **D, PU, 4x4, Trk, Fm; B3, AMC**
Granville; Terry's Auto Parts, *see Late Vintage*
Independence; West Edge Auto Salvage, *see Late Vintage*
Iowa City; Ace Auto Recyclers, 2752 S Riverside Dr, 52246; 319-338-7828, FAX 319-337-3234, 800-223-2886; Sp; 1000+; **D, F, PU, 4x4; B**3
Jesup; Clayton Auto Salvage, *see Late Vintage*
Keokuk; E & E Auto & Truck Salvage, *see Vintage*
  Rairden's Auto Salvage, *see Late Vintage*
Kimballton; D & L Salvage, *see Vintage*

Malvern; Malvern Body & Salvage, 1308 Main, 51551; 712-624-8459, FAX 712-624-8109, 800-432-9244; CC, Sp, Wr; 500+; **D, PU, 4x4; B**3
Muscatine; Island Auto Salvage, *see Late Vintage*
  Muscatine Used Parts, 2407 Industrial Connector, 52761; 319-263-3821, FAX 319-263-6746, 800-397-2787; CC, Sp; 1500; **D, F, PU, 4x4; B**3**, VW**
Nashua; Wilken Auto Wrecking, *see Late Vintage*
Oelwein; Key's Motor Company Salvage, *see Late Vintage*
Osceola; East Side Auto Recyclers, 714 E McLane St, 50213; 515-342-4833, 800-775-7381; CC, Sa; 400; **D, PU, 4x4, Trk; B**3**, AMC, Jp, IH**
Oto; Lyle's Auto Salvage, *see Late Vintage*
Palo; Hayes Salvage, *see Vintage*
Perry; Billy's Sales & Salvage, *see Late Vintage*
Pleasantville; Mid State Truck & Auto Salvage, *see Vintage*
Rome; Pulse Auto Salvage, *see Late Vintage*
Russell; Pollard Salvage, *see Vintage*
Sandyville; Phillips Jim Auto Salvage, *see Late Vintage*
Sioux Center; B & B Salvage, *see Late Vintage*
Spencer; Hurst Salvage, 4019 4 Av W, 51301; 712-262-3011, 800-286-3011; Sa, Sp, UR; 2000+; **D, F, PU, 4x4, Trk, Fm; B**3
  VanderHaag's Inc, *see Vintage*
Spirit Lake; Hawn's Salvage Co, *see Vintage*
Tama; Sand Hill Auto Salvage, *see Late Vintage*
Urbana; Mid-State Salvage, *see Vintage*
Van Meter; Hawkeye Auto Salvage, *see Late Vintage*
Washington; Piper Auto Salvage, *see Vintage*
Waterloo; Chase Auto Parts Co, 1041 Sheffield Av, 50702; 319-234-2445, FAX 319-234-1977, 800-728-2568; CC, Sa, Sp; 10ac; **89+, few earlier; D, F, PU, 4x4; B**3**, AMC, Jp, IH, VW**
  Northside Auto Salvage, *see Late Vintage*
  Waterloo Auto Parts Inc, *see Late Vintage*
  Wilber Auto Salvage, *see Late Vintage*
Waverly; Walker's Auto Salvage, 2220 4th St SW, 50677; 319-352-2535, FAX 319-352-3105, 800-772-2088; CC, Sa, Sp; 500; **D, F, PU, 4x4; B**3

Never stand on cars. Dents ruin salable body parts & greatly increase the risk of getting hurt.

Yard Operators Tell us...

135

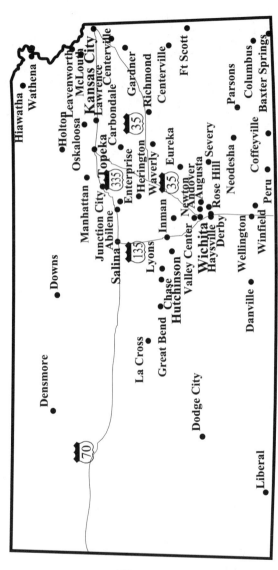

Kansas

Please mention you saw'em in Ray's wReckingyard Roster when contacting these yards

KANSAS

Baxter Springs; CRS Garage & Wrecker Svc, 66713; 316-856-3368; CC, Sa, Sp; 400; **28+; D, few F; B3; Ford Model A**

Carbondale; Weekleys Auto Slvg, 66414; 785-836-7375; Sa, Sp; 1000; **50+, few 90s; D; B3, Edsel**

Centerville; Morse's Auto Salvage & Tow Svc, RR 1 Box 121, 66014; 913-898-4455, FAX 913-898-2685; Sa, Sp, PL; 1000; **50+; D, F, PU, 4x4; B3, AMC, Jp, IH, VW**

Chase; Patterson's Auto Salvage, 758 US Hwy 56, 67524; 316-938-2557; Sa; 10ac; **39-86; D, F, PU; B3, AMC, St, VW; Spc: Corvair; Open Sunday**

Coffeyville; Purkey's Auto Salvage, RR 1 Box 303, 67337; 316-251-5200; Sa, Sp; 60ac; **50+; D, F, PU, 4x4; B3, AMC, Jp, IH, Hd, Ns, St, Pk, VW**

Columbus; Larison's Classics, 66725; 316-674-8449, 800-539-8449; Sa, Sp, Br; 450; **50-75; D, F, PU; B3, Hd, Ns, Other Independents**

Danville; Bob Lent Motor Shop, PO Box 87, 101 Main, 67036; 316-962-5247; Sa, Sp, Wr; **70 D, PU, Fm; B3, St; Spoke Wheels, many loose parts, Ford Model A & T**

Densmore; Keiswetter Brothers Salvage, HC 63 Box 157, 67645; 785-622-4298; Sa; 450+; **60-85; D, F, PU, 4x4; B3, AMC**

Dodge City; Stapleton Salvage, 11525 Lariat Way, 67801; 316-225-5557; 16ac, 5000; **40-85; D, PU, 4x4; B3, AMC, Hd, Ns, St, Pk, Ks, Fr**

Downs; Sumpter Farm Salvage, 541 W 47th Dr, 67437; 785-454-3858, sumpfarmsalv. nckcn.com; Sa, Sp; **60+; D, PU, 4x4, Trk; B3; Spc: Pickup & 4x4; Front wheel drive GM**

Enterprise; Enterprise Auto Salvage, 901 S Bluff St, 67441; 785-263-8573, 800-466-8573; CC, Sp, PL; 600; **30-79; D, F, PU, Mil; B3, AMC, Hd; Spc: 70s Buick**

Fort Scott; Bolin & Sons Auto Salvage, RR 3 Box 394, 66701; 316-223-3193; Sa; 250+; **65-85; D, F; B3, AMC, VW**

Great Bend; Two Eighty One Auto Salvage, 5 1/2 Mile N GRT BND Hwy 281, 67530; 316-793-8469, FAX 316-793-7791, 800-282-9017; Sa, Sp; 1000; **39+; D, F, PU, 4x4; B3, AMC, Jp, IH, VW**

Herington; B C Salvage, 424 S 5th St, 67449; 785-258-2899; CC, Sa, Sp; 900; **60+; D, PU, 4x4, Trk; B3, AMC, Jp**

Holton; Robinsons Auto Salvage, 600 Illinois Av, 66436; 785-364-2161; Sp; 19ac; **70-80s, few 50-60s; D, F, PU, 4x4, few Trk; B3**

Hutchinson; Pifer's Auto Salvage, 6809 E 17th Av, 67501; 316-662-8564; Sa; **56-89; D, PU; B3, AMC**

Inman; Jim's Auto Sales, Rt 2, 67546; 316-585-6648; Sa, Sp, Br; 250+; **30-79; D; B3, St; Open Sunday by appointment**

Junction City; Easy Jack & Sons Antique Auto, 2725 S Milford Lake Rd, 66441; 785-238-7161 or 238-7541; CC, Sa, Sp; 35ac, 2500; **00-85; D, F, PU, 4x4; B3, Hd, Ns, St, Pk, Ks, Cr, Whippet, Franklin, Graham, Ford Model T**

   McDonald Auto Sales & Salvage, 305 Hoover Rd, 66441; 785-238-2583; Sa; 200; **60+; D, F, PU; B3; Open Sun; Some older; Spc: Edsel**

Kansas City; Muncie Auto Salvage Inc, 6345 Kansas Av, 66111; 913-287-6185; Sa, Br; 12ac; **48-89, few 90s; D, F, PU, 4x4; B3, Pk**

   Thibodo Auto Salvage, 941 S 26th St, 66106; 913-281-1843; CC, Sa, Sp; 200; **60+; D, F, PU, 4x4, Trk; B3, AMC, Jp, IH, VW; Open Sun**

Leavenworth; Wiley's Auto Salvage, 16779 Michals Rd, 66048; 913-682-7600; Sa, Sp; **50+; D, F, PU; B3**

Liberal; Crosby's Salvage, RR 2, 67908; 316-624-5306; Sa, Sp; **60-80; D, F, 4x4; B3, AMC**

   Friesen Salvage One, Salvage Rd, 67901; 316-624-2388; Sa, Sp; 5ac; **50+, few prewar; D, F, PU, Fm; B3, AMC, St, Ks, VW, motorcycles; Some whole cars**

McLouth; Edmonds Old Car Parts, PO Box 303, 66054; 913-796-6529; Sa, Sp, Br; **50+; 28-66; D, PU; Chevy only; mescil parts**

Oskaloosa; Robbins Salvage & Used Cars, Hwy 16-92 E, 66066; 785-863-2216; CC, Sa; 850; **50+; D, F, PU; B3, AMC, VW**

Peru; Peru Auto Wrecking, 817 S Merchant St, 67360; 316-725-5287; Sa, Sp; 400; **25-75; D, PU; B3, Ns**

137

Richmond; T T & T Auto & Truck Salvage, 2937 Allen Ter, 66080; 785-835-6284, FAX 785-835-6678, 800-748-7625; CC, Sa, Sp; 8ac, 1000; **75-90; D, PU, 4x4; B**3**; Spc: Corvair**

Salina; Charlie Heath West 40 Salvage, 2600 W Old Hwy 40, 67401; 785-823-8919; Sa, Sp; 400; **40-90; D, F, PU, 4x4, Trk, Fm, Mil; B**3**, AMC, Jp, IH, VW**

Topeka; Massey & Son Auto & Truck Slvg, 1628 NW Gordon, 66608; 785-232-5708; Sa; 17ac, 3000; **60-89; D, F, PU, 4x4; B**3**, AMC, Jp, IH, VW**

   Northland Auto Salvage, 5249 NW Topeka Blvd, 66617; 785-246-1866; Sa, Sp; 650; **60-89; D, PU, 4x4; B**3**, AMC, Jp, IH**

Valley Center; Les Truck & Salvage, 8217 N Broadway St, 67147; 316-755-1784, 800-817-1784; Sp; 100; **60-89; D, PU; B**3**; Some older, 40 years in business**

   Watkins Auto Salvage Inc, 8127 N Broadway St, 67147; 316-755-1216; CC, Sa; 2000; **50+; D, PU, 4x4, Trk; B**3**, Hd, Ns, Edsel**

Wathena; Schuster Auto Wrecking, 406 Benton Byp 31, 66090; 913-989-4719; Sa, Sp, Br; 38-82; **D, PU; B**3**; Spc: Ford & Chevy Pickup**

Waverly; Terry's Auto Sales & Salvage, 66871; 785-733-2231; Sa, Sp; 100; **D, F; B**3**, VW, DeSoto**

Wellington; Wellington Auto Salvage, 2001 E 20th St S, 67152; 316-326-8022, 800-871-8022; CC, Sp, Br, PL; 400; **50+; D, PU; B**3

Wichita; B & W Auto Salvage, 2540 S West St, 67217; 316-942-3727; Sa; 200; **D; B**3

   Kruse Parts & Salvage, 3501 S Broadway St, 67216; 316-522-2251; CC, Sa; 10ac, 1000; **80s, few 60-70s; D, PU; B**3**, AMC; Spc: Ford**

   Northwest Auto Salvage, 3059 N Hoover Rd, 67205; 316-942-8366 , FAX 316-942-7107, 800-491-6529; CC, Sa, Sp, PL; 700+; **60+; D, F, PU, 4x4; B**3**, AMC, Jp, IH, VW**

LATE VINTAGE

Abilene; Picking & Goodwin Auto Salvage, 626 2300 Av, 67410; 785-263-2403; Sa; 400+; **79-89; D, F, PU, 4x4; B**3**, Jp**

   Sutton Auto Salvage, 206 S Washington St, 67410; 785-263-2672; Sa; 300; **69-89; D, PU, 4x4; B**3**, AMC, IH**

Andover; Charlie's Truck Salvage, 517 W Hwy 54, 67002; 316-733-1317, FAX 316-733-9806, 888-733-2171; CC, Sp, Br; 1000; **D, F, PU, 4x4, Trk; B**3**; Trucks only**

Baxter Springs; CRS Garage & Wrecker Svc, *see Vintage*

Carbondale; Weekleys Auto Salvage, *see Vintage*

Centerville; Morse's Auto Salvage & Tow Svc, *see Vintage*

Chase; Patterson's Auto Salvage, *see Vintage*

Coffeyville; Purkey's Auto Salvage, *see Vintage*

Columbus; Larison's Classics, *see Vintage, see Vintage*

Densmore; Keiswetter Brothers Salvage, *see Vintage*

Derby; Access Imports, 5025 S 143rd St E, 67037; 316-733-1561; Sa, Sp; 2ac, 130+; **75-89; F, PU; mostly Jpa**

Dodge City; Dodge City Salvage, 1402 Minneola Rd, 67801; 316-227-8606, 800-955-8733; CC, Sa, Sp; 5.5ac; 70+; D, PU, 4x4; B3

   Stapleton Salvage, *see Vintage*

Downs; Sumpter Farm Salvage, *see Vintage*

Enterprise; Enterprise Auto Salvage, *see Vintage*

Eureka; Eureka Auto Salvage & Sales, PO Box 525, E Hwy 54, 67045; 316-583-5959; Sp; 300; **78+; D, PU, 4x4; B**3**, AMC**

Fort Scott; Bolin & Sons Auto Salvage, *see Vintage*

   Nevada Used Auto Parts & Cars, 66701; 316-223-4275, 417-667-7050, 800-201-7050; CC, Sa; 500+; **80+; D, PU, 4x4; B**3**; Yard is just across border in Nevada, MO**

Gardner; Cowden Used Car & Salvage, 32055 W Hwy 56, 66030; 913-884-8879; Sa; 4ac; **70-89; D, F, PU; B**3**, AMC**

Great Bend; Two Eighty One Auto Salvage, *see Vintage*

Herington; B C Salvage, *see Vintage*

Hiawatha; Roy Spicer's Used Cars & Salvage, 1010 Miami St, 66434; 785-742-3677; Sa; 250+; **70-89; D, F, PU, 4x4; B**3**, AMC, IH, VW; Spc: GM**

Holton; Robinsons Auto Salvage, *see Vintage*

138

Hutchinson; Doc's Auto Salvage, 914 N Chemical St, 67501; 316-665-7244; Sa; 300; **65-92; D, PU; B**3

Gary's Auto & Truck Salvage, 520 E. Osborne St, 67501; 316-662-3029; SA; 400; **70-90; D, PU; B**3

J D's Auto Salvage, 510 N Poplar St, 67505; 316-665-5527, 800-371-5527; CC, Sp, PL; 750; **80+; D, F, PU; B**3

Pifer's Auto Salvage, *see Vintage*

Inman; Jim's Auto Sales, *see Vintage*

Junction City; Easy Jack & Sons Antique Auto, *see Vintage*

McDonald Auto Sales & Salvage, *see Vintage*

Kansas City; B & H Auto Salvage, 769 S 26th St, 66106; 913-321-3994; Sa; 3ac, 300; **78-93; D, PU, 4x4, Trk; B**3**, few AMC; Tail lights & glass from older cars; Spc: Ford & GM**

Bud's Auto Wrecking, 1000 S 26th St, 66106; 913-321-5771; Sa; 100+; **70+; D, F, PU; B**3**, AMC, IH; Foreign mostly Japanese, few European**

Crumby Auto Salvage & Hauling, 901 Cheyenne Ave, 66105; 913-321-3602, FAX 913-321-5490; CC, Sa; 2500; **67-91; D, F, PU, Trk; B**3**, AMC, Jp, IH**

Gard's Yard, 800 S 26th St, 66106; 913-621-1709; Sa, Sp; 0.5ac; **79-89; D, F, 4x4; B**3

Griffith Foreign Car Salvage, 1025 S 11th St, 66105; 913-342-0602; CC, Sp; 100; **70-90; F; VW, Spc: Volvo 240**

Muncie Auto Salvage Inc, *see Vintage*

South Valley Auto Salvage, 529 S Valley St, 66105; 913-281-3836; Sa; 500+; **69-85; D, Trk; B**3

Thibodo Auto Salvage, *see Vintage*

La Crosse; R K Svc Salvage & Towing, N Hwy 183, 67548; 785-222-3322, 800-352-4812 KS only; Sa, Sp; 140; **77-88; D, PU, 4x4; B**3

Lawrence; 19th Street Auto Recyclers, 2005 E 19th St, 66046; 785-842-1480, FAX 785-842-8176, 800-888-1480; CC, Sa, Sp; 1200; **80+; D, PU; B**3**, AMC**

Mid-America Auto Recycling, 2001 E 19th St, 66046; 785-842-5300, FAX 785-842-0668, 800-289-5300; CC, Sp, PL; 1000; **80+; D, F, PU, 4x4; B**3**; Spc: Mustang, Camaro, pullout motors**

Leavenworth; Lake's Auto Salvage, 235 Marion St, 66048; 913-682-3191; Sa, PL; 350+; **83-93; D, F, PU, 4x4; B**3

Wiley's Auto Salvage, *see Vintage*

Liberal; Crosby's Salvage, *see Vintage*

Friesen Salvage One, *see Vintage*

Sam's Salvage & Sandblasting, RR 2 Box 430, 67901; 316-624-0443, 800-491-0443; Sa; 650; **D; B**3**, AMC**

Neodesha; 75 Auto Salvage & Body Shop, RR 2 Box 178, 66757; 316-325-5281; CC, Sa, Sp; 700+; **68-92; D, F, PU, 4x4, Trk; B**3**, AMC, Jp, IH, VW**

Newton; Partridge Auto Supply, 613 N Meridian Rd, 67114; 316-283-1588, FAX 316-283-1599, 800-303-3373; CC, Sa, Sp; 350+; **D; B**3

Oskaloosa; Robbins Salvage & Used Cars, *see Vintage*

Peru; Peru Auto Wrecking, *see Vintage*

Richmond; T T & T Auto & Truck Salvage, *see Vintage*

Rose Hill; Diehl Salvage, 6141 S 159th St E, 67133; 316-776-2534; Sa; **79+; F, PU, 4x4; Toyota Pickup only**

Salina; Central Kansas Salvage, 2303 W Old Hwy 40, 67401; 785-827-5801; Sa, Sp, Br; 3.5ac, 500; **70-89, few 50-60s; D, F, PU, 4x4, Trk; B**3**, Wy, VW**

Charlie Heath West 40 Salvage, *see Vintage*

Fuller's Auto & Truck Recycling, 501 E Pacific Ave, 67401; 785-825-0234, FAX 785-825-1814, 800-848-5068; CC, Sp; 7ac; **83+; D, F, PU, 4x4; B**3

Severy; Severy Auto Salvage, W Hwy 96, 67137; 316-736-2900, 800-362-0062; Sp; 550+; **79+; D, F, PU, 4x4; B**3**, Jp, IH; Spc: Pickup, 4x4**

Topeka; M & M Auto & Salvage, 841 NW Tyler St, 66608; 785-233-7719, FAX 785-232-1267, 800-748-7117; CC, Sa, Sp; 500; **77+; D, F, PU; B**3**, VW**

Massey & Son Auto & Truck Slvg, *see Vintage*

Northland Auto Salvage, *see Vintage*

Valley Center; Broadway Auto Slvg, 8159 N Broadway St, 67147; 316-755-1127, FAX 316-755-3797, 800-947-0994; CC, Sa, Sp; 500+; **80-93; D, F, PU, 4x4, Trk; B3, AMC, Jp, VW**

Les Truck & Salvage, *see Vintage*

Watkins Auto Salvage Inc, *see Vintage*

Wathena; Schuster Auto Wrecking, *see Vintage*

Waverly; Terry's Auto Sales & Salvage, *see Vintage*

Wellington; Wellington Auto Salvage, *see Vintage*

Wichita; A & K & R Salvage, 420 E 20th St N, 67214; 316-262-4006, akr@wichita.fn.net; Sa, Sp; 450+; **78-92; D, F, PU, 4x4, Trk; B3, VW, Jpa**

B & W Auto Salvage, *see Vintage*

Beckel Imports Auto Salvage, 5963 N Broadway St, 67219; 316-744-0489, 888-755-5539; CC, Sa, Sp; 700; **D, F, PU, 4x4, Trk; B3**

Big Jakes Truck & Auto Salvage, 1855 E 68th St S, 67233; 316-524-3800; Sa, Sp; 2ac; **80-89; D, F, PU, 4x4; B3, AMC, Jp, IH, VW**

Chrisman's Auto Salvage, 3703 Maple St, 67216; 316-943-8231; CC, Sp; 500; **70-90; D, F, PU, 4x4; B3, AMC, Jp, IH, VW**

D C Auto Salvage, 3246 S Broadway St, 67216; 316-529-2366, 800-264-8766; CC, Sp, Br; 400; **80-95; D, PU; Spc: Mini Trucks & Vans**

Instant Auto & Truck Salvage, 421 E 20th St N, 67214; 316-262-0468, 800-884-6055; Sa, Sp, PL; **66-90; D, F, PU; B3**

Kruse Parts & Salvage, *see Vintage*

Marshall Auto Salvage, 2536 S West St, 67217; 316-943-9221; Sa; 2ac; 70-86; **D; B3, AMC; Open Sunday, Closed Monday**

Northwest Auto Salvage, *see Vintage*

Southwest Salvage, 2756 S West St, 67217; 316-942-2031, FAX 316-942-2834; Sa; 1000; **70-89, few older; D, F, PU; B3; Also: Truck Shop, Tire Recycle, Trash service**

Winfield; Winfield Auto Recycling, 311 Manning St, 67156; 316-221-2995; Sa; 200; **70-89; D, PU; B3**

LATE MODEL

Andover; Charlie's Truck Salvage, *see Late Vintage*

Augusta; Augusta Auto Salvage, PO Box 249, 1604 Custer Ln, 67010; 316-775-1113, FAX 316-775-7949, 800-333-0951; CC, Sp, Br; 7.5ac, 750+; **D, PU, 4x4; B3, AMC, Jp**

Baxter Springs; CRS Garage & Wrecker Svc, *see Vintage*

Carbondale; Weekleys Auto Salvage, *see Vintage*

Centerville; Morse's Auto Salvage & Tow Svc, *see Vintage*

Coffeyville; Purkey's Auto Salvage, *see Vintage*

Dodge City; Dodge City Salvage, *see Late Vintage*

Mid-West Salvage, 1000 Minneola Rd, 67801; 316-225-2222, FAX 316-225-4537, 800-825-0234; CC, Sa, Sp; **D, F, PU, 4x4; B3, Spc: Toyota**

Downs; Sumpter Farm Salvage, *see Vintage*

Eureka; Eureka Auto Salvage & Sales, *see Late Vintage*

Fort Scott; Nevada Used Auto Parts & Cars, *see Late Vintage*

Great Bend; Nobody's Auto Recycling, 332 N US Hwy 281, 67530; 316-793-3557; CC, Sp; 2500; **D, F, PU, 4x4; B3, Spc: Mercedes**

Two Eighty One Auto Salvage, *see Vintage*

Haysville; A-One Auto Salvage, 7335 S Broadway St, 67060; 316-524-3273, FAX 316-524-2566, 800-342-9921; CC, Sa, Sp; 800; **D, F, PU, 4x4, Trk; B3, AMC, Jp**

Herington; B C Salvage, *see Vintage*

Hutchinson; Doc's Auto Salvage, *see Late Vintage*

J D's Auto Salvage, *see Late Vintage*

Junction City; Hess & Son's Salvage, 1209 Perry St, 66441; 785-238-3382, FAX 785-238-6809, 800-825-4377; Sa, Sp; 800+; **D, F, PU, 4x4, Trk; B3, Jp; Spc: 4x4**

McDonald Auto Sales & Salvage, *see Vintage*

Kansas City; Alamo Auto Salvage, 451 S 14th St, 66105; 913-371-5941; 15; **D, PU; Ford & Chevy trucks only**

140

B & H Auto Salvage, *see Late Vintage*

Bud's Auto Wrecking, *see Late Vintage*

Gross Auto Salvage, 705 S 26th St, 66106; 913-371-5008; Wr; **D; Chrysler only**

JGs Auto Wrecking, 1128 Pawnee Av, 66105; 913-321-2716; Sa, Br; 120; **D, PU, 4x4; B3**

Muncie Auto Salvage Inc, *see Vintage*

Thibodo Auto Salvage, *see Vintage*

Lawrence; 19th Street Auto Recyclers, *see Late Vintage*

Mid-America Auto Recycling, *see Late Vintage*

Leavenworth; Lake's Auto Salvage, *see Late Vintage*

Wiley's Auto Salvage, *see Vintage*

Liberal; Friesen Salvage One, *see Vintage*

Lyons; D M Auto Sales & Salvage, 709 N Grand Ave, 67554; 316-257-2151, FAX 316-257-3665, 800-215-4817; Sa, Sp; 400; **D, PU, 4x4; B3**

Manhattan; Superior Salvage, 2801 W 56th Av, 66502; 785-539-9511, FAX 785-539-1276; CC, Sa, Sp; 7ac; **D, F, PU, 4x4, Trk; B3, Buses**

Neodesha; 75 Auto Salvage & Body Shop, *see Late Vintage*

Oskaloosa; Al's 4x4 Salvage, 9081 Wellman Rd, 66066; 785-863-2814, 800-657-2880; Sa; **D, PU, 4x4 only**

Robbins Salvage & Used Cars, *see Vintage*

Parsons; Parsons Auto Salvage, 1780 US Hwy 160, 67357; 316-421-3110, FAX 316-421-9095; CC, Sa, Sp; 500; **D, PU, 4x4; B3**

Rose Hill; Diehl Salvage, *see Late Vintage*

Salina; Fuller's Auto & Truck Recycling, *see Late Vintage*

Severy; Severy Auto Salvage, *see Late Vintage*

Topeka; M & M Auto & Salvage, *see Late Vintage*

Topeka; Mid-America Import Salvage, 5725 SW Topeka Blvd, 66619; 785-862-8888, FAX 785-862-2329, 800-627-2100, www.recyclersgroup.com; CC, Sp, PL; 3000; **D, F, PU, 4x4; mostly Japanese**

Valley Center; Broadway Auto Salvage, *see Late Vintage*

Watkins Auto Salvage Inc, *see Vintage*

Wellington; Wellington Auto Salvage, *see Vintage*

Wichita; Northwest Auto Salvage, *see Vintage*

Wichita; A & A Auto & Truck Salvage, 700 E 21st N, 67214; 316-263-0099, 800-566-9572; CC, Sa, Sp; 3ac; **D, F; B3**

A & K & R Salvage, *see Late Vintage*

A J's Salvage & Used Cars, 2510 S West St, 67210; 316-943-7844; CC, Sa; 300+; **88+. Few older; D; B3, AMC, Jp**

A-Plus Parts & Salvage, 2865 S Broadway St, 67216; 316-524-8644; CC, Sp, Br; 450; **D, F, PU, 4x4; B3, AMC, Jp**

AAron's Mid Town Salvage, 1716 S Richmond St, 67213; 316-942-7379; Sa; **D, F, PU, 4x4; B3, AMC, Jp, IH, VW**

Beckel Imports Auto Salvage, *see Late Vintage*

Beeline Salvage, 4754 S Madison St, 67216; 316-522-4343, FAX 316-522-4610; **D, F, PU, 4x4; B3, AMC, Jp**

Cook's Auto Salvage, 3059 N Hoover Rd, 67205; 316-943-6529; Sa, Sp; **D, F, PU, 4x4, Trk; B3, AMC, Jp**

D C Auto Salvage, *see Late Vintage*

Don Schmid Auto Salvage, 225 E 31st St S, 67216; 316-522-2275, FAX 316-522-3139, 800-362-2426, jwswing@aol.com; CC, Sa, Sp; 500+; **D, PU; B3**

Koons Salvage, 713 Leonine St, 67213; 316-943-2229; Sa, Sp; 200; **D; B3**

Meyer Auto Recycling, 3527 N Broadway St, 67219; 316-838-3261, 800-838-3275; CC, Sp; 150; **D; GM only**

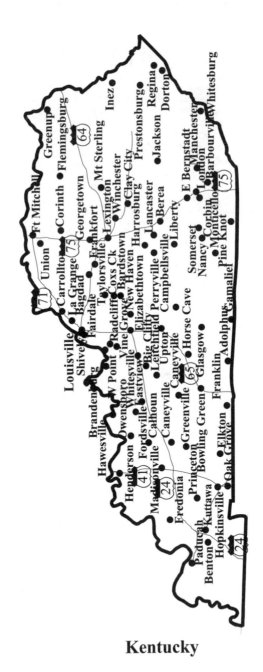

Kentucky

KENTUCKY

VINTAGE

Berea; Madison Auto Salvage, 1452 Paint Lick Rd, 40403; 606-986-8009; 700+; **50+; D, F, PU; B3, AMC**

Big Clifty; Hornback Salvage, 922 Clifty Church Rd, 42712; 270-242-2551; Sa, Sp, Br; 500+; **55+; D, F, PU, 4x4; B3, Jp, VW**

Campbellsville; Nolley auto Sales, 42718; 270-465-2306; Sa; **50-69; D; B3, St**

Coxs Creek; Lee's Auto Salvage, 931 Louisville Rd, 40013; 502-538-7707; Sa; 250+; **63+; D, PU, 4x4; B3, AMC, Jp**

Fairdale; A-1 Used Auto Parts, 1515 Fairdale Rd, 40118; 502-368-8905; Sa, Wr; 200; **50-89; D, PU; B3**

Fordsville; Brown's Auto Salvage, Hwy 261, 42343; 270-276-5129; Sa, Sp, UR; 2000; **50-89; D, PU; B3**

Gamaliel; Proffitt's Auto Salvage, 1640 Freetown Emberton Rd, 42140; 270-457-4675; Sp, UR; 30+; **49+; D, PU; Chevy, IH; Spc: Chevelle; body & frame work**

Georgetown; B & D Towing & Used Auto Parts, 4128 Cincinnati Rd, 40324; 502-863-0335, FAX 502-863-1513, 888-329-6567, templedoll@aol.com; Sp; 800; **39+; D, F, PU, 4x4; B3, AMC, Jp, IH, VW**

Henderson; Laughary's Auto Salvage, 3892 Melody Ln, 42420; 502-826-1718; Sp; 250+; **50-60s, 88+; D; B3; Spc: Chey, Ford, Cadillac**

Liberty; Jerry Rodgers Auto Salvage, 145 Hwy 1547, 42539; 606-787-8440; Sa, UR; 6000; **28+; D, F, PU, 4x4; B3, AMC, Jp, IH; Spc: 50s**

Liberty; Jimmy's Auto Salvage, 11000 Hwy 7 W, 42539; 606-743-7967; Sa; Sa; 300; **63-89; D, F, PU, 4x4; B3, AMC, Jp, IH**

Wrigley Auto Salvage, 9662 Hwy 7 W, 41472; 606-743-1774; CC, Sa, UR; **60+; D, F, PU; B3, AMC, VW**

Louisville; Morton's Auto Wreckers, 2931 Greenwood Ave, 40211; 502-776-8061, 800-776-8061; CC; 1.5ac; **60-89; D, PU, 4x4; B3**

Monticello; Quality Wrecking, N Hwy 90, 42633; 606-348-5372, FAX 606-348-3161; 1000; **30+; D, F; B3**

Oak Grove; Mick's Auto Salvage, 111 Wilson Dr, 42262; 270-439-3773, FAX 270-439-5486; CC, Sa; 350+; **60-89; D, F, PU; B3, VW; few 50's**

Oak Grove Auto Salvage, 424 Walter Garrett Ln, 42262; 270-439-4040; Sa, UR, PL; 350+; **34-87; D, F, PU; B3, AMC, Ks, VW; open Sunday; will locate whole cars**

Perryville; Boynton Auto Salvage, Rt 2 Hwy 442, 40468; 606-336-7259; Sa; 200; **55+; D, F, PU; B3, AMC, VW**

Princeton; B & C Used Auto Parts, 75 Murray St, 42445; 270-365-2099; CC, Sa, Sp; 1500+; **40+; D, F, PU, 4x4; B3, AMC, Jp, IH**

Radcliff; Dennis Auto Wrecking, 1990 Illinois Rd, 40159; 270-351-5740; Sa; **60-89; D; B3**

Union; Boone Country Auto & Truck Slvg, 3902 Hathaway Rd, 41091; 606-384-1164; CC, Sp, Wr; 12ac; **80+, few 50-60s; D, F, PU, 4x4, Trk; B3, IH, Hd, Ns, St, Pk, VW; some parts for 60 and older**

Vine Grove; B & W's Auto Slvg, 165 Fort Av, 40175; 270-828-2838; Sa; 600+; **60-90; D, PU; B3**

West Point; A A Archway Auto Salvage, 16416 Dixie Hwy, 40177; 502-922-9234, FAX 502-922-9232, 888-335-3026; CC, Sa, Sp, PL; 400; **30-69 & 90+; D, F, PU, 4x4; B3, IH**

West 44 Used Auto Parts, 12712 Hwy 44 W, 40177; 502-922-4542; Sa, UR; 5ac; **46+; D, F, PU, 4x4, Trk; Ford & Chevy**

LATE VINTAGE

Adolphus; J & J Auto Slvg, 1991 Walkers Chapel Rd, 42120; 502-622-4329; **70+; D, F; B3**

Bagdad; Brewer Salvage, 9051 Vigo Rd, 40065; 502-747-8753; Sa, Sp; 16ac; **70-95; D, F, PU; B3, AMC, VW**

Barbourville; Buttery Auto Salvage, Pineville Rd, 40906; 606-546-4507; Sa, Sp; 1800; **70+; D, F, PU, 4x4; B3, AMC, Jp, IH, VW**

Bardstown; Bardstown Auto Wreckers, 3205 Springfield Rd, 40004; 502-348-8613, FAX 502-348-8002; Sp; 1000; **77+; D, PU, 4x4; B3, Jp**

Berea; Madison Auto Salvage, *see Vintage*

143

Big Clifty; Cooper's 62 Auto Recycling, 16639 Leitchfield Rd, 42712; 270-862-5053, 800-282-8205; CC, Sa, Sp, PL; 1200+; **67+; D, F, PU, 4x4; B3, AMC, Jp, VW; Spc: front wheel drive Chrysler**

Hornback Salvage, *see Vintage*

Bowling Green; Hooper Auto Salvage, 900 Barren River Rd, 42101; 270-796-4040; Sa, UR; 1ac, 200; **70-89; D, F, PU; B3**

Brandenburg; Watt's Auto Salvage, Hwy 448, 40108; 502-422-2409; Sa, Sp, UR; 1000+; **65+; D, F, PU, 4x4, In; B3, AMC, Jp, VW**

Calhoun; Phillips Auto Salvage, 608 Hwy 81 N, 42327; 270-273-5654; Sa, UR; 600; **80-92; D, F, PU, 4x4; B3, AMC**

Carrollton; Berts Auto Body & Slvg, 100 Clay St, 40018; 502-732-6201; Sa; **80-95; D, F; B3**

Clay City; Richardson's Used Auto Parts, 8330 Winchester Rd, 40312; 606-663-0360; Sa; 20ac; **70+; D, F, PU, 4x4, Trk, Fm, In, Cn; B3, Jp, IH, VW**

Corbin; Hightop Used Parts, 406 Hightop Rd, 40701; 606-526-0971, FAX 606-526-0735; Sa, Sp, 100; **80-92; D, F, PU; B3, AMC**

Corinth; Mike's Auto Salvage, 1000 Corinth Rd, 41010; 606-823-2401; Sa, UR; 400; **70+; D, F, PU, 4x4, Trk; B3, Jp, IH, VW**

Coxs Creek; Lee's Auto Salvage, *see Vintage*

Dorton; Potters Used Parts, 18400 US Hwy 23 S, 41537; 606-639-4244; Sa, Sp; 100; **85+; D, PU, 4x4; B3; Spc: Chevy**

Elkton; Clifton's Auto Salvage, 1942 W Jeff Davis Hwy, 42220; 270-265-2334, 888-883-4707; Sa, Sp; 900; **70+; D, F, PU; B3**

Fowler Bro Auto Salvage, 1616 W Jefferson Davis Hwy, 42220; 270-265-0959; Sa, Sp, Br; 400+; **70+; D, F, PU, 4x4, Trk; B3, AMC, IH**

Fairdale; A-1 Used Auto Parts, *see Vintage*

Flemingsburg; JR's Salvage, Rt 1 Box 712, Convict Pike, 41041; 606-845-6060, 888-650-9009, jrlogan@kih.net; CC, Sa, Sp, Wr; **68+; D, PU, 4x4; B3**

Fordsville; Brown's Auto Salvage, *see Vintage*

Frankfort; L & M Salvage, 1509 Benson Valley Rd, 40601; 502-223-0229, FAX 502-223-2201; Sa, Sp, PL; 3000; **80-89; D, F, PU, 4x4, Trk; B3, AMC, Jp, VW; Spc: 4x4**

Franklin; J's Auto Salvage, 2196 Nashville Rd, 42134; 270-586-0130; Sa; 350+; **70+ D, F, PU; B3, AMC**

Fredonia; Harper Bro Salvage, 44 Livingston Cemetery Rd, 42411; 270-545-3907, FAX 270-545-7753, 800-405-3117 KY only; CC, Sa, Sp, Br; 1300; **70-96; D, F, PU; B3, VW; Spc: GM**

Gamaliel; Proffitt's Auto Salvage, *see Vintage*

Georgetown; B & D Towing & Used Auto Parts, *see Vintage*

Greenup; Scaff's Used Parts, RR 2, 41144; 606-473-7355; CC, Sa, Sp; 250+; **80+; D, F, PU, 4x4; B3, Jp; Spc: Fiero, Sunfire**

Greenville; Dukes Auto Salvage, PO Box 3636 State Rt 176, 42345; 270-338-3544; Sa; 500; **72-87; D, F, PU; B3**

Harrodsburg; Whitehouse Salvage, 3139 Harrodsburg Rd, 40330; 606-262-5553; Sa, Sp, UR; 300; **68-94; D, F, PU; B3, VW**

Hawesville; Pellville Auto Salvage, 1035 State Rt 144 W, 42348; 502-927-8786; Sa; 200+; **73-90; D, PU, 4x4; B3, AMC, Jp; Spc: Pickup**

Hopkinsville; Hilltop Auto Salvage, 529 Grand Orchard Dr, 42240; 270-886-9369; Sa, Sp, UR; **80-90; D, F; B3**

Horse Cave; Jeffries Auto Salvage, 4211 Hiseville Center Rd, 42749; 270-565-4343, FAX 270-453-4081, 800-962-2393; Sp; **80+; D, F, PU; B3**

Inez; Maynard's Used Auto Parts, P.O. Box 869, Rt 40, 41224; 606-298-7365, FAX 606-298-3941; Sa, Sp, UR; 100; **80+; D, PU, Trk; B3**

Jackson; Coal Tipple Salvage, 6160 Ky Hwy 15 N, 41339; 606-666-2277; CC, Sa, Sp; 5000+; **75+; D, F, PU, 4x4; B3, AMC, Jp, IH**

Kuttawa; Travis & Sons Auto Salvage, 3518 State Rt 295 N, 42055; 270-388-7728; **80-89; D, F, PU; B3**

144

La Grange; Newman's Auto Salvage, 1111 Dawkins Rd, 40031; 502-222-1325, FAX 502-222-4043; CC, Sa, Sp, UR; 500; **80+; D, PU; B3**

Lancaster; Turner's Wrecking Yard, 737 Stanford Rd, 40444; 606-792-3259; Sa, UR; 500+; **65-89; D, F, PU; B3**

Liberty; Jerry Rodgers Auto Salvage, *see Vintage*

Jimmy's Auto Salvage, *see Vintage*

Wrigley Auto Salvage, *see Vintage*

London; P & P Wrecking Yard, 578 Morentown Rd, 40741; 606-864-4490, 800-682-0401; CC, Sa, Sp; 2000; **80+; D, F, PU, 4x4; B3, AMC, Jp**

Louisville; Bob Collett Auto Wreckers, 1630 Frankfort Av, 40206; 502-582-2863, FAX 502-587-0213; Sa; 150+; **70+; D, F, PU; B3**

Evans Auto Salvage, 354 Farmington Av, 40219; 502-636-2880, 800-446-6221; CC, Sp; 1000; **80+; D, F, PU, 4x4; B3, VW; Spc: Toyota Pickup & 4x4**

Morton's Auto Wreckers, *see Vintage*

Sadler's Auto Parts & Salvage, 735 N 31st, 40212; 502-772-3160; Sa, UR; 300+; **76-89; D, F, PU, vans; B3**

Manchester; D & M Wrecking Yard, Sexton Creek Rd, 40962; 606-598-1232; Sa; 250+; **80-89; D, F, PU; B3**

Monticello; Quality Wrecking, *see Vintage*

Mt Sterling; Camargo Salvage, 4046 Camargo Rd, 40353; 606-498-2247, FAX 606-498-5891, 800-345-1847; CC, Sa, Sp, UR; 500+; **69+; D, F, Pickup only, 4x4; B3**

Nancy; Foster Wrecking CO, 11346 W Hwy 80, 42544; 606-871-7493, FAX 606-871-7429; 3500; **80+; D, F, PU, 4x4; B3, AMC, Jp, IH**

Stevenson Wrecking, 2435 Hwy 235, 42544; 606-636-6553; Sa, Sp; **80+; D, PU & Trk only; B3**

New Haven; Culver's Auto Salvage, 8295 New Haven Rd, 40051; 502-549-3470, FAX 502-549-6727; CC, Sa, Br; 300+; **70+; D, PU; B3**

Oak Grove; Mick's Auto Salvage, *see Vintage*

Oak Grove Auto Salvage, *see Vintage*

Owensboro; Grider's Auto Salvage, 4841 US Hwy 60 W, 42301; 270-684-1373; Sa, Sp, Br; 300; **75-88; D, PU; B3**

Paducah; Beasley's Used Parts, 4711 Cairo Rd, 42001; 270-442-3765; Sa, Br; 2000; **70-84; D; B3, AMC**

Perryville; Boynton Auto Salvage, *see Vintage*

Pine Knot; Stanley's Auto Salvage, S of Pine Knot, 42635; 606-354-3770; Sa; 300; **74+; D, F, PU, 4x4; B3, AMC, VW**

Princeton; B & C Used Auto Parts, *see Vintage*

Radcliff; Dennis Auto Wrecking, *see Vintage*

Shively; Elmwood Auto Salvage, 3729 Elmwood Ave, 40216; 502-447-4135; Sa, Br, Wr; 1000+; **60-90; D, F, PU; B3, AMC, VW**

Somerset; Buie's Wrecking, 356 Mark Shopville Rd, 42503; 606-274-4330, 800-682-8437; Sa; 400; **70-90; D, F, PU; B3, AMC; Spc: Toyota, Oldsmobile Cutlass Supreme**

Taylorsville; Elk Creek Auto Salvage & Parts, 5895 Elk Creek Rd, 40071; 502-477-8395; Sa, UR; **80+; D, F; B3, VW**

Union; Boone Country Auto & Truck Slvg, *see Vintage*

Upton; Wheeler's Auto Salvage & Svc, 1885 Layton Turner Rd, 42784; 502-531-3783; Sa; 1000+; **70-89; D, F, PU, 4x4; B3, Jp; Spc: Chevelle, Camaro**

Vine Grove; B & W's Auto Salvage, *see Vintage*

Fannin's Auto Salvage, Hwy 60, 40155; 502-828-3912; 4ac; **80+; D, F, PU; B3, VW**

Warren's Auto Salvage, 746 Shot Hunt Rd, 40175; 502-828-2299; Sa, Br; 300; **80-89; D, F, PU; B3**

West Point; West 44 Used Auto Parts, *see Vintage*

Whitesburg; Morton's Salvage, Rt 7, 41858; 606-855-9005; Sa; 3.5ac; **80+; D, PU, 4x4; B3**

Whitesburg Auto Salvage, Craft Colly Creed Rd, 41858; 606-633-1912; Sa, Sp, UR; 300+; **60+; D, F, PU; B3; Spc: Ford Ranger, Escort, Chevy S-10**

145

Winchester; Clark Auto Recycling, 200 Browning Ln, 40391; 606-744-2310, 800-816-6782; CC, Sa; 600+; **86-91; D, F, PU; B3**

King Brothers Auto Salvage, 317 W Broadway St, 40391; 606-744-3328, 800-633-5325; CC, Sa, Sp, Br, PL; 1200; **60+; D, F, PU, 4x4; B3, AMC, Jp, IH**

LATE MODEL

Adolphus; J & J Auto Salvage, *see Late Vintage*

Bagdad; Brewer Salvage, *see Late Vintage*

O'Nan's Auto Salvage, 7345 Elmburg Rd, 40003; 502-747-8804, 888-747-8804; CC, Sa, Sp, UR; 3000; **D, F, PU,** 4x4

Barbourville; Buttery Auto Salvage, *see Late Vintage*

Bardstown; Bardstown Auto Wreckers, *see Late Vintage*

Benton; Universal Auto Recycling, 8123 Brewers Hwy, 42025; 270-527-8225, 800-443-8578; Sa, Sp; 1000+; **D, F, PU, 4x4, Trk, Fm; B3**

Berea; Madison Auto Salvage, *see Vintage*

Big Clifty; Cooper's 62 Auto Recycling, *see Late Vintage*

Hornback Salvage, *see Vintage*

Bowling Green; Hayes Auto Salvage, 4498 Richardsville Rd, 42101; 270-843-4889; Sa; **D, F, PU; B3**

Brandenburg; Watt's Auto Salvage, *see Late Vintage*

Calhoun; Phillips Auto Salvage, *see Late Vintage*

Caneyville; Hack's Auto Sales & Salvage, 8601 Love Lee Rd, 42721; 270-879-9274, 888-397-8000; Sa; 350+; **D, PU; B3**

Carrollton; Berts Auto Body & Salvage Shop, *see Late Vintage*

Clay City; Richardson's Used Auto Parts, *see Late Vintage*

Corbin; Davis Salvage, Cumberland Falls Rd, 40701; 606-528-3951, 800-442-7876; 877-528-5741; CC, Sp; 2000; **D, F, PU, 4x4; B3, Jp, Jpa, Corvette; 70% PU & SUV**

Hightop Used Parts, *see Late Vintage*

S & H Salvage Co, 1054 Hwy 26, 40701; 606-528-3200; CC, Sa, Br; 100; **D, F; B3**

Corinth; Mike's Auto Salvage, *see Late Vintage*

Coxs Creek; Lee's Auto Salvage, *see Vintage*

Dorton; Potters Used Parts, *see Late Vintage*

East Bernstadt; London Auto Salvage & Frame, 243 Fields Rd, 40729; 606-843-9889, FAX 606-843-6272, 888-846-4363; CC, Sa, Sp; 500; **D, PU; B3**

Eastview; 84 Auto Recyclers, 12208 Sonora Hardin Springs Rd, 42732; 502-862-3450, 800-868-3450; Sa, Sp, UR; 400; **D, F, PU; B3, AMC**

Elizabethtown; 1135 Auto Salvage, 1999 Roundtop Rd, 42701; 502-360-8600, 800-262-9127; Sa, UR; 500 **D, F, PU, 4x4; B3**

Elkton; Clifton's Auto Salvage, *see Late Vintage*

Fowler Bro Auto Salvage, *see Late Vintage*

Flemingsburg; JR's Salvage, *see Late Vintage*

Fort Mitchell; Highland Motors, 3650 Madison Pike, 41017; 606-331-6659; Sa, Sp; 30+; **F**

Franklin; J's Auto Salvage, *see Late Vintage*

Jimmy's Auto Repair & Salvage, 517 Lemon St, 42134; 270-586-8272, 800-699-7818; CC, PL; 10ac; **D, PU; B3**

Fredonia; Harper Bro Salvage, *see Late Vintage*

Gamaliel; Proffitt's Auto Salvage, *see Vintage*

Georgetown; B & D Towing & Used Auto Parts, *see Vintage*

Glasgow; US 68 Auto Salvage, 4340 Bowling Green Rd, 42141; 270-678-2470; Sa, UR; 200; **D, F; B3**

Greenup; Scaff's Used Parts, *see Late Vintage*

Hawesville; Dave's Auto Sales & Salvage, 7970 Hwy 2181, 42348; 270-927-6752, FAX 270-927-8455, 800-927-6752; CC, Sa, Sp, Br; 1000+; **D, F, PU, 4x4; B3, Jp, IH; Spc: Pickup & GM; some 60's**

Henderson; Laughary's Auto Salvage, *see Vintage*

Horse Cave; Jeffries Auto Salvage, *see Late Vintage*

Inez; Maynard's Used Auto Parts, *see Late Vintage*

146

Jackson; Coal Tipple Salvage, *see Late Vintage*

La Grange; Newman's Auto Salvage, *see Late Vintage*

Leitchfield; Young's Auto Recycler, 702 W White Oak St, 42754; 270-259-4156, FAX 270-259-5346; CC, Sp; 1000+; **D, F, PU, 4x4; B3; Spc: Pickup**

Lexington; Lexington Auto & Truck Recyclers, 1107 Manchester St, 40508; 606-255-1085, FAX 606-255-6206, 800-942-2137; CC, Sp; 500; **D, F, PU, 4x4; B3, VW**

Liberty; Jerry Rodgers Auto Salvage, *see Vintage*

    Wrigley Auto Salvage, *see Vintage*

London; Collett Wrecking Yard, Hwy 1956 W, 40741; 606-878-7389, FAX 606-877-1661; Sa; 200+; **D, F, PU, 4x4; B3; Spc: GM**

    P & P Wrecking Yard, *see Late Vintage*

    Reed Brothers Auto Salvage, 2333 Somerset Rd, 40741; 606-864-6990, FAX 606-877-4291, 800-525-6689; 3000+; **D, F, PU; B3**

Louisville; Abell Auto Parts & Salvage, 7119 Grade Ln, 40213; 502-361-8861, FAX 502-361-8865, 800-922-0590; CC, Sa, Sp, UR; 1200; **D, F, PU, 4x4; B3**

    Allstate Auto Parts, 7301 Grade Ln, 40213; 502-367-8788; Sa, Sp, Br, PL; 1000; **D, F, PU, 4x4; B3**

    Bob Collett Auto Wreckers, *see Late Vintage*

    Evans Auto Salvage, *see Late Vintage*

    Gilbert & Mitchell Inc, 1001 Outer Loop, 40219; 502-366-0323, 800-624-0915; CC, Sp; 14ac; **D, F, PU, 4x4**

    Grade A, 4556 Melton, 40213; 502-361-9466, 800-342-0713; CC, Sp, PL; 400; **D, F, PU, 4x4; B3**

Madisonville; Cates Auto Parts Inc, 819 S Main St, 42431; 502-821-5456, FAX 502-825-2372, 800-462-2357; CC, Sp; 3000; **D, F, PU, 4x4; B3**

Monticello; Quality Wrecking, *see Vintage*

Mt Sterling; Camargo Salvage, *see Late Vintage*

Nancy; Foster Wrecking CO, *see Late Vintage*

    Stevenson Wrecking, *see Late Vintage*

New Haven; Culver's Auto Salvage, *see Late Vintage*

Perryville; Boynton Auto Salvage, *see Vintage*

Pine Knot; Stanley's Auto Salvage, *see Late Vintage*

Prestonsburg; Stapleton Used Auto Parts, 8 Ky Rt 1428, 41653; 606-874-2350; Sa; 300; **D, F, PU, 4x4; B3, AMC, Jp, VW**

Princeton; B & C Used Auto Parts, *see Vintage*

Radcliff; Frakes Auto Salvage, Box 412, S Dixie Blvd, 40159; 270-351-4438, FAX 270-351-4358, 800-535-1703; Sp; 7ac; **D, F, PU, 4x4; B3**

Regina; East Kentucky Salvage, 458 Marrowbone Creek Rd, 41567; 606-754-9513; Sa; 250+; **D, F, PU, 4x4; B3**

Somerset; Slate Branch Wrecking, 315 Shafter Shepola Rd, 42503; 606-678-0485, FAX 606-679-3747, 800-421-5310; Sa, UR; 700; **D, F, PU, 4x4; B3**

    West Somerset Used Cars, 345 Race Track Rd, 42503; 606-679-2511, FAX 606-678-5343, 800-345-0460; CC, Sp, UR; **60ac; D, F, PU, 4x4; B3**

Taylorsville; Elk Creek Auto Salvage & Parts, *see Late Vintage*

Union; Boone Country Auto & Truck Slvg, *see Vintage*

Vine Grove; Fannin's Auto Salvage, *see Late Vintage*

West Point; A A Archway Auto Salvage, *see Vintage*

    West 44 Used Auto Parts, *see Vintage*

Whitesburg; Morton's Salvage & Auto Sales, *see Late Vintage*

    Whitesburg Auto Salvage, *see Late Vintage*

Whitesville; West Side U-Pull-It-Yard, 5669 State Rt 764, 42378; 270-275-9381; Sa, UR; 900; **D, F, PU; B3, VW**

Winchester; King Brothers Auto Salvage, *see Late Vintage*

Louisiana

Please use the cards in the back to let us know about yards we may have missed, or any other comments or information for future editions of Ray's wRreckingyard Roster

LOUISIANNA

VINTAGE

Basile; Roger's Classic Restoration, P.O. Box 760, 70515; 318-432-5760, FAX 318-432-6044; CC, Sp, Br; 90+; **64-89; D, PU, 4x4, Trk; GM, Fd; Spc: Camaro**

Bossier City; B & B Auto Salvage, 4725 E Texas St, 71111; 318-742-2087, FAX 318-742-0673; Sa, Sp, UR; 200+; **50-90; D, PU; B3; Spc: Classic Chevy**

Chalmette; L & L Auto Salvage, 4141 Paris Rd, 70043; 504-271-9800, FAX 504-271-9795; Sa, Sp; 600; **60+; D, F, PU; B3, VW; Spc: Mustang**

Denham Springs; A A Auto Salvage, 23968 Walker South Rd, 70726; 225-667-2020, FAX 225-664-3434; Sp; 4ac, 500+; **60+; D, F, PU, 4x4; B3, AMC, IH, VW**

Haughton; Red Chute Auto Ctr Inc, 1831 Hwy 80, 71037; 318-949-2467, FAX 318-949-4935, 800-829-3535; CC, Sa, Sp, UR; 700; **65+; D, F, PU, 4x4; B3, AMC, Jp**

Houma; Bayou Black Wrecking Yard, 201 Billy Ln, 70360; 504-879-4389; Sa; 30ac, 600+; **60+; D, F, PU, 4x4; B3**

Kaplan; Le Maires Towing & Wrecker, 300 S Lemaire Av, 70548; 318-643-7200, FAX 318-643-1452; CC, UR; **65-89; D, PU; B3**

Lafayette; A Lafayette Auto Salvage, 134 Galbert Rd, 70506; 318-233-9687, 800-737-6700; CC, Sa, Sp, Br; 6000; **60+; D, F, PU, 4x4, Trk; B3, AMC, Jp, IH, VW; Spc: MG, Triumph, Peugeot**

Lake Charles; L J Auto Salvage, 5825 Hwy 90 E, 70615; 318-439-3374, FAX 318-439-3317; Sa, Br; 1.5ac, 250+; **30+; D, F, PU, 4x4; B3**

New Iberia; Courreges Wrecking Yard, 1130 W Main St, 70560; 318-369-6416, FAX 318-369-6416, 800-375-6416; CC, Sp; 6ac, 3000; **65+; D, F, PU, 4x4; B3, AMC, Jp; Spc: Chrysler**

New Orleans; Charlies Auto Wreckers, 9025 Old Gentilly Rd, 70127; 504-242-3431; Sa, Sp, UR; 75; **60+; D, F, PU; B3**

   Industrial Auto Wreckers, 11661 Old Gentilly Rd, 70128; 504-242-0854; UR; 13ac, 1500+; **60+; D, F, PU, 4x4; B3, Jp, IH, VW**

Ponchatoula; Fannaly's Auto Exchange, PO Box 23, 70454; 504-386-3714; CC, Sa, Sp; 300; **40-79; D; B3, St, Pk, Ks, Fr, Cr, DeSoto; NOS parts & glass; By Appointment Only**

Saint Rose; Mac's Wrecking Yard, 10519 Airline Hwy, 70087; 504-468-3690, FAX 504-469-1466; Sa; 6ac, 800; **66+; D, F, PU, 4x4, Trk; B3, AMC, Jp, IH; Makes driveshafts, modifies 4x4s, rebuilds rear ends & transmissions**

Zwolle; Eddie's Auto Salvage, 251 Hamlin St, 71486; 318-645-6409; UR; 50; **60-79; D, F, PU; B3; Spc: Pickup**

LATE VINTAGE

Basile; Roger's Classic Restoration, *see Vintage*

Baton Rouge; Insurance Wrecking, 8125 Airline Hwy, 70815; 225-927-8000; Sp; **80+; D, F, PU, Spc: 4x4; B3**

Bossier City; B & B Auto Salvage, *see Vintage*

Chalmette; L & L Auto Salvage, *see Vintage*

De Ridder; South Side Auto Salvage Inc, 891 Pleasant Hill Rd, 70634; 318-462-1373, FAX 318-462-1374, 800-523-4241; Sp; 400; **75+; D, F, PU; B3**

Denham Springs; Brown's Salvage, 9430 Forrest Delatte Rd, 70726; 225-665-2083, FAX 225-667-0257, 800-293-1980; CC, Sa, Sp, Br; 1300; **80+; D, F, PU; B3**

   A A Auto Salvage, *see Vintage*

Franklin; Lee Clark Salvage, 1204 Irish Bend Rd, 70538; 318-828-2146; Sa, UR; 2ac; **75-89; D, F, PU, 4x4; B3**

Gueydan; La Pointe Wrecking Yard, 33610 Veteran Memorial Dr, 70542; 318-536-6303; **70-89; D, F, PU; B3; no phone inquiries**

Haughton; Red Chute Auto Ctr Inc, *see Vintage*

Holden; A to Z Auto Salvage & Used, 30028 Connie Dr, 70744; 225-567-2550, FAX 225-567-2815; 1000+; **69+; D, F, PU, 4x4, Trk; B3, AMC, Jp, VW**

Houma; Bayou Black Wrecking Yard, *see Vintage*

Kaplan; Le Maires Towing & Wrecker, *see Vintage*

Lafayette; A Lafayette Auto Salvage, *see Vintage*

Lake Charles; L J Auto Salvage, *see Vintage*

149

Louisiana – Late Vintage

Lake Charles Auto Salvage, 2644 N Hwy 171, 70611; 318-436-3389; Sa, Sp, UR; 1.5ac; **70+; D, F, PU; B3**

Mamou; Gahn Auto Salvage, 6452 Veteran Memorial Hwy, 70554; 318-468-5594; Sa, Sp; 500+; **80+; D, F, PU, 4x4; B3**

LaVergne Salvage, 6088 Veteran Memorial Hwy, 70554; 318-468-2636; Sa; 300+; **80-95; D, F, PU; B3**

Mansfield; 175 Salvage, 142 Marr Rd, 71052; 318-872-1907; Sa; 2ac; **70+; D, F, PU, 4x4, Trk, Fm, In, Cn, Mil; B3, AMC, JP, IH, VW**

New Iberia; Courreges Wrecking Yard, *see Vintage*

New Orleans; Charlies Auto Wreckers, *see Vintage*

Industrial Auto Wreckers, *see Vintage*

Opelousas; Doucet's Salvage, 332 Hwy 744, 70570; 318-948-3933; CC, Sa, Sp; 400; **70+; D, F, PU; B3**

Ponchatoula; Fannaly's Auto Exchange, *see Vintage*

Port Allen; Auto Salvage, 3022 Hwy 190 W, 70767; 225-383-6000, 800-406-9359; CC, Sa, Sp, UR, PL; 700+; **80+; D, F, PU; B3**

West Baton Rouge Auto Salvage, 6937 Hwy 190W, 70767; 225-344-1288; Sa, Br; 150+; **70+; D, F, PU; B3**

Ruston; Ben's Wrecking Yard, 7344 Hwy 80, 71270; 318-247-8222, 800-276-2367; UR; 10ac; **75+; D, PU, 4x4; B3**

Saint Rose; Mac's Wrecking Yard, *see Vintage*

Shreveport; American Auto Salvage, 9530 Linwood Av, 71106; 318-686-0476, 800-297-6393 LA TX AR MS only; Sa; 450+; **80+; D, PU; B3; Spc: Pickup**

Gattis Wrecking Yard, 7150 Mansfield Rd, 71108; 318-686-5211; Sa, UR; 7.5ac; **70-89; D, F, PU, 4x4; B3**

Thibodaux; Schriever Auto Recyclers, 320 Schriever Hwy, 70301; 504-446-5740; Sa, Sp, PL; 550; **82+; D, F, PU, 4x4; B3**

Ville Platte; American Auto Salvage, 2102 W Main St, 70586; 318-363-7226, 800-298-5287; Sa, Sp; 450+; **75-95; D, F, PU; B3**

Zachary; Cox's auto Salvage, 19511 Plank Rd, 70791; 504-654-4591, 800-325-8273; CC, Sp, PL; **80+; D, F, PU, 4x4; B3**

Zwolle; Eddie's Auto Salvage, *see Vintage*

LATE MODEL

Alexandria; Henry's Auto Salvage, 5880 Old Boyce Rd, 71301; 318-443-2536, FAX 318-443-9908, 800-256-1356; CC, Sp; 3000+; **D, F, PU, 4x4; B3, Jp, VW**

Baker; A Hemco Salvage, 15240 Brown Rd, 70704; 225-261-8801, FAX 225-261-9915; CC, Sa, Sp, UR, PL; 550; **D, F, PU, 4x4; B3; few older Pickups**

Baton Rouge; Harris & Son Auto Salvage, 1402 Mengel Rd, 70807; 225-355-1789; Sa, UR; **open Sunday**

Insurance Wrecking, *see Late Vintage*

Bossier; Greenwood Auto Salvage, 3801 Shed Rd, 71111; 318-938-6941, FAX 318-938-6943; CC, Sa; 11ac, 600; **D, F, PU; B3**

Breaux Bridge; Robbo's Auto Salvage, 1694 Mills Hwy, 70517; 318-332-6702, 800-960-1260; CC, Sp, UR; 2000; **D, F, PU, 4x4; B3; Spc: Chevy Pickup**

Brusly; Black's Auto Salvage, 6025 Hwy 1 S, 70719; 225-749-3161, 800-234-5063; CC, Sp, Wr; 3ac; **D, F, PU; B3**

Chalmette; L & L Auto Salvage, *see Vintage*

De Ridder; South Side Auto Salvage Inc, *see Late Vintage*

Denham Springs; A A Auto Salvage, *see Vintage*

Brown's Salvage, *see Late Vintage*

Haughton; Red Chute Auto Ctr Inc, *see Vintage*

Roy's Auto Salvage, 546 Parker Rd, 71037; 318-949-1699; Sa; **D, F, PU**

Holden; A to Z Auto Salvage & Used, *see Late Vintage*

Houma; Bayou Black Wrecking Yard, *see Vintage*

Kenner; Kenner Auto Salvage, 101 W 27th St, 70062; 504-468-2692; Sa, Sp, UR; 500; **D, F, PU, 4x4; B3; Crusher yard-sells some parts**

Lafayette; A Lafayette Auto Salvage, *see Vintage*

Dien's Auto Salvage, 6157 Johnston St, 70503; 318-988-0462; Sa, Sp; **D, F, PU, 4x4; B3**

Lake Charles; L J Auto Salvage, *see Vintage*

Lake Charles Auto Salvage, *see Late Vintage*

Livingston; A-1 National Auto Salvage, 12716 Florida Blvd, 70754; 225-686-7700, 800-828-5545; CC, Sp; 300+; **D, F, PU; B3**

Mamou; Gahn Auto Salvage, *see Late Vintage*

LaVergne Salvage, *see Late Vintage*

Mansfield; 175 Salvage, *see Late Vintage*

Marrero; Buddy's Auto Salvage, 6514 4th St, 70072; 504-341-6304, FAX 504-348-7019, 800-828-4290; CC, Sa, Sp; 8ac, 750; **D, F, PU, 4x4; B3, Jp**

Monroe; Perry Auto Ranch Inc, 711 Hwy 80 E, 71203; 318-343-0352; 5ac, 400; **D, PU; B3**

New Iberia; Courreges Wrecking Yard, *see Vintage*

New Orleans; Almonaster Auto Wreckers, 7979 Almonaster Av, 70126; 504-246-2563; Sa, Br; **D, F, PU, 4x4; B3; some older cars**

Car Crushers Inc, 10301 Old Gentilly Rd, 70127; 504-242-1265, FAX 504-242-1723; CC, Sa, Br; 2500+; **D, F, PU, 4x4, Trk; B3**

Charlies Auto Wreckers, *see Vintage*

Garrett Auto Parts & Salvage, 11441 Almonaster Av, 70128; 504-245-9054, FAX 504-245-9159, 800-875-9054; CC, Sa, Sp, UR, PL; 8ac, 1400+; **D, F; B3**

Industrial Auto Wreckers, *see Vintage*

Opelousas; Doucet's Salvage, *see Late Vintage*

Ponchatoula; Bennett Towing & Recovery, 18272 Sisters Rd, 70454; 504-386-3242; CC, UR; 150; **D, F; B3**

Port Allen; Auto Salvage, *see Late Vintage*

West Baton Rouge Auto Salvage, *see Late Vintage*

Ruston; Ben's Wrecking Yard, *see Late Vintage*

Saint Rose; B & C Auto Wreckers, 10501 Airline Hwy, 70087; 504-464-9559; Sa; **D, F, PU, Trk; B3**

Mac's Wrecking Yard, *see Vintage*

Shreveport; American Auto Salvage, *see Late Vintage*

Thibodaux; Schriever Auto Recyclers, *see Late Vintage*

Ville Platte; American Auto Salvage, *see Late Vintage*

Zachary; Cox's auto Salvage, *see Late Vintage*

You may be a car nut if

Half your shirts and all your hats have pictures of cars on them

MAINE

VINTAGE
Canaan; Jenness's Auto Salvage, Nelson Hill Rd, 04924; 207-474-3041; Sa, Sp; **37+; D, F, PU, 4x4, Trk; B3, AMC, Jp, IH, VW**
Caribou; Beaulieu's Auto Salvage, 168 High St, 04736; 207-496-1281; Sp, Wr; 30+; **30-89; D, F; B3, AMC, Hd, St, Pk, VW**
Houlton; Stevens Salvage Corp, Main Rd, 04760; 207-538-9521; Sa, Sp; 300; **50+; D, F; B3**
Machias; Machias Auto Salvage, Box 253, W Kennebec Rd, 04654; 207-255-4069; Sa; 1ac, 50+; **60+; D, F, PU, 4x4; B3; Many running cars; open Sunday**
Monmouth; Phil's Garage & Salvage Yard, 360 S Monmouth Rd, 04259; 207-933-4364; Sa; 250+; **30+; D, F, PU; B3, Hd, Pk, VW**
Winn; Soucie Junk Yard, Rt 2 Box 91, 04495; 207-736-3500; Sa, Sp; 3000; **60+; D, F, PU, 4x4, Trk; B3, AMC, Jp, IH, VW; Call aft 5pm; open Sunday**
LATE VINTAGE
Acton; Lake Region Auto Salvage, H Rd, 04001; 207-636-1800; Sa, Sp; 200+; **80+; D, F, PU, 4x4; B3**
Alfred; J & J Auto Salvage, 276 Jordan Spring Rd, 04002; 207-324-6566, 800-281-6566; CC, Sa, UR; 450+; **81-93; D, F, PU; B3**
   M & J Auto Salvage, 23 Mountain Rd, 04006; 207-490-1142, 800-490-1142; CC, Sa, Sp; **70-93; D, F, PU, 4x4; B3**

Biddeford; Gary's Auto Salvage, 258 River Rd, 04046; 207-967-5160, 800-540-5160; CC, Sa, Sp, Br, PL; 500; **80+; D, F, PU, 4x4; B**3**, VW**

Canaan; Jenness's Auto Salvage, *see Vintage*

Caribou; Beaulieu's Auto Salvage, *see Vintage*

Chelsea; Bob's Used Auto Parts, RR 2 Box 2600, 04330; 207-582-3559; Sa; 150+; **80-93; D, PU, 4x4; B**3

Freeport; John E. Ingerson, 33 Allen Range Rd, 04032; 207-865-3967; Sa, UR; 2000; **70-90; D, F; B**3

Houlton; Stevens Salvage Corp, *see Vintage*

Lisbon; Campbell's Used Auto Parts, 36 River Rd, 04250; 207-353-2331; CC, Sa; 800; **75-88; D, F, PU, 4x4; B**3**, AMC, Jp, VW**

Machias; Machias Auto Salvage, *see Vintage*

Monmouth; Barrow's Used Auto Parts, 49 Town Farm Rd, 04259; 207-268-4262; Sa; 200; **75-90; D, F, PU; B**3

Phil's Garage & Salvage Yard, *see Vintage*

Oakland; Reggie Bickford Auto Salvage, Broomhandle Rd, 04963; 207-465-7235, FAX 207-465-2756; UR; 600; **80-88; D, F, PU, 4x4; B**3**, Jp; Spc: Toyota Camry**

Oxford; Lashin's Auto Sales & Salvage, 1 Route 121, 04270; 207-539-2905, 800-696-5274; CC, Sa, UR, Wr, PL; 1000; **90+; D, F, PU, 4x4; B**3**; few older Chrysler Mopar & Mustang**

Palmyra; K & K Auto Salvage, 229 Oxbow Rd, 04965; 207-368-2264; CC, Sa; 400; **80-94; D, F, PU, 4x4; B**3**, AMC, Jp, VW**

Palmyra; Shaw's Used Auto Parts, Wyman Rd, 04965; 207-938-2811; Sa, UR; 2ac, 250; **70-89; D, few F, PU, Trk; B**3

Westbrook; Larson's Auto Salvage, 740 County Rd, 04092; 207-772-5289; Sa; 100; **80-89; D, F, PU, 4x4, Trk**

Winn; Soucie Junk Yard, *see Vintage*

LATE MODEL

Acton; Lake Region Auto Salvage, *see Late Vintage*

Alfred; J & J Auto Salvage, *see Late Vintage*

M & J Auto Salvage, *see Late Vintage*

Auburn; M & P Used Auto Parts, 227 Merrow Rd, 04210; 207-786-3030, FAX 207-786-3797, 800-244-0663; CC, Sa, Sp; 500; **D, F, PU, 4x4; B**3**, Jp, VW**

Biddeford; Gary's Auto Salvage, *see Late Vintage*

Canaan; Jenness's Auto Salvage, *see Vintage*

Chelsea; Bob's Used Auto Parts, *see Late Vintage*

Fairfield; Bill's Auto Salvage, 56 Middle Rd, 04937; 207-453-2143, FAX 207-453-7174; CC, Sa, Sp; 1000; **D, F, PU, 4x4; B**3**, AMC, VW**

Freeport; Allen Range Rd Used Auto Parts, 13 Allen Range Rd, 04032; 207-865-4702, 800-775-4702 ME only; Sa; 5000; **D, F; B**3**; Mostly GM & Ford**

Gorham; Gorham Used Auto Parts Co, 176 Narragansett St, 04038; 207-839-3080, FAX 207-839-5431; CC, Sp; 1500; **D, F, PU, 4x4; B**3**, Jp, VW, Saab, Volvo**

Houlton; Stevens Salvage Corp, *see Vintage*

Machias; Machias Auto Salvage, *see Vintage*

Monmouth; Phil's Garage & Salvage Yard, *see Vintage*

Orrington; J & J Auto Salvage, 333 Brewer Lake Rd, 04002; 207-825-3061, FAX 207-825-8874, 800-660-3061; CC, Sa, Sp; 20ac; **D, F, PU, 4x4; B**3**; Spc: GM Pickup**

Oxford; Lashin's Auto Sales & Salvage, *see Late Vintage*

Palmyra; K & K Auto Salvage, *see Late Vintage*

Presque Isle; Cowett's Used Auto Parts Wrhse, 75 Davis St, 04769; 207-762-3048; CC, Sa, Sp; 500; **D, F, PU, 4x4; B**3**, VW**

Scarborough; Scarboro Used Auto Parts, 40 Holmes Rd, 04074; 207-883-4161, 800-427-0632, www.scarboroautoparts.com; CC, Sa, Sp; 800; **D, F, PU, 4x4; B**3**, Jp, VW**

Windham; Auto & Truck Used Parts Inc, 1011 Roosevelt Trl, 04062; 207-892-6334, 800-974-6334; CC, Sa, Sp, Wr; 100+; **D, F, PU, 4x4; B**3**, VW; Spc Pickup & 4x4**

Winn; Soucie Junk Yard, *see Vintage*

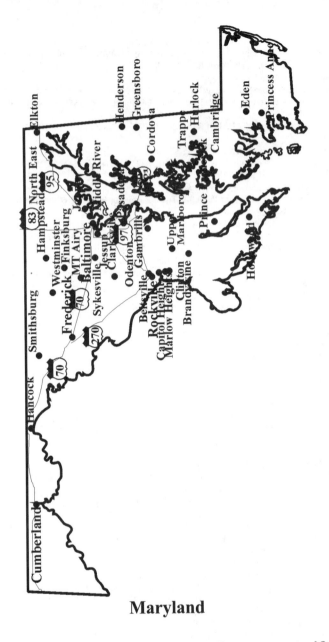

Maryland

Ray's wReckingyard Roster makes a great gift for the "car nut" on your shopping list. To order, Call Toll Free: 877-4RAYS BOOKS

MARYLAND

VINTAGE

Baltimore; A-Plus Auto Recyclers, 216 Earls Rd, 21220; 410-335-2998; Sa, UR; 550+; **60+; D, F, PU; B3, VW; Open Sun**

The Mercedes Connection, 5817 Park Heights Av, 21215; 410-922-1410 or 367-4490, FAX 410-466-3566, tmcpub@jagunet.com; CC, Sp, Wr; 100; **57-85; F; Mercedes only**

Tom's Car & Truck Removal, 2723 N Point Blvd, 21222; 410-284-7040, FAX 410-284-0888; Sa, Sp; 3ac, 900; **65-92; D, F, PU, Trk; B3**

Clarksville; Ellis Wise Junkyard & Towing, 12046 Hall Shop Rd, 21029; 410-531-5000; Sa, UR; 9ac; **60+, few 50s; D, F, PU, Trk; B3**

Finksburg; Buzzy Shamer Used Car Parts, 2943 Patapsco Rd, 21048; 410-848-1545; Sa, Sp, UR; 3ac; **48-94; D, F, PU, 4x4; B3; only a few older cars**

Vogt Parts Barn, 2239 Old Westminster Pike, 21048; 410-848-1300 or 876-1300 FAX 410-876-1630, 800-492-1300; CC, Sa, Sp, UR; 17ac, 3000+; **35+; D, F, PU, 4x4; B3, AMC, Jp, IH, Hd, Ns, St, Pk, Ks, Fr, VW**

Frederick; Schroyers Recycling Center, 8005 Reichs Ford Rd, 21704; 301-663-6022, FAX 301-663-3720, 800-214-8144, mdbsr@aol.com; CC, Sa, Sp, UR; 17ac, 700+; **30+; D, PU, 4x4, Trk; B3, AMC, Jp, IH, Ns, Peterbilt**

Greensboro; Foy's Auto Salvage, 24985 Harrington Rd, 21639; 410-482-8544, 800-378-1264; Sa, Sp, PL; 2500; **60+; D, F, PU, 4x4; B3, AMC, Jp, IH, VW; Spc: Chrysler**

Hampstead; Smith Brother's Auto Parts, 2316 Snydersburg Rd, 21074; 410-374-6781 or 239-8514; Sa, Sp, UR; 4ac; **40-85; D, F, PU, 4x4; B3, AMC, Jp, IH, St, Pk**

Hurlock; Era's Auto Salvage, 6012 Hurlock Shiloh Rd, 21643; 410-943-3089; Sa, UR; 6ac, 1000+; **50+; D, F, PU, 4x4, Trk, Fm, In; B3, AMC, Jp, VW**

Marlow Heights; Chuck's Used Auto Parts, 4722 St Barnabas Rd, 20748; 301-423-0007, www.chucksusedautoparts.com; CC, Sa, Sp; 250; **53+; D; all GM, Spc: Cadillac, Corvette**

Mount Airy; Mt Airy Auto Wrecking Inc, 5510 Woodville Rd #A, 21771; 410-795-6633 FAX 301-663-3720, 800-214-8144, mbowie5000@aol.com; CC, Sa, Sp; 2200; **35+; D, F, PU, 4x4, Trk, Fm; B3, Jp, IH, Hd, Ns, St, Pk, Ks, Fr, Wy, VW**

Smithsburg; Elwood's Auto Exchange, 21411 Jefferson Blvd, 21783; 301-739-7159; CC, Sa, UR; 75ac; **40+; D, F, PU, 4x4, Trk, Fm, In, Cn; B3, Hd, Ns, St, Pk**

Sykesville; Yesterday's Chevrolet, 4801 Bushey Rd, 21784; 410-549-6631; Sp; 567; **58-64; D: Chevy only; Call for appointment**

Trappe; Thomas's Junk Yard, 4479 Ocean Gtwy, 21673; 410-820-7428; Sa, UR; 4ac; **50+; D, F, PU, 4x4; B3**

LATE VINTAGE

Baltimore; A-Plus Auto Recyclers, *see Vintage*

Arriva Automotive Recycling, 1401 Fleet St, 21231; 410-558-1400, FAX 410-522-1726, 800-735-5831; CC, Sp, Wr; **82+; F; Japanese only**

Curtis Recyclers Inc, 6212 Pennington Av, 21226; 410-761-4222, FAX 410-768-6862; Sa, Sp, Wr; 350; **66+; D, F, PU, 4x4; B3, Jp, VW**

The Mercedes Connection, *see Vintage*

Tom's Car & Truck Removal, *see Vintage*

Brandywine; Brandywine Auto Parts Inc, 20613; 301-372-1000, FAX 301-248-7981; CC, Sa, Sp, Br, PL; 400; **75-92; D, F, PU, 4x4, Trk; B3**

Cambridge; Cambridge Auto Recyclers, 2057 Church Creek Rd, 21613; 410-228-4053, FAX 410-228-4053, 800-346-3423; Sa, Sp, Wr, PL; 800+; **70+; D, F, PU, 4x4; B3, Jp**

Clarksville; Ellis Wise Junkyard & Towing, *see Vintage*

Cordova; Ewing Motors, 11766 Cordova Rd, 21625; 410-364-5200; Sa; 6ac; **70-89; D, F, PU, 4x4; B3**

Cumberland; Lewis Junkyard, 14515 Jesse Ln, 21501; 301-722-5559; Sa; 0.3ac; **79-90; D, F, PU, 4x4; B3**

Elkton; Country Boys Used Auto Parts, 201 Johnstown Rd, 21921; 410-392-4495; Sa, UR; 150+; **70-85; D; B3, AMC**

Wright's Used Auto Parts, 826 Union Church Rd, 21921; 410-398-9548, FAX 410-392-7844, 800-559-7317; Sa, Sp, Br; 10ac; **80+; D, F, PU, 4x4; B3**

155

Finksburg; Buzzy Shamer Used Car Parts, *see Vintage*

Vogt Parts Barn, *see Vintage*

Frederick; AMG Used Auto Parts, 706 East St, 21701; 301-662-4028, 800-368-3864; Sa; 1ac; **80-94; F; Jpa**

Potomac Classic Pontiac, 7311 Grove Rd Unit S, 21704; 301-668-0101, FAX 301-668-0102, mdpontiacs@aol.com; CC, Sp, Wr; **64-81; D; Pontiac only, GTO, Firebird, LeMans, Tempest**

Potomac German Auto, 4305 Lime Kiln Rd, 21703; 301-831-1111, FAX 301-874-2450, 800-831-8901, www.pgauto.com; CC, Sp; 8ac, 600+; **75+; F; Mercedes**

Schroyers Recycling Center, *see Vintage*

Greensboro; Foy's Auto Salvage, *see Vintage*

Hampstead; Smith Brother's Auto Parts, *see Vintage*

Hancock; J & S Salvage Co, 14204 White Oak Rdg, 21750; 301-678-6806; Sa, UR; 4ac; **75+; D, PU, 4x4; B3**

Henderson; Henderson Auto Salvage, 327 Henderson Rd, 21640; 410-482-7264, FAX 410-482-7349, 877-712-8686; Sa, Sp; 10ac; **79+; D, F, PU, 4x4; B3**

Hurlock; Era's Auto Salvage, *see Vintage*

Jessup; Capitol Used Auto Parts, 7451 Montevideo Rd, 20794; 410-799-7900; CC; **70-90; F**

Joppa; Banks Auto Wrecking, 908 Pine Rd, 21085; 410-679-1118; Sa, UR; 2ac; **70-89; D, F, PU; B3**

Marlow Heights; Chuck's Used Auto Parts, *see Vintage*

Middle River; Doug's Auto & Truck Recycler, 516 Earls Rd #C, 21220; 410-335-3626; Sa, Sp, Br; 4500; **D, F, PU, 4x4, Trk; B3, AMC, Jp, IH, VW**

Mount Airy; Mt Airy Auto Wrecking Inc, *see Vintage*

North East; King Salvage, 3105 Pulaski Hwy, 21901; 410-287-8430; Sa; 500; **78+; D, F, PU, 4x4, Mil; B3**

Odenton; Buz's Used Auto Parts, 1553 Meyers Station Rd, 21113; 410-721-7552, 888-793-0400; CC; 6ac; **70+; D, F, PU, 4x4; B3**

Pasadena; Smitty's Auto Parts, 8229 Baltimore Annapolis Blvd, 21122; 410-437-3100, 800-773-3101; Sa, Sp; 10ac, 1000; **75+; D, F, PU, 4x4, Trk; B3**

Prince Frederick; Seymour Inc, 20678; 410-535-5296, FAX 301-884-5767; CC, Sp; 2500; **80+; D, F, PU, 4x4, Trk; B3**

Princess Anne; Smullen Salvage & Towing Inc, 12570 Recycle Dr, 21853; 410-651-1503, FAX 410-651-3249, 800-331-0786; CC, Sa, Sp, PL; 700+; **80+; D, F, PU, 4x4; B3**

Rockville; AAA Gene's Used Auto Parts, 14900 Dover Rd, 20850; 301-279-5596, FAX 301-279-9613; Sa, Sp, UR; 200; **80+; D, F, PU, 4x4; B3**

Smithsburg; Elwood's Auto Exchange, *see Vintage*

Trappe; Thomas's Junk Yard, *see Vintage*

Westminster; Jones Auto & Salvage, 111 E Nicodemus Rd, 20847; 410-876-3382; Sp; 3ac; **60-89; D, F, PU, 4x4; B3; Mustang, Peugeot; Does restorations**

Shifflett's Used Auto Parts, 724 Gorsuch Rd #R, 21157; 410-876-3277; Sa; 450+; **78-88; D, F, PU, 4x4; B3, AMC, Jp, VW**

<u>*LATE MODEL*</u>

Baltimore; A-Plus Auto Recyclers, *see Vintage*

Arriva Automotive Recycling, *see LateVintage*

Curtis Recyclers Inc, *see LateVintage*

Eastside Auto Recycling Inc, 4725 Erdman Av, 21231; 410-276-2000, FAX 410-522-1388; CC, Sa, Sp; 200; **D, F, PU, 4x4; B3**

Tom's Car & Truck Removal, *see Vintage*

Beltsville; Allstat Used Auto Parts Inc, 11501 Maryland Av, 20705; 301-595-5595, FAX 301-595-7069; CC, Sa, Sp, Br; 60; **F; Jpa**

Brandywine; Brandywine Auto Parts Inc, *see LateVintage*

Cambridge; Cambridge Auto Recyclers, *see LateVintage*

Capitol Heights; Downtown Auto Wreckers Inc, 5612 J St, 20743; 301-925-8882, 800-870-8191; CC, Sp; 1ac, 10; **F, PU, 4x4; Spc: Pickup & Van**

Clarksville; Ellis Wise Junkyard & Towing, *see Vintage*

Clinton; B & M Used Foreign & American, 11700 Brandywine Rd, 20735; 301-868-7440, FAX 301-868-5291, 800-333-2621; CC, Sa, Sp, Br; 5ac; **F; Jpa, Mercedes**

Eden; Eden Used Auto Parts, 14661 Mercer Rd, 21822; 410-749-5116, FAX 410-742-3930, 800-982-3589, www.brandywineparts.com; CC, Sa, Sp, PL; 1200; **D, F, PU, 4x4; B3, AMC, Jp, IH**

Elkton; Wright's Used Auto Parts, *see LateVintage*

Finksburg; Buzzy Shamer Used Car Parts, *see Vintage*
  Vogt Parts Barn, *see Vintage*

Frederick; AMG Used Auto Parts, *see LateVintage*
  Potomac German Auto, *see LateVintage*
  Schroyers Recycling Center, *see Vintage*

Gambrills; Henry's Auto Dismantlers Inc, 781 Maryland Route 3 N, 21054; 410-987-5800, FAX , 800-891-6677; CC, Sa, Sp; **D, F; B3**

Greensboro; Eagle Auto Salvage Inc, 216 S Main St, 21639; 410-482-8991, 800-638-4991, www.lkqparts.net; CC, Sp; 650+; **D, F, PU, 4x4; B3, VW**
  Foy's Auto Salvage, *see Vintage*

Hancock; J & S Salvage Co, *see LateVintage*

Henderson; Henderson Auto Salvage, *see LateVintage*

Hollywood; Hollywood Used Auto Parts, 43900 Commerce Av, 20636; 301-373-6964, FAX 301-373-3162, 800-764-1007; CC, Sa, Sp, PL; 10ac; **D, F, PU, 4x4, Buses; B3**

Hurlock; Era's Auto Salvage, *see Vintage*

Joppa; Joppa Auto Salvage, 420 Pulaski Hwy, 21085; 410-679-0766; Sa, UR; 50; **D, F; B3**

Marlow Heights; Chuck's Used Auto Parts, *see Vintage*

Middle River; Doug's Auto & Truck Recycler, *see LateVintage*

Mount Airy; Mt Airy Auto Wrecking Inc, *see Vintage*

North East; King Salvage, *see LateVintage*

Odenton; Buz's Used Auto Parts, *see LateVintage*

Pasadena; Smitty's Auto Parts, *see LateVintage*

Prince Frederick; Seymour Inc, *see LateVintage*

Princess Anne; Smullen Salvage & Towing Inc, *see LateVintage*

Rockville; AAA Gene's Used Auto Parts, *see LateVintage*
  Rockville GM Used Auto Parts, 212 Mason Dr, 20850; 301-279-5834; CC, Sa, Sp, UR; 3ac; **D, F, PU, 4x4; B3**

Smithsburg; Elwood's Auto Exchange, *see Vintage*

Trappe; Thomas's Junk Yard, *see Vintage*

Upper Marlboro; Central Small Car Salvage, 104 N Crain Hwy Rte 301, 20772; 301-249-3200, 800-638-3446, www.brandywine.com; CC, Sa, UR, PL; 2500; **F; Jpa, Acura, Sterling**
  Ripples Service, 4904 Largo Rd, 20772; 301-627-3639, 800-590-2218, rippsaprt@aol.com; CC, Sa, Sp; 3ac, 600; **D, F, PU, 4x4, Trk; B3; mostly Domestic**

You may be a car nut if

You spend your whole vacation visiting wrecking yards

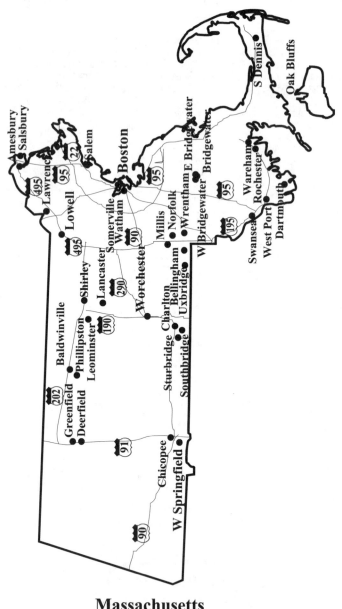

Massachusetts

**Please mention you saw'em in
Ray's wReckingyard Roster when
contacting these yards**

MASSACHUSETTS

VINTAGE

Bellingham; John's Used Auto Parts, 85 Hartford Av, 02019; 508-966-0135, 800-649-5033; Sa, Br; 400+; **40+; D, F, PU, 4x4; B3, Jp, Hd, St, VW**

Charlton; Stevens Auto Wrecking, 162 Freeman Rd, 01507; 508-248-5539, FAX 508-248-4894, 888-382-5941; CC, Sa, Sp, UR; 50ac, 2000+; **40+; D, F, PU, 4x4; B3**

Dartmouth; Will & Sons Auto Wrecking, 1342 N Hixville Rd, 02747; 508-995-8032; Sa; 3ac, 600; **60-90; D, F, PU; B3, AMC, Jp, VW**

Deerfield; East Deerfield Auto Wrecking, 727 River Rd, 01342; 413-773-7303; Sa; 28ac, 450; **23-91; D, F, PU, Trk; B3, Hd, St, Pk, VW**

Oak Bluffs; M D Auto Salvage, 12 Washington St, 02557; 508-693-0763, FAX 508-696-7733, 800-371-0763; Sa, Sp; 1500; **50+; D, F, PU, 4x4, Trk; B3, AMC, Jp, IH, VW**

Somerville; Nissenbaum's Auto Parts, 480 Columbia St, 02143; 617-776-0194, FAX 617-776-0197; CC, Sa, Wr; **65+; D, F, PU, 4x4; B3**

Sturbridge; Curboy's Used Auto Parts, 71 Meshapaug Rd, 01566; 508-347-9650, FAX 508-347-3202, 800-424-2014; Sa, Sp, UR; 3000; **40+, few 30s; D, F; B3, AMC, Hd, Ns, St, Pk, Ks, Fr, Wy**

West Bridgewater; Perry's Auto Sales & Parts, 640 East St, 02379; 508-697-4836; Sa, Wr; **30-69; D, PU; B3, AMC, St; parts for many older models**

Westport; Lantic Salvage, 58 Charlotte White Rd, 02790; 508-636-6959; Sa; 300; **60+; D, F, PU, 4x4; B3, AMC, Jp, VW**

Worchester; Standard Auto Wrecking, 257 Grant St, 01600; 508-755-8631, FAX 508-798-8445, 800-922-8281; CC, Sa, Sp, Br; 40ac; **60+; D, F, PU, 4x4; B3**

Wrentham; Tosy's Ford Mustang Farm, 714 South St, 02093; 508-384-8777, FAX 508-384-0591; Sa, Sp, UR, Wr; 900+; 15-89; **D, Trk; B3, AMC, Hd, St, Pk, Ks, Fr, Wy; Spc: 64-89 Mustang**

LATE VINTAGE

Amesbury; Martin Road Salvage Inc, 37 S Martin Rd, 01913; 978-388-5810; Sa, Sp, PL; 2000; **75+; D, F, PU, 4x4, Trk; B3, AMC, Jp, VW; Exports outside US**

Baldwinville; MBW Salvage Inc, 411 Baldwinville Rd, 01436; 978-939-5601; CC, Sa, Sp; 700+; **80+; D, F, PU, 4x4; B3**

Bellingham; John's Used Auto Parts, *see Vintage*

Boston; B Street Junk Car Removal, 183 W 1st St, 02127; 617-269-9732; Sa; 30; **70+; D, F; B3, AMC, Jp, IH**

Bridgewater; Jameson's Auto Salvage, 288 Pond St, 02324; 508-697-9621; Sa, Sp, UR; 150+; **80s, few 70s & 90s; D, F; B3, AMC, VW**

Charlton; Stevens Auto Wrecking, *see Vintage*

Chicopee; Fairview Auto Salvage Inc, 781 Ludlow Rd, 01020; 413-532-7463; Sa; 300; **70-89; D, PU; B3**

Dartmouth; Will & Sons Auto Wrecking, *see Vintage*

Deerfield; East Deerfield Auto Wrecking, *see Vintage*

East Bridgewater; A Regal Used Auto Parts, 358 Thatcher St, 02333; 508-583-1041, FAX 508-583-3386, 800-421-1041; CC, Sa, Sp, UR; 250+; **68+; D, F, PU, 4x4, Trk; B3, Jp, VW; Open Sunday; Spc: Muscle cars**

   All Foreign Auto Salvage Inc, 300 Thatcher St, 02333; 508-587-0222, FAX 508-580-0499, 800-831-0222; **CC, Sa, Sp; 1.5ac, 450; 83+; F, PU, 4x4**

Lawrence; Anchor Used Auto Parts, 140 West St, 01841; 978-687-2328, 800-829-2328; Sa, Sp, UR; 10000; **80+; D, F, PU, 4x4, Trk; B3, AMC, Jp, IH, VW**

Oak Bluffs; M D Auto Salvage, *see Vintage*

Phillipston; Fred's Used Parts, 300 Templeton Rd, 01468; 978-939-8061, 800-300-8061; Sa, Sp; 400; **80+; D, F, 4x4; B3, Jp**

Salem; Naumkeag Used Auto Parts, 50 Broadway St Rear, 01970; 978-744-8505; **70+; D, F**

Somerville; Aaple Used Auto Parts, 51 Allen, 02143; 617-282-1077; Sa, Sp; 100+; **80+; D, F; B3**

   Nissenbaum's Auto Parts, *see Vintage*

South Dennis; Center Street Auto Salvage, 550 Center St, 02660; 508-398-8988, 800-698-8988; CC, Sa, Sp, Br; 10ac, 2000; **80+, few 60-70s; D, F, PU, 4x4; B3**

Sturbridge; Curboy's Used Auto Parts, *see Vintage*
Uxbridge; Mill Street Auto Parts, 194 Mill St, 01569; 508-278-5157; Sa; 550; **80-89; D, PU, 4x4; B3, Jp**
Waltham; Route 128 Used Auto Parts, 40 Green St, 02154; 781-890-0025, FAX 781-466-8480, 800-698-4050; CC, Sa, Sp, UR; 300; **80-93; D, F, PU, 4x4; B3, AMC**
Wareham; Robertson's Auto Salvage, 2680 Cranberry Hwy, 02571; 508-295-9444, FAX 508-291-0695, 800-551-7000; CC, Sa, Sp, UR; 3000; **80+; D, F, PU, 4x4, Trk; B3, Jp, IH, VW**
West Springfield; Auto Salvage-West Springfield, 157 Agawam Av, 01089; 413-733-6948, FAX 413-788-5441, 888-447-4433; CC, Sa, Sp; 3000; **80+; few D, F, PU; Spc: Honda, Toyota, Mazda**
Westport; Lantic Salvage, *see Vintage*
   Thad's Auto Salvage, 37 Charlotte White Rd, 02790; 508-636-3301; Sa, Sp; 2500; **71+; D, F, PU, 4x4, Trk; B3, Jp, VW**
   Westport Auto Recycling Inc, 443 American Legion Hwy, 02790; 508-636-8201; Sa; **70-79; D, F, PU; B3, AMC, Jp, IH, VW**
Worchester; Standard Auto Wrecking, *see Vintage*
Wrentham; Armitage Auto Parts, 1143 South St, 02093; 508-384-5358; Sa; 400; **79-90; D, F; B3**
   Tosy's Ford Mustang Farm, *see Vintage*

LATE MODEL
Amesbury; Martin Road Salvage Inc, *see Late Vintage*
Baldwinville; MBW Salvage Inc, *see Late Vintage*
Bellingham; John's Used Auto Parts, *see Vintage*
Boston; B Street Junk Car Removal, *see Late Vintage*
Bridgewater; Jameson's Auto Salvage, *see Late Vintage*
Charlton; Stevens Auto Wrecking, *see Vintage*
Chicopee; Pasterczyk's Used Car Parts, 1737 Donohue Rd, 01020; 413-593-9200; Sa, Sp; 300; **D, PU, 4x4; B3, Jp; Spc: S-10**
Dartmouth; Sylvia's Auto Parts Inc, 73 Milton St, 02748; 508-994-5151, FAX 508-992-7059, 800-642-7598; CC, Sp; 10ac, 300; **D, F, PU, 4x4; B3**
East Bridgewater; A Regal Used Auto Parts, *see Late Vintage*
   All Foreign Auto Salvage Inc, *see Late Vintage*
Greenfield; Greenfield Auto Salvage, 392 Deerfield St, 01301; 413-774-4758, 800-322-3046; CC, Sa, Sp; 500; **D, F, PU, 4x4; B3, Jp, VW**
Lancaster; Crawford Quality Used Auto, 2176 Main St, 01523; 978-534-6855, FAX 978-840-6414, 800-322-2310; CC, Sa, Sp, UR; 3500; **D, F, PU, 4x4, Trk; B3, Jp, VW; Spc: SUV, vans**
Lawrence; Anchor Used Auto Parts, *see Late Vintage*
Leominster; Ollie's I-190 Used Auto Parts, 250 Lancaster St, 01453; 978-537-4742; CC, Sa, Sp, UR; **800+; D, F, PU, 4x4; B3, Jp, VW, Jpa**
   Route 2 Used Auto Parts, 56 Crawford St, 01453; 978-534-4221, FAX 978-534-8286, 800-922-8173, ; CC, Sa, Sp, UR; 600; **D, F, PU, 4x4; B3, Jp, VW**
Lowell; Atlantic Used Auto & Truck Parts, 12 Baldwin St, 01851; 978-459-2544, 800-225-0812, www.atlanticsalvage.com; CC, Sa, Sp; 1500; **D, F, PU, 4x4; B3**
   Kazanjians Used Auto Parts, 651 Dutton St, 01854; 978-970-4900, FAX 978-934-0001, 800-648-0034; CC, Sa, Sp, UR; 2ac; **D, F, PU, 4x4**
Miles; Millis Used Auto Parts Inc, 1465 Main St, 02054; 508-879-4100, 800-962-4100; CC, Sa, Sp, UR; **D, F, PU, 4x4; B3; Spanish**
Norfolk; Call & Wait Auto Svc, 15 Lincoln Rd, 02056; 508-528-1119, FAX 508-528-6808; Sa, Sp, Wr; **Trk, In, Cn; IH**
Oak Bluffs; M D Auto Salvage, *see Vintage*
Phillipston; Fred's Used Parts, *see Late Vintage*
Rochester; High Street Auto & Truck Salvage, 54 High St, 02770; 508-763-8990; Sa, Sp; **D, F, PU, 4x4, Trk; B3**
Salem; Naumkeag Used Auto Parts, *see Late Vintage*

160

Salisbury; Salisbury Auto Salvage, 16 Main St, 01952; 978-462-8262, 800-343-0327; CC, Sa, Sp, Br; 250+; **D, F, PU, 4x4; B3, Jp, VW**

Shirley; Burlington Used Auto Parts Inc, 127 Hazen Rd, 01464; 978-425-9132, FAX 978-425-4399, 800-228-5544; CC, Sa, Sp; 4000; **D, F, PU, 4x4; Spc: Foreign**

Somerville; Aaple Used Auto Parts, *see Late Vintage*
    Nissenbaum's Auto Parts, *see Vintage*

South Dennis; Center Street Auto Salvage, *see Late Vintage*

Southbridge; Plaza Used Auto Parts, 475 E Main St, 01550; 508-764-2773; Sa; **D, F**
Sturbridge; Curboy's Used Auto Parts, *see Vintage*

Swansea; Al's Auto Parts, 566 Bark St, 02777; 508-673-3519; Sa, Sp; 400; **D, F; B3, AMC**

Uxbridge; Universal Auto Salvage, 852 Millville Rd, 01569; 508-278-5600, FAX 508-278-6354, 800-441-6000, usainc@earthlink.net; CC, Sa, Sp; 1000; **D, PU, 4x4, Trk; B3, Jp**

Waltham; Route 128 Used Auto Parts, *see Late Vintage*

Wareham; Robertson's Auto Salvage, *see Late Vintage*

West Springfield; Auto Salvage-West Springfield, *see Late Vintage*

Westport; Lantic Salvage, *see Vintage*

Westport; Thad's Auto Salvage, *see Late Vintage*

Worchester; Standard Auto Wrecking, *see Vintage*

**Clyde, Assistant Manager
In Charge of Customer
Inspection & Mooching
Speedway Wreckers
Erie, CO**

MICHIGAN

VINTAGE
Battle Creek; Whispering Oaks Salvage, 523 Bowers Av, 49014; 616-962-9652; Sa, Sp; 1800+; **40+; D, F, PU, 4x4; B3, AMC, Jp, IH, VW**
Brighton; Rasmussen's Automotive Salvage, 9040 Spicer Rd, 48116; 734-449-2002; 150; **60+; D, PU; B3**
Carsonville; Carsonville Salvage, 355 Old 51, 48419; 810-657-9840, FAX 810-657-9227; Sa, UR, PL; 10ac; **65+; D, F, PU, 4x4; B3**

Cedar Springs; J & R Auto Salvage, 15730 Northland Dr, 49319; 616-696-1520, FAX 616-696-8388, 800-696-1720; CC, Sa, Sp, UR, PL; 20ac; **50+; D, F, PU, 4x4; B3; Spc: Corvair 60-69**

Chase; J & J Used Auto Parts, 8685 E US Hwy 10, 49623; 616-832-9013; CC, Sa, Sp, UR; 20ac; 1200; **60+; D, F, PU, 4x4, Trk; B3, AMC, IH, VW**

Clifford; La Blanc Auto Salvage, 9310 Lake Pleasant Rd, 48727; 517-761-7182; Sa, UR; 50ac, 5000+; **40+; D, F, PU, 4x4, Trk, Fm; B3 AMC, Jp, IH, St, Pk, VW; Open Sunday**

Crystal; Crystal Mike's Salvage Yard, 8643 Sidney Rd, 48818; 517-235-4663; Sa, Sp, Wr; 30ac; 3**0-95; D, F, PU, 4x4, Fm; B3, Jp, Wy; Spc: Chrysler Mopar**

Detroit; John's Auto Salvage, 5166 Grand River Av, 48209; 313-898-2332; Sa, Sp, Wr; 250; **65+; D, F, PU, 4x4; B3, VW**

Fenton; Fenton Auto Salvage, 1200 Torrey Rd, 48430; 810-629-1297; Sa, Sp, UR; 700; **46+; D, PU, 4x4; B3, AMC, Jp, IH, DeSoto**

Flint; Doyle's Auto Salvage, 5130 N Dort Hwy, 48505; 810-785-6535; CC, Sa, Sp; 600+; 6**0-93; D, F, PU, 4x4; B3, AMC**

Flint Auto Salvage, 5901 N Dort Hwy, 48505; 810-787-1166; Sa; 500+; **50+; D, F, PU, 4x4, Trk; B3, AMC, Jp, IH, VW; Open Sunday**

Fostoria; Bob's Auto Parts, 6390 N Lapeer Rd, 48435; 810-793-7500; Sa, Sp; 2000; **30+; D, PU, 4x4; B3, AMC, Jp, IH, Hd, St, Pk; By appointment only**

Gladwin; Frank's Auto Salvage, 5160 Eagleson Rd, 48624; 517-426-8789; Sa, UR; 300; 6**0-89; D, F, PU, 4x4; B3, AMC, IH**

Lapeer; Lapeer Auto & Truck Salvage, 2610 Imlay City Rd, 48446; 810-664-6608, FAX 810-664-4230; CC, Sa, Sp, UR; 10ac; **47+; D, F, PU, 4x4, Trk, Cn; B3, AMC, Jp, Wy, VW, Rambler, Edsel, Corvair, Mercedes, Ford Falcon**

North Pine River; Pine River Salvage, PO Box 30, Hwy 371 N, 56474; 218-587-2700, FAX 218-587-2094, 800-337-2705; Sa, Sp, UR; 200; **40-80; D, F, PU, 4x4, Trk, Fm; B3, AMC, Jp, IH, Wy**

Onaway; Croad Salvage, 439 State Hwy 33 S, 49765; 517-733-8221; Sa, UR; 10ac; **50+; D, few F, PU, 4x4; B3, AMC, Jp, IH**

Pierson; Zimmerman's Auto Wrecking, 103 Superior, 49339; 616-636-8285; Sa, UR; 4ac; 6**0-95; D, PU, 4x4; B3**

Richmond; Richmond Salvage, 31895 32 Mile Rd, 48062; 810-727-5554; Sa, Sp, Br; 350+; **60+; D, PU, 4x4; B3, Jp**

Riga; Michigan Corvette Recyclers, 11995 US Hwy 223, 49276; 517-486-4650, FAX 517-486-4124, 800-533-4650; CC, Sa, Sp, Wr; **68+; D; Corvette only**

Smiths Creek; Dave's Auto & Truck Slvg, 6449 Dove Rd, 48074; 810-367-3561, FAX 810-367-6905; CC, Sa; 800+; **40+; D, F, PU, 4x4, Trk, Fm; B3, AMC, Jp, IH, St; Closed Monday**

Southfield; Midwestern Motors & Dismantlers, 19785 W 12 N Mi Bldg 404, 48076; 248-559-8848, www.midwesternmotors.com; CC, Sa, Sp, UR; 100; **50+; F; Mercedes only**

Vestaberg; Hillard's Scrapyard, 11301 Crystal NE, 48891; 517-268-5262; Sa, UR; 10000; **30+; D, F; B3, AMC**

Westphalia; Westphalia Auto Salvage, 407 W Main St, 48894; 517-587-3060; UR; 100; 6**0-94 D, F, PU; B3**

Williamsburg; Erickson's Salvage, 3992 Moore Rd, 49690; 616-267-5955; Sa, UR, 300+; 6**1-88; D, F, PU, 4x4; B3, AMC**

Ypsilanti; Michigan Avenue Auto Salvage, 2494 E Michigan Av, 48198; 734-483-4980; Sa, Sp; 500; **65+; D, F, PU, 4x4, Cn; B3, AMC, Jp, VW**

LATE VINTAGE

Ada; Ada Auto Salvage & Parts, 6766 4 Mile Rd NE, 49301; 616-676-0644; Sa, Sp; 3ac; **75-93; D, F, PU, 4x4; B3**

Almont; P & L Auto Salvage, 504 Cherry St, 48003; 810-798-3393; Sa, UR; 500; **70+; D, PU; B3**

Bannister; Bill's Country Auto Salvage, 8491 S Woodbridge Rd, 48807; 517-862-5087; Sa, UR; 10ac; **70-90; D, F, PU, 4x4; B3**

Battle Creek; Whispering Oaks Salvage, *see Vintage*

Benton Harbor; A-1 Auto Salvage Co, 4478 Red Arrow Hwy, 49022; 616-849-3300, 800-870-0714; Sa; **70-89; D, F, PU; B3**

August Pohl Auto Wreckers, 2670 Territorial Rd, 49022; 616-925-3800; CC, Sa, Sp; 10ac; **85-90; D, F; B3**

Brighton; Jeff's Bronco Graveyard, 7843 Lochlin Dr, 48178; 248-437-5060, FAX 248-437-9354, www.broncograveyard.com; CC, Sa, Sp, Wr, PL; 66-**79; D; Fd Bronco only**

Rasmussen's Automotive Salvage, *see Vintage*

Burton; Southend Auto Salvage, G3360 Kleinpell St, 48529; 810-744-1200; Sa; 800; **70+; D, PU, 4x4; B3**

Canton; E & M Used Auto Parts, 42800 Yost Rd, 48188; 734-397-2200; Sa; 100; **80+, few 70s; D, PU; B3**

T & M Auto Salvage, 5405 S Sheldon Rd, 48334; 734-397-0000; Sa; 500+; **80+; D, F, PU, 4x4; B3**

Carsonville; Carsonville Salvage, *see Vintage*

Cass City; Bartnik Sales & Service, 6524 Van Dyke, 48726; 517-872-3541; Sa, Br; 375; **70+; D, F, PU, 4x4, Trk, Fm; B3, AMC, Jp, IH**

Cedar Springs; J & R Auto Salvage, *see Vintage*

Chase; J & J Used Auto Parts, *see Vintage*

Chesaning; Chesaning Auto Salvage, 10572 Baldwin Rd, 48616; 517-845-3076, FAX 517-845-3077; CC, Sa, Sp, Br; 2000; **70+; D, PU; B3; Spc: Fiero**

Clifford; La Blanc Auto Salvage, *see Vintage*

Coloma; Coloma Auto Wreckers, 5901 Red Arrow Hwy, 49038; 616-468-3183, FAX 616-468-4753; CC, Sa, Sp; 5.5ac; **75+; D, F, PU, 4x4; B3**

Crystal; Crystal Mike's Salvage Yard, *see Vintage*

Detroit; F & A Autos & Salvage, 5784 Rosa Parks Blvd, 48208; 313-873-8421; Sa; 100; **69+; D; B3**

John's Auto Salvage, *see Vintage*

Dorr; Dorr Auto Salvage Inc, 2311 141st Av, 49323; 616-681-2268; CC, Sa, Sp, PL; 1000+; **70+; D, F, PU, 4x4; B3, AMC, Jp, IH, VW**

Fenton; Fenton Auto Salvage, *see Vintage*

Flint; Doyle's Auto Salvage, *see Vintage*

Flint Auto Salvage, *see Vintage*

Fostoria; Bob's Auto Parts, *see Vintage*

Gladwin; Frank's Auto Salvage, *see Vintage*

JVS Auto Salvage Inc, 1445 S State Rte 30, 48624; 517-426-6710; CC, Sp, PL; 300; **70+; D, F, PU, 4x4, Trk; B3, AMC, Jp**

Grand Rapids; Easy Russ' Auto Salvage, 1952 Tamarack Av, 49504; 616-364-7626; Sa; 700; **80-93; D, F, PU; B3**

Harrison; Fox Used Cars & Parts, 3265 E Hamilton Dr, 48625; 517-539-7119; Sa, UR; 5000; **75+; D, F, PU, 4x4, Trk; B3, AMC, VW**

Howell; Miechiels Auto Salvage Inc, 405 S National St, 48843; 517-546-4111, 800-429-8506; Sa, UR; 2000+; **80+, few 60-70s; D, PU, 4x4; B3, Jp; Spc: Pickup**

Inkster; Bishops Auto Wrecking, 2780 Spring Hill Av, 48141; 734-722-9030, FAX 734-729-4081; Sa, UR; 2ac; **80+. Few 70s; D; B3**

Murphy Auto Wrecking, 2615 Bayhan St, 48141; 313-562-5100; Sa, UR; 150; **80-93; D, F, few PU, Trk; B3**

Lansing; Macs, 1800 Glenrose Av, 48915; 517-482-3885, FAX 517-487-8995; CC, Sa, UR; 700; **80s, few 70s; D, F, PU; B3**

Lapeer; Lapeer Auto & Truck Salvage, *see Vintage*

Mount Pleasant; W W Wing Used Parts, 4517 Packard Rd, 48858; 517-772-1528; 250; **80-89; D; B3**

North Pine River; Pine River Salvage, *see Vintage*

Onaway; Croad Salvage, *see Vintage*

Owosso; American Metal Buyers Inc, 1700 Cornell Rd, 48867; 517-725-7131; Sa, UR; 300; **70-89; D, PU; B3**

Pierson; Zimmerman's Auto Wrecking, *see Vintage*

Pinconning; C & L Auto Salvage, 1809 E Coggins Rd, 48650; 517-879-4689; Sa; 10ac; **70-89; D, F, PU, 4x4; B3**

Ravenna; R & R Auto Salvage, 11700 Bailey Rd, 49451; 616-853-2079; 50; **70-89; D; B3; Mostly repair**

Richmond; Richmond Salvage, *see Vintage*

Riga; Michigan Corvette Recyclers, *see Vintage*

Saginaw; Asher Auto Salvage, 1150 Butler Rd, 48601; 517-755-3484, FAX 517-755-0603; CC, Sp, PL; 500+; **75-93; D, F, PU, 4x4; B3**

   Fredd's Auto Salvage, 70 W Center St, 48602; 517-799-3415, FAX 517-799-1219, 888-324-4470; CC, Sa, Sp, Br; 300+; **75+; D, F, PU, 4x4; B3, AMC**

Sheridan; Armock's Auto Salvage, 2670 W Carson City Rd, 48884; 517-248-3202; Sa; 5ac; **70-89, few 60s; D, F, PU, 4x4; B3**

Smiths Creek; Dave's Auto & Truck Salvage, *see Vintage*

Southfield; Midwestern Motors & Dismantlers, *see Vintage*

Taylor; Taylor Auto Salvage Inc, 16211 Pardee Rd, 48180; 734-281-1342; Sa; UR; 10ac, 2500; **70-90; D, F, PU; B3, AMC**

Three Oaks; Zabel's Auto Salvage, 6288 W Kruger Rd, 49128; 616-756-3841, FAX 616-756-3124; Sa, Sp; 300+; **75+; D, F, PU; B3, VW**

Vestaberg; Hillard's Scrapyard, *see Vintage*

Westphalia; Westphalia Auto Salvage, *see Vintage*

Williamsburg; Erickson's Salvage, *see Vintage*

Ypsilanti; Harry's Towing & Auto Parts, 2600 Coolidge Rd, 48199; 734-481-2237; CC, Sa, Sp; 3.5ac; **80+; D, F, PU, 4x4; B3**

   Keb Inc, 2280 E Michigan Av, 48198; 734-484-0508, FAX 734-484-1210; CC, Sa, Sp, UR; 5.5ac, 850+; **70+; D, F, PU, 4x4; B3**

   Michigan Avenue Auto Salvage, *see Vintage*

LATE MODEL

Ada; Ada Auto Salvage & Parts, *see Late Vintage*

Almont; P & L Auto Salvage, *see Late Vintage*

Battle Creek; Whispering Oaks Salvage, *see Vintage*

Brighton; Rasmussen's Automotive Salvage, *see Vintage*

Burton; Southend Auto Salvage, *see Late Vintage*

Canton; E & M Used Auto Parts, *see Late Vintage*

   T & M Auto Salvage, *see Late Vintage*

Carson City; Carson City Auto Salvage, 7190 S Garlock Rd, 48811; 517-584-3219; Sa; 350+; **D, PU, 4x4; B3; Spc: GM**

Carsonville; Carsonville Salvage, *see Vintage*

Cass City; Bartnik Sales & Service, *see Late Vintage*

Cedar Springs; J & R Auto Salvage, *see Vintage*

Chase; J & J Used Auto Parts, *see Vintage*

Chesaning; Chesaning Auto Salvage, *see Late Vintage*

Clifford; La Blanc Auto Salvage, *see Vintage*

Coloma; Coloma Auto Wreckers, *see Late Vintage*

Crystal; Crystal Mike's Salvage Yard, *see Vintage*

Detroit; Ace Auto Wrecking, 6462 Miller St, 48211; 313-922-6150; Sa, Sp, UR; **D, F; B3**

   F & A Autos & Salvage, *see Late Vintage*

   John's Auto Salvage, *see Vintage*

Dorr; Dorr Auto Salvage Inc, *see Late Vintage*

Dowagiac; Allen's Wrecking Yard, 54290 State Rte 51 N #M, 49047; 616-782-8128; **D**

Dundee; Bonnie & Clyde's Auto Salvage, 425 Roosevelt, 48131; 734-529-2181; Sa, UR; 4.5ac; **D, PU, 4x4, Trk, Cn; B3**

   Dundee Truck & Trim, 500 Roosevelt, 48131; 734-529-5934; Sa, Sp; 100; **D, PU; Chevy Pickup & Suburban only**

Fenton; Fenton Auto Salvage, *see Vintage*

Flint; Doyle's Auto Salvage, *see Vintage*

   Flint Auto Salvage, *see Vintage*

165

Fostoria; Bob's Auto Parts, *see Vintage*
Fremont; Leo's Auto Parts, 2392 South Stone Rd, 49412; 616-924-6562; CC, Sa; 37ac, 200+; **D, F, PU, 4x4**
Gladwin; JVS Auto Salvage Inc, *see Late Vintage*
Grand Rapids; Easy Russ' Auto Salvage, *see Late Vintage*
Harrison; Fox Used Cars & Parts, *see Late Vintage*
Harrison Township; Ernie's Auto Parts Inc, 42449 Irwin Dr, 48045; 810-465-0091, FAX 810-465-1324, 877-775-9550; CC, Sa, Sp; 400; **D, PU, 4x4; B3**
    Shaw Brothers Auto Salvage, 25350 Joy Blvd, 48045; 810-468-8244, FAX 810-468-5491; CC, Sa, Sp, UR; 600; **D, F, PU, 4x4; B3**
Howell; Miechiels Auto Salvage Inc, *see Late Vintage*
Inkster; Bishops Auto Wrecking, *see Late Vintage*
    Murphy Auto Wrecking, *see Late Vintage*
Iron Mountain; Wally's Auto Salvage Inc, W8094 S US Hwy 2, 49801; 906-774-5503; CC, Sp, PL; 1500+; **D, F, PU; B3, AMC, VW**
Lansing; Cats Part-S-Mart Auto Salvage, 5405 W Mount Hope Rd, 48917; 517-322-2350; CC, Sa, UR; 1000; **D, F, PU, 4x4; B3**
Lapeer; Lapeer Auto & Truck Salvage, *see Vintage*
Mancelona; R & S Auto & Truck Parts, 3011 Leonard Rd, 49659; 616-587-5511, 800-462-7074; Sp; 600; **D, F, PU, 4x4; B3**
Marquette; Mattson Auto Ctr, 534 Co Rd 553, 49855; 906-249-1010, FAX 906-249-1022; Sa; 300; **D, F, PU, 4x4; B3**
Millington; Shulty's Auto Salvage, 10101 N Belsay Rd, 48746; 517-871-3165, FAX 517-871-4672; Sa, Sp, Br; 750+; **D, PU, 4x4; B3, AMC**
Naubinway; Cut River Auto Salvage, 57 US 2 W, 49762; 906-292-5636, FAX 906-292-0013; Sp, PL; 400+; **86+, few 60s; D, F, PU, 4x4, Trk; B3**
Onaway; Croad Salvage, *see Vintage*
Pierson; Zimmerman's Auto Wrecking, *see Vintage*
Richmond; Richmond Salvage, *see Vintage*
Riga; Michigan Corvette Recyclers, *see Vintage*
Romulus; Co-Part Auto Salvage, 19845 Telegraph Rd, 48174; 734-479-2500; **Auction Weds**
    Van Born Auto Wrecking, 28527 Van Born Rd, 48174; 734-722-8680, FAX 734-722-0211; CC, Sa, Sp; 200; **D; B3**
Saginaw; Asher Auto Salvage, *see Late Vintage*
    Fredd's Auto Salvage, *see Late Vintage*
Shepherd; Oil City Auto Salvage, 1316 S Dickenson Rd, 48883; 517-772-5859; Sp; **D, F; B3**
Smiths Creek; Dave's Auto & Truck Salvage, *see Vintage*
South Lyon; Bears Auto Salvage, 22675 Griswold Rd, 48178; 248-437-2010; CC, Sa, Sp, UR; 500; **D, PU, 4x4, Trk; B3, AMC, Jp, IH**
Southfield; Midwestern Motors & Dismantlers, *see Vintage*
Spring Lake; Joe's Auto Wrecking, 14718 M 104, 49456; 616-842-6940, FAX 616-842-9889, 800-442-3508; Sa, UR; 36ac; **D, F, PU, 4x4, Trk; B3, AMC, Jp, VW**
Three Oaks; Zabel's Auto Salvage, *see Late Vintage*
Vestaberg; Hillard's Scrapyard, *see Vintage*
Warren; Macomb Auto Salvage Inc, 26600 Bunert Rd, 48089; 810-778-6530, FAX 810-778-7078, 800-837-7735; CC, Sa, Sp; 11ac, 1000; **D, F, PU, 4x4; B3**
Westphalia; Westphalia Auto Salvage, *see Vintage*
Willis; Abbot Auto Salvage, 10339 Willis Rd, 48191; 734-461-9600, FAX 734-461-1344; Sa, Sp, UR; 125; **D, few PU; B3**
Ypsilanti; Harry's Towing & Auto Parts, *see Late Vintage*
    Keb Inc, *see Late Vintage*
    Michigan Avenue Auto Salvage, *see Vintage*

1949 Hudson Commodore Convertible
Ray Harvey
Cheyenne, WY

D

Crookston

Bimidji

Grand Rapids

94

Park Rapids

Duluth

Brainerd

35

Wadena

Pierz

Royalton
Henriette
Alexandria   Pine City
Milaca

Browns Valley   Melrose
                              Sauk Rapids North Branch
Paynesville   St Francis
New London   Big Lake   E Bethel

Litchfield   Silver Lake
Hutchinson   Roseville Anoka
                        Shakopee   St Paul
                        Rosemount   Newport
                                      Hastings
Green Isle   Jordan   Lakeville
Marshall   Redwood Falls
                                   35
            Sleepy Eye
Balaton   Sanborn
                        Byron   Winona
Pipestone   St Charles
            90   Albert Lee   Peterson
Worthington   Glenville Austin
    Ellsworth   Fairmont

MINNESOTA

VINTAGE
Austin; Crews Auto Salvage, 2700 11 St NE, 55912; 507-433-5182, 800-658-7001; CC, Sa, Sp, Br; 1600; **50-94; D, F, PU, 4x4; B3, Hd, Ns, St, VW**
Bemidji; Aassee's Auto Salvage Inc, 1718 Sunnyside Rd SE, 56601; 218-751-7260, FAX 218-751-2010, 800-862-7260; Sa, Sp, UR, PL; 40ac, 5000; **50+; D, F, PU, 4x4; B3, AMC, Jp, IH, VW, Porsche, Mercedes**

Brainerd; Kohl's Auto Salvage "Bob", 220 Nokasippi River Rd SE, 56401; 218-829-1947; 4ac; 65-91; **D, F, PU, 4x4; B3**

Browns Valley; Brown's Valley Auto Salvage, 56219; 320-695-2107; Sa, Sp; 100ac; **55+; D, F, PU, 4x4; B3**

Byron; Dillon's Auto Salvage, 7507 10 St SW, 55920; 507-281-3872, FAX 507-281-4723, 800-898-3872; CC, Sa, Sp; 30ac; 60+; D, F, PU, 4x4; B3

Crookston; Crookston Auto Salvage, 800 S Minnesota St, 56716; 218-281-2452; www. salvage@northernet.com; Sa, Sp, UR; 500; **40+; D, F, PU, 4x4; B3, AMC, Jp, IH, St, VW**

Glenville; Bridley Auto Slvg, RR 2, 56036; 507-448-2905, 800-584-9458; Sa, Sp, UR; 2500+; 11-**85; D, F, PU, 4x4, Trk, Fm, Mil; B3, AMC, Jp, IH, Hd, Ns, St, Pk, Ks, Fr, Wy, VW, Jpa**

Grand Rapids; Chuck's Auto Salvage, 5011 E Bass Lk Rd, 55744; 218-328-6281, 800-300-6281; Sa, Sp, UR; 2000; **50+; D, F, PU, 4x4; B3, AMC, Jp, IH, VW**

Hastings; Joe's Auto Sales, 5849 - 190th St E, 55033; 651-437-6787, 800-359-0970; CC, Sa, Sp, Br, PL; 1300+; 39-**89; D; Fd, Lincoln, Mercury only; PL #: 800-831-0820**

Marshall; Doug's Auto Parts, 900 Hwy 59 N Box 811, 56258; 507-537-1487, FAX 507-537-0519; CC, Sp, Wr; 10ac; 1000; **32-70; D, PU, 4x4; Fd, Chevy; Sells whole cars; Spc: Coupes & Convertibles**

Melrose; Skunk's Auto Salvage & Part, 30655 County Rd 17, 56352; 320-256-3827; Sa, Sp, UR; 2000; **50-95; D, F, PU, 4x4, Trk, Mil; B3, AMC, Jp, IH, VW; Snowmobiles**

Milaca; Freyholtz Auto Salvage, 13436 140th St, 56353; 320-983-6990; Sa, Sp, UR; 75ac; 500; **30+; D, F, PU, 4x4, Trk; B3, AMC, Jp, IH, St; Older Chevys & Panel Trucks**

New London; Windy Hill Auto Parts, 9200 240th Av NE, 56273; 320-354-2201, FAX 320-354-2229, 800-398-0566; CC, Sa, Sp, Br; 160ac, 12000; **30+; D, F, PU, 4x4, Trk, Fm, In, Cn, Mil; B3, AMC, Jp, IH, Hd, Ns, St, Pk, Ks, Fr, Cr, Wy, VW**

Newport; Bill's Auto Parts, 310-7th Av, 55055; 651-459-9733, www.billsauto.8m.com; Sa, Sp; **30-89; D, F, 4x4; B3, AMC, Jp, Ns, St, Edsel, Hillman**

Park Rapids; Dick's Auto Wrecking, Hwy 71 S, 56470; 218-732-4220, FAX 218-732-4220, 800-492-4835; CC, Sa, Sp; 30ac; 60+; D, F, PU, 4x4; B3

Peterson; Chiglo's Auto Salvage, County Road 107, 55962; 507-875-2323, 800-360-1398; Sa, Sp; 60+; D; B3

Pierz; Okroi's Auto Salvage Inc, RR 1, 56364; 320-468-2810; Sa, Sp; 1000; **53-96; D, F, PU, 4x4; B3, AMC, Jp, IH, VW, DeSoto**

Sauk Rapids; Countryside Auto Salvage, 2714 Mayhew Lake Rd NE, 56379; 320-251-2979, FAX 320-255-0526; Br; 1000; **50-92; D, F, PU, 4x4; B3, AMC, Jp, IH, VW**

Silver Lake; R & R Auto & Truck Salvage, 8506 180th St, 55381; 320-327-3164; CC, Sa, Sp; 5ac, 300+; **20-85; D, PU, 4x4, Trk, Fm; B3, Jp, IH, Pk**

Sleepy Eye; Sleepy Eye Salvage Co, RR 4 Box 60, Hwy 4S, 56085; 507-794-6673; Sa, Sp; 1500; **54+; D, F, PU, 4x4; B3, St; Also sells whole cars**

Winona; Papenfuss Salvage, RR 1 Box 120, 55987; 507-643-6745, FAX 507-643-6928, 800-866-9864; CC, Sa, Sp; 2000+; **20+; D, F, PU, 4x4; B3, AMC, Jp, IH, St, Wy, VW**

LATE VINTAGE

Alexandria; Budget Auto Salvage, 5111 State Hwy 27 E, 56308; 320-763-4231, FAX 320-763-0564, 800-450-6500; CC, Sa, Sp; 12ac, 1400; 69-**94; D, PU, 4x4; B3**

Anoka; Anoka Auto Wrecking, 1775 NW Bunker Lk Blvd, 55304; 612-755-4580, FAX 612-755-9346; CC, Sa, Sp, UR; 23ac; **70+; D, F, PU, 4x4; B3**

Austin; Crews Auto Salvage, *see Vintage*

Balaton; Balaton Auto Slvg, RR 1 Box 420, 56115; 507-734-6381; Sp; 15ac; **80+; D, PU, 4x4; B3**

Bemidji; Aassee's Auto Salvage Inc, *see Vintage*

Brainerd; Kohl's Auto Salvage "Bob", *see Vintage*

Browns Valley; Brown's Valley Auto Salvage, *see Vintage*

Byron; Dillon's Auto Salvage, *see Vintage*

Crookston; Crookston Auto Salvage, *see Vintage*

Duluth; Calvary Auto & Salvage Inc, 4825 Rice Lake Rd, 55803; 218-723-1294, FAX 218-723-1122; Sa, Sp, UR, PL; 1500; **80+; D, F, PU, 4x4; B3, AMC, Jp, VW**

Chesney Auto Salvage, 6250 Beaver River Rd, 55803; 218-721-4874, FAX 218-721-4140, 800-826-2941; CC, Sa, Sp, UR; 40ac, 5000+; 70+; **D, F, PU, 4x4; B3, AMC, Jp, IH, VW**

East Bethel; North Metro Auto Salvage Inc, 20418 Hwy 65 NE, 55011; 612-434-5229, FAX 612-434-9575, 800-422-5229; CC, Sa, Sp, UR; 25ac; **80+; D, F, PU, 4x4; B3**

Ellsworth; Ellsworth Auto Salvage, 401 W Sherman Av, 56129; 507-967-2525, FAX 507-967-2526, 800-801-4073; CC, Sa, Sp; 600; **78-96; D, F, PU, 4x4; B3; Spc: GM**

Fairmont; B & K Auto Salvage, 1775 90th St, 56031; 507-238-1934; Sa, Sp; 15ac; **75-95; D, PU, 4x4; B3**

Glenville; Bridley Auto Salvage, *see Vintage*

Grand Rapids; Chuck's Auto Salvage, *see Vintage*

Green Isle; Green Isle Auto Salvage, N Hwy 5 & 25, 55338; 507-326-5791; Sa, UR; 300; **80+; D, F, PU, 4x4, Trk; B3**

Hastings; Joe's Auto Sales, *see Vintage*

Henriette; B & J Auto Salvage, 237 Main St S, 55036; 320-679-3886, FAX 320-679-9038, 800-570-3886; CC, Sa, Sp, UR; 200; 70-**89; D, F, PU, 4x4; B3**

Hutchinson; Hutch Auto & Truck Salvage, 13396 Hwy 7, 55350; 320-587-5839, 800-685-5839; CC, Sa, Sp, Br, PL; 30ac; **75+; D, F, PU, 4x4; B3**

Litchfield; Mies Auto Salvage, 62805 MN Hwy 24, 55355; 320-693-2546; Sa, UR; 500; 70+; **D, F, PU, 4x4, Trk, Fm, In, Cn; B3**

Marshall; Doug's Auto Parts, *see Vintage*

Melrose; Skunk's Auto Salvage & Part, *see Vintage*

Milaca; Freyholtz Auto Salvage, *see Vintage*

New London; Windy Hill Auto Parts, *see Vintage*

Newport; Bill's Auto Parts, *see Vintage*

North Branch; Auto Truck & Van Salvage, 8410 St Croix Trl, 55056; 651-674-0000, FAX 651-674-0289, 800-800-8393; CC, Sa, Sp; 10ac; **75-89; D, F, PU, 4x4; B3; Rebuilds steering & drive trains**

Park Rapids; Dick's Auto Wrecking, *see Vintage*

Peterson; Chiglo's Auto Salvage, *see Vintage*

Pierz; Okroi's Auto Salvage Inc, *see Vintage*

Pipestone; Hubers Salvage, RR 4 Box 119, 56164; 507-825-4676, FAX 507-825-2628; CC, Sa, Sp; 14ac; 77-**96; D, F, PU, 4x4; B3; Spc: Pickup**

Redwood Falls; Nelson's Salvage, 30806 360th Av, 56283; 507-641-3061, FAX 507-641-5087; Sa, Sp; 15ac; **80+; D, F, PU, 4x4; B3**

Roseville; RX7 Heaven, 1743 W Co Rd C, 55113; 651-639-9460, FAX 651-639-0351, 888-571-2472; CC, Sa, Sp, Wr; **79-95; F; Mazda RX-**7 only

St Charles; Timm's Auto Salvage, 936 W 12 St, 55972; 507-932-4464, FAX 507-932-0217, 800-234-4464; CC, Sa, Sp, Br; 14ac; **80+; D, F, PU, 4x4, Trk, Cn; B3**

Sanborn; Hilltop Auto & Truck Slvg, Rt 1 Box 2A, 56083; 507-648-3398, FAX 507-648-3898, 800-348-6403; Sa, Sp; 6ac; **80-95; D, F, PU, 4x4, Trk, Fm; B3; Spc: Pickup**

Sauk Rapids; Countryside Auto Salvage, *see Vintage*

Shakopee; Hwy 101 Auto Salvage Inc, 9099 13 Av E, 55378; 612-445-7020, FAX 612-496-2441, 888-449-9101; CC, Sa, Sp, UR; 9ac; 77-**90; D, F, PU, 4x4; B3**

Silver Lake; R & R Auto & Truck Salvage, *see Vintage*

Sleepy Eye; Sleepy Eye Salvage Co, *see Vintage*

Wadena; Ward's Auto Salvage, RR 1 Box 144, 56482; 218-631-9273; Sp; 1000; **75-93; D, F, PU, 4x4; B3**

Winona; Papenfuss Salvage, *see Vintage*

LATE MODEL

Albert Lea; Albert Lea Auto Salvage Inc, County Rd 46 E, 56007; 507-256-7201, FAX 507-256-7203, 800-950-4644, www.albertleaauto.com; CC, Sa, Sp; 4500; **D, F, PU, 4x4; B3**

Alexandria; Budget Auto Salvage, *see Late Vintage*

Crosstown Auto & Truck Salvage, 8066 State Hwy 29 S, 56308; 320-762-1011, FAX 320-762-5645, 800-658-3431, www.mypartsshop.com; CC, Sa, Sp; 10ac; **D, F, PU, 4x4; B3; Spc: GM, Ford**

Anoka; Anoka Auto Wrecking, *see Late Vintage*

Austin; Crews Auto Salvage, *see Vintage*

Balaton; Balaton Auto Salvage, *see Late Vintage*

Bemidji; Aassee's Auto Salvage Inc, *see Vintage*

Big Lake; Jerry's Auto Salvage Inc, 20798 Hwy 10, 55309; 612-263-2600, FAX 612-263-8505, 800-223-1817; CC, Sa, Sp; 40ac; **D, F, PU, 4x4; B3**

Browns Valley; Brown's Valley Auto Salvage, *see Vintage*

Byron; Dillon's Auto Salvage, *see Vintage*

Crookston; Crookston Auto Salvage, *see Vintage*

Duluth; Calvary Auto & Salvage Inc, *see Late Vintage*
  Chesney Auto Salvage, *see Late Vintage*

East Bethel; North Metro Auto Salvage Inc, *see Late Vintage*

Ellsworth; Ellsworth Auto Salvage, *see Late Vintage*

Fairmont; B & K Auto Salvage, *see Late Vintage*

Grand Rapids; Chuck's Auto Salvage, *see Late Vintage*

Green Isle; Green Isle Auto Salvage, *see Late Vintage*

Hutchinson; Hutch Auto & Truck Salvage, *see Late Vintage*

Jordan; Cedar Auto Parts, 1100 Syndicate St, 55352; 612-492-3303, FAX 612-492-3303, 800-755-3266; CC, Sa, Sp, Br; 5.5ac, 750; **D, PU, 4x4; B3; Spc: Corvette**

Lakeville; Metro Auto Salvage, 11710 263 St E, 55044; 612-461-2186, FAX 612-461-2184, 800-252-5831; CC, Sa, Sp; 8ac; **D, F, PU, 4x4; B3**

Litchfield; Mies Auto Salvage, *see Late Vintage*

Melrose; Skunk's Auto Salvage & Part, *see Vintage*

Milaca; Freyholtz Auto Salvage, *see Vintage*

New London; Windy Hill Auto Parts, *see Vintage*

Park Rapids; Dick's Auto Wrecking, *see Vintage*

Paynesville; Paynesville Auto Salvage, 448 E Hoffman St, 56362; 320-243-5000; Sa, Sp, UR, Wr, PL; 3ac; **D, F, PU, 4x4; B3**

Peterson; Chiglo's Auto Salvage, *see Vintage*

Pierz; Okroi's Auto Salvage Inc, *see Vintage*

Pine City; Pine Auto Salvage, Rt 4 Box 237, 55063; 320-629-2593, FAX 320-629-3703, 800-338-4591, www.pineautosalvage.com; CC, Sa, Sp; 8ac; **D, F, PU, 4x4; B3**

Pipestone; Hubers Salvage, *see Late Vintage*

Redwood Falls; Nelson's Salvage, *see Late Vintage*

Rosemount; AAA Auto Salvage, 2871 160th W, 55068; 651-423-2432, FAX 651-423-2808, 800-238-6664, www.parts@AAAparts.com; CC, Sa, Sp; 800; **D, F, PU, 4x4; B3; 2 locations**

Roseville; RX7 Heaven, *see Late Vintage*

Royalton; Rick's Towing Auto Parts & Sales, Box 92, 56373; 320-584-5586, FAX 320-584-8040, 800-245-5588; CC, Sa, Sp, Br; 300; **D, F, PU, 4x4, Trk; B3**

St Charles; Timm's Auto Salvage, *see Late Vintage*

St Francis; Bourke Auto Salvage, 4058 Hwy 47, 55070; 612-753-9535; Sa, Sp, UR; 10ac; **D, F, PU; B3**

St Paul; Crosstown Auto Inc, 1440 Marshall, 55104; 651-645-7715, FAX 651-645-5183; CC, Sa, Sp, UR; 1ac; **D, F, PU, 4x4; B3**

Sanborn; Hilltop Auto & Truck Salvage, *see Late Vintage*

Sauk Rapids; Countryside Auto Salvage, *see Vintage*

Sleepy Eye; Sleepy Eye Salvage Co, *see Vintage*

Wadena; Ward's Auto Salvage, *see Late Vintage*

Winona; Papenfuss Salvage, *see Vintage*
  Whetstone Auto & Truck Salvage Inc, RR 3 Box 2856, 55987; 507-452-2040, FAX 507-452-5725, 800-328-7754; CC, Sp; 40ac; **D, F, PU, 4x4; B3; Rebuilds digital controls & speedometers**

Worthington; Dyke's Auto Salvage, Hwy 59 & 60, 56187; 507-372-2936, FAX 507-372-2938, 800-658-2424; CC, Sa, Sp; 10ac; **D, F, PU, 4x4**

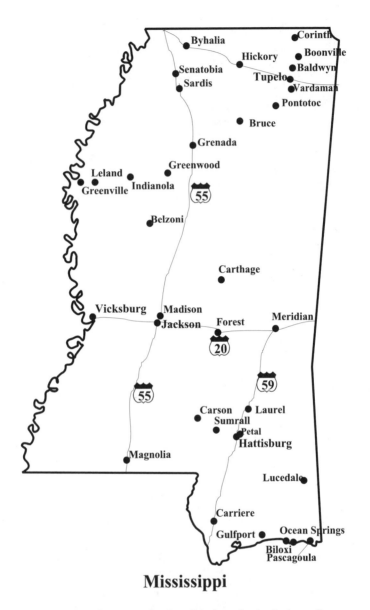

Mississippi

Please use the cards in the back to let us know about yards we may have missed, or any other comments or information for future editions of Ray's wReckingyard Roster

MISSISSIPPI

VINTAGE

Bruce; Patterson's Garage & Salvage, PO Box 134, 38915; 662-983-2133; Sa, Sp, UR; 1200; **50-89; D, F, PU, 4x4, Trk, Fm; B3, AMC, Jp, IH**

Forest; Forest Auto Salvage, 19207 Hwy 80, 39074; 601-469-1996; Sa, Sp, Br; 1000+; **60+; D, F, PU, 4x4, Trk; B3, AMC, Jp, VW**

Hickory; Harrison Auto Salvage & Garage, 8949 Hwy 503, 39332; 601-646-2210, 800-287-1272; Sa, Sp, UR; 1100; **36+; D, F, PU, 4x4, Trk, Fm; B3, AMC, Jp, IH, VW**

Magnolia; Sandifer Auto Salvage, 6062 Osyka Progress Rd, 39652; 601-542-3684; Sa, Sp, UR; 5500+; **50+; D, F, PU, 4x4, Trk, Fm, In; B3, AMC, Jp, IH, St, Pk, VW**

Ocean Springs; Meyers Auto Salvage, 9113 Hwy 57, 39565; 228-826-5792; Sa, UR; 200; **50+; D, PU, 4x4; B3**

LATE VINTAGE

Belzoni; Forty Nine Auto Salvage, Hwy 49 W, 39038; 601-247-2178; Sa, UR; 300; **75+; D, F, PU; B3**

Biloxi; F & M Auto Salvage, 4220 Lickskillet Rd, 39532; 228-392-4939; Sa, UR; 350; **75-90; D, few F, few PU, few 4x4, Trk; B3, AMC, few Jp, few VW**

Holley's Wrecking Yard, 15813 Lemoyne Blvd, 39532; 228-392-3599; Sa, UR; 4ac, 250; **77-90; D, F, PU, 4x4, Trk; B3, AMC, VW**

Bruce; Patterson's Garage & Salvage, *see Vintage*

Byhalia; A A Foreign Auto Parts Salvage, 9279 Hwy 78 W, 38661; 662-838-5189, 800-200-4292; Sa, Sp; 350+; **81+; F, PU, 4x4; Jpa**

Carriere; Fleming's Auto Salvage, 29 Fleming Rd, 39426; 601-798-4129; Sa, UR; 1300; **70-91; D, F, PU, 4x4; B3, AMC, VW**

Carson; D & G Auto Salvage, Rt 1 Box 211, 39427; 601-943-5758; Sa, Br; **80-95; D, F, PU, 4x4; B3, Jp**

Carthage; City Auto Salvage, 808 Hwy 35 N, 39051; 601-267-4593, 800-748-8987; Sp; 950+; **70-90; D, F, PU, 4x4, Trk; B3, AMC, Jp; Spc: GM & Ford**

Forest; Forest Auto Salvage, *see Vintage*

Greenville; C & W Salvage, 827 Hwy 82, 38701; 662-335-9828; Sa, Sp, UR; 3ac; **65+; D, F, PU; B3**

Greenwood; 49 Auto Salvage, 2900 US Hwy 49 E, 38930; 662-453-1843; Sa; 350+; **80+; D, F, PU, 4x4; B3, VW**

Grenada; Jack's Auto Salvage, 25555 Hwy 8 E, 38901; 662-226-7744; CC, Sp; 10ac; **80+; D, F, PU, 4x4, Trk; B3, AMC, Jp, IH**

Gulfport; Affordable Auto Salvage, 13203 Three Rivers Rd, 39503; 228-832-2014; CC, Sa, Sp; 3ac, 400+; **75-95; D, F, PU, 4x4; B3, AMC, Jp, VW**

Hickory; Harrison Auto Salvage & Garage, *see Vintage*

Indianola; Cobb's Salvage, 1847 Hwy 82 W, 38751; 662-887-4015; Sa, UR; 250+; **70-89; D, F, PU; B3**

Jackson; Rankin County Auto Parts, 654 Casey Ln, 39208; 601-939-3699, 800-234-3699; CC, Sa, Sp; **80+; D, F; B3, AMC, VW**

Staring Auto Salvage, 6765 I 55 S, 39212; 601-372-5152, FAX 601-373-1677; Sp; 21ac; 800; **65+; D, F, PU, 4x4, Trk; B3, AMC, Jp, IH**

Laurel; Mack's Auto Wrecking Used Parts, 5 Williams Rd, 39443; 601-649-1249; Sa, Sp, UR; 500; **70-95; D, F, PU; B3, AMC**

Magnolia; 48 Salvage, 2073 Hwy 48 E, 39652; 601-783-3777, FAX 601-783-3001; Sp, UR; 1000; **65+; D, F, PU, 4x4, Trk; B3, AMC, Jp, IH**

Sandifer Auto Salvage, *see Vintage*

Ocean Springs; Meyers Auto Salvage, *see Vintage*

Pascagoula; Delmas Salvage, 5901 Orchard Av, 39581; 228-769-1927; Sa, UR; 500+; **65+; D, F, PU, Fm; B3, VW**

M & Z Auto Salvage, 8401 Old Stage Rd, 39581; 228-475-555, FAX 228-475-2483, 888-475-6455; CC, Sa, Sp, UR; 600+; **80+; D, F, PU, 4x4, Trk; B3, AMC, Jp, IH, VW**

Pascagoula Auto Salvage Inc, 10600 Hwy 90 E, 39581; 228-475-6730, FAX 228-475-2007, 800-277-2788; Sp; 30ac, 3000; **D, F, PU, 4x4, Mil, Trk, Fm; B3, AMC, Jp, IH, VW**

Petal; Petal Auto Parts, 831 Hwy 11, 39465; 601-584-8838, FAX 601-584-8839, 800-844-1227, papi@netdoor.com; CC, Sp, Br; 1000; **80+; D, F, PU, 4x4; B3, AMC, Jp, IH**

Sardis; Davis Auto Salvage, 100 S Main St, 38666; 662-487-1871; Sa; 2ac; **75-89; D, PU; B3; Also used car sales**

Sumrall; Lamar Auto Salvage Exchange, 8575 US Hwy 98 W, 39482; 601-264-7992, FAX 601-261-2608, 800-844-2886; CC, Sp; 15ac, 3500+; **80+; D, F, PU, 4x4, Trk; B3, AMC, Jp, IH, VW**

Tupelo; Garrison's Auto Salvage, 2648 Sims Gin Rd, 38801; 601-680-5194; Sa; **75-92; D, F, PU; B3**

Vardaman; Parker Auto Salvage, 416 Hwy 8E, 38878; 662-682-7800; Sa, UR; 450+; **80-95; D, PU, 4x4; B3, AMC**

Vicksburg; Matthews Auto Parts, 4404 Hwy 61 S, 39180; 601-638-9393, 800-777-9394; CC, Sp; 20ac, 3000; **90s, few 60s & 70s; D, F, PU, 4x4, Trk; B3, AMC, Jp, IH**

LATE MODEL

Baldwyn; R & S Auto Salvage, Hwy 45 S, 38824; 662-365-2198; 800; **D, PU; B3, AMC**

Belzoni; Forty Nine Auto Salvage, *see Late Vintage*

Biloxi; Barry's Import Auto Salvage, 13464 Hwy 15, 39532; 228-392-4980, FAX 228-392-7978, 800-647-8842; CC, Sp; 500; **D, F, PU, 4x4, Trk; B3, AMC, Jp, IH, VW**

Booneville; Lambert Auto Sales & Salvage, 2412 S 2nd St, 38829; 662-728-0409, FAX 662-728-0489, 877-728-0409; CC, Sp, Br; 250; **D; Camaro, Trans Am, sports cars**

Byhalia; A A Foreign Auto Parts Salvage, *see Late Vintage*

Carson; D & G Auto Salvage, *see Late Vintage*

Corinth; Corinth Auto Salvage, 1202 Old Hwy 45 S, 38834; 662-286-2966; CC, Sp, UR; 8000+; **D, F, PU, 4x4, Trk; B3, AMC, Jp**

   Wilbanks Import Salvage & Used, County Rd 605, 38834; 662-287-2626; CC, Sp, Br; 1500+; **F, PU, 4x4**

Forest; Armadillo Auto Salvage, 2669 Hwy 21, 39074; 601-469-2705, FAX 601-469-1895, 800-287-7105; CC, Sp; 20ac, 750; **D, F, PU, 4x4, Trk; B3, AMC**

   Forest Auto Salvage, *see Vintage*

Greenville; C & W Salvage, *see Late Vintage*

Greenwood; 49 Auto Salvage, *see Late Vintage*

Grenada; Jack's Auto Salvage, *see Late Vintage*

Gulfport; Affordable Auto Salvage, *see Late Vintage*

Gulfport; J & B Auto Parts & Salvage, 11239 Dobson Rd, 39503; 228-831-1744, FAX 228-831-0155, 800-366-3018; CC, Sa, Sp; 300; **D, F, PU, 4x4; B3, AMC**

Hattiesburg; Shemper Auto Parts, 901 Bouie St, 39401; 601-582-7000; Sa; **D, F, PU, 4x4; B3, AMC, VW**

Hickory; Harrison Auto Salvage & Garage, *see Vintage*

Jackson; Jones Used Auto Parts, 9377 Hwy 49, 39209; 601-366-4277; Sa, Sp, UR; **D, F**

   Mid-State Auto Parts & Cars, 900 Hwy 475 S, 39208; 601-939-2131, 800-222-7685; CC, Sp, Br; 400; **D, F, PU, 4x4; B3, AMC**

   Murray Auto Parts Inc, 4640 Medgar Evers Blvd, 39213; 601-362-1585, 800-247-9396; Sp; 8ac; **D, F, PU, 4x4; B3, AMC**

   Rankin County Auto Parts, *see Late Vintage*

   Staring Auto Salvage, *see Late Vintage*

Laurel; Mack's Auto Wrecking Used Parts, *see Late Vintage*

Leland; Rodgers Salvage Inc, Black Bayou Rd, 38756; 662-686-9624; Sa, Sp, UR; 15ac, 1000; **D, F, PU, 4x4, Trk, Mil; B3, AMC, Jp, IH, VW**

Lucedale; South Mississippi Dismantling, 118 Grady Brown Rd, 39452; 601-947-7171; Sa; **D, F, PU, 4x4; B3, AMC**

Madison; Madison Foreign Auto Parts, 347 Distribution Dr, 39110; 601-853-2112; CC, Sa; **F, PU, 4x4**

Magnolia; 48 Salvage, *see Late Vintage*

   Sandifer Auto Salvage, *see Vintage*

Meridian; Meridian Auto Salvage, 1461 Hwy 19 S # A, 39301; 601-485-7080; Sa; **D, F**

Ocean Springs; Meyers Auto Salvage, *see Vintage*

Pascagoula; Delmas Salvage, *see Late Vintage*
  M & Z Auto Salvage, *see Late Vintage*
  Pascagoula Auto Salvage Inc, *see Late Vintage*
Petal; Petal Auto Parts, *see Late Vintage*
Pontotoc; Keith Auto Salvage, 189 Dalton Ln, 38863; 662-844-6586, FAX 662-844-4714, 800-550-6586; CC, Sp, UR, PL; 10ac; **D, F, PU, 4x4, Trk; B3**
Pontotoc; Larry Keith Garage & Salvage, 392 Pontocola Rd, 38863; 662-489-7006; Sa, Sp, UR; 200; **D, F, PU, 4x4; B3, AMC, IH**
Senatobia; Scott Auto Wrecking, 1000 Stage Rd, 38668; 662-562-9928; Sp; 1000; **D, F, PU, 4x4, Trk; B3, AMC, Jp, IH, VW**
Sumrall; Lamar Auto Salvage Exchange, *see Late Vintage*
Tupelo; Garrison's Auto Salvage, *see Late Vintage*
Vardaman; Parker Auto Salvage, *see Late Vintage*
Verona; B & M Auto Salvage, Hwy 145 S, 38879; 662-566-2313, 800-530-6418; Sp; 1000+; **D, F, PU, 4x4, Trk; B3, AMC, Jp**
Vicksburg; Matthews Auto Parts, *see Late Vintage*

1941 Packard
Fresno, CA

175

Missouri

You may be a car nut if

When asked about your hard drive, you tell 'um about the car club trip last week end

Ray's wReckingyard Roster makes a great gift for the "car nut" on your shopping list. To order, Call Toll Free: 877-4RAYS BOOKS

MISSOURI

VINTAGE

Barnhart; Auto Wrecker & Transport Svc, 7164 Hwy 21, 63012; 314-942-4154; Sa, Sp; 60+;
79-89, few 60s; D, F, PU; B3

Bourbon; I-44 Auto Salvage, 530 N Outer Rd, 65441; 573-732-5582; Sa, Sp, UR; 2000; **70+,
few 40-60s; D, F; B3, DeSoto**

Camdenton; Green View Garage, Rt 71 Box 1389, 65020; 573-873-5393; Sp, Br; 20; **35-77;
D, PU; B3; Closed Tuesday**

Cassville; Slinkard's Auto Salvage, , 65625; 417-847-3005; CC, Sa, Sp, UR; 75+; **49-79; D;
B3, IH**

Chillicothe; Nick Anderson Auto Salvage, 120 Batta St, 64601; 660-646-2518; UR; **30-79;
D; B3, St, Ford Model A & T**

Clever; Midwest Auto Salvage, 774 Schupbach Rd, 65631; 417-743-2363; Sa, Sp; 50; **60-90;
D, PU, 4x4; B3, Spc: Pickup**

Columbia; Kemper's Used Cars & Salvage, 2710 E Clays Fork Rd, 65202; 573-474-5814; Sa,
Sp, UR; 150+; **50-69; D; Fd, Chevy, Cadillac**

Fairview; West Salvage, 307 N Linebarger St, 64842; 417-632-4606; Sa, Sp, UR, Wr; 350;
49-91; D, F, PU; B3; Parts for 50-60s

Goodman; J & M Vintage Auto, PO Box 297, 64843; 417-364-7203; Sa, Sp, Br; 20ac, 2500;
36-72; D, PU; B3, AMC, Jp, IH, Hd, Ns, St, Pk, Ks, Fr, Cr, Wy

Kansas City; Automotive Wholesale Inc, 2908 Southwest Blvd, 64108; 816-931-2886; Sa,
Sp; 200; **80+, few 60-70s; D, F, PU; B3**

 C & D Auto Salvage Inc, 814 E 19th St, 64108; 816-421-3802, FAX 816-421-3802; CC,
Sa, Sp, Wr; **80+, few 60-70s; D; B3**

 C & H Auto Salvage, 7604 E Truman Rd, 64126; 816-231-0008; CC, Sp; 3000; **60+; D, F,
PU; B3**

 Dependable Auto Salvage, 6600 E US Hwy 40, 64129; 816-921-6939; Sp; **70+, few 60s;
D, 4x4; B3, IH**

 Little Wills Auto Salvage, 7900 E 17th St, 64126; 816-483-6814; 500; **50-79, few 40s; D,
4x4; B3, Jp, Hd, St, Pk**

Kirksville; S & H Salvage, N State Hwy 63, 63501; 660-665-3997, 800-491-3997; CC, Sa,
Sp, UR; 300; **70-89, few 60s; D, F, PU; B3**

Lebanon; Ronnie Melton Salvage, 65536; 417-532-6107, FAX 417-532-8216; Sp, Br; 2500;
60+, earlier; D, F, 4x4; B3, IH

Lewistown; Webster's Salvage, 63452; 573-497-2332; Sa, Sp; 300; **60-89, few earlier; D,
PU; B3**

Piedmont; German's Auto Salvage, 63957; 573-223-2383, FAX 573-223-2383, 800-
223-2383; Sa, Sp, UR; 100+; **50-89; D, F, PU; B3; Spc: Ford Pickup**

Rolla; Telle VW Air-Cooled, , 65402; 573-364-3376; Sa, Wr; **30-79; F; VW only**

St Charles; Just Corvettes, 1630 N 2nd, 63301; 314-947-6060, FAX 314-947-9676,
800-886-8388; CC, Sa, Sp, Wr; **68+; D; Corvette only**

 Verona; R & R Auto Salvage, Rt 2 Box 196G, 65769; 417-678-5551, FAX 417-678-6403,
800-426-HEMI; CC, Sa, Sp, UR; 1600; **42-90; D, PU, 4x4; Chrysler only**

LATE VINTAGE

Barnhart; Auto Wrecker & Transport Svc, *see Vintage*

Belton; M & M Auto Wrecking Co, 215 N Scott Av, 64012; 816-331-5313; Sa, Sp, Br; 300;
70+; D, PU; B3

Bourbon; I-44 Auto Salvage, *see Vintage*

Camdenton; Green View Garage, *see Vintage*

Cassville; Slinkard's Auto Salvage, *see Vintage*

Chillicothe; Nick Anderson Auto Salvage, *see Vintage*

Clever; Midwest Auto Salvage, *see Vintage*

Columbia; Algiere Salvage & Excavating, 1650 Old US Hwy 40, 65202; 573-474-4000, FAX
573-474-1775; CC, Sa, Br; 800; **75+, few 60s; D, F, PU; B3**

Elsberry; Kinion Salvage, Deer Run Dr, 63343; 573-898-5039; Sa, Sp, Br; 1000; **70-89; D, F,
PU; B3**

Fairview; West Salvage, *see Vintage*

177

Goodman; J & M Vintage Auto, *see Vintage*

Hannibal; Bob's Auto Slvg, 2713 Market St, 63401; 573-221-5499; 300; **80+, few earlier; D, F, Trk; B3**

Independence; Davis Auto Wrecking, 27403 E Flynn Rd, 64057; 816-229-3636; Sa; 2000; **80+; D; B3**

Kansas City; A-1 Auto Parts, 3621 Stadium Dr, 64129; 816-921-9826; Sa; 400; **80+; D; B3**

    Able Auto Salvage, 6601 E US Hwy 40, 64129; 816-923-1234; CC, Sa; 1000; **80+; D, F, PU; B3**

    Automotive Wholesale Inc, *see Vintage*

    C & D Auto Salvage Inc, *see Vintage*

    C & H Auto Salvage, *see Vintage*

    Dependable Auto Salvage, *see Vintage*

    Little Wills Auto Salvage, *see Vintage*

    Midway Auto Parts Inc, 4210 Gardner Av, 64120; 816-241-0501, FAX 816-241-7708; CC, Sp; 1500; **70+; D, F, PU; B3**

    Midway Auto Salvage, 4919 NW Gateway Av, 64151; 816-741-1600; UR; 200; **70-93; D, PU; B3**

Kirksville; S & H Salvage, *see Vintage*

Lebanon; Mott Auto Inc, 65536; 417-532-3914, FAX 417-532-9662, 800-226-6887; CC, Sp, PL; **80s, few 90s; D; B3**

    Ronnie Melton Salvage, *see Vintage*

Lewistown; Webster's Salvage, *see Vintage*

Nevada; Nevada Used Auto Parts & Cars, 901 E Highland, 64772; 417-667-7050, 316-223-4275, FAX , 800-201-7050; CC, Sa; 500+; **80+; D, PU, 4x4; B3**

Piedmont; German's Auto Salvage, *see Vintage*

Poplar Bluff; Berry's Salvage Yard, Hwy 67 S, 63901; 573-785-0585; CC, Sa, Sp, UR; 500; **80+; D, F, PU; B3**

    Clifford & Steve Browning Auto, 1445 W State Rte 53, 63901; 573-785-6002; **80+; D**

    Spencer's Auto Sales & Salvage, Hwy 53, 63901; 573-686-2267; Sa, Br; 500; **70-89; D; B3**

Sedalia; Jack's Auto Slvg & Parts, 1680 Honda Rd, 65301; 660-827-1379; Sa; **80+, few 70s; D, F; B3**

Springfield; Howard's Auto Salvage, 1962 N Hillcrest Av, 65802; 417-869-8109; Sa, UR; 300; **70-89; D; B3; parts for 50-60s**

St Charles; Jack's Auto Salvage, 2106 N Main St, 63301; 636-947-6005, FAX 636-949-0161; Sa, Sp, Br; 250; **80+; D, F; B3**

    Just Corvettes, *see Vintage*

St Louis; Opal's Salvage Yard, 1216 S 7th St, 63104; 314-621-2104; Sa; **70+; D, F; B3**

Trenton; Jim's Auto Salvage & Repairs, 64683; 660-359-3888, 800-433-1847; Sp; 5ac; **80+; D, F, PU, 4x4, Trk; B3**

Verona; R & R Auto Salvage, *see Vintage*

LATE MODEL

Belton; M & M Auto Wrecking Co, *see Late Vintage*

Bourbon; I-44 Auto Salvage, *see Late Vintage*

Columbia; Algiere Salvage & Excavating, *Late Vintage*

DeSoto; De Soto Auto Parts Inc, Hwy 110, 63020; 636-586-3222; Sp; 1000; **D, F; B3**

Doniphan; Bargain Auto Salvage, State Rt 142 E, 63935; 573-996-3746; Sa, Sp, UR; 1000; **D, F, PU, 4x4, Trk, Fm, Mil; B3, AMC, Jp, IH; 70+ Pickup & Truck**

Grovespring; Griffins Auto Sales & Salvage, 10637 Hwy TT, 65662; 417-462-3928; Sp; 4500; **D, F, PU; B3**

Hannibal; Bob's Auto Salvage, *Late Vintage*

Independence; Davis Auto Wrecking, *Late Vintage*

    Tri-State Auto Salvage, 11405 E Truman Rd, 64050; 816-461-4145; **F**

Kansas City; A-1 Auto Parts Inc, *Late Vintage*

    Able Auto Salvage, *Late Vintage*

    Automotive Wholesale Inc, *see Vintage*

    C & D Auto Salvage Inc, *see Vintage*

C & H Auto Salvage, *see Vintage*

Dependable Auto Salvage, *see Vintage*

Economy Auto Salvage, 3135 Stadium Dr, 64128; 816-921-3700; Sa; 200; **D, F, PU; B3**

Frogs Import Salvage, 3701 E US Hwy 40, 64129; 816-924-7788, 816-924-8435; CC, Sa, UR; 9ac, 900; **D, F, PU; B3**

Midway Auto Parts Inc, *see Late Vintage*

Midway Auto Salvage, *see Late Vintage*

U-Wrench-It Auto Parts, 8012 E Truman Rd, 64126; 816-231-0600; Sa, UR; 1000; **D, F; $1 admission**

Lebanon; Mott Auto Inc, *see Late Vintage*

Rogers Wrecking & Salvage Inc, Hwy 66 W, 65536; 417-532-3731, 800-798-0105; Sp; 5000; **D, F, PU; B3**

Ronnie Melton Salvage, *see Vintage*

Nevada; Nevada Used Auto Parts & Cars, *see Late Vintage*

O'Fallon; Goodfellow Auto Salvage, 1415 W Terra Ln, 63366; 636-946-7872, FAX 636-980-1797; CC, Sa, Sp; Br; 800; **D, F, PU; B3**

Poplar Bluff; Berry's Salvage Yard, *see Late Vintage*

C & F Auto Salvage, 1401 W State Rte 53, 63901; 573-785-3311, 800-235-3106; Sa, Sp; 3000; **D, F, PU; B3**

Clifford & Steve Browning Auto, *see Late Vintage*

Sedalia; Askins Auto Slvg, Rte 1 S Hwy 65, 65301; 660-827-2576; Sp; 1000; **D, F, PU; B3**

Jack's Auto Salvage & Parts, *see Late Vintage*

Springfield; B & W Auto Salvage, 1462 N Warren Av, 65802; 417-865-0324, FAX 417-865-8019, 800-743-0282; CC, Sa, Sp, UR; 1500; **D, PU; B3**

St Charles; Jack's Auto Salvage, *see Late Vintage*

Just Corvettes, *see Vintage*

St Louis; Modern Imports, 7928 Alaska Av, 63111; 314-638-1040, 638-6040, FAX 314-638-4445, 800-200-9277; CC, Sp; **F**

St Louis; Opal's Salvage Yard, *see Late Vintage*

Trenton; Jim's Auto Salvage & Repairs, *see Late Vintage*

Wright City; Quality Auto Parts & Salvage, 983 Westwoods Rd, 63390; 636-745-3302, 800-483-8921; Sa, Sp; 1000; **D, F, PU, 4x4, Trk; B3**

Respect yard hours.
Your staying late could
cause paying overtime
upping the over all costs.

*Yard Operators
Tell us...*

MONTANA

Remember not to copy, reproduce or distribute this list in any way without the written permission of Ray's wReckingyard Roster

Butte; Zimp's Enterprises, 2800 S Montana, 59701; 406-782-5674; Sa, Br; 5ac, 200+; **20-69; D; B3, Hd, Ns; Spc: Dodge, Cadillac; Whole Cars available**

Charlo; Smiths Auto Wrecking & Svc, 200 Kicking Horse Rd, 59824; 406-644-2633; Sp, UR; 2ac, 100+; **40+; D, PU; B3**

Columbia Falls; American Auto Towing & Salvage, 295 4th St East N, 59912; 406-892-8111; Sa, Sp, Br; 1500; **50+; D, PU, 4x4, Trk; B3, AMC, IH, St; Spc: Dodge**

Cut Bank; Jim's Auto, US Hwy 2, 59427; 406-873-2015; Sp, Br; 4ac; **30-89; D, F, PU, 4x4; B3, AMC, Jp, IH, Ns, St, Pk, Ks, VW**

Ennis; M & B Used Auto Parts & Towing, , 59729; 406-682-7212, FAX 406-682-7771, 800-823-7325; CC, UR; 10ac, 300; **60+; D, F, PU, 4x4; B3; Spc: 4x4**

Florence; Medicine Bow Motors, 343 One Horse Creek Rd, 59833; 406-273-0002; CC, Sa, Sp, Wr; **46-51 D; Fd; Street Rods**

Glendive; Glendive Auto Parts, 1021 W Bell St, 59330; 406-365-4480, FAX 406-365-6788; Sa, Sp, UR; 1500+; **40+; D, PU, 4x4; B3, AMC, Jp, IH, Hd, Ns, St, Pk, Ks, Fr**

Great Falls; Ralph Ward & Sons Auto Parts, 1020 Franklin Ave, 59405; 406-452-7332; Sa; 4000; **40+; D, F, PU; B3**

  S & C Repair-Wrecker Svc, 1925 32nd Av S, 59405; 406-453-6950; Sa; 200+; **50+; D, F, PU; B3, Hd, Ns, St, Pk**

Greycliff; Greycliff Salvage, PO Box 43, 59033; 406-932-6609; 50; **60+; few D, F, PU, 4x4, Trk**

Hamilton; Dutton's Restorables, 179 Ricketts Rd, 59840; 406-363-3380; **10-69; D; B3; Pre-War Fords**

Helena; Al & Buzz Rose Wrck Yard, 8290 Applegate Dr, 59602; 406-458-5524; Sa, Sp, UR; 23+ac, 3000+; **40-89; D, F, PU, 4x4; B3, AMC, Jp, IH, Hd, Ns, St, Pk, Ks, Cr, Wy, VW**

Kalispell; R & J Wrecking, 2758 US Hwy 93 S, 59901; 406-755-3077; Sa, Sp, UR; 4.5ac; **40+; D, F, PU, 4x4, Trk, Fm; B3, Hd**

  Swartzenberger Wrecking, 2745 US Hwy 93 S, 59901; 406-755-6009, FAX 406-755-6011, 800-624-6009; Cc, Sa, Sp; 8ac; **60+; PU, 4x4; Spc: Pickup and 4x4**

  Tri-City Wrecking, 3900 US Hwy 2E, 59901; 406-752-5565, FAX 406-752-7466, 800-626-3088, eagle@dogisys.net; CC, Sp, UR; 10ac; **50+; D, F, PU, 4x4, Trk; B3**

  Wishers Salvage Frame & Body, 2190 Airport Rd, 59901; 406-752-2461; Sa; 1200; **50-88; D; B3**

  Young's Enterprises, 2870 Hwy 2 W, 59901; 406-755-6043; Sp, UR; 2ac; **50-60; D, PU; GM; Spc: Chevy**

Libby; Jim's Auto Wrecking, 5600 US Hwy 2 S, 59923; 406-293-6634; Sa, Sp, Br; 6.5ac, 500; **50-90; D, F, PU, 4x4, Trk; B3, AMC, Jp, IH, Ns, St, Wy**

Miles City; Auto Dismantlers, 2700 Edgewood St, 59301; 406-232-4024, 800-660-4024; CC, Sp, Br; 1000; **mid 60-89; D, F, PU, 4x4, Trk; B3, AMC, Jp, IH, few VW**

Missoula; Missoula Auto Salvage, 9905 Inspiration Dr, 59802; 406-542-0600; Sa, Sp, UR; 55ac, 6000+; **60-88; D, F, PU, 4x4, Trk; B3, AMC, Jp, St, Wy, Corvair**

Opportunity; S & S Salvage, Crackerville, 59711; 406-797-3586; 1200; **40-93; D, F, PU, 4x4, Fm; B3, AMC, Jp, St, Wy, VW**

Ronan; Timberlane Auto, 41 Timberlane Rd, 59864; 406-676-8111; CC, Sa, Sp, Br; **60+; D, few F, PU, 4x4, Trk; B3, AMC, Jp, IH; Spc: Chrysler Mopar & 4x4**

Sidney; Sidney Auto Wrecking, , 59270; 406-482-1406, 800-282-9870; Sa, Sp; 10ac; **50+; D, F, PU, 4x4; B3, AMC, Hd**

Somers; Flathead Salvage & Storage, 495 State Hwy 82, 59932; 406-857-3791, FAX 406-857-2129; CC, Sa, Sp, UR; 10ac, 600; **32-50 & 70+; D, F, PU, Trk; B3 AMC, Jp, IH, St, Wy, VW**

Whitehall; Freeman's Auto, 138 Kountz Rd, 59757; 406-287-5436, FAX 406-587-9103, marsha@bigplanet.com; Sp; 12000; **50-80; D, F, PU, 4x4; B3**

<u>*LATE VINTAGE*</u>

Arlee; Kelly's Auto Salvage, *see Vintage*

Belgrade; A F & T Salvage, 6125 Jackrabbit Ln, 59714; 406-388-4735; **70-89; D; B3**

Billings; A-1 Johnson Auto Wrecking, *see Vintage*

Blue Creek Salvage, 4843 Bollinger Ln, 59101; 406-259-6611, 800-380-6611; CC, Sa, Sp, Br; 6ac; **70+; D, F, PU, 4x4; B3, AMC, Jp, IH Spc: Pickup**

Dietz Auto & Truck Salvage, 1104 Bench Blvd, 59105; 406-248-1124, FAX 406-248-1204; CC, Sa, Sp, UR; 9ac; **70+; D, F, PU, 4x4; B3, AMC, Jp, VW; snowmobile, motorcycle & RV**

Hansers Automotive, 5539 Keller Rd, 59101; 406-248-6073, FAX 406-248-6180, 800-345-1754; CC, Sa, Sp, Br; 12ac, 1200; **75+; D, F, PU, 4x4; B3, AMC, Jp, IH, VW, Jpa**

Lockwood Auto & Truck, *see Vintage*

Butte; Summit Valley Auto Wrecking, 705- E Iron, 59701; 406-782-6358, 800-823-6358; Sa, Sp, UR, PL; 250; **68+; D, F, PU, 4x4; B3, AMC, Jp, VW, Subaru**

Charlo; Smiths Auto Wrecking & Svc, *see Vintage*

Columbia Falls; American Auto Towing & Salvage, *see Vintage*

Cut Bank; Jim's Auto, *see Vintage*

East Missoula; Mountain Auto Dismantlers & Towing, 6705 Juniper Dr, 59802; 406-258-6141, FAX 406-258-5255, 800-452-5125; CC, Sp; 5ac; **80+; D, F, PU, 4x4; B3**

Ennis; M & B Used Auto Parts & Towing, *see Vintage*

Glasgow; Glasgow Auto Wrecking, 53999 Hwy 2 W, 59230; 406-228-2715, FAX 406-228-4524; CC, Sa, Sp, UR; 6ac; **80-89; D; B3**

Glendive; Glendive Auto Parts, *see Vintage*

Great Falls; Auto Parts & Recycling, 2635 9th Ave NW, 59404; 406-454-1917; CC, Sp, Br; 6ac; **70-85 D, F, PU, 4x4; Trk; B3**

Moltzan's Auto, 2209 Vaughn Rd, 59404; 406-452-8675, FAX 406-453-1829, 800-422-8675; Cc, Sp; 17ac; **80+; D, F, PU, Trk; B3, Jp, IH**

Northwest Truck, 2513 Vaughn Rd, 59404; 406-452-2101; Sp; 3.5ac, 300+; **80+; D, F, PU; Pickup only**

Ralph Ward & Sons Auto Parts, *see Vintage*

S & C Repair-Wrecker Svc, *see Vintage*

Greycliff; Greycliff Salvage, *see Vintage*

Helena; Al & Buzz Rose Wrecking Yard, *see Vintage*

Green Meadow Auto Salvage, 7313 Green Meadow Dr, 59601; 406-458-9204, FAX 406-458-9940, 800-345-5695, grnmeadow@initco.net; CC, Sp; 5ac, 600+; **70+; D, F, PU, 4x4; B3, Jp, Jpa**

Myrl rose Auto Salvage, 5320 N Montana Av, 59602; 406-458-9510, FAX 406-458-3940; Sa, Sp, UR; 300; **73+; D, F, PU, 4x4, Trk; B3, AMC, Jp, IH, VW**

Huntley; G T Auto Salvage, 348 Squaw Creek Rd, 59037; 406-348-2039; Sa, Sp, UR; 400+; **70+; D, F, PU, 4x4; B3**

Kalispell; R & J Wrecking, *see Vintage*

Stan's Parts Locating Svc, 203 E Evergreen Dr, 59901; 406-756-8946; Sa, Sp, UR; 25; **70+; D, F, PU, 4x4; B3**

Swartzenberger Wrecking, *see Vintage*

Tri-City Wrecking, *see Vintage*

Wishers Salvage Frame & Body, *see Vintage*

Libby; Carrs Towing, 4063 US Hwy 2 S, 59923; 406-293-3988; CC, Sa, Sp; **50; D, Trk; B3, AMC, Jp, IH**

Jim's Auto Wrecking, *see Vintage*

Miles City; Auto Dismantlers, *see Vintage*

Missoula; AC Auto Recycling, 6705 Juniper, 59802; 800-452-5125; CC, Sa, Sp, Br; 6.5ac; **70+; D, F, PU, 4x4; B3**

Ace Auto Salvage, 10131 Garry More Lane, 59802; 406-543-7614, 888-500-7614; Sa, Sp, Br, PL; 10ac; **70+; D, F, PU, 4x4; B3**

Missoula Auto Salvage, *see Vintage*

Opportunity; S & S Salvage, *see Vintage*

Polson; Polson Auto Salvage, 54826 Hwy 93, 59860; 406-883-6860, FAX 406-883-6776, 888-421-6921; CC, Sa, Sp, UR; 7ac, 600+; **70-89; D, few F, PU, 4x4; B3, AMC, Jp, IH; Spc: Minivans**

Ronan; Timberlane Auto, *see Vintage*

Montana – Late Vintage

Sidney; Sidney Auto Wrecking, *see Vintage*
Somers; Flathead Salvage & Storage, *see Vintage*
Stevensville; United Auto & Truck Dismantlers, 280 Middle Burnt Fork Rd, 59870; 406-777-3900, FAX 406-777-7064; CC, Sa, Sp; 300; **75+; D, F, PU, 4x4; B**3; **Spc: Pickup, S-10**
Whitehall; Freeman's Auto, *see Vintage*

LATE MODEL

Arlee; Kelly's Auto Salvage, *see Vintage*
Billings; A-1 Johnson Auto Wrecking, *see Vintage*
  Blue Creek Salvage, *see Late Vintage*
  Dietz Auto & Truck Salvage, *see Late Vintage*
  Hansers Automotive, *see Late Vintage*
  Lockwood Auto & Truck, *see Vintage*
  Louies & Deans Montana Truck, 516 Scott St, 59101; 406-245-6621; **D, Trk; B**3
Bozeman; Bullwhacker Industries, 34246 Frontage Rd, 59715; 406-587-2106; Sa; **D, F, PU; B**3**, Jpa**
Butte; Summit Valley Auto Wrecking, *see Late Vintage*
Charlo; Smiths Auto Wrecking & Svc, *see Vintage*
Choteau; Johnson's Auto Repair-Recycling, 22 3rd St NE, 59422; 406-466-2290; CC, Sa; 300+; **D; B**3
Columbia Falls; American Auto Towing & Salvage, *see Vintage*
Comumbia Falls; A Plus Western Towing, 1030 Jensen Rd, 59912; 406-892-5423; 3ac; **D; B**3
East Missoula; Mountain Auto Dismantlers & Towing, *see Late Vintage*
Ennis; M & B Used Auto Parts & Towing, *see Vintage*
Glendive; Glendive Auto Parts, *see Vintage*
Great Falls; Moltzan's Auto, *see Late Vintage*
  Northwest Truck, *see Late Vintage*
  Ralph Ward & Sons Auto Parts, *see Vintage*
  S & C Repair-Wrecker Svc, *see Vintage*
  Sports & Imports LTD, 4427 2nd Av N, 59405; 406-452-5722; Cc, Sp, UR; **D, F, PU, 4x4; B**3**, Jp**
  Woyth Wrecking Yard & Body, 1801 Vaughn Rd, 59404; 406-452-2350; Sp, UR; 300+; **D, F, PU, 4x4; B**3**, AMC; Spc: GM**
Greycliff; Greycliff Salvage, *see Vintage*
Havre; M & M Auto Parts Salvage, 1823 13th St, W of Havre, 59501; 406-265-1322, FAX 406-262-2023, 800-287-1323; CC, Sa, Sp, UR; 2000; **D, F, PU, 4x4, Trk, Fm, Cn, In; B**3**, AMC, Jp, IH, VW**
Helena; Green Meadow Auto Salvage, *see Late Vintage*
  Myrl rose Auto Salvage, *see Late Vintage*
Huntley; G T Auto Salvage, *see Late Vintage*
Kalispell; R & J Wrecking, *see Vintage*
  Stan's Parts Locating Svc, *see Late Vintage*
  Swartzenberger Wrecking, *see Vintage*
  Tri-City Wrecking, *see Vintage*
Miles City; Auto Dismantlers, *see Vintage*
Missoula; AC Auto Recycling, *see Late Vintage*
  Ace Auto Salvage, *see Late Vintage*
Opportunity; S & S Salvage, *see Vintage*
Ronan; Timberlane Auto, *see Vintage*
Sidney; Sidney Auto Wrecking, *see Vintage*
Somers; A-1 Salvage, 915 Mt Hwy 82, 59932; 406-857-3638; Sa, Sp, Br; 6ac; **D, F, PU, 4x4**
  Flathead Salvage & Storage, *see Vintage*
Stevensville; United Auto & Truck Dismantlers, *see Late Vintage*

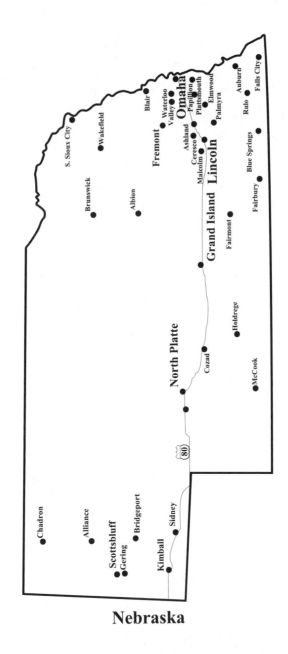

Nebraska

**Please mention you saw'em in
Ray's wReckingyard Roster when
contacting these yards**

184

NEBRASKA

VINTAGE

Alliance; Taylor's Auto Repair & Salvage, 6971 Otoe Rd, 69301; 308-762-7208; Sa, Sp, UR; 20acc 800+; **30-89; D, F, PU, 4x4, Trk; B3, Jp, IH, Hd, St, Pk, VW, Austin Cooper; Jeepster, Ford Model A & T; Early V-8; Open Sunday**

Ashland; M & M Salvage, 1/2 Mile North of Ashland, 68003; 402-944-2186; Sa, UR; 60+; **60-80, few 50s; D, PU, Trk; B3; Spc: Pickup**

Blue Springs; Antique Cars, Trucks & Parts, 526 E 2nd, 68318; 402-645-3546; Sp; Br; 3.5ac; 80+; **12-53; D, PU; B3, Hd, Ns, St, Maxwell, Lafayette, Rio; '17-'27 Ford T & A; '29-'48 Chevy; Prewar V-8, Touring Cars; By Appointment Only**

Bridgeport; B J's Auto Salvage & Towing, RR 1 Box 107, 69336; 308-262-0477; Sa, Br; 5ac; **49-89; D, F, PU, 4x4; few Trk; B3, Cadillac**

Brunswick; S & S Salvage, RR1 Box 157B, 68720; 402-842-3055; Sp, Br; 600; 50-87; **D, PU, 4x4; B3, IH**

Ceresco; Swanson Auto Co & Salvage, 105 E Main St, 68017; 402-665-3911, FAX 402-665-2498; Sp; 25+; **60+; D, PU; Spc: Ford**

Elmwood; Eastern Nebraska Auto Sales, PO Box 260, 68349; 402-994-4555; Sp; 10ac, 1400+; **40+ D, F, PU, 4x4; B3, Hd, St, Ns, Vauxhall; few Buses**

Fairbury; Paneitz Salvage, 56730 Crystal Springs Rd, 68352; 402-729-2958; Sa, Sp; 1000+; **40+; D, F, PU, 4x4, Cn; B3, Jp, Hd, St, VW**

Falls City; Falls City Auto Salvage, E 14th St, 68355; 402-245-3947; Sa, Sp, UR; 6ac, 500+; **60+; D, F; B3, Jpa, VW; few 50s**

Fremont; Bernheisel Salvage Yard, 1510 S Main St, 68025; 402-727-1860; Sa, Sp, UR; 5ac; **60+, few 50s; D, F, PU, 4x4, few Trk; B3**

Holdrege; Richardson & Son Auto Wrecking, 911 Maberly St, 68949; 308-995-4212; CC, Sp; 200; **30-85; D, F, PU; B3, Jp, St, Ks; some whole cars**

Malcolm; Walkies Auto Salvage, 9605 NW 112th St, 68402; 402-796-2482; Sa, Sp, UR; 40ac, 3000+; **20+; D, F, PU, 4x4; B3, AMC, Jp, St, VW**

McCook; Marin Auto Salvage, RR 1 Box 92, 69001; 308-345-3919; Sp; 2ac; **20-80; D, F, PU, 4x4; B3, AMC, Jp**

North Platte; ABC Auto Salvage, 3400 W Hwy 30, 69101; 308-532-4571, 800-422-4683; CC, Sa; 22ac; **80+, few 50s; D. F, PU, 4x4; few 50s**

Papillion; Roger's Foreign Auto & Recyclers, 226 N Adams, 68046; 402-331-6666, FAX 402-331-2867; Sa, Sp; 6.5ac, 1500; **60-89; F, PU**

Rulo; Koelzer Salvage, 68431; 402-245-4986; Sa, Sp, Wr; 5ac, 200+; **60-89; D, F, PU, few 4x4, few Trk, Fm; B3; Few Pre-War**

Scottsbluff; Goodro Auto Salvage, 240426 County Rd G, 69361; 308-635-1119; Sa, Sp, Br; 300; **28+; D, F, PU, 4x4; B3, AMC, IH, Hd, St, Ks; Spc: Ford 50s**

Sidney; Dan's Auto & Metal, E Elm St, 69162; 308-254-2255, FAX 308-254-2255, 800-231-0226; CC, Sa, Sp, Br; 10ac, 1000+; **50+; D, F, PU, 4x4, Buses; B3, Jp, IH, VW, Jpa, Puegeot; Most 50s Ford & GM; 70+ Chrysler**

Waterloo; C & C Salvage & Auto Sales, 24540 Hwy 275, 68069; 402-779-4968, pazracebb@aol.com; Sa, Br; 1200; **60+; D, PU, 4x4; B3, Jp**

Papio Valley, 68069; 402-731-4841; CC, Sa, Sp; 600+; **50+; D, PU, 4x4, few Trk; B3, AMC, Jp, IH**

LATE VINTAGE

Albion; Albion Auto Parts & Salvage, S Hwy 14, 68620; 402-395-2814; Sa, Sp; 250; 84+; **D, PU, 4x4; B3**

Alliance; Taylor's Auto Repair & Salvage, *see Vintage*

Ashland; M & M Salvage, *see Vintage*

Auburn; Auburn Auto Salvage, RR1, 68305; 402-274-3499; Sa, Sp; 100; 80+; **D; B3, AMC**

Bridgeport; B J's Auto Salvage & Towing, *see Vintage*

Brule; B & J Salvage, 69127; 308-287-2244, 800-774-2244; Sa, Sp; 2000; **72+; D, F, PU, 4x4; B3, AMC**

Brunswick; S & S Salvage, *see Vintage*

Ceresco; Swanson Auto Co & Salvage, *see Vintage*

Chadron; Ed's Auto Slvg & Rebuilders, 5793 Hwy 20, 69337; 308-432-3696, 800-253-5415; Sa, Sp, Br; 400+; **70+ D, F, PU, 4x4; B3, AMC, IH, Jpa, Eur; Few 60s parts**

Cozad; H & H Auto Salvage, 41835 Hwy 30, 69130; 308-784-2305 or 534-4685, 800-627-3006; CC, Sa, Sp, Br; 22ac, 700+; **80+; D, F, PU, 4x4; B3, AMC, Jp, IH, VW, Jpa**

Elmwood; Eastern Nebraska Auto Sales, *see Vintage*

Fairbury; Paneitz Salvage, *see Vintage*

Falls City; Falls City Auto Salvage, *see Vintage*

Fremont; Bernheisel Salvage Yard, *see Vintage*

Gering; Rich's Wrecking & Salvage, 925 Lockwood Rd, 69341; 308-632-7625, 800-439-9082; CC, Sp; 1400; **85+, few earlier; D, F, PU, 4x4; B3; Spc: 4x4**

Holdrege; Richardson & Son Auto Wrecking, *see Vintage*

Lincoln; Capital City Auto Recyclers, 140 W P St, 68628; 402-475-2982; CC, Sa, UR; 5ac; 850+; **72+ D, F, PU, 4x4; B3, AMC, Jp, VW**

Kendle's Auto Salvage, 100 W Sumner St, 68522; 402-477-9702; Sa, UR; 250+; **70+; D, F, PU, 4x4; B3, AMC, Jp, VW; Vans**

Star City Auto Salvage, 2705 N 33rd St, 68504; 402-464-7009; Br; 350+; **70-90; D, PU; B3, AMC**

Malcolm; Walkies Auto Salvage, *see Vintage*

McCook; Marin Auto Salvage, *see Vintage*

North Platte; ABC Auto Salvage, *see Vintage*

Omaha; Bradley Salvage, 3903 N 16th St, 68110; 402-451-2226; Sa; 1ac; **80+; D; B3**

Hansen's Truck Salvage, 5702 S 60, 68117; 402-734-7016, FAX 402-734-1729, 800-228-2845; CC, Sa, Sp, UR, Wr; 55ac, 500+; **D, PU, 4x4, Trk; B3, IH**

Papillion; Roger's Foreign Auto & Recyclers, *see Vintage*

Plattsmouth; Montgomery's Salvage Yd, 615 N 18th St, 68048; 402-296-3427, gomery@juno.com; Sa, Sp; 200; **70-85; D; B3, AMC**

Rulo; Koelzer Salvage, *see Vintage*

Scottsbluff; Goodro Auto Salvage, *see Vintage*

Sidney; Dan's Auto & Metal, *see Vintage*

Valley; Long's Salvage, 25858 Hwy 275, 68064; 402-359-4221; CC, Sa, Sp; 5ac; **82-92; D, F, PU; B3, AMC, VW**

Wakefield; Ekberg Auto Salvage, RR 1, 68784; 402-287-2950; CC, Sa, Sp, Br; 400+; **70-89 D, PU, 4x4; B3**

Waterloo; C & C Salvage & Auto Sales, *see Vintage*

Papio Valley, *see Vintage*

LATE MODEL

Albion; Albion Auto Parts & Salvage, *see Late Vintage*

Auburn; Auburn Auto Salvage, *see Late Vintage*

Blair; Nebraska Porsche Recyclers, 13153 Co Rd 16, 68008; 402-426-3597, FAX 402-426-8066, 800-279-5185; CC, Sa, Sp; **F; Porsche only-900, 914, 911**

Brule; B & J Salvage, *see Late Vintage*

Ceresco; Swanson Auto Co & Salvage, *see Late Vintage*

Chadron; Ed's Auto Salvage & Rebuilders, *see Late Vintage*

Cozad; H & H Auto Salvage, *see Late Vintage*

Elmwood; Eastern Nebraska Auto Sales, *see Vintage*

Fairbury; Paneitz Salvage, *see Vintage*

Fairmont; Boon's Auto Salvage, 68354; 402-759-4411, 888-768-4411, boonsauto@yahoo.com; CC, Sp; 500+; **D, PU, 4x4**

Falls City; Falls City Auto Salvage, *see Vintage*

Fremont; Bernheisel Salvage Yard, *see Vintage*

Gering; Rich's Wrecking & Salvage, *see Late Vintage*

Grand Island; Oakleaf Auto Crushing, 1913 Eldorado St, 68801; 308-381-2870; Sa, UR;

Kimball; Richs Wrecking & Salvage, Hwy 71, 69145; 308-235-2331, FAX 308-235-2331, 800-439-9082 or 422-6643; CC, Sa, Sp; 20ac, 1000+; **D, F, PU, 4x4; few older PU. 2nd yard in Gering**

Lincoln; Capital City Auto Recyclers, *see Late Vintage*

G M Auto Parts, 5440 N 70th St, 68507; 402-467-3531, FAX 402-467-4935, 800-535-4787, gmauto@ink.goexcel.net; CC, Sa, Sp; 5.5ac, 250+; **D, PU, 4x4**

Kendle's Auto Salvage, *see Late Vintage*

Olston's Import Auto Salvage, 3450 N 35th St Circle, 68504; 402-467-4541, FAX 402-467-4548, 800-223-7020, olstons@olstons.com; CC, Sa, Sp; 1500+; **F, PU, 4x4; VW, Jpa, Eur**

Malcolm; Walkies Auto Salvage, *see Vintage*

North Platte; ABC Auto Salvage, *see Vintage*

Omaha; All Foreign Auto & Truck Slvg, 5800 S 60th St, 68117; 402-734-2460, FAX 402-731-8335, 800-323-2947; CC, Sa, Sp; 5ac, 500; **F, PU, 4x4; Jpa; few Ford Probe & Geo Metro**

Bradley Salvage, *see Late Vintage*

Hansen's Truck Salvage, *see Late Vintage*

Palmyra; Boon's Auto Salvage & Sales, 68418; 402-780-5383, FAX 402-780-6642; CC, Sp; 18ac, 400; **D, PU, 4x4**

Scottsbluff; Goodro Auto Salvage, *see Vintage*

Sidney; Dan's Auto & Metal, *see Vintage*

South Sioux City; Garvin Used Auto Sales & Salvage, W Hwy 20, 68776; 402-494-4011; Sa, Sp; 200+; **D, PU, 4x4, Trk, Fm; B3**

Valley; Long's Salvage, *see Late Vintage*

Waterloo; C & C Salvage & Auto Sales, *see Vintage*

Papio Valley, *see Vintage*

An example of damage to be avoided! This trunk lid was destroyed to get the mechanism

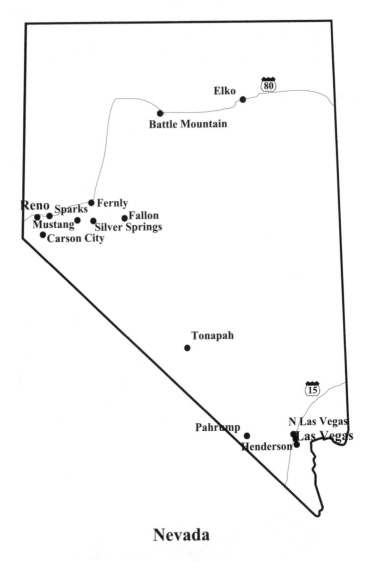

Nevada

Please use the cards in the back to let us know about yards we may have missed, or any other comments or information for future editions of Ray's wReckingyard Roster

NEVADA

VINTAGE

Carson City; Ace Auto & Truck Wrecking, 38 Newman Ln, 89706; 775-246-3900; Sa, Br; 2.5ac; **65+; D, F, PU, 4x4; B3, AMC, Jp, IH**

Buena Vista Auto Recyclers, 7 Martin Dr, 89706; 775-246-3535; Sa, Sp; 4.5ac; **40-69; D, few F, PU, Trk, Cn, Mil; B3, buses**

D & L Auto Dismantlers, 11 Martin Dr, 89706; 775-246-3444; Sa, Sp; 2.5ac, 500; 19-**60 & 85+; D, F, PU; Spc: late model Ford**

Elko; Clint's Auto Salvage, 5345 Manzanita Ln, 89801; 775-753-5290; Sa, Sp, Br; 150; **35-80s; D; B3**

Fallon; Western Salvage & Recycling, 13900 Bango Rd, 89406; 775-867-2507, FAX 775-867-3202; Sa, Sp, UR, PL; 1500; **80+; D; B3**

Fernley; Speedway Salvage Auto Wrecking, 30 Speedway Rd, 89408; 775-575-1040; Sa, Sp, Br; 40+ac; **50-89; D, F; B3**

Henderson; A Any & All Auto Wrck, 755 W Sunset Rd, 89015; 702-564-1212, FAX 702-564-3330; CC, Sa, Sp, Wr; 500; **D, F, PU, 4x4; B3; also Radiator repair; Vintage parts**

Nevada Pic-A-Part, 110 W Rolly St, 89015; 702-565-1414, FAX 702-565-1130; Sa, UR; 900+; **60+; D, F, PU, 4x4; B3; few Vintage**

Las Vegas; Bert's Main Gate Wrecking, 5070 Copper Sage St, 89115; 702-644-6007, FAX 702-644-5465; Sa, Sp, UR; 500; **60+; D, F, PU, 4x4; B3, AMC, Jp, IH, VW; Open Sunday**

Fords Only, 3793 Kolanut Lane, 89115; 702-644-0159, 888-829-5359; CC, Sa, Sp; 5ac; **20+; D; Ford only; Prewar Ford Model A & T**

K & L Auto Wrecking, 4540 E Hammer Ln, 89115; 702-644-5544; Sa, Br; 700+; **60-79; D; mostly GM**

Larry's Auto Wrecking, 4860 E La Mancha Av, 89115; 702-644-1671; CC, Sa, Sp, Br, Wr; 600; **40-90; D, F, PU, 4x4; B3, Pk, Ks, Fr; also loose Parts**

Nevada Differential, 63 N 30th St, 89101; 702-382-1310, FAX 702-471-1011; Sp; **60+; D; B3; Spc: Differential parts & repair**

Vegas Valley Auto Wrecking, 6019 N Hollywood Blvd, 89115; 702-644-1484; Sa; 450+; **30-93; D, F, PU, 4x4, Trk; B3, AMC, Jp, IH, VW**

Mustang; Mustang Auto Wreckers, RR1, 89434; 775-342-0225, 888-343-0228; CC, Sa, Sp; 750+; **55+; D, F, PU, 4x4; B3; Spc: Mopar & Cadillac**

North Las Vegas; Aboco VW Svc & Salvage, 1900 N Commerce St, 89030; 702-642-5219; Sa, Sp; 10ac, 400; **60+; F; VW; some VW bugs & buses**

Pahrump; Smart Auto Salvage & Recycling, 3850 China St, 89048; 702-727-0993; 300; **50+; D, F, PU, 4x4; B3**

Reno; North Valley Wreckers, 9915 N Virginia St, 89506; 775-972-0404, FAX 775-972-6433; CC, Sa, Sp, UR; 2.5ac; **40-80; D, F, PU, 4x4, Trk, Cn; B3**

Shamrock Auto Parts Inc, 2560 E 4th, 89512; 775-329-1606, FAX 775-329-5607; CC, Sa, Sp, Wr; **50+; Wheels & Used Tires**

Sparks; D & D Foreign Dismantlers, 1408 Pittman Av, 89431; 775-359-1851, FAX 775-359-5347; CC, Sa, Sp; 650+; **56+; F, PU, 4x4; VW, Porsche, Audi, Jpa**

D & S Auto & Truck Dismantlers, 1705 Marietta Way, 89431; 775-331-3344 or 329-8044, FAX 775-331-2891, ds3344@aol.com; CC, Sa, Sp, Wr, PL; 250+; **60+; D, F, PU, 4x4; B3; Spc: Muscle cars**

LATE VINTAGE

Battle Mountain; Atlas Towing Svc, 1339 Clydesdale Rd, 89820; 775-635-2112, FAX 775-635-8617; CC; 1500; **70+; D, few F, PU, 4x4; B3**

Carson City; Ace Auto & Truck Wrecking, *see Vintage*

All Parts Car & Truck Wrecking, 53 Newman Ln, 89706; 775-246-7361; Sp; 2ac; **70-85, few 60s; D, F, PU, 4x4; B3**

CAR, 17-A Martin Dr, 89403; 775-246-3640, FAX 775-246-9302, 800-435-7251; CC, Sa, Sp; 275; **80-92; D, F, PU, 4x4; Spc: GM**

Little John Auto Wrecking, 45 Newman Ln, 89706; 775-246-3531, FAX 775-246-5639; CC, Sa, Sp, UR; 450+; **80+; D, PU, 4x4, Trk, Cn; B3**

Elko; Clint's Auto Salvage, *see Vintage*
Fallon; Western Salvage & Recycling, *see Vintage*
Fernley; Speedway Salvage Auto Wrecking, *see Vintage*
Henderson; A Any & All Auto Wrecking, *see Vintage*
    Nevada Pic-A-Part, *see Vintage*
Las Vegas; Abbie's Nevada Pic-A-Part, 6351 Vegas Valley Dr, 89122; 702-457-8077; Sa, UR; 350+; **70+; D, F, PU, Trk; B3; Pickup & Truck only**
    Bert's Main Gate Wrecking, *see Vintage*
    Fords Only, *see Vintage*
    K & L Auto Wrecking, *see Vintage*
    Ken's Auto Wrecking, 5051 Copper Sage St, 89115; 702-644-5665; 350; **64+; D, F, PU, 4x4; B3, VW**
    Larry's Auto Wrecking, *see Vintage*
    M & R Auto Wrecking, 4630 E Ann Rd, 89115; 702-644-4774, FAX 702-644-6342; 2ac; **80+; D, F; B3**
    Mellis Auto Dismantlers, 5150 N Lamb Blvd #C, 89115; 702-651-8961; Sa, Sp, UR; 450+; **70+; D, F, PU, Trk; B3**
    Nevada Differential, *see Vintage*
    Nevada Pic-A-Part, 5090 N Lamb Blvd, 89115; 702-643-1776 or 565-1414; Sa, UR; 600; **70+; D, few F; B3, AMC, VW; Open Sunday**
    Vegas Valley Auto Wrecking, *see Vintage*
    Walton's Salvage, 4904 Copper Sage St, 89115; 702-644-2110; CC, Sa, Sp; 500+; **61+; D, PU; B3, IH; Spc: GM Pickup & IH Scouts**
Mustang; Mustang Auto Wreckers, *see Vintage*
North Las Vegas; Aboco VW Svc & Salvage, *see Vintage*
    Snap Auto Wrck, 2221 Losee Rd, 89030; 702-643-1776, FAX 702-649-9255; **70+; D; B3**
Pahrump; Smart Auto Salvage & Recycling, *see Vintage*
Reno; North Valley Wreckers, *see Vintage*
    Shamrock Auto Parts Inc, *see Vintage*
Sparks; A Auto Recker & Radiator, 11985 Interstate 80E, 89434; 775-342-0426; CC, Sa, Sp; 600; **66+; D, F, PU, 4x4; B3; Spc: Ford, Pickup, Radiators**
    D & D Foreign Dismantlers, *see Vintage*
    D & S Auto & Truck Dismantlers, *see Vintage*
Tonopah; Tonopah Auto Wrckr, 622 Depot St, 89049; 775-482-5900, FAX 775-482-5679; CC, Sp, UR; 200; **75-85; D, F; B3; By Appointment Only**

LATE MODEL

Battle Mountain; Atlas Towing Svc, *see Late Vintage*
Carson City; Ace Auto & Truck Wrecking, *see Vintage*
    D & L Auto Dismantlers, *see Vintage*
    Little John Auto Wrecking, *see Late Vintage*
Henderson; A Any & All Auto Wrecking, *see Vintage*
    All Foreign Auto Parts, 651 W Sunset Rd, 89015; 702-566-8082; CC, Sa, Sp; 100; **F**
    B & E Auto Auction, 1239 N Boulder Hwy, 89015; 702-565-8795, FAX 702-564-6553; Sa; 425; **D, F, PU, 4x4, Trk; B3; Only open to registered dealers, mostly wrecked cars**
    Nevada Pic-A-Part, *see Vintage*
Las Vegas; Abbie's Nevada Pic-A-Part, *see Late Vintage*
    Bert's Main Gate Wrecking, *see Vintage*
    Fords Only, *see Vintage*
    Ken's Auto Wrecking, *see Late Vintage*
    King Auto Parts, 4995 Copper Sage St, 89115; 702-644-7723, FAX 702-644-1648; CC, Sa, Sp; 20ac; **D, PU 4x4, few Trk; B3; Spc: Domestic**
    M & R Auto Wrecking, *see Late Vintage*
    Mellis Auto Dismantlers, *see Late Vintage*
    Nevada Differential, *see Vintage*
    Nevada Pic-A-Part, *see Late Vintage*

Southwest Auto Wrecking, 4510 Smiley Rd, 89115; 702-643-1771, FAX 702-644-2331; CC, Sa, Br; 15ac; **D, F, PU, 4x4; B3**

T N H Auto Wrecking, 5380 Novak St, 89115; 702-642-8086, FAX 702-643-8228; CC, Sa, Sp, UR; 300; **F; Jpa**

Tiger Auto Parts & Salvage, 3019 Meade Av, 89102; 702-642-1533 or 362-5511; CC; **D, F, PU, 4x4; B3; after market sheet metal**

Vegas Valley Auto Wrecking, *see Vintage*

Walton's Salvage, *see Late Vintage*

Mustang; Mustang Auto Wreckers, *see Vintage*

North Las Vegas; AA-Row Wrecking & Salvage, 125 Miller Av, 89030; 702-649-2222, FAX 702-649-2245; **D; B3**

Aboco VW Svc & Salvage, *see Vintage*

City Auto Pick-A-Part, 2220 N Commerce St, 89030; 702-649-3366; Sa; **D; B3**

Las Vegas Auto Truck Salvage, 2000 N Commerce St, 89030; 702-649-3111; **D; B3**

R & R Salvage, 2224 Crestline Loop, 89030; 702-649-1360; 200; **D; B3**

Ray's Auto Wrecking, 228 W Owens Av, 89030; 702-384-1414; 1ac; **D; B3; few 50-60s Body Parts**

Snap Auto Wrecking, *see Late Vintage*

Southern Nevada Auto Parts, 2221 Losee Rd, 89030; 702-642-5500; CC, Sa; 100+; **D; B3**

Vegas Valley Auto Dismantlers, 2048 N Commerce St #A, 89030; 702-642-2228; CC, Sa; **F; Honda only**

Pahrump; Smart Auto Salvage & Recycling, *see Vintage*

Reno; Airport Auto & Truck Wreckers, 1416 Gentry Way, 89502; 775-825-6761, FAX 775-825-2172; CC, Sa, Br; 2ac, 250+; **F, PU; Japanese only**

American Auto Wreckers, 495 Parr Cir, 89512; 775-322-9092, FAX 775-786-8885, 888-397-3581; Sa, Sp; 7ac, 800+; **D; B3**

Great Basin Enterprises, 5425 Alpha Av, 89506; 775-972-0800; **D; B3**

Reno Auto & Truck Wrecking, 2429 W 4th St, 89503; 775-329-8671, FAX 775-329-9210; CC, Sa, Sp, Br; 1000+; **D, PU, 4x4; B3, Jp; 2 other locations**

Shamrock Auto Parts Inc, *see Vintage*

Silver Springs; B & R Automotive Machine Shop, 3001 Opal Av, 89429; 775-577-2127; 50; **D, F, PU, 4x4; B3**

Sparks; A Auto Recker & Radiator, *see Late Vintage*

D & D Foreign Dismantlers, *see Vintage*

D & S Auto & Truck Dismantlers, *see Vintage*

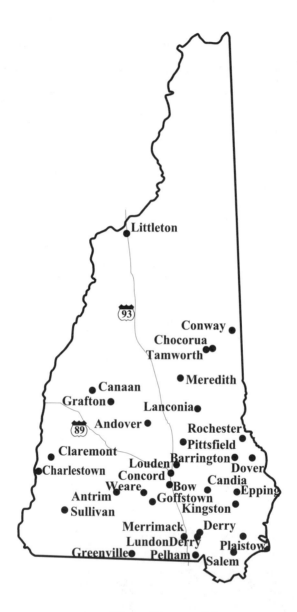

Littleton

93

Conway
Chocorua
Tamworth

Meredith

Canaan
Grafton
Lanconia

89 Andover

Rochester
Claremont
Pittsfield
Louden Barrington
Charlestown
Concord Dover
Candia
Weare Bow
Antrim Goffstown Epping
Sullivan Kingston

Merrimack Derry
LundonDerry Plaistow
Greenville Pelham
Salem

New Hampshire

**Remember not to copy, reproduce or distribute this list in
any way without the written permission of
Ray's wReckingyard Roster**

192

NEW HAMPSHIRE

<u>*VINTAGE*</u>

Andover; Andover Auto Wrecking, 153 Main St, 03216; 603-735-5313; Sa; 7ac; **50-89; D, F, PU, 4x4, Trk; B**3**, Ks, Checker**

Antrim; Hugrons Auto Salvage, 33 Depot St, 03440; 603-588-2817; Sa, Sp, Br; 400; **60-92; D, F, PU, 4x4; B**3**, AMC, Jp, IH, VW**

Canaan; Parts of the Past, Rt 2 Box 118 A, 03741; 603-523-4524, FAX 603-523-4524*49; Sp, Br, Wr; 1200+; **24-72; D, PU, 4x4; B**3**, AMC, Jp, IH, Hd, St, Pk, Ns, Wy, Ks, Fr, Graham, Lincoln, LaSalle, Edsel**

Charlestown; Morway's Auto Salvage, Oxbrook Rd N, 03603; 603-543-1466; Sa; 7ac; **46-89; D, F, PU, 4x4, Fm; B**3**, Jp, VW; Vintage mostly Ford & Chevy**

Chocorua; Ricker Auto Salvage, 112 Maple Rd, 03817; 603-323-7363; Sa, Sp, UR; 2000; **40+; D, F, PU, 4x4, Trk; B**3**; 40s mostly Chevy Pickup**

Concord; Little's Auto Parts, 426 Deer Meadow Rd, 03303; 603-746-4657; Sa, UR; 600; **29-86; D, F, PU, 4x4, Trk, Fm; B**3**, Jp, Hd, VW, Model A Ford**

Conway; Plum Potter Automotive, Box 964, 03818; 603-447-5561; Sp; 3000; **30+; D, F; B**3**; Does restorations & street rods**

Epping; Epping Auto Salvage, 49 Jenness Rd, 03042; 603-679-8010, FAX 603-679-4343, 800-637-7109; CC, Sa, Sp; 500; **50-94; D, F, PU, 4x4; B**3

Grafton; V H McDow & Sons Salvage, Sargent Hill Rd, 03240; 603-523-4555, FAX 603-523-4397; Sa, Sp, UR, Wr; 5ac; **40+; D, few F, PU, 4x4, few Trk, In; B**3**, AMC, Jp, IH**

Louden; Lane's Garage & Auto Body, RFD 8 Box 365, 03301; 603-783-4752, FAX call first, oldcar366 @aol.com; Sa, Sp; 20ac; **30-69; D, F, PU, 4x4, Trk, Cn; B**3**, AMC, Jp, IH, Hd, Ns, St, Pk, Ks, Fr, Cr, Wy, VW; Spc: Chevelle, GM, Henry J, Alstate**

Pelham; Jean-Guy's Used Cars & Parts, RR 111A, 03076; 603-635-2661, FAX 603-635-7117, 800-535-7171, www.jeanguys.com; CC, Sa, Sp; 24ac; **60+; D, F, PU, 4x4; B**3

Sullivan; Northeast Ford & Mustang Parts, Route 9, 03445; 603-847-9956, FAX 603-847-9691, 800-562-3673; CC, Sp; UR; **28-79; D; Ford Model A & Mustang only; By appointment on weekends**

Tamworth; GP Auto Salvage, 729 Turkey St, 03886; 603-323-8080; Sa, Sp, UR; 100ac; **55-90; D, F, PU, 4x4, Trk; B**3**; Spc: Chevy**

<u>*LATE VINTAGE*</u>

Andover; Andover Auto Wrecking, *see Vintage*

Antrim; Hugrons Auto Salvage, *see Vintage*

Canaan; Parts of the Past, *see Vintage*

Charlestown; Morway's Auto Salvage, *see Vintage*

Chocorua; Ricker Auto Salvage, *see Vintage*

Claremont; R Bly & Sons Used Auto Parts, Bowker St, 03743; 603-542-7661; Sa; 2ac; **80+; D, F, PU, 4x4; B**3

Concord; Little's Auto Parts, *see Vintage*

Conway; Plum Potter Automotive, *see Vintage*

Derry; Watts Auto Salvage, 109 Rockingham Rd, 03038; 603-432-2171; Sa, UR; **70+; D, F, PU, 4x4; B**3

Epping; Epping Auto Salvage, *see Vintage*

Grafton; V H McDow & Sons Salvage, *see Vintage*

Kingston; John's Truck & Auto Salvage, 71 New Boston Rd, 03848; 603-642-8748, 800-952-0810; CC, Sa, Sp; 2ac; **70+; D, F, PU, 4x4; B**3**; Spc: 4x4**

Laconia; Reed's Auto Wrecking Co, 89 Frank Bean Rd, 03246; 603-524-1622, FAX call first; Sa, UR; 4ac; **70-90; D, F, PU, 4x4; B**3

Littleton; Red's Auto Wrecking, Manns Hill Rd, 03561; 603-444-5884; Sa, Sp; 3ac; **70-89; D, F, PU, 4x4, Trk, Cn; B**3**; Spc: Pickup & Truck**

Londonderry; Murray's Auto Recycling Ctr, 55 Hall Rd, 03053; 603-425-2562, 877-JUNK BOX; CC, Sa, Sp, UR; 13ac; **83+; D, F, PU, 4x4; B**3

Meredith; Royea's Auto Wrecking, E Holderness Rd, 03253; 603-279-4421; Sa, Sp, UR; 2000; **70+; D, F, PU, 4x4, Fm, In, Cn, Mil; B**3

Merrimack; Matt's Salvage, 54 Baboosic Lake Rd, 03054; 603-424-3376; Sa, UR; 400; **70+; D, F, PU, 4x4, few Trk; B**3

Pelham; Jean-Guy's Used Cars & Parts, *see Vintage*

Pittsfield; Roy's Auto Slvg, Rt 107, 03263; 603-435-5115; Sa; **70-89; D, F, PU, 4x4; B3**

Rochester; American Used Auto Parts, 40 Little Falls Bridge Rd, 03867; 603-330-0370; Sa, Sp, PL; 750; **80+; D, F, PU, 4x4; B3**

    Camaro Heaven, 64 River St, 03867; 603-332-7495, FAX 603-332-3297, 800-CAMARO-1, cambird@acornworld.net; CC, Sa, Sp, Wr; 70; **67+; D; Camaro & Firebird only**

Salem; A J's Used Auto Parts, 89 Lowell Rd, 03079; 603-425-7938, FAX 603-894-5577, 800-894-4361, 888-JUNKCAR; Sa, Sp, UR; 400+; **70+; D, F, PU, 4x4; B3**

Sullivan; Northeast Ford & Mustang Parts, *see Vintage*

Tamworth; GP Auto Salvage, *see Vintage*

Weare; Allied Auto Wrecking, 32 Dustin Tavern Rd, 03281; 603-529-7211, FAX 603-529-0134, 800-529-5865; CC, Sa, Sp, UR; 25ac; **70-96; D, F, PU, 4x4, Trk, Buses; B3; Spc: Chevy**

LATE MODEL

Antrim; Hugrons Auto Salvage, *see Vintage*

Barrington; Landry's Auto Salvage, 3 Greenhill Rd, 03825; 603-332-4937, 800-332-4937, www.landrysauto.com; CC, Sa, Sp, Br; 3ac; 600; **D, F, PU, 4x4; B3**

Bow; Bow Auto Salvage, 663 Route 3A, 03301; 603-224-8400, FAX 603-224-4042, 800-464-3141; CC, Sa, Sp, UR; 400+; **D, F, PU, 4x4; B3**

Candia; Car World Used Parts, 134 Raymond Rd, 03034; 603-483-2366, FAX 603-483-2165, 800-500-8733, www.carworldused.com; CC, Sa, Sp, UR; 1000; **D, F, PU, 4x4; B3**

Chocorua; Ricker Auto Salvage, *see Vintage*

Claremont; General Auto Salvage Co, Old Newport Rd, 03743; 603-542-9595, FAX 603-542-2978, 800-562-3845; CC, Sa, Br; 20ac; **D, F, PU, 4x4; B3**

    R Bly & Sons Used Auto Parts, *see Late Vintage*

Concord; Central New Hampshire Parts, 54 Basin St, 03301; 603-224-5329; CC, Sa, Sp; 600; **D, F, PU, 4x4, Trk; B3**

Conway; Plum Potter Automotive, *see Vintage*

Derry; Watts Auto Salvage, *see Late Vintage*

Dover; Mid-Way Auto Salvage Inc, 120 Route 108 N, 03820; 603-742-5151; CC, Sa, Sp, PL; **D, F, PU, 4x4; B3; Spc: Pickup**

Epping; Epping Auto Salvage, *see Vintage*

Goffstown; Herbert's Used Auto Parts, 516 Shirley Hill Rd, 03045; 603-623-3573, FAX 603-623-8679, 800-499-3573; CC, Sa, Sp, UR; 12ac; **D, F, PU, 4x4; B3**

Grafton; V H McDow & Sons Salvage, *see Vintage*

Greenville; Fitchburg Rd Sales & Salvage, 549 Fitchburg Rd, 03048; 603-878-1172, 800-874-1172, jessl3@prodigy.net; Sa, Sp; 3.5ac; **D, F, PU, 4x4, Trk, Fm; B3; Spc: Pickup**

Kingston; John's Truck & Auto Salvage, *see Late Vintage*

    Ken's Auto Sales & Salvage Inc, 18 Powwow River Rd, 03848; 603-642-3636, FAX 603-642-5151, 800-927-4702; CC, Sp; 25ac; **D, F, PU, 4x4**

Londonderry; Murray's Auto Recycling Ctr, *see Late Vintage*

Meredith; Royea's Auto Wrecking, *see Late Vintage*

Merrimack; Matt's Salvage, *see Late Vintage*

Pelham; Jean-Guy's Used Cars & Parts, *see Vintage*

Plaistow; Anchor Used Auto Parts, 233 Main St, 03865; 603-382-5235, FAX 603-382-2292, 800-382-5235; Sa, Sp, Br; 10ac; **D, F, PU, 4x4; B3**

Rochester; American Used Auto Parts,

    Camaro Heaven, *see Late Vintage*

    Colony Used Auto Parts, 181 Milton Rd, 03868; 603-335-3600, 800-439-6101; CC, Sa, Sp; 800; **D, F, PU, 4x4; B3**

Salem; A J's Used Auto Parts, *see Late Vintage*

Weare; Allied Auto Wrecking, *see Late Vintage*

Mercedes Specialist
Onager Corp
Chula Vista, CA

New Jersey

Please mention you saw'em in Ray's wReckingyard Roster when contacting these yards

NEW JERSEY

VINTAGE

Avenel; Homestead Auto Wreckers, 1019 Homestead Av, 07001; **20s; D; No phone calls**
  Riverside Auto Parts, Leesville Av, 07001; 732-388-1081, FAX 732-388-0416; Sa, Sp;
100ac; **53-80; D, F, PU, 4x4, Trk; B3, AMC, Jp, IH, Hd, Ns**
Bayville; Cosmos Green Acres Recycling, 23 Double Trouble Rd, 08721; 732-349-0112; Sa,
Sp, UR; 13ac, 1000+; **50+; D, F, PU, 4x4; B3, AMC, Jp, IH, VW**
Berlin; Albion Auto Parts, 110 Cross Keys Rd, 08009; 609-768-2250; Sa; 14ac; **30-90; D, F;
B3, AMC, Hd, Ns, St, Pk, Cr, Wy, VW, Alfa Romeo**
Browns Mills; Buster's Garage, 34 Pepper Rd, 08015; 609-893-5575; Sa, Sp, Wr; 18ac;
30-88; D, F, PU, 4x4, Trk, Fm, In, Cn; B3, AMC, Jp, IH, VW
Clementon; A White Auto Parts, 81 Hickstown Rd, 08021; 609-783-0879; Sa, Sp; 900+; **60+**
Elizabeth; Midtown Auto Wreckers, 221 Catherine St, 07201; 908-355-8020; Sa; 500+; **60+;
D; B3**
Freehold; A & A Truck Parts, 80 Hendrickson Rd, 07728; 732-780-4962, FAX
732-780-0573, www.a-atruckparts.com; CC, Sa, Sp; 8ac; **50+; D, PU, 4x4, Trk, In, Cn,
MIL; Pickup and 4x4 only**
Hoboken; Hoboken Auto Body Repair, 620 Jackson St, 07030; 201-798-1915, FAX
201-798-2775; Sa; 3ac; **60+; D, F; B3**
Jamesburg; Jack's Auto Wreckers, 568 Old Bridge Rd, 08831; 732-446-6021, FAX
732-446-6337; Sa, Br; 700; **60+; D, F, PU, 4x4; B3; "anything is possible"**
Jersey City; A T Auto Wreckers, 400 Sip Av, 07306; 201-333-3242; Sa; 2ac; **60-90; D, F; B3**
  Turnpike Auto Inc, 931 Garfield Av, 07305; 201-434-1400, 800-606-0359; Sa; 300; **50+;
D, F, PU, 4x4, Trk; B3**
Lanoka Harbor; Fine Auto Inc, 602 Rte 9, 08734; 973-672-2290, FAX 609-693-6935,
800-298-8233; CC, Sa, Sp, Br; 500; **60+; D, F, PU, 4x4; B3, AMC, Jp, IH, VW**
  Lacey Used Auto Parts Inc, 602 US Hwy 9, 08734; 609-693-0898, FAX 609-693-6935,
800-298-8233, www.laceyusedauto.qgp.com; CC, Sa, Sp, UR; 2ac; **60+**
Middlesex; Absolute Auto Truck Salvage Co, 245 Mountain Av, 08846; 732-469-2202, FAX
732-469-8230, 800-870-3202, www.absoluteautotruck.com; CC, Sa, Sp; 20ac, 1000; **55+; D,
F, PU, 4x4, Trk; B3, VW; preserves collectible cars**
Morganville; Barons Auto Wrecking, 230 Texas Rd, 07751; 732-591-1250, FAX
732-591-5529; CC, Sa, Sp; 3ac; **60+; D, F, PU, 4x4, vans; B3**
  Tennent Road Automotive Inc, 147 Tennent Rd, 07751; 732-591-0006, FAX 732-591-
0252, tennentauto@monmouth.com; CC, Sa, Sp, Wr; 7ac, 800; **65+; D, F, PU, 4x4, Trk; B3**
New Egypt; Price's Auto Recyclers, 831 Rte 539, 08533; 609-758-8035; CC, Sa, Sp; 5ac;
50+; D, F, PU, 4x4; B3, Hd, Pk, Cr, Edsel, Cadillac, Ford Model A
Newark; Heavy Metal Industries, 318 Roseville Av, 07107; 973-485-0198, FAX
973-485-4049; Sa, Sp, Wr; **50-90; D, F, PU, 4x4; B3, Jpa**
Passaic; American Scrap Iron & Metal, 201 Market St, 07055; 973-365-1100, 800-992-0538;
Sa, Sp; 1000+; **60+; D, F; B3**
Pennsauken; Certi-Fit Body Parts, 9160 Pennsauken Hwy, 08110; 609-661-9500, FAX
609-665-7799, 800-619-0003; CC, Wr; **64+; D, F, PU, 4x4; B3, AMC, Jp, VW; Spc:
Mustang; outside body parts only**
Roselle; Linden Car Care Ctr, 111 Saint George Av, 07203; 908-862-7890, FAX
908-620-9233; CC, Sa, Sp; 1.5ac, 85+; **66-95; D, F, PU, 4x4; B3, AMC, IH, VW**
Toms River; Tice Brothers, 132 Cedar Grove Rd, 08753; 732-349-1371, FAX 732-349-1351;
Sa, Sp; 15ac; **40+; D, F, PU, 4x4, Trk; B3, AMC, Jp, IH, Hd, Ns, St, few VW**
Vincentown; Friendship Auto Parts, 58 New Rd, 08088; 609-268-0365; Sa, UR; 10ac; **30+;
D, F, PU, 4x4, Trk; B3, AMC, Jp, IH, VW**
Vineland; Forest Grove Motors, 4 N Main Rd, 08360; 609-691-4669, FAX 609-691-2516;
CC, Sa, Sp, Br; 29ac; **65-92, few earlier; D, F, PU, 4x4; B3, AMC, Jp, IH, VW**
Washington; Kober's Used Truck Parts, 470 Montana Rd, 07882; 908-689-6464, FAX
908-689-4787; Sp; 30ac; **37+; D, F, Trk; Peterbilt, Mack, Volvo, Iveco, Isuzu, Mitsubishi;
1 ton & larger only; dual wheel & larger; rebuilds transmissions**

Washington; Studebaker Sanctuary, 425 Washburn Av, 07882; 908-689-3509; Sa, Sp, Wr; 3ac, 300; **27-83; D, Trk; B3, AMC, Jp, IH, Hd, St, Pk, Ns, Fr; By Appointment Only; "This is not a wrecking yard... I have several collector cars in the mid 30s. This is the time period I enjoy most."**
Westfield; John Bosco Enterprises, 123 Park St, 07090; 908-233-8019; CC, Sa, Sp; 100; **50+; D, PU, 4x4; B3, St**
Whiting; J & S Auto Wreckers, 530 Lacey Rd, 08759; 732-350-4493; CC, Sa, Sp; 7ac; **60s; D, F, PU, 4x4, Trk, Mil; B3, AMC, Jp, IH, VW**
Wrightstown; B & B Auto Wrecking & Towing, 361 Jacobstown Cookstown Rd, 08562; 609-758-8850; Sa, Sp, UR; 8ac; **60+; D, F, PU, 4x4, Trk; B3**

LATE VINTAGE

Avenel; Jim's Auto Wrecking, 100 Ralph Av, 07001; 732-574-3292; Sa, Br; 35; **80+; D, PU, 4x4; B3**

Riverside Auto Parts, *see Vintage*

T & E Auto Wreckers Inc, US 1, 07001; 732-381-2131; Sp; **70+; D, PU, 4x4; B3**
Barnegat; Barnegat Auto Wreckers, 866 Rte 72, 08005; 609-698-2244; Sa, UR; 12ac; **80-90; D, F, PU, 4x4; B3, AMC**
Bayville; Cosmos Green Acres Recycling, *see Vintage*
Belvidere; S & L Used Auto Parts, 492 County Rd 519, 07823; 908-475-2168, FAX 908-475-8277; CC, Sa, Sp; 550+; **70-90; D; B3**
Belmar; Wall Auto Wreckers Inc, 1822 State Rte 71, 07719; 732-681-4200, FAX 732-681-6049; CC, Sa, UR; 1500+; **D, F, PU, 4x4; B3**
Berlin; Albion Auto Parts, *see Vintage*

Albion Auto Parts-U Pull It, 114 Cross Keys Rd, 08009; 609-768-7855; CC, Sa, Sp, UR; 500+; **70-89; D, F, PU, 4x4; B3, AMC, Jp, IH**
Browns Mills; Buster's Garage, *see Vintage*
Caldwell; One A Auto, 194 Ruckers Ln, 07006; 973-228-7500; Sa, Br; 100; **75-90; D, F; B3, Jpa**
Cape May; Cape May Used Auto Parts, 1024 Shunpike Rd, 08204; 609-884-4258; CC, Sa, Sp; 8ac; **70+; D, F, PU, 4x4; B3**
Clementon; A White Auto Parts, *see Vintage*
Dover; Dover Foreign Cars, 286 Rt 15, 07801; 973-328-1663; Sa; 5+; **80+; D, F, PU, 4x4; B3**
Elizabeth; J & L Used Auto Pt, 73 S Front St, 07202; 908-354-3836; Sa; 500+; **70+; D, F; B3**

Midtown Auto Wreckers, *see Vintage*

Security Auto Wreckers, 214 S 1st St, 07206; 908-352-2291; Sa; 400+; **70-91; D, F; B3**

Spencer Distributing Inc, 312 Atlantic St, 07206; 908-352-8076; CC, Sa, Sp; **70+; D, F, PU, 4x4; B3**
Emerson; Petrows Auto Body Svc Inc, 50 Chestnut St, 07630; 201-262-3333, FAX 201-634-9190, jzr&nj@att.net; Sp; 500+; **70+; D, F; B3; Spc: Lincoln Town Car**
Freehold; A & A Truck Parts, *see Vintage*
Hackensack; Hackensack Auto Wreckers, 308 2nd St, 07601; 201-342-0116, FAX 201-342-9404; Sa, UR; 100; **70-90; D, F; B3, AMC**
Hammonton; Caruso's Auto Parts, 1199 S White Horse Pike, 08037; 609-567-3474, 800-567-3475; 800; **80+; D, F, PU, 4x4; B3**
Hightstown; A OK Auto Wreckers, State Hwy 33, 08520; 609-443-6200; Sp; 1000+; **70+; D, F, PU, 4x4; B3**

Madison Auto Sales, 403 Monmouth St, 08520; 609-371-1918; Sa; 1000+; **70+; D, F, PU, 4x4; B3**
Hoboken; Hoboken Auto Body Repair, *see Vintage*
Howell; John Blewett Inc, 2250 US Hwy 9, 07731; 732-780-0880, 800-675-5331; Sa, Sp, Wr; **65+; D, F, PU, 4x4, Trk; B3, Jp, IH; Pickup & Truck parts only**

John Blewett Inc, 246 Herbertsville Rd, 07731; 732-938-5331, FAX 732-919-1912, 800-675-5331; CC, Sa, Sp, UR; 50ac, 1000; **60+; D, F; B3, VW; car parts only**
Jackson; Childs Auto Wrecking Yard, 390 W Commodore Blvd, 08527; 732-928-0624; Sa; 1.75ac, 200; **70+; D, F, PU, 4x4; B3**

Jamesburg; Jack's Auto Wreckers, *see Vintage*
   Red & Black Auto Parts, 60 Lincoln Av, 08831; 732-521-9856, FAX 732-521-0313; CC, Sa, UR; 2000; **70-90; D, F, PU, 4x4, Trk; B3, AMC, Jp, IH, VW**

Jersey City; A T Auto Wreckers, *see Vintage*
   Star Auto Sales, 6 County Rd #A, 07307; 201-656-5850, FAX 201-656-7488; CC, Sa, Sp; 200+; **80+; D, F, PU; B3**
   Turnpike Auto Inc, *see Vintage*

Kearny; A-OK Auto Glass, 54 Stover Av, 07032; 201-997-8899; UR; 700+; **75+**

Lafayette; Lafayette Salvage Inc, 20 Van Sickle Rd, 07848; 973-579-7428, 800-579-5458; CC, Sa, Sp; 8ac, 400; **70+; D, F, PU, 4x4; B3, AMC, Jp, VW**

Lakewood; Tilton Used Auto Parts, 685 Squankum Rd, 08701; 732-363-1217, FAX 732-905-8777, 800-531-1180; CC, Sa, Sp, PL; 9.5ac, 1800; **70+; D, F, PU, 4x4; B3; Spc: Nova 70-72**

Lanoka Harbor; Fine Auto Inc, *see Vintage*
   Lacey Used Auto Parts Inc, *see Vintage*

Lodi; Academy Auto Recyclers Inc, 1 Park Pl, 07644; 973-773-4580; Sa, Sp, UR; 150; **80-93; D, PU, 4x4; B3**
   Duke's Auto Salvage & Recycling, 99 Dell Glen Av, 07644; 973-478-6522, FAX 973-478-4924; Sa; 300; **80+; D, F, PU, 4x4; B3, VW**

Mantua; Pontes Auto Parts, 55 New York Av, 08051; 609-468-3325; Sa; 500; **80+; D, F; B3**

Metuchen; AMP Auto Parts, 225 Liberty St, 08840; 732-632-8882, FAX 732-632-8886, 800-882-2888; CC, Sp, UR, Wr; **80+; D, F, PU, 4x4; B3, AMC, Jp, VW**

Middlesex; Absolute Auto Truck Salvage Co, *see Vintage*

Montville; V & V Recycling, 144 Main Rd, 07045; 973-334-0073, FAX 973-334-1571, 800-894-0073; CC, Sa, Sp, Wr; **70+; D, F, PU, 4x4**

Morganville; Barons Auto Wrecking, *see Vintage*
   P & J Auto Salvage & Towing, 162 Greenwood Rd, 07751; 732-591-1028; Sa, UR; 50+; **80+, few 70s; D, F, PU, 4x4, Trk; B3**
   Tennent Road Automotive Inc, *see Vintage*

Mount Holly; Dennings Garage, 765 Rancocas Rd, 08060; 609-267-5555, FAX 609-267-5526; CC, Sp; 5.5ac; **70+; D, F, PU, 4x4; B3**

New Brunswick; Jersey Ave Auto & Truck Sales, 121 Jersey Av, 08901; 732-249-2048; **80+; D, PU, 4x4, Trk; B3**

New Egypt; Price's Auto Recyclers, *see Vintage*

New Gretna; Kaszuba & Sons Auto Recycling, Oak Av, 08224; 609-296-3944; Sa, Sp; 5ac; **75+; D, F, PU, 4x4; B3**

Newark; Airport Used Auto Parts, 561 Avenue P, 07105; 973-817-8859, FAX 973-589-3062; CC, Sa; 150; **75-90; D, F, PU, 4x4, Trk; B3, AMC**
   Bryans Auto Wrck, 567 Wilson Av, 07105; 973-344-3113; Sa, Sp; 1ac; **74+; D, F; B3, AMC**
   Heavy Metal Industries, *see Vintage*
   Kar King USA Inc, 555 Avenue P, 07105; 973-589-8400; CC, Sa, UR, Wr; **80+; D, F, PU, 4x4; B3, AMC**
   M & N Used Auto Parts, 3856 Stockton St #56, 07105; 973-344-4211, FAX 973-344-1560; Sa, UR; **78+; D, F, PU, 4x4; B3, AMC, Jp, IH, VW**
   Newark Motor & Export Corp, 249 Ave P, 07105; 973-589-7456, FAX 973-589-0167, www.newarkmotors.com; CC, Sa, Sp; 3ac; **70+; D, F, PU, 4x4; B3**

North Arlington; Meadowlawns Auto Wreckers Inc, 317 River Rd, 07031; 201-991-0180; 50; **80+; D, F, PU, 4x4; B3; closed Monday, small amount of older cars**

North Bergen; Deb-Dot Enterprises Inc, 9524 Railroad Av, 07047; 201-861-4704; Sa, Wr; **83-89; D, F; B3**
   Dewland Service, 1710 Tonnelle Av, 07047; 201-866-3400, FAX 201-866-3460; Sa; 100; **72+; D, F, PU, 4x4; B3, AMC, Jp, VW**

Orange; Daloia Auto Sales, 32 Main St, 07050; 973-676-4272; Sa; 200; **70+; D, F, PU, 4x4, Trk; B3, AMC, Jp, IH**

Passaic; American Scrap Iron & Metal, *see Vintage*

Michael's Towing & Auto, 70 Jefferson St, 07055; 973-471-5791; Sa; 1ac; **82+; D, F, PU, 4x4; B3**

Paterson; Auto Connection Towing & Svc, 164 Michigan Av, 07503; 973-345-8560; Sa, Sp, Wr; 75+; **75-91; D, F, PU, 4x4, Trk; B3, AMC, VW**

CFS Auto Wreckers, 16 Bloomfield Av, 07503; 973-684-3500; CC, Sa, Sp, Br; 1ac; 125; **80+; D, F, PU, 4x4; B3, AMC, Jp, VW; Spc: Camaro**

Pennsauken; Certi-Fit Body Parts, *see Vintage*

Pine Brook; G I Auto Salvage Co, 85 Old Bloomfield Av, 07058; 973-227-1100, FAX 973-808-4393; Sa, UR; 1500; **76-90; D, F; B3**

Port Murray; Washington Auto Salvage, 517 State Rte 57, 70865; 908-689-0013, FAX 908-689-0072; Sa, Br; 300; **80s, few 70s & 90s; D, PU; B3**

Red Bank; Red Bank Recycling & Auto Wrck, 64 Central Av, 07701; 732-747-7779; Sa, Wr; **80+; D, F; B3, AMC, Jp, IH**

Riveredge; Bergenfield Auto Parts, 550 Hackensack Av, 07661; 201-342-0923; Sa, UR; 300; **80-90; D, F; B3, AMC, VW**

Roselle; Linden Car Care Ctr, *see Vintage*

Somerset; Somerset Recycling & Wreckers, 921 Somerset St, 08873; 732-545-5050; Sa; 3ac; **80-90; D, F, PU, 4x4; B3, AMC, VW**

South Plainfield; Auto Salvage, 138 Ryan St, 07080; 908-756-3355, FAX 908-753-8449; CC, Sa, Sp, Wr; 200; **80+, few 60-70s; D, F, PU, 4x4, Trk, Mil; B3, AMC, few Jp, VW**

Spotswood; Big A Auto Salvage, 192 Manalapan Rd, 08884; 732-251-1400; Sa, Sp; 100; **D, F; B3, AMC, Jp, VW; Spc: older Ford & Chevy**

Stanhope; North Jersey Auto Wrck, 287 Lackawanna Dr, 07874; 973-347-5800, FAX 973-347-4320; CC, Sa, Sp, Br; 9ac; 750+; **70-97; D, F, PU, 4x4, Trk; B3, AMC, Jp, IH, VW**

Sussex; Beemerville Auto Wrecking Inc, 268 County Rd 519, 07461; 973-875-4900, FAX 973-875-6750; CC, Sa, UR; 1500; **80+; D, F, PU, 4x4, Trk; B3, AMC, few Jp, few IH, few VW; some 70s trucks**

Toms River; Tice Brothers, *see Vintage*

Trenton; Hamilton Auto Recycling Inc, 225 Turnbull Av, 08610; 609-587-8522, FAX 609-890-6596, 800-839-7124, hamiltonauto@aol.com; CC, Sa, Sp; 2ac; **70+; D, F, PU, 4x4; B3**

Vincentown; Friendship Auto Parts, *see Vintage*

Vineland; Forest Grove Motors, *see Vintage*

Washington; Kober's Used Truck Parts, *see Vintage*

Studebaker Sanctuary, *see Vintage*

Waterford Works; Myers Auto Wrecking, 250 Chew Rd, 08089; 609-767-1248, FAX 609-767-4715; Sa, Sp; 60ac; **D, F, PU, 4x4, Trk; B3, AMC, Jp, IH, VW**

Westfield; John Bosco Enterprises, *see Vintage*

Wharton; Valley Auto Wreckers, 217 Berkshire Valley Rd, 07885; 973-366-0058; **78-89; D, few F; B3, AMC**

Williamstown; Manuel's Auto Parts Inc, 1041 Morgan Rd, 08094; 609-629-1703, FAX 609-728-0626, 800-422-7784; CC, Sa, Sp, Br; 1000; **80+; D, F, PU, 4x4, Trk; B3, AMC, Jp, IH, VW**

Williamstown Auto & Truck, 468 Huber Av, 08094; 609-728-2018; Sa, Sp; 7ac; 750+; **77-93; D, F, PU, 4x4, Trk; B3, AMC, Jp, IH, VW**

Whiting; J & S Auto Wreckers, *see Vintage*

Wrightstown; B & B Auto Wrecking & Towing, *see Vintage*

LATE MODEL

Allamuchy; B & J Auto Salvage-Sussex, 77 Gibbs Rd, 07820; 908-852-7444, FAX 908-852-2336, 800-452-9329; CC, Sa, Sp; 7ac; **D, F, PU, 4x4; B3**

Avenel; Frank's Auto Wrecking, Rt 1, 07001; 732-381-3911; Sa, Sp, UR; 4ac; **D, F, PU, 4x4, Trk, In, Cn; Spc: rebuilt transmissions; across from Rahway State Prison**

Horbaly's Auto Wreckers Inc, 1 Dudley Ct, 07001; 732-381-2546; CC, Sa, Sp; 3ac; **D, F; cars only**

Jim's Auto Wrecking, *see Late Vintage*

Lige Auto Salvage, 189 Elliot St, 07001; 732-396-0666, FAX 732-396-9713; CC, Sa, Sp, UR, Wr; **D, F, PU, 4x4, Trk; B3**

200

T & E Auto Wreckers Inc, *see Late Vintage*

Bayville; Cosmos Green Acres Recycling, *see Vintage*

Ocean County Auto Wreckers, 176 Rte 9, 08721; 732-349-0332, FAX 732-286-9486; CC, Sa, Sp, Wr; 5ac; **D, F, PU, 4x4; B3**

Belmar; Wall Auto Wreckers Inc, *see Late Vintage*

Bridgewater; Price Auto Wreckers, 4 Edgewater Av, 08807; 908-725-4800, FAX 908-725-4436; Sa, Sp; 4ac; **D, F; B3**

Cape May; Cape May Used Auto Parts, *see Late Vintage*

Clementon; A White Auto Parts, *see Vintage*

Dover; Dover Foreign Cars, *see Late Vintage*

Wharton Auto Wreckers, 22 Trenton, 07801; 973-366-2149; Sa, UR; 50; **D, F; B3, AMC**

East Rutherford; A A Auto Recycling, 808 Paterson Av, 07073; 201-438-1670, FAX 201-438-2715; Sa; 650+; **D, F, PU; B3**

Egg Harbor; Pro Auto Recycler, 3037 Ocean Heights Av, 08221; 609-927-7337, FAX 609-653-8067, 800-962-7337, www.proautorecycler.com; CC, Sa, Sp; 1200; **D, F, PU; B3**

Elizabeth; Abcar Autowreckers Inc, 409 South St, 07202; 908-351-5858; **D, PU, 4x4; B3**

J & L Used Auto Parts, *see Late Vintage*

Midtown Auto Wreckers, *see Vintage*

Spencer Distributing Inc, *see Late Vintage*

Emerson; Petrows Auto Body Svc Inc, *see Late Vintage*

Forked River; Bamber Lake Auto Recycling, 2834 W Lacey Rd, 08731; 609-693-6500; 300+; **D, F; B3**

Freehold; A & A Truck Parts, *see Vintage*

Hackensack; Carr Auto Wrecking & Towing, 36 Jersey Pl, 07601; 201-489-5545; CC, Sp; 60; **D, F; B3**

Hammonton; Caruso's Auto Parts, *see Late Vintage*

Hampton; Cozze Brothers, 49 Race St, 08827; 908-735-7126, FAX 908-735-9287, 800-452-9112; Sa, Sp; 300+; **D, F, 4x4; B3**

Hightstown; A OK Auto Wreckers, *see Late Vintage*

Madison Auto Sales, *see Late Vintage*

Hoboken; Hoboken Auto Body Repair, *see Vintage*

Howell; John Blewett Inc, *see Late Vintage*

Jackson; Childs Auto Wrecking Yard, *see Late Vintage*

Jamesburg; Jack's Auto Wreckers, *see Vintage*

Jersey City; Necma Auto Repair, 318 Sip Av, 07306; 201-333-4796; Sa; 300+; **D, F; B3**

Star Auto Sales, *see Late Vintage*

Turnpike Auto Inc, *see Vintage*

Kearny; A-OK Auto Glass, *see Late Vintage*

Lafayette; Lafayette Salvage Inc, *see Late Vintage*

Lakewood; Tilton Used Auto Parts, *see Late Vintage*

Lanoka Harbor; Fine Auto Inc, *see Vintage*

Lacey Used Auto Parts Inc, *see Vintage*

Lodi; Academy Auto Recyclers Inc, *see Late Vintage*

Duke's Auto Salvage & Recycling, *see Late Vintage*

Mantua; Pontes Auto Parts, *see Late Vintage*

Metuchen; AMP Auto Parts, *see Late Vintage*

Middlesex; Absolute Auto Truck Salvage Co, *see Vintage*

Montville; V & V Recycling, *see Late Vintage*

Morganville; Barons Auto Wrecking, *see Vintage*

Marlboro Auto Wreckers, 153 Tennent Rd, 07751; 732-591-1400, FAX 732-591-8762, 800-223-9900; Sa, Sp, UR, Wr; 2500+; **D, 4x4; Jp; Spc: gears, windshields, door parts, glass distributor**

Midway Auto Wreckers, 456 Texas Rd, 07751; 732-591-1652, FAX 732-591-2751, 800-870-1652, www.newjerseyparts.com; CC, Sa, Sp; 8ac, 800; **D, F, PU, 4x4; B3**

P & J Auto Salvage & Towing, *see Late Vintage*

Tennent Road Automotive Inc, *see Vintage*

Mount Holly; Dennings Garage, *see Late Vintage*

New Brunswick; Jersey Ave Auto & Truck Sales, *see Late Vintage*

New Brunswick Auto Exchange, 81 Joyce Kilmer Av, 08901; 732-828-5110; CC, Sa, UR; 0.5ac; **D, F; B3**

New Egypt; Price's Auto Recyclers, *see Vintage*

New Gretna; Kaszuba & Sons Auto Recycling, *see Late Vintage*

Newark; American Auto Sales, 28 Avenue C, 07114; 973-623-2479; Sa, Sp; 1ac, 150+; **D, F, PU; B3, AMC, Jp, VW**

Avenue P Auto Wreckers, 553 F Avenue P #A, 07105; 973-344-2221; Sa, UR; 200; **D, F, PU, 4x4; B3**

Boss Salvage, 259 Av C, 07114; 973-642-5595, FAX 973-642-0209; Sa; **D, F; B3, AMC**

Bryans Auto Wreckers, *see Late Vintage*

Cowboy's Auto Salvage, 62 Avenue C, 07114; 973-242-8981; Sa, Br; 80; **D, F, PU, 4x4; B3, Jp, IH, VW**

Discount Auto Wreckers, 539 Avenue P, 07105; 973-344-4030, www.discountautosalvage. net.usrc; Sa, Br; 350+; **D, F; Spc: Foreign**

Jersey Junk Auto Wrck, 964 Frelinghuysen Av, 07114; 973-621-8775; Sa; **D, F; B3, AMC**

Kar King USA Inc, *see Late Vintage*

Lacey Used Auto Parts, 305 Wilson Av, 07105; 973-465-7553; CC, Sa, Br; 100; **D, F, PU, 4x4; B3, AMC**

M & N Used Auto Parts, *see Late Vintage*

Mendez Auto Sales, 88 Avenue C, 07114; 973-824-9775, FAX 973-824-2565; Sa, Sp, UR; 200; **D, F, PU, 4x4, Trk; B3; mostly cars**

Newark Motor & Export Corp, *see Late Vintage*

Primero Used Auto Parts, 2 Riverside Av, 07104; 973-481-7272, FAX 973-481-5560; CC, Sa; 3.5ac; **D, F; B3, AMC, Jp, VW**

South Street Auto Salvage, 320 South St, 07114; 973-344-2083; CC, Sa; **D, F, PU, 4x4; B3, AMC, VW**

Newton; Newton Auto Salvage LLC, 79 Mount View St, 07860; 973-383-1753; Sa, Sp; 3ac; **D, F, PU, 4x4; B3**

North Arlington; Meadowlawns Auto Wreckers Inc, *see Late Vintage*

North Bergen; Dewland Service, *see Late Vintage*

Dottinos Used Parts Co, 9526 Railroad Av, 07047; 201-868-5884; Sa, UR; 40; **D, F, PU, 4x4; B3, AMC, Jp, IH, VW**

West Side Auto Wreckers, 1900 Tonnelle Av, 07047; 201-865-8333, FAX 201-865-5567; Sa, Sp, Br; 120; **D, F, PU, 4x4; B3, AMC, VW**

Orange; Daloia Auto Sales, *see Late Vintage*

Holiday Salvage & Wrecking, 185 S Jefferson St, 07050; 973-673-5145; Sa, Br; 50+; **D, F; B3, AMC**

Passaic; American Scrap Iron & Metal, *see Vintage*

Michael's Towing & Auto, *see Late Vintage*

Paterson; CFS Auto Wreckers, *see Late Vintage*

Harry & Phil's Auto Wrecking, 45 Montgomery St, 07501; 973-345-1861; Sa; 55+; **D, few F; B3, AMC**

Hill Auto Parts, 785 Main St, 07503; 973-754-0022, FAX 973-881-8054; CC, Sa, Sp, PL; 2.5ac, 200; **D, F, PU, 4x4; B3, AMC, Jp, IH, VW**

Johnstone's Used Auto Parts, 354 Marshall St, 07503; 973-684-2763, jsused@aol.com; Sa, Br; 250; **D, F, PU, 4x4; B3, AMC, Jp**

Magic Auto Sales, 11 Bergen St, 07522; 973-790-1620, FAX 973-684-1122; CC, Sa, Sp, UR; 100+; **D, F, PU, 4x4; B3, AMC, Jp**

North East Auto Sales Inc, 330 River St, 07524; 973-742-8804; Sa, Wr; 0.75ac; **D, F; B3, AMC**

Pike Motors Auto Parts, 88-92 Montgomery St, 07501; 973-345-7184, FAX 973-881-0977, pike@eclipse.net; CC, Sa, Sp; **F; few 90s – mostly late 80s**

R & S Recycling, 40 Holsman St, 07522; 973-942-2213, FAX 973-942-6593; CC, Sa, Sp, UR, Wr; 100; **D, F, PU, 4x4; B3, AMC, Jp, VW**

Pennsauken; Certi-Fit Body Parts, *see Vintage*
Port Murray; Port Murray Auto Salvage, 89 Brickyard Rd, 07865; 908-689-3152, FAX 908-689-7676; Sp; 4ac; **D, F, PU, 4x4; B3, AMC, Jp, VW**
   Washington Auto Salvage, *see Late Vintage*
Rahway; Avenel Auto Wrecker, 20 Leesville Av, 07065; 732-381-7575; Sa; **D, F, PU, 4x4; B3, AMC, Jp**
   Leesville Auto Wreckers, 186 Leesville Av, 07065; 732-388-0783, www.leesvilleauto.com; CC, Sa, Sp, Br; 300; **D, F, PU, 4x4; B3, VW**
   Riverside Scrap, Leesville Av, 07065; 732-381-3355, FAX 732-381-7919; Sa, Sp, Br; 14ac; **D, F, PU, 4x4; B3, AMC, VW**
Red Bank; Red Bank Recycling & Auto Wrck, *see Late Vintage*
Somerset; King Parts Auto Wreckers III, 201 Cover Rd, 08873; 732-220-1177, FAX 732-329-3161; Sa, Sp, Wr; **D, PU, 4x4; B3, AMC; At the shore**
Somerville; Vinnie's Auto Salvage, 2124 W Camplain Rd S, 08876; 908-685-9503, FAX 908-526-6708; CC, Sa; 4000; **D, F, PU, 4x4; B3, AMC, Jp, IH, VW**
South Amboy; Mid-Jersey Stadium Auto Parts, Main & Scott St, 08879; 732-721-0746, 800-624-0529; CC, Sa, Sp; 150; **D, F, PU, 4x4; B3, AMC, Jp, VW**
South Plainfield; Auto Salvage, *see Late Vintage*
South River; Michaelsons Foreign Car Parts, 56 Causeway St, 08882; 732-254-0043, FAX 732-234-5075; CC, Sa, Sp, Br; 1000; **F**
Stanhope; North Jersey Auto Wreckers, *see Late Vintage*
Stockton; Locktown Auto Salvage, 1 Old Mill Rd, 08559; 908-996-2867, FAX 908-996-0987; Sa; **D, F, PU, 4x4; B3**
Sussex; Beemerville Auto Wrecking Inc, *see Late Vintage*
Tenafly; Tenafly Auto Parts Co, 66 W Railroad Av, 07670; 201-568-0851, FAX 201-568-9813, jydog@aol.com; Sa, Sp; 1ac; **D, F, PU, 4x4; B3, AMC, Jp, VW**
Toms River; Tice Brothers, *see Vintage*
   Toms River Auto Recyclers, 15 Cox Cro Rd, 08755; 732-341-5110, FAX 732-341-8049, 800-392-6978; CC, Sa, Sp, Br; 12ac; 300; **D, F, few PU; B3, AMC, Volvo, BMW**
   Vincentown; Friendship Auto Parts, *see Vintage*
Trenton; Acres Auto Inc, 74 Youngs Rd, 08619; 609-586-3225, FAX 609-588-8896; CC, Sa; 4ac; **F; VW**
   Hamilton Auto Recycling Inc, *see Late Vintage*
Union; B & A Towing Svc, 1170 Morris Av #A, 07087; 908-688-7420, FAX; **D, F; B3**
   Union Auto Wreckers, 2345 Rte 22 W, 07083; 908-687-1051, FAX 908-687-7807; CC, Sa, Sp; 2ac; **D, F, PU, 4x4, Cn; B3, AMC, VW**
Voorhees; Micciche Auto Parts, Route 73, 08043; 609-767-4460, FAX 609-767-5925, 800-310-4460; CC, Sa, Sp; 8ac; 1200; **D, F, PU, 4x4; B3, AMC, Jp, VW; few 80s**
Washington; Kober's Used Truck Parts, *see Vintage*
Waterford Works; Myers Auto Wrecking, *see Late Vintage*
West Milford; Concours Automotive Recycling, 1894 State Rte 23, 07480; 973-492-1262, FAX 973-492-8271, 800-624-0141; CC, Sa, Sp; 150; **D, F, PU, 4x4; B3, AMC, Jp, VW**
Westfield; John Bosco Enterprises, *see Vintage*
Whippany; A A Auto Wreckers, 146 Parsippany Rd, 07981; 973-887-1096; Sa; **D, F; B3**
   Cobra Auto Wreckers, 156 Parsippany Rd, 07981; 973-884-5777, FAX 973-884-5080; Sa, UR; 2ac; 500; **D, F, PU, 4x4; B3, AMC, Jp, VW**
Whiting; J & S Auto Wreckers, *see Vintage*
Williamstown; Manuel's Auto Parts Inc, *see Late Vintage*
   Midway Auto Parts, 1623 Glassboro Rd, 08094; 609-881-8568, FAX 609-881-7904; Sa, Sp, PL; 13ac; **D, F; B3**
   Williamstown Auto & Truck, *see Late Vintage*
Woodbine; Woodbine Auto Repair Works, 301 Washington Av, 08270; 609-861-3891; CC, Sa; **D, F; B3**
Woodbury; Advanced Slvg, 2207 County 7, 08096; 609-227-1133, 800-932-3797; **D, F; B3**
Wrightstown; B & B Auto Wrecking & Towing, *see Vintage*

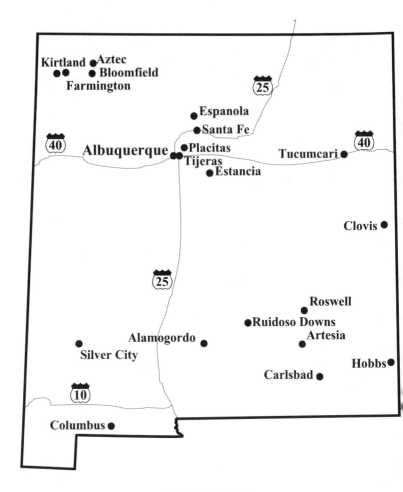

NEW MEXICO

VINTAGE

Alamogordo; North Fifty-Four Salvage, 7066 Hwy 54 70, 88310; 505-437-4188, FAX 505-437-5029, 800-624-4941; CC, Sa, Sp, Br; 2000; **35+; D, F, PU, 4x4, Trk; B3, Jp IH, Hd, Ns, St, Pk, Ks, Fr; some parts, some restorable cars**

Southside Salvage & Used Cars, Hwy 54 S, 88310; 505-437-2850; Sa, Sp, UR; 10ac; **30-73; D, F, PU, Trk; B3, St, Pk, VW**

Walker Towing & Slvg, 1520 Indiana Av, 88310; 505-434-2500; CC; 2ac; **60+; D, F; B3**

Wild Bills Auto Wrecking, 7030 Hwy 54 70, 88310; 505-437-5400, FAX 505-437-7400, 800-861-5472; CC, Sa, Sp, UR; 2500; **44+; D, F, PU, 4x4, Trk; B3, Hd, Ns, St, Pk, Cr**

Albuquerque; Chavez Auto Parts, 922 Atrisco Dr SW, 87105; 505-247-0533, FAX 505-243-2870; CC, Sa, Sp, Br; 2ac; **70+, few 30-60s; D, F, PU, 4x4; B3, AMC, Ns, St, VW; Spanish**

Chevy Connection, 2600 Broadway Blvd SE, 87102; 505-242-0101, FAX 505-242-3044; CC, Sa, Sp, Br; 1ac; 600+; **50-89; D, PU, 4x4; B3 Spc: Chevy**

Complete Auto & Truck Parts, 4510 Broadway Blvd SE, 87105; 505-877-5960, 800-423-3732; CC, Sa, Sp, Br; 10ac; **60+; D, F, PU, 4x4, Trk; B3, AMC, Jp, IH, Jpa, Eur**

204

Discount Auto Parts, 4703 Broadway Blvd SE, 87105; 505-877-6782, 800-748-1537; CC, Sa, Sp, Br; 1400; 55+; F; VW, Audi; VW from day one!

J & E Auto Salvage, 203 Prosperity Av SE, 87105; 505-877-7573; CC, Sa, UR; 500; 60+; D, F; B3

South Coors Truck Salvage, 1125 Coors Blvd SW, 87121; 505-242-1144, FAX 505-242-2620; CC; Sp; 700; D, PU, Trk; B3, Jp, IH; No cars

Artesia; Clark Auto, 2305 S 1st, 88210; 505-746-4607; Sa, UR; 7ac; 40+; D, F, PU, Trk, Cn; B3, Jp, IH

Clovis; American Auto Salvage, 513 S Prince, 88101; 505-763-4812, 888-851-8697; Sa, Sp, UR; 500; 68-85; D, F, PU; B3, Jp, IH, VW

Thompson's Auto Salvage, S Swift Plant Rd, 88101; 505-763-6557; Sa, Sp, UR; 400; 55-85; D, F, PU, 4x4, Trk; B3

Wholesale Wrecking, 2112 W 7th St, 88101; 505-762-9850, 800-571-9850; CC, Sp, UR; ac, 250; 10-91; D, F, PU, 4x4, Trk; B3, St

Estancia; Hooker Salvage, 87016; 505-384-3162; Sa, Sp, UR; 2.5ac; 70+, few 49-69; D, F, PU, 4x4, Trk, Fm, Cn, In; B3, Jpa; Mostly 70s

Hobbs; Hobbs Wrecking Co, 1717 S Dal Paso St, 88240; 505-397-1571, 800-353-1571; CC, Sa, Wr; 4ac, 250; 88+, few 60s; D, PU, 4x4; B3; Pickups only

Placitas; Placitas Auto Wrecking, 87043; 505-867-5310; Sa, Br; 2.5ac, 150; 49+; D, F, PU, 4x4; B3 AMC, Jp, IH, VW

Roswell; Diamond Auto, 5100 SE Main St, 88201; 505-347-5589; Sp; 6ac, 650+; D; B3, AMC, Hd, Ns, Wy

Roswell Auto Salvage, 201 Wooldridge Margaret Rd, 88201; 505-623-2256; Sp; 5ac, 100; 29+; D, PU, 4x4; B3, Jp, IH; some '29 models & DeSoto

Silver City; Arenas Valley Auto Salvage, 2075 N Pinos Altos Rd, 88061; 505-388-1234; Sa, Sp, UR; 1ac, 160+; 60-89, few 50s; D, F, PU; B3, VW

Tijeras; Route 66 Reutillization, 1357 Historic Rt 66 E, 87059; 505-286-2222; Sp, UR; 20ac; Pre-War-60s; D; B3, St; By Appointment Only

Tucumcari; Quay Valley Salvage, 6358 Quay Rd AM, 88401; 505-461-2077, 800-814-2077; CC, Sa, Sp, UR; 17ac, 1500; 40+; D, F, PU, 4x4; B3, IH, Hd, Ns, St

LATE VINTAGE

Alamogordo; Auto Shop, 501 1st St, 88310; 505-434-0661, FAX 505-434-4720; CC, Sp, UR; 100; 70-83; D, F, PU, 4x4; B3

North Fifty-Four Salvage, see Vintage

Southside Salvage & Used Cars, see Vintage

Walker Towing & Salvage, see Vintage

Wild Bills Auto Wrecking, see Vintage

Albuquerque; A & A Cervantes Auto Salvage, 111 Hill St SW, 87105; 505-242-9358; Sa; 1.5ac; 80+; D, F; B3

A-Foreign Auto Parts, 4520 Williams St SE, 87105; 505-877-4750; CC, Sa; 2ac, 350; 78-88; F; Spc: Japanese

Antonio's Auto Parts, 800 Commercial St SE, 87102; 505-247-8431; Sa; 300; 80+; D, F, PU, 4x4, Trk

Chavez Auto Parts, see Vintage

Chevy Connection, see Vintage

Complete Auto & Truck Parts, see Vintage

Coronado Auto Recyclers, 9320 San Pedro Dr NE, 87113; 505-821-0440, FAX 505-821-4965, 800-444-0414; CC, Sa, Sp; 1000; 80+; D, PU, Trk; B3

Discount Auto Parts, see Vintage

East Central Auto Wrecking, 401 Conchas St SE, 87123; 505-299-8725; Sa; 2ac; 80+; D, F, PU; B3

El Mexicano Auto Salvage, 1200 Coors Blvd SW, 87121; 505-242-2131; 800-249-3569; CC, Sa; 3ac; 80+; D, PU; B3; Pickups only

Five Foreign Auto Parts, 601 Haines Av NW, 87102; 505-247-2227; CC, Sp; 300; 80+; F, PU; Foreign Only

J & E Auto Salvage, *see Vintage*

San Diego Wrecking, 7909 Central Av NW, 87121; 505-836-1566; Sa; 3ac; **D, F; B3**

South Coors Truck Salvage, *see Vintage*

Artesia; Bulldog Wrecking, 4136 W Main St, 88210; 505-746-4655; CC, Sa, Sp; 20ac; **70-90; D, PU; B3**

Clark Auto, *see Vintage*

Aztec; Huskey Auto, 905 N Hwy 550, 87410; 505-334-9816, 888-881-8404; UR; **70-90; D, F**

Bloomfield; Tri-Cities Truck & Auto, 31 Rd 4915, 87413; 505-632-3770; Sa; **70+; D, F; B3**

Carlsbad; Carlsbad Wrecking Co, 1822 Railroad Av, 88220; 505-885-6923, FAX 505-885-0587, 800-658-2068; CC, Sa, UR; 5ac, 300+; **80+; D, F, PU, Trk; B3**

Landreth Wrecking Co, 1604 Radio Blvd, 88220; 505-887-2532; CC, Sa; 6ac; **70+; D, F, PU, 4x4; B3**

Clovis; American Auto Salvage, *see Vintage*

Discount Auto Wrecking, 609 S Prince St, 88101; 505-762-9614; UR; 4ac; **80-90; D, F, PU, Trk; B3**

Quality Auto Salvage, 515 S Prince St, 88101; 505-763-4454, 800-303-4454; CC, Sa, Sp, UR; 200; **80+; D, F, PU, 4x4, Trk; B3**

Thompson's Auto Salvage, *see Vintage*

Wholesale Wrecking, *see Vintage*

Columbus; Columbus Car Sales & Trucking, Hwy 11, 88029; 505-531-2454; Sa, Sp, Br; 30; **70+; D, F; B3**

Espanola; Boneyard Auto Salvage, 87532; 505-753-3786; Sa, UR; 7ac, 200; **70-89; D, F, PU; B3**

Estancia; Hooker Salvage, *see Vintage*

Farmington; A-1 Auto Salvage, 99 Rd 6100, 87401; 505-325-1994, FAX 505-325-1273, 800-530-8571; CC, Sa, Sp; 25ac, 4000; **70+; D, F, PU, 4x4; B3**

A 550 Truck & Auto Salvage, 62 Rd 6100, 87401; 505-326-3464; CC, Sa; 300; **73+; D, PU, 4x4; B3 AMC**

Off Again Auto, 508 E Murray Dr, 87401; 505-325-5761, FAX 505-326-1552, 888-633-2424; CC, Sa, Sp, Br; 2ac, 300; **90+, few 77-89; D, F, PU, 4x4, Trk; B3, AMC, Jp Mostly 90s**

Hobbs; Hobbs Wrecking Co, *see Vintage*

Jerry's Auto Salvage, 2026 N Cottrell St, 88240; 505-397-1541, 800-657-9341; Sa, Sp, UR; 8ac, 600; **75-94; D, F, PU, 4x4; B3**

Kirtland; Gilmores Truck & Auto Salvage, 4306 Hwy 64, 87417; 505-598-5584, 800-239-5584; CC, Sa, Sp, UR; 1200; **72+, few earlier; D, F, PU, 4x4, Trk; B3, AMC, Jp, IH, St**

Placitas; Placitas Auto Wrecking, *see Vintage*

Roswell; Clyde's Auto Parts & Wrecking, 4500 S Main St, 88201; 505-623-3632, FAX 505-623-8006; CC, Sp; 10ac, 500; **70+; D, F, PU; B3, AMC, Jp**

Roswell Auto Salvage, *see Vintage*

Roswell Wrecking Co, 5700 N Main, 88201; 505-622-2831, 800-624-0656; CC, Sa; 20ac, 2000+; **80+; D, F, PU, 4x4; B3**

Western Wrecking Co of Roswell, 3504 W 2nd St, 88201; 505-622-5716; Sa, UR; 10ac, 400; **80s; D, F, PU, 4x4; B3, AMC**

Santa Fe; A-1 Towing, 87501; 505-983-1616; Sa; 1ac, 40; **79+; D, PU, 4x4; B3; Spanish**

Airport Auto Acres, Airport Rd, 87501; 505-471-0123; Sa, UR; 18ac, 2000; **70+; D, F, PU, 4x4, Trk; B3, AMC, Jp, IH; Spanish**

Capital Scrap Metals, 1162 Cooks Ln, 87505; 505-471-0740, FAX 505-438-4639, 800-369-5020; Sa; 1.5ac, 400; **80-93; D, F, PU, 4x4; B3, AMC, Jp**

Padillas Auto Sales, Rt 6 Box 26 Aqua Fria, 87501; 505-471-2685; Sa, UR; 2.5ac, 10+; **80+; D, PU, 4x4, B3; Spanish**

Silver City; Arenas Valley Auto Salvage, *see Vintage*

Tucumcari; Allrite Towing & Salvage, 6351 Quay Rd AM, 88401; 505-461-1934, FAX 505-461-0727, 800-696-8691, allrite@srbb.com; CC, Sp; 10ac, 300; **68-89; D, PU; B3, AMC, IH**

206

Quay Valley Salvage, *see Vintage*

LATE MODEL

Alamogordo; North Fifty-Four Salvage, *see Vintage*

Walker Towing & Salvage, *see Vintage*

Wild Bills Auto Wrecking, *see Vintage*

Albuquerque; A & A Cervantes Auto Salvage, *see Late Vintage*

Albuquerque Foreign Auto Parts, 5028 Broadway Blvd SE, 87105; 505-877-4856, FAX 505-877-5822, abqfor@aol.com; CC, Sp; 1200; **F, PU, 4x4, Trk**

Antonio's Auto Parts, *see Late Vintage*

Chavez Auto Parts, *see Vintage*

Complete Auto & Truck Parts, *see Vintage*

Coors Auto Dismantlers, 1905 Coors Blvd SW, 87121; 505-877-2075; CC, Sa; 500; **D**

Coronado Auto Recyclers, *see Late Vintage*

Discount Auto Parts, *see Vintage*

East Central Auto Wrecking, *see Late Vintage*

El Mexicano Auto Salvage, *see Late Vintage*

Five Foreign Auto Parts, *see Late Vintage*

Four Twenty Two Foreign Auto, 6115 Alameda Blvd NE, 87113; 505-821-1010, 800-422-5575; CC, Sa, Sp; 2500; **F, PU**

J & E Auto Salvage, *see Vintage*

Jack's Auto Parts, 4320 Broadway Blvd SE, 87105; 505-877-6293, 800-654-7116 NM only; CC, Sa, Sp; 700+; **D, F, PU**

Lujans Auto, 2920 Isleta Blvd SW, 87105; 505-877-0642; Sa; **D, F, few Trk**

M & M Body, 5925 Edith Blvd NE, 87107; 505-345-7300, FAX 505-343-8445; Sa, Br; 350; **D, F, PU, Trk**

Olguins Auto Sales & Salvage, 4220 Broadway Blvd SE, 87105; 505-877-5929, 888-465-4846; Sa, Sp; 300; **D**

Artesia; Clark Auto, *see Vintage*

Bloomfield; Tri-Cities Truck & Auto, *see Late Vintage*

Carlsbad; Carlsbad Wrecking Co, *see Late Vintage*

Landreth Wrecking Co, *see Late Vintage*

Clovis; CBS Auto Recyclers, 2024 S Prince St, 88101; 505-769-2324, 800-748-2528; CC, Sp, UR; 500; **D, F, PU**

Quality Auto Salvage, *see Late Vintage*

Columbus; Columbus Car Sales & Trucking, *see Late Vintage*

Estancia; Hooker Salvage, *see Vintage*

Farmington; A-1 Auto Salvage, *see Late Vintage*

A 550 Truck & Auto Salvage, *see Late Vintage*

Bumper to Bumper Auto Salvage, 5418 Hwy 64, 87401; 505-325-7600, FAX 505-325-6958, 800-932-9764; Cc, Sa, Sp, Br, PL; 15ac; **D, PU, 4x4**

Off Again Auto, *see Late Vintage*

Hobbs; Hobbs Wrecking Co, *see Vintage*

Jerry's Auto Salvage, *see Vintage*

Kirtland; Gilmores Truck & Auto Salvage, *see Late Vintage*

Placitas; Placitas Auto Wrecking, *see Vintage*

Roswell; Clyde's Auto Parts & Wrecking, *see Late Vintage*

Roswell Auto Salvage, *see Vintage*

Roswell Wrecking Co, *see Late Vintage*

Ruidoso Downs; D & S Sales & Salvage, 1620 Hwy 70E, 88346; 505-257-2924; Sa, Sp; 450; **D, F, PU, 4x4; B3, Jp, IH**

Santa Fe; A-1 Towing, *see Late Vintage*

Airport Auto Acres, *see Late Vintage*

Capital Scrap Metals, *see Late Vintage*

Padillas Auto Sales, *see Late Vintage*

Tucumcari; Quay Valley Salvage, *see Vintage*

207

New York state map with locations:

Massena, Burke, Norwalk, Watertown, Youngstown, Newfane, Sanborn, Lockport, Webster, Oswego, Queensbury, Niagra Falls, Brockport, Macedon, Tonawanda, Rochester, Buffalo, Caledonia, Weedsport, Bernhards Bay, Cicero, Utica, Clarence, Frankfort, Hamburg, Holland, Elma, Livonia, Syracuse, Mohawk, Irving, Lancaster, Bliss, Angola, Scipio, Schenectady, Dunkirk, Yorkshire, Homer, Mechanicville, Fredonia, Gowanda, Arkport, Ithica, Amsterdam, Ballston Lake, Brocton, Great Valley, Belfast, Schoharie, Albany, Mayville, Jamestown, Franklinville, Middleburgh, Athens, Stephentown, Frewsburg, Pine City, Waverly, Kingston, Pleasant Valley, Hyde Park, Woodridge, Poughkeepsie, Vingdale, Mongaup Valleys, Fishkill, Roughquag, Rock Hill, Monticello, Newburgh, Wurtsboro, Campbell Hall, Cuddebackville, Beacon, Central Valley, Brewster, Middletown, Old Spr, Croton Falls, Monrose, Peekskill, W Haversh

Metro New York

Amityville	Flushing	New Hyde Park
Bay Shore	Freeport	Oceanside
Bellmore	Glen Cove	Patchogue
Bellport	Hempstead	Riverhead
Bethpage	Holbrook	Rockville Center
Bronx	Huntington Station	Ronkonkoma
Brooklyn	Island Park	Seaford
Center Moriches	Islip	Southampton
Centereach	Jamaica	Speonk
Copiague	Kings Park	Spring Valley
Deer Park	Lindenhurst	Staten Island
E Meadow	Mamaroneck	Westbury
E Northport	Massapequa	Yonkers
E Quogue	Medford	
Elmsford		
Far Rockaway		

Metro New York

NEW YORK

<u>*VINTAGE*</u>
Albany; Jim Meisner Auto Parts, 1918 Central Av, 12205; 518-456-2263, FAX 518-456-3437, 800-MEISNER, www.meisner.com; CC, Sa, Sp; 17.5ac, 2500; **40+; D, F, PU, 4x4, Trk; B3, AMC, Jp, IH, Hd, Ns, St, Pk, Ks, Fr, Wy ; motorcycles**
Angola; Evans Auto Wrecking & Repair, 9612 Hardpan Rd, 14006; 716-549-7522; Sa, Sp; 300; **50-91; D, F, PU, 4x4; B3; Spc: Cadillac**
Athens; Muffucci Sales Company, Rd 1 Box 60, 12015; 518-943-0100, FAX 518-943-4534, 888-295-4184, maffuccisales@mindspring.com; CC, Sp, Wr; 7.5ac, 150; **50-79; D; Mercury, Lincoln only; Mail Order Only**
Ballston Lake; Glenville Auto Wrecking, 1130 Rt 146 A, 12019; 518-399-5321; **D, F, PU, 4x4; B3, AMC**
Bay Shore; Poppy's North Clinton Auto, 1384 N Clinton Av, 11706; 516-665-1575, FAX 516-665-1596, 800-286-1575; CC, Sa, Sp; 6ac, 300; **50+; D, F, PU, 4x4; B3, AMC**
Bellmore; Used Auto Glass, 1933 Bellmore Av, 11710; 516-785-8889, FAX 516-781-1933; CC, Sa, PL; **40+; D, F, PU, 4x4; B3, AMC, Jp, IH, Hd, Ns, St, Pk, Ks, Fr, Cr, Wy, VW; can get any glass**
Bellport; D & D Used Truck Parts, 32 Shaw Rd, 11713; 516-286-1616, FAX 516-286-0648; CC, Sa, Sp, PL; 1.5, 500; **50+; D, F, PU, 4x4; B3, AMC, Jp, IH**

Ray's wReckingyard Roster makes a great gift for the "car nut" on your shopping list. To order, Call Toll Free: 877-4RAYS BOOKS

Brooklyn; Lou's Auto Wrecking, 634 Johnson Av, 11237; 718-821-4040; Sa; **65-8**9; **D, F, PU, 4x4; B3, AMC, VW**

Buffalo; Carpenters Auto Parts, 1455 Niagra St, 14213; 716-883-4733; Sa, Sp, Wr; 3ac; **30+; D, F, PU, 4x4, Trk; B3, AMC, Jp, Hd, Ns, St, Pk, Ks, Fr, Cr, Wy, VW; few loose parts**

    Skyway Auto Parts, 637 Tifft St, 14220; 716-824-4348; Sa, UR; 3000; **60-92; D, F, PU, 4x4, Trk; B3, AMC, Jp, IH, VW**

Burke; Tuckers Auto Slvg, 5121 State Rt 11, 12917; 518-483-5478; Sa, Sp, Br; **39-90; D; B3**

Center Moriches; Moriches Used Auto Parts, 210 Brookfield Av, 11934; 516-878-8988; CC, Sa, Sp, Br; 15ac, 4000; **40+; D, F, PU, 4x4, Trk; B3, AMC, Jp, IH, Hd, St, Wy, VW**

Cold Spring; Cold Spring Auto Parts, Route 9, 10516; 914-265-2252; CC, Sa, Sp, Br; 143ac; **30+; D, F, PU, 4x4, Trk; B3, AMC, St, Pk, Ks, Fr, Cr, Wy, Tucker**

East Rochester; Northside Salvage, 954 W Linden Av, 14445; 716-381-9667, FAX 716-264-0868, 888-999-5865; CC, Sa, Sp, Br; 500; **60+; D, F, PU, 4x4, Trk; B3, AMC, Jp, IH, VW**

Flushing; Hitch King, 18903 Northern Blvd, 11358; 718-353-6078, FAX 718-353-6163; CC, Sa, Sp; 200; **60+; D, F, PU, 4x4, Trk; B3, AMC, Jp, IH, VW**

Franklinville; Lamberts Auto Parts, 8552 Route 16 N, 14737; 716-676-3061; Sa; **50+; D, F, PU, 4x4; B3**

Freedom; Previty's Auto Wrck, 11075 Galen Hill Rd, 14065; 716-492-3936, FAX 716-496-5185, 800-675-7738; Sp, PL; 1000+; **50+; D, F, PU, 4x4, Trk, Fm; B3, AMC, Jp, IH, VW**

Glen Cove; Glen Cove Auto Salvage, 232 Glen Cove Av, 11542; 516-759-1400, FAX 516-674-0433; Sa, Sp; 350; **65+; D, F, PU, 4x4; B3, Mercedes, BMW, Porsche**

Gowanda; Good Door Store, 2 S Water St, 14070; 716-532-9906, 800-367-9906; CC, Sa, Wr, PL; **60+; D, PU, 4x4; body parts only**

Hyde Park; Molt's Used Auto Parts, 54 Honeywell Ln, 12538; 914-471-2377, FAX 914-485-1701; Sa, UR; 20ac, 2000+; **60+; D, F, PU, 4x4; B3, AMC**

Ithaca; Danby Motors, 1675 Danby Rd, 14850; 607-273-8049; Sa, Sp; **50+; D, F, PU, 4x4, Trk; B3, AMC, Jp, IH, St, Pk, Ks, VW; Holds car shows, call or write for info**.

Jamaica; A J Minutello, 11507 Guy R Brewer Rd, 11434; 718-297-8410; UR; 2ac, 140; **65-87; D, F; B3; everyday cars, family business.**

    Liberty Auto Wrecking, 10001 Rockaway Blvd, 11417; 718-843-0770, FAX 718-843-3494, www.libertyautowrecking.com; CC, Sa, Sp, PL; 130; **65-89; D, F; Spc: GM & some Chrysler muscle cars**

Lancaster; A Js Auto Wrecking, 955 Ransom Rd, 14086; 716-681-5454, FAX 716-681-5048, 800-AJS-AUTO; CC, Sa, Sp; **65+; D, F, PU, 4x4; B3**

Lindenhurst; Albin Auto Salvage, 807 Albin Av, 11757; 516-422-9491, FAX 516-669-4113; Sa, Sp; 1ac, 200; **65-89; D; B3; Spc: Muscle cars**

    Romano Brothers Scrap Metal Co, 600 Muncy St, 11757; 516-669-7915; Sa; 50; **60s-89, few 50s; D; B3, Fire Engines; will sell whole cars**

    Tri-State Auto, 200 Reid St, 11757; 516-661-2875, FAX 516-661-8132; Sa, Sp, Br; 1000; **60+; D, F, PU, 4x4; B3, Jp; Spc: Muscle cars**

Lockport; Vince's Auto Wrck & Sales, 8440 Akron Rd, 14094; 716-434-6238, FAX 716-434-6287, 800-462-7954; CC, Sa, Sp; 20ac, 3500; **30+; D, F, PU, 4x4; B3, AMC, Jp, IH, VW**

Macedon; British Auto, 600 Penfield Rd, 14502; 315-986-3097, FAX 315-986-9262, 800-458-4575, part@britishauto.com; CC, Sa, Sp, Br; 800; **50+; F; British only**

Mayville; A Automotive, 6251 Honeysette Rd, 14757; 716-753-2367, FAX 716-753-2330, 800-873-2886; CC, Sa, Sp; 30ac, 2000+; **60+; D, F, PU, 4x4; B3; Spc: Pickup**

Mohawk; Reardon Enterprises, 1633 Rte 28, 13407; 315-866-3072; **27-70; D, PU; B3, Hd, Pk, Ks; motorcycles; "All offers considered, even the stupid ones"**

Monticello; Fast Eddie's Auto Wreckers, 201 Harris Rd, 12701; 914-794-5089, FAX 914-796-1398, www.ntntop.net; CC, Sa, Sp, Br; 27ac, 3500; **64+; D, F, PU, 4x4; AMC, Jp, IH, VW; Spc: Corvette, early Mustang**

Newburgh; Fleetline Automotive, 181 N Drurury Ln, 12550; 914-566-4557; CC, Sa, Sp, Br; 6ac; **36-87 PU; D, PU, few Trk; Spc: GM; open by appointment**

Newfane; Newfane Auto Parts, 6481 Dale Rd, 14108; 716-778-7833; Sa, Sp, UR; 20ac, 200; **50+; D; B3, St; Building older car inventory & will do installation on older**

Patchogue; Chapel Avenue Autoparts, 36 Chapel Av, 11772; 516-475-0604, FAX 516-475-8204, www.chapelauto.com; CC, Sa, Sp, UR; 200; **62+; D, F, PU, 4x4; B3; Spc: Impala 62-67**

   Wards Used Auto Parts, 86 Barthold Av, 11772; 516-475-8805; Sa, Sp; 0.5ac; **40-88; D; B3, St**

Peekskill; Marcy Junk Car Removal Svc, ROA Hook Rd, 10566; 914-739-6769; CC, Sa, Wr; **60+; D, F, PU, 4x4; B3, AMC, Jp, VW**

Poughkeepsie; Body Part Intl, 13 Davis Av, 12603; 914-471-0800, FAX 914-471-0862, bpi-ltd@prodigy.net; Sp; **65+; D, F, PU, 4x4; B3, VW**

Queensbury; Ray's Salvage, 15 Pasco Av, 12804; 518-798-8902, FAX 518-798-8146; Sa; 750; **70+, some 30's; D, F, PU, 4x4, Trk, Mil; B3, IH**

Riverhead; We Got It Auto Parts, 1577 Flanders Rd, 11901; 516-727-1811; Sa; 6ac, 800; **80s, few 50-60s; D, F, PU, 4x4; B3, AMC**

Sanborn; A Able Auto Wrecking, 5396 Chew Rd, 14132; 716-297-0010, FAX 716-297-8654; Sa; 1000; **50-89; D, F, PU, 4x4, Fm; B3, St**

Schenectady; Williams Auto Parts, 2837 Aqueduct Rd, 12309; 518-382-9623; Sa, Sp, UR; 21ac, 1500; **36-91; D, F, PU, 4x4; B3**

Speonk; Outpost Automotive, 33 High, 11972; 516-325-0011, FAX 516-325-7769; 5ac; **32-92; D, F, PU, 4x4, Trk; B3, AMC, Hd, Ns, St, Pk**

Stephentown; Adler's Antique Auto, 801 NY Rt 43, 12168; 518-733-5749, advdesign1@aol.com; Sa, Sp, Br, Wr; 10ac, 700; **31-80; D, PU, 4x4; Spc: Chevy Cars & Pickups; Complete restoration facilities**

Syracuse; ABC Auto Sales, 2424 Lodi St, 13208; 315-474-0111; 40; **60s-94; D, F, PU, 4x4; B3**

Tonawanda; INS Scrap Processors, 4111 River Rd, 14150; 716-875-7988; Sa, UR; 450+; **60s-90; D, F, PU, vans; B3; Spc: Impala; open Sunday by appointment**

Troy; Jack's Auto Wreckers, 1 Ingalls Ave, 12180; 518-272-5591, FAX 518-272-7187; CC, Sa, Sp, PL; 2000; **50+; D, F, PU, 4x4; B3, AMC, Jp, IH, VW**

Waverly; Williams Auto Salvage, 161 Tinkham Rd, 14892; 607-565-4432; Sa, UR; 650; **30+; D, F, PU, 4x4, Trk; B3, Pk**

Webster; Elmer's Auto Parts, 137 Donovan St, 14580; 716-872-4402, FAX 716-872-2519; Sa, Sp, Wr; **50-79; D; B3; Spc: Muscle cars, Corvette**

Weedsport; Nash Auto Parts, 8631 Pump Rd, 13166; 315-252-5878, 800-272-6274, jcarnash@aol.com; CC, Sa, Sp, Br, Wr; 3000; **50+, few prewar; D, PU; B3, AMC, Hd, Ns, St, Pk; Closed Saturday in summer**

Westbury; Nassau Suffolk Recycling Corp, 1 Hopper St, 11590; 516-334-2274; Sa, PL; 1ac, 100; **30+; D, F, PU, 4x4, Trk, Fm; B3**

Woodridge; AAA Auto Salvage, 320 Glenwild Rd, 12789; 914-434-3800, FAX 914-434-1437; Sa, Sp; 33ac; **55-69; D, F, PU, 4x4; B3**

Yorkshire; Tidds Auto Parts, 3234 W Yorkshire Rd, 14173; 716-492-4700, FAX 716-492-1030; Sa; 1000; **40-89; D, F, PU, 4x4; B3, AMC, Jp, IH, Hs, Ns, St, Pk, Ks, Wy, VW**

Youngstown; J & T Auto Salvage & Recycling, 1209 Balmer Rd, 14174; 716-745-7079; Sa, Br; 1500; **50+; D, PU, 4x4; B3**

LATE VINTAGE

Albany; Branch Auto Parts, 5 Norton St, 12205; 518-459-2787, 888-282-2780; CC, Sa, Sp; 1.5ac, 1000; **D, PU, 4x4; B3, AMC, VW**

   Jim Meisner Auto Parts, *see Vintage*

Amityville; Accurate Auto Salvage, 139 Dixon Av, 11701; 516-789-3737, FAX 516-789-3830; Sa, Sp; 500; **80+; D, F, PU, 4x4; B3**

Angola; Evans Auto Wrecking & Repair, *see Vintage*

Athens; Muffucci Sales Company, *see Vintage*

Bay Shore; Poppy's North Clinton Auto, *see Vintage*

Bellmore; Used Auto Glass, *see Vintage*

Bellport; D & D Used Truck Parts, *see Vintage*

   Lou's Auto Wrecking, *see Vintage*

Three Sons Auto Wrecking, 1485 Montauk Hwy, 11713; 516-286-6825, FAX 516-286-6879, 800-852-0845; CC, Sa, Sp, PL; 1.5ac, 500; **70+; D, F, few PU, few 4x4; B3, AMC**

Bernhards Bay; Hardy's Auto, 1159 County Rte 17, 13028; 315-675-3006, 800-404-2880; CC, Sp; 12ac, 1000; **80+; D, F, PU, 4x4; B3, AMC, VW**

Bliss; Bliss Auto Wreckers, 4191 Rte 39, 14024; 716-496-5588, 800-870-2938; Sa, Sp; 10ac, 1000; **80+; D, F, PU, 4x4; B3, AMC, Jp, VW**

Brewster; Simon Auto Wreckers, 10509; 914-279-2988, FAX 914-279-4222; CC, Sa; 5ac; **D, F, PU, 4x4; B3, AMC, Jp, IH, VW; Spc: Corvette**

Bronx; A C Auto Wrecking Co, 475 Gerard Av, 10451; 718-292-3274; CC, Sp, Br, PL; 0.25ac; **80-93; D, F, PU, 4x4; B3**

Alicea Auto Wreckers, 1330 Oakpoint Av, 10474; 718-893-6283; Sa; 200; **79+; D, F; B3**

Apex Auto Parts, 1235 Bronx River Av, 10472; 718-328-7200; CC, Sa, Sp; 3ac; **80+; D, F, PU, 4x4; B3, AMC**

Boston Road Auto Wreckers, 4171 Boston Rd, 10466; 718-324-3500, FAX 718-231-3242; CC, Sa, UR; 100; **80+; D, F, PU, 4x4; B3, AMC, Jp, IH, VW**

D G Auto Wreckers, 1365 Spofford Av, 10474; 718-893-3211; Sa; 50; **70-89; D, F; B3**

Point Wrecking & Salvage Corp, 1380 Spofford Av, 10474; 718-328-3737, FAX 718-542-1095; CC; **80-93; D, F; B3**

US 1 Auto Wreckers, 206 Drake St, 10474; 718-589-5852, FAX 718-991-4524; CC, Sa, Br; 1000; **80+; D, F, PU, 4x4; B3, AMC, Jp, VW**

Brooklyn; A-Best Used Auto Parts, 1074 Grand St, 11211; 718-599-2300; Sa; **80+; D, F, PU, 4x4; B3, AMC, Jp, IH**

A1A Auto Co, 8014 Preston Ct, 11236; 718-531-8625; Sa, Sp; 500+; **70+; D, F, PU, 4x4, Trk; B3**

Ace Auto Wreckers, 835 61st St, 11220; 718-438-8789, FAX 718-382-5305, 800-449-3886; Sa, Sp; **80; 70+; D, F, PU, 4x4; B3, AMC, Jp, VW**

Al-Fred Auto Salvage, 1440 Ralph Av, 11236; 718-444-9075; Sa; 0.25ac; **80-90; D, F, PU, 4x4; B3**

Auto Gobbler Parts, 5601-21 Preston Ct, 11234; 718-251-2140, FAX 718-251-4641, sertiflink.net; CC, Sp; 5000; **70+; D, F, PU, 4x4, Trk; B3, AMC, Jp, VW**

Big Apple Auto, 1934 Pitkin Av, 11207; 718-495-1774; Sa, Sp; **70+; D, F, PU, 4x4; B3, AMC, Jp, IH**

Carboys, 87 Walton St, 11206; 718-388-5289, FAX 718-599-0232, 800-830-7186; Sa, Sp; 0.75ac, 200; **70+; D, F; B3, VW; Buy & sell export items, motors, trans.**

Century Salvage Ltd, 8109 Foster Av, 11236; 718-763-8000, FAX 718-763-8099, 888-763-8005, www.centurysalvage.com; CC, Sa, Sp, Br, PL; 1ac; **90s, few 80s; D, F, PU, 4x4; B3**

FJR Auto Wreckers, 822 Rockaway Pkwy, 11236; 718-272-3217; Sa; 60; **78-87; D, F; B3, AMC, VW**

G & K Auto Wrecking, 202 Varick Av, 11237; 718-821-3034, FAX 718-821-6642; UR; 1ac, 60; **80+; D, F, PU, 4x4; B3, VW**

Mattie's Auto Parts, 325 Avenue Y, 11223; 718-336-6200, FAX 718-336-6292; CC, Sa, Sp; 0.5ac; **70+; D, F, PU; B3**

Parts R Us, 428 Johnson Av, 11237; 718-366-6272; Sa; 45+; **70+; D, F, PU, 4x4; B3**

Satellite Auto Parts, 1096 Rockaway Av, 11236; 718-495-4949, FAX 718-927-1219; CC, Sa; 1ac; **70+; D, F, PU, 4x4; B3**

Straightway Auto Slvg, 475 E 58th St, 11203; 718-251-6598; Sa, Sp, Br; 250+; **75+; F**

Buffalo; 2060 Auto Parts, 2060 William St, 14206; 716-894-2060, FAX 716-895-0547, 800-955-7445; CC, Sa, Sp, Br; 30ac; **75-90; D, F, PU, 4x4, Trk; B3, AMC, Jp, VW**

Auto City-Buffalo, 276 Military Rd, 14207; 716-877-4237, FAX 716-871-1937, 800-877-3607; CC, Sa, Sp; 3.5ac; **80-90; D, F, PU, 4x4, Trk; B3, AMC, Jp, IH, VW**

Bens, 540 E Delavan Av, 14211; 716-894-1483, FAX 716-894-7629; CC, Sa, Sp, Br; 6ac; **70+; D, F, PU, 4x4, Trk; B3, AMC, Jp, VW**

Bob & Dons Auto Parts, 49 Hopkins St, 14220; 716-825-2700; Sa, Br; 300; **80+; D, F, PU, 4x4, Trk; B3, AMC, Jp**

Buffalo Auto Wrecking, 229 Hertel Av, 14207; 716-873-3699; CC, Sa, Sp, UR; 400; **80-92; D, F, PU, 4x4, Trk; B3, Jp, VW**

Carpenters Auto Parts, *see Vintage*

Clinton Auto Wrecking, 1125 Clinton St, 14206; 716-856-3016; CC, Sa, Hr, Sp; 500; **70+; D, F, PU, 4x4, Trk; B3, AMC, Jp, VW**

Delavan Auto Parts, 505 E Delavan Av, 14211; 716-892-3312, FAX 716-892-3326; CC, Sa, Sp; 100; **84+; D, F; B3, AMC**

Kenmore Auto Wrecking, 32 Skillen St, 14207; 716-873-7276; Sa, Sp, Br; **80-89; D, F, PU, 4x4; B3, AMC, Jp, VW**

R & R Salvage, 1329 William St, 14206; 716-853-1735; CC, Sa, UR; **80-90; D, F, PU, 4x4; B3, AMC, Jp, VW**

Skyway Auto Parts, *see Vintage*

Tuckers Auto Salvage, *see Vintage*

United Auto Parts, 180 Lehigh St, 14218; 716-826-8400, FAX 716-826-8403; Sa, Sp; **80+; D, PU, 4x4; B3, AMC**

Center Moriches; Moriches Used Auto Parts, *see Vintage*

Central Valley; Bergs Auto Towing, Laura Ln, 10917; 914-928-7272, FAX 914-928-7913, 800-724-BERG, bergauto@frontiernet.net; CC, Sa, Sp, Wr; 4ac, 500; **79+; D, F, PU, 4x4, Trk; B3, AMC, Jp, IH**

Clarence; United 4 Wheel Drive Parts Ctr, 10187 Main St, 14031; 716-759-7420; CC, Sa, Sp; **D, F, 4x4 only; Drive lines only**

Cold Spring; Cold Spring Auto Parts, *see Vintage*

Croton Falls; Brysons Auto Repair Parts, Mahopac Croton Falls Rd, 10519; 914-277-3201; CC, Sa, Sp; 4ac, 100; **80-90; D, F**

Deer Park; A & J Used Auto Parts, 1033 Long Island Av, 11729; 516-667-3700, FAX 516-667-0108, 800-667-0085, www.ajautoparts.baweb.com; CC, Sa, Sp, Br, Wr; 7ac, 1500; **67+; D, F, PU; B3, AMC, Jp**

C & S Auto Parts, 992 Long Island Av, 11729; 516-586-0707; Sa, Br; 100; **80-95; D, F, PU, 4x4; B3, AMC, Jp, VW**

DPA Auto Parts, 999 Long Island Av, 11729; 516-667-8232, FAX 516-595-9829; CC, Sa, Sp, Br; 200; **85-92; D, F, PU, 4x4; B3, Jp**

Mid-Island Auto Wreckers, 1013 Long Island Av, 11729; 516-586-6599, FAX 516-586-6649, 800-414-9726; CC, Sa, Sp, Br; 10ac, 1000; **80+; D, F, PU, 4x4; B3, AMC, Jp, IH, VW**

Dunkirk; Moore Auto Salvage, 3767 Franklin Av, 14048; 716-366-3563; Sa, UR; 500; **70+; D, F, PU, 4x4, Trk; B3, AMC**

East Quogue; Westhampton Auto Salvage, 30 County Rd 104, 11942; 516-653-4055; Sa, Br; 2ac, 400; **80+; D, F, PU, 4x4, Trk; B3, AMC, Jp, VW**

East Rochester; Northside Salvage, *see Vintage*

Elma; Howbill Auto Parts, 550 Pound Rd, 14059; 716-652-1651; CC, Sa, Sp, UR; 30ac; **80+; D, few F, PU, 4x4, Trk; B3, Jp, IH, VW**

Elmsford; Brookfield Metal Co, 280 Lamont St, 10523; 914-592-5250; CC, Sa, Sp, UR; **80s, few 70s; D, F, PU, 4x4; B3, AMC, Jp**

Flushing; Hitch King, *see Vintage*

Jamaica Auto Salvage, 12680 Willets Point Blvd, 11368; 718-639-7400; **80-90; D, F, PU**

Jon-Carlo Foreign Auto Parts, 1252 150th St, 11357; 718-358-0500, FAX 718-358-1741, 888-487-9292; CC, Sa, Sp; 3000; **70+; D, F, PU, 4x4, Trk; B3, AMC, Jp, VW; Open Sun**

Master Used Parts, 12630 Willets Point Blvd, 11368; 718-397-5555, FAX 718-397-1431, www.couponpage.com; Sa, UR; **82+; D, F, PU; B3, VW**

Roosevelt Auto Wrecking, 12743 Willets Point Blvd, 11368; 718-424-2008; Sa, UR; 500+; **70+; D, F, PU, 4x4; B3**

Sacco Auto Sales & Parts, 175 Woodward Av, 11385; 718-417-3555, FAX 718-417-5021; CC, Sa, Sp; 50+; **75+; D, F, PU, 4x4, vans; B3; Spc: PU & vans**

Shop 4, 12615 Roosevelt Av, 11368; 718-426-0917; Sa, UR; **80+; D, F**

Steering Wheel Rentals, 18903 Northern Blvd, 11358; 718-353-6848, FAX 718-353-6163; CC, Sa, Sp, Br; 1000; **70+; D, F, PU, 4x4, Trk; B3**

212

Willets Point Auto Salvage, 12661 Willets Point Blvd, 11368; 718-803-2792, FAX 516-794-3987; Sa, Br; 300; **73+; D, F, PU; B**3

Franklinville; Lamberts Auto Parts, *see Vintage*

Fredonia; Clemens Sales, 9558 Stone Rd, 14063; 716-672-8054; Sa, Sp, Wr; **67+; D, F, PU, 4x4; Body parts only, rust free**

Freedom; Previty's Auto Wrecking, *see Vintage*

Glen Cove; Glen Cove Auto Salvage, *see Vintage*

Gowanda; Good Door Store, *see Vintage*

Great Valley; Triple S Auto Dismantling, Rte 98, 14741; 716-699-4608, FAX 716-699-4793, 800-545-8500; Sa, Sp, UR; 350; **80+; D, F, PU, 4x4; B**3**, AMC, Jp**

Hamburg; Calkins Used Auto Parts, 5661 Camp Rd, 14075; 716-649-2294; Sa, Sp; 12ac; **70+; D, F, PU, 4x4; B**3**, Cadillac**

Hempstead; Hempstead Used Auto & Truck, 627 Peninsula Blvd, 11550; 516-485-0800; Sa, Sp; **80+; D, F, PU, 4x4; B**3

Holbrook; Suffolk Auto Recycling, 912 Lincoln Av, 11741; 516-589-2384, FAX 516-589-7317; CC, Sa, Sp; 2.5ac; **82+; D, F, PU, 4x4; B**3**; Spc: PU**

Holland; Kloiber Auto Recycling, 10353 Darien Rd, 14080; 716-655-4012, FAX 716-655-3414; Sa, Sp, UR; 500; **83+; D, PU, 4x4; B**3

Homer; Contentos, 163 Main St, 13077; 607-749-2676, FAX 607-749-3124, 800-660-2674; CC, Sa, Sp, UR; 1000; **80s, few 90s; D, F, PU, 4x4; B**3

Huntington Station; Gardiners Auto Parts, 189 W 9th St, 11746; 516-427-5147; Sa; 150; **70+; D, F, PU, 4x4; B**3

Hyde Park; A & T Auto Parts, 271 Cardinal Rd, 12538; 914-229-8855, FAX 914-229-9541, 800-284-0987; CC, Sa, UR; 1000; **75+; D, F, PU, 4x4; B**3**, AMC, Jp**

Molt's Used Auto Parts, *see Vintage*

Irving; J W Used Auto Parts, Rte 5 and 20, 14081; 716-934-2774; CC, Sa; 5ac, 400; **80-90; D, F, PU, 4x4, Trk; B**3**, AMC**

Island Park; Auto Undertaker, 4370 Austin Blvd, 11558; 516-432-8770, 800-354-8770; Sa, Sp; **80+; D, F**

Islip; Sils Foreign Auto Parts, 1498 Spur Dr S, 11751; 516-581-7624, FAX 516-581-0063, 800-244-7457; CC, Sa, Sp; 2ac, 350; **80+; F**

Ithaca; Auto Salvage of Ithaca, 129 Hornbrook Rd, 14850; 607-272-8061, 800-468-8858; CC, Sa, Sp; 50ac, 3500; **75-90; D, F, PU, 4x4; B**3**, Jp, VW**

Danby Motors, *see Vintage*

Jamaica; A J Minutello, *see Vintage*

A Rite Auto Parts, 16874 93rd Av, 11433; 718-658-8833; Sa, UR; 30; **80+; D, F; B**3

Citywide Auto Parts, 14836 Liberty Av, 11435; 718-297-9797, FAX 718-297-2866, www.newyorkcityautosalvage.com; CC, Sa, Sp, PL; 1ac, 30; **80+; D, F, PU, 4x4; B**3

Do-Rite Auto Slvg, 15519 Liberty Av, 11433; 718-739-1218; CC, Sa; 100; **80+; D, F; B**3

East Coast Auto Salvage, 9550 Tuckerton St, 11433; 718-739-2025, FAX 718-291-6016, 800-669-1746; CC, Sa, Sp, UR; 450+; **75+; D, F, PU, 4x4; B**3

Jamaica Auto Wreckers, 10618 148th St, 11435; 718-291-7464; Sa, UR; **70-89; D, F**

Liberty Auto Wrecking, *see Vintage*

Marino's Auto Salvage, 15010 Beaver Rd, 11433; 718-526-5100, 800-283-7340; Sa, Sp, Wr; **80+; D, F, PU; B**3

Roth's Auto Wrck, 13431 Merrick Blvd, 11434; 718-525-6300, FAX 718-978-7508, 800-348-8848, www.rothautowrecking.com; CC, Sa, Sp; 150; **75+; D, F, PU, 4x4; B**3**, Jp, VW**

Jamestown; Townline Auto Parts, 2877 Fluvanna Av, 14701; 716-484-2353, 800-734-8557; Sa, Sp; 6ac, 500+; **80+; D, F, PU, 4x4; B**3

Kingston; Burton Deitz, 436 State Rt 28, 12401; 914-331-8420; CC, Sa, UR; 2ac, 200; **80-93; D, F, PU, 4x4; B**3

Lancaster; A Js Auto Wrecking, *see Vintage*

Ed's Auto Parts, 911 Ransom Rd, 14086; 716-683-5174, FAX 716-651-9759; Sa; **80+; D, PU, 4x4; B**3

Ransom Auto Parts, 867 Ransom Rd, 14086; 716-684-1520; Sa; **80-89, few 70s; D, PU, 4x4**

Lindenhurst; Act Auto Wrecking, 650 W Hoffman Av, 11757; 516-225-5865, FAX 516-225-6901; Sa, Sp; 100; **70+; D, F, PU, 4x4; B3**

Albin Auto Salvage, *see Vintage*

All Stop Used Auto Parts, 858 N Queens Av, 11757; 516-888-8850, 800-210-2155; Sa, Sp, Wr, PL; **70+; D, F, PU, 4x4; B3**

Elite Auto Parts, 120 Albany Av, 11757; 516-226-1003, FAX 516-226-1056, 800-439-1003, www.eliteautoparts.com; CC, Sa, Sp, PL; 400+; **80+; D, F, PU, 4x4; B3**

J & C Auto Salvage, 550 S Railroad Av, 11757; 516-669-0220; CC, Sa, Sp; 500; **70-85, few 60s; D, F, PU, 4x4; B3, Jp; Spc: Muscle cars**

Romano Brothers Scrap Metal Co, *see Vintage*

Tri-State Auto, *see Vintage*

Lockport; Dave Spencer Auto Repair, 385 Mill St, 14094; 716-434-6402; 5ac; **80-91; D, F, PU, 4x4; B3**

Gothard Auto Wrecking, 7264 Akron Rd, 14094; 716-439-9037; Sa, Sp, Br; 5ac; 300; **75-91; D, F, PU, 4x4; B3; Spc: GM**

Vince's Auto Wrecking & Sales, *see Vintage*

Macedon; British Auto, *see Vintage*

Mamaroneck; Blood Bro Wrck, 270 Waverly Av, 10543; 914-698-5200, FAX 914-698-1509, getrag@aol.com; CC, Sa, Sp, UR; 2ac; 300; **80+; D, F, P, 4x4; B3, AMC, Jp, VW**

Massena; LaFlesh Garage, Massena Winthrop Rd, 13662; 315-769-6544; CC, Sa, Sp, UR; 10ac; 1000+; **82-93; D, F, PU, 4x4; B3**

Mayville; A Automotive, *see Vintage*

Mechanicville; ABC Recycled Auto Parts, 250 Walnut Rd, 12118; 518-399-3500; Sa, Sp; 20ac, 1500+; **75+; D, F, PU, 4x4; B3, AMC**

Medford; Medford Auto Wrecking, 171 Peconic Av, 11763; 516-289-1772; CC, Sa, Sp; 4000; **77+; D, F, PU, 4x4; B3**

Middletown; Martines Service Ctr, 487 Route 211 E, 10940; 914-342-3998, FAX 914-343-3699; CC, Sa, Sp; 400+; **70+; D, F, PU, 4x4, Trk; B3, VW; Open Sunday**

Mohawk; Reardon Enterprises, *see Vintage*

Monticello; Fast Eddie's Auto Wreckers, *see Vintage*

New Hyde Park; July Auto Wrecking, 20 1st Av, 11040; 516-746-0297, FAX 516-747-1394; Sa, UR; 500; **72+; D, F, PU, 4x4; B3**

Newburgh; Fleetline Automotive, *see Vintage*

Newfane; Newfane Auto Parts, *see Vintage*

Niagra Falls; A-1 Walmore Rd Recycling, 6510 Walmore Rd, 14304; 716-695-0294; CC, Sa, Sp, Br; 33ac; **68-89; D, F, few PU, 4x4; B3; buses**

Airport Auto Wrecking, 4401 Hyde Park Blvd, 14305; 716-284-0040, FAX 716-282-7898; CC, Sa, Sp; 2500; **70+; D, F, PU, 4x4, Fm; B3, Jp, IH, VW; Open Sunday**

Dave's Auto Wrecking, 2998 Delaware Av, 14305; 716-285-9790; Sa, Sp, UR; 2ac; 200; **70-89; D, PU, 4x4; B3**

R Pera Auto Wrecking, 2304 Maryland Av, 14305; 716-285-9077; Sa; **75-85; D, F**

Norfolk; Butch's of Norfolk, Raymondville Rd, 13667; 315-384-4251, FAX 315-384-4252, 888-ALWRECK; Sa; 10ac, 500; **80+; D, PU, 4x4; B3**

North Tonawanda; L & M Auto Salvage, 1273 & 4001 River Rd, 14120; 716-694-2175, FAX; 2.5ac; **70-89; D, F, PU, 4x4; B3**

N T Auto Parts, 435 Payne Av, 14120; 716-694-1731, FAX 716-694-1732, 888-819-4455; Sa, Sp, Wr, PL; 300+; **72+; D, PU, 4x4; B3**

Oceanside; Anchor Auto Parts, 44 New St, 11572; 516-766-9206; Sa; 50+; **70-91; D, F; B3**

Oswego; Fred's Used Auto Parts, 2541 Co Rte 7, 13126; 315-343-2064; CC, Sp, Br; 200; **80-90; D, PU; B3**

Patchogue; Chapel Avenue Autoparts, *see Vintage*

South Shore Auto Wreckers, 1350 Montauk Hwy, 11772; 516-286-5865; Sa; 300; **80+; D, F, PU, 4x4; B3**

Wards Used Auto Parts, *see Vintage*

Peekskill; Marcy Junk Car Removal Svc, *see Vintage*

214

Pine City; Rubin Auto Parts, 36 Christian Hollow Rd, 14871; 607-733-5557, FAX 607-733-4282, 800-247-8246, www.rubins.com; CC, Sa, Sp; 10ac, 1000; **75+; D, F, PU, 4x4; B3, Jp, VW**

Poughkeepsie; Body Part Intl, *see Vintage*

   Poughquag Auto Wreckers, Beekman Poughquag Rd, 12570; 914-724-5362; CC, Sa, UR; 2ac; **80+; D, F, PU, 4x4; B3**

   Rube & Sons Auto Shop, 505 South Rd, 12601; 914-462-5100, FAX 914-462-8632; CC, Sa; 5ac, 300; **80+; D, F, PU, 4x4; B3**

Queensbury; Ray's Salvage, *see Vintage*

Riverhead; We Got It Auto Parts, *see Vintage*

Rochester; RPM Performance Auto Parts, 67 Warehouse St, 14608; 716-235-8440, FAX 716-546-8944; CC, Sa, Sp; 7ac, 800; **75+; D, F; B3**

Rockville Centre; John Bruzzo, 458 Princeton Rd, 11570; 516-766-4660; 20; **80s; D; B3**

Sanborn; A Able Auto Wrecking, *see Vintage*

Schenectady; Williams Auto Parts, *see Vintage*

Schoharie; Coach Works, RD 1 Box 331, State Rt 30, 12157; 518-827-5160, FAX 518-827-7760, 800-851-6005; CC, Sa, Sp, UR; 7ac, 700; **75-92; D, F, PU; B3**

Seaford; Garrett Auto, 3627 Bayview St, 11783; 516-826-2778; CC, Sa; 20; **70-89; D, F; B3**

Speonk; Outpost Automotive, *see Vintage*

   Peconic Auto Wreckers, Montauk Hwy, 11972; 516-325-0022; CC, Sa, Sp; 5ac, 500; **80-93; D, F, PU; B3**

Spring Valley; Ampex Auto Wreckers, 8 Hoyt St, 10977; 914-352-5100, FAX 914-352-5116, 800-564-6161, www.ampex.qpg.com; CC, Sp; 200; **80+; D, F; B3**

Springville; Kohler Auto Repair Svc, 13008 Dowd Rd, 14141; 716-592-2150; CC; 10ac, 1000; **70-94; D, F, PU, 4x4, Trk; B3**

Staten Island; Bayview Auto Wreckers, 3333 Richmond Ter, 10303; 718-273-6060, FAX 718-448-6767; CC, Sa, Sp; **80+; D, F, PU, 4x4, Trk; B3**

   Ben Francesco Auto Wrecking, 422 Chelsea Rd, 13014; 718-761-3636; Sa, UR; 1ac; **85-90; D, F, PU, 4x4; B3**

   Edkins Auto Scrap, 2265 Richmond Ter, 10302; 718-442-7582, FAX 718-876-9795, 800-433-5467; Sa, Sp, UR; 23ac, 500+; **77+; D, F, PU, 4x4; B3, AMC, Jp, VW**

   Edkins Foreign Auto Parts, 2267 Richmond Ter, 10302; 718-273-8519, 800-445-1818; CC, Sa, UR; **70+; F; Porsche, Jaguar, exotics**

   Henry's Service Ctr, 4414 Arthur Kill Rd, 10309; 718-948-3337; CC, Sa, UR; 2ac, 200; **78+; D, F, PU, 4x4, Trk; B3**

   RCL Auto Corp, 2777 Arthur Kill Rd, 10309; 718-984-1900, FAX 718-984-1901; Sa, Sp; 850; **65+; D, F, PU, 4x4; B3**

Stephentown; Adler's Antique Auto, *see Vintage*

Syracuse; ABC Auto Sales, *see Vintage*

   Kassel Auto Parts-Syracuse, 121 Teall Av, 13210; 315-472-2321, FAX 315-472-3256; CC, Sa, Sp, UR; 10ac, 900+; **80+; D, F, PU, 4x4, Trk; B3**

Tonawanda; INS Scrap Processors, *see Vintage*

Troy; Jack's Auto Wreckers, *see Vintage*

Waverly; Williams Auto Salvage, *see Vintage*

Webster; Elmer's Auto Parts, *see Vintage*

Weedsport; Nash Auto Parts, *see Vintage*

Westbury; Nassau Suffolk Recycling Corp, *see Vintage*

Westfield; Joe's Auto Wrecking, 150 N Portage St, 14787; 716-326-2822, FAX 716-326-7822; Sa, Sp; 400; **75+; D, F, PU, 4x4; B3**

Wingdale; Southeast Auto Recycle, State, 12594; 914-832-9448, FAX 914-832-3973, 800-471-2276, req@southeastny.com; CC, Sa, Sp, Br; 6ac; **80+; D, F, PU, 4x4; B3**

Wurtsboro; G & H Auto Salvage, Old Route 17M, 12790; 914-888-4171; Sa; 350+; **80-90; D, F, PU, 4x4; B3**

Yorkshire; Tidds Auto Parts, *see Vintage*

Youngstown; J & T Auto Salvage & Recycling, *see Vintage*

LATE MODEL

Albany; Branch Auto Parts, *see Late Vintage*
    Jim Meisner Auto Parts, *see Vintage*
Amityville; Accurate Auto Salvage, *see Late Vintage*
Amsterdam; Bills Auto Parts, 12010; 518-842-6050; CC, Sa, Sp; 40ac, 4000; **D, F; B3, AMC,VW**
Arkport; Michael's Auto Parts, 8740 Burns Rd, 14807; 607-295-7091; Sa; 4ac, 400; **D, F, PU, 4x4; B3, AMC, Jp, VW**
Bay Shore; Moffitt Auto Wrecking, 34 Moffitt Blvd, 11706; 516-665-5266; CC, Sa; 3.5ac, 1500; **D, F, PU, 4x4, Trk; B3, AMC**
    Phoenix Foreign & American, 7 Macadam St, 11706; 516-666-0630, FAX 516-666-0695, 800-427-0630; CC, Sa, Sp; 2.5ac, 500; **D, F, PU, 4x4; B3, AMC, Jp, VW**
    Poppy's North Clinton Auto, *see Vintage*
Bellmore; Used Auto Glass, *see Vintage*
Bellport; D & D Used Truck Parts, *see Vintage*
    Three Sons Auto Wrecking, *see Late Vintage*
Beacon; Beacon Auto Salvage, 8 Churchill St, 12508; 914-831-8230, FAX 914-831-0517, 800-838-3591; Sa, Sp; 4ac, 500; **D, F, PU, 4x4; B3, AMC, Jp, VW**
Belfast; Howe Auto Parts, 6680 Rte 305, 14711; 716-365-2828; Sp; 1ac, 100; **D, F, PU, 4x4; B3**
Bernhards Bay; Hardy's Auto, *see Late Vintage*
Bethpage; Garrett Auto Parts, 145 Stewart Av, 11714; 516-735-2886, FAX 516-735-2359, 888-201-2886; CC, Sa, Sp; 2ac, 200; **D, F, PU, 4x4; B3, AMC, VW**
Bliss; Bliss Auto Wreckers, *see Late Vintage*
Brewster; Simon Auto Wreckers, *see Late Vintage*
Brockport; Performance Auto Parts, 2069 Drake Rd, 14420; 716-637-5000; CC, Sa, Sp, Br; 14ac; **D, F, PU, 4x4, Trk; B3, AMC, Jp, VW**
Brocton; R & R Dismantling, 125 Highland Av, 14716; 716-792-4842; Sa, Sp; 7ac, 500; **D, PU, 4x4; B3, AMC**
Bronx; A C Auto Wrecking Co, *see Late Vintage*
    Active Auto Wreckers, 2317 Clementine St, 10466; 718-324-9400, 800-224-9494; Sa; 1ac, 250; **D, F; B3**
    Alicea Auto Wreckers, *see Late Vintage*
    Allied Used Auto Parts, 1371 Spofford Av, 10474; 718-542-7300, FAX 718-542-8438; CC, Sa; **D, F; B3**
    American Auto Wrecking, 530 Drake St, 10474; 718-542-6028; Sa; **D, F; B3**
    Apache Auto Salvage, 638 Longfellow Av, 10474; 718-617-5555, FAX 718-328-1796, 800-339-2739; CC, Sa, Sp; **75+; D, F, PU, 4x4; B3, AMC, Jp, VW**
    Apex Auto Parts, *see Late Vintage*
    Bacher Auto Salvage, 1383 Spofford Av, 10474; 718-328-9200; CC, Sa, Sp; 1ac, 100; **D, F, PU, 4x4; B3, AMC, Jp, VW**
    Boston Road Auto Wreckers, *see Late Vintage*
    Hilltop Auto Salvage, 4157 Boston Rd, 10466; 718-324-0706, 888-339-PART, www.hilltopautosalvage.com; **D, F, PU, 4x4; B3, AMC, VW**
    Ideal Auto Parts, 1340 Lafayette Av, 10474; 718-991-4444; Sa, Wr; 100; **D, F, PU, 4x4; B3, AMC, VW**
    Salient Auto Salvage Corp, 1400 Blondell Av, 10461; 718-931-2666, 800-842-3287 Metro only; CC, Sa, Sp, Br; **80; D, F, PU, 4x4, vans; B3, AMC, Jp, VW**
    Telia-What Auto Parts, 2351 Hollers Av, 10475; 718-325-7211; Sa, Wr; **D, F; B3, AMC**
    US 1 Auto Wreckers, *see Late Vintage*
Brooklyn; A-Best Used Auto Parts, *see Late Vintage*
    A1A Auto Co, *see Late Vintage*
    Ace Auto Wreckers, *see Late Vintage*
    Art's Automotive Parts, 499 Hamilton Av, 11232; 718-768-6100, FAX 718-965-9898; **D, F**
    Auto Gobbler Parts, 681 E 56th St, 11234; 718-251-8193, FAX 718-251-4641; CC, Sa, Sp, Br; 2.5ac, 200; **D, F, PU, 4x4; B3, AMC, Jp, few VW**
    Big Apple Auto, *see Late Vintage*

216

Brooklyn Auto Salvage, 257 Hegeman Av, 11212; 718-498-0111, FAX 718-498-1111; Sp; 1ac; **D, F; B3, AMC**

Carboys, *see Late Vintage*

Century Salvage Ltd, *see Late Vintage*

D'Angelo Auto Sales & Parts, 582 Johnson Av, 11237; 718-381-0010, FAX 718-417-7801, 800-305-4559; Sa, Sp; **D, F; B3, AMC, VW**

Erebuni Corp, 158 Roebling St, 11211; 718-387-0800, FAX 718-486-7957; CC, Sp; **D, F, PU, 4x4; B3, AMC, Jp, VW; Spc: all new spoilers**

G & K Auto Wrecking, *see Late Vintage*

Henry's Service Ctr, 6209 9th Av, 11220; 718-745-2727; CC, Sa, UR; 1ac; **D, F, PU, 4x4; B3**

Mattie's Auto Parts, *see Late Vintage*

Parts R Us, *see Late Vintage*

Satellite Auto Parts, *see Late Vintage*

Straightway Auto Salvage Sales, *see Late Vintage*

T & J Salvage Corp, 2647 Stillwell Av, 11223; 718-946-6200, FAX 718-946-7687, 800-640-8810; Sa, Br; 3ac; **D, F, PU, 4x4; B3**

Buffalo; AA-1 Auto Wrecking, 40 Hopkins St, 14220; 716-823-0515; Sa, Sp, Br; 1500; **D, F, PU, 4x4, Trk; B3, AMC, Jp, IH, VW**

Bens, *see Late Vintage*

Best Door Store, 797 Seneca St, 14210; 716-854-3617, FAX 716-854-3640, 800-854-6352; CC, Sa, Sp, Wr; **D, F; Spc: refinish gas tanks**

Bob & Dons Auto Parts, *see Late Vintage*

Buffalo Auto Wrecking, *see Late Vintage*

Carpenters Auto Parts, *see Vintage*

City Line Auto Parts, 2070 William St, 14206; 716-893-2957, FAX 716-894-3358; Sa, UR; **D, PU, 4x4, Trk; B3, AMC, Jp**

Clinton Auto Wrecking, *see Late Vintage*

Delavan Auto Parts, *see Late Vintage*

Erie Auto Parts, 1055 William St, 14206; 716-852-3735, FAX 716-852-3461; CC, Sa, Sp, UR; **F**

Gregs Auto Parts, 1980 William St, 14206; 716-893-6910; CC, Sa; 300; **D, F; B3, AMC**

Mark's Auto Parts, 1970 William St, 14206; 716-896-1616, FAX 716-896-3986, 800-866-0275; CC, Sp; 2500; **D, F, PU, 4x4, Trk; B3, AMC, Jp, VW**

South Buffalo Auto Parts, 654 Elk St, 14210; 716-822-1111; Sa, UR; 2000; **D, F, PU, 4x4, Trk; B3, AMC, Jp, VW**

United Auto Parts, *see Late Vintage*

Caledonia; PJs Used Cars & Auto Parts, 2708 W Main Rd, 14423; 716-538-2391, FAX 716-538-6192, 800-946-5787; Sa, Sp; **D, F, PU, 4x4; B3, AMC, Jp, VW**

Campbell Hall; C H Auto Salvage, 10916; 914-457-1420, FAX 914-427-5371, 800-359-5998; CC, Sa, Sp; 12ac; **D, F, PU, 4x4; B3, AMC, Jp**

Candaigua; Chappell's Auto Salvage, 4630 Co Rd 46, 14424; 716-394-9450; Sa; 75+; **D, F, PU, 4x4; B3**

Center Moriches; Moriches Used Auto Parts, *see Vintage*

Centereach; Middle Country Auto Wreckers, 1379 Middle Country Rd, 11720; 516-698-1550; CC, Sa, Sp; 700; **D, F; B3, VW**

Central Valley; Bergs Auto Towing, *see Late Vintage*

Cicero; Stosh's Auto Parts, 5796 Crabtree Ln, 13099; 315-699-7715; Sa; 10; **D, F; B3, AMC**

Clarence; United 4 Wheel Drive Parts Ctr, *see Late Vintage*

Cold Spring; Cold Spring Auto Parts, *see Vintage*

Expressway Auto Parts, RR 9, 10516; 914-265-2251; CC, Sa, Sp; 800; **D, F, PU, 4x4, Trk; B3, AMC, Jp, VW**

Copiague; South Shore Auto Corp, 1120 Marconi Blvd, 11726; 516-842-7440; Sa, Sp, Br; 150; **D, F, PU; B3, AMC, VW**

Cuddebackville; Brim Recyclers, 12729; 914-754-7671; CC, Sa, Sp, Br; 100; **D, F, PU, 4x4; B3, AMC, Jp, VW**

Deer Park; A & J Used Auto Parts, *see Late Vintage*
Ace Overseas Corp, 1028 Long Island Av, 11729; 516-667-3331; Sp, Wr; **F**
J & P Auto Wrecking, 987 Long Island Av, 11729; 516-595-9617; Sa; 3ac, 300; **D, F, PU, 4x4, Trk; B3, AMC, Jp, IH**
Mid-Island Auto Wreckers, *see Late Vintage*

Dunkirk; Moore Auto Salvage, *see Late Vintage*

East Meadow; East Meadow Used Auto Parts, 2623 N Jerusalem Rd, 11554; 516-785-6066, FAX 516-785-0452; CC, Sa, Sp, Br; 150; **D, F; B3, AMC**

East Northport; Marty's Auto Wrecking, 1007 3rd St, 11731; 516-261-3604; Sp; 0.5ac, 50; **D, F, PU, 4x4; B3, AMC, Jp**

East Quogue; Westhampton Auto Salvage, *see Late Vintage*

East Rochester; Northside Salvage, *see Vintage*

East Setauket; Setauket Auto Wreckers, 91 Gnarled Hollow Rd, 11733; 516-689-8401, FAX 516-689-6746; Sa, Sp, Br; 1ac, 75; **F, PU, 4x4; Jpa**

Elma; Howbill Auto Parts, *see Late Vintage*

Far Rockaway; Bay Used Auto Parts & Sales, 356 Beach 80th St, 11693; 718-474-1114; **D, F**
Garas Auto Wrecking, 6222 Alameda Av, 11692; 718-945-3682; CC, UR; 300; **D, F, PU, 4x4; B3, AMC**

Fishkill; Double Z Motors, 2895 Route 9, 12524; 914-896-7930, FAX 914-896-4594; CC, Sa, Sp; 350+;

Flushing; Aalba Auto Wrecking, 151 Woodward Av, 11385; 718-386-3953; **D, F**
Alliance Auto Parts, 5016 72nd St, 11377; 718-672-3800, FAX 718-672-2388; CC, Sa, Sp; 400; **D, F, PU, 4x4; B3, AMC, Jp, VW**
Express Used Auto Prt, 12616 37th Av, 11368; 718-565-1234; Sa; 150; **D, F; mostly Japanese**
F & F Auto Salvage, 12634 Willets Point Blvd, 11368; 718-639-3736; Sa; 600; **D, F**
Flushing Auto Salvage, 12636 34th Av, 11368; 718-672-0700; Sa; 150+; **D, F; B3, AMC**
Glen Used Auto Parts, 1937 Flushing Av #A, 11385; 718-381-2240, FAX 718-386-3335; CC, Sa, Sp; 150+; **D, F, PU, 4x4; B3, AMC, VW**
Good Luck Used Auto Parts, 12633 34th Av, 11368; 718-672-0254; CC, Sa, Sp, Br; 450; **D, F, vans; B3, AMC**
H & S Auto Repair Corp, 12727 Willets Point Blvd, 11368; 718-779-4156; Sa, Br; 150+; **D, F; B3, AMC, VW**
Hitch King, *see Vintage*
Jon-Carlo Foreign Auto Parts, *see Late Vintage*
Master Used Parts, *see Late Vintage*
Metro Auto Salvage, 4646 Metropolitan Av, 11385; 718-381-2727, 888-381-6634; Sa, Sp, UR; **D, F, PU, 4x4; B3**
Prevete Brothers Co, 12515 Roosevelt Av, 11368; 718-899-2022; Sa; 2.5ac; **D, F, 4x4; B3**
Roosevelt Auto Wrecking, *see Late Vintage*
Sacco Auto Sales & Parts, *see Late Vintage*
Sambucci Brothers, 12602 36th Ave, 11368; 718-446-9752, FAX 718-899-8265, 800-990-7278, www.sambuccibros.com; CC, Sa, Sp, Br; 1200; **D, F, PU**
Select Auto Parts, 3323 127th St, 11368; 718-458-3300; Sa, Wr; 15; **F**
Shop 4, *see Late Vintage*
Steering Wheel Rentals, *see Late Vintage*
Stop #4 Auto Parts, 12668 Willets Point Blvd, 11368; 718-898-5653; Sa; **D, F; American transmissions & engines only, Foreign whole cars**
US Auto Salvage, 12620 35th Av, 11368; 718-507-2697, FAX 718-507-5995; CC, Sa, Sp; 100; **D, F; B3, AMC**
Willets Point Auto Salvage, *see Late Vintage*

Frankfort; Givo's Used Auto Parts, 106 Broad St, 13340; 315-724-8424; Br; **D; B3, AMC**

Franklinville; Lamberts Auto Parts, *see Vintage*

Fredonia; Clemens Sales, *see Late Vintage*

Freedom; Previty's Auto Wrecking, *see Vintage*

Freeport; Freeport Auto Parts & Wrecking, 122 Buffalo Av, 11520; 516-378-9463, FAX 516-867-5865, 800-285-9930; CC, Sa, Sp, Wr, PL; 2ac; **D, F; open Sunday**

Frewsburg; Twin Auto Sales, 125 W Main St, 14738; 716-569-5232, FAX 716-569-5233; Sa, UR; 700+; **D, F, PU, 4x4, Trk, Fm; B3, AMC, Jp, IH, VW**

Glen Cove; Glen Cove Auto Salvage, *see Vintage*

Gowanda; Good Door Store, *see Vintage*

Great Valley; Triple S Auto Dismantling, *see Late Vintage*

Hamburg; Calkins Used Auto Parts, *see Late Vintage*

Hempstead; Hempstead Used Auto & Truck, *see Late Vintage*

Holbrook; Suffolk Auto Recycling, *see Late Vintage*

Holland; Kloiber Auto Recycling, *see Late Vintage*

    Nuwer Auto Parts, 7178 Vermont Hill Rd, 14080; 716-537-2800, FAX 716-537-9182, 800-333-3031; CC, Sa, Sp; 22ac, 5000; **D, F, PU, 4x4; B3**

Huntington Station; Fat City Auto Wreckers, 100 W 11th St, 11746; 516-673-2966; Sa; **D, F, PU, 4x4**

    Gardiners Auto Parts, *see Late Vintage*

    Pete's Auto Parts, 150 W 10th St, 11746; 516-423-7825; Sa; 2.5ac, 300; **D, F, PU, 4x4; B3**

    S & S Auto Wrecking, 100 Railroad St, 11746; 516-423-2735, FAX 516-423-8943; CC, Sa, Sp; 4ac, 500; **D, F, PU, 4x4; B3**

Hyde Park; A & T Auto Parts, *see Late Vintage*

    East Park Auto Recycling, PO Box 24, Cty Rd 41, 12538; 914-229-2104, FAX 914-229-7224, 800-BUY-USED; CC, Sa, Sp; 1000; **F, PU, 4x4; Japanese mostly**

    Molt's Used Auto Parts, *see Vintage*

Island Park; Auto Undertaker, *see Late Vintage*

Islip; Sils Foreign Auto Parts, *see Late Vintage*

Ithaca; Danby Motors, *see Vintage*

Jamaica; A Rite Auto Parts, *see Late Vintage*

    Antonelli's Auto Parts, 12002 Sutphin Blvd, 11434; 718-322-7179, 800-463-2787; CC, Sa, Sp, PL; **D, F**

    Citywide Auto Parts, *see Late Vintage*

    Do-Rite Auto Salvage Corp, *see Late Vintage*

    East Coast Auto Salvage, *see Late Vintage*

    Easy Does It Auto Salvage, 15020 Beaver Rd, 11433; 718-291-2048; Sa, Sp; 100; **D, F**

    Jamaica Auto Salvage, 15037 Liberty Av, 11433; 718-657-2851, FAX 718-291-6016, 800-643-9619; CC, Sa, Sp, UR; 2ac; **D, F**

    Marino's Auto Salvage, *see Late Vintage*

    Nelson's Auto Salvage, 12280 Montauk St, 11413; 718-276-1234, FAX 718-276-5897; CC, Sa, Sp, UR; 300; **D, F, PU, 4x4; B3**

    Richmond Auto Salvage, 8771 130th St, 11418; 718-805-6136; Sa; **D, F**

    Roth's Auto Wrecking, *see Late Vintage*

    Springfield Auto Wreckers, 18436 147th Av, 11413; 718-525-5885, FAX 718-276-5897; CC, Sa, Sp, UR; 300; **D, F, PU, 4x4; B3**

Jamestown; Busti Auto Sales, 3385 Busti Stillwater Rd, 14701; 716-484-8930; Sa, Sp; 10ac, 1000; **D, PU, 4x4; Ford, Lincoln, Mercury only**

    Townline Auto Parts, *see Late Vintage*

Kings Park; Greg's Auto Body & Salvage Liquidators, 141 Old Northport Rd, 11754; 516-544-0497; Sa, Sp, UR; 300; **D, F, PU; B3**

Kingston; Burton Deitz, *see Late Vintage*

Lancaster; A Js Auto Wrecking, *see Vintage*

    Ed's Auto Parts, *see Late Vintage*

Lindenhurst; A-Plus Auto Salvage, 640 W Hoffman Av, 11757; 516-226-0580; CC, Sa, Sp; **D, F, PU, 4x4; B3**

    Act Auto Wrecking, *see Late Vintage*

    All Stop Used Auto Parts, *see Late Vintage*

    Elite Auto Parts, *see Late Vintage*

John Spinelli Auto Salvage, 638 W Hoffman Av, 11757; 516-226-9630, FAX 516-226-3645, 800-649-1245; CC, Sa, Sp, PL; 350+; **D, F, PU; B3**

Lakewood Used Auto Parts, 1070 Farmingdale Rd, 11757; 516-957-3200; CC, Sa, Sp, UR; 3.5ac, 400+; **D, F, PU; B3**

Michaels Auto Recycling, 100 Bahama, 11757; 516-661-6910; Sa, Sp; **D, F**

Tri-State Auto, *see Vintage*

Livonia; Fugles Auto Parts, 5278 S Livonia Rd, 14487; 716-346-3658, FAX 716-346-6211; Sa, Sp, Br; 30ac, 3000; **D, F, PU, 4x4, Trk; B3, AMC, Jp, VW**

Lockport; Vince's Auto Wrecking & Sales, *see Vintage*

Macedon; British Auto, *see Vintage*

Mamaroneck; Blood Brothers Wreckers, *see Late Vintage*

Massapequa; Massapequa Auto Salvage, 50 Sunrise Hwy, 11758; 516-541-8504, FAX 516-541-4098, 800-244-8504; CC, Sa, Sp, Wr; 1ac, 150; **D, F, PU, 4x4, vans; B3, Jp**

Massena; LaFlesh Garage, *see Late Vintage*

Mayville; A Automotive, *see Vintage*

Mechanicville; ABC Recycled Auto Parts, *see Late Vintage*

Medford; Aaron Auto Supply Corp, 136 Peconic Av, 11763; 516-289-3434, FAX 516-289-3655, 800-616-8319, www.aaronauto.com; CC, Sa, Sp; 1000; **F**

Medford Auto Wrecking, *see Late Vintage*

Sonny's Auto Wrecking, 139 Peconic Av, 11763; 516-758-6366; Sa, Sp; 700; **D, F, PU, 4x4; B3**

Middleburgh; Bill's Auto & Commercial Towing, Route 145 S, 12122; 518-827-8007

Middletown; Martines Service Ctr, *see Late Vintage*

Middletown Auto Wreckers, 106 California Av, 10940; 914-343-8011; Sa, UR; **D, F, PU, 4x4; B3**

Mongaup Valley; Seven-X Motors, Route 17B, 12762; 914-583-5110, FAX 914-583-5133; CC, Sa, Sp, UR; 500; **D, F, PU, 4x4, Trk; B3, AMC, Jp**

Monticello; Fast Eddie's Auto Wreckers, *see Vintage*

Montrose; Kaufman Auto Parts, 135 Albany Post Rd, 10548; 914-737-2393; Sa, Sp; 500; **D, F, PU, 4x4; B3**

New Hyde Park; F & S Auto Parts, 1 Denton Av, 11040; 516-747-0250, FAX 516-747-5446; CC, Sa, Sp; 200; **D, F, PU, 4x4; Spc: Mercedes**

July Auto Wrecking, *see Late Vintage*

Newfane; Newfane Auto Parts, *see Vintage*

Niagra Falls; Airport Auto Wrecking, *see Late Vintage*

Auto Reclaim Scrap Ctr, 5509 Lockport Rd, 14305; 716-297-4055; Sa, UR; 250+; **D, F, PU; B3**

Garlock's Auto Wrecking, 2360 Maryland Av, 14305; 716-282-6551, FAX 716-282-0747; CC, Sa, Sp, PL; 10ac, 1500; **D, F, PU; B3**

Kachs Auto Svc, 4800 Witmer Rd, 14305; 716-282-3455, FAX 716-285-8296; CC, Sa; 6ac, 350+; **D, F, PU, 4x4; B3**

Norfolk; Butch's of Norfolk, *see Late Vintage*

North Tonawanda; N T Auto Parts, *see Late Vintage*

Oceanside; Novak Auto Corp, 4 Hampton Rd, 11572; 516-764-5562, www.usedautoparts .com; Sa, Sp; 200; **D, F, PU, 4x4; B3**

Patchogue; All American Auto Wreckers, 1383 Montauk Hwy #A, 11772; 516-286-5500, FAX 516-286-5549, 888-748-5924; CC, Sa, Sp; 300; **D, F, PU, 4x4; B3**

Chapel Avenue Autoparts, *see Vintage*

South Shore Auto Wreckers, *see Late Vintage*

Peekskill; Marcy Junk Car Removal Svc, *see Vintage*

Pine City; Rubin Auto Parts, *see Late Vintage*

Pleasant Valley; Hankamp Auto Parts, Rte 44, 12569; 914-635-3026; **PL service only**

Poughkeepsie; Body Part Intl, *see Vintage*

Redls Parkway Auto Parts, 171 Freedom Plains Rd, 12603; 914-452-7715, FAX 914-452-6032, 800-245-0555; CC, Sa, Sp; 17ac, 1000; **D, PU, 4x4, vans; B3**

Rube & Sons Auto Shop, *see Late Vintage*
Poughquag; Poughquag Auto Wreckers, *see Late Vintage*
Queensbury; Ray's Salvage, *see Vintage*
Riverhead; Fred J Gallo Used Auto Parts, 27 Hubbard Av, 11901; 516-727-6490; Sa, Sp; 700; **D, F, PU, 4x4; B3**
Rock Hill; Gildick Auto Wrecksperts, Box 357, Foss Rd, 12775; 914-794-5310, FAX 914-794-1585, www.gildick.com; CC, Sp; 100ac, 1000; **D, F, PU, 4x4; B3**
Rochester; RPM Performance Auto Parts, *see Late Vintage*
Ronkonkoma; Rigs Used Auto Parts, 2164 Pond Rd, 11779; 516-467-9413; Sa; 15; **D; B3**
Southampton; J & V Auto Salvage, 375 Majors Path, 11968; 516-283-5111; **D, F, PU, 4x4**
Spring Valley; Ampex Auto Wreckers , *see Late Vintage*
Springville; Kohler Auto Repair Svc, *see Late Vintage*
Staten Island; Ace Auto Salvage, 1335 Castleton Av, 10310; 718-448-5900, FAX 718-442-1351, 800-843-0301; CC, Sa, Sp; 450+; **D, F, PU, 4x4; B3**
    Ace Auto Salvage, 95 Rector St, 10310; 718-273-4100, FAX 718-442-1351, 800-843-0301; CC, Sa, Sp; 65+; **D, F, PU, 4x4; B3**
    Bayview Auto Wreckers, *see Late Vintage*
    Brothers Foreign Car Specs, 2151 Forest Av, 10303; 718-448-0300, FAX 718-448-0301, 800-207-2787, www.plentyparts.com; CC, Sa, Sp, Wr; **F; Porsche only, mostly 944, 924**
    Edkins Auto Sales, 2239 Richmond Ter, 10302; 718-442-4866, FAX 718-876-9795, 800-433-5467; Sa, Sp, UR; 14ac, 350+; **D, F, PU, 4x4; B3**
    Edkins Auto Scrap, *see Late Vintage*
    Edkins Foreign Auto Parts, *see Late Vintage*
    Henry's Service Ctr, *see Late Vintage*
    Motorcade Auto Corp, 1641 Richmond Ter, 10310; 718-273-3000; CC, Sa; **D, F, PU**
    RCL Auto Corp, *see Late Vintage*
Syracuse; ABC Auto Sales, *see Vintage*
    Kassel Auto Parts - Syracuse, *see Late Vintage*
Tonawanda; Frontier Auto Wrecking, 493 Young St, 14150; 716-693-2240, FAX 716-695-0369; CC, Sa; 2ac, 100; **D, F; B3**
Troy; Jack's Auto Wreckers, *see Vintage*
Utica; A-1 Auto Parts, Barnes Av, 13502; 315-735-2233, FAX 315-735-0959; CC, Sa, Sp, UR; 23ac, 800; **D, F, PU, 4x4; B3**
Watertown; Eiss Brothers, 28250 State Rte 37, 13601; 315-629-4370, FAX 315-629-1025, 800-698-3477; CC, Sa, Sp; 500; **D, F, PU, 4x4; B3**
Waverly; Williams Auto Salvage, *see Vintage*
Weedsport; Nash Auto Parts, *see Vintage*
West Haverstraw; Keahon Auto Wreckers, 210 Beach Rd, 10993; 914-429-3737, FAX 914-429-1411; Sa, UR; **D, F, PU, 4x4, Trk**
Westbury; Frank & Sons Auto Wrecking, 132 Hopper St, 11590; 516-997-5736; Sa; **D, F, PU, 4x4; B3**
    Nassau Suffolk Recycling Corp, *see Vintage*
Westfield; Joe's Auto Wrecking, *see Late Vintage*
Wingdale; Southeast Auto Recycle, *see Late Vintage*
Wurtsboro; M & R Quickway Svc, Box 216, 12790; 914-888-4013; Sa; 100; **D, PU, 4x4; B3**
Yonkers; Saw Mill Auto Wrecking, 12 Worth St, 10701; 914-968-5300 CC, Sa, Sp; **D, F**
    Yonkers Auto Parts, 435 Roberts Ave, 10702; 914-968-3800; Sa, Sp, UR, Wr; 2ac; **D, F, PU, 4x4**
Yorkshire; 1490 Motors, 11253 Old Olean Rd, 14173; 716-492-5210, FAX 716-496-7300; Sa, Sp; 150; **D, F, PU, 4x4; B3, AMC, VW**
Youngstown; J & T Auto Salvage & Recycling, *see Vintage*

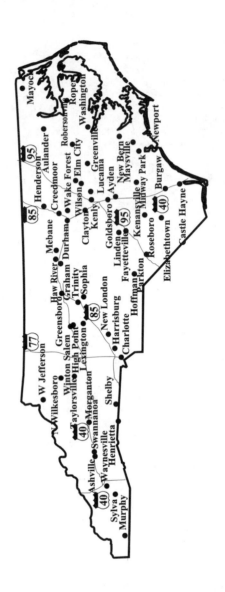

North Carolina

Please use the cards in the back to let us know about yards we may have missed, or any other comments or information for future editions of Ray's wReckingyard Roster

NORTH CAROLINA

VINTAGE

Asheville; I-26 Auto Salvage, 80 Pond Rd, 28806; 828-667-1001; Sa, Sp; 600+; **40+; D, F, PU, 4x4; B**3**, AMC, VW; Spc: Chevy Impala, VW**

Aulander; Drennan's Antique Auto Parts, PO Box 508, 27805; 252-345-8191; Sp UPS only; 31ac, 1400; **50-79; D, F, PU; B**3**, AMC, Jp, VW, Jpa; No sport, expensive or rare; Mail Order, Call ahead for appointment**

Ayden; Carolina Cadillacs, Rt 2 Box 212, 28513; 252-746-2594, FAX 252-746-2826; Sp, Wr; 56-80; **D; Cadillac only**

Clayton; Johnston County Auto Salvage, 4417 US Hwy 70 Business E, 27520; 919-553-8161, FAX; Sa, UR; 500; **50+; D, F, PU, 4x4, Trk, vans; B**3**, VW, MG, Volvo, Saab, Peugeot; ambulances**

Creedmoor; Bullock Salvage Co, 2696 Sam Moss Hayes Rd, 27522; 919-528-0094, FAX 919-528-3337, 800-262-1358; CC, Sp, UR; 700+; **60+; D, F, PU, 4x4, Trk; B**3

Elm City; Cox Auto Salvage, 7622 E Langley Rd, 27822; 252-236-4127, 800-437-2456; Sp, UR; 5ac; **29+; D, F, PU, 4x4, Trk; B**3**, AMC, Jp, IH, St**

Fayetteville; Bishop Auto Wrecking, 714 Dunn Rd, 28301; 910-483-5156, FAX 910-483-1604, 877-655-3219; CC, Sa, Sp; 64ac; **48+; D, F, PU, Trk; B**3**, AMC, Jp, IH; Ford & Chevy Pickup, Rambler**

   Diffin's Auto Salvage, 663 Horseshoe Rd, 28303; 910-864-3565, FAX 910-864-5172; CC, Sa, UR; 5ac; **60+; D, F, PU; B**3**; some muscle cars**

Kenly; Holland's Salvage, 9580 US Hwy 301 N, 27542; 919-284-4561; Sa, Sp; 6ac; **60+; D, F, PU, 4x4; B**3**, few AMC, few Jp, few IH**

Linden; K & S Salvage, Slocomb Rd, 28356; 910-488-2230; Sa; 79ac; **50+; D, F, PU, 4x4, few Trk; B**3**, AMC, Jp, VW**

Midway Park; Piney Green Auto Salvage, 2264 Piney Green Rd, 28544; 910-353-1386, FAX 910-353-7159; CC, Sa, Sp; 10ac; **67+; D, F, PU, 4x4; B**3**, AMC, Jp, IH, VW, Jpa**

Moyock; Robert Cannon's Corvette Parts, PO Box 900, Hwy 168, 27958; 252-435-2212, FAX 252-435-6944, 800-523-2090; CC, Sa, Sp, Wr; **53+; D; Corvette only**

Murphy; Murphy Auto Salvage, RR 2, 28906; 828-837-6692; Sa, Sp; 10ac; **47+; D, F, PU, 4x4, Trk; B**3**, AMC, Jp, IH, VW; Spc: Corviar**

New Bern; Tuscarora Auto Salvage, 280 Tuscarora Rhems Rd, 28562; 252-638-1232; Sa; 400; **50+; D, F, PU, 4x4, Trk; B**3

North Wilkesboro; Thunderbird Barn, 2919 Elkin Hwy 268, 28659; 336-667-0837; Sa, Sp, Br; 50; **58-69; D, F; Spc: Ford Thunderbird; also whole cars**

Parkton; Simpkins Auto Salvage, 225 Davis Bridge Rd, 28371; 910-875-4405; Sa; 300; **60-89; D, F, PU; B**3**, VW**

Robersonville; Jim's Auto & Salvage, 24471 NC Hwy 903 S, 27871; 252-795-4488; Sa, UR; 13ac; **56+; D, F, PU, 4x4; B**3**, AMC, Jp, St, VW; school buses**

Shelby; Sundell Auto Specialties, 1105 Mooresboro Rd, 28150; 704-434-6759, FAX 704-434-7071; CC, Sa, Sp; 500+; **64-85; D; GM only; Spc: Malibu, Cutlass, El Camino**

Sophia; Hooker's Auto Sales, 1944 Groom Rd, 27350; 336-498-2542, FAX 336-495-5540, 877-495-5540, lutherhouse-1@att.net; CC, Sa, Sp, UR; 500; **50-69; D, F, PU; B**3**, Hd, Renault**

Swannanoa; Blake's Auto Salvage, 1108 US Hwy 70, 28778; 828-298-8600, FAX 828-298-1150; CC, Sa; 3ac; **67-87; D, F, PU, 4x4; B**3**, AMC**

Trinity; Prospect Auto Parts, 5243 Snyder Country Rd, 27370; 336-861-5007, FAX 336-861-6509, www.tvilleclassics.com; CC, Sp, UR; 14ac+; 2000; **46-80; D; Pontiac, Olds, Buick, Nash; By Appointment Only**

Washington; Perry's Auto Salvage, 2884 Harvey Rd #1, 27889; 252-946-7644; Sa; 10ac; **52+; D, F, PU, 4x4; B**3**, VW**

West Jefferson; Barkers Automotive & Salvage, 656 Orville Barker Rd, 28694; 336-877-4895; Sa, Sp, UR; 30ac, 300+; **60-90; D, F, PU; B**3**, St**

Winston-Salem; Mid-South Auto Sales, 2700 Nieman Industrial Dr, 27103; 336-768-6251; Sp; **60-89; D, 4x4; B**3**, IH**

LATE VINTAGE

Asheville; I-26 Auto Salvage, *see Vintage*

Aulander; Drennan's Antique Auto Parts, *see Vintage*

Ayden; Carolina Cadillacs, *see Vintage*

Burgaw; Babson Auto Salvage Svc, 6951 NC Hwy 53 E, 28425; 910-259-4678; CC, Sa, Sp, PL; 10ac; **77+; D, PU, 4x4, Trk; B3**

Charlotte; City Salvage, 3700 Statesville Av, 28206; 704-375-1234, FAX 704-375-7878, 800-532-0116; Sp, UR; 800; **80+, few 50-70s; D, F, PU, 4x4, Trk; B3**

Hunter Salvage, 5310 David Cox Rd, 28269; 704-596-5891; UR; 30ac; **80+; D, F, PU, 4x4; B3**

Clayton; Johnston County Auto Salvage, *see Vintage*

Creedmoor; Bullock Salvage Co, *see Vintage*

Durham; Wagner's Auto Salvage Inc, 4115 S Alston Av, 27713; 919-544-1729, 800-669-1673; CC, Sa, Sp; 20ac; **75+; D, F, PU, 4x4, Trk; B3, Jp, VW**

Elizabethtown; Elizabethtown Salvage Yard, 1003 White Lake Dr, 28337; 910-862-8809, 800-222-9847; Sa, Sp; 41ac; **67+; D, PU, 4x4, Trk; B3, Jp, IH**

Elm City; Cox Auto Salvage, *see Vintage*

Fayetteville; Bishop Auto Wrecking, see Vintage

Diffin's Auto Salvage, *see Vintage*

R C Auto Salvage, PO Box 293, 28348; 910-484-9713; Sa, UR; **70+; D, F, PU, Fm; B3**

Graham; Graham Auto Salvage, 4747 NC Hwy 54 #B, 27953; 336-376-3144; Sp, UR; 200; **70+, few 60s; D, few F, few PU; B3**

Greensboro; Welch's Auto Salvage, 2530 Alamance, 27406; 336-274-0946; Sa, UR; 400; **70-90; D, F, PU, Trk; B3**

Harrisburg; K & C Auto Salvage, 2609 Hwy 49 N, 28075; 704-455-2526, FAX 704-455-5209, 800-422-6512 NC & SC only; CC, Sa, Sp; 10ac; **82-94; D, F, PU, 4x4; B3, Jp, VW**

Henrietta; Robbins Used Cars, 1891 Harris Henrietta Rd, 28076; 828-657-5732, FAX 828-657-6554, 800-726-0275; CC, Sa, Sp, UR; 20ac, 1000+; **80+; D, F, PU, 4x4, Trk; B3, Jp, IH; rebuild & restoraton**

High Point; Guil-Rand Wrecker Svc, 1411 Foust Av, 27260; 336-889-2100; Sa; 2000; **80s, few 70s; D, F, PU; B3**

Hoffman; Wallace Parts & Salvage, US Hwy 1 S, 28347; 910-281-3151, FAX 910-281-4289, 800-682-4064; CC, Sa, Sp; 800; **80+; D, F, PU; B3, Jp, VW**

Kenansville; Rackley Auto Salvage, 964 E NC 24 Hwy, 28349; 910-296-0351; Sa, UR, Wr; 60+; **80-90; D, F, PU; B3; Spc: Mustang**

Kenly; Holland's Salvage, *see Vintage*

Linden; K & S Salvage, *see Vintage*

Lucama; Hinnant's Auto Salvage, 7027 NC Hwy 42 W, 27851; 252-237-1036, 800-848-8040; CC, Sp; 750+; **70+; D, F, PU, 4x4; B3, Jpa**

Maysville; Pala-Alto Auto Salvage, 1731 Belgrade Swansboro Rd, 28555; 910-743-2902; Sa, UR; 500; **77+; D, F, PU, 4x4; B3**

Mebane; Crutchfield's Mobile Crusher, 1639 US Hwy 70 #A, 27302; 336-578-2088; Sa; 1000; **80+; D, F, PU; B3**

Midway Park; Piney Green Auto Salvage, *see Vintage*

Moyock; Robert Cannon's Corvette Parts, *see Vintage*

Murphy; Murphy Auto Salvage, *see Vintage*

New Bern; Tuscarora Auto Salvage, *see Vintage*

New London; Richfield Auto Salvage, 48460 Ingram Rd, 28127; 704-463-5989, 800-438-1248, www.richfield.com, GTE Superpages; CC, Sp, UR; 600; **80+; F; Honda only**

Parkton; Simpkins Auto Salvage, *see Vintage*

Robersonville; Jim's Auto & Salvage, *see Vintage*

Roper; Taylor Auto Salvage, 3595 W Mill Pond Rd, 27970; 252-793-5744, FAX 252-793-2431, taylor3595@coastalnet.com; Sa, Sp; 300; **80+; D; B3**

Roseboro; Royal Auto Salvage, 9117 Roseboro Hwy, 28382; 910-525-4029; Sa, UR; 300; **80-92; D, F, PU; B3, VW**

Shelby; Sundell Auto Specialties, *see Vintage*

Swannanoa; Blake's Auto Salvage, *see Vintage*

Sylva; Sylva Salvage, 5 Elders Rd, 28779; 828-586-9019, 888-532-4153; Sa, UR; 250+; **70+; D, F, PU; B3, AMC, VW**

Taylorsville; Little Egypt Salvage, 219 Three Forks Rd NW, 28681; 828-632-3923; CC, Sp; 12ac; **80+; F, PU, 4x4**

Trinity; Prospect Auto Parts, *see Vintage*

Wake Forest; T E Nines Auto Parts, 3679 Bruce Garner Rd, 27587; 919-528-2513, 800-200-2844; CC, Sa, Sp, UR; 2000; **80+, few 70s; D, F, PU, 4x4; B3**

Washington; Perry's Auto Salvage, *see Vintage*

Waynesville; Schulhofer's Inc, 525 Howell Mill Rd, 28786; 828-456-9408, FAX 828-456-8742, 800-457-9408; Sp, UR; 100; **77+; D, F, PU; B3**

West Jefferson; Barkers Automotive & Salvage, *see Vintage*

Winston-Salem; A-1 Auto Salvage, 6571 Old Lexington Rd, 27107; 336-784-0021; Sa; 500+; **88+; D, F, PU; B3; Spc: hub caps, 70+**

   Mid-South Auto Sales, *see Vintage*

LATE MODEL

Asheville; I-26 Auto Salvage, *see Vintage*

Burgaw; Babson Auto Salvage Svc, *see Late Vintage*

Castle Hayne; Wilmington Auto Salvage, 4614 N College Rd, 28429; 910-675-9400, 800-722-6451; CC, Sp; 700; **D, F, PU; B3**

Charlotte; City Salvage, *see Late Vintage*

   Daves Auto Slvg, 5416 Mt Holly Huntersville Rd, 28216; 704-393-7064; Sa; 300; **D; B3**

   Hunter Salvage, *see Late Vintage*

Clayton; Johnston County Auto Salvage, *see Vintage*

Creedmoor; Bullock Salvage Co, *see Vintage*

Durham; City Auto Salvage, 1301 S Miami Blvd, 27703; 919-596-8191, FAX 919-596-7250, 800-672-8550; CC, Sp; 15ac; **D, F, PU, 4x4; B3**

   Wagner's Auto Salvage Inc, *see Late Vintage*

Elizabethtown; Elizabethtown Salvage Yard, *see Late Vintage*

Elm City; Cox Auto Salvage, *see Vintage*

Fayetteville; Bishop Auto Wrecking, *see Vintage*

   Diffin's Auto Salvage, *see Vintage*

   Fayetteville Auto Salvage, 4429 Murchison Rd, 28311; 910-488-4141; CC, Sp; 5ac; **D, F, PU; B3**

   Goodfellas Auto Salvage, Hwy 87 S, 28306; 910-484-4035; Sa, UR; 1ac; **D, PU, 4x4; B3**

   McLamb's Auto Salvage, 315 Pelt Dr, 28301; 910-488-5255, FAX 910-822-2247, 800-682-5238; CC, Sp; 3000; **D, F, PU, 4x4; B3**

   R C Auto Salvage, *see Late Vintage*

Goldsboro; Wayne Auto Salvage, 1911 US Hwy 117 S, 27530; 919-734-3959, FAX 919-735-9684, 800-672-5887, dale@waynes.actual/america.com; CC, Sp; 4000+; **D, F, PU, 4x4; B3**

Graham; Graham Auto Salvage, *see Late Vintage*

Greensboro; Gate City Auto Salvage Inc, 6020 High Point Rd, 27407; 336-299-4937, 800-331-4660; CC, Sp, UR; 1000; **D, F, PU; B3**

   Greensboro Auto Parts Co, 3720 Burlington Rd, 27405; 336-375-5809, FAX 910-621-8522, 800-632-4008; CC, Sp; 25ac; **D, F, PU, 4x4, Trk; B3**

   Tri-City Auto Salvage Inc, 3848 Burlington Rd, 27405; 336-375-5871, 800-451-0693; CC, Sp; 5000; **D, F, PU, 4x4; B3, Jp, VW**

Greenville; J & P Auto Salvage, 27858; 252-355-4631

Harrisburg; K & C Auto Salvage, *see Late Vintage*

Haw River; Crutchfield Auto Parts, 1638 US Hwy 70E, 27258; 336-578-1681, 800-289-8179; Sa, Sp; 2000; **D, F, PU, 4x4; B3**

Henderson; Mike's Auto Salvage Inc, 541 Industry Dr, 27536; 252-438-5376; Sp; 1000; **D, F, PU, 4x4; B3; Spc: Pickup & 4x4**

Henrietta; Robbins Used Cars, *see Late Vintage*

High Point; Guil-Rand Wrecker Svc, *see Late Vintage*

Hoffman; Wallace Parts & Salvage, *see Late Vintage*

Kenly; Holland's Salvage, *see Vintage*
Lexington; Campbell's Auto Parts & Sales, 9029 Old US Hwy 52, 27295; 336-764-5655; Sp; 250; **D, F, PU; B3**
Linden; K & S Salvage, *see Vintage*
Lucama; Hinnant's Auto Salvage, *see Late Vintage*
Maysville; Pala-Alto Auto Salvage, *see Late Vintage*
Mebane; Crutchfield's Mobile Crusher, *see Late Vintage*
Midway Park; Piney Green Auto Salvage, *see Vintage*
Morganton; Hightower Auto Salvage, 101 1/2 Tabernacle Church Rd, 28655; 828-437-9071, 800-542-1893; Sa, Sp; 1100; **D, F, PU, 4x4; B3**
Moyock; Robert Cannon's Corvette Parts, *see Vintage*
Murphy; Murphy Auto Salvage, *see Vintage*
New Bern; Tuscarora Auto Salvage, *see Vintage*
New London; Richfield auto Salvage, *see Late Vintage*
Newport; Atlantic Auto Parts & Salvage, 5871 Hwy 70, 28570; 252-223-4151, FAX 252-223-4423, 800-950-9443; CC, Sp; 35ac; **D, F, PU, 4x4; B3**
Robersonville; Jim's Auto & Salvage, *see Vintage*
Roper; Taylor Auto Salvage, *see Late Vintage*
Roseboro; Royal Auto Salvage, *see Late Vintage*
Sylva; Sylva Salvage, *see Late Vintage*
Taylorsville; Little Egypt Salvage, *see Late Vintage*
Wake Forest; T E Nines Auto Parts, *see Late Vintage*
Washington; Perry's Auto Salvage, *see Vintage*
Waynesville; Schulhofer's Inc, *see Late Vintage*
Wilson; Auto Salvage of Wilson Inc, 2328 Womble Brooks Rd, 27893; 252-243-6155, FAX 252-243-9526, 800-672-4227; CC, Sp; 12ac; **D, F, PU, 4x4; B3, Spc: Jeep**
Winston-Salem; A & J Salvage, 7224 Old Lexington Rd, 27107; 336-785-0045, FAX 336-785-2486, 800-908-4636; CC, Sp; 12ac; D, F, PU, 4x4; B3; 2 locations
A-1 Auto Salvage, *see Late Vintage*

Watch your children and companions - Remember you may be held responsible for any damage they do.

Yard Operators Tell us...

1973 Lemans GTO
Lincoln Valley Auto Salvage
Cheyenne, WY

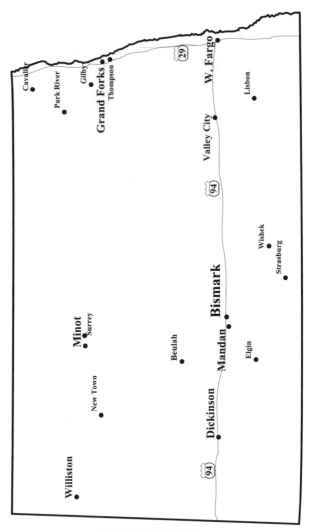

NORTH DAKOTA

<u>*VINTAGE*</u>
Beulah; Walker's Garage, HC3 Box 38, 58523; 701-873-4489; Sa, Sp, Br; 37ac, 3500+;
49-70; D; B3; Edsel
Cavalier; I & H Auto Repair & Salvage, RR2, 58220; 701-265-4563; Sa, Sp, UR; **60-90; D;
GM, Chr, Hd**
Grand Forks; Swangler Auto Wrecking, Hwy 2 W, 58201; 701-775-4044; Sa, Sp; 1200; **65+;
D, PU, 4x4; B3**
Mandan; Berg's Used Auto & Truck Parts, 1818 40 Av SE, 58554; 701-663-6492, FAX
701-663-2552, 800-654-6491; CC, Sp; 3ac; **60-90; D, F, PU, 4x4, Trk; B3; 60-70s Pickup**
   Johnson's Wrecking Used & Rebuilt Auto & Truck Parts, 2295 Hwy 10, 58554;
701-663-3957; Sa, Sp, UR, PL; 20ac; **50+; D, F, PU, 4x4, Trk; B3, AMC, Jp, VW**
New Town; LA Wrecking/Salvage, PO Box 815, 58763; 701-862-3363; Sp; 500+; **60-89; D,
F, PU; B3, AMC, Jp, St, VW**

228

Park River; Porter Auto Repair & Salvage, Rt 1 Box 180, 58270; 701-284-6517; Sa, Sp, Br; 15ac, 2000+; **50-75; D, PU, 4x4, Trk; B3, Hd, Ns, St, Pk, Ks, Fr; some Ford Model A & T**
Surrey; Swartwout Auto Salvage, 3301 153rd St NE, 58785; 701-728-6572; Sa, UR; 2500+; **55-90; D, F, PU, 4x4, Trk; B3, AMC, Jp, IH; Spc: Pickup**
West Fargo; Hazer's Auto & Truck Slvg, 811 9 St NE, 58078; 701-282-0441, FAX 701-277-9296, 800-343-6673; CC, Sa, Sp, UR; 10,000+; **50+; D, F, PU; B3, AMC, Ns, St, Pk, Wy**
Williston; Pete's Truck & Salvage, Hwy 2 W, 58801; 701-572-2373, FAX, 800-735-5983; Sa, Sp, Wr; **50+; D, F, PU, 4x4, Trk, Fm; B3, IH; Foreign in Pickup & Truck only**
Wishek; Martell's Salvage, 8045 Hwy 3 SE, 58495; 701-452-2339; Sa, Sp; 3000; **20-89; D, PU, 4x4, Trk, Fm; B3, AMC, Jp, IH, Hd, Ns, St, Ks, Fr, Wy; Antique Tractor**
　Railes Auto & Parts, Hwy 13, 58495; 701-452-2726; Sp; **55-83 D, PU, Trk; B3 Pickup & Truck only**

LATE VINTAGE

Bismark; Don's Auto Salvage, 3312 Franklin Av, 58501; 701-258-2166; Sa, UR; 50; **70-85; D, PU, 4x4, Trk, Fm; B3**
Cavalier; I & H Auto Repair & Salvage, *see Vintage*
Dickinson; Rummel's Auto Wrecking, 1132 W Villard St, 58601; 701-225-3362, FAX 701-225-1064; Sa, Sp; 8ac, 500+; **75-90; D, F, PU; B3, AMC, Jp, VW**
Elgin; Hank's General Repair & Used Auto Parts, RR 1 Box 61, 58533; 701-584-2640; Sa, Sp, UR; 75+; **70-85; D, PU, 4x4; B3**
Grand Forks; Swangler Auto Wrecking, *see Vintage*
Lisbon; Wil's Body Shop & Auto Salvage, 6807 Hwy 32 S, 58054; 701-683-4848, FAX 701-683-5364, 800-640-7751; CC, Sa, Br; 12ac; **78+; D, PU, 4x4; B3; Cougar, T-Bird, Pickup**
Mandan; Berg's Used Auto & Truck Parts, *see Vintage*
　Johnson's Wrecking Used & Rebuilt Auto & Truck Parts, *see Vintage*
New Town; LA Wrecking/Salvage, *see Vintage*
Park River; Porter Auto Repair & Salvage, *see Vintage*
Surrey; Swartwout Auto Salvage, *see Vintage*
Thompson; J & S Auto Wrecking, 208 Pacific Av, 58278; 701-599-2711; 30; **80-90; D, PU, Trk, Fm; B3**
Valley City; Truck & Auto Salvage, Exit 292 S Frontage Rd, 58072; 701-845-3080, FAX 701-845-3080, 800-922-8733; CC, Sa, Sp, UR; 900+; **70+; D, PU, 4x4; B3, AMC, Jp**
West Fargo; Hazer's Auto & Truck Salvage, *see Vintage*
Williston; Pete's Truck & Salvage, *see Vintage*
Wishek; Martell's Salvage, *see Vintage*
　Railes' Auto & Parts, *see Vintage*

LATE MODEL

Gilby; Freeberg Auto Salvage, RR 1 Box 55-D, 58235; 701-869-2409; Sa; 7ac, 250; **D, PU, 4x4; B3; some older parts**
Grand Forks; Swangler Auto Wrecking, see *Vintage*
Lisbon; Wil's Body Shop & Auto Salvage, see *Late Vintage*
Mandan; Johnson's Wrecking Used & Rebuilt Auto & Truck Parts, see Vintage
Minot; Action Auto, 1215 Valley St, 58701; 701-852-2470, FAX 701-838-7627, 800-533-5904; CC, Sa, Sp, Br; 4ac, 250+; **D, F, PU, 4x4; B3, AMC, Jp, IH, VW, Eur, Jpa**
New Town; Lakeview Wrck, Hwy 23E, 58763; 701-627-3898; Sa, UR; 100+; **D, PU, 4x4**
Park River; Porter Auto Repair & Salvage, *see Vintage*
Strasburg; Ken's Auto Body & Sales, 95 N 2nd St, 68573; 701-336-7563, FAX 701-336-7792, 800-950-1402; CC, Sa, PL; 30ac, 300+; **D, F, PU, 4x4, Trk; Spc: Big GM cars**
Valley City; Truck & Auto Salvage, see *Late Vintage*
West Fargo; Hazer's Auto & Truck Salvage, *see Vintage*
　Seventh Av Auto Salvage, 402 42nd St NW, 58078; 701-282-6315, FAX 701-281-8688, 800-729-5130; CC, Sa, Sp, UR; 2000+; **D, F, PU, 4x4**
Williston; A 1 New & Used Auto Parts, 58801; 701-774-8315, FAX 701-774-0310, 800-735-4907; CC, Sa, Sp, UR; 14ac, 1500; **D, F, PU, 4x4**
　Pete's Truck & Salvage, *see Vintage*

Ohio

Please use the cards in the back to let us know about yards we may have missed, or any other comments or information for future editions of Ray's wReckingyard Roster

OHIO

VINTAGE

Ashtabula; Budget Auto Parts, 6015 Woodman Av, 44004; 440-992-1111, FAX 440-998-3600, budget@alltel.net; CC, Sa, Sp, Br; 500; **60-90; D, F, PU, 4x4, Trk; B3, AMC, Jp, IH, VW**

Bedford; Berger Scrap Metal Auto Parts, 23659 Broadway Av, 44146; 440-232-3177, FAX 440-468-5892; Sa, Sp, UR; 75; **56-74; D; B3; Muscle Car**

Burbank; Burbank Automotive & Salvage, 15586 Franchester Rd, 44214; 330-948-2384; Sa, Br; 7ac; **37-93; D, F, PU, 4x4; B3, few AMC, Jp, IH, VW**

Cleveland; Davis Salvage, 54456 Lake Ct, 44114; 216-391-1051; Sa, Sp; .75ac; **40-88; D, few F, PU, 4x4; B3, AMC, Jp, IH, VW**

Fulton Auto Wrecking, 2300 Fulton Rd, 44113; 216-651-2727; CC, Sa, Sp, UR; 300; **59-94; D, F, PU, 4x4, Fm; B3, AMC, Jp, IH, VW**

Miles Av Auto Wrecking, 14114 Miles Av, 44128; 216-921-7171; Sa, Sp, Br; 500; **53-90; D, F, PU, 4x4, Trk; B3, AMC, Jp, IH, VW**

Columbia Station; Chink's Auto Wrecking, 27133 Sprague Rd, 44028; 440-235-4100; Sa, Sp, UR; 3ac; **50-93; D, F, PU, 4x4; B3, AMC, Jp, IH**

Columbus; All City Auto Wrecking, 1547 Joyce Av, 43219; 614-294-2556, FAX 614-294-8566; CC, Sa, Br; 2000; **30-95; D, F, PU, 4x4, Trk; B3, AMC, Jp, IH, Hd, Ns, St, Pk, Ks, Cr, Wy, VW**

Columbus Grove; Steel's Wrecking Yard, 8143 State Rt 12, 45830; 419-659-5992; Sa, Sp Br; 1200; **60+; D, few F, PU, 4x4, Trk; B3, AMC, Jp, IH**

Conneaut; Ed Matt Auto Wreckers, 4399 E Center St, 44030; 440-593-4714; Sa, UR; 670+; **47+; D, F, PU, 4x4, Trk; B3, AMC, Jp, IH**

Crestline; Moyer's Auto Wrckng, 731 Bauer Av, 44827; 419-683-2255, FAX 419-683-4726; CC, Sa, Sp, Br; 5000; **30+; D, F, PU, 4x4, Trk; B3, AMC, Jp, IH, Hd, Ns, St, Pk**

Dayton; Mr Mustang, 5088 Wolf Creek Pike, 45426; 937-275-7439, FAX 937-275-4346, 800-543-9195; CC, Sa, Sp; 80; **64.5+; D; Ford Mustang only; Used, NOS & Reproduction parts; Restoration done**

Delaware; Colonial Automotive Recycling, 5427 State Rt 37 E, 43015; 740-369-9886, FAX 740-363-3734, 800-369-9274; CC, Sa, Sp, UR; 11ac, 800; **66+; D, F, PU, 4x4, Trk, Cn, In, Mil; B3, AMC, Jp, IH, VW**

Dover; Speedie Auto Salvage, 6995 Eberhart Rd NW, 44622; 330-878-5531, FAX 330-878-5532, 800-334-9683; CC, Sa, Sp; 26ac; **50+, few prewar; D, F, PU, 4x4, Trk; B3, AMC, Jp, IH, VW**

Elyria; Universal Joint Auto Wrckng, 411 Oberlin Rd, 44035; 440-322-5220, FAX call first, 800-776-9711; Sa, Sp, UR; 17ac **60+; D, F, PU, 4x4; B3, AMC, Jp, IH, VW; few Muscle cars**

Fostoria; Boneyard, 401 Columbus Av, 44830; 419-435-5717; Sa by appointment, UR; 300; **50-79; D, few F, PU; B3; Spc: Ford Pickup**

Frazeysburg; Minnich Auto Wrecking, 6840 Hedge Ln, 43822; 740-828-2091; Sa, UR; 1200+; **40-79, few 80s; D, few F, PU, 4x4, Trk; B3, AMC, Jp, IH, Hd, Pk, Ks, Fr**

Garrettsville; Kohler Auto Wrecking, 10545 Bancroft Rd, 44231; 440-548-5817; CC, Sa, Sp, UR; 1ac; **60-89; D, few F, PU, 4x4; Trk, In, Cn; B3; Spc: Domestic Pickup & 4x4**

Geneva; American Auto Tow & Slvg, 2630 Walter Main Rd, 44041; 440-466-1619, FAX 440-474-4948, 800-436-4256; CC, Sa, Sp, UR, PL; 11+ac; **50+; D, F, PU, 4x4; B3, AMC, Jp**

Harlem Springs; Moe's Auto Wrecking, 5041 Parlay Rd SE, 44631; 330-739-3141, 800-416-3416; Sa, UR; 12.5ac; **60+; D, F, PU, 4x4, Trk; B3, AMC, Jp, IH, VW**

Holland; Spud's Auto Parts, 614 S Crissey Rd, 43528; 419-865-5755; CC, Sa, Sp, Br; 50ac; **65-91; D, F, PU, 4x4; B3**

Kent; Boyles Automotive, 1641 Brady Lake Rd, 44240; 330-673-5891; Sa; 7ac; **70+, few 60s; D, F, PU, 4x4; B3**

Lancaster; Derr's Auto Salvage, 670 S Columbus St, 43130; 740-681-9689; Sa, UR; 500; **75-90, few 40-74; D, F, PU, 4x4; B3, AMC**

Lima; Belmont Auto Wrecking, 901 Findlay Rd, 45801; 419-222-4961, FAX 419-224-2530, 800-398-3487; CC, Sa, Sp, Br; 200; **80+, few 50-70 ; D, few F, PU, 4x4; B3**

231

Hartman's Wrecker Svc, 1596 Neubracht Rd, 45801; 419-229-8342; Sa, UR; 15ac; **45+; D, F, PU, 4x4, Trk, Fm, Cn, Mil; B**3**, AMC, Jp, IH, Hd, St, VW**

T & T Auto Parts, 1530 Neubrecht Rd, 45801; 419-228-3551, FAX 419-228-4432; Sa, Sp, Br; 3ac; **31+; D, PU; B**3**, Pk, Ks; Spc: 47-61 Cadillac; Does restoration**

Lodi; Tons of Parts, 9400 Jamison Rd, 44254; 330-948-2567; UR; 100+; **30+; D, few F, PU, 4x4; B**3

Lorain; City View Auto Wrecking, 3705 Elyria Av, 44055; 440-233-8953, FAX 440-327-3066, dwcater99@hotmail.com; Sa, Sp, UR; 5ac; **40+; D, F, PU, 4x4; B**3

Lowellville; Ruozzo's Auto Salvage, 51 Lowellville Rd, 44436; 330-536-8140; Sa, Sp, UR, PL; 100; **50-85; D, F, PU, 4x4; B**3

Macedonia; Michael's Auto Parts, 9566 N Bedford Rd, 44056; 330-467-3159, FAX 330-468-2332, 800-327-6492; CC, Sa, Sp, Br; **50+; 40-89; D, PU; B**3

Mansfield; 4-H Auto Salvage, 501 Cairns Rd, 44903; 419-524-1566; Sa, Sp, UR; 500; **50-90; D, PU, 4x4, Trk; B**3**, AMC**

Maple Heights; Deneman's Automotive, 5401 Dunham Rd, 44137; 216-662-6103; Sa, Sp, UR; 150; **55+; D, F, PU, 4x4, Mil; B**3**, AMC**

Miamisburg; Alotta Auto Parts, 8426 Upper Miamisburg Rd, 45342; 937-866-1849, FAX 937-866-6431; Sa, Sp, UR; 6ac; **50-89; D, few F, PU; B**3**; Spc: Chevy & Ford**

Stark Wrecking, 7081 Germantown Pike, 45342; 937-866-5032; Sa, Sp, UR; 50ac; **30-90; D, PU, 4x4, Trk, Fm, Cn; B**3**, AMC, Jp, IH**

Milian; Bob's Auto Wrecking, 12602 Rt 13, 44846; 419-499-2415, bobsauto@accnorwalk. com; Sa, Sp, UR; 40ac; 5000; **60+; D, F, PU, 4x4; B**3

Mount Gilead; Beck's Auto Wrecking, 6983 Township Rd 91, 43338; 419-362-3551; Sa, UR; 50ac; **50-90; D, F, PU, 4x4, few Trk; B**3

Nelsonville; Valley View Auto Parts, 16480 Pancake Rd, 45764; 740-753-2364; CC, Sa, Sp; 11ac; **60-89; D, F, PU, 4x4, Trk; B**3**, AMC, Jp, few VW bus**

New Lexington; 13 Auto Salvage, 4161 State Rt 13 NE, 43764; 740-342-5000; Sa; 200; **60+; D, F, PU, 4x4; B**3**, AMC, Jp, IH, VW**

New Philadelphia; Howenstine Auto Salvage, 1396 Steele Hill Rd NW, 44663; 330-339-1606; Sp, Br; 500; **38+; D, few F, PU, Trk, Fm, Cn; B**3**, Jp, IH, VW**

Wainwright Auto Parts, 562 Wainwright Rd SE, 44663; 330-339-2703; Sp, Br; 1000; **49+; D, few F, PU, 4x4; B**3

New Vienna; AAA Collins Towing & Salvage, 256 Elm, 45159; 937-987-2873, FAX 937-987-0128, kcollins@intouch.net; UR; 3ac; **57+; D, F, PU, 4x4; B**3

North Ridgeville; Burnworth Auto Wrecking, 7218 Case Rd, 44039; 440-327-3066; Sa, UR; 100; **60-90; D, F, PU, 4x4; B**3**, AMC, Jp, IH, VW**

Painesville; A-1 Auto Recycling, 1580 N Ridge Rd, 44077; 440-357-7593, FAX 440-357-1810, 800-357-7593; CC, Sa, Sp, UR; 6ac, 500+; **85+m few 60-84; D, F, PU, 4x4; B**3**, AMC, Jp, IH, VW**

Perry; Great Lakes Auto, 4990 Lane Rd, 44081; 440-951-4000, FAX 440-953-4906; Sa, Sp, UR; 25ac, 3000; **70-90, few 30-60s; D, F, PU, 4x4, Trk, Fm, Cn; B**3**, AMC, Jp, IH, VW**

Rockford; Ketchum Auto Wrecking, 5159 Shelley Rd, 45882; 419-363-2007; CC, Sa, UR; 150+; **80+, few 40-70s; D, few F, PU, 4x4; B**3**; Spc: GM & Ford**

Saint Marys; Fisher Auto Wrecking, 3520 Celina Rd, 45885; 419-394-4704; Sa, Sp, Br; 2ac; **80+; D, few F, PU, 4x4; B**3

St Marys Auto Salvage, 14974 State Rt 116, 45885; 419-394-3418; Sa, UR; 4ac; **50+; D, F, PU, 4x4, Trk; B**3**, AMC, Jp, IH, VW; boats; Open Sunday**

Salem; All Chevy Auto, 3772 Conkle Rd, 44460; 330-332-9830; CC, Sa, Sp; 200; **64-72; D; Chevy; Spc: Chevelle, El Camino, Monte Carlo**

Hilltop Auto Wrecking, 3544 McCracken Rd, 44460; 330-332-1998; Sa; 6ac; **40-85; D, PU, 4x4; B**3**, St; Spc: Chevy**

Sandusky; Big Krome Auto, 4219 W Bogart Rd, 44870; 419-626-4433; Sa, Sp; 8ac; **63+; D, few F, PU, 4x4, Motorhomes; B**3**, Jp**

Sidney; B & B Truck & Auto Parts, 2470 Tawawa Maplewood Rd, 45365; 937-492-7330 or 492-7965; Sa, Br; 1000; **50-88; D, few F, PU, 4x4, Trk; B**3**, Jp, IH, few Wy; Spc: 4x4**

232

Strongsville; B & O Auto Parts, 21487 Royalton Rd, 44136; 440-238-7391, FAX 440-238-2822; CC, Sa, Sp, UR; 500; **60-90; D, F, PU, 4x4, Trk; B**3**, Jp, IH, VW**

Swanton; Shaffer Road Auto Parts, 12055 Shaffer Rd, 43558; 419-826-8246; Sa, Sp, UR; 5ac; **60-90; D, PU, 4x4, Trk; B**3

Toledo; A & D Auto Parts & Repair, 5846 N Detroit Av, 43612; 419-476-4772, FAX 419-269-1182; Sa, UR; 15ac; **65+; D, F, PU; B**3**; Spc: Late Model Chevy Pickup**

Ray's Wrecking Auto & Truck, 998 Whittier St, 43609; 419-243-7327, FAX 419-389-1628; Sa; 3ac; **57-89; D, F, PU, 4x4, Trk, Fm, Cn; B**3

Washington Court House; Cartwright Salvage, 839 Bogus Rd NE, 43160; 740-335-0357; Sa, Sp; 30+ac; **50-87; D, F, PU, 4x4, In, Cn; B**3**, AMC, Jp, IH, Ns, Wy, VW**

West Manchester; American Parts Depot, 409 N Main St, 45382; 937-678-7249, FAX 937-678-5886, www.americanpartsdepot.com; CC, Sp; 180; **60-88; D; AMC & Rambler only**

Westerville; Del-Car Used Auto Parts, 6650 Harlen Rd, 43081; 614-882-0777, FAX 614-895-1399, 800-732-8502; CC, Sp, Br, Wr; 12ac, 700; **65+; D, F, PU, 4x4; B**3**, AMC, Jp, VW**

Windham; A-1 Auto Wrckng, 8466 Freedom Rd, 44288; 330-297-1842, FAX 330-297-1847; Sa, UR; 800+; **77-89, few 3**5**-76; D, F, PU, 4x4; B**3**, Pk, Saab, Corvair, Javalin**

Wooster; Tom's Salvage, 4499 E Lincoln Way, 44691; 330-264-4747; Sa, UR; 15ac; **63+; D, F, PU, 4x4, Trk; B**3**, AMC, Jp, IH**

Xenia; Dayton Xenia Auto Parts, 1094 Cincinnati Av, 45385; 937-426-3807; CC, Sa; 28ac; **60+; D, F, PU, 4x4; B**3**, AMC, Jp, IH**

Youngstown; Chuck's Auto Wrecking, 1849 Waverly Av, 44509; 330-799-6204; Sa, UR; **34+; D, few F, PU; B**3

Schulte Auto Wrecking, 3737 Logangate Rd, 44505; 330-759-9500; Sa, UR; 35ac; **40+; D, F, PU, 4x4; B**3**, AMC, Jp, Hd, Ns, St, Pk; Spc: Chrysler & Cadillac**

Tippers-Tipron Auto, 1685 Cherry St, 44506; 330-744-2518; Sa; 300+; **50-90; D, F, PU, few 4x4; B**3

Zanesville; Ron's Auto Parts, 3590 Center Rd, 43081; 740-453-7234, FAX 740-453-0048, ahall@msmisp.com; Sa, Sp, Br; 3000; **60+; D, F, PU, 4x4, Trk, In, Cn; B**3

LATE VINTAGE

Akron; Akron Airport Auto Parts, 1493 Triplett Blvd, 44306; 330-733-2254, FAX 330-733-7891; CC, Sa; 300+; **78-90; D, F, PU; B**3

East Side Auto Recycling, 2915 Mogadore Rd, 44312; 330-784-6029, FAX 330-784-0044; CC, Sa, Sp; 300+; **70+; D, F, PU; B**3

Kenmore Auto Parts & Wrecking, 1554 Kenmore Blvd, 44314; 330-753-4211; Sa; 100; **80-93; D, F; B**3

Lakes Auto Recycling, 566 Kenmore Blvd, 44314; 330-753-2286, FAX 330-753-0341, 800-441-3317; CC, Sa; 1500; **67+; D, F, PU; B**3**, VW**

Moon's Auto Recycling, 1958 Firestone Pky, 44301; 330-724-1560; Sa, Sp, UR; 600; **80+; D, F, PU; B**3

Morgan Auto Wrecking, 838 S Arlington St, 44306; 330-724-2713; CC, Sa; **80+; D, F; B**3

Alger; Henderson's Country Auto Supply, 677 Township Rd 100, 45812; 419-757-6840; CC, Sp; 300+; **70+; D, F, PU, 4x4, Trk; B**3**, Jp**

Alliance; A & J Riverside Auto Ctr, 22150 Alliance Sebring Rd, 44601; 330-823-2022; Sa; 300+; **70-90; D, F, PU; B**3

Conrand's, 22650 Alliance Sebring Rd, 44601; 330-823-2555; **70-89; D, F; B**3

Andover; A Ds Auto Wrecking, 2290 Pymatuning Lake Rd, 44003; 440-293-7531; CC, Sa, Sp, UR; 400; **70+; D, F, PU, 4x4, Trk, Fm, In, Cn, Mil; B**3**, AMC, Jp, IH, VW**

Ashley; Rusk Auto Parts, 6677 State Rt 229 E, 43003; 740-747-2231, FAX 740-747-2458, 800-843-3537 or 686-8811; CC, Sp, Br; 3000; **80+; D, F, PU, 4x4, Trk; B**3**, AMC, Jp, VW**

Ashtabula; Budget Auto Parts, *see Vintage*

G & H Motor Sales & Wrck, 2021 Maryland Av, 44004; 440-997-1541, FAX 440-997-2006, 800-526-8999; CC, Sa, Sp, Br; 350+; **80+; D, F, PU, 4x4, Trk; B**3**, AMC, Jp, VW**

Barberton; Chuck's Auto Wrecking, 338 S Van Buren Av, 44203; 330-745-6632; Sa, UR; 5ac, 400; **70-94; D, F, PU, 4x4; B**3**, AMC**

Bedford; Berger Scrap Metal Auto Parts, *see Vintage*

Bowling Green; E & M Recycling, 12795 S Dixie Hwy, 43402; 419-352-0019; Sa, Br; 50; **70-89; D; B3**
Brookville; Overpass Auto Parts, 11794 National Rd, 45309; 937-833-4808; Sa, UR; 400; **80+; D, F, PU, 4x4, Trk; B3, AMC**
Bucyrus; Knecht's Auto Recycling, 1045 W Mansfield St, 44820; 419-562-9932; CC, Sa, UR; 100+; **79-89; D; B3, AMC**
Burbank; Burbank Automotive & Salvage, *see Vintage*
Burghill; Horodyski Bro, 5137 Youngstown Conneticut Rd, 44404; 330-772-3714, FAX 330-772-9009, 800-669-4512; CC, Sa, Sp, Br; 15; **80+; D, F, PU, 4x4; B3, AMC, Jp, IH, VW**
Cadiz; Cadiz Drive-In Used Auto Parts, 45700 Cadiz Harrisville Rd, 43907; 740-942-3607; CC, Sp; 200; **80-90; D, F, PU, 4x4; B3, AMC, Jp, IH, VW**
Canton; Canton Auto Salvage, 1434 7th St NE, 44704; 330-453-3888; CC, Sa, UR; 500; **80+; D, F, PU, 4x4, Trk; B3, AMC**
    Fosnaught Auto Parts, 6025 Whipple Av NW, 44720; 330-494-1251, FAX 330-494-8570; CC, Sa, Sp, Br; 300; **80+; D, F, PU, 4x4; B3, AMC, Jp**
Cincinnati; Carthage Auto Prt, 433 W North Bend Rd, 45216; 513-761-4887, FAX 513-761-0209, 800-437-5715, www.carthageauto.com; CC, Sa, Sp, Br; 18ac; **80+; D, F, PU, 4x4; B3**
Circleville; Circleville Auto Wrecking, 21239 US Hwy 23 N, 43113; 740-474-3125, FAX 740-474-3083, 800-257-1548; CC, Sa, Sp; 40ac; **80+; D, F, PU, 4x4, Trk; B3, AMC, Jp, IH**
Cleveland; Buckeye Woodland Auto Wrecking, 8322 Buckeye Rd, 44104; 216-421-2500, FAX 216-421-1663; Sa, UR; 200; **80-90; D, F, PU, 4x4; B3, AMC, Jp, IH, VW**
    Cleveland American Auto Co, 17201 Saint Clair Av, 44110; 216-531-6444, FAX 216-531-3447; CC, Sa, Sp, Br; 300; **77-90; D, F; B3, AMC; Cars only**
    Collinwood Auto Wrecking, 17605 Saint Clair Av, 44110; 216-486-1220, FAX 216-338-7244; CC, Sa; 4ac; **70+; D, PU, 4x4; B3, AMC**
    Davis Salvage, *see Vintage*
    Door-Man, 7591 Cecelia Dr, 44134; 440-845-3667, FAX 330-273-8505; Sa, Sp; **80+; D; GM & Ford doors only for body shops**
    Eddies Towing Svc, 10223 Miles Av, 44105; 216-883-6605; Sa, Sp, UR; 100; **80-91; D, F, PU, 4x4; B3, AMC, Jp, IH, VW**
    Fulton Auto Wrecking, *see Vintage*
    Lexington Towing, 4900 Lexington Av, 44103; 216-391-2225; Sa, Sp, Br, Wr; 35+; **80+; D, PU, 4x4; B3, AMC**
    McMahans Wrecking, 3378 W 65th St, 44102; 216-961-8500, FAX 216-961-8249; CC, Sa, UR; 7.5ac, 3000+; **80+; D, F, PU, 4x4, Trk; B3, AMC, Jp, IH**
    Miles Av Auto Wrecking, *see Vintage*
    Republic A-1 Auto Parts, 3210 E 65th St, 44127; 216-271-4200; CC, Sa, Sp, Br; 6.5ac, 450+; **80-94; D, F, PU, 4x4; B3, AMC, Jp, IH, VW**
    Sass Auto & Wrecking, 2487 W 25th St, 44113; 216-696-7636; CC, Sa, Sp; **80-90; D, F, PU, 4x4; B3, VW**
    Tim's Cars & Parts, 5307 Denison Av, 44102; 216-391-3050; Sa; **70-90; D; B3, AMC**
Clyde; B & K Auto Svc, 983 N Woodland Av, 43410; 419-547-9843; Sa, Sp, UR; **80+; D, F, PU, 4x4, Trk, Fm, Cn, Mil; B3, AMC, Jp, IH**
Coldwater; Graveyard II Auto Parts, 3383 Kuhn Rd, 45828; 419-586-1367; Sa; 4000; **80-93; D, F, PU, 4x4, Trk, In; B3, AMC, Jp, IH**
Columbia Station; Chink's Auto Wrecking, *see Vintage*
    D & B Auto Wrecking, 11097 Jaquay Rd, 44028; 440-236-8247; CC, Sa, Sp, UR; 3.5ac, 200+; **82+, few 70s; D, F, PU, 4x4; B3, AMC, few Jp; Spc: 70s Ford SUV**
Columbiana; Ohio Auto Sales & Salvage, 42083 State Rt 344, 44408; 330-482-4100, FAX 330-482-1231, 800-332-1980; CC, Sa, Sp; 1500; **80+; D, F, PU, 4x4, Trk; B3, AMC**
Columbus; Ace Iron & Metal, 2515 Groveport Rd, 43207; 614-443-5196; CC, Sa, UR; 700; **70-90; D, F, PU, 4x4; B3, AMC, Jp, IH**
    All City Auto Wrecking, *see Vintage*
    All Foreign Used Auto Parts, 1559 McKinley Av, 43222; 614-276-9359, FAX 614-276-9932, 800-541-6344, all4nauto@aol.com; CC, Sa, Sp, Wr; **80-90; F; Foreign only**

234

Parsons Auto Parts, 2250 Parsons Av, 43207; 614-443-7451; CC, Sa, Sp, Br; 1000; **70-95; D, F, PU, 4x4; B**3, **AMC, Jp, IH**

Columbus Grove; Steel's Wrecking Yard, *see Vintage*

Conneaut; Ed Matt Auto Wreckers, *see Vintage*

Conneaut; Northeast Auto Recyclers, 412 Middle Rd, 44030; 440-599-7078, FAX 440-593-6152; CC, Sa, Sp, Br; 8ac, 250; **70+; D, F, PU, 4x4; B**3, **AMC**

Cortland; Bob Karl's Auto Wrecking, 2315 Elm Rd NE, 44410; 330-372-4145; Sa; 600; **81+; D, F, few PU, few 4x4, few Trk; B**3, **AMC, Jp, IH**

Coshocton; Hilltop Auto Sales, 46200 State Rt 541, 43812; 740-622-4201, FAX 740-622-5555; CC, Sa, Sp; 1500; **80+; D, F, PU, 4x4, Trk; B**3, **AMC, Jp, IH; Spc: Minivan & SUV**

Crestline; Frank's Auto Wrecking, 939 E Main St, 44827; 419-683-3096; Sa, Br; 25ac, 200; **67+; D, F, PU, 4x4; B**3

Moyer's Auto Wrecking, *see Vintage*

Creston; Creston Auto Recycling, 9144 Cleveland Rd, 44217; 330-435-4441, FAX 330-435-1032, 800-210-3349; CC, Sa, Sp, Br; 1200; **80-96; D, F, PU, 4x4, Trk; B**3, **AMC, Jp, IH, VW**

Ramsier Motors, 11441 Cleveland Rd, 44217; 330-435-6351; CC, Sa; **80-90; D, F, PU, 4x4, Trk; B**3, **AMC, Jp, IH**

Dayton; Al's Auto Parts, 5940 W 3rd St, 45427; 937-263-3512, FAX 937-363-2485, 888-455-5185, elsalvage@ameritec.net; CC, Sa, Sp, Br; 22ac; **80+; D, F, PU, 4x4; B**3, **AMC, Jp, VW**

Mr Mustang, *see Vintage*

De Graff; Springhills Auto Wrecking, 9519 Carlisle Pike, 43318; 937-465-8585; Sa, UR; **74-89; D, F; B**3, **AMC**

Defiance; Vaughns Auto Salvage, 201 Hill St, 43512; 419-782-8176, FAX 419-782-1426; CC, Sa, Sp; 6ac; **80+; D, PU, 4x4; B**3; **Spc: GM**

Delaware; Colonial Automotive Recycling, *see Vintage*

Delphos; County Line Auto Wrecking, 24957 Pohlman Rd, 45833; 419-692-5853; Sa; 300; **75-90; D, F, PU, 4x4, Trk; B**3, **AMC, Jp, IH, VW**

Dover; Speedie Auto Salvage, *see Vintage*

Elyria; Butternut Ridge Wrecking, 40346 Butternut Ridge Rd, 44035; 440-458-5220; Sa, Sp, Br; 5ac; **80+; D, PU, 4x4; B**3

Sugar Ridge Auto & Truck, 41850 Oberlin Rd, 44035; 440-244-9618, FAX 440-323-5257; CC, Sa, Sp, Br; 17ac; **80+; D, F, PU, 4x4, Trk; B**3

Universal Joint Auto Wrecking, *see Vintage*

Findlay; Dick's Automotive Salvage, 4404 Township Rd 142, 45840; 419-422-7434, FAX 419-424-0034, 800-252-4712; CC, Sa, Sp, Br; 10ac; **80+; D, few F, PU, 4x4; B**3

Findlay Auto Parts, 3333 County Rd 140, 45840; 419-299-3336, FAX 419-299-1220; CC, Sa, Sp; 13ac; **78+; D, F, PU, 4x4; B**3

Fostoria; Boneyard, *see Vintage*

Frazeysburg; Minnich Auto Wrecking, *see Vintage*

Fremont; Mike's Auto Wrecking, 2430 Hayes Av, 43420; 419-332-7600; CC, Sa, Sp, UR; 2300; **70-89; D, few F, PU, 4x4; B**3

Galion; Bowman Salvage, 8687 State Rt 19, 44833; 419-468-6670; Sa, Br; 300; **68+; D, PU, 4x4; B**3

St James Auto & Truck Wrecking, 3852 County Rd 51, 44833; 419-468-1541, FAX 419-462-8832; Sa, Sp, Br; 10ac; **66+; D, F, PU, 4x4; B**3

Garrettsville; Kohler Auto Wrecking, *see Vintage*

Geneva; American Auto Towing & Salvage, *see Vintage*

Grafton; Reed's Salvage, 36521 Royalton Rd, 44044; 440-748-2016; Sa; 58ac; **80+; D, F, PU, 4x4, few Trk; B**3

Greenville; Trent Auto Parts, 6496 US Rt 36, 45331; 937-548-1308, 800-206-5605; Sa, Sp; 6ac; **80+; F, PU; 2 yards**

Harlem Springs; Moe's Auto Wrecking, *see Vintage*

Hillsboro; C & G Towing, 239 W North St, 45133; 937-393-5609; Sa; 4ac; **70+; D, F, PU, 4x4; B**3

235

Holland; Spud's Auto Parts, *see Vintage*
Hopewell; Mt Sterling Auto Wrecking, 565 Flint Ridge Rd, 43746; 740-452-7313, 800-559-5893; Sa, UR; 2ac; **70+; D, F, PU, 4x4, Trk; B**3
Jefferson; Roy's Auto Recycling, 941 S Chestnut, 44047; 440-576-9525, FAX 440-576-6111, 888-576-9526; CC, Sa, Sp, Br; 12ac; **70-90; D, F, PU, 4x4**
Johnstown; Jim Houck's Auto Parts & Garage, 3634 Sportsman Club Rd, 43031; 740-967-5116; Sa; 14ac; **78-90; D, PU, 4x4, Trk; B**3
Kent; Boyles Automotive, *see Vintage*
Kinsman; Countryside Salvage, 6542 Orangeville Kinsman Rd, 44428; 330-876-6700; Sa; 200; **70-92, few earlier; D, few F, PU, 4x4, Trk, Fm, Cn; B**3
Lancaster; Derr's Auto Salvage, *see Vintage*
 Hines Auto Wrecking, 7005 Hopewell Church Rd SW, 43130; 740-969-2014; Sa, UR; 400+; **68+; D, F, PU, 4x4; B**3
Leavittsburg; Chet's Auto Wrecking, 561 N Leavitt Rd, 44430; 330-898-1030; Sa, Sp, Wr; 150; **70-89; D, PU, 4x4; B**3
Lima; Belmont Auto Wrecking, *see Vintage*
 Bible Road Auto Wrck, 505 Bible Rd, 45801; 419-222-7955; Sa; 11ac; **80s; D, few F; B**3
 Hartman's Wrecker Svc, *see Vintage*
 Midwest Ohio Auto Parts, 4893 S Dixie Hwy, 45806; 419-991-0908, 800-589-6830; Sa, Wr; **73+; D, F; After Market Parts: Sheet metal, glass, lights etc**
 Perry Auto Wrecking, 4185 Saint Johns Rd, 45806; 419-221-2886, FAX 419-222-7904, 800-356-4586; CC, Sp; 22ac; **75-94; D, F, PU, 4x4, Trk; B**3
 T & T Auto Parts, *see Vintage*
Lisbon; Bower's Auto Salvage, 14011 E Liverpool Rd, 44432; 330-385-3380, FAX 330-385-5144; Sa, Sp, Br; 1200; **70+; D, few F, few PU**
Lodi; Tons of Parts, *see Vintage*
Lorain; American Auto Wrecking, 3618 Elyria Av, 44055; 440-233-6131, FAX 440-233-4588; CC, Sa, Sp; 300; **80+, few 70s; D, F, PU, 4x4; B**3
 Lowes Auto Wrck, 4276 Maple rd, 44055; 440-277-4533; Sa, Sp; **77+; D, F, PU, 4x4; B**3
 Top Notch Auto Wrecking, 3761 Ada Av, 44055; 440-233-7445; Sa, UR; 100; **70+; D, F, PU, 4x4, few Trk; B**3
 City View Auto Wrecking, *see Vintage*
Lowellville; Ruozzo's Auto Salvage, *see Vintage*
Macedonia; Michael's Auto Parts, *see Vintage*
Malvern; Fox Auto Salvage & Parts, 7140 Alliance Rd NW, 44644; 330-863-1011, 800-228-6159, foxautosalvage.com; CC, Sa, Sp, Br; 36ac; **80+, few 70s; D, F, PU, 4x4; B**3, **AMC, Jp, IH**
Mansfield; 4-H Auto Salvage, *see Vintage*
 Bowman Auto Recycling, 1501 Bowman St, 44903; 419-747-6615; CC, Sa, Sp, Br; 400+; **70+; D, F, PU, 4x4, Trk, Fm (trk); B**3, **AMC, Jp, IH, VW, Jpa**
 Tucker Brothers Auto Wrecking, 760 Hickory Ln, 44905; 419-589-6464, 800-628-6464; CC, Sa, Sp, Br; 4000; **75+; D, F, PU, 4x4, Trk; B**3, **AMC, VW**
Maple Heights; Deneman's Automotive, *see Vintage*
Marengo; Auto & Truck Recycling, 5724 State Rt 229, 43334; 419-253-0403; Sa, UR; 2000; **75-93; D, F, PU, 4x4, Trk; B**3, **AMC, Jp, IH, VW**
 General Auto Sales, 3349 State Rt 229, 43334; 419-253-6175; CC, Sa, Sp, Br; 22ac; 1000+; **70-89; D, F, PU, 4x4; B**3, **AMC, Jp, IH, VW**
Marion; Bill Johnson's Auto Wrecking, 1701 White Oaks Rd, 43302; 740-382-1516; CC, Sa, Sp, Br; 500; **80+; D, F, PU, 4x4, Trk; B**3, **AMC, Jp, VW**
Miamisburg; Alotta Auto Parts, *see Vintage*
 Stark Wrecking, *see Vintage*
Middlefield; Rolland Auto Sales-Parts, 15600 Old State Rd, 44062; 440-632-0909, FAX 440-632-9007; Sa, Sp, UR; 1000; **79-89; D, F; B**3
Milian; Bob's Auto Wrecking, *see Vintage*
Mount Gilead; Beck's Auto Wrecking, *see Vintage*
Nelsonville; Valley View Auto Parts, *see Vintage*

New Lexington; 13 Auto Salvage, *see Vintage*

New Paris; G W Pierce Auto Parts, 9118 US Rt 40E, 45347; 937-437-2461, FAX 937-437-5632, 800-762-2951; CC, Sa, UR; 13ac; **84+; D, PU, 4x4; B**3, **AMC, Jp**

New Philadelphia; Howenstine Auto Salvage, *see Vintage*

Wainwright Auto Parts, *see Vintage*

New Vienna; AAA Collins Towing & Salvage, *see Vintage*

Newark; Crispin Auto Wrecking, 629 New Haven Av, 43055; 740-345-4730, FAX 740-345-9240; Sa, Sp; 400+; **80+; D, F, PU, few 4x4, few Trk, Fm; B**3, **AMC, Jp, IH, few VW**

Niles; Main Auto Wrecking, 1793 N Main St, 44446; 330-652-6441, FAX 330-652-9686; CC, Sa, Sp, UR; 500+; **70-90; D, F, PU, 4x4, Trk; B**3, **AMC, Jp, IH, VW**

North Ridgeville; Burnworth Auto Wrecking, *see Vintage*

Norwalk; Auto Wrecking 601, 4460 State Rt 601, 44857; 419-668-4949; Sa, UR; 5ac; **80-93; D, few F, PU, few 4x4; B**3, **AMC, Jp, VW**

Norwalk; US 20 Auto Parts, 1640 US Hwy 20 E, 44857; 419-668-4891; CC, Sp; 850; **80-90; D, F, PU, 4x4, Trk; B**3, **AMC**

Painesville; A-1 Auto Recycling, *see Vintage*

Perry; Great Lakes Auto Recycling, *see Vintage*

Piqua; Miami Auto Salvage, 200 Hemm Av, 45356; 937-773-3025, FAX 937-773-3089; Sa, Sp, UR; 350; **70+; D, F, PU, 4x4; B**3, **AMC, Jp, IH, VW**

Plymouth; Plymouth Auto Salvage, 8274 State Rt 61, 44865; 419-933-4923; Sa, Sp, UR; 400+; **70-90; D, PU, 4x4; B**3, **AMC, Jp, IH**

Ravenna; Kurkey Auto Wrecking, 3666 Sandy Lake Rd, 44266; 330-297-1178, FAX 330-297-9114, 800-489-8441; CC, Sa, Sp; 200; **80-93; D, F, PU, 4x4; B**3, **AMC, Jp, IH, VW**

Midway Auto Sales & Wrecking, 5824 Newton Falls Rd, 44266; 330-297-9498; Sa, UR; 300+; **78-90, few earlier; D, F, PU, 4x4; B**3, **AMC, Jp, IH**

Rockford; Ketchum Auto Wrecking, *see Vintage*

Rogers; Millrock Auto Sales & Wrecking, 48173 State Rt 154, 44455; 330-227-3444, FAX 330-325-3325; Sa, Sp; 500; **73+; D, PU; B**3

Saint Marys; Fisher Auto Wrecking, *see Vintage*

St Marys Auto Salvage, *see Vintage*

Salem; All Chevy Auto, *see Vintage*

B & E Auto Wrecking, 12550 State Rt 62 N, 44460; 330-332-0512, FAX 330-332-2141, 800-377-0587; CC, Sa, Sp, some Wr, some UR; 1000; **80+; D, F, PU; B**3; **Spc: GM & Chrysler Pickup & Van**

Hilltop Auto Wrecking, *see Vintage*

Smith Auto, 30604 Hartley Rd, 44460; 330-537-3227, FAX 330-537-3547; Sa, UR; 20ac; **67+; D, F, PU, 4x4; B**3

Sandusky; Big Krome Auto, *see Vintage*

J & D Auto Wrecking, 4605 Tiffin Av, 44870; 419-625-0673; Sa; **82+; D, PU, 4x4; B**3

Sidney; B & B Truck & Auto Parts, *see Vintage*

Spencer; Country View Auto Recycling, 12561 Chatham Rd, 44275; 330-648-2584; **75-90; D, F, PU, 4x4; B**3, **AMC, Jp, IH, VW**

Springfield; A-1 Auto Parts, 935 Dayton Rd, 45506; 937-325-5771; **70-89; D, F, PU; B**3

Strongsville; B & O Auto Parts, *see Vintage*

Sugarcreek; Sugarcreek Auto & Truck Parts, 623 Dover Rd NE, 44681; 330-852-2266, FAX 330-852-4175; CC, Sa, Sp; 2ac; **80-88; D, F, PU, 4x4; B**3

Swanton; Shaffer Road Auto Parts, *see Vintage*

Toledo; A & D Auto Parts & Repair, *see Vintage*

Bill's City Auto Parts, 106 City Park Av, 43602; 419-241-8902; CC; 2.5ac; **70+, few 60s; D, few F, PU, few 4x4; B**3; **few 60s**

Cherry Auto Parts, 5650 N Detroit Av, 43612; 419-476-7222, FAX 419-470-6388, 800-537-8677, www.cherry-auto.com; CC, Sp; 800; **70+; D, F, PU, 4x4; B**3, **Jpa, Eur; Spc: Imports & Chrysler, Jeep, Eagle**

Ray's Wrecking Auto & Truck, *see Vintage*

237

Spud's Auto Parts, 4440 N Holland Sylvania Rd, 43623; 419-882-2095; CC, Sa; **70+; D, F, PU, 4x4, Trk; B**3

Vermilion; Inter City Auto Wrecking, 8712 Cherry Rd, 44089; 440-327-3066, dwcater99@hotmail.com; Sa, Sp, UR; 1000; **76-93; D, F; B**3, **AMC, VW**

Wapakoneta; D & B Auto Parts, 17349 National Rd, 45895; 419-645-4108; 7ac; **80+; D, PU, 4x4; B**3

Washington Court House; Cartwright Salvage, *see Vintage*

West Lafayette; Sharier Auto Wrecking & Slvg, 22265 State Rt 751, 43845; 740-545-9042; Sa, UR; 7ac; **70+; D, PU, 4x4, Trk; B**3, **AMC, Jp, IH**

West Manchester; American Parts Depot, *see Vintage*

Westerville; Del-Car Used Auto Parts, *see Vintage*

Windham; A-1 Auto Wrecking & Sales, *see Vintage*

Wooster; Abe Auto Parts, 1080 S Honeytown Rd, 44691; 330-264-7793, FAX 330-262-4198; Sa, Sp; 5ac; **70+; D, few F, PU, 4x4; B**3; **Spc: Chrome bumpers from Arizona**

Tom's Salvage, *see Vintage*

Wayco Automotive, 7679 Burbank Rd, 44691; 330-345-8829, FAX 330-345-7490 call first; Sa, Sp, UR, PL; 25ac; **67+; D, F, PU, 4x4, Trk, Fm, In, Cn; B**3

Xenia; Dayton Xenia Auto Parts, *see Vintage*

Youngstown; Al's Auto Salvage, 1127 Poland Av, 44502; 330-744-3720, FAX 330-744-3747, alsautosalvage1@aol.com; Sa, Sp; 2ac; **75+; D, F, PU, 4x4, Trk, Cn; B**3

B & M Auto Wrecking, 2608 Hubbard Rd, 44505; 330-759-2541, FAX 330-759-2651, 800-450-1500; CC, Sa, Sp; 1800; **70+; D, F, PU, 4x4; B**3

Center Street Auto, 1411 Wilson Av, 44506; 330-743-1492, FAX 330-743-9902; Sa, Sp, UR; 40ac, 2500; **80+; D, F, PU, 4x4, Trk; B**3, **AMC, Jp, IH; 80+ PU in Foreign**

Chuck's Auto Wrecking, *see Vintage*

Interstate Auto Salvage, 1214 Poland Av, 44502; 330-743-6113; Sa; 15ac; **70+; D, F, PU, few 4x4; B**3

Lous Auto Wrecking, 1715 Waverly Av, 44509; 330-799-6598; Sa; **80s; D, F, PU; B**3

Passarelli Brothers Auto, 2530 Hubbard Rd, 44505; 330-747-9200; Sa; 8ac; **78-90; D, F, PU, 4x4; B**3; **Spc: GM**

Schulte Auto Wrecking, *see Vintage*

Texas Auto Wrecking, 1381 Poland Av, 44502; 330-743-2911, FAX 330-743-3991; CC, Sa, Sp; 2ac; **75-90; D, F, PU, few 4x4; B**3, **VW, Jpa**

Tippers-Tipron Auto, *see Vintage*

Zanesville; Ron's Auto Parts, *see Vintage*

LATE MODEL

Akron; Akron Auto Wrecking, 336 Kenmore Blvd, 44301; 330-434-5188, 800-458-5188; CC, Sa, Sp; 300+; **D, F, PU, 4x4**

East Side Auto Recycling, *see Late Vintage*

Kenmore Auto Parts & Wrecking, *see Late Vintage*

Lakes Auto Recycling, *see Late Vintage*

Moon's Auto Recycling, *see Late Vintage*

Morgan Auto Wrecking, *see Late Vintage*

Alger; Henderson's Country Auto Supply, *see Late Vintage*

Alliance; Broadway Auto Parts & Repair, 300 S Mahoning Av, 44601; 330-821-7278; Sa; 200+; **D, F, PU**

Andover; A Ds Auto Wrecking, *see Late Vintage*

Ashley; Rusk Auto Parts, *see Late Vintage*

Ashtabula; G & H Motor Sales & Wrecking, *see Late Vintage*

Barberton; Action Auto, 263 31st St SW, 44203; 330-825-0855, FAX 330-825-5051, 800-526-1111; CC, Sa, Sp, UR; 1000; **D, F, PU, 4x4, Trk**

All American Auto Wrecking, 111 E Tuscarawas Av, 44203; 330-753-2271; CC, Sa, Sp; 500; **D, F, PU, 4x4**

Camp Auto Salvage, 59 Snyder Av, 44203; 330-745-5579, FAX 330-745-2774, 800-745-0655; CC, Sa, Sp, Br; 200+; **D, F, PU, 4x4**

Chuck's Auto Wrecking, *see Late Vintage*

Bedford; Bedford Auto Wrecking, 7270 Division St, 44146; 440-232-6474, FAX 440-232-3140, 800-589-6474; CC, Sa, Sp, Br; 8ac, 600+; **D, F, PU, 4x4; B3, few AMC, Jp**

Frank's Automotive Supply, 5969 Lehman Dr, 44146; 440-883-4466, FAX 440-232-5631; Sp; **D, F, PU, 4x4**

Intercity Auto Wrecking, 7140 Northfield Rd, 44146; 440-439-8100, FAX 440-439-8104, 800-GET-Used, interc:tyauto@buckeyacb.com; CC, Sp; 4ac, 600+; **F**

Bloomingburg; Bennett Brothers Salvage, 66 Biddle Blvd, 43106; 740-437-7442; Sa, UR, Wr; **D, F, PU, 4x4**

Bowling Green; Dixie Auto Parts, 17581 N Dixie Hwy, 43402; 419-353-8681; CC, Sa, Sp; 150; **D, F, few PU & 4x4, few Trk**

Brookville; Overpass Auto Parts, *see Late Vintage*

Burbank; Burbank Automotive & Salvage, *see Vintage*

Burghill; Horodyski Brothers, *see Late Vintage*

Byesville; Bartholow Auto Wrecking, 59200 Marietta Rd, 43723; 740-685-2158; Sa, Sp; 23ac; **D, F, PU, 4x4, Trk, Mil, Fm, Cn, In**

Cambridge; Rayburn's Auto Wrecking, 7153 Manila Rd, 43725; 740-432-6433; CC, Sa, Sp; **D, F, PU, 4x4**

Canton; Canton Auto Salvage, *see Late Vintage*

Danny's Auto Parts, 4015 Georgetown Rd NE, 44704; 330-488-2050; Sa, UR; **D, F**

Fosnaught Auto Parts, *see Late Vintage*

Slesnick Auto Salvage, 1100 Warner Rd SE, 44707; 330-489-6690, FAX 330-489-6692, 877-284-0688; CC, Sa, Sp, UR; 2.5ac; **D, F, PU, 4x4; B3, AMC, Jp**

Carrollton; B W Auto Wrecking, 1040 Canton Rd NW, 44615; 330-627-2055; **D**

Chardon; Chardon Auto Wrecking, 10144 Old State Rd, 44024; 440-951-9163, 800-682-2959; Sp; 500; **D, F, PU, 4x4**

Chardon; Whitright Towing & Salvage, 12846 Chardon Windsor Rd, 44024; 440-285-1765; 600; **D, F**

Cincinnati; Carthage Auto Parts, *see Late Vintage*

Duck Creek Auto Parts, 4538 Kellogg Av, 45226; 513-321-9278, FAX 513-321-1060; CC, Sa, Sp; 10ac; **D, F, PU, 4x4; B3, Jp, VW**

Circleville; Circleville Auto Wrecking, *see Late Vintage*

Clarksville; Dares Clarksville Auto Parts, 9011 E State Rt 22, 45113; 937-289-2657; Sa, Sp; 12ac; **D, few F, PU, 4x4, Trk; B3**

Cleveland; A & H Auto Salvage & Towing, 13030 Broadway Av, 44125; 216-587-4942, FAX 216-587-5403; CC, Sa, Sp; 4.5ac, 500; **D, F, PU, 4x4**

ABC Auto Parts & Wrecking, 3920 Valley Rd, 44109; 216-661-3015, FAX 216-749-4965; Sa, Sp, Br; 50+; **D, F, PU, 4x4, Trk; B3, AMC**

Aetna A1 Parts & Wrck, 14312 Miles Av, 44128; 216-561-1009; CC, Sa; **D, F, PU, 4x4**

Automobile Repair Center, 14900 Miles Av, 44128; 216-751-1200; CC, Sa, Sp; 50; **D, PU, 4x4; B3, AMC, Jp**

Bessemer Auto Wrecking, 7225 Bessemer Av, 44127; 216-883-0024; Sa, UR; 1000; **D, PU, 4x4, Trk**

Broken Wheel Auto Prt, 4343 W 130 St, 44135; 216-941-4488, FAX 216-941-5004; **D, F**

Carnegie Auto Parts, 2070 E 61st St, 44103; 216-432-1530, FAX 216-432-3460, info@carnegieauto.com; CC, Sa, Sp, UR; 1ac, 200; **D, F, PU**

Collinwood Auto Wrecking, *see Late Vintage*

Denison Auto Parts, 4500 W 130th St, 44135; 216-671-9000, FAX 216-252-7033, 800-328-9001; CC, Sa, Sp; 1500; **D, F, PU, 4x4**

Door-Man, *see Late Vintage*

Eddies Towing Svc, *see Late Vintage*

Fulton Auto Wrecking, *see Vintage*

John's Towing & Used Auto Parts, 10012 Meech Av, 44105; 216-271-8555, FAX 216-271-7125; Sa, Sp, Br; 2ac; **D, F, PU, 4x4**

Lexington Towing, *see Late Vintage*

McMahans Wrecking, *see Late Vintage*

Perkin's Auto Service, 6401 Grand Av, 44104; 216-881-5444; Sa, Sp; **D, F, PU, 4x4**

Republic A-1 Auto Parts, *see Late Vintage*

Republic Auto Recycling, 14700 Miles Av, 44128; 216-561-0580; CC, Sa, Sp; 12ac, 150; **D; B3, AMC**

Ridge Road Automobile Parts, 3741 Ridge Rd, 44144; 216-281-1400, FAX 216-281-7956, 800-837-7283; CC, Sa, Sp, Br; **D, F, PU, 4x4**

Stan-Ford Motors, 13511 Miles Av, 44105; 216-751-5100, FAX 216-751-5102, 800-900-5122; CC, Sa, Sp, Br, Wr; **D, few F, PU, 4x4**

Clyde; B & K Auto Svc, *see Late Vintage*

Coldwater; Graveyard II Auto Parts, *see Late Vintage*

Columbia Station; Chink's Auto Wrecking, *see Vintage*

Cleveland Pick-A-Part, 12420 Station Rd, 44028; 440-236-5031, FAX 440-236-6150, clevelandpickapart.com; CC, Sa, Sp; 25ac; **D, F, PU, 4x4, Trk**

D & B Auto Wrecking, *see Late Vintage*

Columbiana; Ohio Auto Sales & Salvage, *see Late Vintage*

Columbus; Abe's Used Auto Parts, 1049 Joyce Av, 43219; 614-257-0800; Sa, Sp, UR; 200; **D, PU, 4x4**

All City Auto Wrecking, *see Vintage*

Buckeye Auto Parts, 2474 McKinley Av, 43204; 614-488-9773; CC, Sa, Sp; 55ac; **D, F, PU, 4x4, Trk, Cn; B3, AMC, Jp**

Cantley's Auto Salvage, 1301 Little Av # Rear, 43223; 614-274-7419; CC, Sa, Sp, UR; 6000; **D, F**

Central City Auto Parts, 1930 McKinley Av, 43222; 617-276-9617, FAX 617-276-7722, 800-357-7969, pres265@aol.com (Att: Greg); CC, Sa, Sp; 1500; **D, F, PU, 4x4**

Edison Automotive, 1529 McKinley Av, 43222; 614-274-1118, FAX 614-274-6886; CC, Sa, UR; 900; **D, F**

Parsons Auto Parts, *see Late Vintage*

Wirthman Brothers, 3515 E Main St, 43213; 614-231-2752, FAX 614-231-1968, 800-433-4364; CC, Sa, Sp, Br; 18ac, 3500; **D, F, PU, 4x4**

Woody's Auto Salvage, 1988 McKinley Av, 43204; 614-276-2597; CC, Sa, UR; 12.5ac; **D, F, PU, 4x4, Trk, Fm, Cn**

Columbus Grove; Steel's Wrecking Yard, *see Vintage*

Conneaut; Ed Matt Auto Wreckers, *see Vintage*

Conneaut; Northeast Auto Recyclers, *see Late Vintage*

Convoy; Auto Salvage, 7167 Lincoln Hwy, 45832; 419-749-2710, 800-635-8378; CC, Sa, Sp, Br; **D, PU, 4x4**

Cortland; Bob Karl's Auto Wrecking, *see Late Vintage*

Coshocton; Hilltop Auto Sales, *see Late Vintage*

Nelson's Auto Wrecking, 51118 State Rt 541, 43812; 740-622-2566; Sa, Br; 200+; **D, F, PU, 4x4, Trk, Mil**

Crestline; Frank's Auto Wrecking, *see Late Vintage*

Crestling; Moyer's Auto Wrecking, *see Vintage*

Creston; Creston Auto Recycling, *see Late Vintage*

Dayton; Al's Auto Parts, *see Late Vintage*

Moraine Auto Parts & Towing, 2833 Northlawn Av, 45439; 937-293-0703, FAX 937-278-9327; Sa, UR; 2ac; **few D, F, few PU & 4x4; Spc: Foreign**

Mr Mustang, *see Vintage*

Westside Auto Wreckers, 4167 Freudenberger Av, 45427; 937-263-2654; Sa, Sp, Br; 1500+; **D, F**

Defiance; Vaughns Auto Salvage, *see Late Vintage*

Delaware; Colonial Automotive Recycling, *see Vintage*

Dover; All Quality Import Auto Parts, 524 River St, 44622; 330-602-6751, FAX 330-602-7101, 800-251-8023, aqiparts@aol.com; CC, Sp, Wr; 300; **F; Import only; Cars dismantled and parts on shelf**

Speedie Auto Salvage, *see Vintage*

Doylestown; City Recycling, 11776 Black Diamond Rd, 44230; 330-658-6808; CC, Sa, Br; 50+; **D, F, PU, 4x4**

240

Elyria; Butternut Ridge Wrecking, *see Late Vintage*
  Sugar Ridge Auto & Truck, *see Late Vintage*
  Universal Joint Auto Wrecking, *see Vintage*
Findlay; Dick's Automotive Salvage, *see Late Vintage*
  Findlay Auto Parts, *see Late Vintage*
Galion; Bowman Salvage, *see Late Vintage*
  Carroll's Truck Parts, 2064 Nazor Rd, 44833; 419-683-2448, FAX 419-683-3665; Sa, Sp; 75ac; **Trk; Trucks only; Spc: over 2 ton**
  St James Auto & Truck Wrecking, *see Late Vintage*
Gallipolis; Tommy's Enterprises, 244 Thivener Rd, 45631; 740-446-0745; Sa, Sp, Br; 125ac; **D, F, PU, 4x4**
Geneva; American Auto Towing & Salvage, *see Vintage*
  South Western Auto Parts, 6211 N Ridge Rd W, 44041; 440-466-6819; CC, Sa, Sp; 100+; **D, F, PU, 4x4, Trk; Pickup & Truck only**
Genoa; D & R Auto Parts, 26 Main St, 43430; 419-855-7800; Sa, Br; 4ac; **D, F; Spc: GM & Ford**
Grafton; Jim's Sales, 16978 State Rt 83, 44044; 440-926-2120; Sa, UR; 7ac; **D, PU, 4x4**
  Reed's Salvage, *see Late Vintage*
Grand Rapids; Howard's Auto Parts, 1085 State Rt 65, 43522; 419-832-2853; **D, F, PU, 4x4; Spc: Domestic**
Greenville; Trent Auto Parts, 201 S Ohio St, 45331; 937-548-5605, 800-206-5605; Sa, Sp; 2.5ac; **D, PU; 2 yards**
  Trent Auto Parts, *see Late Vintage*
Grove City; Darbydale Auto Salvage, 5880 Harrisburg Georgesville Rd, 43123; 614-877-3072; Sa, Sp, UR; 100+; **D, few F, PU, 4x4; B3, AMC, few Jp**
Harlem Springs; Moe's Auto Wrecking, *see Vintage*
Hillsboro; C & G Towing, *see Late Vintage*
Holland; Dave's Crissey Road Auto Parts, 211 N Crissey Rd, 43528; 419-865-2329, FAX 419-855-1231; CC, Sa, Sp, PL; 24ac; **D, few F, PU, 4x4**
Hopewell; Miller's Auto Wrecking, 4355 Pleasant Valley Rd, 43746; 740-452-2971, FAX 740-452-1470; Sa, UR; 50ac; **D, PU, 4x4**
  Mt Sterling Auto Wrecking, *see Late Vintage*
Kent; Boyles Automotive, *see Vintage*
Kinsman; Countryside Salvage, *see Late Vintage*
  Hunter Auto Wrecking, 6908 Beach Smith Rd, 44428; 330-772-4861, FAX 330-772-5417, 800-567-1427; Sa, Sp, Br; 6ac; **D, few F, PU, 4x4; Spc: Domestic**
Kirtland; Mike's Auto Salvage, 7887 Chillicothe, 44094; 440-942-7201; Sa, UR; 400; **D, F, PU, 4x4, Trk**
Lancaster; Hines Auto Wrecking, *see Late Vintage*
  Mattox Auto Parts, 541 S Broad St, 43130; 740-654-1853; 300; **D, PU**
Lima; Auto Barn, 1635 E State Rd, 45801; 419-641-4853, FAX 419-641-7002, 800-541-5462; CC, Sp, Br; 500; **D, few F, PU, 4x4**
  Belmont Auto Wrecking, *see Vintage*
  Five Acre Auto Recycling, 1608 Findlay Rd, 45801; 419-224-5721, FAX 419-224-8294; Sa, Sp, Br; 5ac; **D, PU**
  Hartman's Wrecker Svc, *see Vintage*
  Kenny's Auto Wrecking, 1401 Findlay Rd, 45801; 419-223-0836, FAX 419-222-0037, 800-686-1871; CC, Sp, Br, PL; 5ac; **D, F, PU, 4x4**
  Midwest Ohio Auto Parts, *see Late Vintage*
  Perry Auto Wrecking, *see Late Vintage*
  T & T Auto Parts, *see Vintage*
Lisbon; Bower's Auto Salvage, *see Late Vintage*
Lodi; Tons of Parts, *see Vintage*
Lorain; American Auto Wrecking, *see Late Vintage*
  City View Auto Wrecking, *see Vintage*
  Lowes Auto Wrecking, *see Late Vintage*

241

Top Notch Auto Wrecking, *see Late Vintage*

Lowellville; Stanley's Automotive Wrecking, 5400 Center Rd, 44436; 330-536-6281; CC, Sa, Sp; 500; **D, few F, PU, 4x4, few Trk**

Malvern; Fox Auto Salvage & Parts, *see Late Vintage*

Mansfield; Bowman Auto Recycling, *see Late Vintage*

Mansfield; Milliron Industries, 2384 State Rt 39, 44903; 419-747-4566, FAX 419-747-1539; CC, Sa, Sp, Br; 400+; **D, few F, PU, 4x4, few Trk**

Tucker Brothers Auto Wrecking, *see Late Vintage*

Mantua; Geauga Lake Auto Body, 9801 State Rt 44, 44255; 330-274-3250, FAX 330-274-3665; CC, Sa, Sp, Br; 500; **D, few F, PU, 4x4; B3, AMC**

Maple Heights; Deneman's Automotive, *see Vintage*

Marengo; Auto & Truck Recycling, *see Late Vintage*

Marion; Bill Johnson's Auto Wrecking, *see Late Vintage*

Marshallville; J & J Auto Wrecking, 8558 Black Diamond Rd, 44645; 330-855-2951, FAX 330-855-2940, 800-425-1555; Sp; Br; 400+; **D, F, PU, 4x4, Trk; B3, Jp**

Massillon; Augie's Import America, 11816 Lincoln Way NW, 44647; 330-833-7300, FAX 330-833-7743, 800-950-5752; CC, Sa, Sp; 600; F, PU, 4x4

Grand Central Auto Recyclers, 12192 Lincoln Way NW, 44947; 330-833-6001, FAX 330-833-4503, 800-843-1010, sales@grandcentralauto.com; CC, Sa, Sp, Br; 13ac; **D, F, PU, 4x4, Trk; B3, AMC, Jp, VW**

Massillon Auto Salvage, 145 Walnut Rd SW, 44646; 330-833-3336, FAX 330-833-7005; CC, Sa, Sp, PL; 8ac; **D, F, PU, 4x4, Trk, Cn; Spc: Foreign**

McArthur; Zimmerman Auto Wrecking, 65101 Meeksville Rd, 45651; 740-596-4263, FAX 740-596-1026; Sa, Br; 500; **D, PU, 4x4, Trk; B3, AMC; Spc: Ford & Chevy**

Miamisburg; Mel's Auto Parts, 7080 Germantown Pike, 45342; 937-866-8512; Sa, UR; 200; **D, F, PU, 4x4**

Middletown; Hydes Auto Enterprises, 221 Oxford State Rd, 45044; 513-423-4685, 888-423-2000; Br; 500; **D, F, PU, 4x4, Trk**

Milian; Bob's Auto Wrecking, *see Vintage*

Mineral City; Honey Road Auto Salvage, 10195 Honey Rd NW, 44656; 330-859-2304, FAX 330-859-2004, 888-302-2928; CC, Sa, Sp, Br; 500; **F, few PU**

Mingo Junction; Flesher Auto Salvage, 360 County Rd 74, 43938; 740-283-3778, FAX 740-283-4143, 800-670-2054; CC, Sa, Sp, UR; 300+; **D, F, PU, 4x4**

Rocky's Auto Wrecking, Mingo Jct Goulds Rd, 43938; 740-282-1364, FAX 740-535-1751, 800-966-9114; Sa; 3000+; **D, F, PU, 4x4, Trk**

Mogadore; Mogadore Auto Wrecking, 508 S Cleveland Av, 44260; 330-628-9909, FAX 330-628-4006, 800-310-1834; CC, Sa, Sp, UR; 800; **D, F, PU, 4x4, Trk; B3, AMC, Jp**

New Lebanon; Mike's Auto Parts, 8201 W 3rd St, 45345; 937-835-5670; CC, Sa, Br; 200; **D, F, PU, 4x4; B3, AMC**

New Lexington; 13 Auto Salvage, *see Vintage*

New Paris; G W Pierce Auto Parts, *see Late Vintage*

New Philadelphia; Howenstine Auto Salvage, *see Vintage*

New Philadelphia; Route 39 Auto Salvage, 2799 State Rt 39 NE, 44663; 330-343-4686; Sa, UR; 8ac, 400+; **D, F, PU, 4x4, Trk; B3, AMC, IH, VW**

Tuscarwas Auto Parts, 1037 W High Av, 44663; 330-339-3369, FAX 330-339-6694, 888-832-0066, fhr224@aol.com; CC, Sa, Sp, UR; 23ac, 1000+; **D, F, PU, 4x4, Trk; B3, AMC, Jp, IH, VW**

Wainwright Auto Parts, *see Vintage*

New Richmond; Mahaffey Auto Salvage, 2760 Laurel Lindale Rd, 45157; 513-797-4999; Sa, UR; 45ac; **D, F, PU, 4x4, Trk, Cn**

New Vienna; AAA Collins Towing & Salvage, *see Vintage*

Newark; Crispin Auto Wrecking, *see Late Vintage*

Newport; Tom's Auto Wrecking, Sheets Run Rd, PO Box 229, 45768; 740-374-9199; Sa, UR; 2000; **D, F, PU, 4x4, Trk; B3, AMC, Jp, IH, VW**

North Lima; A-1 Auto Parts, 10398 Woodworth Rd, 44452; 330-549-3936, 1import @aol.com; CC, Sa, Sp, UR, Wr; 15ac; **F, PU, 4x4; Import only; Most parts on shelf**

242

Norwalk; Auto Wrecking 601, *see Late Vintage*

Painesville; A-1 Auto Recycling, *see Vintage*

Patriot; L & L Auto Sales, 5760 State Rt 325, 45658; 740-379-2726, FAX 740-379-2734; Sa, Sp; 200; **D; Spc: Chrysler & GM**

Piqua; Miami Auto Salvage, *see Late Vintage*

Steve's Used Cars & Auto Parts, 8435 N Dixie Dr, 45356; 937-773-7261; Sa, UR; 600; **D, F, PU, 4x4**

Ravenna; 44 Auto Parts & Wrecking, 517 E Lake St, 44266; 330-297-1415, FAX 330-297-1417, rt44auto@aol.com; CC, Sa, Sp; 7ac, 600; **D, F, PU, 4x4**

Cleveland Road Auto Wrecking, 6720 Cleveland Rd, 44266; 330-296-3056, FAX 330-296-7992, 800-245-8755, www.clevelandroad.com; CC, Sa, Sp; 7ac; **D, F, PU, 4x4**

Kurkey Auto Wrecking, *see Late Vintage*

Northeast Auto Recycling, 6651 Cleveland Rd, 44266; 330-296-2177; Sa; 6ac, 400; **D, PU, 4x4; B3, AMC**

Reedsville; Barber's Auto Parts, 2443 State Rt 124, 45772; 740-378-6346; Sa, UR; 400; **D, F, PU, 4x4, Trk; B3, AMC, Jp, IH, VW**

Reynoldsburg; K & K Auto Parts & Salvage, 13141 National Rd SW, 43068; 740-927-5384, FAX , 888-4FAT-KAT; Sp, UR; 400; **D, F, PU, 4x4, Trk; B3, AMC**

Rockford; Ketchum Auto Wrecking, *see Vintage*

Rogers; Millrock Auto Sales & Wrecking, *see Late Vintage*

Saint Marys; St Marys Auto Salvage, *see Vintage*

Salem; B & E Auto Wrecking, *see Late Vintage*

Diamond Auto Wrecking, 12300 State Rt 62 N, 44460; 330-337-3556, 800-533-4440; Sa, Sp; 40ac; **D, F, PU, 4x4**

Lesicks, 7350 Salem Unity Rd, 44460; 330-332-2200, FAX 330-332-2714; Sa, Sp, Wr; **D, F, PU, 4x4; B3, Jp; Spc: Jeep**

Smith Auto, *see Late Vintage*

Sandusky; Big Krome Auto, *see Vintage*

Country Imported Motors, 3303 Venice Rd, 44870; 419-625-7082; CC, Sa, Sp; 4ac; **F, PU**

J & D Auto Wrecking, *see Late Vintage*

Sebring; Hughes Auto Wrecking, 886 N Johnson Rd, 44672; 330-938-9132; Sp; 200+; **D, PU, 4x4**

Slyvania; Alexis Auto Prt, 8061 Sylvania Av, 43560; 419-882-7168; CC; **D, few F, PU, 4x4**

Steubenville; Stateside Auto Recycling, 500 N 3rd St, 43952; 740-282-3337, 800-282-4020; CC, Sp, PL; 1500+; **D, F, PU**

Toledo; A-1 Auto Parts, 4105 N Detroit Av, 43612; 419-478-5100, FAX 419-478-4448, 800-449-7773; CC, Sa, Sp, PL; 6ac; **D, F, PU, 4x4**

A-Northtowne Auto Parts, 5206 N Detroit Av, 43612; 419-478-1111

A & D Auto Parts & Repair, *see Vintage*

Bill's City Auto Parts, *see Late Vintage*

Cherry Auto Parts, *see Late Vintage*

Spud's Auto Parts, *see Late Vintage*

Westwood Auto Parts, 130 S Westwood Av, 43607; 419-535-1116, 800-720-1116; CC, Sp, Wr; 20ac; **D, F, PU, 4x4**

Troy; Polings Auto Parts, 2226 N County Rd 25A, 45373; 937-335-7855, FAX 937-339-1159, 800-998-2152; Sa; 30ac; **D, few F, PU, 4x4**

Vermilion; Inter City Auto Wrecking, *see Late Vintage*

Vinton; Vinton Auto Salvage, 308 Frank Rd, 45686; 740-388-9062; Sa; **D, F, PU, 4x4**

Wapakoneta; D & B Auto Parts, *see Vintage*

Warren; Four-Twenty-Two Auto Wrecking, 4858 Parkman Rd NW, 44481; 330-898-4420, 800-233-8234; CC, Sa, Sp; 40ac, 8000+; **D, few F, PU, 4x4**

Union Auto Parts, 2174 Austintown Warren Rd SW, 44481; 330-652-5973, FAX 330-392-4378, 800-638-6466; CC, Sa, Sp; **D, F, PU**

Wellsville; M & S, 17892 State Rt 45, 43968; 330-532-2660; Sa, Br; 500+; **D only**

West Lafayette; Sharier Auto Wrecking & Slvg, *see Late Vintage*

Sharrocks Auto Wrecking, 56988 Township Rd 261, 43845; 740-545-7790, FAX 740-545-7733; Sp; 30ac; **D, few F, PU, few 4x4; campers & motorcycles**
Westerville; Del-Car Used Auto Parts, *see Vintage*
Wooster; Abe Auto Parts, *see Late Vintage*
   Tom's Salvage, *see Vintage*
   Wayco Automotive, *see Late Vintage*
Xenia; Dayton Xenia Auto Parts, *see Vintage*
   Kil Kare Auto Wrecking, 1170 Dayton Xenia Rd, 45385; 937-426-5233, FAX 937-427-2001, 800 KIL KARE, www.kilkare.auto.com; CC, Sp; 34ac; **D, F, PU; B3; Spc: Front Wheel Drive**
Youngstown; Al's Auto Salvage, *see Late Vintage*
   B & M Auto Wrecking, *see Late Vintage*
   Center Street Auto, *see Late Vintage*
   Chuck's Auto Wrecking, *see Vintage*
   Cleveland Auto Wrecking, 2700 Hubbard Rd, 44505; 330-759-2820, FAX 330-759-3530, 800-362-2773; CC, Sa, Sp; 50ac; **D, F, PU**, 4x4
   Interstate Auto Salvage, *see Late Vintage*
   Schulte Auto Wrecking, *see Vintage*
Zanesville; Ron's Auto Parts, *see Vintage*

The customer did not use the proper name for the part resulting in time invested in removing the wrong part.

Yard Operators Tell us...

Hauf's Antique & Classic Salvage
Stillwater. OK

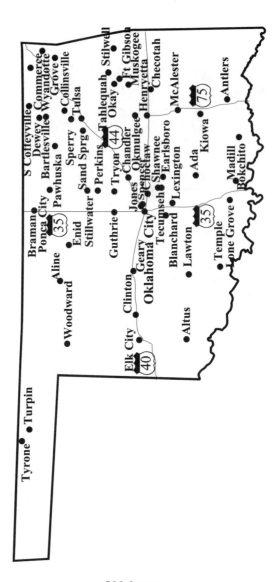

Oklahoma

Please mention you saw'em in Ray's wReckingyard Roster when contacting these yards

246

OKLAHOMA

VINTAGE

Aline; Bud's Salvage, Hwy 8, 73716; 580-463-2204, FAX 580-463-2503, 800-375-2837; Sp, UR; 60ac, 5000; **30+; D, F, PU, 4x4, Trk; B3, AMC, Jp, Hd, St, Pk, Ns, Ks, Fr, Wy; Vintage cars sold whole only**

Bartlesville; Bartlesville Auto Salvage, 16582 State Hwy 123, 74003; 918-336-0532, 800-881-2343; Sp; 1000; **60+; D, F, PU, 4x4; B3, VW**

Blanchard; County Line Salvage, County Line Rd, 73010; 405-392-2630, FAX call first; Sa; 5ac; **70+, few 50-60s; D, F, PU, 4x4, Trk, Fm; B3, Jpa**

Chandler; Country Auto, Rt 4 Box 125 A, 74834; 405-258-0957, www.expage. com/page/country; Sp, UR, Wr; 6ac, 300+; **50-69; D, F; B3, St, Pk, VW, Mercedes, Opel, Fiat, Mopar, Jpa; Whole cars & parts; Open Saturday by appointment**

Commerce; Don's Auto Salvage, 620 N Jefferson St, 74339; 918-675-4118; Sa, UR; 10ac; **20+; D, PU; B3**

Earlsboro; Willie's Salvage, RR 1 Box 125, 74840; 405-997-5782; Sa, Sp; 800+; **40-89; D, PU; B3, AMC, Ns, St, Pk**

Elk City; C & C Auto Salvage, P.O. Box 1928, S of City Hwy 6, 73648; 580-225-6314; CC, Sa, Sp; 400+; **50+; D, PU, 4x4; B3, AMC, Jp**

Enid; Guthrie's Auto Salvage, RR 4 Box 120B5, 73701; 580-233-0901; **40-85; D, F, PU; B3**

Geary; American Horse Salvage, Rt 1 Box 32A, Hwy 281, 73040; 405-884-2730; Sa, UR; 150+; **50-92; D, F, PU, 4x4, vans; B3**

Grove; Ten & Fifty Nine Salvage, Hwy 59 S, 74346; 918-786-3221; Sa, UR, Wr; **30+, few 20s; D, F, PU, 4x4; B3, AMC, IH, Hd, Ns, St, Pk, Ks; Restores antiques**

Jones; J T's Auto & Pickup Salvage, 9413 N Hiwassee Rd, 73049; 405-399-3784; Sa; 5ac; **60+; D, F, PU, 4x4, Trk; B3; Spc: Pickup**

Kiowa; Larry's Auto & Truck Salvage, Box 359, Hwy 69 N, 74553; 918-432-5547; Sa, UR; 400+; **40-85; D, PU; B3, IH, St**

Lawton; C & W Auto Salvage Inc, 1404 SW 2nd St, 73501; 580-357-1820, FAX 580-353-3539, 800-375-1820; CC, Sa, Sp; 1000; **60+; D, F, PU, 4x4, Trk, Fm; B3, Jp D, F, PU, 4x4, Trk, Fm; B3, Jp**

Lexington; Idlett Salvage & Wrecker Svc, 815 N Main St, 73051; 405-527-6608; CC, Sa, Sp; 500; **60-93; D, F, PU, 4x4, Trk; Jp, IH; Has a Classic section**

Lone Grove; Gunter Salvage, Enterprise Dr., 73443; 580-657-3229; Sa, Sp, UR; 350+; **60+; D, PU; B3**

McAlester; 31 Auto Salvage, Rt 5, 74554; 918-423-2022; Sa, Sp, Br; 10ac, 250+; **60+; D, PU; B3; Spc: Chevy 60-72**

Okay; McDaniel Salvage & Wrecking, PO Box 36, 74446; 918-683-5371 or 6675; Sa, Sp; 31ac, 1000+; **50+; D, F, PU, 4x4; B3, AMC, Jp, IH, VW, Morris Minor, Triumph, Metro, Mustang, Falcon; Spc: Ford; open Sunday by appointment**

Oklahoma City; Aabar's Cadillac & Lincoln Slvg, 9700 NE 23rd, 73141; 405-769-3318, FAX 405-769-9542, 800-749-3318; CC, Sa, Sp, Br; 7ac, 600; **40+; D; Cadillac & Lincoln only**

   Leonard's Auto Salvage, 1400 S Robinson Av, 73109; 405-239-2726; CC, Sa, Sp, UR, PL; 300; **33-88; D, F, PU, 4x4; B3, AMC**

   Steve's Classic Chevy & Ford, 1010 W Main St, 73106; 405-232-1972, klassikars @aol.com; CC, Sp, PL, Wr; 150; **50+; D, 4x4, Trk; B3, AMC, Jp, IH, Wy**

   West Auto Salvage, 2408 NW 10th St, 73107; 405-528-5537; CC, Sa, Sp; 600; **59-90; D, F, PU; B3, AMC**

Pawhuska; Pawhuska Auto Salvage, Hwy 99-11 S, 74056; 918-287-3450, 800-375-3472; CC, Sp, PL; 30ac, 700+; **50+; D, F, PU; B3, AMC**

Sand Springs; Grigsby's Auto Salvage, 312 Broad St, 74063; 918-245-1586; Sp, UR; 1500; **40-89; D, PU, 4x4; B3, AMC, Hd, St, Pk, Ks, Cr, Wy; Spc: 55-67 Chevy**

Shawnee; Bugg Pickup Salvage, 45 Bristow Ln, 74801; 405-273-1045; Sa; 50-85; **D, PU only; B3**

   S & S Auto, 815 N Harrison St, 74801; 405-275-0606; Sp, UR; 7ac, 1000; **70-93, few 40-60s; D, PU; B3, AMC, Jp, IH, St, Pk, Wy**

South Coffeyville; Collins Auto Salvage, 824 Oklahoma, 74072; 918-255-6203; UR; **30+; D, F, PU, 4x4; B3, Jp, IH, Triumph, MG**

Sperry; North Yale Auto Parts, Rt 1 Box 707, 74073; 918-288-7218, FAX 918-288-7223, 800-256-6927; CC, Sa, Sp, UR; 10ac, 1000; **60-89; D, PU; B3**

Stillwater; Hauf Auto Supply, Box 547, 74076; 405-372-1585, FAX 405-372-1586; Sp; 1500; **20-80; D, F, PU; B3, AMC, IH, St, Pk, Ns, Ks, Fr, VW, Hr; Spc: Classic, Antique & Pickup; Closed Sunday & Monday**

Stilwell; Collins Salvage, RR 4, 74960; 918-456-4753; Sa, UR; **60-94; D, PU, Fm; B3, AMC; Spc: Ford Tempo**

Tecumseh; Rath's Auto Salvage, Hwy 9 E, 74873; 405-598-5005, FAX 405-598-8331; Sa; 2000; **50+; D, PU; B3, Hd, St**

Tulsa; A-1 Chrysler Auto Parts, 13521 E Apache Av, 74116; 918-234-4022, FAX 918-234-4017, 800-330-5523; Sp; Br; 5ac, 800+; **80+, few 40-70s; D, PU, 4x4; B3, Jp; Spc: Chrysler & Mini Vans**

   Allstate Auto Salvage, 13603 E Apache St, 74116; 918-437-5445; CC, Sa, Sp, UR; 1000; **57+; D, F; B3, VW**

   East West Auto Parts, 4605 Dawson Rd, 74115; 918-832-7077, FAX 918-832-7900, 800-447-2886; CC, Sp; 15ac, 1000; **40-89; D, F; B3, few Eur; Spc: GM; Mail order only**

   Goat Man, 7758 E 106th St, 94133; 918-493-1966; Sp; 200+; **80s, few 40-70s; D, PU; B3, AMC, Jp, IH; Spc: Pontiac; motorcycles; MAIL ORDER ONLY**

   J C Morgan Truck & Auto Slvg, 3901 N Lewis Av, 74110; 918-425-4779; CC; **75+; 50-89; D, PU; B3**

Tyrone; Jim's Auto & Salvage, Hwy 54 E, 73951; 580-854-6828, 800-292-7476; Sa, UR; 750+; **48+; D, F, PU, 4x4; B3**

LATE VINTAGE

Aline; Bud's Salvage, *see Vintage*

Altus; Altus Auto Salvage, Hwy 62, 73521; 580-482-0708, 800-886-0708; Sa, Sp, PL; 600+; **80+; D, F, PU; B3**

Antlers; B J's Auto Salvage, HC 67 Box 595, 74523; 580-298-6788; Sa, UR; **60+; 70-89; D, PU; B3, AMC**

Bartlesville; Bartlesville Auto Salvage, *see Vintage*

   Lee's Auto Salvage, 1823 W 14th St, 74003; 918-337-2777; Sa, Br; 350+; **67-90; D, F, PU, 4x4; B3, VW**

Blanchard; County Line Salvage, *see Vintage*

Bokchito; Phillips Auto Salvage, Hwy 70, 74726; 580-295-3456; CC, Sp, PL; 800+; **67+; D, F, PU, 4x4; B3**

Braman; T & B Auto Salvage, 5772 N 29th St, 74632; 580-363-1386; Sa; 500; **70-95; D, PU, 4x4; B3**

Chandler; Country Auto, *see Vintage*

Checotah; Checotah Used Cars & Salvage, Old Hwy 69 S, 74426; 918-473-6062, FAX 918-473-0423; CC, Sa, Sp; 150; **67-94; D, PU, 4x4; B3; Spc: GM**

Choctaw; Dollar & Salvage, 13500 NE 10th St, 73020; 405-769-2211; Sa, Sp; 450+; **67+; D, PU, 4x4; Ford, Mercury & Lincoln only; Spc: Mustang 67-93**

Clinton; Sixty Six Salvage, E of City IH 40, 73601; 580-323-2338; Sp, PL; 300; **80+; D, F, PU, 4x4; B3**

Commerce; Don's Auto Salvage, *see Vintage*

Dewey; AAR & K Salvage, 716 Moore Ln, 74029; 918-534-2034; Sa, UR; 900; **67+; D, F, PU; B3, VW, Jpa**

Earlsboro; Willie's Salvage, *see Vintage*

Elk City; C & C Auto Salvage, *see Vintage*

Enid; Guthrie's Auto Salvage, *see Vintage*

Fort Gibson; A A Country Salvage, RR 2 Box 509, 74434; 918-478-2529; Sa, Br; 5ac, 250; **70-85; D, F, PU, 4x4, Trk; B3**

Geary; American Horse Salvage, *see Vintage*

Grove; Ten & Fifty Nine Salvage, *see Vintage*

248

Henryetta; Terrapin's Auto Salvage, RR 1 Box 200, 74437; 918-652-3934; Sa, Br; 800; **70-89; D, PU; B3, AMC**

Jones; J T's Auto & Pickup Salvage, *see Vintage*

Kiowa; Larry's Auto & Truck Salvage, *see Vintage*

Lawton; C & W Auto Salvage Inc, *see Vintage*

Lexington; Idlett Salvage & Wrecker Svc, *see Vintage*

    Lexington Truck/Auto Salvage, 831 N Main St, 73051; 405-527-6039, www.members. xoom.com/lewreck/; Sa, Sp, UR; 350+; **68+; D, F, PU, 4x4; B3, AMC, Jp; Spc: Pickup**

Lone Grove; Gunter Salvage, *see Vintage*

    Langs Auto Salvage & Wrecker, HC 62 Box 4280, Cheek Rt, 73443; 580-657-3292, FAX 580-657-2434; Sa, Sp; 200; **70+; D, F, PU, 4x4; B3 Spc: Pickup**

Madill; Buddy's Crushed Cars, S of City, 74446; 580-795-2750, FAX 580-795-7003; Sa, UR; **80-91; D, F, PU, 4x4, Trk, Fm; B3**

McAlester; 31 Auto Salvage, *see Vintage*

Muskogee; B D Salvage, 610 Mooney Dr, 74401; 918-683-6033; 2ac; 79-92; **D, F, PU, few 4x4; B3, AMC, Jp**

Ponca City; Weld-All Welding & Auto Salvage, 2030 Tonkawa Rd, 74601; 580-762-2065; Sa, UR; 1000+; **70-89; D, F, PU; B3, AMC**

Okay; McDaniel Salvage & Wrecking, *see Vintage*

Oklahoma City; Aabar's Cadillac & Lincoln Salvage, *see Vintage*

    American Camaro & Firebird, 5932 NW 39th St, 73122; 405-495-9114, 888-833-4582; CC, Sa, Sp, Wr; 200; **82+, few 60-70s; D; Firebird & Camaro only**

    Leonard's Auto Salvage, *see Vintage*

    R & T Salvage, 901 NE Sunnyland Rd, 73117; 405-232-1313, 888-880-2834; Sa, Sp, UR; 400; **70+; D, F, PU, 4x4; B3; some 60s whole cars**

    Southwest Pickup & Truck Slvg, 300 S May Av, 73108; 405-232-1020; Sa, Sp, Br; 1ac; **70+; D, PU, 4x4, vans; B3**

    Steve's Classic Chevy & Ford, *see Vintage*

    West Auto Salvage, *see Vintage*

Okmulgee; Okmulgee, Loop 56 E, 74447; 918-756-2990; Sa, UR; 2500; **70-94; D, F, PU, 4x4; B3, AMC, Jp**

Pawhuska; Pawhuska Auto Salvage, *see Vintage*

Perkins; J W La Follette Auto Salvage, Rt 2 Box 1165, 74059; 405-547-2580; 350+; **70-89; D, F, PU; B3, AMC**

Sand Springs; Grigsby's Auto Salvage, *see Vintage*

Shawnee; Bugg Pickup Salvage, *see Vintage*

    S & S Auto, *see Vintage*

    Shawnee Imports Salvage, RR 5 Box 137, 74801; 405-273-8174; Sp; 300+; **70-91; F, PU, 4x4; all Jpa**

South Coffeyville; Collins Auto Salvage, *see Vintage*

    Southtown Auto Salvage, 820 Oklahoma, 74072; 918-255-6350; Sp; 9ac; **80-92; D, F, PU, 4x4; B3**

Sperry; North Yale Auto Parts, *see Vintage*

Stillwater; Hauf Auto Supply, *see Vintage*

Stilwell; Collins Salvage, *see Vintage*

    Bruner's Salvage Yard, Rt 4 Box 1470, Hwy 59 S, 74960; 918-696-2541; Sa, Sp, UR; 600; **70-89; D, F, PU, 4x4; B3, Jp**

Tecumseh; Rath's Auto Salvage, *see Vintage*

Tryon; Green Acre Auto Salvage, Oklahoma St, 74875; 918-374-2787, 800-598-4899; CC; 400+; **80+; D, F, PU, few 4x4; B3**

Tulsa; A-1 Chrysler Auto Parts, *see Vintage*

    Allstate Auto Salvage, *see Vintage*

    East West Auto Parts, *see Vintage*

    Goat Man, *see Vintage*

    J C Morgan Truck & Auto Slvg, *see Vintage*

Mingo Auto Salvage, 13605 E Apache St, 74116; 918-437-2374; Br; 1100+; **70-94; D; B3, AMC**

Standard Auto Salvage, 6100 New Sapulpa Rd, 74131; 918-446-6353; CC, Sa; 200; **80-92; D, F, PU; B3**

Turpin; Randy's Salvage, RR 2 Box 284S, 73950; 580-778-3665; Sa; 100+; **80-96; D, PU, 4x4; Ford, Chevy**

Tyrone; Jim's Auto & Salvage, *see Vintage*

LATE MODEL

Ada; A G Sanders Auto Salvage, Hwy 1, 74820; 580-332-7977; **D, PU**

Aline; Bud's Salvage, *see Vintage*

Altus; Altus Auto Salvage, *see Late Vintage*

Bartlesville; Bartlesville Auto Salvage, *see Vintage*

Blanchard; County Line Salvage, *see Vintage*

Bokchito; Phillips Auto Salvage, *see Late Vintage*

Braman; T & B Auto Salvage, *see Late Vintage*

Checotah; Checotah Used Cars & Salvage, *see Late Vintage*

Choctaw; Dollar & Salvage, *see Late Vintage*

Clinton; Sixty Six Salvage, see *Late Vintage*

Collinsville; Lambert's Auto Salvage, 15107 N 137th East Av, 74021; 918-371-4444, 800-441-4133; Sp; **D; Ford, Chevy only**

Commerce; Don's Auto Salvage, *see Vintage*

Dewey; AAR & K Salvage, *see Vintage*

Elk City; C & C Auto Salvage, *see Vintage*

Enid; Stanleys, 325 E Ash Av, 73701; 580-242-1984, FAX 580-237-7524, 800-749-1984, stanleys@enid.com; CC, Sa, Sp, PL; 300; **D, F, PU, 4x4, Trk**

Geary; American Horse Salvage, *see Vintage*

Grove; Ten & Fifty Nine Salvage, *see Vintage*

Guthrie; Morgan Auto World, 4024 S Division St, 73044; 405-282-5675; CC, Sa, Sp, UR, PL; 200; **D, PU; B3**

Jones; J T's Auto & Pickup Salvage, *see Vintage*

Lawton; C & W Auto Salvage Inc, *see Vintage*

Corley's South Plains Salvage, 1502 SW 2nd St, 73501; 580-355-0627, FAX 580-353-6271, 800-375-3673; CC, Sp; 300; **D, PU; Ford & Chrysler only**

Lexington; Idlett Salvage & Wrecker Svc, *see Vintage*

Lexington Truck/Auto Salvage, *see Late Vintage*

Lone Grove; Gunter Salvage, *see Vintage*

Langs Auto Salvage & Wrecker, *see Late Vintage*

McAlester; 31 Auto Salvage, *see Vintage*

Muskogee; B D Salvage, *see Late Vintage*

Okay; McDaniel Salvage & Wrecking, *see Vintage*

Oklahoma City; A & D Metal Co, 10820 NE 23rd St, 73141; 405-769-4144, 888-845-6415; CC, Sp; 300; **D, F, PU; B3**

Aabar's Cadillac & Lincoln Salvage, *see Vintage*

American Camaro & Firebird, *see Late Vintage*

R & T Salvage, *see Late Vintage*

Southwest Pickup & Truck Slvg, *see Late Vintage*

Okmulgee; Okmulgee, *see Late Vintage*

Pawhuska; Pawhuska Auto Salvage, *see Vintage*

Shawnee; S & S Auto, *see Vintage*

South Coffeyville; Collins Auto Salvage, *see Vintage*

Spencer; Productive Auto Wrck, 3701 N Westminster Rd, 73084; 405-769-4818; UR; **D, F**

Stilwell; Collins Salvage, *see Vintage*

Talequah; B & J Auto Salvage, Hwy 51 E, 74464; 918-456-2481, FAX 918-456-7102; Sa, Sp; 800; **D, F, PU; B3**

Tecumseh; Rath's Auto Salvage, *see Vintage*

Temple; Smith & Sons Salvage, S Hwy 5, 73568; 580-342-6218; Sa, Sp; 1500; **D, PU, 4x4; B3; mostly PU**

Tryon; Green Acre Auto Salvage, *see Late Vintage*

Tulsa; A-1 Chrysler Auto Parts, *see Vintage*

   Allstate Auto Salvage, *see Vintage*

   Mingo Auto Salvage, *see Late Vintage*

   Standard Auto Salvage, *see Late Vintage*

Turpin; Randy's Salvage, *see Late Vintage*

Tyrone; Jim's Auto & Salvage, *see Vintage*

Woodward; Jim's Auto Salvage, SE Hwy 270, 73801; 580-256-6047, 800-725-8733; CC, Sp; 1200; **D, PU, 4x4; B3**

Wyandotte; State Line Salvage, Rt 1 Box 320, 74370; 918-666-1777, FAX 918-776-2204; Sa; 5ac; **D, PU, 4x4, Trk, Cn; Travel Trailers; rebuilders**

If you wish to have the part shipped, be sure to get a detailed description so you are not disapointed on arrival.

Yard Operators Tell us...

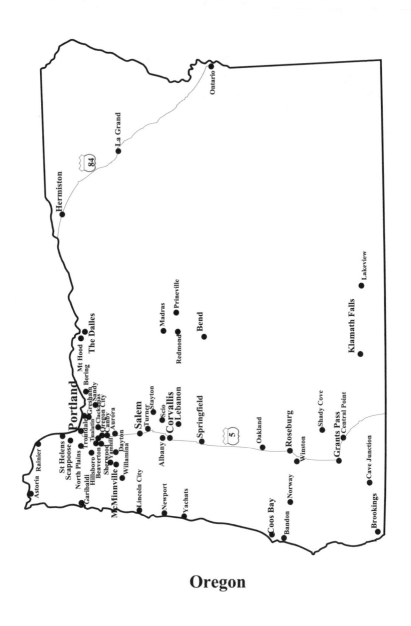

Oregon

Ray's wReckingyard Roster makes a great gift for
the "car nut" on your shopping list. To order,
Call Toll Free: 877-4RAYS BOOKS

OREGON

VINTAGE

Albany; Albany Engine Exchange, 3275 Knox Butte Av NE, 97321; 541-928-7865, 800-676-2912; CC, Sp, Wr, PL; **D, F; Engines only**

D & J Auto Salvage Inc, 34150 Hwy 20 SE, 97321; 541-928-4566, 800-801-4566; Sa, Sp, UR; 600; **80+, few 50-70s; D, F, PU; B3**

Linn Auto Salvage, 4646 Santiam Hwy SE, 97321; 541-926-5855, FAX 541-926-3556; CC, Sp; 300; **80s, few 50-70s; D, F, PU, Fm; B3**

Loops Auto Wrecking & Salvage, 30811 Ehlen Dr SW, 97321; 541-928-5111; Sp; 10ac; **40-69; D, few F; B3, Hd, Ns, St, Pk, Renault, Peugeot**

R & S Mustang Supply, 250 Queen Av SE, 97321; 541-926-5383; CC, Sa, Sp, UR; 60+; **65-73; D; Mustang only**

Aurora; Aurora Wreckers & Recyclers, 21111 Hwy 99E NE, 97002; 503-678-1107; Sa, Sp; 7ac; **40-79; D, PU; B3, AMC, Jp, IH, Hd, Ns, St, Pk, Wy, VW**

Beaverton; Beaverton Auto Wrecking, 4350 SW 142nd Av, 97005; 503-644-3121; Sa; 1ac; **70-89, few 60s; D, F, PU, 4x4; B3, AMC**

Bend; Bend Salvage & Auto Wrecking, 64154 N Hwy 97, 97701; 541-382-1987, 800-754-1987; CC, Sa, Sp, UR; 19ac; **70-89, few 50-60s; D, F, PU, 4x4, few Trk, Fm, Cn; B3, AMC, Jp, IH, Hd, St, VW**

George Merricks, 3090 NE 27th St, 97701; 541-382-6134; Sp, Wr; **50-69; D; B3, AMC; Spc: Chrysler; by Appt. Only or Mail Order**

Tired-Iron, 63545 N Hwy 97, 97701; 541-382-8377; Sp; 10ac; **70-89, few 50-60s; D, F, PU, 4x4; B3, AMC, Jp, IH, St, VW; tries to keep older cars**

Boring; Alpha Engines & Transmission, 12900 SW Richey Rd, 97009; 503-663-9703, FAX 503-280-9892, 800-223-7961; CC, Sa, Sp, Wr; **50+; D, F, PU, 4x4; engine & trans only**

Damascus U Pull It, 19510 SE Sunnyside Rd, 97009; 503-658-3191, 800-978-5548; CC, Sa, UR; **50+; D, F, PU, 4x4; B3**

U-Pull It U-Save, 30545 SW Hwy 212, 97009; 503-663-2211; Sa, UR; 1500; **60+; D, F, PU, 4x4; B3 only**

Canby; South Canby Auto Wreckers, 7925 S Zimmerman Rd, 97013; 503-651-2116; Sa, UR; 700; **50-90; D, F, PU, 4x4; B3, Jp, IH, St, VW**

Yoder Garage at Yoder, 32471 S Kropf Rd, 97013; 503-651-2192; Sa, Sp, UR; 2ac; **70+, few 50-60s; D, F, PU; B3, VW**

Cave Junction; Phillips Auto Wrecking, 27752 Redwood Hwy, 97523; 541-592-2516; Br; 5.5ac; **50-80; D, F, PU, 4x4, Mil; B3**

Central Point; Ben's Auto Wrecking & Towing, 5393 Table Rock Rd, 97502; 541-664-2567; Sa; **50-69; D; B3**

Clackamas; Drive Train Four Wheel Drive, 13621 SE Ambler Rd, 97015; 503-659-8589; Sa, Sp; **30+; D, few F, PU, 4x4; B3, Jp; Spc: Vintage 4x4**

Coos Bay; A-101 Auto Salvage & Towing, 515 Eckles Way, 97420; 541-269-0425, 800-590-1100; CC, Sa, Sp, PL; 7ac; **70-94, few 60s & earlier; D, F, PU, 4x4; B3**

Greenacres Auto Wrecking, 600 Luscombe Dr, 97420; 541-269-0252; Sa, Sp, UR; 2ac; **50-89; D, F, PU; B3, IH, Ks, VW, DeSoto**

Shinglehouse Auto Wreckers, 5333 Hwy 42, 97420; 541-269-1975, FAX 541-269-0481, 800-327-1975; Sa, Sp, UR; 10ac; **50+; D, F, PU, 4x4; B3**

Corvallis; Corvallis Auto Wrecking & Sls, 4075 SE 3rd St, 97333; 541-758-2700, 800-422-7081; CC, Sa, Sp; 1000+; **40+; D, F, PU, 4x4; B3, IH, Wy, VW**

Dayton; Dayton Auto Wrecking, 10825 SE Amity Dayton Hwy, 97114; 503-864-2262; Sa, UR; 5ac, 700; **70+, few 50-60s; D, F, PU, 4x4; B3**

Grants Pass; Caveman Auto Parts-Recyclers, 440 NE Agness Av, 97526; 541-476-8816; CC, Sa, Sp, UR; 3000; **70+, few 50-60s; D, F, PU, 4x4; B3, AMC**

Hermiston; D & R Auto Sales, 80361 Hwy 395 N, 97838; 541-567-8048, FAX 541-567-1463; CC, Sa, Sp, Br; 500; **60+; D, F, PU, 4x4; B3, AMC, Jp, IH, VW**

Klamath Falls; Axel-Rods Auto Parts & Salvage, 2941 Laverne Av, 97603; 541-882-8858; Sa, Sp; **60-89; D, F, PU, 4x4, vans; B3, IH**

Klamath Auto Wreckers, 3315 Washburn Wy, 97603; 541-882-1677, FAX 541-882-0180, 800-452-3301; Sp, UR; 6ac; **40-79; D, PU; B3, IH; Spc: Ford, Chevy**

One Stop Auto Parts & Svc, 247 Gage Rd, 97601; 541-882-7978; Sa, Sp; **60s & 90s; D, F, PU; B3, IH; some 60s Pickup**

Lakeview; Lakeview Auto Wrecking, 1084 S J St, 97630; 541-947-2703; CC, Sa, Sp, Br; 200; **40-89; D, F, PU, 4x4; B3, Jp, IH, VW**

Lebanon; Cascade Auto Body, 5597 S Santiam Hwy, 97355; 541-451-1797, FAX 541-451-1664, 800-452-2466; CC, Sp, UR; 3ac; **50+; D, F, PU, 4x4; B3, Jp, IH**

Lincoln City; 23rd Auto Wrecking & Towing, 2560 SE 23rd Dr, 97367; 541-994-9000; Sa, Sp; 5ac; **70-89, few 50-60s; D, F, PU; B3**

McMinnville; McMinnville Auto Wrecking, 13341 SE Old Station Rd, 97128; 503-835-2661, FAX 503-835-5700, 800-322-9771; CC, Sa, Sp, UR; 10ac; **60+; D, F, PU, 4x4; B3; Pickup 60+, cars 90+**

Mount Hood Parkdale; Mt Hood Motors Inc, 6635 Cooper Spur Rd, 97041; 541-352-7118; Sa, Sp; 5ac; **80+, few 40-60s; D, F, PU, 4x4; B3; also restore cars**

North Plains; Abacus Pickup Parts Inc, 31625 NW Hillcrest St, 97133; 503-647-5785; CC, Sa, Sp, UR; **40-69 & 85+; D, F PU; B3 Spc: PU, vans; uninventoried misc parts 40-69**

Norway; Norway Auto Recycling, Hwy 42, 97460; 541-572-4040, 800-809-7705; Sa, Sp, UR; 17ac; **55-69; D, F, PU, 4x4; B3, IH, Wy, VW; Spc: 4x4 & Classics**

Oakland; Union Gap Recyclers Inc, 112 Union Gap Loop, 97462; 541-459-2750; Sa, UR; 0.5ac; **60-89; D, F, PU, 4x4; B3, IH**

Oregon City; Dales Auto Wrecking, 1367 Molalla Av, 97045; 503-656-2010; Sa, Sp, UR; 8ac; **30+; D, F, PU, 4x4, Trk, Fm, In, Cn; B3**

Portland; A to Z Auto Wrecking, 1209 SE 190th Av, 97233; 503-665-6914; CC, Sp; 15ac; **50s & 60s, mostly 80+; D, F, PU, 4x4; B3, AMC**

A-1 Light Trucks & Vans, 12010 N Columbia Blvd, 97203; 503-283-2925, 800-735-3429; CC, Sa, Sp; 500+; **60+; D, F, PU; B3; Pickup & Vans only**

Bob's Ford Parts, 2103 SE 190th Av, 97233; 503-492-4566, 888-439-0400; Sp; 350; **64+; D, Ford only; Mustangs 64+**

Bud's Auto Wrecking, 7100 SE Fern Av, 97206; 503-771-2095; Sa, UR; 200; **50-89; D, F, PU; B3, AMC**

Burnside Used Auto Parts, 9245 E Burnside St, 97216; 503-252-0268; CC, Sa, Sp; 1ac; **68+; D, F, PU, 4x4; B3, AMC; Pickup & vans only**

Chevy Store, 8705 SE Stark St, 97216; 503-256-0098, FAX 503-256-0105, 800-232-6472; CC, Sa, Sp; **62-81; D, PU; Chevy only; Spc: Camaro, Corvette**

Cliffs Classic Chevy Parts Co, 619 SE 202nd Av, 97233; 503-667-4329, FAX 503-669-4268; CC, Sa, Sp, Wr; **55-59; D, Pickup; Chevy only**

Columbia Light Truck Parts, 9087 N Columbia Blvd, 97203; 503-286-1194, FAX 503-285-3238, 877-691-7269; CC, Sa, Sp, PL; **60+; D, F, PU; B3, AMC, Jp, IH; Pickup only**

Discount Pickup Parts, 7625 NE Killingsworth St, 97218; 503-254-5325, FAX 503-261-1560; CC, Sa, Sp, Wr, PL; **40+; D, F, PU, 4x4; B3; Spc: Pickup, vans, SUV**

Division Street Auto Wrecking, 13231 SE Division St, 97236; 503-760-7423; Sa, Sp; **50-79; D, PU; B3; Mustang & Camaro; Spc: GM**

GM Toys, 11305 NE Marx Pl, 97220; 503-252-9028; Sa, Sp; **65-88; D; Spc: Corvette**

Import Auto Salvage & Repair, 511 N Columbia Blvd, 97217; 503-285-2611, 800-578-6787; CC, Sa, Sp; 600; **67+; F, PU; Jpa, BMW**

J & H 4-Wheel Drive Specialty, 7057 SE Powell Blvd, 97206; 503-777-2993, 800-628-8602; CC, Sa, Sp, Wr; **60+; D, F, PU, 4x4; B3, IH; 4x4 only, no bodies**

Michael's Auto Parts, 5875 NW Kaiser Rd, 97229; 503-690-7750, FAX 503-690-7735, www.mercedesusedparts.com, CC, Sa, Sp, Wr; 500; **55-93; F; Mercedes only**

Mustang Specialties, 4511 NE 148th Av, 97230; 503-255-4065; Sa, Sp; 1.5ac, 250; **65-93; D; Mustang only**

Northwest Classic Falcons, 1964 NW Pettygrove St, 97209; 503-241-9454, FAX 503-241-1964; CC, Sp, Wr, PL; **60-79; D; Ford Falcon, Fairlane, Comet**

Northwest Recycling, 12122 N Columbia Blvd, 97203; 503-286-6262; CC, Sa, UR; **70+, few 50s & 60s; D, F, PU, 4x4; B3;**

Old Car Parts, 7525 SE Powell Blvd, 97206; 503-771-9416, FAX 503-771-1981, 800-886-7277; CC, Sp, Wr; 5ac; **36-69; D; GM**

Pacific West Imports, 11315 SE Foster Rd, 97266; 503-760-6989, FAX 503-760-8727, 800-575-8655; CC, Sa, Sp, UR; 2ac; **70+, few 60s VW bugs; F, PU; VW; Imports only**

River-Gate Auto Wrecking, 9061 N Columbia Blvd, 97203; 503-286-5861, 877-767-0880; CC, Sa, Sp; 5ac; **70+, parts for 50-60s; D, F, PU, 4x4; B3**

Rose City Mustang Ltd, 2335 NW Thurman St, 97210; 503-243-1938, FAX 503-222-7720; Sa, Sp, Wr; **64-70; D; Mustang only**

Truck Wrecking Yard Inc, 7941 SE 82nd Av, 97266; 503-771-7684; Sa, Sp; 2ac; **30-89; D, PU, Trk, Mil; B3, IH**

Prineville; Dave's Auto Wrecking, 3595 NE 3rd St, 97754; 541-447-1739; CC, Sa, Sp; 2ac; **60-89; D, F, PU, few 4x4; B3; Spc: Ford & Chevy**

Rainier; Bob's Towing, 26171 Pellham Hill Rd, 97048; 503-556-3439, FAX 503-556-8038, 888-556-3439, bobtow@columbia-center.org; CC, Sa, Sp, UR; 700; **70+, few 50s & 60s; D, F, PU; B3;**

Redmond; Brad's Auto & Truck Parts, 2618 S Hwy 97, 97756; 541-923-2723, FAX 541-923-3113, 800-232-2723; CC, Sa, Sp; **60+; D, F, PU, 4x4, Trk, Cn; B3; motorcycles**

Roseburg; Walker Sales & Svc, 2666 NE Diamond Lake Blvd, 97470; 541-672-5751; Sa, Sp, UR; 7ac; **60+; D, F, PU, 4x4; B3, IH; Spc: Pickup**

Sandy; Pat's Auto, 34909 SE Gunderson Rd, 97055; 503-668-6033; CC, Sa, Sp, UR, Wr; 87; **60-88; F; VW only**

Wildcat Auto Wrecking, 46827 SE Wildcat Mountain Dr, 97055; 503-668-7786; CC, Sa, Sp, UR; 700+; **55-80; D; Chrysler only**

Scio; West Scio Auto Wreckers, 38130 Jefferson Scio Dr, 97374; 503-394-2230; Sa, Sp; 2ac; **60-80s; D, F, PU; B3, AMC, Jp, IH; Spc: Pickup**

Shady Cove; European Auto-Winch-Em Towing, 21425 Hwy 62, 97539; 541-878-3377, FAX 541-826-9168; Sp; 100; **50-79; F; VW, Jpa, Volvo, English, Midget, Triumph**

Springfield; Springfield Auto Recyclers Inc, PO Box 127; 750 S 28th St, 97477; 541-747-9601, 800-733-9601; CC, Sa, Sp, UR; 13ac; **40-90; D, F, PU, 4x4; B3, St**

Stayton; Stayton Auto Wreckers, 200 Jetters Wy, 97383; 503-769-3525, FAX 503-769-9420, 800-699-6682; CC, Sa, Sp; 1ac; **60-89; D, F, PU only; B3, IH**

Tualatin; T Bird Sanctuary, 9997 SW Avery, 97062; 503-625-5555, FAX 503-692-9849, 800-275-2661; CC, Sa, Sp, Wr; **58-79; D; Spc: Ford Thunderbird**

Willamina; Mishler Wreckers, 22705 Business 18, 97396; 503-876-2432, FAX 503-876-2616, 800-832-7779 OR only; CC, Sa, Sp, UR; **8ac; 80+, few 60-70s; D, F, PU, 4x4; B3; Spc: Pickup & 4x4**

Winston; Winston Towing, 380 SE Main St, 97496; 541-679-5625, FAX 541-679-1190, 888-679-5625, CC, Sp, UR; 5ac; **50+; D, F, PU, 4x4; B3, AMC, IH**

LATE VINTAGE

Albany; AA Auto Wrecking, 260 Queen Av SE, 97321; 541-926-2725, FAX 541-967-2334; CC, Sp, UR; 250; **67-96; D, F, PU; B3**

Albany Engine Exchange, *see Vintage*

D & J Auto Salvage Inc, *see Vintage*

Linn Auto Salvage, *see Vintage*

R & S Mustang Supply, *see Vintage*

Albany; Riverside Salvage, 36139 Riverside Dr SW, 97321; 541-967-3904; Sa, Sp, UR; 150; **70-89; D, F, PU; B3; Spc: Pickups**

Astoria; Astoria Auto Wrecking, 850 Hwy 101, 97103; 503-325-3782, FAX 503-325-5145, 800-456-4406; CC, Sa, Sp; 500; **70-95; D, F, few PU; B3**

Aurora; Aurora Wreckers & Recyclers, *see Vintage*

Bandon; South Coast Auto Wrecking, Hwy 101, 97411; 541-347-3101, 800-399-3101; CC, Sa, Sp, UR; 2.5ac; **70+; D, F, PU, 4x4; B3, AMC, IH, VW**

Beaverton; Beaverton Auto Wrecking, *see Vintage*

Bend; Bend Salvage & Auto Wrecking, *see Vintage*

Tired-Iron, *see Vintage*

Boring; Alpha Engines & Transmission, *see Vintage*

Damascus U Pull It, *see Vintage*

Oregon – Late Vintage

German Auto Salvage, 30495 SE Hwy 212, 97009; 503-663-3006; CC, Sa, Sp; 1ac; **70+; F; VW, BMW, Audi, Porsche; German only**

U-Pull It U-Save, *see Vintage*

Brookings; Phil's Auto Recycling, 207 King, 97415; 541-469-7489; CC, Sp; 0.5ac; **70-89; D, PU; Ford & Chevy only; Spc: Pickup**

Canby; South Canby Auto Wreckers, *see Vintage*

Yoder Garage at Yoder, *see Vintage*

Cave Junction; Phillips Auto Wrecking, *see Vintage*

Clackamas; Drive Train Four Wheel Drive, *see Vintage*

Coos Bay; A-101 Auto Salvage & Towing, *see Vintage*

Greenacres Auto Wrecking, *see Vintage*

Shinglehouse Auto Wreckers, *see Vintage*

Corvallis; Corvallis Auto Wrecking & Sls, *see Vintage*

Dayton; Dayton Auto Wrecking, *see Vintage*

Garibaldi; Dons Auto Wrecking & Towing, Hwy 101, 97118; 503-322-3303; Sa, Sp, UR; 3ac; **70-80; D, F, PU, 4x4; B3**

Grants Pass; Caveman Auto Parts-Recyclers, *see Vintage*

Gresham; Orient Auto Parts & Recycling, 28425 SE Orient Dr, 97080; 503-663-1909, FAX 503-663-9711, 800-332-1909; CC, Sa, Sp, UR; 2ac; **80-94; D, F, PU, 4x4; B3**

Hermiston; D & R Auto Sales, *see Vintage*

Hillsboro; Hillsboro Auto Wrecking, 2845 NW Glencoe Rd, 97124; 503-648-8944, FAX 503-640-5809, 800-547-5415; CC, Sa, Sp; 2ac; **80+, few 70s; D, F; B3**

Klamath Falls; Altamont Auto Wreckers, 2805 Altamont Dr, 97603; 541-882-2035; Sa, Sp, UR; 100; **80-89; D, few PU; B3**

Axel-Rods Auto Parts & Salvage, *see Vintage*

Klamath Auto Wreckers, *see Vintage*

Smash Auto Wrecking, 7242 Hilyard Av, 97603; 541-884-0710; Sa, Sp; 2ac; **70+; D, F, PU, 4x4; B3; Spc: Foreign, SUV**

Weatherford Salvage, 7330 Hilyard Av, 97603; 541-882-1554, FAX 541-884-3234; CC, Sa, Sp, Br; 2ac; **70-95; D, F, few PU, few 4x4; B3, IH**

La Grande; B & K Auto Salvage, 64190 Hwy 203, 97850; 541-963-6744, 800-233-9640; CC, Sp; 10ac; **85+; D, F, PU; B3; some IH**

Lakeview; Lakeview Auto Wrecking, *see Vintage*

Lebanon; Cascade Auto Body, *see Vintage*

Lincoln City; 23rd Auto Wrecking & Towing, *see Vintage*

McMinnville; McMinnville Auto Wrecking, *see Vintage*

Mount Hood Parkdale; Mt Hood Motors Inc, *see Vintage*

Oakland; Union Gap Recyclers Inc, *see Vintage*

Ontario; North Verde Auto Salvage, 2001 N Verde Dr, 97914; 541-889-5451; CC, Sp, UR; 6ac; **70-90; D, F, PU, 4x4; B3**

Oregon City; Dales Auto Wrecking, *see Vintage*

Portland; A & B Auto Wrecking, 11930 N Columbia Blvd, 97203; 503-286-4405, FAX 503-286-6193, 800-304-4405; CC, Sa, Sp; 2ac; **80+; D, F; B3**

A to Z Auto Wrecking, *see Vintage*

A-1 Light Trucks & Vans, *see Vintage*

Airport Auto Salvage, 4623 NE Buffalo St, 97218; 503-281-9788; CC, Sa; **75-91; D, F, PU, 4x4; B3**

Bob's Ford Parts, *see Vintage*

Bud's Auto Wrecking, *see Vintage*

Burnside Used Auto Parts, *see Vintage*

Chevy Corner Light Truck Slvg, 9101 SE Stanley Av, 97206; 503-771-3128, 888-771-3128; CC, Sp, Wr; **78+; D, PU; Chevy Pickup only**

Chevy Store, *see Vintage*

Columbia Light Truck Parts, *see Vintage*

Crystal Lane Auto Salvage Inc, 4545 NE Crystal Ln, 97218; 503-282-3452, FAX 503-282-0660; Sa, Sp, UR; 300; **80-92, few earlier; D; Spc: Camaro, Taurus**

256

Discount Pickup Parts, *see Vintage*
Division Street Auto Wrecking, *see Vintage*
GM Toys, *see Vintage*
Import Auto Salvage & Repair, *see Vintage*
J & H 4-Wheel Drive Specialty, *see Vintage*
John's Import Auto, 4701 SE 24th Av, 97202; 503-231-1601, 800-230-8116; CC, Sa, Sp, PL; 500+; **79+; F, PU**
Light Truck Parts, 10815 SE Foster Rd, 97266; 503-760-2468, 800-452-8004; CC, Sa, Sp, Wr; **80+, few 70s; D, F, PU; B3; Pickup only**
Michael's Auto Parts, *see Vintage*
Mustang Specialties, *see Vintage*
Northwest Classic Falcons, *see Vintage*
Northwest Recycling, *see Vintage*
Oregon Auto Wrecking, 14428 SE McLoughlin Blvd, 97267; 503-653-8181, 800-666-2412; CC, Sp; 350; **70+; D, F, PU, 4x4; B3, vans**
Pacific West Imports, *see Vintage*
Portland Auto Wrecking, 12122 N Columbia Blvd, 97203; 503-286-6262, FAX 503-735-4952, 800-821-6518; CC, Sa, UR; 500+; **70-89; D, F, PU, Trk; B3, AMC**
Ram Light Truck Salvage, 3546 NE Columbia Blvd, 97211; 503-284-4171, 800-359-6017; CC, Sa, Sp; 2ac; **70-90; D, F, PU; B3; Pickup only**
Reubens Import Auto Wrecking, 9501 N Columbia Blvd, 97203; 503-286-8349, 800-978-3276; CC, Sa, Sp, UR; 1ac; **70-89; Foreign only**
River-Gate Auto Wrecking, *see Vintage*
Rose City Classic Car Emporium, 1626 NW Thurman St, 97209; 503-294-7020; **68-73; D; Ford & Mercury only**
Rose City Mustang Ltd, *see Vintage*
Star Auto Wrecking, 9711 SE 82nd Av, 97266; 503-777-1477; Sa; 1ac; **80-89; D, F; B3**
Truck Wrecking Yard Inc, *see Vintage*
U-Pull-It Auto Wrecking, 6241 SE 111th Av, 97266; 503-760-5820; CC, Sa, UR; 5ac; **70+; D, F; B3**
Prineville; Dave's Auto Wrecking, *see Vintage*
Rainier; Bob's Towing, *see Vintage*
Redmond; Brad's Auto & Truck Parts, *see Vintage*
Schneider's Auto Wrecking, 906 NW 6th St, 97756; 541-923-6434, FAX 541-923-0353, 800-923-6434; CC, Sa, Sp, UR; 5ac; **70+, few 60s & earlier; D, F, PU; B3**
Roseburg; Walker Sales & Svc, *see Vintage*
Saint Helens; Ralph's Auto & Truck Wrecking, 1955 Old Portland Rd, 97051; 503-366-0957; Sa, Sp; 15ac; **80+, few 70s, parts for 60s & earlier; D, F, PU, 4x4, Trk, Cn; B3**
Salem; Economy Auto Wrecking, 11030 Portland Rd NE, 97305; 503-371-8963; Sa, Sp; 3ac; 300; **70-89, few 60s; D, F, PU; B3**
Mac's Jeeparts, 2484 Delany Rd SE, 97306; 503-371-3957, FAX 503-365-0702; CC, Sp; 30; **70+; D; Jeep only**
Sandy; Pat's Auto, *see Vintage*
Wildcat Auto Wrecking, *see Vintage*
Scappoose; Far West Auto Wrecking, 53635 Columbia River Hwy, 97056; 503-543-7118; Sp, Wr; 5ac; **70+; D, F, PU, 4x4; B3**
Scio; West Scio Auto Wreckers, *see Vintage*
Shady Cove; European Auto-Winch-Em Towing, *see Vintage*
Sherwood; Aries Truck Parts, 11535 SW Tonquin Rd, 97140; 503-692-5090; Sa, Sp, Wr; **80+, few 70s; D, F, PU, 4x4; B3**
Springfield; Springfield Auto Recyclers Inc, *see Vintage*
Stayton; Stayton Auto Wreckers, *see Vintage*
The Dalles; AFD Auto Salvage, 707 Snipes St, 97058; 541-298-4168; CC, Sa, Sp; **70+; D, F, PU; B3**
Jones Auto Wrecking, 749 Snipes St, 97058; 541-296-5222; UR; **80+; D, F; B3**
Troutdale; Burns Marsh Twin Lakes Jag, 97060; 503-669-8475; Sp; 72-**90; F; Spc: Jaguar**

Tualatin; T Bird Sanctuary, *see Vintage*
Willamina; Mishler Wreckers, *see Vintage*
Winston; Winston Towing, *see Vintage*
Yachats; Pop's Pre-Owned Parts & Slvg, 500 Camp One St, 97498; 541-547-3808; Sp, UR; 10ac; **70-89, few 50-60s parts; D, F, PU, 4x4; B3, AMC, IH**
Yamhill; Yamhill Auto Wrecking, 19455 NW Reservoir Rd, 97148; 503-662-3233; Sa, UR; 7ac; **70+; D, F, PU, 4x4; B3, IH**

LATE MODEL

Albany; AA Auto Wrecking, *see Late Vintage*
  Albany Engine Exchange, *see Vintage*
  B & R Auto, 1052 Goldfish Farm Rd SE, 97321; 541-967-8241, FAX 541-926-1990, 888-325-8469; CC, Sa, Sp, UR; 5ac, 800; **D, F, PU; B3; also in Springfield & Corvallis**
  D & J Auto Salvage Inc, *see Vintage*
Astoria; Astoria Auto Wrecking, *see Late Vintage*
Bandon; South Coast Auto Wrecking, *see Late Vintage*
Boring; Alpha Engines & Transmission, *see Vintage*
  Damascus U Pull It, *see Vintage*
  German Auto Salvage, *see Late Vintage*
  U-Pull It U-Save, *see Vintage*
Canby; Yoder Garage at Yoder, *see Vintage*
Clackamas; Drive Train Four Wheel Drive, *see Vintage*
Coos Bay; Shinglehouse Auto Wreckers, *see Vintage*
Corvallis; B & R Auto Wrecking Co, 3065 SE 3rd St, 97333; 541-757-0456, FAX 541-757-7720, 800-325-8469; CC, Sa, Sp; 12ac, 2000; **D, F, PU, 4x4; B3**
  Corvallis Auto Wrecking & Sls, *see Vintage*
Dayton; Dayton Auto Wrecking, *see Vintage*
Grants Pass; Caveman Auto Parts-Recyclers, *see Vintage*
  Indian Creek Import Parts, 1098 SE M St, 97526; 541-479-7203, FAX 541-476-4758, 800-289-7325; CC, Sa, Sp, UR; 2ac; **F, PU, mini vans**
  Peach Street Auto Recycling, 2851 Highland Av, 97526; 541-476-9575, FAX 541-476-7620, 800-365-2341; CC, Sa, Sp; 5ac; **F, PU**
Gresham; All Z East Auto Recycling, 1721 NW Eleven Mile Av, 97030; 503-666-5659
  Orient Auto Parts & Recycling, *see Late Vintage*
  Section Line Auto Wrecking, 3105 NE Division St, 97030; 503-665-8059; CC, Sa, Sp; **D, F, PU, 4x4; B3**
Hermiston; D & R Auto Sales, *see Vintage*
Hillsboro; All Foreign Auto Wrecking, 2995 SW 221st Av, 97123; 503-649-5691; CC, Sa, Sp; 350; **F, PU; VW, Jpa**
  Hillsboro Auto Wrecking, *see Late Vintage*
Klamath Falls; One Stop Auto Parts & Svc, *see Late Vintage*
  Smash Auto Wrecking, *see Late Vintage*
  Weatherford Salvage, *see Late Vintage*
La Grande; B & K Auto Salvage, *see Late Vintage*
Lebanon; Cascade Auto Body, *see Vintage*
  Petersons Auto Wrecking, 4330 S Santiam Hwy, 97355; 541-451-1557; CC, Sa, Sp, UR; **D, F, PU, 4x4; B3, Jp**
Madras; Ira's Sales & Svc, 181 SW Merritt Ln, 97741; 541-475-3861; CC, Sp; 20ac; **D, F, PU, 4x4, Trk, Mil; B3, Jp**
McMinnville; McMinnville Auto Wrecking, *see Vintage*
Mount Hood Parkdale; Mt Hood Motors Inc, *see Vintage*
Newport; Kings Towing, 109 King Place Rd, 97365; 541-265-8583; Sp; 5ac; **D, F, PU, 4x4, Trk, Cn; B3**
North Plains; Abacus Pickup Parts Inc, *see Vintage*
Oregon City; Dales Auto Wrecking, *see Vintage*
Portland; A & B Auto Wrecking, *see Late Vintage*
  A to Z Auto Wrecking, *see Vintage*

A-1 Light Trucks & Vans, *see Vintage*

Airport Auto Salvage, *see Late Vintage*

American Auto Wrecking Inc, 626 N Columbia Blvd, 97217; 503-289-5528; Sa, Sp; 4ac; **D, F; B3**

Auto Adventure, 125 SE Clay St, 97214; 503-238-6218; CC, Sa, Sp; 500+; **F; Honda only**

Auto Salvage 205, 5605 NE 105th Av, 97220; 503-256-3232; CC, Sa, Sp; 5.5ac; **D, PU, 4x4; GM only**

Bob's Ford Parts, *see Vintage*

Burnside Used Auto Parts, *see Vintage*

Chevy Corner Light Truck Slvg, *see Late Vintage*

Columbia Light Truck Parts, *see Vintage*

Crystal Lane Auto Salvage Inc, *see Late Vintage*

Discount Pickup Parts, *see Vintage*

Economy Auto Parts, 6909 NE 47th Av, 97218; 503-282-9067; CC, Sp; 300; **D, F; B3**

Foster Auto Parts Paint Supls, 10355 SE Foster Rd, 97266; 503-777-4531, www.fosterauto.com; CC, Sa, Sp, Wr; 150; **D, F; B3**

Import Auto Salvage & Repair, *see Vintage*

J & H 4-Wheel Drive Specialty, *see Vintage*

John's Import Auto, *see Late Vintage*

Light Truck Parts, *see Late Vintage*

Michael's Auto Parts, *see Vintage*

Mustang Specialties, *see Vintage*

Northwest Recycling, *see Vintage*

Oregon Auto Wrecking, *see Late Vintage*

Pacific West Imports, *see Vintage*

Portland Import Auto Parts, 13126 NE Whitaker Way, 97230; 503-255-8735, 800-547-3682; CC, Sa, Sp; 3ac; **F, PU; Imports only**

River-Gate Auto Wrecking, *see Vintage*

Rose Auto Wrecking Inc, 8140 N Commercial Av, 97217; 503-283-1164; CC, Sa, Sp; 50+; **D, F, PU, 4x4; B3**

Rainier; Bob's Towing, *see Vintage*

Redmond; Brad's Auto & Truck Parts, *see Vintage*

Schneider's Auto Wrecking, *see Late Vintage*

Roseburg; Roseburg Auto Wrecking, 220 Speedway Rd, 97470; 541-679-8786; CC, Sa, Sp; **D, F, PU, 4x4; B3**

Walker Sales & Svc, *see Vintage*

Saint Helens; Ralph's Auto & Truck Wrecking, *see Late Vintage*

Salem; Mac's Jeeparts, *see Late Vintage*

Scappoose; Far West Auto Wrecking, *see Late Vintage*

Sherwood; Aries Truck Parts, *see Late Vintage*

U-Pull-It Auto Wrecking, 19135 SW Pacific Hwy, 97140; 503-625-6141; Sa, UR; **D, F, PU; B3; inventory posted daily**

Terrebonne; Ike Abbas Automotive, 925 Central, 97760; 541-548-4540; CC, Sa, Sp, UR; 500; **F, PU**

The Dalles; AFD Auto Salvage, *see Late Vintage*

Jones Auto Wrecking, *see Late Vintage*

Troutdale; Mazda-Toyota Auto Recycling, 3611 NW Marine Dr, 97060; 503-667-6818, FAX 503-366-7810, 800-628-0918; CC, Sp, Wr; **F, PU; Jpa**

Turner; Pick-A-Part, 677 Turner Rd SE, 97392; 503-743-7425; CC, Sa, UR; 500; **D, F, PU; B3**

Willamina; Mishler Wreckers, *see Vintage*

Winston; Winston Towing, *see Vintage*

Yamhill; Yamhill Auto Wrecking, *see Late Vintage*

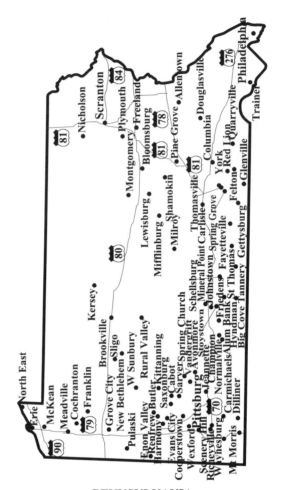

PENNSYLVANIA

VINTAGE

Big Cove Tannery; Shives Auto Salvage, HCR 81 Box 70A, Pittman Rd, 17212; 717-294-3485; Sa, UR; 300+; 60+; **D, F, PU, 4x4, Fm; B3**

Winfield Salvage Co, HCR 81 Box 225, 17212; 717-294-6064, wsc@nb.net; CC, Sa, Sp, UR; 3000; **46+; D; B3; closed Sunday & Monday**

Butler; James Winters Auto Wrecking, 310 Mushrush Rd, 16001; 724-283-0689; Sa; 2400; **40-89; D, PU, 4x4; B3, AMC, Pk; Spc: Rambler 5**2-73

Soose Auto Wrecking, 104 Swamp Run Rd, 16001; 724-283-0700; Sa, UR; 550+; 60-**89; D; B3, AMC, St**

Carlisle; Failors Salvage Yard, 452 Crossroad School Rd, 17013; 717-776-5200; Sa, Sp; 20ac, 2000; **50-89; D, PU; B3, AMC, Pk**

Columbia; Earl & Jack's Auto Parts, 4350 Marietta Av, 17512; 717-684-2556; CC, Sa, UR; 33ac, 2000; **39+; D, F, PU, 4x4; B3, AMC, St, Wy**

Enon Valley; Feezle Auto Wrecking, RD 1 Box 215, 16120; 724-336-5512, FAX 724-336-3630; CC, Sa, Sp, UR; 20ac, 5000; **60+; D, F, PU, 4x4, Trk, Fm; B3, AMC, Jp, IH, St, VW**

260

Erie; Carl's Auto Parts, 5250 Knoyle Rd, 16510; 814-899-1412; Sa; 3000; **50-89; D, PU, 4x4; B3, AMC, Jp, St, Ks**

Fayetteville; Beechers Auto Salvage Inc, 7287 Lincoln Way E, 17222; 717-352-2246, FAX 717-352-0042; CC, Sa, Sp, UR; 1200; **50+; D, F, PU, 4x4; B3, Jp, Hd, Pk, VW**

Felton; Barry L Eckert & Sons, 7025 S Church Rd, 17322; 717-993-2786; Sa, UR; 50; **50-89; D, F, PU, 4x4; B3**

Franklin; Lowrey's Auto Wrecking, RD 3 Lamberton Rd, 16323; 814-437-5708, FAX 814-437-2333, 800-955-8554; Sa, Sp, PL; 1000; **19+; D, F, PU, 4x4; B3, AMC, Jp, IH, VW**

Gettysburg; Corvair Ranch Inc, 1079 Bon-Ox Rd, 17325; 717-624-2805, FAX 717-624-1196; CC, Sa, Sp, Wr; 400+; **60-69; D; Corvair only; used & new parts**

Road Rangers Towing, 1936 Biglerville Rd, 17325; 717-337-9633, FAX 717-337-1055; CC, Sa; 1ac; **60+; D, F, PU, 4x4; B3; Spc: muscle cars**

Glenville; Ed Lucke's Auto Parts, RR 2 Box 2883, 17329; 717-235-2866; Sa, Sp, UR; 2000+; **30-85; D; B3, AMC, Hd, Ns, St, Pk, Fr, Wy; Spc: pre 70**

Grove City; Eperthener Auto Wrecking, 683 Tieline Rd, 16127; 814-786-7173; Sa; 25ac; **60-90; D, F, PU, 4x4; B3**

Johnstown; Auto Wreckers, 704 Pickworth St, 15902; 814-536-5834; Sa, UR; 300; **50+, few 40s; D; B3, St, Pk; 50s mostly**

McKean; Denny's Auto Wrecking, 7243 Thomas Rd, 16426; 814-833-7169; Sa, UR; 3000; **50-94; D, F, PU, 4x4; B3, AMC, IH, VW**

Mifflintown; Aukers Salvage, Rt 4 Box 368, 17059; 717-436-6207; Sa, UR; 500; **50-90; D, F, PU; B3**

Mineral Point; Gillins Auto & Truck Salvage, 1493 Adams Av, 15942; 814-322-4366; Sp; 1000; **60-79, few back to 30s; D, PU, 4x4, Fm; B3, Jp, IH; Spc: Ford**

Normalville; Upton Auto Wreckers, RD 1 Box 142A, 15469; 724-455-2805; Sa, UR; 500; **50+; D, F, PU, 4x4; B3**

Philadelphia; Chuck's Used Auto Parts, 6750 Essington Av, 19153; 215-365-4288; Sa, Sp; 700; **50+; D, F, PU, 4x4; B3, Jp, IH, Wy; Spc: 4x4; shows Hot Rod 4x4s**

Pine Grove; Klinger's Used Auto Sales, RD 3 Box 454, 17963; 717-345-8778; Sa, Sp, UR; 24ac; 2500+; **60-83, few earlier; D, few F, PU, 4x4; B3, AMC, Ns, St; Spc: 41-54 Chevy**

Plymouth; J-L Used Auto Parts Inc, 658 Main St Rear, 18651; 570-779-5101, FAX 570-729-0750; Sa, Sp, UR; 1000; **46+; D, F, PU, 4x4, Trk; B3, AMC, Jp, Wy, VW**

Quarryville; G & R Auto Salvage, 965 Lancaster Pike, 17566; 717-284-2800, FAX 717-284-2540; CC, Sa, UR; 600+; **67+; D, F, PU, 4x4; B3, AMC, Jp, VW**

Scenery Hill; Ritenour & Sons Wreckers, 234 Wherry Rd, 15360; 724-239-2601, FAX 724-239-2603; Sa, Sp; 400+; **60+; D, F, PU, 4x4, Trk, Fm; B3, AMC, Jp, VW**

Scranton; Rudy's Wrecking, 9 E Market St, 18509; 570-969-1330; Sa; 1000; **60+; D, PU; B3, AMC; 2 lots**

Shamokin; Winnick's Auto Sales & Parts, Rt 61 Box 476, 17872; 570-648-6857, FAX 570-648-2767; Sa, Sp, Wr, PL; 500; **65+; D, F, PU, 4x4; B3, AMC, Jp, VW; since 1939; Spc: motors & 65-75 Mustang & Camaro**

Trainer; Joe's Auto Parts, 3305 W 9th St, 19061; 610-494-7901, www.joesautoparts.com; Sa, Sp, UR, Wr; 6ac; 500; **50-87; D; Spc: Cadillac**

Vandergrift; Culps Auto Wrecking, RD 2 Box 108, 15690; 724-567-6669; Sa, UR; 500; **65+; D, F, PU, 4x4; B3, AMC, Jp, IH, VW**

West Sunbury; Renicks Used Auto Parts, 49 West Sunbury Rd, 16061; 724-283-2166; Sa, UR; 2000; **33-90; D, PU, 4x4; B3, Jp, Hd, St, Ks, Fr**

Wexford; Hub Cap City, 11490 Perry Hwy, 15090; 724-935-5380, FAX 724-935-0711; Sa, Sp; 50; **90+; D; B3; mainly Hubcaps back to 30's**

<u>*LATE VINTAGE*</u>

Allentown; The Junkyard, 201 Sumner St, 18102; 610-435-7278; Sa, UR; 1000+; **75-90; D, F, PU, 4x4; B3**

Avonmore; Calandrellas Garage, RD 1 Box 320, 15618; 724-697-4997; Sa; 200; **70+; D, F, PU; B3**

Big Cove Tannery; Shives Auto Salvage, *see Vintage*

W & W Salvage Co, HCR 81 Box 221, Wolf Hollow Rd, 17212; 717-294-6159, 800-484-5213x5213; Sa, UR; 400+; **70-90; D, F, PU, 4x4; B3**

Winfield Salvage Co, *see Vintage*

Bloomsburg; Swartz Salvage Inc, RR 9 Box 201, 17815; 570-458-5109, FAX 570-458-6021; Sa; 3000; **70+; D, F, PU, 4x4, Trk, Fm, In; B3, AMC, IH; Spc: Chevy**

Brookville; Davis Used Cars & Parts, Box 287, Brookville-Davis Rd, 15825; 814-849-2197; Sa, Sp; 1000; **70-90; D, F, PU, 4x4; B3, AMC, Jp**

Butler; Dawson's Auto Wrecking, 113 Protzman Rd, 16001; 724-283-6000; CC, Sa; 1000; **70-93; D, F, PU, 4x4; B3, AMC, VW**

James Winters Auto Wrecking, *see Vintage*

Marshall Offstein Auto Sales, 655 Oneida Valley Rd, 16001; 724-285-8800; Sa, UR; 2000; **80+; D, F, PU, 4x4; B3, AMC**

Reges Auto Wrck, 696 Glenwood Wy, 16001; 724-285-5113; CC, Sa; 850+; **80-93; D, F**

Soose Auto Wrecking, *see Vintage*

Cabot; Ambrose Auto Wrck, 117 Ambrose Ln, 16023; 724-352-4354; Sa; 250+; **70-89; D**

Carlisle; Failors Salvage Yard, *see Vintage*

Carmichaels; Marty's Auto, RD 1, 15320; 724-966-7832; Sp; 200; **80-89; D, F, PU, 4x4; B3**

West End Auto Wreckers, RR 2, 15320; 724-966-5537; Sa; 5ac, 500; **70-88; D, F, PU; B3**

Champion; William A. Durstine Auto, Box 62, 15662; 724-455-3342; 2ac, 200; **70-89; D, F**

Cochranton; Peterson Brothers Salvage, Custards Rd, 16314; 814-425-2411; Sa, UR; 300+; **70-89; D, F, PU, 4x4, few Trk; Fm; B3**

Columbia; Earl & Jack's Auto Parts, *see Vintage*

Cooperstown; Bucholz Auto Salvage & Parts, RD 1 Box 295, Dempseytown Rd, 16317; 814-676-6563; Sa; 2ac, 200; **70-89; D, F, PU, 4x4; B3**

Dilliner; Jordan Auto Parts, Rt 1 Box 289A, 15327; 724-943-3522, FAX 724-943-4196, 800-448-3522, www.jordanautoparts.com; CC, Sa, Sp, Wr; 70ac, 8000+; **70+; D, F, PU, 4x4, Trk; B3, AMC, Jp, VW**

Enon Valley; Feezle Auto Wrecking, *see Vintage*

Erie; American & Foreign Auto, 1020 W 19th St, 16502; 814-456-0041; Sa, Wr; 100; **86-93; D, F, PU, 4x4; B3**

Bizzarro's Towing & Used Parts, 1130 W 16th St, 16502; 814-459-0953, FAX 814-452-2384; CC, Sa; 1500; **70-91; D, F, PU, 4x4; B3**

Carl's Auto Parts, *see Vintage*

Community Auto Recycling, 2540 Manshester Rd, 16506; 814-833-8518; Sa, UR; 500; **70+; D, F, PU, 4x4; B3, AMC, VW**

Kendall Auto Parts Inc, 802 Perry St, 16503; 814-456-7075, FAX 814-456-0851, 800-898-PART, autopart@velocity.net; Sa, Sp, Wr; **70+; D, PU, 4x4; B3, AMC**

Mother's Auto Sales & Parts, 10320 Wattsburg Rd, 16509; 814-825-3731, FAX 814-825-1018, 877-530-5992, www.citiesites.com/mothers; CC, Sa, Sp; 200; **70+; D, F, PU, 4x4; B3, Jp**

Fayetteville; Beechers Auto Salvage Inc, *see Vintage*

Felton; Barry L Eckert & Sons, *see Vintage*

Franklin; Lowrey's Auto Wrecking, *see Vintage*

Freeland; Masley's Auto Wreckers, RR 1 Box 199C, 18224; 570-636-2690; Sa; 1200; **75+; D, PU; B3, AMC, IH**

Gettysburg; Corvair Ranch Inc, *see Vintage*

Road Rangers Towing, *see Vintage*

Glenville; Ed Lucke's Auto Parts, *see Vintage*

Grove City; Eperthener Auto Wrecking, *see Vintage*

Hyndman; Jim Sacco Auto Wreckers, Cook's Mill Rd, 15545; 814-842-3482; CC, Sa, Sp, UR; 1000; **80+; D, F, PU, 4x4; B3, AMC, Jp; some 70s**

Jeannette; Gombach Towing & Auto Salvage, Gombach Rd, 15644; 412-744-4430; Sa; 2000; **70+; D, F, PU, 4x4; B3, AMC, Jp, IH, VW**

Johnstown; Auto Wreckers, *see Vintage*

William Penn Auto, 837 William Penn Av, 15906; 814-539-0610; Sa; 300+; **70+; D, F, PU, 4x4; B3**

262

Kersey; Elk County Recycling Ctr, 1388 Million Dollar Hwy, 15846; 814-834-2089; Sa, Sp, UR; 120; **79-86; D, PU, 4x4; B**3

Kittanning; Rupps Auto Wrecking, RD 6, 16201; 724-543-3187; Sa; 250+; **70-89; D, F; B**3, **AMC, Jp**

   Zimmerman's Auto Wrecking, RD 2 Box 186B, 16201; 724-545-7102; Sa, Sp, PL; 27ac; 1000; Car: **85-95, PU: 68-93; D, F, PU, 4x4; B**3, **AMC, Jp, IH, VW**

McKean; Denny's Auto Wrecking, *see Vintage*

Meadville; Merle Hayes Auto Wrecking, 16379 Valley Rd, 16335; 814-763-4008; Sa, Sp; 650+; **80+; D, PU, 4x4; B**3, **AMC, Jp**

Mifflinburg; Hartman's Junk & Auto Wrecking, RR 2 Box 503, 17844; 717-966-0672; Sa; 300; **80s, few 70s; D, F, PU; B**3

Mifflintown; Aukers Salvage, *see Vintage*

   Goshorn Auto Salvage, RR5 Box 552, 17059; 717-436-2576; Sa; 100; **70-79; D, F; B**3

Mineral Point; Gillins Auto & Truck Salvage, *see Vintage*

Montgomery; B & C Auto Wreckers, 4867 Rt 15 Hwy, 17752; 570-547-1040, FAX 570-547-7051; CC, Sa, Sp, PL; 3000; **70+; D, F, PU, 4x4; B**3, **AMC, Jp, VW**

Mount Morris; Shannon Run Auto Salvage, RD 1 Box 342A, 15349; 724-324-2886; **50+; 80+, few 70s; D, F, PU, 4x4; Jp**

New Bethlehem; Mc Cauley's Auto Wrecking, Rt 66 RD 3, 16242; 814-275-2025; Sa; 450+; **87-95; D, F, PU, 4x4; B**3

   Rhodes Auto Salvage Inc, PO Box 273, Rt 28N, 16242; 814-275-1095; Sa; 1000; **75-94; D, F, PU, 4x4**

Nicholson; C B Auto Salvage, Martin Creek Rd, 18446; 570-942-6337; Sa; 1000; **70+; D, F, PU, 4x4; B**3, **AMC, VW**

Normalville; Robert E Platt Auto Wreckers, RD 1 Box 16, 15469; 724-455-3878; Sa; 700+; **70+; D, PU, 4x4; B**3, **AMC, Hp, IH**

   Upton Auto Wreckers, *see Vintage*

North East; North East Auto, 10224 W Main Rd, 16428; 814-725-1253, 800-222-6109; CC, Sa, Sp; 1600; **82+; D, F, PU, 4x4; B**3

Philadelphia; American Auto Parts & Slvg, 3501 S 61st St, 19153; 215-724-4912, FAX 215-729-4888, www.americanautoparts.baweb.com; CC, Sa, Sp; 250; **78+; D, F, PU, vans; B**3

   Chuck's Used Auto Parts, *see Vintage*

Pine Grove; Klinger's Used Auto Sales, *see Vintage*

Pittsburgh; Baldwin Auto Parts & Wreckers, 900 Horning Rd, 15236; 412-653-9090; Sa, Wr; 45+; **70+; D, PU, 4x4; B**3, **AMC, Jp**

Plymouth; J-L Used Auto Parts Inc, *see Vintage*

Pulaski; Route 18 Auto Wrecking, 4287 New Castle Rd, 16143; 724-946-2113, 800-927-7818; Sa, Sp, UR; 500; **80-90; D, F, PU, 4x4; B**3, **VW**

Quarryville; G & R Auto Salvage, *see Vintage*

Renfrew; Nolands Auto Salvage, 114 Creek Rd, 16053; 724-586-5812; Sa, Sp; 200; **70-89; D, F, PU, 4x4; B**3

Richeyville; Phillips Auto Salvage, 1134 Maiden St, 15358; 724-632-3393; Sa, UR; **70+; D, PU, 4x4; B**3

Rural Valley; Rankins Auto Wrecking, 16249; 724-354-2647, FAX 724-354-3609; Sa, Br; 30ac; **80-89; D, PU, 4x4, Trk; B**3

Scenery Hill; Ritenour & Sons Wreckers, *see Vintage*

Scranton; Anthracite Auto Wreckers, 900 S 5th Av, 18504; 570-346-3309, 800-606-2002; CC, Sa, Sp, UR; 2500+; **80-95; D, F, PU, 4x4, Trk, Fm, Cn; B**3, **AMC, IH, VW**

   Keyser Valley Auto Wreckers, 2300 Washburn St, 18504; 570-347-6062; CC, Sa, UR; 28ac; **78-85; D, F, PU, Trk; B**3

   Rudy's Wrecking, *see Vintage*

Shamokin; Winnick's Auto Sales & Parts, *see Vintage*

Spring Grove; Eichelberger Auto Salvage, Rt 1, 17362; 717-225-5610; 400; **85-94; D, F, PU, 4x4; B**3

Stoystown; A-1 Auto Wreckers, 3265 Whistler Rd, 15563; 814-893-5750, 800-826-1903; Sa, Sp; 1200; **78+; D, F, PU, 4x4; B**3

263

Pennsylvania – Late Vintage

Ray's Auto Sales & Parts, 3179 Lincoln Hwy, 15563; 814-629-7411, FAX 814-629-6031, 800-626-5775 PA only; Sa, Sp; **80+; D, F; B3**

Stoystown Auto Wreckers, P.O. Box 240, 15563; 814-893-5418, FAX 814-893-6262, 800-358-8770; CC, Sa, Sp; 30ac; **80+; D, F, PU, 4x4; B3**

Thomasville; Christine Auto Salvage, Box 131, 17364; 717-792-4465; Sa; 800; **70-89; D, PU; B3, AMC**

Trainer; Joe's Auto Parts, *see Vintage*

Vandergrift; Culps Auto Wrecking, *see Vintage*

West Sunbury; Renicks Used Auto Parts, *see Vintage*

Wexford; Hub Cap City, *see Vintage*

York; Christine's Auto Recycling, 5100 N Susquehanna Trl, 17402; 717-266-1347; Sa; 150; **70-89; D, F, PU, 4x4; B3; Spc: Camaro**

Hap Gemmill's Junkyard, 1563 Camp Betty Washington Rd, 17402; 717-755-8211; Sa, Wr; 13; **70+; D, F; B3, AMC, Jp, VW**

LATE MODEL

Allentown; CARS Inc, 299 Cedar St, 18102; 610-439-8641, FAX 610-770-1031; CC, Sp; 1000; **D, F, PU, 4x4; B3**

Alum Bank; Dull's Auto Wreckers, Main St, 15521; 814-839-2941, FAX 814-839-9311; Sa, Sp; **D, F, PU, 4x4**

Avonmore; Calandrellas Garage, *see Late Vintage*

Big Cove Tannery; Shives Auto Salvage, *see Late Vintage*

Winfield Salvage Co, *see Vintage*

Bloomsburg; Swartz Salvage Inc, *see Late Vintage*

Brockport; Cristinis Auto Wrecking, RD 1 Box 164, Boone Mountain Rd, 15823; 814-268-6685, FAX 814-265-1353, 800-672-7160; CC, Sa, Sp; 1000+; **D, PU, 4x4; B3**

Butler; Dawson's Auto Wrecking, *see Late Vintage*

Lockaton Auto Wreckers, 330 Herman Rd, 16001; 724-287-5830; Sa, Sp; **D; B3**

Marshall Offstein Auto Sales, *see Late Vintage*

Milich Auto Wrecking, 423 Oneida Valley Rd, 16001; 724-287-1001, FAX 724-287-7444, 800-MILICH1; CC, Sa; 500; **D, PU, 4x4; B3**

Reges Auto Wrecking, *see Late Vintage*

Carmichaels; Whiteley Auto Wreckers, RD 1 Box 84, 15320; 724-966-7191; Sa; 2ac, 200; **D**

Cochranton; Patterson Auto Wrecking Inc, 1973 Old 322, 16314; 814-425-7415, FAX 814-425-1110, 800-822-2028; 40ac, 2000; **D, F, PU, 4x4; B3**

Columbia; Earl & Jack's Auto Parts, *see Vintage*

Dilliner; Jordan Auto Parts, *see Late Vintage*

Douglassville; Chuck's Auto Salvage, 6867 Boyertown Pike, 19518; 610-385-6310, FAX 610-689-4072; CC, Sp; 7ac, 600; **D, F, PU, 4x4; B3**

Enon Valley; Feezle Auto Wrecking, *see Vintage*

Erie; American & Foreign Auto, *see Late Vintage*

Community Auto Recycling, *see Late Vintage*

Kendall Auto Parts Inc, *see Late Vintage*

Mother's Auto Sales & Parts, *see Late Vintage*

Evans City; A-1 Automotive, 429 May Ln, 16033; 724-538-9865, 888-538-9233; CC, Sa, Sp, UR; 450+; **D; B3; rebuilds cars**

Walters Auto Wrecking, 364 Old Route 68, 16033; 724-538-9317; CC, Sa, Sp

Fayetteville; Beechers Auto Salvage Inc, *see Vintage*

Franklin; Eakin Auto, RD 1 Box 10, 16323; 814-432-3153, FAX 814-437-2811, 800-352-3543; Sa, Sp; 600; **D; B3**

Lowrey's Auto Wrecking, *see Vintage*

Freeland; Masley's Auto Wreckers, *see Late Vintage*

Friedens; Hemminger Auto & Truck Parts, 15541; 814-445-9603; **D, PU, 4x4, Trk; B3**

Gettysburg; Road Rangers Towing, *see Vintage*

Harmony; Ed Wagner Pickup & Van Parts, 727 Perry Hwy, 16037; 724-368-9585, FAX 724-368-9696, 800-366-8196, truckparts@webtv.net; CC, Sa, Sp, UR; 600+; **D, PU, 4x4; B3; Spc: Pickup & vans**

Harmony; John Wagner & Sons Auto Wrkg, 735 Perry Hwy, 16037; 724-368-8831, FAX 724-368-9501, 800-472-2830; CC, Sa, Sp, UR; 1500; **F, PU, 4x4; mostly Japanese**

Hyndman; Jim Sacco Auto Wreckers, *see Late Vintage*

Jeannette; Gombach Towing & Auto Salvage, *see Late Vintage*

Johnstown; Auto Wreckers, *see Vintage*
    William Penn Auto, *see Late Vintage*

Kittanning; Zimmerman's Auto Wrecking, *see Late Vintage*

Lewisburg; Milton Auto Parts Inc, 901 Ziegler Rd, 17837; 717-568-5131; Sa; 600+; **D, PU**

McKean; Denny's Auto Wrecking, *see Vintage*

Meadville; Merle Hayes Auto Wrecking, *see Late Vintage*

Milroy; Aumiller's Auto Wreckers Inc, 45 Mechanic St, 17063; 717-667-2191, FAX 717-667-6780, 800-642-8323; Sa, Sp; 67ac, 5000; **D, F, PU, 4x4; B3, VW, Mercedes, BMW, Audi**

Montgomery; B & C Auto Wreckers, *see Late Vintage*

Mount Morris; Burnside Auto Salvage, PO Box 429, 15349; 724-324-5126; Sa; 500+; **D; B3**
    Shannon Run Auto Salvage, *see Late Vintage*

New Bethlehem; Mc Cauley's Auto Wrecking, *see Late Vintage*
    Rhodes Auto Salvage Inc, *see Late Vintage*

Nicholson; C B Auto Salvage, *see Late Vintage*

Normalville; Robert E Platt Auto Wreckers, *see Late Vintage*
    Upton Auto Wreckers, *see Vintage*

North East; North East Auto, *see Late Vintage*

Philadelphia; American Auto Parts & Salvage, *see Late Vintage*
    Chuck's Used Auto Parts, *see Vintage*

Pittsburg; Baldwin Auto Parts & Wreckers, *see Late Vintage*

Plymouth; J-L Used Auto Parts Inc, *see Vintage*

Quarryville; G & R Auto Salvage, *see Vintage*

Red Lion; Red Lion Auto Salvage Inc, 5433 Rippling Run Rd, 17356; 717-244-8579, FAX 717-246-2777; CC, Sa, Sp; 1100+; **D, PU, 4x4; B3**

Richeyville; Phillips Auto Salvage, *see Late Vintage*

Saint Thomas; Dave Shockey Used Auto Parts, 472 Saint Thomas Williamson Rd, 17252; 717-369-3113, 800-522-1145; 600+; **D; B3**

Sarver; Cash Auto & Truck Salvage Inc, 306 Coal Hollow Rd, 16055; 724-353-1680; 2ac; **D**

Saxonburg; Saxonburg Blvd Auto Parts Inc, 1140 Saxonburg Blvd, 16056; 724-265-3011; Sa, Sp; 10ac; **D; B3**

Schellsburg; A J Self Storage, RD 1, 15559; 814-733-4669; Sa, Sp; **D, F, PU, 4x4; B3**

Scenery Hill; Ritenour & Sons Wreckers, *see Vintage*

Scranton; Anthracite Auto Wreckers, *see Late Vintage*
    Rudy's Wrecking, *see Vintage*

Shamokin; Winnick's Auto Sales & Parts, *see Vintage*

Sligo; Sligo Auto Salvage, 16255; 814-745-3300; Sa, Sp, PL; **D, F**

Spring Church; Spring Church Auto Wrecking, Box 59A, 15686; 724-478-1110; Sa; 40; **D**

Spring Grove; Eichelberger Auto Salvage, *see Late Vintage*

Stoystown; A-1 Auto Wreckers, *see Late Vintage*
    Ray's Auto Sales & Parts, *see Late Vintage*
    Stoystown Auto Wreckers, *see Late Vintage*

Vandergrift; Culps Auto Wrecking, *see Late Vintage*

Waynesburg; Barton Auto Wrecking, 175 School Dr, 15370; 724-627-3351, www.bartonautowrecking.com; Sa; 600; **D, F; B3**

Wexford; Hub Cap City, *see Vintage*
    Wexford Auto Parts, 11490 Perry Hwy, 15090; 724-935-2764; Sa, Sp, Wr; 2ac; **D; B3; hub caps 40+ D & F most models**

York; Hap Gemmill's Junkyard, *see Late Vintage*

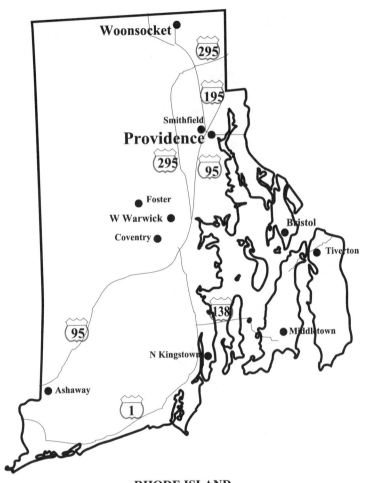

RHODE ISLAND

Rhode Island - Vintage

North Kingstown; Oak Hill Auto Salvage, 381 Oak Hill Rd, 02852; 401-295-0585, FAX 401-295-3260; Sa, Sp, U-Pk; 3ac; **60+; D, F, PU, 4x4; B3; Boats**

Providence; ABC Auto Truck & Bus Parts, 120 Plympton St, 02904; 401-353-2100; CC, Sa, Sp, Br; 4ac; **65+; Mostly 90+; D, F, PU, 4x4, Trk, Bus; B3**

North Providence Auto Salvage, 940 Smithfield Rd, 02904; 401-353-6720; CC, Sa, Sp; 3ac; **60+; D, F, PU, 4x4; B3**

LATE VINTAGE

Bristol; Jack's Salvage & Auto Parts, *see Vintage*

Coventry; Capozzi's Auto Sales & Salvage, 2015 New London Tpke, 02816; 401-821-5793; Sa, Sp, U-Pk; 3ac; **70+; D, F, PU, 4x4; B3**

Cumberland; Bill's Auto Parts, *see Vintage*

Foster; Wilson's Auto Parts, 40 Mill Rd, 02825; 401-647-3554, FAX 401-647-2920, 800-334-4273; CC, Sa, Sp, U-Pk; 36ac; **80+; D, F, PU, 4x4, few Trk; B3**

Middletown; Gold Auto Wrecking, *see Vintage*

North Kingstown; Oak Hill Auto Salvage, *see Vintage*

Providence; A & A Auto, 381 Huntington Av, 02909; 401-943-6625; CC, Sa; 100; **80+; D, F; B3**

ABC Auto Truck & Bus Parts, *see Vintage*

AMP Auto Salvage, 186 Sisson St, 02909; 401-353-9714; 40; **80-86; D, F**

International Auto Salvage, 385 Huntington Av, 02909; 401-942-1165; Sa; 300; **83-93; F; Jpa & Eur**

North Providence Auto Salvage, *see Vintage*

Zavota Auto Salvage, 255 Chalkstone Av, 02908; 401-274-5010; CC, Sa, U-Pk; **80+; D, F, PU, 4x4; B3**

Smithfield; Five Star Auto Salvage, 1348 Douglas Pike, 02917; 401-231-2916, FAX 401-231-9849; Sa, Sp; 5ac 2000; **70+; D, F, PU, 4x4; B3**

Tiverton; General Auto Recycling, 384 King Rd, 02878; 401-624-6687, FAX 401-625-1040, 800-556-7316; CC, Sa, Sp, U-Pk, PL; 25ac; **F=75+, D=88+; D, F, PU, 4x4; B3**

Woonsocket; Woonsocket Auto Salvage, Madison Av, 02895; 401-769-2323, FAX 401-769-7190, 800-924-2303; CC, Sa, Sp; 12ac; **70+; S, D, PU, 4x4; B3**

LATE MODEL

Bristol; Franco Brothers Salvage, 25 Tower St, 02809; 401-253-1030; 1ac; **D, F, PU, 4x4**

Jack's Salvage & Auto Parts, *see Vintage*

Coventry; Capozzi's Auto Sales & Salvage, *see Late Vintage*

Cumberland; Advanced Auto Recycling, 290 Curran Rd, 02864; 401-334-2000, FAX 401-334-0137, 800-447-1034, www.advancedautoparts.com; CC, Sa, Sp; 20ac; **D, F, PU, 4x4**

Bill's Auto Parts, *see Vintage*

Foster; Wilson's Auto Parts, *see Late Vintage*

Middletown; Gold Auto Wrecking, *see Vintage*

North Kingstown; Oak Hill Auto Salvage, *see Vintage*

Providence; A & A Auto, *see Late Vintage*

ABC Auto Truck & Bus Parts, *see Vintage*

Allen's Avenue Auto Salvage, 75 Ellenfield St, 02905; 401-461-4200, FAX 401-461-6130, 800-343-9399; CC, Sa, Sp; 2ac; **D, F, PU, 4x4, Trk**

K & R Auto Salvage, 950 Smithfield Rd, 02904; 401-353-9200, FAX 401-353-8668, 800-638-8089 New England only; CC, Sa, Sp; 700; **D, F, PU, 4x4**

North Providence Auto Salvage, *see Vintage*

Zavota Auto Salvage, *see Late Vintage*

Smithfield; Five Star Auto Salvage, *see Late Vintage*

Tiverton; General Auto Recycling, *see Late Vintage*

West Warwick; J & D Auto Salvage, 1 Bridal Av, 02893; 401-826-0618, FAX 401-826-0657, mikebec@aol.com; Sa, Sp; 2ac; **D, F, PU,4x4**

Woonsocket; Woonsocket Auto Salvage, *see Late Vintage*

267

South Carolina

Please use the cards in the back to let us know about yards we may have missed, or any other comments or information for future editions of Ray's wReckingyard Roster

SOUTH CAROLINA

VINTAGE

Anderson; Ed Powell's Auto Salvage, 3715 Mabry St, 29624; 864-296-9722, FAX 864-296-2370, 888-889-3122; CC, Sa, Sp, Br; 40ac, 5000+; **64-93; D, F, PU; B3, AMC, VW**

Bamberg; Hutto's Salvage, Hwy 601, 29003; 803-245-5573; Sa; 300; **60+; D, PU, 4x4; B3, AMC**

Chesnee; Vick's Classic Auto Parts, 815 Rutherfordton Hwy, 29323; 864-461-9071; Sa, Sp, UR; 14ac; **50-90; D, F, PU, 4x4, Trk; B3, AMC, Jp, IH, VW; Spc: Chevelle, Fairlane, Monte Carlo, Nova**

Easley; Bruce O'Shields Used Auto Parts, 136 O'Shields Rd, 29640; 864-859-1558; Sa; 2500+; **40+; D, F, PU; B3, AMC, St, Pk**

Fort Mill; Miller's Auto Salvage & Garage, 2231 Dam Rd, 29715; 803-548-5970; Sa, UR; 200+; **60-89; D, F, PU; B3, VW**

Greenville; Vintage Auto, 605 Pine Knoll Dr, 29609; 864-292-8785, FAX 864-967-0195, www.vintageonline.com; CC, Sa, Sp, UR; 60; **60+; F; VW 60-95 & Honda 85+ only**

Hodges; Martin Quarles Used Parts, 318 Daniel Rd, 29653; 864-374-3418; Sa; 150; **51-89; D, F, PU; B3**

Iva; A to Z Auto Salvage, 936 Audrey Hardy Rd, 29655; 864-348-3878; Sa, Sp; 200; **60-85; D, F, PU; B3**

Laurens; Kellett's Auto Salvage, RR 3, 29360; 864-575-3293; Sa; 1500; **60+, few 40-50s; D, F, PU, 4x4; B3, AMC; Spc: Pontiac**

Lexington; Brock's Camaro & Firebird Prts, 1737 S Lake Dr, 29073; 803-951-3063; Sa; 100; **75+, few 40-73; D; B3, Camaro, Firebird, some other Vintage cars**

North; K & W Auto Salvage, 3651 Savannah Hwy, 29112; 803-247-2167; Sa, UR; 375; **60-93; D, F, PU; B3; AC rework**

Prosperity; Mid-Carolina Parts & Salvage, 3950 Bethel Church Rd, 29127; 803-364-4350, FAX 803-364-2205; Sa; 50ac, 500+; **39+; D, F, PU; B3, AMC; Mostly 60s Pickup**

St Matthews; Franks Auto Salvage, Rt 1 Box 158-G, Hwy 6, 29135; 803-655-5335; Sa, UR; 200+; **50-80; D, F; B3**

Waterloo; Burdette Auto Salvage Svc, 3588 Riverfork Rd # F, 29384; 864-677-2122, FAX 864-677-3434; Sa, Sp, UR; 1000; **40+; D, F, PU, 4x4; B3, AMC, Jp, Ns, St, Wy**

Williams; Garris Auto Salvage Inc, 1425 Garris Av, 29493; 843-562-2111, 800-922-6809; Sp; 10ac; **60+; D, F, PU, 4x4; B3, AMC, Jp, VW**

LATE VINTAGE

Aiken; Graves Auto Salvage, 1360 Edgefield Hwy, 29801; 803-648-9012, FAX 803-648-6111, 800-922-8849; CC, Sp; 3000+; **76+; D, F, PU, 4x4; B3, AMC, Jp, VW**

Anderson; Ed Powell's Auto Salvage, *see Vintage*

Bamberg; Hutto's Salvage, *see Vintage*

Beaufort; Coastal Auto Salvage, 130 Laurel B0ay Rd, 29906; 843-846-6688; Sa, Sp; 500+; **70-92; D, F, PU; B3, AMC; Spc: Chrysler - Mopar**

Charleston; BBDS Used Parts, 1951 Horne Rd, 29406; 843-553-8836; CC, Sa, Sp; 1500; **80-89; D, F, PU; B3, VW**

Chesnee; Vick's Classic Auto Parts, *see Vintage*

Cottageville; April's Used Auto Parts, Rd 242, 29435; 843-835-2613; Sa, UR; 100+; **80-92; D, F, Fm; B3**

Easley; Bruce O'Shields Used Auto Parts, *see Vintage*

Fair Play; Layton Brown Used Cars & Parts, 221 Browns Rd, 29643; 864-972-3814; Sa; 800; **75-92; D, F, PU, 4x4; B3**

Fort Mill; Miller's Auto Salvage & Garage, *see Vintage*

Greenville; Vintage Auto, *see Vintage*

Greer; Auto Salvage & Country Repair, 3688 N Hwy 14, 29651; 864-895-8002; Sa, Sp, UR; 300; **72-89; D, PU; B3**

Hartsville; Galloway's Used Cars, 1725 W Billy Farrow Hwy, 29550; 843-332-0434; Sa; **85-93; D, F; B3**

Hodges; Greenwood Auto Salvage, 3810 Hwy 25N, 29653; 864-374-3303, 800-633-4531; Sp; 3000; **70+; D, F, PU, 4x4; B3, Jp**

　Martin Quarles Used Parts, *see Vintage*

Iva; A to Z Auto Salvage, *see Vintage*
Lancaster; Bowers Used Parts Inc, 1208 Jonathan Ln, 29720; 803-283-9311, FAX 803-286-6454, 800-328-4769; Sp; 1500; **80+; D, F, PU, 4x4; B3**
Laurens; Kellett's Auto Salvage, *see Vintage*
Lexington; Brock's Camaro & Firebird Prts, *see Vintage*
North; K & W Auto Salvage, *see Vintage*
Orangeburg; C & R Auto Salvage Inc, 690 Cannon Bridge Rd SW, 29115; 803-536-2211, 800-922-1935; CC, Sa, Sp; 5500+; **80+; D, F, PU, 4x4; B3, AMC, Jp, VW**
    J & K Auto Salvage, 495 Canon Bridge Rd, 29115; 803-531-7582; Sa, Sp; 500+; **70+ D, F, PU, 4x4; B3**
    Tri-Bet Auto Salvage, 641 Canaan Rd, 29115; 803-531-5450, FAX 803-531-5625; Sp; 300+; **75-89; D, F, PU; B3, VW**
Pelzer; H & H Auto Salvage, 308 Courtney St, 29669; 864-847-7861; Sp, UR; 1500; **75-95; D, F, PU, 4x4; B3, AMC, Jp, VW**
Prosperity; Ackerman's Used Parts, 9206 Hwy 76, 29127; 803-364-3011, 800-822-9898; CC, Sp; 6ac; **69+; D, F, PU; B3, VW**
    Mid-Carolina Parts & Salvage, *see Vintage*
Rock Hill; Carolina Salvage, 234 Porter Rd, 29731; 803-324-7510, FAX 803-324-5894, 800-845-7098; CC, Sp; 3000; **80+; D, F, PU, 4x4; B3, AMC, Jp, VW**
St Matthews; Franks Auto Salvage, *see Vintage*
Spartanburg; Tony's Auto Salvage, 412 Monks Grove Church Rd, 29303; 864-578-9725, FAX 864-578-4007, 800-964-8669; CC, Sa, Sp; 500; **75+; D, F, PU, 4x4; B3, Jp**
Timmonsville; Turner's Auto Salvage, 4634 W Palmetto St, 29161; 843-665-9443, FAX 843-346-2296, 800-922-2384; Sp; 55ac; **80+; D, PU, 4x4, Trk; B3**
Waterloo; Burdette Auto Salvage Svc, *see Vintage*
Williams; Garris Auto Salvage Inc, *see Vintage*
LATE MODEL
Aiken; Graves Auto Salvage, *see Late Vintage*
Anderson; Ed Powell's Auto Salvage, *see Vintage*
Bamberg; Hutto's Salvage, *see Vintage*
Belton; Anderson Auto Salvage, 3500 Hwy 29 N, 29627; 864-226-7076, 800-327-2736; Cc, Sa; 3000; **F, PU, 4x4; Jpa, Peugeot, Mercedes**
Easley; Bruce O'Shields Used Auto Parts, *see Vintage*
    Dixie Auto Salvage, 1439 Old Easley Hwy, 29640; 864-295-8782; Sa; 1500; **D, F, PU, 4x4; B3, AMC, Jp**
Fair Play; Layton Brown Used Cars & Parts, *see Late Vintage*
Georgetown; Drayton Auto Salvage, N Santee, 29440; 843-546-5605; Sa, Sp, UR; 2ac, 600; **D, F, PU, 4x4; B3, VW; Some School Buses**
Greenville; Vintage Auto, *see Vintage*
Greer; A-1 Import Salvage Inc, 1681 E Wade Hampton Blvd, 29651; 864-879-3034, 800-888-3034; Sp; 3500; **F, PU, 4x4; VW, Peugeot, Volvo**
Hardeeville; McGraw's Auto & Salvage, Hwy 17 S, 29927; 843-784-6651, 800-346-6810; CC, Sp, PL; 30ac; **D, F, PU; B3**
Hartsville; Galloway's Used Cars, *see Late Vintage*
Hemingway; Watford's Nissan Salvage, Hwy 261 E, 29554; 843-558-9283; 50; **F; Nissan only**
Hodges; Greenwood Auto Salvage, *see Late Vintage*
Ladson; Auto Salvage Co, 230 Royle Rd, 29456; 843-821-1989; CC, Sp, Br, PL; 400+; **D, F, PU, 4x4; B3, VW**
Lancaster; Bowers Used Parts Inc, *see Late Vintage*
Laurens; Kellett's Auto Salvage, *see Vintage*
Lexington; Brock's Camaro & Firebird Prts, *see Vintage*
North; K & W Auto Salvage, *see Vintage*
Orangeburg; C & R Auto Salvage Inc, *see Late Vintage*
    G & J Salvage Co, 5979 North Rd Hwy 178, 29118; 803-536-3282, FAX 803-536-0732, 800-541-7768; Sp; 450+; **F, PU, 4x4; VW, Jpa**

J & K Auto Salvage, *see Late Vintage*

Pelzer; H & H Auto Salvage, *see Late Vintage*

Prosperity; Ackerman's Used Parts, *see Late Vintage*

Mid-Carolina Parts & Salvage, *see Vintage*

Rock Hill; Carolina Salvage, *see Late Vintage*

Frank Bobo's Used Auto Parts, 904 Albright Rd, 29730; 803-329-3038, FAX 803-328-3040, 800-329-3037; CC, Wr; **D, F, PU, 4x4, Trk; B3; Motors and Transmissions only**

Spartanburg; M & M Auto Salvage, 1358 Goldmine Rd, 29307; 864-579-7817, 800-570-4825; 100+; **D, F; Spc: Chrysler**

Tony's Auto Salvage, *see Late Vintage*

Timmonsville; Turner's Auto Salvage, *see Late Vintage*

Union; Union Auto Salvage Inc, 1370 Jonesville Hwy, 29379; 864-427-8760, 800-521-9798; Sp; 5000; **D, F, PU, 4x4; B3**

Waterloo; Burdette Auto Salvage Svc, *see Vintage*

Williams; Garris Auto Salvage Inc, *see Vintage*

Fiat Convertible
Lincoln Valley Auto Salvage
Cheyenne, WY

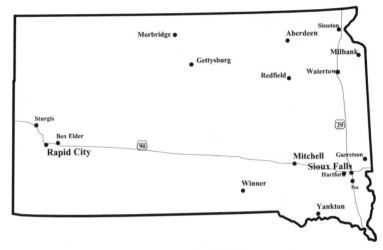

SOUTH DAKOTA

272

Watertown; Roger's Salvage, 1507 S Broadway St, 57201; 605-886-2475, FAX 605-886-3741, rogers@willinet.net, www.valuparts.com; Sa, Sp; 1300+; **60+; D, F, PU, 4x4, Trk; B**3, **AMC, Jp, IH, VW**

Winner; Wayne's Auto Salvage, RR3 Box 41, 57580; 605-842-2054; UR; 20ac, 1700+; **40-60; D; B**3, **AMC, Jp, Hd, St, Pk, Ns, Wy, Ks, Fr; Few Mopar**

Yankton; Merrigan's Auto Salvage, 1102 Ferdig, 57078; 605-665-3162, FAX 605-665-2230; Sa, Sp, UR; 5ac; **30-90; D, F, PU, 4x4; B**3 **Jp, Ns, Wy, VW**

LATE VINTAGE

Box Elder; Lefler Auto Salvage, *see Vintage*

Garretson; Nordstroms Auto Recycling, 25513 480th Av, 57030; 605-594-3910, FAX 888-818-PART, 800-272-0083, www.nordstromsauto.com; CC, Sa, Sp, UR; 30ac, 5000; **75+; D, F, PU, 4x4, Trk; B**3

Gettysburg; A G Sales & salvage, *see Vintage*

Milbank; Berkner Auto Repair & Salvage, *see Vintage*

Mitchell; Dakota Salvage, *see Vintage*

Morbridge; Meidinger Auto Salvage, *see Vintage*

Rapid City; A & A Auto Salvage, *see Vintage*

　Angel Bros Auto Salvage, *see Vintage*

　B & B Auto Salvage, *see Vintage*

　Rapid Import Salvage, 2855 Flack Ln, 57701; 605-348-7169, FAX 605-348-1880, 800-252-2498, radidsd@rapidnet.com; CC, Sa, Sp; 500+; **80+; D, F, PU, 4x4; B**3, **Jp, VW, Jpa**

　S & L Auto Salvage & Repair, 4480 W Sunnyside Dr, 57701; 605-341-8571; Sa, UR; 100+; **70-90; D, F, PU, 4x4; B**3

Sioux Falls; Howard's Corvettes, *see Vintage*

Sisseton; Brooks Auto Slvg, 120 Veterans Av, 57262; 605-698-7331; CC, Sa; 150; **80+, few earlier; D**

　Sisseton Salvage Auto Parts, RR 2 Box 55, 57262; 605-698-7251; Sp, Br; **70-90; D, B**3

Sturgis; Jim's Auto Salvage, *see Vintage*

　Langin Auto Salvage, *see Vintage*

　Westside Dismantlers, *see Vintage*

Tea; Johnson's Salvage, *see Vintage*

Watertown; Roger's Salvage, *see Vintage*

Yankton; Merrigan's Auto Salvage, *see Vintage*

LATE MODEL

Aberdeen; AAA Auto Parts, 4155 6th Av SE, 57401; 605-225-8200, FAX 605-229-4407, 800-456-5383; CC, Sa, Sp, Wr; 20ac; **D, F, PU, 4x4; B**3, **Jpa**

Garretson; Nordstroms Auto Recycling, *see Late Vintage*

Hartford; Oakleaf Auto Slvg, 26246 463 Av, 57033; 605-528-3244; Sa, Sp; 30ac; **D, F, PU**

Mitchell; Dakota Salvage, *see Vintage*

Morbridge; Meidinger Auto Salvage, *see Vintage*

Rapid City; A & A Auto Salvage, *see Vintage*

　A-1 Auto Salvage, 7804 S Hwy 79, 57701; 605-348-8442, FAX 605-348-8167, 800-456-0715; CC, Sa, Sp, UR; 35ac, 2000+; **D, F, PU, 4x4; few boats, RVs & Motorcycles**

　Angel Bros Auto Salvage, *see Vintage*

　B & B Auto Salvage, *see Vintage*

　Rapid Import Salvage, *see Late Vintage*

Redfield; Redfield Salvage, 519 E 9 Av, 57469; 605-472-2796; Sp, UR; 200; **D, F, PU, 4x4**

Sioux Falls; Barneys Auto Salvage, 2700 N Cliff, 57104; 605-338-7041, FAX 605-338-9629, 800-662-8032; CC, Sa, Sp; 40ac, 6000; **D, F, PU, 4x4, Cn, In**

Sisseton; Brooks Auto Salvage, *see Late Vintage*

Tea; Johnson's Salvage, *see Vintage*

Watertown; Roger's Salvage, *see Vintage*

Winner; B & D Auto Salvage, W Hwy 18, 57580; 605-842-2877; Sa, Sp, UR; 12ac, 600+; **D, PU, 4x4**

Yankton; Syds Auto Salvage, 57078; 605-665-5119, FAX 605-668-0941; 6ac, 400+; **D, PU**

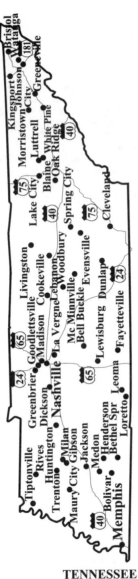

TENNESSEE

Please mention you saw'em in
Ray's wReckingyard Roster when contacting
these yards

Blaine; Sonny's Auto Parts, PO Box 252, Hwy 11 W, 37709; 423-932-2610 or 933-9137; CC, Sa, Sp, Br; 82ac, 3000+; **40-69; D, F, few PU, few 4x4; B3, AMC, Jp, IH**

Evensville; D & K Auto Salvage, 13587 Rhea County Hwy, 37332; 423-775-5309, FAX; Sa; 1000+; **65+; D, F, PU, 4x4; B3**

Fayetteville; Bradford's Auto Salvage, 21 Round Square Ln, 37334; 931-433-1133; Sa; 200+; **60-93; D, F, PU; B3; Spc: Camaro**

Goodlettsville; C & C Auto Salvage, 1840 Slaters Creek Rd, 37072; 615-851-0612; Sa, Sp; 600+; **60+; D, F, PU, 4x4, Trk; B3, Jp**

Greenbrier; Volunteer State Chevy Parts, 2414 Hwy 41 S, 37073; 615-643-4583, FAX 615-643-5100; CC, Sp; 60+; **60-75; D; Chevy only; Call for Appointment**

Jackson; Hwy 18 Salvage, 2000 Hwy 18, 38301; 901-424-8364; Sp; **40-90; D, F, PU, 4x4, Trk; B3, AMC, Jp, IH**

La Vergne; Waldron Auto Salvage, 5356 Murfreeshore Rd, 37086; 615-793-2791; Sa, Br; 1200; **75+; D, F, PU, 4x4, Trk; B3, AMC, Jp, IH**

Lake City; A-1 Auto Body Specialists, 130 Bolin Rd, 37769; 423-426-4371, FAX 423-426-4372; CC, Sa, Sp; 900; **70+, few 40-60s; D, F, PU; B3, IH**

Luttrell; Allen & Roberts Auto Salvage, 190 Roberts Rd, 37779; 423-992-3802, FAX 423-992-6276; 400+; **50+; D, F, PU; B3, VW**

Medon; Highway 18 Slvg, 2000 St Rt 18, 38356; 901-424-8364; Sp, UR, Wr; **70-85, few 40-60s; D; B3**

Memphis; Memphis Auto Salvage, 2610 Fite Rd, 38127; 901-353-9078; Sp; 800; **50-80; D, 4x4, Trk; Fd, Chevy**

South Gibsen; Privitt Garage, 227 Hwy 79, 38338; 901-787-6142; Sa, Sp, UR; 15ac, 2500; **38-94; D, F, PU, 4x4, Trk, Fm; B3, AMC; Spc: Ford**

Spring City; Webb's Auto Salvage, 7283 Toestring Valley Rd, 37381; 423-365-0040; Sa; 4ac; **60+; D, F, PU; B3**

Tiptonville; Choate Brothers Auto Salvage, Keefe Rd, 38079; 901-253-8000; Sa, Br; 15ac; **60+; D, F, PU, 4x4; B3; Cougar, Chevelle**

Woodbury; Smith Truck Salvage, 3370 Jim Cummings Hwy, 37190; 615-563-4343, FAX 615-563-4664, 800-528-1521; Sa, UR; **50+; D, F, PU, 4x4; B3; Pickup only**

LATE VINTAGE

Bell Buckle; Haskins Auto Salvage, *see Vintage*

   Sanders Auto Salvage, 408 Smith Rd #A, 37020; 931-294-5591; Sa; 1200; **70-90; D, F, PU; B3, VW**

Bristol; 421 Auto Slvg, 3149 Hwy 421, 37620; 423-878-5441; Sa, Sp; **70-80; D, PU, Trk; B3**

Cookeville; Kenny's Auto Salvage, 2034 W Broad St, 38501; 931-526-8121, 800-588-8121; Sa, Sp, Br; 1500+; **67+; D, F, PU, 4x4; B3, AMC, Jp, VW**

Dickson; Dickson Auto Salvage, 2249 Hwy 47 E, 37055; 615-446-4414; Sa, UR; 1500; **75-85; D, F, PU; B3**

Dunlap; Roy's Used Cars & Salvage, Cordell Ln, 37327; 423-949-3462; Sa, Sp, UR; 500; **70-90; D, F, PU, 4x4; B3**

Evensville; D & K Auto Salvage, *see Vintage*

Fayetteville; Bradford's Auto Salvage, *see Vintage*

Goodlettsville; C & C Auto Salvage, *see Vintage*

Greenbrier; Volunteer State Chevy Parts, *see Vintage*

Greeneville; Jerry's Salvage & Used Parts, 455 Kidwell School Rd, 37745; 423-639-6854, 800-639-6854; Sp; 800+; **75+; D, F, PU, 4x4; B3, Jp**

Huntington; 22 Auto Salvage, Box 1781, 9110 Hwy 22, 38344; 901-986-2366, 800-759-2366; Sa, Sp; 1000; **70-95; D, PU, 4x4, Trk; B3, AMC, Jp, IH**

Jackson; Hwy 18 Salvage, *see Vintage*

   Jackson Auto Salvage, 769 A Airway Blvd, 38301; 901-424-1112; Sp, Br; 200; **80-89; D, F, PU, 4x4, Trk; B3, AMC**

   Mann's Jackson Auto Exchange, 144 New Deal Rd, 38365; 901-424-7217, FAX 901-427-0156, 800-339-3428; CC, Sa, Sp; **81-96; D, F, PU, 4x4, Trk; B3, AMC, Jp, IH**

Johnson City; Hilltop Auto Salvage, 315 W Main St, 37604; 423-928-4469; Sa; 500+; **85-92; D, F, PU, 4x4; B3, VW**

275

Sweeney's Used Auto Parts, 1906 E Main St, 37601; 423-926-0138, FAX 423-926-0139, 800-232-5268; CC, Sa, Sp; 400; **70+; D, F, PU; B3**

Kingsport; A R Briggs & Son Car Crushing, 230 Bancroft Chapel Rd, 37660; 423-288-5391; Sa, Wr; **70+; D, F; B3**

Nave's Auto Salvage, 1343 Old Gray Station Rd, 37663; 423-477-4124; Sp, UR; 1100+; **75-90; D, F, PU; B3, AMC, VW**

La Vergne; Waldron Auto Salvage, *see Vintage*

Lake City; A-1 Auto Body Specialists, *see Vintage*

Leoma; Kennedy's Auto Salvage & Wreck, 2183 Fall River Rd, 38468; 931-852-2049; Sa, Sp; **70+; D, F, PU, 4x4; B3**

Lewisburg; Pruitt Salvage, 2321 Franklin Pike, 37091; 931-359-7152; Sa, UR; 800; **70+; D, F, PU, 4x4; B3, Jp**

Livingston; Bilbrey's Auto Salvage, 1725 Byrdstown Hwy, 38570; 931-823-4050; CC, Sa, Sp, UR; 500+; **70-90; D, F, PU; B3, AMC; body shop**

Loretto; B & K Auto Salvage, 17 Old Glendale Rd, 38469; 931-853-6379, FAX 931-853-6720, 800-523-7742; Sp; 1600; **78+; D, F, PU, 4x4; B3, AMC, Jp**

Luttrell; Allen & Roberts Auto Salvage, *see Vintage*

Madison; Neelys Bend Auto Sales, 1327 Neelys Bend Rd, 37115; 615-868-9631; CC, Sa, Sp; 270; **80-91, few 70s; D; B3**

Maury City; Hwy 88 Auto Salvage, PO Box 97, 38050; 901-656-2111, FAX 656-4527, 800-287-6144; CC, Sa, Sp; 21ac, 700+; **80+; D, F; B3, Jpa**

McMinnville; Roller's Salvage, 5175 Short Mountain Rd, 37110; 931-939-2971; Sa, Sp, UR; 100+; **68+; D, PU, 4x4; B3, AMC, Jp, IH**

Medon; Highway 18 Salvage, *see Vintage*

Memphis; C & W Auto Sales & Salvage, 966 W Mitchell Rd, 38109; 901-785-9285, FAX 901-789-9750; Sa, UR; 2000+; **80-93; D, F, PU; B3, AMC**

Memphis Auto Salvage, *see Vintage*

Morristown; Hee-Haw Auto Salvage, 4403 Old Hwy 25 E, 37813; 423-581-6205; Sa, Sp; 1000+; **70+; D, F, PU, 4x4; B3, AMC, VW**

Nashville; Abernathy Salvage, 865 W Trinity Ln, 37207; 615-255-7616; 300; **80s, few 70s; D, PU, Trk; B3, IH**

Rives; Younger & Sons Salvage, 1165 Bates Anderson Rd, 38253; 901-536-4958, FAX 901-536-5691; UR; 3ac; **70+, few 60s; D, F, PU; B3**

South Gibsen; Privitt Garage, *see Vintage*

Spring City; Webb's Auto Salvage, *see Vintage*

Tiptonville; Choate Brothers Auto Salvage, *see Vintage*

Trenton; Trenton Auto Salvage, 93 Dyersburg Hwy, 38382; 901-855-2828, 800-924-6578 W TN only; Sp; **80+; D, PU, 4x4; B3, AMC**

Watauga; Watauga Auto Salvage, 279 Cripple Creek Loop, 37694; 423-543-4651; Sa, Sp; 1500; **80+; D, F, PU, 4x4; B3, AMC**

Woodbury; Smith Truck Salvage & Wrecker, *see Vintage*

LATE MODEL

Bell Buckle; Haskins Auto Salvage, *see Vintage*

Bethel Springs; R & R Truck Sales, 93 Redmon Rd, 38315; 901-934-4274, www. hwy54salvage.com; Sa, Sp; **Truck only**

Bolivar; Bolivar Salvage & Auto Pts, 10400 Hwy 64, 38008; 901-658-9468, FAX 901-658-7410, 800-748-9185; CC, Sp, UR; 250+; **D, F, PU, 4x4, Trk; B3, AMC, Jp, IH, VW**

Cleveland; Randy Goins Used Auto Parts, 4578 Waterlevel Hwy, 37323; 423-479-9081; Sa; 8ac; **D, F, PU, 4x4; B3**

Cookeville; Kenny's Auto Salvage, *see Late Vintage*

Evensville; D & K Auto Salvage, *see Vintage*

Fayetteville; Bradford's Auto Salvage, *see Vintage*

Goodlettsville; AAA Auto Salvage, 1050 Buck Hill Rd, 37152; 615-859-7981; Sa; 3.5ac; **D, F, PU; B3, VW**

C & C Auto Salvage, *see Vintage*

276

Greenbrier; Tennessee Auto Salvage, 1932 Tom Austin Hwy, 37073; 615-384-5033; Sp; 100ac; **D, F, PU; B3**

Greeneville; Jerry's Salvage & Used Parts, *see Late Vintage*

Henderson; Drue's Used Cars & Parts, 1629 Hwy 45 N, 38340; 901-989-5493, FAX 901-983-0541; Sa, Sp, UR; 700; **D, F, PU, 4x4, Trk; B3, AMC, Jp, IH, Jpa**

Huntington; 22 Auto Salvage, *see Late Vintage*

    Holland's Auto Salvage, 8405 Hwy 22 S, 38344; 901-986-4434, FAX 901-986-2911, 800-372-3885; CC, Sp; 1000; **D, F, PU, 4x4, Trk; B3, AMC, Jp**

Jackson; 70 Auto Salvage, 1589 Hwy 70 E, 38301; 901-423-1001; Sp, UR; 150; **D, F, PU, 4x4, Trk; B3, AMC, Jp, IH**

    Carmon's Rock & Axles, 32 Miller Av, 38301; 901-664-7119, 800-254-3794; Sp, Wr; **Spc: CV axles, steering parts; some after market**

    Mann's Jackson Auto Exchange, *see Late Vintage*

Johnson City; A-1 Auto Slvg, 1918 E Main St, 37601; 423-543-7277; Sa, Sp; 600; **D, PU**

    Hilltop Auto Salvage, *see Late Vintage*

    Sweeney's Used Auto Parts, *see Late Vintage*

Kingsport; A R Briggs & Son Car Crushing, *see Late Vintage*

    Midway Auto Salvage, 253 Dogwood Ln, 37663; 423-239-7231, 800-344-4804; CC, Sp; 500+; **D, F, PU, 4x4; B3**

La Vergne; Waldron Auto Salvage, *see Vintage*

Lake City; A-1 Auto Body Specialists, *see Vintage*

Lebanon; A C Hilltop Auto Salvage, 1949 Murfreesboro Rd, 37090; 615-444-9607; CC, Sa; 400; **D, F, PU, 4x4; B3, VW**

Leoma; Kennedy's Auto Salvage & Wreck, *see Late Vintage*

Lewisburg; Pruitt Salvage, *see Late Vintage*

Lexington; Lexington Auto Salvage, 7420 Hwy 200, 38351; 901-967-0954; Sa, UR; 150; **D, PU, 4x4, Trk; B3, AMC, Jp, IH**

Loretto; B & K Auto Salvage, *see Late Vintage*

Luttrell; Allen & Roberts Auto Salvage, *see Vintage*

Madison; Nalley's Bin, 515 Nawakwa Trl, 37216; 615-865-7599; CC, Sa, Sp

Maury City; Hwy 88 Auto Salvage, *see Late Vintage*

McMinnville; Roller's Salvage, *see Late Vintage*

    Turnage Auto Salvage, 5878 Hwy 88, 38050; 901-656-2111, FAX 901-656-4527, 800-287-6174; CC, Sa, Sp; 600; **D, F, PU; B3**

Memphis; C & W Auto Sales & Salvage, *see Late Vintage*

    Morristown; Hee-Haw Auto Salvage, *see Late Vintage*

    Mustin Auto Parts, 5700 Lamar Av, 38118; 901-363-7457; 500+; **D, few F, PU; B3**

Milan; 45 Auto Salvage, 176 Bradford Hwy, 38358; 901-686-7491, 800-372-3925; CC, Sp; 35ac, 2000; **D, F, PU, 4x4, Trk; GM, Chr, AMC, Jp, IH**

Morristown; Lakeway Auto Salvage, 3795 Old Hwy 25 E, 37814; 423-586-6350, 800-347-0949; CC, Sp; 1000; **D, F, PU, 4x4; B3, Jp**

Oak Ridge; Fox Auto Salvage, 110 Melton Lake Dr, 37830; 423-482-2468, 888-482-4411; CC, Sa, Sp; 200; **D, F, PU; B3**

Rives; Younger & Sons Salvage, *see Late Vintage*

South Gibsen; Privitt Garage, *see Vintage*

Spring City; Webb's Auto Salvage, *see Vintage*

Tiptonville; Choate Brothers Auto Salvage, *see Vintage*

Trenton; Compact Car Parts, 128 Alamo Hwy, 38382; 901-855-0110, FAX 901-855-9781; CC, Sp, Br, Wr; 1000; **D, F, PU, 4x4, Trk; B3, Jp**

    Trenton Auto Salvage, *see Late Vintage*

Watauga; Watauga Auto Salvage, *see Late Vintage*

White Pine; Strange Auto Salvage, 3513 Roy Messer Hwy, 37890; 423-235-2850, FAX 423-674-2987, 800-445-2091; CC, Sp, PL; 102ac; **D, F, PU, 4x4; B3**

Woodbury; Smith Truck Salvage & Wrecker, *see Vintage*

Texas

Ray's wReckingyard Roster makes a great gift for the "car nut" on your shopping list. To order, Call Toll Free: 877-4RAYS BOOKS

TEXAS

VINTAGE

Acton; Hernandez Automotive Inc, 5617 Gee Rd, 76049; 817-326-5846; Sa, Sp, Wr; 600; **47-88; D**

Amarillo; Cherry Avenue Auto Parts, 309 W Cherry Av, 79108; 806-383-7859; Sa, UR; 25ac; **50+; D, F, PU, 4x4; B3, AMC, Jp, IH, VW**

Amarillo; Clark's Auto Sales Parts, 112 W Cottonwood St, 79108; 806-383-3157; Sa, UR; 8ac; **50+; D, F, PU; B3, AMC; Spc: Chevy, Malibu, Mercury, Ford**

Bertram; David's Auto Parts, 1644 E State Hwy 29, 78605; 512-355-2071, FAX 512-355-3208, 800-835-2972; Sa, Sp, Br; 500; **30+; D, F, PU; B3, AMC, IH, Hd, Ns, St, Pk, VW**

Bowie; Phillips Auto Salvage, Hwy 287 S, 76230; 940-872-1513, 888-729-2277; CC, Sa, Sp; 550; **40+; D, F, PU, 4x4; B3, Jp; Spc: Pickup**

Breckenridge; Seller's Auto Salvage, 3223 Hwy 180 E, 76424; 254-559-7267, 800-984-3465; Sa, Sp, PL; **50+; D, F, PU; B3**

Brownwood; Hi-Way Auto Parts, 2708 Belle Plain St, 76801; 915-646-825, FAX 915-646-5332, 800-447-0611; CC, Sp; 10ac; **70+, few 40-60s; D, PU, 4x4; B3**

Corpus Christi; Best Deal Auto Salvage, 5537 Agnes St, 78405; 361-289-1677, FAX 361-985-6705; CC, Sa, Sp, PL; 450+; **50+; D, F, PU, 4x4; B3, AMC, Jp, VW; Spc: Glass**

    Mike's Auto Salvage, 5453 Greenwood Dr, 78417; 361-857-8926; CC, Sa, Sp; 250+; **55-89; D, F, PU; B3**

    Vic's Salvage, 1705 N Clarkwood Rd, 78409; 361-241-7171, FAX 361-241-0495; Sa, Sp; 700; **59+; D, F, PU, 4x4; B3, AMC, VW**

Dallas; Dallas Auto Salvage & Used Car, 14057 Skyfrost Dr, 75253; 972-286-5644; Sp, UR; 500+; **39-90; D, F**

    Nabors Auto Wrecking, 2775 Dowdy Ferry Rd, 75217; 972-286-2543; Sa, Sp; 350+; **60-93; D, PU, 4x4, Trk, In; B3, AMC; Forklifts**

El Paso; Ramirez Auto Parts, 600 S Stonton, 79901; 915-542-3114, FAX 915-533-3050; Sa, Sp; **60-95; D, F, PU, 4x4, Trk; B3, AMC, Jp, IH, VW**

    U Pull It, 9663 Alameda Av, 79927; 915-860-8282, FAX 915-859-3300, 800-553-1103; Sa, Sp, UR; 10.5ac; **55-89; D, F, PU, 4x4; B3**

Elm Mott; Elm Mott Auto Salvage, 14401 N IH 35, 76640; 254-829-2795, 800-810-2795; CC, Sa, Sp; 5500+; **50+; D, F, PU, 4x4; B3, AMC, Jp, IH, St, VW**

Fort Worth; James Pack's Auto Wrck, 5721 Elliott Reeder Rd, 76117; 817-838-0192, 800-383-7225; CC, Sa, Sp, Br; 400; **60-90; D, F, PU, 4x4, Trk to 1.5T; B3, AMC, Jp, IH, VW**

Gainesville; Wayne Gilbert Auto Salvage, 2916 E Hwy 82, 76240; 940-668-8501, FAX 940-668-8502; CC, Sa, UR; 6ac; **30+; D, F, PU, 4x4; B3, St**

Grand Prairie; Dallas County Auto Salvage, 2300 Meyers Rd, 75050; 972-263-3051, FAX 972-262-4873; Sa, Sp, Br; 20000; **40+; D, F, PU, 4x4, Trk; B3, AMC, Jp, IH, VW**

Houston; Absolutely Ford Chrysler, 222 Holmes Rd, 77045; 713-726-0077, FAX 713-726-0254; CC, Sp, Br; 21ac; **61+; D, F, PU, 4x4, Trk; B3, AMC, Jp**

    Ernest G Musquiz Wrecker Svc, 6231 Carson Rd, 77048; 713-991-0610, FAX 713-991-4458; Sa, Sp, UR; 40ac; **47-85; D, PU; B3, AMC, Jp**

Jacksonville; A & A Auto Salvage, Hwy 175 W, 75766; 903-586-7216; Sa, Br; 200; **63+; D, PU, 4x4; B3**

Justin; Honest John's Caddy Corner, PO Box 741, 76247; 940-648-3330, FAX 940-648-9135, 888-592-2339, www.honestjohn.com; CC, Sp; 300; **41-91; D; Cadillac only; Mail Order; Call for Appointment**

Kaufman; Henderson Auto Parts, 307 Ball St, 75159; 972-287-4787, 932-6803; Sa, Sp, Br; 10ac, 750; **30-96; D, F, PU; B3, AMC, Jp, Hd, St, Pk, Ks, Fr, Wy, VW; Spc: Pickup**

Killeen; Texas Acres, 1130 Martin Luther King Jr, 76543; 254-698-4555, FAX 254-698-4393, 800-667-2764, www.texasacres.com; CC, Sa, Sp, Wr; **46-80; D; Chr only**

Lubbock; Auto Salvage Co, 9103 Tahoka Hwy, 79412; 806-745-2202, FAX 806-748-0385, 800-451-2202; CC, Sa, Sp, Br; 12ac; **60-92; D, F, PU, 4x4, Trk; B3, AMC, Jp, IH**

    Chevy Craft, 3400 Quirt, 79404; 806-747-4848, FAX 806-747-9037, www.chevycraft. com; Sp, Wr; 5ac, 350; **55-72; D; Chevy only**

San Angelo; Chatham Salvage Co, 1224 Pulliam St, 76903; 915-658-1387; Sa, Sp, Br; 250; **50-92; D, PU, 4x4, Trk, In; B3, AMC**

Texas - Vintage

Clark Auto Wrecking, 901 N Cecil St, 76903; 915-655-9936, FAX 915-653-2330, 800-655-9936, casey711@wcc.net; CC, Sa, UR; 5ac, 1000+; **55-95; D, F, PU, 4x4; B3, Jp, Edsel**

Menchaca Wrck, 1700 Center St, 76905; 915-651-9674; Sa, UR; **49-89; D, PU, 4x4; B3**

Temple; Action Auto Recyclers, PO Box 352, 76503; 254-773-6201, FAX 254-742-0395, www.traderonline.com/dactionauto; CC, Sa, Sp; 10ac, 300; **30-89; D, few F, Spc: Pickup, Mustang**

Texarkana; Rabbit's Salvage Yard, 3618 Buchanan Rd, 75501; 903-793-0477; Sa, Sp; 13ac, 1100; **57+; D, F, PU, 4x4, Trk; B3, VW; Restoration of Chrysler**

Tyler; D G Auto Salvage, 10009 FM 14, 75706; 903-595-6499, 800-760-6499; CC, Sa, Sp, UR; 700; **62+; D; B3**

Waco; Best Value Used Auto Parts, 1704 New Dallas Hwy, 76705; 254-799-3285; Sp, UR; **50+; 57-89; D, PU; B3**

Weatherford; Johnny's Auto & Truck Salvage, 10602 Mineral Wells Hwy, 76088; 940-682-4802, 800-776-3066; Sp, UR; 2ac, 200+; **60-95; D, F, PU, 4x4; B3**

Wellington; South Side Salvage, Rt 2 Box 8, 79095; 806-447-2391; Sa; 9ac, 900; 20-**93; D, PU; B3, AMC, Hd, Ns, St, Pk, Ks, Fr, Cr**

LATE VINTAGE

Abilene; Abilene Auto Wrecking, 4001 Pine St, 79601; 915-672-8542; CC, Sa; 7ac, 800; **70-89; D, F, PU; B3**

FM 600 Wrecking, 9402 W Lake Rd, 79601; 915-672-2597; Sp, UR; **70+; D, F; B3, IH**

Acton; Hernandez Automotive Inc, *see Vintage*

Alvin; Highway 35 Auto Slvg, 6402 N Hwy 35, 77511; 281-585-5034; Sa, UR; 100; **80+; D, F**

S & S Auto Salvage, 3610 Hwy 6 E, 77511; 281-331-6591; Sa, UR; 140; **80+; D**

Amarillo; Amarillo Salvage, 4310 E Amarillo Blvd, 79107; 806-373-0002; Sa, Sp; 14ac, 1100; **77+, few 60-76; D, F, PU, 4x4; B3, Jp, IH**

B & P Salvage, 2500 S Lakeside, 79118; 806-372-6577, 800-657-7157; CC, Sa, Sp, UR; 7ac; **80-89; D, F, PU, 4x4; B3**

Cherry Avenue Auto Parts, *see Vintage*

Clark's Auto Sales Parts, *see Vintage*

Amarillo; Complete Auto Recyclers, 240 SE 58th, 79118; 806-622-3161, 888-295-4947; Sa, Sp, UR; 10ac, 600; **65+; D, F, PU, 4x4, Trk; B3; Has transmission shop**

Arlington; A A Auto Parts, 7751 Hwy 287 Business, 76001; 817-572-5262; CC, Sa, Sp, Br; 400; **65+; D, F, PU, 4x4, Trk; B3; Spc: Pickup & vans**

Ace Auto Salvage, 7701 Mansfield Way, 76001; 817-483-6711; CC, Sa; 80+**, few 70s**

Atascosa; All Bimmers & Benzes, 17444 IH 35 S, 78002; 210-622-5700, FAX 210-622-5815, 888-622-7066; CC, Sa, Sp, UR, Wr, PL; 75+; **70+; F; BMW, Mercedes only**

Austin; Aaron's Auto Parts, 8409 S Congress Av, 78745; 512-282-1715; CC, Sa, Sp, UR; 12ac; **70-89, few 60s; D, F, PU, 4x4; B3**

Bertram; David's Auto Parts, *see Vintage*

Bowie; Phillips Auto Salvage, *see Vintage*

Breckenridge; Seller's Auto Salvage, *see Vintage*

Brownsville; 511 Auto & Truck Salvage, 4275 FM 511, 78521; 956-838-6900; Sa; 500+; **75+; D, F, PU; B3, VW**

Brownwood; Hi-Way Auto Parts, *see Vintage*

Bryan; Highway 6 Auto Salvage, 1805 E Byp N, 77803; 409-778-0921, FAX 409-778-0638, 800-460-1558; CC, Sp, UR; 7ac; **83+; D, F, PU, 4x4, Trk; B3, AMC**

Carrollton; Hi-Way Auto Parts II, 1910 E Hwy 121, 75006; 972-492-0919, FAX 972-492-4096, 800-492-1039; CC, Sa, Sp, PL; 5.5ac, 500; **83+; D, F, PU, 4x4; B3, Jp**

Conroe; McCulloch Auto Slvg, 606 N Loop 336 E, 77301; 409-760-1333, FAX 409-760-1307, 800-833-2587; CC, Sa, Sp, Br; 5ac, 1200; **80+; D, F, PU, 4x4, Trk; B3, AMC, Jp, few VW; Spc: Jeep**

Corpus Christi; All-State Auto & Truck Wrecker, 3540 Agnes St, 78405; 361-888-9444; Sa; 20; **85-89; D, F, PU; B3, VW**

Corpus Christi; Best Deal Auto Salvage, *see Vintage*

Mike's Auto Salvage, *see Vintage*

Vic's Salvage, *see Vintage*

Dallas; Chuck Taylor Auto Parts, 10815 C F Hawn Fwy, 75217; 972-286-4707; CC, Sa, Sp, Br; 6ac, 600; **75+; D, F, PU, 4x4; B3, AMC, Jp**

Dallas Auto Salvage & Used Car, *see Vintage*

Nabors Auto Wrecking, *see Vintage*

Dallas; Office Auto Salvage, 4211 Loop 12, 75241; 214-371-8681; Sa, UR; 500; **70-92; D, PU, 4x4; B3**

Denton; W W Auto Salvage, 5075 Barthold Rd, 76207; 940-566-6536; CC, Sa, UR; 12ac, 800; **75+; D, F, PU, 4x4; B3, AMC, Jp, IH, VW**

El Paso; CC Auto Parts, 1913 Magoffin Av, 79901; 915-532-5971; Sa, Sp; 3ac, 300; **70-95; D, PU, 4x4; B3, AMC**

Fiesta Auto Salvage, 13300 Montana Av, 79938; 915-855-7999, FAX 915-856-2400; CC, Sa; 50ac, 750+; **70-90; D, F; B3, AMC**

Ramirez Auto Parts, *see Vintage*

U Pull It, *see Vintage*

Rio Grande Parts, 5900 Doniphan Dr, 79932; 915-584-2877, FAX 915-833-6259; Sp; 250+; **80+; D, PU, 4x4; B3, AMC, Jp, IH**

Elm Mott; Elm Mott Auto Salvage, *see Vintage*

Ennis; Ennis Auto Salvage, 3511 Ensign Rd, 75119; 972-875-8691; CC, Sp; 1000; **80-95; D, F, PU, 4x4, Trk; B3, AMC**

Fort Worth; Azle Avenue Wrecking Co, 5103 Azle Av, 76114; 817-626-8851; Sa, UR; 100; **70-89; D, F; B3, AMC**

Chrysler Heaven, 5808 Elliott Reeder Rd, 76117; 817-834-1711, FAX 817-834-2456, www.chrhavn.com; CC, Sa, Sp; 2ac, 400; **78+; D, F, PU, 4x4; Chr, Jp; some Maserati**

Frank's Wrecking Yard, 5700 Elliott Reeder Rd, 76117; 817-834-0711; CC, Sa, UR; 1500+; **70-90; D, F, PU, 4x4, Trk; B3, Jp, IH; Open Sunday**

James Pack's Auto Wrecking, *see Vintage*

Gainesville; Wayne Gilbert Auto Salvage, *see Vintage*

Gladewater; Choctaws Bone Yard, Hwy 271, 75647; 903-845-6648; Sa, Br; 900; **70-90; F**

Grand Prairie; Dallas County Auto Salvage, *see Vintage*

Hamilton; Galindo Slvg, Hwy 36 W, 76531; 254-386-5282; Sa, UR; 2ac; **80-89; D, F, PU**

Hereford; Dearing Wrecking, N Progressive Rd, 79045; 806-364-2754, FAX 806-363-6202; Sp, Br; 550; **65-90; D, F, PU; B3, AMC, IH, VW**

Holland; Snyder's Salvage, S Hwy 95, 76534; 254-657-2747, FAX 254-657-2583, 800-460-8025; CC, Sp, Br; 30ac, 7000; **80+; D, F, PU, 4x4; B3; Spc: Pickup**

Houston; Absolutely Ford Chrysler, *see Vintage*

Auto World, 5711 W Montgomery Rd, 77091; 713-691-5285, FAX 713-619-5312, 800-248-2095; CC, Sa, Sp, Br; 5ac, 500; **75+; D, PU, 4x4; B3, AMC, Jp**

Bronco Truck Salvage Inc, 900 Aldine Mail Rd, 77037; 281-448-2792, FAX 281-448-2796, 800-383-1961; Sp, Br; 250; **68+; D, PU, 4x4; Pickup only**

Ernest G Musquiz Wrecker Svc, *see Vintage*

Houston Auto Recycling, 1520 Upland Dr, 77043; 713-465-0290; CC, Sa, Sp, UR; 150; **80+; D, F, PU, 4x4; B3, AMC, IH**

Model Automotive Enterprises, 6011 Liberty Rd, 77026; 713-672-1614; **78+; D, PU**

Pick A Part Auto Wrecking, 1100 Nothville St, 77038; 281-448-8897, FAX 281-999-2125, 800-675-5924, www.houstonpickapart.com; CC, Sa, UR; **80+; D, F, PU, 4x4; B3; Open Sunday; Other locations: 723 N. Drennan, 9314 Wallaceville Rd**

Take-A-Part & Save, 5431 Crawford Rd, 77041; 713-896-6696; CC, Sa, UR; 5ac, 700; **80-93, few 70s; D, F, PU, 4x4; B3; Open Sunday**

Volvo Parts Independent, 11020 Old Katy Rd, 77043; 713-722-0505, FAX 713-722-0528, 800-303-6544, vpiparts@wt.net, www.swedishparts.com; CC, Sp, PL, Wr; **F; Volvo only, 200 to 900 series**

Williams Auto Salvage, 5431 N Shepherd Dr, 77091; 713-691-2015, FAX 713-691-3365, 800-969-2015; CC, Sa, Sp; 3ac; **70+; D, PU, 4x4; B3**

Jacksonville; A & A Auto Salvage, *see Vintage*

Justin; Honest John's Caddy Corner, *see Vintage*

Kaufman; Henderson Auto Parts, *see Vintage*

Killeen; Do-Rite Wrecking Yard, Rt 7 Box 100, Hwy 195 S, 76542; 254-634-7715; CC, Sa, UR; 1000; **80-93; D, F, PU; B3**

    Moore's Auto Salvage, 3704 Old Copperas Cove Rd, 76542; 254-526-6272; CC, Sa, Sp; 300; **70+; D, F; B3**

    Speedway Auto Salvage Inc, 3502 Old Copperas Cove Rd, 76542; 254-526-5723, 888-526-5665; CC, Sa, Sp, PL; 700; **72+; D, F, PU, 4x4; B3, VW**

    Texas Acres, *see Vintage*

Longview; Smiddy's Wrecker Svc, 2108 SE Eastman, 75603; 903-236-4693, FAX 903-236-3336; CC; **70-89; D, F; B3**

Lubbock; American Pickup Salvage, 4213 E 4th St, 79403; 806-741-0201, 800-693-2299; Sa, Sp, Br; 300; **65+; D, PU, 4x4; B3, AMC, Jp**

Lubbock; Auto Salvage Co, *see Vintage*

    Burgess Auto Salvage Inc, 9416 Hwy 87, 79423; 806-745-1212, FAX 806-745-4371, 800-473-7172; CC, Sa, Sp, Br; 17ac, 1000; **80+; D, F, PU, 4x4; B3, AMC, Jp, VW**

Lufkin; Redland Auto Salvage, Rt 7 Box 2324, 75904; 409-639-2851, FAX 409-639-9301; CC, Sa, Sp; 750; **65+; D, PU; B3; Spanish**

Midland; Benny's Auto Parts Inc, 4560 W Hwy 80, 79703; 915-381-2401; Sa, Br; 1000; **73+; D, PU, 4x4, Trk; B3, AMC, IH**

Mineral Wells; Jack's Auto Salvage, 107 SW 14th Av, 76067; 940-325-3146; CC, Sa, UR; **70+; D, F, PU, 4x4, Trk, Fm, In, Cn; B3**

Mount Pleasant; Hwy 67 Auto Salvage, 512 E 16th St, 75455; 903-572-3375; Sa, Sp, UR; 400; **75-95; D, F, PU, Trk; B3**

Nacogdoches; American Auto Salvage, 5208 South St, 75964; 409-564-0272; CC, Sa, Sp, Br; 400; **80-95; D, F, PU, 4x4; B3**

Nevada; C & H Wrecking, 1021 W FM 6, 75173; 972-843-2667; Sa, UR; 5ac, 400; **60s+; D, F, PU, 4x4; B3, AMC, Jp, IH, VW**

New Braunfels; Comal Auto Salvage Inc, 5135 FM 482, 78132; 830-629-6965; Sa; 800; **65+; D, F, PU, 4x4; B3, AMC; Closed Monday**

Odessa; James Truck & Auto Parts, 500 N Moss Av, 79763; 915-385-0453; CC, Sa, Sp, UR; 1000; **70+; D, F, PU, 4x4; B3**

    John's Auto Salvage, 318 Georgia St, 79764; 915-368-4353; Wr; 100; **80-90; D, F, PU, 4x4, Trk; B3, AMC, Jp, IH, VW**

    P & P Auto, 9371 W Dunn St, 79763; 915-381-5211; Sa, UR; 250+; **80-90; D, PU, 4x4; B3, AMC**

Pharr; Vic's Auto Slvg, S Hwy 281, 78577; 956-781-0676; 100; **80-92; D, F; B3; Spanish**

Quinlan; A-1 Metroplex Auto, 880 FM 751, 75474; 903-356-4575, FAX 903-560-1337; CC, Sa, Sp, Br; 500; **80-93; D, F, PU; B3, AMC**

    AAA Auto Salvage, 6952 FM 2947, 75474; 903-883-3029, 800-776-4917; CC, Sa, Sp, Br; 400; **80+, few 70s; D, PU, 4x4; B3, AMC, Jp**

Rowlett; G & E Wrecking Yard, Hwy 276, 75088; 972-412-3852; Sa, Sp; **80+; D, F, PU, 4x4; B3, AMC, VW**

Royse City; Blackland Car & Truck Parts, 1117 State Hwy 276, 75189; 972-771-6847; CC, Sa, Br; 20ac, 2000; **D, F, PU, 4x4, Trk; B3**

San Angelo; A Better Buy Auto Parts, 2539 W FM 2105, 76901; 915-658-2881, FAX 915-658-8236, 800-299-2881; CC, Sp, Br, PL; 600; **65+; D, F; B3, AMC**

    Chatham Salvage Co, *see Vintage*

    Clark Auto Wrecking, *see Vintage*

    Jim Hall Sales, 1402 W Loop 306, 76904; 915-651-9300; CC, Sa, Sp, UR; 600; **70-95; D**

    Menchaca Wrecking, *see Vintage*

San Antonio; A-1 Auto & Truck Parts, 9635 S US Hwy 81, 78211; 210-623-5555; **76+; D, F, PU, 4x4, Trk; B3, AMC, Jp**

    Alamo Auto Parts, 3223 SW Military Dr, 78211; 210-924-6651, FAX 210-924-6652; Sa, Br; **64+; D, PU, 4x4; B3, AMC; Spc: Mustang**

    All Foreign Auto Parts Inc, 9604 New Laredo Hwy, 78211; 210-623-5000, FAX 210-623-5156, 800-833-4941; CC, Sa, Sp; 800; **79-96; F, PU**

Allied Auto Parts Co, 6112 W Old US Hwy 90, 78227; 210-674-0310; CC, Sa, Sp, Br; 550+; **80-90; D, F, PU, 4x4; Trk; B**3, **AMC, Jp, IH, VW**

Laredo Auto & Truck Salvage, 9545 New Laredo Hwy, 78211; 210-623-4880, 888-482-0057; Sa; 200; **80+; D, F, PU; B**3

Pick-N-Pull Inc, 11795 Applewhite Rd, 78224; 210-624-2830, FAX 210-628-1194; Sa, UR; 35ac, 3500; **65-89; D, F, PU, 4x4; B**3; **Open Sun**

Ram's Auto Salvage, 1531 Somerset Rd, 78211; 210-924-2233; CC, Sa, Sp; 200; **82+; D, F, PU, 4x4; B**3, **Jp**

Temple; Action Auto Recyclers, *see Vintage*

Texarkana; Rabbit's Salvage Yard, *see Vintage*

Tyler; D G Auto Salvage, *see Vintage*

Waco; Best Value Used Auto Parts, *see Vintage*

J Ds Auto Parts, 2224 S 3rd St, 76706; 254-753-3726; Sa, UR; 270; **73-87; D, F, PU; B**3

Weatherford; Johnny's Auto & Truck Salvage, *see Vintage*

Wellington; South Side Salvage, *see Vintage*

LATE MODEL

Abilene; FM 600 Wrecking, *see Late Vintage*

Grape Street Wrecking, 4242 Grape St, 79601; 915-672-5511, FAX 915-677-0152, 800-592-4424; CC, Sa, Sp; 3ac; **D, PU, 4x4; B**3; **Spc: Pickup**

Mike's Wrecking, 4005 Pine St, 79601; 915-673-6542, 800-592-4676, mikes@camalott. com; CC, Sp, Wr; **D, F, PU, 4x4; B**3

Alvin; Highway 35 Auto Slvg, *see Late Vintage*

S & S Auto Salvage, *see Late Vintage*

Amarillo; ABA Texas Truck Parts Inc, 11015 E Interstate 40, 79118; 806-335-1862; CC, Sa, Sp; **few PU, few 4x4, Truck only**

Amarillo Salvage, *see Late Vintage*

Cherry Avenue Auto Parts, *see Vintage*

Clark's Auto Sales Parts, *see Vintage*

Complete Auto Recyclers, *see Late Vintage*

Dulaney Auto & Truck Parts, 6600 Canyon Dr, 79109; 806-352-4111, 800-858-2277; CC, Sp; 45ac, 450; **D, PU, 4x4; B**3, **Jp; Spc: Jeep Wagoneer & Cherokee**

Texas Auto Parts, 10501 E I-40, 79103; 806-335-2277; CC, Sa, Sp; **D, F, PU, 4x4; B**3

Aransas Pass; Pruitt's Auto Salvage, Hwy 1069 NW, 78336; 361-758-3695, 800-758-3695; CC; 400; **D, PU, 4x4; B**3; **Spc: Pickup**

Arlington; A A Auto Parts, *see Late Vintage*

Ace Auto Salvage, *see Late Vintage*

Snider's Auto Salvage, 4015 W Division St, 76012; 817-275-0351; CC, Sa, Sp; 500; **D, F, PU, 4x4; B**3

Atascosa; All Bimmers & Benzes, *see Late Vintage*

Austin; Allied Auto Parts Co, 8534 S Congress Av, 78745; 512-282-1682; CC, Sa, Sp, Br; 3ac, 400; **D, F, PU, 4x4; B**3

Big 4 Auto Parts, 8601 Cullen Ln, 78748; 512-282-4546; CC, Sp; 10ac; **D, F, PU, 4x4; B**3

Bertram; David's Auto Parts, *see Vintage*

Big Spring; Westex Auto Parts Inc, 1511 Hwy 350 N, 79720; 915-263-5000, FAX 915-267-1680, 800-622-1888; CC, Sa, Sp; **D, F, PU, 4x4; B**3

Bonham; A-1 Auto Parts Inc, Hwy 121 S, 75418; 903-583-9519; CC, Sa, Sp; 400; **D, PU; B**3

Bowie; Phillips Auto Salvage, *see Vintage*

Breckenridge; Seller's Auto Salvage, *see Vintage*

Brownsville; 511 Auto & Truck Salvage, *see Late Vintage*

Brownwood; Hi-Way Auto Parts, *see Vintage*

Bryan; Doggett Auto Parts, 3601 Old Kurten Rd, 77809; 409-778-7536, FAX 409-778-1338, 800-877-9949, doggett@myriad.net; CC, Sp; 500; **D, F, PU, 4x4, Trk; B**3, **AMC, Jp**

Highway 6 Auto Salvage, *see Late Vintage*

Canton; Myers Auto Salvage, Rt 5 Box 316, 75103; 903-567-4671, FAX 903-567-1485, 800-404-4143; CC, Sp; 850+; **D, F, PU, 4x4, Trk; B**3, **AMC, Jp, IH**

Carrollton; Hi-Way Auto Parts II, *see Late Vintage*

Celeste; Area Celeste Body Shop, FM 903 Rd, 75423; 903-568-4280; Sa, Sp, UR; **75+; D, F, PU, 4x4, Trk; B3, AMC**

Cleburne; Prine's Auto Salvage, 1902 N Main St, 76031; 817-645-9412; Sa, Sp, UR; 100; **D, few F**

Conroe; McCulloch Auto Salvage, *see Late Vintage*

Corpus Christi; Ace Auto Parts, 5649 State Hwy 44, 78406; 512-289-0187, 800-225-0136; Sp; 200+; **D, F, PU, 4x4, Trk, Fm; B3, AMC, Jp, IH, few VW**

    Best Deal Auto Salvage, *see Vintage*

    Deluxe Auto Parts, 230 Omaha, 78405; 512-883-2581, 800-654-3589; CC, Sp, Br; 13ac; **D, F, PU, 4x4, Trk; B3, AMC, Jp, VW**

    International Foreign Auto, 3232 Agnes St, 78405; 512-882-1755, FAX 512-884-7463, 800-256-7300; CC, Sa, Sp, Br; 300; **F**

Corpus Christi; Vic's Salvage, *see Vintage*

Corsicana; Dowd & Sons Auto Salvage, 416 S 7th St, 75110; 903-872-3081, FAX 903-872-6463; CC, Sa, Sp, Br; **D, F, PU, 4x4, Trk; B3, Jp**

Dallas; Atomic Pick U Part, 8835 S Centr Expy, 75241; 214-375-5555; Sa, UR; 1000; **D, F**

    B & C Auto Wrecking, 5419 S R L Thornton Fwy, 75232; 214-372-9700; Sa, Sp, Br; 5ac; **D, F; B3, AMC, Jp, VW**

    B & W Auto Salvage & Car Crusher, 10328 Rylie Rd, 75217; 972-286-7104, FAX 972-286-7304; Sa; 5ac; **D, F, PU, 4x4; B3, AMC, VW**

    C & D Auto Parts & Salvage, 1753 S Belt Line Rd, 75253; 972-286-3577, FAX 972-286-3795; CC, Sa, Sp; 1500; **D, Spc: Pickup**

    Chuck Taylor Auto Parts, *see Late Vintage*

    Office Auto Salvage, *see Late Vintage*

    Nabors Auto Wrecking, *see Vintage*

    Rylie Auto Parts, 1115 Ellenwood St, 75217; 972-286-0004, FAX 972-286-0003; Sa, Sp; **D, F; B3; Spc: Foreign**

Denison; Bill's Auto Salvage, Hwy 69 E, 75020; 903-463-1970; Sa, Sp, Br; 6ac, 250; **D, F**

Denton; Denton County Auto Salvage, 1715 Fort Worth Dr, 76205; 940-387-5202, FAX 940-387-6715, 800-245-0647, www.dentoncountryautosalvage.com; CC, Sa, Sp, Br, PL; 300; **D, F, PU, 4x4, Trk, Fm; B3**

    W W Auto Salvage, *see Late Vintage*

Eagle Pass; Eagle Pass Auto Wrecking Inc, 100 Big River Rd, 78852; 830-773-1515, FAX 830-757-6736, 800- 292-5519, www.eaglepassauto.com; CC, Sa, Sp, Br, Wr; 17ac, 1000; **D, PU; B3, AMC, Jp**

    Las Brisas Auto Salvage, 150 Big River Rd, 78852; 830-757-0374; Sa; 100; **D, PU, 4x4, Trk; B3, AMC**

Ector; James Cobb Wrecking Yard, Hwy 82 W, 75439; 903-961-2855; Wr; **D, Fm**

El Paso; Aguirre Car Salvage, 11231 Alameda Av, 79927; 915-858-2884; Sa; **D, F, PU, 4x4; B3, AMC, Jp, IH, VW**

    CC Auto Parts, *see Late Vintage*

    Ramirez Auto Parts, *see Vintage*

    Rio Grande Parts, *see Late Vintage*

Elm Mott; Elm Mott Auto Salvage, *see Vintage*

Ennis; Ennis Auto Salvage, *see Late Vintage*

Fort Worth; American Auto Salvage Co, 928 N Henderson St, 76107; 817-335-3328, FAX 817-335-2711, 800-562-5986, mrautosalvage@americanautosalvage.com; CC, Sp; 1000; **D, F, PU, 4x4; B3, AMC, Jp**

    Auto Recyclers, 5806 Elliott Reeder Rd, 76117; 817-831-6356, FAX 817-831-6366, 800-322-4892; CC, Sa, Sp; 2000; **D, F, PU, 4x4, Trk; B3, AMC, Jp, IH, VW**

    Chrysler Heaven, *see Late Vintage*

    North Main Auto Salvage, 3014 N Main St, 76106; 817-625-5351; Sa, Sp; **D**

Gainesville; Wayne Gilbert Auto Salvage, *see Vintage*

Galveston; City Auto Salvage, PO Box 4402, 520 44th St, 77550; 409-765-9788; Sa; **D, F**

Grand Prairie; ABC Truck & Auto Parts, 4007 E Jefferson St, 75051; 972-263-1014; Sa, Br; 2000; **D, PU, 4x4; B3, AMC, Jp; Jeep Cherokee only**

Affordable Auto Salvage, 4111 E Jefferson St, 75051; 972-642-0400; Sa, Sp, Br; 350+; **F**

Dallas County Auto Salvage, *see Vintage*

Texas Auto Salvage, 3925 E Jefferson St, 75051; 972-263-3306, FAX 972-664-4745; **D, F**

YourFord, 4001 E Jefferson St, 75051; 972-263-3303; CC, Sa, Sp, Br; 800; **D; Ford, Lincoln, Mercury only**

Haltom City; Auto Recyclers of Fort Worth, 5806 Elliott Reeder Rd, 76117; 817-831-3585, FAX 817-831-6366, 800-322-4819, autorftw@aol.com; CC, Sa, Sp, Br; 12ac, 1700; **D, F, PU, 4x4; B3**

Harlingen; Carter's Foreign Car Slvg, 2901 Expressway 77, 78550; 956-428-4673; 450+; **F**

Holland; Snyder's Salvage, *see Late Vintage*

Houston; Absolutely Ford Chrysler, *see Vintage*

    Auto World, *see Late Vintage*

    Bottom Line Honda Salvage, 6702 Chippewa Blvd, 77086; 281-820-9933, FAX 281-448-5738, 888-454-3693; CC, Sa, Sp, PL; 1ac, 75+; **F; Honda & Acura only**

    Bronco Truck Salvage Inc, *see Late Vintage*

    Houston Auto Recycling, *see Late Vintage*

    Jim's Auto Parts, 12415 Tomball Pky, 77086; 281-999-4990; Sa; 175; **D, PU, 4x4; B3, AMC, Jp**

    Johnny Franks Auto Parts, 1225 Sawyer St, 77007; 713-869-6200, FAX 713-869-6326, 800-553-3810; CC, Sa, Sp; 400; **D, F, PU, 4x4; B3, AMC**

    Leroy's Parts, 5430 Washington Av, 77007; 713-802-1185, 877-453-7697; Sa, Sp, Br; 2.5ac, 100; **D, F, PU, 4x4, SUV; B3, Explorer, GMC**

    Model Automotive Enterprises, *see Late Vintage*

    Patkes Auto Parts Inc, 13130 Cullen Blvd, 77047; 713-734-1621, FAX 713-734-1633, 800-392-1810; Sp; 7ac; **D, PU, 4x4; B3**

    Pick A Part Auto Wrecking, *see Late Vintage*

    Price Lo Auto Imports Salvage, 10905 Airline Dr, 77037; 281-847-3400, FAX 281-847-1077, 800-351-0151, www.pricelo.com; Sa, Sp, Br; 800+; **F**

    Scott Street Auto Parts, 7115 Scott St, 77021; 713-747-0212, FAX 713-747-1348, 800-955-0210; CC, Sa, Sp; 800; **D, PU, 4x4, Trk; B3, AMC**

    Take-A-Part & Save, *see Late Vintage*

    Volvo Parts Independent, *see Late Vintage*

    Williams Auto Salvage, *see Late Vintage*

Jacksonville; A & A Auto Salvage, *see Vintage*

Kaufman; Henderson Auto Parts, *see Vintage*

Kennedale; Apple Auto Salvage, 7002 Mansfield Hwy, 76060; 817-478-4899; CC, Sa, Sp, UR; 1500; **F, PU, 4x4**

    B & B Foreign Car, 7301 Mansfield Hwy, 76060; 817-478-4451, FAX 817-478-4827, 800-242-6019; CC, Sa, Sp, Br; 550+; **F, PU, 4x4**

    Barry's Auto Sales, 7701 US Hwy 287 Business, 76060; 817-572-5142; CC, Sa, Sp, PL; 3ac; **D, few PU, few 4x4; B3**

    Budget American & Import Auto, 1208 Mansfield Hwy, 76060; 817-483-4497, FAX 817-561-2980, 800-624-9880; CC, Sa, Sp, Br; 1000+; **D, F, PU, 4x4; B3, AMC, Jp, IH, VW**

Killeen; Do-Rite Wrecking Yard, *see Late Vintage*

    Moore's Auto Salvage, *see Late Vintage*

    Speedway Auto Salvage Inc, *see Late Vintage*

Longview; Wreck Out Auto Salvage, 3120 N Eastman Rd, 75605; 903-663-1942, FAX 903-663-5121, 800-222-1638; Sp; 1300; **D, F, PU, 4x4, Trk; B3, AMC, Jp**

Lubbock; American Pickup Salvage, *see Late Vintage*

    Auto Salvage Co, *see Vintage*

    B & R Auto Parts Inc, 4401 Avenue A, 79404; 806-762-0319, FAX 806-744-1027, 800-692-4492; CC, Sp, Wr; 3ac; **D, F, PU, 4x4; B3, AMC, Jp, IH**

    D C Wrecking, 4720 Hwy 84, 79416; 806-762-8738, FAX 806-762-8765, 800-692-4418; CC, Sp, PL; 44ac, 3000; **D, F, PU, 4x4; B3**

    Jerry Burgess Used Auto Parts, 2722 Texas Av, 79405; 806-744-2244, 800-462-2240; CC, Sa, Sp; 5ac, 1500; **D, F, PU, 4x4; B3, AMC**

Lufkin; Redland Auto Salvage, *see Late Vintage*
Midland; Benny's Auto Parts Inc, *see Late Vintage*
Mineral Wells; Jack's Auto Salvage, *see Late Vintage*
Mount Pleasant; Hwy 67 Auto Salvage, *see Late Vintage*
Nacogdoches; American Auto Salvage, *see Late Vintage*
Nederland; Lawson's Auto Slvg, Hwy 69 N, 77627; 409-722-3481; **D, F, PU, 4x4; B3, AMC**
Nevada; Action Auto Salvage, 1021 W FM 6, 75173; 972-442-3412; Sa, Br; 400; **D, F, PU, 4x4, Trk; B3, AMC, Jp, IH, VW**
 C & H Wrecking, *see Late Vintage*
New Braunfels; Comal Auto Salvage Inc, *see Late Vintage*
Odessa; James Truck & Auto Parts, *see Late Vintage*
Pharr; Texano Salvage Yard, Rt 3 Box 77 F, S Hwy 281, 78577; 956-781-5641; Sa, UR; 20; **D, F, PU; B3; Open Sunday**
 Vic's Auto Salvage, *see Late Vintage*
Plainview; D Js Auto Salvage, 401 E 24th St, 79072; 806-293-3662, 800-692-4471; CC, Sp; 8ac; **D, F; B3**
 Dulaney Auto Parts-Plainview, 311 S Columbia St, 79072; 806-296-7456, FAX 806-293-8304, 800-858-2277; Sp, Br; **D, PU, 4x4; B3, AMC, Jp**
Quinlan; A-1 Metroplex Auto, *see Late Vintage*
 AAA Auto Salvage, *see Late Vintage*
Rowena; Halfmann Bro, S US Hwy 67, 76875; 915-442-2026; CC, Sp, Br, Wr; 3ac; **D, PU**
Rowlett; G & E Wrecking Yard, *see Late Vintage*
Royse City; Blackland Car & Truck Parts, *see Late Vintage*
Saltillo; Eddy Auto Salvage & Sales, PO Box 163, 75478; 903-588-2491; CC, Br; 150; **D, F, PU, 4x4; B3, AMC, Jp**
San Angelo; A Better Buy Auto Parts, *see Late Vintage*
 Chatham Salvage Co, *see Vintage*
 Clark Auto Wrecking, *see Vintage*
 Earl Bowman Auto Wrecking Inc, 2020 S Chadbourne St, 76903; 915-655-6417; CC, Sp; 900; **D, PU, 4x4, Trk; B3, AMC**
 Jim Hall Sales, *see Late Vintage*
San Antonio; A-1 Auto & Truck Parts, *see Late Vintage*
 Acme Auto Parts Inc, 1573 Somerset Rd, 78211; 210-927-2021, FAX 210-924-3447, 800-638-2263; Sp; **D; B3, AMC**
 Alamo Auto Parts, *see Late Vintage*
 All Foreign Auto Parts Inc, *see Late Vintage*
 American Auto Salvage, 8524 S US Hwy 81, 78211; 210-977-9301, FAX 210-977-8777, 877-812-0287; Sp; 100; **D, PU; B3**
 Insurance Auto Salvage Co, 5814 E IH 10 E, 78219; 210-661-2339, FAX 210-661-9527; CC, Sp; 12ac; **D, F, PU, Trk; B3, AMC, Jp; few earlier than 90**
 Laredo Auto & Truck Salvage, *see Late Vintage*
 Ram's Auto Salvage, *see Late Vintage*
San Juan; Flores Wrecking Yard, 2 Mi North 1 Rd, 78589; 956-781-2772, 800-781-3039; CC, Sa, Sp, Br; 750+; **D, PU, 4x4, Trk; B3, AMC, Jp**
Silsbee; Armour J Inc, Hwy 327 W, 77656; 409-385-4108, FAX 409-385-7426, 800-460-4108; CC, Sp; 3500; **D, F, PU, 4x4; B3, AMC, Jp**
Sulphur Springs; Sulphur Springs Auto Salvage, Rt 6 Box 585, 75482; 903-885-6961, 888-439-0044; CC; 650; **D, F, PU, 4x4; B3, AMC, Jp, IH, VW**
Texarkana; Rabbit's Salvage Yard, *see Vintage*
Tyler; D G Auto Salvage, *see Vintage*
Vidor; Aldridge Auto Slvg, 2555 Mansfeld Ferry Rd, 77662; 409-768-1079; Sa, UR; **D, F**
Weatherford; Johnny's Auto & Truck Salvage, *see Vintage*
Wellington; South Side Salvage, *see Vintage*

1933 836 Pierce Arrow
Club Sedan
Dan Greer
Cheyenne, WY

Before

After

UTAH

VINTAGE

American Fork; Kurt's Auto Wrck & Rcvry, 1075 W Main St, 84003; 801-756-5878, FAX 801-763-0628, 800-662-6552; CC, Sa, Sp, UR, PL; 5.5ac; **60+; D, F, PU, 4x4; B3, Jp, VW**

Aurora; Country Auto Salvage, 4800 W 3550 S, 84620; 435-529-3211, FAX 435-529-4153; CC, Sp; 35ac; **60+, few 50s; D, F, PU, 4x4; B3, Jp, IH; 50s Chevy & Ford**

Chester; Johansen Auto Wrecking, 12070 N 4000 E, 84623; 435-436-8236, FAX 435-436-8237, jo@cut.net; CC, Sa, Sp, Br; 1000+; **mid 60+; D, F, PU, 4x4; B3, AMC**

Grantsville; Westside Auto Wrecking, 519 W Main St, 84029; 435-884-6602; CC, Sa, Sp, Br; 5ac; **80+, few 50-70s; D, F, PU, 4x4; B3**

Ivins; St George Auto Recycling, 595 W Hwy 91, 84738; 435-673-7679, FAX 435-652-4232; CC, Sa, Sp, UR; 1.5ac; **80+, few 50-70s; D, F, PU; B3, Jp, IH**

Midvale; All Small Auto Wrecking, 72 E 8000 S, 84047; 801-561-2221; Sa, Sp; 400; **60+; F; VW; Foreign only**

Nephi; Nephi Auto Wrecking & Towing, N US Hwy 91, 84648; 435-623-2200; Sa, UR; 6ac; **30-70; D; B3, St, Wy, VW, DeSoto**

Ogden; AAA Auto Salvage & Auto Body, 262 W 20th St, 84401; 801-399-2982; Sa, UR; 3ac; **60-87; D, F; B3, AMC, Wy, VW**

 B & R Old Car Parts, 770 W 17th St, 84404; 801-399-5203; Sp, Br; 5ac; **30-80; D, few PU, few Trk, Fm, In, Cn; B3, AMC, Jp, IH, Ns, St, VW; few Edsel; By Appoint. Only**

 Joes Towing & Parts, 1873 Stephens Av, 84401; 801-399-1106, FAX 801-399-1132, 800-385-8062; CC, Sa, Sp; 5ac; **70+, few 50-60s; D, F, PU; B3, IH**

288

Orem; Rawlings Auto Wrecking, 255 S 1600 W, 84058; 801-225-2308, 800-658-8447; UR; 4ac; **60-79; D, PU, 4x4; B3, IH; Spc: Chrysler**

Salt Lake City; A-1 Truck Parts, 2223 N Redwood Rd, 84116; 801-521-2002, 877-521-2002; CC, Sa, Sp; 2ac; **60+; Truck only, 2T & bigger**

Acme Salvage & Recycling, 1240 Wallace Rd, 84104; 801-972-3116; 1200; **50+; D, F, PU, 4x4, Trk; B3, AMC, Jp, IH, VW**

Chick's Auto Wrecking, 5645 W 2300 S, 84128; 801-972-8924, FAX 801-975-9736, 888-972-8924; CC, Sp; **80+, few 50-79; D, few F, PU, 4x4; B3**

Hansen Auto Wrecking, 2340 S 5700 W, 84128; 801-972-6905; Sa, Sp, UR; 2ac; **80+, few 40-70s; D, PU; B3, IH, St, VW**

King Size Auto & Truck, 5130 W 700 S, 84104; 801-973-8666; Sa, Sp; 5ac; **40+; D, F, PU, 4x4, Trk; B3, Hd, St, Pk, VW**

S & B Foreign Car Parts, 2401 N Redwood Rd, 84116; 801-531-9400; Sp, UR; 5ac; **70+, few 50-60s; D, F, PU, 4x4; Trk; B3, AMC, IH, Ns, VW; Bus**

Sommers Auto Wrecking, 647 W 3300 S, 84119; 801-262-0340; Sa, UR; 5.5ac, 2000; **70+, few 50-60s; D, F, PU, 4x4; B3, IH, St, VW**

Special Editions, 68 E 3300 S, 84115; 801-487-2177; Sa, Sp, UR; **70+, few 40-60s; D, F, PU, 4x4, Fm; B3, AMC, Hd, Pk**

TLW Auto, 1761 S Main St, 84115; 801-463-1916; Sp; 15ac; **67+; D, F, PU, 4x4, Trk; B3**

W W Auto Wrecking & Sales, 2300 S 5800 W, 84128; 801-972-8923, FAX 801-972-8928, 800-670-8034; Sp; 5ac, 2000; **30+; D, F, PU, 4x4; B3, AMC, Hd, Ns, Pk**

Sigurd; Dwights Auto Wrecking, 5375 N Stake Farm Rd, 84657; 435-896-8031, FAX 435-836-2881, 800-300-8031; Sa, Sp, UR; 60ac; **40+; D, F, PU, 4x4, Fm; B3, AMC, Jp, IH, St, Wy, VW**

Springville; Anderson's Auto Wrecking, 3448 S State St, 84663; 801-489-3729; Sa, UR; 11.5ac; **70+, few 40-60s; D, F, PU, 4x4, Fm; B3, AMC, IH, St, VW**

JRJ Auto Wrecking, 595 W 1600 S, 84663; 801-489-9373, 800-627-4575; CC, Sa, Sp, UR; **30+; D, F, PU, 4x4, Trk; B3**

Tooele; Moore Auto Shop, 7720 Hwy 36, 84074; 801-250-0396; CC, Sa, Sp; 40ac; **70+, few 40-60s; D, F, PU, 4x4; B3, IH, Ns, St**

Tremonton; Hathaways Towing-Auto Salvage, 148 S 1600 E, 84337; 435-257-5084; CC; **40-69; D; B3, St; Prefer to sell whole cars**

West Jordan; Stuarts Sales & Bodyworks, 5442 Wells Park Rd, 84088; 801-280-0444, FAX 801-280-0462, 800-522-0444; CC, Sp; 5ac; **70+, few 50-60s; few D, F, PU, 4x4; B3**

LATE VINTAGE

American Fork; Kurt's Auto Wrecking & Recovery, *see Vintage*

Aurora; Country Auto Salvage, *see Vintage*

Chester; Johansen Auto Wrecking, *see Vintage*

Clearfield; Auto Salvage, 17 N Main St, 84015; 801-825-9779; CC, Sa, UR; 450; **75-85, few 60s; D, F, PU; B3, AMC, IH, VW; Bugs & Rabbits**

Farmington; Haugen Body Shop, 16 W 600 N, 84025; 801-451-9906; Sa, UR; 100; **80+; D, F, few PU; B3**

Grantsville; Westside Auto Wrecking, *see Vintage*

Ivins; St George Auto Recycling, *see Vintage*

Logan; Economy Auto, 1420 N 400 W, 84341; 435-752-5402, FAX 435-752-7143, 800-662-2752; CC, Sp; 20ac; **70+; D, F, PU, 4x4; B3, AMC; Cars 86+; Pickups 70+**

Magna; PM Truck Parts, 7774 W 2100 S, 84044; 801-250-1836; Sa, Sp; 3.5ac; **70+; D, PU; B3; Pickups only**

Midvale; All Small Auto Wrecking, *see Vintage*

Moab; Bert;s Auto Supply, 2591 S Hwy 191, 84532; 435-259-7736; **70-89; D; Chr, Dodge**

Ogden; AAA Auto Salvage & Auto Body, *see Vintage*

B & R Old Car Parts, *see Vintage*

Coy Auto Wrecking, 3586 N Hwy 126, 84404; 801-731-1763, FAX 801-731-2066, 800-453-2006; CC, Sa, Sp, UR; 20ac; **80+, few 60-70s; D, F, PU, 4x4, Trk; B3**

D & B Foreign, 1225 W 3300 S, 84401; 801-627-2713, FAX 801-627-4287; CC, Sa, Sp; 700; **84-94; F, PU; VW; Saab, Volvo; Foreign only**

Joes Towing & Parts, *see Vintage*

Orem; European Only, 802 N Geneva Rd, 84057; 801-224-0859, FAX 801-225-2542, 800-443-6886; CC, Sp; 1ac; **72+; F; European only**

Rawlings Auto Wrecking, *see Vintage*

Provo; State Street Auto Wrecking, 2403 S State St, 84606; 801-377-2886, FAX 801-375-7205, 800-560-2880; CC; 1200; **70-92; D, F, PU, 4x4; B3, AMC, IH, VW**

Salt Lake City; A-1 Truck Parts, *see Vintage*

Acme Salvage & Recycling, *see Vintage*

Butcher Auto Wrecking, 2300 S 5650 W, 84128; 801-973-6696, FAX 801-977-1169, 888-778-6696; CC, Sa, Sp; Br; 6ac; **70+; D, F, PU, 4x4; Spc: GM & Chrysler**

Cal Brown Body Shop, 2067 Indiana Av, 84104; 801-972-1239; **70-89, few 60s; D; B3**

Chick's Auto Wrecking, *see Vintage*

Deseret Recycling Ctr, 1398 Beck St, 84116; 801-364-3484, 800-336-3484; Sa, Sp; 1000; **70-89; D, F, PU, 4x4; B3**

Dick;s Auto Sales Salvage, 1802 Indiana Ave, 84104; 801-973-8355; Sa, Sp; 1ac; **70-89; D, F, PU; B3, AMC, IH**

Foreign Motor Sales, 1775 Chicago St, 84116; 801-355-9161; Sp; **mid 80s; F, few PU**

Hansen Auto Wrecking, *see Vintage*

King Size Auto & Truck, *see Vintage*

Max Auto Wrecking, 5640 W 2300 S, 84128; 801-972-1657; **80+ D, F**

Mc Quaid Towing, 960 Quayle Av, 84104; 801-973-9824; Sa, UR; 100; **70+; D, F, PU, 4x4; B3 AMC, IH, VW**

Penguin Auto Wrecking, 5600 W 2300 S, 84128; 801-972-8926; CC, Sa, Sp; 10ac; **80+; D, F, PU, 4x4**

S & B Foreign Car Parts, *see Vintage*

Sommers Auto Wrecking, *see Vintage*

Special Editions, *see Vintage*

TLW Auto, *see Vintage*

W W Auto Wrecking & Sales, *see Vintage*

Western Sandy Metal, 6580 W 2100 S, 84128; 801-250-7107, 800-224-2216; CC, Sp, UR; 5ac; **80+; D, F, PU, 4x4; B3**

Sigurd; Dwights Auto Wrecking, *see Vintage*

Springville; Anderson's Auto Wrecking, see Vintage

JRJ Auto Wrecking, *see Vintage*

Tooele; Moore Auto Shop, see Vintage

West Jordan; Stuarts Sales & Bodyworks, see Vintage

LATE MODEL

American Fork; Kurt's Auto Wrecking & Recovery, *see Vintage*

Aurora; Country Auto Salvage, *see Vintage*

Chester; Johansen Auto Wrecking, *see Vintage*

Farmington; Haugen Body Shop, *see Late Vintage*

Grantsville; Westside Auto Wrecking, *see Vintage*

Ivins; St George Auto Recycling, *see Vintage*

Lehi; Japanese Auto Wrecking, 10345 N 8800 W, 84043; 801-768-4424, FAX 801-768-2482, 800-359-8211; CC, Sp; 600+; **F; Jpa**

Transwest Auto, 11651 N Frontage Rd, 84043; 801-768-4888, 800-963-0200; **D, F**

Logan; Economy Auto, *see Late Vintage*

Magna; PM Truck Parts, *see Late Vintage*

Midvale; All Small Auto Wrecking, *see Vintage*

Midvale Radiator & Salvage, 153 N Holden St, 84047; 801-255-3341, FAX 801-568-6765; CC, Sa, UR; 1ac; **D; Fd; Ford Escort; Radiators**

Ogden; Coy Auto Wrecking, *see Late Vintage*

Crabtree Auto, 605 W 4600 S, 84405; 801-394-2685, FAX 801-394-2685, 800-888-2685; CC, Sa, Sp; 5ac, 350; **D, F, PU, 4x4**

D & B Foreign, *see Late Vintage*

Foreign Engine Supply, 3192 Midland Dr, 84401; 801-621-4254, FAX 801-621-1595; CC, Sa, Sp; **F; Engines & Transmissions**

J & J Auto Parts, 2390 E 6600 S, 84405; 801-479-3139; Sa; **D, few F**

Joes Towing & Parts, *see Vintage*

Riverside Auto Recyclers, 800 W Wilson Ln, 84401; 801-399-5864; Sa, Sp, UR; 200; **D, F, PU**

Terry's Auto Parts, 1265 W 3300 S, 84401; 801-621-6822; Sa, Sp; 2ac; **D, F, PU, 4x4**

Orem; Duane's Auto Wrecking, 1190 N 1600 W, 84057; 801-225-5586, 800-624-7062; CC, Sp; 1000; **D, F, PU, 4x4**

European Only, *see Late Vintage*

Myron's Auto Wrecking, 650 N Geneva Rd, 84057; 801-225-8140, FAX 801-765-9938, 800-283-1116; CC, Sa, Sp, UR; 1000+; **D, F, PU, 4x4**

Provo; PRTC Performance Products, 1520 N State St, 84604; 801-373-9608, FAX 801-373-9635, 800-742-5734; Sp, UR; 150; **D, few F, PU, 4x4, Trk**

State Street Auto Wrecking, *see Late Vintage*

Saint George; Blakes Auto Rcycl, 4095 S 1630 E, 84790; 435-673-4989; 20ac; **D, F, PU, 4x4**

Salt Lake City; A Partsmart, 5850 W 2300 S, 84128; 801-973-6234, FAX 801-973-0545, 800-286-6234; CC, Sp; 6ac; **D, PU; Suburans, Pickups and minivans**

A-1 National Foreign Auto, 140 S 500 W, 84101; FAX 801-363-2232; Sp; 300; **F, PU; Jpa & Eur**

A-1 Truck Parts, *see Vintage*

Acme Salvage & Recycling, *see Vintage*

All Hyundai Auto Parts, 4195 S 500 W # 68, 84123; 801-261-3305; CC, Sa, Sp; 65; **F; Hyundai only**

All Truck Parts, 7100 W 2100 S, 84128; 801-250-3300, FAX 801-250-3320, 800-828-2559; CC, Sp; 5ac; **D, F, PU, 4x4; Pickup only**

Butcher Auto Wrecking, *see Late Vintage*

Chick's Auto Wrecking, *see Vintage*

Foreign Car Parts, 1009 Beck St, 84103; 801-322-1900; Sa, Sp; 5ac; **F; Jpa, Eur**

Hansen Auto Wrecking, *see Vintage*

King Size Auto & Truck, *see Vintage*

Labrum Auto Wrecking, 3508 S 500 W, 84115; 801-266-3541, 888-522-7862; CC, Sp; 2.5ac; **D, F, PU, 4x4**

Max Auto Wrecking, *see Late Vintage*

Mc Quaid Towing, *see Late Vintage*

Penguin Auto Wrecking, *see Late Vintage*

S & B Foreign Car Parts, *see Vintage*

Sommers Auto Wrecking, *see Vintage*

Special Editions, *see Vintage*

TLW Auto, *see Vintage*

W W Auto Wrecking & Sales, *see Vintage*

Western Sandy Metal, *see Late Vintage*

Sigurd; Dwights Auto Wrecking, *see Vintage*

Springville; Anderson's Auto Wrecking, *see Vintage*

JRJ Auto Wrecking, *see Vintage*

Tooele; Moore Auto Shop, *see Vintage*

Washington; Dixie Foreign Auto Wrecking, 1795 E Washington Dam Rd, 84780; 435-674-1272, FAX 435-674-4673, 800-967-8894; CC, Sp, Br; 5.5ac; **D, F, PU, 4x4**

Southwest Auto Recycling, 1750 E Washington Dam Rd, 84780; 435-628-1649, 800-292-2607; Sp; 600; **D, F, PU, 4x4**

West Jordan; Stuarts Sales & Bodyworks, *see Vintage*

Woods Cross; South Bountiful Auto Parts, 847 W 1500 S, 84087; 801-292-2489, FAX 801-294-5912, 800-517-2489; Sp; 8ac; **D, F, PU, 4x4**

Vermont

**Please mention you saw'em in
Ray's wReckingyard Roster when
contacting these yards**

VERMONT

VINTAGE
Bennington; Le Blanc's Auto Salvage, East Rd, 05201; 802-442-2308, FAX 802-442-8847, 800-444-2308; CC; 5ac; **64+; D, F, PU, 4x4; B**3; **Spc: 64-68 Mustang & 68+ Ford & Chevy Pickup**
Grafton; Auto Salvage of Grafton, Fisher Hill Rd, 05146; 802-843-2200; Sa, Sp, UR; 800; **50+; D, F; B**3; **Few teens cars**
Lyndonville; C & M Used Auto Parts, Sutton Rd, 05851; 802-626-3320; Sa, Sp; 2ac; **60+; D, F, PU, 4x4, Trk; B**3 **VW**
Morrisville; Morrisville Used Auto Parts, Rt 15, 05661; 802-888-4981, FAX 802-888-9266, 800-287-4981; **20+; B**3 **Call for specific car information**

LATE VINTAGE
Bennington; Le Blanc's Auto Salvage, *see Vintage*
Bomoseen; Green Mountain Used Auto Parts, Rt 4A, 05732; 802-468-5206; CC, Sa, Sp, Br; 500; **80+; D, F, PU, 4x4; B**3
Chester; McDermott's Auto Salvage, RR2 Box 322, 05143; 802-875-2364, FAX 802-875-4144, 800-524-8839; CC, Sp, Br, PL; 5ac; **80+; D, F, PU, 4x4; B**3
Colchester; Rathe's Salvage, 1 Rathe Rd, 05446; 802-655-0651, FAX 802-655-1448; CC, Sa, UR; 1500; **75+; D, F; B**3, **AMC**
Grafton; Auto Salvage of Grafton, *see Vintage*
Hancock; Betti's Autoland & Salvage Yard, Rt 100, 05748; 802-767-3311, 888-224-0027; CC, Sa, Sp, Br, PL; 500+; **80+; D, F, PU, 4x4, Trk; B**3
Hardwick; Gates Salvage Yard, Craftsbury Rd, 05843; 802-472-5058, FAX; 500 **70+; D, F, PU, 4x4, Trk; B**3, **VW**
Lyndonville; C & M Used Auto Parts, *see Vintage*
Morrisville; Morrisville Used Auto Parts, *see Vintage*

LATE MODEL
Bennington; Le Blanc's Auto Salvage, *see Vintage*
Bomoseen; Brown's Auto Salvage, Rt 4A, 05748; 802-265-4548; Cc, Sa, Sp, Wr; **D, F, PU, 4x4**
   Green Mountain Used Auto Parts, *see Late Vintage*
Chelsea; Allen Auto Salvage, Rt 113, 05038; 802-685-7799; Sa; **Spc: 4x4**
Chester; McDermott's Auto Salvage, *see Late Vintage*
Colchester; Rathes Salvage, *see Late Vintage*
Eden; Jewett's Salvage Yard, 336 Warren Rd, 05652; 802-635-2649; CC, Sa, Sp; 5ac; **D, F, PU, 4x4; B**3; **Spc: Pickup**
Grafton; Auto Salvage of Grafton, *see Vintage*
Hancock; Betti's Autoland & Salvage Yard, *see Late Vintage*
Hardwick; Gates Salvage Yard, *see Late Vintage*
Lyndonville; C & M Used Auto Parts, *see Vintage*
   Mt View Auto Restoration, 45 Pinehurst St, 05851; 802-626-9251, FAX 802-626-6110, 800-639-1591; Cc, Sa; 200; **D, F, PU, 4x4**
Morrisville; Morrisville Used Auto Parts, *see Vintage*

You may be a car nut if

Your garage has a TV, Stereo, phone. computer & a BED

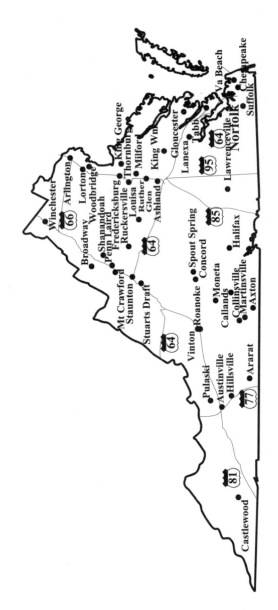

Virginia

Ray's wReckingyard Roster makes a great gift for the "car nut" on your shopping list. To order, Call Toll Free: 877-4RAYS BOOKS

VIRGINIA

VINTAGE

Ashland; Old Dominion Mustang, 509 S Washington Hwy Rt 1, 23005; 804-798-3348, FAX 804-798-5105, www.oldominion.com; CC, Sa, Sp, UR; 2ac, 200+; **60-89; D; Mustang, Camaro, Chevelle, Falcon**

Austinville; B & B Auto Sales & Salvage, RR 1, 24312; 540-699-6281; Sa, Sp; 200; **50+; D, F, PU; B3**

Broadway; Auto Krafters Inc, 5228 Main St Box 8, 22815; 540-896-5910, FAX 540-896-6412, 800-228-7346, www.autokrafters.com; CC, Sa, Sp, Wr; 14ac; **50-79; D, PU, 4x4; Ford only**

Castlewood; B & B Auto Salvage, 24224; 540-762-7834; UR; 5ac, 300+; **F; Spc: Mercedes**

Chesapeake; Edmonds Corner Salvage Yard, 2040 Campostella Rd, 23324; 757-545-8425, FAX 757-545-4514, 800-603-7278; CC, Sa, Sp, UR; 10.5ac; **80-95, few 40-70s; D, F, PU, 4x4; B3, Saab, Jpa**

   Johnson's Mustang & Truck Parts, 4513 Bainbridge Blvd, 23320; 757-545-8370; Sa, Sp, UR; 12ac; **64+; D, PU, 4x4; B3, Jp; Spc: Mustang**

Concord; Concord Salvage, State Rte 609, 24511; 804-993-9668; Sa, Sp; 300; **60-93; D, PU, 4x4; B3, Jp**

Fredericksburg; Fredericksburg Auto Salvage, 11045 Claiborne Crossing Rd, 22408; 540-898-8630, 800-582-2749; CC, Sa, Sp; 5000; **49-90; D, F, PU, few 4x4; B3, St**

Gloucester; Dickey's Auto Slvg, 9243 George Washington Mem Hwy, 23061; 804-693-5860, FAX 804-693-7481, 800-533-4101; Sa, Sp; 10ac; **60+; D, F, PU, 4x4, Trk; B3**

Lanexa; Philbates Auto Wrecking Inc, Box 178 Rt 1, Hwy 249, 23089; 804-843-9787; Sa, Sp, UR; 50ac, 8000+; **60-89, few 30-50s; D, F, PU, 4x4, Trk, Fm; B3, AMC, Jp, Hd, Ns, St, Pk, Ks, Fr, Wy, VW, Edsel, Graham, Airflow, Farmall, John Deere**

Louisa; Dave's Ferncliff Auto Parts, Hwy Rte 250E, 23093; 804-589-3642; Sa; 5ac; **50+; D; B3; Spc: Pontiac, Fiero, Firebird**

Martinsville; A & B Used Auto & Truck Parts, Rte 220 N, 24055; 540-629-1224; Sa, UR; 12ac; **50-89; D, PU, 4x4, Trk; B3, AMC, Jp, IH, St, Wy; Spc: standard transmission**

Milford; Milford Salvage, 14302 Devils Three Jump Rd, 22514; 804-633-2401; Br; 20ac; **50+; D, F, PU, 4x4, Trk; B3**

Moneta; Bill Thomasen, 1118 Wooded Acres Lane, 24121; 540-297-1200; Sp; 50; **53-73; D, PU; Full size Chevy only; By Appointment Only**

Mount Crawford; Harold Ludholtz's, Rt 2 Box 63, 22841; 540-828-3348; Sp, UR; 15ac; **40-60, few newer; D, F, PU, 4x4; Be, AMC, Hd, Ns, St, Pk, Ks; Call Ahead**

Norfolk; Antique Auto Parts, , 23501; 757-455-5551; 30ac, 1500;, 50-80; **D, PU; B3, AMC, St; yard in NC, By Appointment Only**

Ruckersville; Carr Svc Ctr, 22968; 804-985-3554; Sa, UR; 5ac; **30-59; D, F; B3, St, VW**

Staunton; Byrd's Wrecking Yd, 3169 Morris Mill Rd, 24401; 540-885-1445; Sp, UR; 6000+; **40+; D, F, PU, 4x4, Trk, Fm; B3, AMC, Jp, IH, St, Wy; open Sun; Spc: muscle cars**

   Staunton Wrecking Co, 133 National Av, 24401; 540-942-2873, FAX, 800-476-5970; Sa, Sp; 35ac, 2500; **40+; D, F, PU, 4x4; B3, AMC, Jp, VW**

Stuarts Draft; Shields Auto Salvage, RR 2 Box 404H, 24477; 540-949-5922; Sa, UR; 17ac; **30+; D, F, PU, 4x4, Trk; B3, Jp, IH**

Tabb; Bottom Line Salvage, 2110 George Washington Mem Hwy, 23693; 757-591-0750; Sa, Sp, Wr; 4ac; **30+; D, F, PU; B3; Spc: muscle cars**

Vinton; Auto Salvage & Sales Inc, 1001 Hill Ave, 24179; 540-982-8777, FAX 540-982-6931, 800-982-8778; Sa; 600; **47+; D, F, PU, 4x4; B3, St(PU), Jaguar**

LATE VINTAGE

Ararat; Barnard's Used Auto Parts, Kibler Valley, 24053; 540-251-5212; UR; **75+; 60-79; D; B3; some F & PU**

Ashland; Old Dominion Mustang, *see Vintage*

Austinville; B & B Auto Sales & Salvage, *see Vintage*

Broadway; Auto Krafters Inc, *see Vintage*

Castlewood; B & B Auto Salvage, *see Vintage*

Chesapeake; Edmonds Corner Salvage Yard, *see Vintage*

   Johnson's Mustang & Truck Parts, *see Vintage*

Concord; Concord Salvage, *see Vintage*

Fredricksburg; Fredricksburg Auto Salvage, *see Vintage*

Gloucester; Dickey's Auto Salvage, *see Vintage*

Halifax; Big John's Used Auto Parts, Hwy 615, 24558; 804-476-6014; Sa, Sp, UR; 500+; 67+; **D, F, PU, 4x4, Trk; B3**

King George; Accurate Foreign Car Parts Inc, 6269 Caledon Rd, 22485; 540-775-5300, 800-635-5330; CC, Sa, Sp; 300; **70-89; F; Jpa, VW, Mercedes, Volvo**

Lanexa; Philbates Auto Wrecking Inc, *see Vintage*

Lawrenceville; Central Auto Salvage, 939 Rose Dr, 23868; 804-848-4245, 800-813-6785; Sp; 200; **75-89; D, F, PU; B3**

Louisa; Dave's Ferncliff Auto Parts, *see Vintage*

Martinsville; A & B Used Auto & Truck Parts, *see Vintage*

Milford; Milford Salvage, *see Vintage*

Moneta; Bill Thomasen, *see Vintage*

Mount Crawford; Harold Ludholtz's, *see Vintage*

Norfolk; Antique Auto Parts, *see Vintage*

Pulaski; Taylor Salvage, RR 1 Box 396A5, 24301; 540-994-0129; 200; **70-89; D, PU; B3; Call for Appointment**

Ruther Glen; Ladysmith Auto Salvage, 16223 Jefferson Davis Hwy, 22546; 804-448-4300; Sa, Sp, UR; 10ac; **80+; D, F, PU, 4x4; B3**

Shanandoah; Richard Auto Salvage, 484 Comertown Rd, 22849; 540-652-1111, FAX 540-652-3332; Sa; 14ac; **75-95; D, PU, 4x4; B3**

Spout Spring; Smith's Foreign Used Auto Parts, Hwy 647 S, 24593; 804-352-5371, FAX 804-352-9305; CC, Sa; 10ac; **82-94; F; Jpa, Eur**

Staunton; Byrd's Wrecking Yard, *see Vintage*
Staunton Wrecking Co, *see Vintage*

Stuarts Draft; Shields Auto Salvage, *see Vintage*

Suffolk; B & B Auto Parts & Crushing, 1326 Portsmouth Blvd, 23434; 757-539-2821, FAX 757-934-7884; Sa, Sp; 27ac; **70-90; D, F, PU, 4x4, Trk; B3, AMC, Jp, IH, VW**

Tabb; Bottom Line Salvage, *see Vintage*

Thornburg; Lew's Auto & Salvage, 6516 S Roxbury Mill Rd, 22565; 540-582-5475, 800-874-0620; CC, Sa; 14ac; **82-93; D; B3**

Vinton; Auto Salvage & Sales Inc, *see Vintage*

Virginia Beach; Oceana Salvage, 1040 S Oceana Blvd, 23454; 757-425-7930, FAX 757-425-3233; CC, Sa, Sp, UR; 15ac, 1000+; **70+; D, F, PU, 4x4; B3, AMC, Jp, IH, VW; open Sunday; also auto glass**

Winchester; Main Salvage Inc, 202 Cedar Grove Rd, 22601; 540-665-0133; Sa; 7ac; **77+; D, F, PU, 4x4; B3**

Woodbridge; American Auto Salvage Inc, 14210 Jefferson Davis Av, 22191; 703-494-7184; Sa, UR; 500; **80+; D, F, PU; B3, VW**

LATE MODEL

Arlington; Hercules Guaranteed Auto, 4000 S Four Mile Run Dr, 22206; 703-671-7200; Sa, UR; 3ac, 150; **F; Jpa**

Austinville; B & B Auto Sales & Salvage, *see Vintage*

Axton; Barker's Auto Salvage, State Hwy 620, 24054; 540-650-2318, 800-762-3620; 20ac, 800+; **F; Jpa**

Callands; B & W Auto Salvage, 14001 Callands Rd, 24530; 804-724-4718; **D; B3**

Castlewood; B & B Auto Salvage, *see Vintage*

Chesapeake; Al Rudd Used Auto Parts, 5411 W Military Hwy, 23321; 757-488-4451; **D, F**
Edmonds Corner Salvage Yard, *see Vintage*
Johnson's Mustang & Truck Parts, *see Vintage*

Collinsville; Auto Salvage Co, Reed Creek Dr, 24078; 540-647-8679, 800-468-1383; Sa, UR; 2ac; **D; B3**

Concord; Concord Salvage, *see Vintage*

Gloucester; Dickey's Auto Salvage, *see Vintage*

Halifax; Big John's Used Auto Parts, *see Late Vintage*

Virginia – Late Model

Carr's Used Parts, 2182 Dudley Rd, 24558; 804-476-6715; Sa, UR; 300+; **D, F; B3**

Hillsville; Blue Ridge Auto Salvage Inc, 3132 Fancy Gap Hwy, 24343; 540-728-3116, 888-309-6599; Sp; 300; **D, F, PU, 4x4; B3**

King William; Fleetwood Motor Co, , 23086; 804-643-6826; CC, Sa; **D; B3**

Lorton; AAAA Co Auto Parts Inc, 10212 Richmond Hwy, 22079; 703-643-2221; Sa; 200+; **D, F; B3, Jpa**

Louisa; Dave's Ferncliff Auto Parts, *see Vintage*

Milford; Milford Salvage, *see Vintage*

Mount Crawford; Harold Ludholtz's, *see Vintage*

Penn Laird; Crawford's Used Auto & Truck, , 22846; 540-434-3227; 100+; **D; B3**

Roanoke; Star City Auto Parts, 3372 Shanandoah Av NW, 24017; 540-982-0811; Sa; **D; B3**

Ruckersville; M & M Salvage Yard, Rte 617, 22968; 804-985-2559; Sp; **F, PU, 4x4**

Ruther Glen; Ladysmith Auto Salvage, *see Late Vintage*

Shanandoah; Richard Auto Salvage, *see Late Vintage*

Spout Spring; Smith's Foreign Used Auto Parts, *see Late Vintage*

Staunton; Byrd's Wrecking Yard, *see Vintage*

Staunton Wrecking Co, *see Vintage*

Stuarts Draft; Shields Auto Salvage, *see Vintage*

Tabb; Bottom Line Salvage, *see Vintage*

Thornburg; Lew's Auto & Salvage, *see Late Vintage*

Vinton; Auto Salvage & Sales Inc, *see Vintage*

Virginia Beach; Oceana Salvage, *see Late Vintage*

Winchester; Main Salvage Inc, *see Late Vintage*

Woodbridge; American Auto Salvage Inc, *see Late Vintage*

Sometimes only small parts can be customer removed. Find out the rules of removal ahead of time

Yard Operators Tell us...

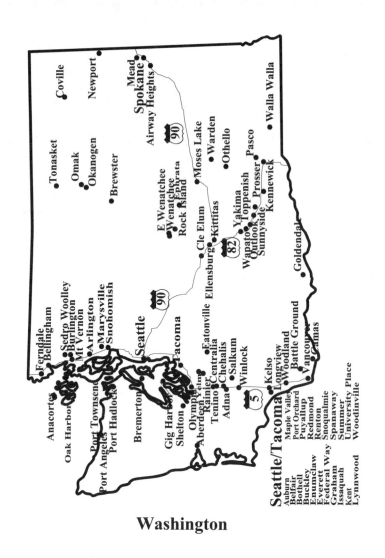

Washington

Please use the cards in the back to let us know about yards we may have missed, or any other comments or information for future editions of Ray's wReckingyard Roster

WASHINGTON

VINTAGE

Adna; Audi Volkswagon Specialist, PO Box 210, 98522; 360-748-8578; CC, Sa, Sp, Wr; **57+; F; VW, Audi only**

Airway Heights; Auto Parts Barn, 15910 W Hwy 2, 99001; 509-244-5566; CC, Sa, Sp, UR; 800; **50-90; D, F, PU, 4x4; B3, AMC, Jp, IH; Jpa**

Arlington; Campbell Nelson Auto Wrecking, 18021 59th Av NE, 98223; 360-403-9800, FAX 360-403-9377, 888-337-7757, www.campbellnelson.com/cnar.htm; CC, Sa, Sp, Br, Wr, PL; **59+; F, PU; VW, Audi, BMW, Porsche, Saab, Jpa**

Belfair; Belfair Truck & Auto Wrecking, 25603 NE State Hwy 3, 98528; 360-275-6677; CC, Sa, Sp, UR, Wr; 1000+; **20-90; D, F, PU, 4x4; B3, AMC, Hd, Ns, St, Pk**

Bothell; American & Japanese Cascade, 18412 Bothell Everett Hwy, 98012; 425-338-1922, FAX 425-672-1101, 800-326-1922; CC, Sa, Sp, UR; 4.5ac, 300; **50-72; D, F, PU, 4x4; B3, Jpa; Spc: Muscle cars**

Cascade Auto Wrecking Inc, 18412 Bothell Everett Hwy, 98012; 425-481-1922, FAX 425-672-1101, 800-326-1922; CC, Sa, Sp, UR; 5ac; **60+; D, F, PU, 4x4; B3**

Bremerton; Eastside Auto Wrck, 6068 State Hwy 303 NE, 98311; 360-377-7651, FAX 360-792-1318, 800-726-7651; CC, Sa, Sp, Wr; 7ac; **63+; D, F, PU, 4x4, Trk; B3, AMC, Jp**

Burlington; Larry's Auto & Truck Parts, 199 Pease Rd, 98233; 360-757-7444, FAX 360-757-7449; CC, Sa, Br; 2500; **49-89; D, PU, 4x4, Trk, Fm, In, Cn; B3, AMC, Jp, IH**

Camas; Downs Classic Auto, 2518 NE 252nd Av, 98607; 360-834-6181, FAX 360-834-3273, www.pacifier.com/~wrecking; Sp, Br; 200+; **60+ D, F, PU, Trk; B3**

Centralia; Grasser Auto Wrecking, 2705 N Pearl St, 98531; 360-736-5467; Sa, Br; 1300; **16-90; D, F, PU, 4x4, Trk; B3, AMC, Jp, IH, Hd, Ns, St, Pk, Ks, Fr, Cr, Wy, VW**

Chehalis; Carter & Son Volkswagen, 2669 Jackson Hwy, 98532; 360-748-3008; CC, Sp, Br; 800; **59-89; F; VW only**

I-5 Auto & Truck Parts, 190 Estep Rd, 98532; 360-262-3550, 800-551-4489; CC, Sa, Sp, UR; 3000+; **40-90; D, F, PU, 4x4, Trk; B3, AMC, Jp, IH, VW**

Cle Elum; A & A Auto Wreckers, 5461 Hwy 970, 98922; 509-674-7106, 800-925-8410; CC, Sa, UR; 5.5ac, 1000; **39+; D, F, PU, 4x4, Trk; B3, AMC, Jp, IH, VW**

Colville; A-Z Auto Parts, 371 Dominion View Rd, 99114; 509-684-6137; Sa, Sp, Br, PL; 7ac; **49-80; D, F, PU, 4x4; B3, AMC, St, VW; Spc: Chevy Pickup**

Eatonville; Highway Auto Wrecking, 32416 Mountain Hwy E, 98328; 253-847-1164; Sa, UR; 0.5ac; **60-85; D, PU, 4x4; B3 only**

Edmonds; Campbell Nelson Volkswagen, 24329 Hwy 99, 98026; 425-778-1131, 888-337-7757, www.campbellnelson.com; CC, Sa, Sp, Br, Wr, PL; 3000; **59+; F, PU; VW, Audi, BMW, Porsche, Saab, Jpa**

Ephrata; Burck's Auto Wrck, 2083 Basin St SW, 98823; 509-754-4641, FAX 509-754-4643, 888-818-7257; CC, Sa, Sp; 800; **36-96; D, F, PU, 4x4; B3, AMC, Jp, IH, VW**

Everett; A-1 Fleury Auto & Truck Parts, 13303 Hwy 99, 98204; 425-355-0554, FAX 425-787-8712, 800-353-1468, fleurys@aol.com; CC, Sa, Sp, Br; 2000+; **63+; D, F, PU, 4x4; B3, AMC; Spc: 4x4**

Alseth Auto Wrecking, 618 105th St SW, 98204; 425-353-3303, FAX 425-348-4873; CC, Sa, Sp; 150; **57-94; F, PU; VW only**

Randy's Ring & Pinion Svc, 11630 Airport Rd #300, 98204; 425-347-1199, FAX 425-347-1440, 800-347-1188, www.ring-pinion.com; CC, Sp, Wr; **55+; D, F, PU, 4x4; B3; Differentials only; Street Rod parts; Spc: 4x4**

Ray's Auto Wrecking, 2707 100th St SE, 98202; 425-337-4656, 337-4056; Sa, UR; 700; **25-90; D; B3, St**

Ferndale; A & H Auto Dismantlers, 1887 Newkirk Rd, 98248; 360-384-6932; CC, Sp, UR; 500; **60+; D, F, PU, 4x4, Trk; B3, AMC, Jp, IH**

Kent; Green River Auto Wrecking, 25923 78th Av S, 98032; 253-863-7080, FAX 253-850-8436, 800-577-2885, fishin69@aol.com; CC, Sa, Sp, UR; 1800; **57+; D, F, PU, 4x4, Trk; B3, AMC, Jp, IH, VW; Spc: older Pickup**

Lynnwood; Schaffner Motors Inc, 21705 Hwy 99, 98036; 425-778-6900, FAX 425-774-4265, www.biznorthwest.com/schaffner; CC, Sp, Wr; 200; **49+; F; VW only**

Washington– Vintage

Maple Valley; Branris Corp, 26615 Maple Valley Hwy, 98038; 425-255-6200; Sa, Sp, UR; 20ac; **62-89; D, F, PU, 4x4; B3, AMC; Open Sunday**

Mead; Rices, 10713 N Market St, 99021; 509-467-1035, FAX 509-467-4011, 877-236-8869; CC, Sa, Sp; 450; **60-96; D; GM only**

Olympia; John's Radiator & Towing, 411 93rd Av SE, 98501; 360-943-4110, 800-453-8733; CC, Sa, Sp, UR; 16ac, 4000; **50+; D, F, PU, 4x4, Trk, Fm, In, Cn; B3, AMC, Jp, IH, VW**

  Lacey Auto Wrecking, 109 Carpenter Rd NE #B, 98516; 360-456-5555, FAX 360-456-2190; CC, Sa, Sp; 2ac, 400+; **50+; D, F, PU, 4x4; B3, AMC, Jp, IH, VW**

  Nisqually Auto Wrecking, 9319 Martin Way E, 98516; 360-456-6222; Sa, Sp, UR; 400; **60-89; D, F, PU, 4x4; B3, AMC, Jp, IH, VW**

Omak; Byrds Auto Wrecking & Repair, 229 Weatherstone Rd #A, 98841; 509-826-0594, FAX 509-826-5075; Sa, Sp, Br; 7ac, 1300; **50+; D, F, PU, 4x4, Trk; Chevy, Fd**

Outlook; Tee Pee Auto Wreckers, 2201 Outlook Rd, 98938; 509-837-7491; Sa, Br; 4000; **39+; D, F; B3, Hd, St, Wy, VW**

Pasco; Tommy's Steel & Salvage, 904 S Oregon, 99301; 509-547-1221, 800-847-6221; CC, Sa, Sp; **40-89; D, F, PU; B3, Hd, Ns**

Port Angeles; Simpsons Used Parts Truck, 2421 W Hwy 101, 98363; 360-457-4597, 877-246-7278; CC, Sa, Br; 2ac; **62-93; D, F, PU, 4x4; B3**

Port Orchard; Airport Auto Wrecking Too, 4275 State Hwy 3 SW, 98367; 360-674-2544, FAX 360-674-3053, 800-819-2819; CC, Sa, UR; 300; **60-95; D, PU, 4x4, In, Cn, Mil; B3, AMC, Jp, IH**

Port Townsend; RB2 Auto Wrecking, 4711 S Discovery Rd, 98368; 360-385-7603, FAX 360-379-6732, 888-359-7447; Sa, UR; 250; **60-80; D, F, PU, Trk; B3, AMC**

Puyallup; South-Hill Auto Wrecking, 6316 128th St E, 98373; 253-841-0143; CC, Sa, Sp, UR; 8ac, 700; **55-94; D, F, PU, 4x4; B3, Jp**

Salkum; Roberts Repair, 716 Schoen Rd, 98582; 360-985-2402, FAX 360-985-0636; CC, Sa; 1200; **60-80; D, F, PU, 4x4; B3, AMC, Jp, IH, VW**

Seattle; Affordable Auto Wrecking, 9802 M L King Jr Wy S, 98118; 206-723-9820, FAX 206-723-6721; CC, Sa, UR; 650+; **58+PU, 66+cars; D, F, PU, 4x4; B3, Jp**

  Bry's Auto Wrecking, 4017 W Marginal Way SW, 98106; 206-938-3868, FAX 206-923-0082; CC, Sa, Sp, UR, Wr; 100+; **59+; F; VW, Audi only**

  Northern European Auto Recyclers, 1440 NW Leary Wy, 98107; 206-789-7004, FAX 206-789-8408, 800-927-9904; CC, Sa, Sp, Wr; 60+; **F; Volvo only, 122 through 900 series**

Shelton; Highway 3 Auto Wrecking, 8633 E State Rte 3, 98584; 360-426-0809, FAX 360-426-0857, 800-894-0809; CC, Sa, Sp, UR; 1300; **50-90; D, F, PU, 4x4; B3, AMC, VW**

  Mason County Salvage, 1840 W Cloquallum Rd, 98584; 360-426-8626; CC, Sa, PL; 200; **43+; D, F; B3, St, Ks, VW**

  Shelton Auto Parts, 1501 W Dayton Airport Rd, 98584; 360-427-5150, FAX 360-426-4848; Sa, Sp, UR; 13ac, 1000+; **48-96; D, F, PU, 4x4, Trk; B3, AMC, Jp, IH, VW**

Snohomish; Mid-City Towing & Wrecking, 10001 115th Av SE, 98290; 360-568-1288, 888-338-3907; CC, Sa, Sp, UR; 2000; **60-80; D, F, PU, 4x4, Trk, Fm, In, Cn, Mil; B3, AMC, Jp, IH, VW**

  Olympic 4x4 Supply, 520 Pine Av, 98290; 360-568-7728, 425-338-7806, FAX 360-568-9435, 800-752-9979; CC, Sa, Sp; 4.7ac; **60+; D, F, PU, 4x4; B3, Jp, IH, Wy**

  Whiteside Auto Wrecking Inc, 17728 State Rte 9 SE, 98296; 360-668-5248, 800-417-1313, www.whitesideauto.com; CC, Sa, Sp; 650+; **50-90; D, F, PU, 4x4, Vans, Trk; B3**

Snoqualmie; Mc Cuen Auto Wrecking & Towing, 38515 SE 47th St, 98065; 425-888-1224; Sa, Sp, UR; 500; **46+; D, F, PU, 4x4, Trk; B3, Jp, IH, VW**

Spanaway; R & R Auto Wrecking, 20620 Mountain Hwy E, 98387; 253-846-9393, 800-675-9339; CC, Sa, Sp, UR; 5ac, 600; **62+PU, 70+cars; D, F, PU, 4x4; B3**

Spokane; Antique Auto Items, S1607 McCabe Rd, 99216; 509-926-0987; Sp, Wr; **10-69; D, PU; B3, AMC, Hd, Ns, St, Pk, Ks, Fr, Cr, Wy**

  Antique Auto Ranch, 2225 N Dollar Rd, 99212; 509-535-7789, FAX 509-536-7496, 800-327-1469, www.antiqueautoranch.com; CC, Sa, Sp, UR; 200; **00-59; D, PU; B3, AMC, Hd, Ns, St, Pk, Ks, Fr, Cr, Wy; Spc: Model A & T, Repro parts, "Back to the dawn of time"**

Washington - Vintage

Art Santa Rosa's Auto & Truck, 3704 E Everett Av, 99207; 509-483-0040; Sa, Sp; 300+; **40-89; D, PU, 4x4, Trk, Fm, In, Cn, Mil; B**3**, AMC, Jp, IH, St, Wy**

C & T Truck Parts, 9902 N Market St, 99207; 509-466-6211, FAX 509-466-7610, 800-666-6152; CC, Sa, Sp; 5ac, 300; **50+; D, F, PU, 4x4, Trk, Mil; B**3**, AMC, Jp, IH, Ks, Fr, Wy, VW**

Triangle Truck Parts, 3501 E Trent Av, 99202; 509-534-2341, FAX 509-534-5709, 800-444-3633; CC, Sp, Br, PL; **D, F, PU, 4x4, Trk, Fm; B**3**, AMC, Jp, IH, Ks, Fr, Wy; Spc: 4x4**

Sunnyside; Bill's Towing Inc, 1710 Morgan Rd, 98944; 509-837-2704, 800-272-5516; Br; 20ac; **D, F, PU, 4x4, Trk, Fm; B**3**, AMC, Jp, IH, VW; Spc: older Chevy**

Boyd's Auto Sales, 380 S McLean Rd, 98944; 509-837-5698; 5ac; **60-79, few 40-50s; D, Trk; B**3**, St**

Lower Valley Auto Wrecking, 1710 Morgan Rd, 98940; 509-837-2744, 800-272-5516; Sa, UR; 200; **60+; D, F, PU, 4x4; B**3**, AMC, IH, VW**

Tacoma; A-1 Auto Wrecking, 13818 Pacific Av S, 98444; 253-537-3445; Sa, Sp; 100; **40-89; D; B**3**, St, Ks; Spc: B**3** standard transmissions**

Hap's West Side Auto Wrecking, 6802 27th St W, 98466; 253-564-5555, 888-678-8871; Sa; 400+; **60+; D, F, PU, 4x4; B**3**, VW; Spc: Chrysler, VW, brake drums**

Ikan Auto, 1201 Martin Luther King Jr Hwy, 98405; 253-572-0464; Sa, Sp; 5ac; **55-90; D, F; B**3**; Spc: 64-72 Chevelle, GTO, 442**

Mustang Empire, 10721 A St, 98444; 253-531-2629; CC, Sa, Sp, Wr; **65+; D; Mustang only**

Tenino; Columbia Industries Auto Repair, 17005 Old Hwy 99 SE, 98589; 360-264-2622; Sp, Br; 300; **37-92; D, F, PU, 4x4, Trk, Fm, In, Cn; B**3**, St, Pk**

University Place; Bridgeport Auto Wrecking, 5706 Bridgeport Way W, 98467; 253-564-2677; CC, Sa, UR; 1225+; **60+; D, F, PU; B**3**, VW**

Vancouver; All American Classics Inc, 15209 NE Fourth Plain Rd, 98682; 360-254-8850, FAX 360-253-5986, 800-955-4999, www.allamericanclassics.com; CC, Sa, Sp; 3500; **40-75; D, PU; B**3**, Hd, St, Pk, Ks, Camaro, Firebird, Chevelle**

Wade's, 12512 NE Fourth Plain Rd, 98682; 360-892-2222, FAX 360-892-1838, 800-563-6809; CC, Sa, Sp; 3ac; **60+; D, F, PU, 4x4; B**3

Walla Walla; All American Auto Wrecking, 928 N 4th Av, 99362; 509-525-7235; Sa, Sp, UR; 2ac; **60-89; D, F, PU; B**3**; Spc: Foreign**

Wapato; Douglas Wrecking & Scrapping, 1940 Wapato Donald Rd, 98951; 509-877-4700, billsshere@fewa.net; Sa, Sp, UR; 400+; **49-89; D, F, PU, few 4x4, few Trk, Fm; B**3**, AMC, Jp, IH**

Warden; CRC Auto Wrecking, 1405 W 1st, 98857; 509-349-2446; Sa, Br; 900+; **60+; D, F, PU, 4x4, Trk; B**3

Winlock; Cadillac Ville-D Baers, 98596; 360-785-4133; CC, Sp; 1100+; **49-85; D; Cadillac only; Mail Order only**

Woodinville; All Used Auto Parts At Woody's, 23005 State Rte 9 SE, 98072; 425-481-7744, FAX 425-487-6590; CC, Sa, Sp, UR; 3ac, 500; **62+; D, F, PU, 4x4, Trk; B**3

Woodinville; Vintage Auto Parts, 24300 Hwy 9, 98072; 425-486-0777, FAX 425-486-0778, 800-426-5911, www.vapinc.com; CC, Sp, Br, Wr; 6ac, 600; **12-75; D, PU; B**3**, AMC, Jp, IH, Hd, St, Pk, Ns, Wy, Ks, Fr, Cr**

Wild West Mustang Ranch, 22909 State Rte 9 SE, 98072; 425-481-6780, FAX 425-487-1510; CC, Sa, Sp; 300; **64+; D; Mustang, Cougar, Falcon**

Yakima; Big Toe Truck & Auto Sales, 1500 E King St, 98903; 509-457-4114; Sa, Sp; 1.5ac; **41+; D, F, PU, 4x4; B**3**; Spc: Pickup, 4x4**

Poor Boys Auto Wrecking, 6331 W Powerhouse Rd, 98908; 509-965-8680; Sa, Sp, UR; 3ac, 500; **60-85; D, F, PU, 4x4, Trk, Fm; B**3

Yelm; Bill's Yelm Towing & Wrecking, 801 W Yelm Av, 98597; 360-458-5963; CC, Sa, Br; 3ac; **50+; D, F, PU, 4x4, Trk; B**3**, Buses**

Yelm Auto Wrecking & Repair, 14510 93rd Av SE, 98597; 360-458-5366; Sa, Sp; **50+, few earlier; D, F, PU, 4x4, Trk; B**3**, St, Pk, VW**

301

Aberdeen; Aberdeen Auto Wreckers & Towing, 144 State Rt 105, 98520; 360-533-2749, FAX 360-532-6184; CC, Sa, UR; 1500+; **65-90; D, F, PU, 4x4; B**3, **AMC, IH, VW**

Adna; Audi Volkswagon Specialist, *see Vintage*

Airway Heights; Auto Parts Barn, *see Vintage*

Anacortes; Almac Towing & Auto Wrecking, 749 Padilla Heights Rd, 98221; 360-293-7270; CC, Sa, UR; 600; **75-85; D, F, PU, 4x4, Trk; B**3, **AMC, Jp, IH, VW**

Arlington; Campbell Nelson Auto Wrecking, *see Vintage*

Battle Ground; Dollars Corner Auto Wrecking, 7306 NE 219th St, 98604; 360-687-1558, FAX 360-687-5383; CC, Sa, UR; 7ac, 600; **80-90, few 70s; D, F; B**3, **AMC**

    Dollars Corner Truck Salvage, 21919 NE 72nd Av, 98604; 360-687-5128; CC, Sa, Br; 400; **65-90; D, F, PU, 4x4; B**3; **Pickup only**

Belfair; Belfair Truck & Auto Wrecking, *see Vintage*

Bellingham; Gundies, 1283 Mt Baker Hwy, 98226; 360-733-5036, FAX 360-734-6523, 800-444- 4344, www.gundies.com; CC, Sp; 2700; **80+PU, 90+cars; D, F, PU, 4x4, Trk; B**3, **AMC, Jp, IH, VW**

    Wholesale Auto Parts, 1100 Iowa St, 98226; 360-734-1850; CC, Sa, Sp; 600; **80+; D, F, PU, 4x4, Trk; B**3, **AMC, Jp, IH, VW**

Bothell; American & Japanese Cascade, *see Vintage*

    Cascade Auto Wrecking Inc, *see Vintage*

Bremerton; Eastside Auto Wrecking Inc, *see Vintage*

Buckley; Walt & Vern's Pickup Parts, 28520 State Rte 410 E, 98321; 360-829-1263, FAX 360-829-2152, 888-829-1263; CC, Sa, Sp; 5ac; 72+; **D, F, PU & Vans only; B**3

Burlington; Larry's Auto & Truck Parts, *see Vintage*

Camas; Downs Classic Auto, *see Vintage*

Centralia; A A Auto Sales & Parts, 20233 Old Hwy 99 SW, 98531; 360-330-2993, FAX 360-273-2102, 800-207-9331; CC, Sa, Sp; 450+; **70+, few 60s; D, F, PU, 4x4, Trk; B**3, **AMC, Jp, VW**

    Grasser Auto Wrecking, *see Vintage*

Chehalis; Carter & Son Volkswagen, *see Vintage*

    I-5 Auto & Truck Parts, *see Vintage*

Cle Elum; A & A Auto Wreckers, *see Vintage*

Colville; A-Z Auto Parts, *see Vintage*

East Wenatchee; E Z Auto Wrecking & Repair, 1855 Rock Island Rd, 98802; 509-884-5000, 888-558-6767; CC, Sp, UR; 1775+; **70+; D, F, PU, 4x4, Trk; B**3, **AMC, Jp, IH, VW**

Eatonville; Highway Auto Wrecking, *see Vintage*

    Mustang Ranch, 36210 108th Av Ct E, 98328; 253-847-2623, 800-827-2633; CC, Sa, Sp, Wr; 50+; **65-90; D; Mustang, Cougar, Fairlane, Falcon**

Edmonds; Campbell Nelson Volkswagen, *see Vintage*

Ephrata; Burck's Auto Wrecking, *see Vintage*

Everett; A All Foreign Auto Wreck, 4035 Smith Av, 98201; 425-745-1556, FAX 425-252-6608, 800-572-0932, 804nsales@aol.com; CC, Sa, Sp, UR; 400; **82+; F, PU, 4x4**

    A-1 Fleury Auto & Truck Parts, *see Vintage*

    Al's Lynnwood Truck Parts, 13311 Hwy 99, 98204; 425-743-9191; CC, Sp; 300; **73+; D, F, PU, 4x4, Vans; B**3, **Jp**

    Alseth Auto Wrecking, *see Vintage*

    All Nissan Auto Prt, 1202 Chestnut St #6, 98201; 425-259-9315, FAX 425-339-6147, 800-713-3999, www.feltonautoparts.com; CC, Sp; 850; **75+; F, PU; Nissan, Datsun, Infiniti**

    All Z Car Parts, 3532 Smith Av, 98201; 425-259-4691, FAX 425-259-0833, 800-633-3308, www.zsport.com; CC, Sa, Sp, Wr; **F; Datsun Z cars only, all models, 3 warehouses, mail order**

    Ferrill's Auto Parts, 11330 Hwy 99, 98204; 425-355-3147, FAX 425-353-6940, 800-421-3147, ferrills@aol.com; CC, Sp, Br, Wr, PL; 6ac; **80+; F, PU**

    Ferrills Auto Parts Inc, 11310 Hwy 99, 98204; 425-355-3147, FAX 425-771-3147, 800-421-3147; CC, Sa, Sp; 200; 66+; **D, F, PU, 4x4; B**3, **AMC, Jp, IH, VW**

    Randy's Ring & Pinion Svc, *see Vintage*

    Ray's Auto Wrecking, *see Vintage*

Shop Nine-TJ Martin Saab Repair, 2400 Gibson Rd, 98204; 425-353-7969, 888-822-7222, www.shopnine.com; Sa, Sp, Wr; 20+; **75-95; F; Saab only**

Federal Way; Abandoned Auto Parts, 37307 Enchanted Pky S, 98003; 253-927-8000, FAX 253-661-5896, 888-396-2800; CC, Sa, UR; 300; **80-92; D, F, PU, 4x4; B3, AMC, VW**

Ferndale; A & H Auto Dismantlers, *see Vintage*

Goldendale; Goldendale Auto Wrecking, 1590 Hwy 97 N, 98620; 509-773-3922; CC, Sa, Sp, UR; 200; **60-90; D, F, PU, 4x4; B3, AMC, Jp, BW**

Graham; Meridian Auto Wrecking, 20011 Meridian Av E, 98338; 253-847-1922, FAX 253-847-9374, 800-922-6756; CC, Sa, UR; 21ac, 1000+; **D, F, PU, 4x4, Trk; B3, AMC, Jp, IH, VW; Open Sunday**

Issaquah; Hall's Auto Wrecking, 10805 Issaquah Hobart Rd SE, 98027; 425-392-3287; Sa, Sp, Br; 350; **70+; D, F, PU, 4x4; B3; Spc: Chevy 70-90, Japanese 88+**

Kennewick; Big Tow Towing, 213507 Chemical Dr East SR 397, 99337; 509-586-9174, 800-310-9174; Sp; **70+; D, F, PU, 4x4; B3, AMC, Jp, VW**

Dan's Grg, 508 E Bruneau Av, 99336; 509-586-2579; Sa, Sp; 650+; **60-79; D; GM only**

Kent; AAA Auto Wrecking, 26311 78th Av S, 98032; 253-242-2911, FAX 253-854-1099, 800-404-1552; Sa, Sp, UR; 550+; **80-89; D, F, PU, 4x4; B3, AMC, VW**

Budget Auto Wrecking, 26205 78th Av S, 98032; 206-244-4314, FAX 206-854-2774; CC, Sa, Br; 550+; **75+; D, F, PU, 4x4; B3; Open Sunday**

Green River Auto Wrecking, *see Vintage*

Japanese Engines Inc, 23454 30th Av S, 98032; 206-878-5898, FAX 206-878-5991, 800-854-1114; CC, Sp, Wr; **80-96; F, PU, 4x4; Jpa; Engines only**

Kittitas; Gerry's Foreign Auto Parts Ltd, 300 S Main St, 98934; 509-968-4466, FAX 509-968-3313, 800-848-5578, www.gerrys.hypermart.net; CC, Sp; 12ac, 200; **80+; F**

Longview; Ace Auto Wrecking, 742 3rd Av, 98632; 360-423-0370, FAX 360-423-0439, 800-562-8692; CC, Sa, Sp; 0.75ac, 500; **80-90; D, F, PU, 4x4; B3, AMC, Jp, VW**

Hensley's Auto Wrecking & Towing, 616 9th Av, 98632; 360-577-1420; CC, Sa; 30+; **78+; D, F, PU, 4x4; B3, AMC, Jp, IH, VW**

Lynnwood; A Auto Parts-Nix 99, 13718 Mukilteo Speedway, 98037; 425-743-2881, FAX 425-743-0808, 800-782-0682, parts@nix99.com; CC, Sp, Wr; 200; **72+; F, PU, 4x4; Toyota & Lexus only**

Ferrills Auto Parts, 18306 Hwy 99, 98037; 425-778-3147, FAX 425-771-3147, 800-421-3147; CC, Sa, Sp; 300+; **66+; D, PU, 4x4; B3**

Foreign Engines Inc, 6907 216th St SW #A, 98036; 425-774-4546, FAX 425-774-4625, 800-333-9889; CC, Sa, Sp, Wr; **70+; F, PU, 4x4; Japanese & Korean engines only**

Schaffner Motors Inc, *see Vintage*

Maple Valley; Branris Corp, *see Vintage*

Marysville; Eastbury Salvage Metal & Auto, 6805 35th Av NE, 98271; 360-659-1540; CC, Sa, Sp, UR; **70+; D, F, PU, 4x4; B3, AMC, Jp, IH**

Quil Ceda Auto Wrecking, 10118 Smokey Point Blvd, 98271; 360-659-5757; Sa, Sp, Br; 350; **70-89; D, F; B3, AMC**

Mead; Rices, *see Vintage*

Uncle Jims Auto Salvage, 10800 N Market St, 99021; 509-466-1811, FAX 509-467-3777, 800-777-5754; CC, Sa, Sp, UR; 16ac, 250+; **67+PU, 80+cars; D, F, PU, 4x4, Trk; B3, AMC, VW**

Moses Lake; Moses Lake Auto Wrecking Inc, 3645 Broadway Ext NE, 98837; 509-765-7172, FAX 509-766-1298, 800-523-2611; Sp; 30ac; **75+; D, F, PU, 4x4, Trk; B3, AMC, Jp**

Tiffany's Auto Wrecking, 4075 Road E 2 NE #5, 98837; 509-765-8217; Sa, Sp, UR; 500; **70-92; D, F, PU, 4x4; B3, AMC, VW**

Oak Harbor; Christian's Towing, 635 Christian Rd, 98277; 360-675-8442, FAX 360-679-5142; CC, Sa, Sp, UR; 300; **75-85; D, F, PU, 4x4; B3, AMC, Jp, IH, VW Rabbits**

Okanogan; Randy's Auto Wrecking, 2135 Elmway, 98840; 509-422-3170, FAX 509-422-2322, 800-553-4466; CC, Sp, Br; 15ac, 2100; **70+; D, F, PU, 4x4, Trk; B3, AMC, Jp, IH, VW**

Olympia; Allen Auto Parts, 1630 S Bay Rd NE, 98506; 360-943-2800; Sa, Br; 350; **80+; D, F, PU; B3, AMC**

Black Lake Auto Inc, 5612 Black Lake Blvd SW, 98512; 360-357-7650, FAX 360-357-7662; CC, Sa, UR; 200; **80-92; F; Toyota only**

Gerry's Foreign Auto Parts Ltd, 5825 89th Av SE, 98513; 360-923-1633; CC, Sp; 4ac, 650; **80+; F, PU, 4x4**

John's Radiator & Towing, *see Vintage*

Lacey Auto Wrecking, *see Vintage*

Nisqually Auto Wrecking, *see Vintage*

Pick-A-Part Auto Wrecking, 8010 Old Hwy 99 SE, 98501; 360-357-4466; CC, Sa, UR; 1200; **68+; D, F, PU, Trk; B**3

Omak; Byrds Auto Wrecking & Repair, *see Vintage*

Othello; Dick's Repair & Towing, 2151 W Moon St, 99344; 509-488-6370; 500; **65+; D, F PU, 4x4, Trk; B**3**, Jpa**

Outlook; Tee Pee Auto Wreckers, *see Vintage*

Pasco; Tommy's Steel & Salvage, *see Vintage*

Port Angeles; K B Auto Wrecking & Towing, 262 Mount Pleasant Rd, 98362; 360-457-5048; Sa, UR; 2.5ac; **70-85; D, F, PU, few Trk, Mil; B**3

Simpsons Used Parts Truck, *see Vintage*

Port Hadlock; A & G Import Parts Inc, 10565 Rhody Dr, 98339; 360-385-0002, FAX 360-385-3082; CC, Sa, Sp; 200; 65-95; F, PU, 4x4

Port Orchard; Airport Auto Wrecking Too, *see Vintage*

Evergreen Truck Parts, 7360 State Hwy 3 SW, 98367; 360-674-2345, FAX 360-674-3272, 800-622-5181; CC, Sa, Sp, UR; 300; **74+; D, F, PU, 4x4; B**3**; Pickup only**

Evergreen Used Cars, 5003 SE Mile Hill Dr, 98366; 360-871-7500, FAX 360-871-1072, 888-622-5181; CC, Sa, Sp; 1500; **75-93; D, F; B**3**, AMC, Jp**

Kitsap Auto Wrecking Inc, 4949 Mile Hill Dr, 98366; 360-871-1000, 800-509-1001; CC, Sa, Sp, UR, Wr; 5ac, 400; **80-95; D, F, PU, 4x4; B**3**, VW**

Port Townsend; RB2 Auto Wrecking, *see Vintage*

Prosser; Boot Hill Auto Wrecking, 21402 N Williams Rd, 99350; 509-882-2888; Sa, Sp, UR; 300; **75-85; D, F, PU, 4x4, Trk; B**3**, AMC, VW**

Hiway Auto Wrecking, 159101 W County Rd 12, 99350; 509-786-1010, FAX 509-786-7273; Sa, Sp, UR; 2.5ac, 450; **65-93; D, F, PU, 4x4, Trk; B**3**, AMC, Jp, IH, VW**

Puyallup; Grand Forks Auto Wrecking, 5903 Pioneer Way E, 98371; 253-845-0531; CC, Sp, UR; 500; **70-90; D, F, PU, 4x4; B**3**, AMC, Jp, IH, VW**

South-Hill Auto Wrecking, *see Vintage*

Redmond; Eastside Truck Parts, 22647 NE Redmond Fall City Rd, 98053; 425-868-1020; CC, Wr; **73-85; D, PU, 4x4, Trk; B**3

Renton; South End Auto Wrecking, 3400 E Valley Rd, 98055; 425-251-8555, 800-742-9988; CC, Sa, Sp, UR; **65+; D, F, PU; B**3

Rock Island; E Z Auto Wrecking & Repair, 85 S 4th St, 98850; 509-884-9544; CC, Sp, UR; 10ac, 1000; **D, F, PU, 4x4; B**3**, AMC, Jp, IH, VW**

Salkum; Roberts Repair, *see Vintage*

Seattle; Affordable Auto Wrecking, *see Vintage*

Bry's Auto Wrecking, *see Vintage*

Northern European Auto Recyclers, *see Vintage*

Reliable Used Auto Parts, 14032 Interurban Av S, 98168; 206-433-8069, FAX 206-433-7968, 800-720-4599; CC, Sa, Sp; 1200; **80+; D, F, PU, 4x4, Trk; B**3**, AMC, Jp, VW**

Sedro Woolley; Art's Auto Wrecking, 23536 River Rd, 98284; 360-856-1605; Sa, UR; 2000; **70-88; D, F, PU, few 4x4, Trk, Mil; B**3**, AMC, Jp, IH, VW**

Shelton; Highway 3 Auto Wrecking, *see Vintage*

Mason County Salvage, *see Vintage*

Shelton Auto Parts, *see Vintage*

Snohomish; Mid-City Towing & Wrecking, *see Vintage*

Olympic 4x4 Supply, *see Vintage*

Whiteside Auto Wrecking Inc, *see Vintage*

Mc Cuen Auto Wrecking & Towing, *see Vintage*

Spanaway; All Auto Parts, 20917 Mountain Hwy E, 98387; 253-847-1977, FAX 253-847-4276, 800-533-5949; CC, Sa, Sp; 1000; **80-90; D, F, PU, 4x4; B**3, **AMC, Jp**

Dave's Auto Wrecking, 20102 Mountain Hwy E, 98387; 253-847-5150, 888-905-5150; CC, Sa, Sp, UR; 450+; **85+, few 60-70s; D, F, PU, 4x4; B**3, **AMC, Jp, VW**

Garraway's Auto Parts, 19919 Mountain Hwy E, 98387; 253-847-6423, FAX 253-847-6425; CC, Sa, Sp, UR; 900+; **70-80; D, F, PU, 4x4, Trk; B**3, **AMC, Jp, IH**

R & R Auto Wrecking, *see Vintage*

Spokane; A A Auto Salvage Inc, 3504 S Inland Empire Way, 99224; 509-456-4367, FAX 509-455-6381, 800-378-4367; CC, Sa, Sp; 200; **70+, few earlier; D, F, PU, 4x4; B**3, **AMC**

Art Santa Rosa's Auto & Truck, *see Vintage*

Bill's Auto Dismantlers Inc, 4203 E Weile Av, 99207; 509-467-5241, FAX 509-468-0474, 800-482-8480; CC, Sa, Sp, Br; 5ac; 600; **70+; D, PU, 4x4, Trk; Ford only**

C & T Truck Parts Inc, *see Vintage*

Spaldings, 2210 N University Rd, 99206; 509-924-3300, 800-366-2070, www.spaldings. com; CC, Sp; 50ac; **D, F, PU**

Triangle Truck Parts, *see Vintage*

Whitey's Wrecking, 4330 E Francis Av, 99207; 509-489-3850, 800-735-2376; CC, Sp; 5.5ac; 1500; **70+; Foreign**

Sumner; Bowen Auto Wrecking, 20008 State Rte 410 E, 98390; 253-862-9181; Sa, Sp, UR; 4ac; **67-89; D, F, PU; B**3

Sunnyside; Bill's Towing Inc, *see Vintage*

Boyd's Auto Sales, *see Vintage*

Lower Valley Auto Wrecking, *see Vintage*

Tacoma; A-1 Auto Wrecking, *see Vintage*

Ferrill's Auto Parts, 2416 112th St, 98444; 253-588-1776, FAX 253-582-3739, 800-692-2210, ferrills@aol.com; CC, Sa, Sp, PL, Wr; **70+; D, F, PU, 4x4; B**3

Hap's West Side Auto Wrecking, *see Vintage*

Ikan Auto, *see Vintage*

Lake's Auto Wrecking, 4036 100th St SW, 98499; 253-581-2135; CC, Sa, Wr; **75-90; F, PU, 4x4**

Lakeview Auto Wrecking, 11528 Pacific Hwy SW, 98499; 253-582-6000, FAX 253-584-2171; CC, Sa; 4ac; **65+; D; B**3

Midland Auto Wrecking, 10324 Portland Av E, 98445; 253-537-5041; CC, Sa; 30; **75+; D, PU, 4x4; B**3

Mustang Empire, *see Vintage*

Ram Auto & Truck Recycling, 12120 Pacific Hwy SW, 98499; 253-589-1000; CC, Sa, Sp, PL; 50; **70+; D, F, PU, 4x4, Trk; B**3

U-Fix-It Honda, 2520 112th St, 98444; 253-984-1414, FAX 253-984-9438, 800-806-1830; CC, Sp; **81-96; F; Honda only**

Vintage Broncos, 11908 Terry Lake Rd SW, 98498; 253-589-0950; Sp, Br, Wr; **66-77; D, 4x4; Ford Bronco only; Open after 5pm and on weekends, call for appointment**

Tenino; Columbia Industries Auto Repair, *see Vintage*

Toppenish; M & R Sales & Towing, 64491 US Hwy 97, 98948; 509-865-5404; CC, Sa, Sp; 700; **68+; D, F, PU; B**3

Auto Bone Yard, 406 S Division St, 98948; 509-865-3820; Sa, UR; 4.5ac; **74+; D, F, PU, 4x4, Trk; B**3

University Place; Bridgeport Auto Wrecking, *see Vintage*

Vancouver; All American Classics Inc, *see Vintage*

All Truck Parts & Sales, 3113 NE 66th St, 98663; 360-693-9296, FAX 360-696-4371, 800-727-0012; Sa, Sp; 7ac; **67+; D, F, PU, 4x4; B**3

Central Auto Wrecking, 8717 NE 117th Av, 98662; 360-254-3708; Sa; 135+; **78-87; D, F, PU, 4x4; B**3

Smitty's Auto Salvage, 20502 NE 58th St, 98682; 360-254-9160; Sa, Wr; **70+; D, F; B**3

U-Pull-It Auto Wrecking, 9605 NE 76th St, 98662; 360-892-8906; CC, Sa, UR; 850; **80-89; D, F, PU; B**3

Wade's, *see Vintage*

Walla Walla; A Js Auto Parts, 111 George St, 99362; 509-525-9348; UR; 0.5ac **70-89; D, F, PU, 4x4; B**3

   All American Auto Wrecking, *see Vintage*

   C & W Auto Wrecking, 1002 N 4th Av, 99362; 509-525-7973; Sa; 40; **80+; D, F; B**3

Kelty's Auto Parts, 925 N 4th Av, 99362; 509-525-3210, 800-367-0238; CC, Sp; 450+; 67+; **D, F, PU, 4x4; B3, Jpa; Spc: PU, 4x4**

Wapato; Douglas Wrecking & Scrapping, *see Vintage*

   Wofford's Used Cars & Towing, 201 S Frontage Rd, 98951; 509-877-4940; Sa; 50; **80-89; D, F, PU, 4x4; B**3

Warden; CRC Auto Wrecking, *see Vintage*

Winlock; Cadillac Ville-D Baers, *see Vintage*

Woodinville; All Used Auto Parts At Woody's, *see Vintage*

Gerry's Foreign Auto Parts Ltd, 23219 State Rte 9 SE, 98072; 425-481-1313, 800-562-8073, 800-923-1633 Olympia, 800-848-5578 Ellensburg; CC, Sp; 7ac; **70+; F, PU, 4x4; Jpa, Eur**

   Vintage Auto Parts, *see Vintage*

   Wild West Mustang Ranch, *see Vintage*

Yakima; Acme Auto Wrecking, 5607 Postma Rd, 98901; 509-248-5250, 800-274-USED, acem1932@aol.com; CC, Sa, Sp; 20ac; **75+; D, F, PU, 4x4; B**3

   Big Toe Truck & Auto Sales, *see Vintage*

   Buck's Auto Wrecking, 300 Chalmers St, 98901; 509-453-6198; Sa, UR; 2ac; 350; **70+, few 50-60s; D, F, PU; B**3

   Cascade Auto Recycling, 14 E Washington Av, 98903; 509-453-8211, 800-660-8045; CC, Sa, UR; 6ac, 600; **70+; D, F, PU, 4x4, Trk; B3; Spc: new & used auto glass**

   Central Salvage & Auto Wrecking, 8 E Race St, 98901; 509-248-2800; CC, Sa, Sp, UR; 500+; **70+; D, F, PU, 4x4, Fm; B**3

   Chaney's Cars & Parts, 1920 S 11th St, 98903; 509-248-4563; Sa, Sp, Br; 1.5ac; **80+; D, PU, 4x4, Trk; B**3

   Poor Boys Auto Wrecking, *see Vintage*

   Webers Auto Parts, 6410 W Powerhouse Rd, 98908; 509-966-4711, 800-876-4711, tow4u@televar.com; CC, Sp, UR, PL; 10ac; **70+; D, F, PU, 4x4; B**3

Yelm; Bill's Yelm Towing & Wrecking, *see Vintage*

   Yelm Auto Wrecking & Repair, *see Vintage*

LATE MODEL

Adna; Audi Volkswagon Specialist, *see Vintage*

Anacortes; Summit Park Auto Wrecking, 720 S March Point Rd, 98221; 360-293-4658; CC, Sp, UR; 400; **D, F, PU, 4x4, Trk; GM, Fd, Ranger, S-10**

Arlington; Campbell Nelson Auto Wrecking, *see Vintage*

Auburn; South End Auto Wrecking, 3602 A St SE, 98002; 253-939-1000, 800-278-2351; CC, Sa, Sp, UR; 7.5ac, 800; **D, F, PU, 4x4; B3, AMC, VW**

Bellingham; Al's Salvage, 3525 Y Rd, 98226; 360-734-9659, FAX 360-714-1625; CC, Sp; 1000; **D, F, PU, 4x4, Trk; B3, AMC, Jp**

   Gundies Inc, *see Late Vintage*

   Wholesale Auto Parts, *see Late Vintage*

Bothell; Cascade Auto Wrecking Inc, *see Vintage*

Bremerton; Eastside Auto Wrecking Inc, *see Vintage*

Brewster; Shull's Towing & Parts, 25897 S Hwy 97, 98812; 509-689-2292, FAX 509-689-2388, 800-822-5761; CC, Sa, Sp, Br; 1500; **D, F, PU, 4x4; B3, AMC, Jp, IH, VW**

Buckley; Walt & Vern's Pickup Parts, *see Late Vintage*

Camas; Downs Classic Auto, *see Vintage*

Centralia; A A Auto Sales & Parts, *see Late Vintage*

Cle Elum; A & A Auto Wreckers, *see Vintage*

East Wenatchee; E Z Auto Wrecking & Repair, *see Late Vintage*

Edmonds; Campbell Nelson Volkswagen, *see Vintage*

Ellensburg; A & A Auto Wrecking & Towing, 3970 Canyon Rd, 98926; 509-925-5606, FAX 509-933-2797, 800-925-5607; CC, Sa, Sp, UR; 5ac, 1200; **D, F, PU, 4x4, Trk, Cn; B3, AMC, Jp, IH, VW**

Enumclaw; Fred's Towing Svc, 209 Rainier Av, 98022; 360-825-1643; CC, Sa, Sp, UR; 1ac; **D, F, PU, 4x4; B**3

Ephrata; Burck's Auto Wrecking, *see Vintage*

Smith's Auto Wrecking, 2050 Basin St SW, 98823; 509-754-3584, FAX 509-754-4016, 800-572-0111; CC, Sp; 800; **D, F, PU, 4x4; B**3**, AMC**

Everett; A All Foreign Auto Wreck, *see Late Vintage*

A-1 Fleury Auto & Truck Parts, *see Vintage*

Al's Lynnwood Truck Parts, *see Late Vintage*

All Foreign Auto Wrecking, 4035 Smith Av, 98201; 425-339-2663, FAX 425-252-6608; CC, Sa, Sp; 400; **F, PU, 4x4; VW**

All Nissan Auto Parts, *see Late Vintage*

All Z Car Parts, *see Late Vintage*

Alseth Auto Wrecking, *see Vintage*

Downtown Auto Wrecking, 3126 Rucker Av, 98201; 425-259-0734, 800-281-3509; CC, Sa, Sp; **D, PU, 4x4; Chrysler only**

Ferrill's Auto Parts, *see Late Vintage*

Ferrills Auto Parts Inc, *see Late Vintage*

Randy's Ring & Pinion Svc, *see Vintage*

Shop Nine - TJ Martin Saab Repair, *see Late Vintage*

Ferndale; A & H Auto Dismantlers, *see Vintage*

Federal Way; Abandoned Auto Parts Inc, *see Late Vintage*

Gig Harbor; Horseshoe Lake Towing & Auto, 9401 State Rte 302 NW, 98329; 253-857-3866; Sa, UR; 2ac, 300; **D, F, PU, 4x4; B**3**, AMC, Jp, VW**

Issaquah; Hall's Auto Wrecking, *see Late Vintage*

Kelso; Terry's Salvage & Auto, 1124 N Pacific Av, 98626; 360-423-6011; Sa, Sp, UR; 2ac; **D, F, PU, 4x4; B**3**, AMC, Jp**

Kent; Budget Auto Wrecking, *see Late Vintage*

Green River Auto Wrecking, *see Vintage*

Japanese Engines Inc, *see Vintage*

Gerry's Foreign Auto Parts Ltd, *see Late Vintage*

Kennewick; Big Tow Towing, *see Late Vintage*

Longview; Hensley's Auto Wrecking & Towing, *see Late Vintage*

Longview Auto Wreckers, 2001 38th Av, 98632; 360-423-9327; CC, Sa, Sp, UR; 500; **D, F, PU, 4x4; B**3**, AMC, Jp, VW**

Lynnwood; A Auto Parts - Nix 99, *see Late Vintage*

Best Auto Parts, 18100 Hwy 99, 98037; 425-778-2140, 800-562-9174; CC, Sa, Sp; 1000+; **D, F, PU, 4x4; B**3

Ferrills Auto Parts, *see Late Vintage*

Foreign Engines Inc, *see Late Vintage*

Lynnwood Auto Wreckers Inc, 17810 Hwy 99, 98037; 425-743-1111, FAX 425-742-4755, 800-562-9201; CC, Sp; 450+; **D; B**3

Lynnwood; Schaffner Motors Inc, *see Vintage*

Maple Valley; Federal Way Auto Wrecking, 26615 N Maple Valley Hwy, 98038; 253-927-8686; Sa, UR; 2500; **D, F, PU, 4x4, Trk; B**3**, AMC, Jp, IH, VW**

Marysville; All Toyota, 5438 47th Av NE, 98270; 360-653-1105, 800-562-1009; CC, Sa, Sp, UR; 4ac, 1000; **F, PU, 4x4; Japanese only**

Eastbury Salvage Metal & Auto, *see Late Vintage*

Mead; Rices, *see Vintage*

Uncle Jims Auto Salvage Inc, *see Late Vintage*

Moses Lake; Moses Lake Auto Wrecking Inc, *see Late Vintage*

Tiffany's Auto Wrecking, *see Late Vintage*

Mount Vernon; Farrells Auto Wrecking, 215 River Bend Rd, 98273; 360-424-4231; Sa, UR; **D, F, PU, 4x4, Trk, In, Cn, Mil; B**3**, AMC, Jp, IH, VW**

Newport; Shag Nastys Enterprises, 329255 N Hwy 2, 99156; 509-447-4444; Sa, UR; 400; **D, F, PU, 4x4; B**3**, AMC, Jp, IH, VW**

307

Oak Harbor; Oak Harbor Auto Wrecking, 2784 N Goldie Rd, 98277; 360-675-3309, FAX 360-675-2911, 800-673-3309; CC, Sp; 650+; **D, F, PU, 4x4; B**3**, AMC, Jp, IH**

Okanogan; Randy's Auto Wrecking, *see Late Vintage*

Olympia; Allen Auto Parts, *see Late Vintage*

Black Lake Auto Inc, *see Late Vintage*

Gerry's Foreign Auto Parts Ltd, *see Late Vintage*

John's Radiator & Towing, *see Vintage*

Lacey Auto Wrecking, *see Vintage*

Pete's Auto Wrecking & Towing, 8048 Martin Way E, 98516; 360-459-0860, FAX 360-459-2548; CC, Sa, Sp; **D, F, PU, 4x4; B**3**, AMC, VW**

Pick-A-Part Auto Wrecking, *see Late Vintage*

Omak; Byrds Auto Wrecking & Repair, *see Late Vintage*

Othello; Dick's Repair & Towing, *see Late Vintage*

Outlook; Tee Pee Auto Wreckers, *see Vintage*

Pasco; Al's Repair, 900 N Avery Av, 99301; 509-547-8021, FAX 509-547-3434; CC, Sa, Sp, Br; **D, PU, 4x4; B**3**; Repairs**

Bradley's Auto Wrecking, 2904 E Lewis St, 99301; 509-545-1574, 800-922-1574; Sa, UR; 500; **D, F, PU, 4x4, Trk; B**3

Pasco Auto Wrecking, 3602 East, 99301; 509-547-7242, FAX 509-546-5920, 800-572-9624; CC, Sa, Sp, Br; 25ac; **D, F, PU, 4x4, Trk, Fm, In, Cn**

Port Angeles; Simpsons Used Parts Truck, *see Vintage*

Port Hadlock; A & G Import Parts Inc, *see Late Vintage*

Port Orchard; Airport Auto Wrecking Too, *see Late Vintage*

Evergreen Truck Parts, *see Late Vintage*

Evergreen Used Cars, *see Late Vintage*

Kitsap Auto Wrecking Inc, *see Late Vintage*

Port Townsend; Mac's Auto Wrecking & Towing, 13393 Airport Cutoff Rd, 98368; 360-385-3018; Sa, UR; 350+; **D; B**3**, AMC**

Prosser; Hiway Auto Wrecking, *see Late Vintage*

Puyallup; South-Hill Auto Wrecking, *see Late Vintage*

Rainier; Barlow Auto Wrecking, 12833 Vail Cutoff Rd, 98576; 360-446-7800; CC, Sp, UR; 300+; **D, F, PU, 4x4, Trk; B**3**, AMC, Jp, VW, Jpa**

Renton; South End Auto Wrecking, *see Late Vintage*

Rock Island; E Z Auto Wrecking & Repair, *see Late Vintage*

Seattle; Affordable Auto Wrecking, *see Vintage*

Bry's Auto Wrecking, *see Vintage*

King Auto Wrecking, 543 S Monroe, 98108; 206-767-5044, 800-767-5045, www.kingautoandtruck.com; CC, Sp; 300; **D, F, PU, 4x4; B**3**; Pickup & vans only**

Northern European Auto Recyclers, *see Vintage*

Reliable Used Auto Parts, *see Late Vintage*

Shelton; Mason County Salvage, *see Vintage*

Shelton Auto Parts, *see Vintage*

Snohomish; Olympic 4x4 Supply, *see Vintage*

Mc Cuen Auto Wrecking & Towing, *see Vintage*

Spanaway; Action Auto Wrecking, 137 174th St E, 98387; 253-531-4460; CC, Sp, UR; 1.5ac; **D, F, PU, 4x4; B**3**, AMC, Jp, VW**

Dave's Auto Wrecking, *see Late Vintage*

J & J Towing & Auto Wrecking, 5320 224th St E, 98387; 253-847-7275; CC, Sa; 300; **D, F; Spc: GM**

R & R Auto Wrecking, *see Vintage*

Roy Y Auto Wrecking, 19125 Pacific Av S, 98387; 253-847-9191, FAX 253-847-5491, 800-422-5621; CC, Sa, Sp, Br; 1000; **D, F, PU; Fd, Jpa, Mazda including RX-7**

Spokane; A A Auto Salvage Inc, *see Late Vintage*

Bill's Auto Dismantlers Inc, *see Late Vintage*

C & T Truck Parts Inc, *see Vintage*

Spaldings, *see Late Vintage*

Triangle Truck Parts, *see Vintage*

Whitey's Wrecking, *see Late Vintage*

Sunnyside; Bill's Towing Inc, *see Vintage*

Lower Valley Auto Wrecking, *see Vintage*

Tacoma; Ferrill's Auto Parts, *see Late Vintage*

Hap's West Side Auto Wrecking, *see Vintage*

Lake's Auto Wrecking, 4034 100th St SW, 98499; 253-582-6850, FAX 253-582-8997; CC, Sa; 25+; **F, 4x4; Jpa, VW**

Lakeview Auto Wrecking, *see Late Vintage*

Midland Auto Wrecking, *see Late Vintage*

Mustang Empire, *see Vintage*

Ram Auto & Truck Recycling, *see Late Vintage*

U-Fix-It Honda, *see Late Vintage*

Tenino; Columbia Industries Auto Repair, *see Vintage*

Tonasket; Stevens Auto Wrecking & Towing, 31852 US Hwy 97 N, 98855; 509-486-2090,; CC, Sa, Sp; 631; **D, F, PU, 4x4, Trk; B**3

Toppenish; M & R Sales & Towing, *see Late Vintage*

Auto Bone Yard, *see Late Vintage*

University Place; Bridgeport Auto Wrecking, *see Vintage*

Vancouver; All Truck Parts & Sales, *see Late Vintage*

Langleys, 19809 NE 58th St, 98682; 360-892-1560; CC, Sa; 5ac, 250; **D, F**

Smitty's Auto Salvage, *see Late Vintage*

Wade's, *see Vintage*

Walla Walla; Anderson Towing, 1120 W Moore St, 99362; 509-525-3693, 800-359-7163; CC, Sa, Sp, Br; 500; **D, F, PU, 4x4, Trk; B**3

C & W Auto Wrecking, *see Late Vintage*

Kelty's Auto Parts, *see Late Vintage*

Warden; CRC Auto Wrecking, *see Vintage*

Wenatchee; Dick's Towing & Repair, 110 Thurston St, 98801; 509-663-1623, 800-876-9114; CC, Sp, UR; 20; **D, F, PU, 4x4, Trk; B**3

Winlock; Torgerson 4x4, 1730 Hwy 603, 98596; 360-262-9051; Sa, Sp, UR; 5ac; **D, F, PU, 4x4, Trk; B**3**; Spc: 4x4**

Woodinville; All Used Auto Parts At Woody's, *see Vintage*

Fitz Auto Parts, 24000 Hwy 9, 98072; 425-337-3212, FAX 425-486-2400; CC, Sa, Sp; 16ac; **D, F, PU, 4x4, Trk; B**3

Gerry's Foreign Auto Parts Ltd, *see Late Vintage*

U-Fix-It Honda Auto Wrecking, 24115 Hwy 9, 98072; 425-481-1414, FAX 425-485-1240, 800-654-0467; CC, Sp; 500+; **F; Honda, Acura, Sterling**

Wild West Mustang Ranch, *see Vintage*

Woodland; Woodland Auto Wrecking, 9555 Old Pacific Hwy, 98674; 360-225-5946; Sa; 0.5ac; **D, F; B**3

Yakima; Acme Auto Wrecking, *see Late Vintage*

Big Toe Truck & Auto Sales, *see Vintage*

Buck's Auto Wrecking, *see Late Vintage*

Cascade Auto Recycling, *see Late Vintage*

Central Salvage & Auto Wrecking, *see Late Vintage*

Chaney's Cars & Parts, *see Late Vintage*

Nob Hill Auto Wrecking, 2609 W Birchfield Rd, 98901; 509-452-2803, 800-683-2498; Sa, UR; 19ac; **D, F, PU, 4x4; B**3

Webers Auto Parts, *see Late Vintage*

Yelm; B & H Auto Wrecking, 17505 110th Av SE, 98597; 360-458-7938; CC, Sa, Sp, Br; 5ac; **D, F, PU, 4x4, Trk; B**3

Bill's Yelm Towing & Wrecking, *see Vintage*

Yelm Auto Wrecking & Repair, *see Vintage*

West Virginia

Ray's wReckingyard Roster makes a
great gift for the "car nut" on your
shopping list. To order,
Call Toll Free: 877-4RAYS BOOKS

WEST VIRGINIA

VINTAGE

Augusta; Wolfe's Salvage Yard & Parts, HC 71 Box 55A1, 26704; 304-856-3259; Sa, UR; 500+; **40-94; D, F, PU, 4x4; B3**

Core; Ben's Auto Wrecking, Rt 1, 26529; 304-879-5213, FAX 304-879-4003; CC, Sa, Sp; 5ac, 300; **50+; D, F, PU, 4x4; B3, Pk, Cr, Jpa**

Elkview; Antique Auto Parts, PO Box 64, 25071; 304-965-1821; Sa, Sp, Br; 134; **40-50s, few 30s & 60-70s; D; B3, St, Pk; Mostly restorations**

Fairmont; Knoll's Auto Wrecking & Paint, IH 79 Exit 135, 26554; 304-363-7131; UR; 200; 13+; **D, F; B3, Hd**

Fairmont; Morris Auto Wrecking, I-79 Exit 139, 26554; 304-363-1805; Sa, UR; 600; **40-93; D,F, PU, 4x4, Trk; B3, Hd, St, Ks**

Glen Easton; Bungard Used Auto Parts, Rustic Hills, 26039; 304-845-9753, FAX 304-845-2952, 800-320-4819; CC, Sa, Sp; 3100; **58+; D, F, PU, 4x4, Trk; B3, AMC, Jp, IH, VW**

Kearneysville; A & D Auto Parts Inc, PO Box 181, 25430; 304-876-2101; Sa, Sp; **50-89; D, PU, 4x4, Trk; B3, AMC, St**

Leon; Schoonover Auto Salvage, 1525 Arbuckle Creek Rd, 25123; 304-937-2283, 888-434-0115; Sa, Sp, UR; **47+; D, F, PU, 4x4; B3, St; Spc: 60s Muscle cars**

Mathias; Strawderman's Salvage, Route 259, 26812; 304-897-6149; Sa, Br; 250+; **50+; D, F, PU, 4x4, Trk, Fm; B3, Jp; Open Sunday**

Ridgeley; Jump's Recycled Auto Parts, Rt 3 Box 418, Old Furnace Rd, 26753; 301-777-5353, FAX 304-738-3337; Sp; 400; **58 & 85+; D, F, PU, 4x4; B3, Jp; Spc: 58 Cadillac; 3 mi. from Maryland line**

Roceverte; Bill's Repair Shop & Salvage, RR 2 Box 225, 24970; 304-645-6879; Sa, Br; 450+; **50+; D, PU, 4x4; B3, Jp; Towing**

Triadelphia; Orum's Salvage, PO Box 283, Dallas Pike, 26059; 304-547-1741; Sa; 4000; **36+; D, F, PU, 4x4; B3, Jp, IH**

West Columbia; J & D's Auto Parts & Salvage, RR 1 Box 3, 25287; 304-773-5033; Sa, Sp, PL; 600; **46+; D, PU, 4x4, Trk; B3; Spc: Ford Pickup & front wheel drive GM**

LATE VINTAGE

Alderson; J & J Used Parts, Route 3, 24910; 304-445-2135; Sa, Sp; 600; **80-90; D, F, PU, 4x4; B3, AMC, Jp**

Augusta; Wolfe's Salvage Yard & Parts, *see Vintage*

Barboursville; Barboursville Used Auto Parts, 665 Peyton St, 25504; 304-736-4328; Sa; 350+; **80+; D, F, PU; B3, AMC**

Beckley; Vass Branch Salvage & Used, 418 Vass Br, 25801; 304-877-3162; Sa, UR; 1.5ac; **70-88; D, F, PU, 4x4; B3**

Blacksville; Chissy's Auto Wreckers, Route 7, 26521; 304-432-8266; Sa, Sp, PL; 3ac; **70+; D, F, PU, 4x4, Trk; B3, Jp, IH; Mostly Pickup**

Bluefield; Lambert's Used Auto Parts, 310 Cherry St, 24701; 304-327-8316, FAX 304-327-8642, 800-327-8316; CC, Sa, Sp, PL; 200; **75+; D, F, PU, 4x4, Trk; B3, AMC, Jp**

Buckhannon; Central Salvage, 145 Clarksburg Rd, 26201; 304-472-6404, 800-735-0954; CC, Sa; 500; **80-93; D, PU, 4x4; B3, AMC; Spc: Ford & GM**

Bunker Hill; Shane's Auto & Truck Salvage, RR 1 Box 412, 25413; 304-229-3258; CC, Sa, Sp; 2500+; **79+; D, F, PU, 4x4, Trk; B3, AMC, Jp, IH**

Charleston; J & J Auto Salvage & Parts, Rt 1 Box 529, Falcon Dr, 25312; 304-342-5993, FAX 304-342-5992, 800-427-3512; CC, Sa; 3ac; **85-89; D, F, PU, 4x4; B3, Jp**

Smitty's Used Auto Parts, 433 Wolf Pen Dr, 25312; 304-984-3471; CC, Sa, Sp; 300; **80+; D, F, PU, 4x4; B3, AMC, Jp**

Clarksburg; Chip's Auto Parts, Joseph St, 26301; 304-622-7485; Sa, Sp; 500; **78+; D, F; B3, AMC, Mercedes**

Posey's Auto Wrecking Inc, Rt 6 Box 1208, Perry Hollow Rd, 26301; 304-622-6548, 800-287-6548; Sa, Sp, PL; 20ac; **80-93; D, F, PU, 4x4; B3, AMC, Jp, VW**

Core; Ben's Auto Wrecking, *see Vintage*

Fairmont; Haymond's Salvage, Hog Lick Rd, 26554; 304-534-5222; Sa; 500; **75-89; D, F; B3, AMC, VW**

Knoll's Auto Wrecking & Paint, *see Vintage*

Morris Auto Wrecking, *see Vintage*

Gerrardstown; C & J Salvage, PO Box 547, 25420; 304-229-0182; Sa, Sp, Br; 250+; **75-89; D, F; B**3, **AMC**

Glen Easton; Bungard Used Auto Parts, *see Vintage*

Huntington; Cooper's Used Auto Parts, 5040 Guyan River Rd, 25702; 304-522-7003; Sa; 200; **70+; D, F, PU; B**3, **AMC, VW**

Ramey's Auto Salvage Yard, 1855 West Rd, 25701; 304-429-5343; Sa, UR; 250+; **70-89; D; Fd, GM**

Jane Lew; B & G Salvage, Jesses Run, 26378; 304-884-7606, 800-804-7348; CC, Sp; 550+; **80+; D, F, PU, 4x4; B**3, **Jp**

Kearneysville; A & D Auto Parts Inc, *see Vintage*

Cody's Salvage, Rt 1 Box 71, Middleway, 25430; 304-725-8507; Sa, UR; 1500; 65+; D, F, PU, 4x4, Trk; B3, AMC, Jp, IH, VW

Leon; Schoonover Auto Salvage, *see Vintage*

Martinsburg; Ernie's Salvage Yard, RR 11 Williamsport Pike, 25401; 304-274-1133, FAX 304-274-0425; CC, Sa; 30ac; **80+, few 70s; D, F, PU, 4x4; B**3

Martinsburg Auto Salvage, RR 11 N, 25401; 304-263-1234; Sa, Sp, UR; 100; **70-89; D, F, 4x4; B**3

Mathias; Strawderman's Salvage, *see Vintage*

Maysville; Miller's Used Auto Parts, HC 30 Box 256, 26833; 304-749-7346; Sa, Sp; 350+; **76+; D, PU, 4x4; B**3

Moorefield; C & K Salvage Yard, Rig Rd, 26836; 304-434-2485, FAX 304-434-2988; Sa, Sp, Br; 1000; **70+; D, F, PU, 4x4; B**3, **Jp, VW**

Parkersburg; Bear Run Auto Wrecking, 625 Briant St, 26101; 304-422-8437; Sp; 50; **75-85; D, F, PU; B**3, **AMC, Jp, IH**

Eddie's Auto Parts Co, 3415 Murdoch Av Rear, 26101; 304-422-6486, FAX 304-422-3725, 800-784-1128; CC, Sa, Sp, UR; 14ac, 1000; **70+; D, F, 4x4; B**3, **AMC, Jp, IH, VW**

Princeton; Fred & Jack's Auto Salvage, Brickyard Rd, 24740; 304-425-7929, 800-642-7929; CC, Sa, Sp; 2000; **70+; D, F, PU; B**3

Ridgeley; Shanholtz Used Auto Parts, Old Furnace Rd, 26753; 304-738-9378; CC, Sa, Sp; 15ac, 400; **77+; D, PU, 4x4; B**3

Roceverte; Bill's Repair Shop & Salvage, *see Vintage*

Statts Mills; Rhodes Salvage, RR 1 Box 45, 25279; 304-372-8257, 800-474-4221; Sa; 650+; **72-89; D, F, PU, 4x4; B**3, **AMC, IH, VW**

Shepherdstown; Domer's Slvg, Old Ridge Rd, 25443; 304-876-2131; Sa, UR; **80-89; D; B**3

Stephenson; Ron's Salvage & Parts, HC 69 Box 40, 25928; 304-294-5838; Sa; 145; 70-89; D, F, PU, 4x4; B3, AMC, Jp, IH

Triadelphia; Orum's Salvage, *see Vintage*

Wellsburg; Wellsburg Auto Sales & Salvage, 2 & Charles St, 26070; 304-737-0961, FAX 304-737-4555; Sa; 500+; **70+; D, F, PU, 4x4; B**3

West Columbia; J & D's Auto Parts & Salvage, *see Vintage*

LATE MODEL

Augusta; Wolfe's Salvage Yard & Parts, *see Vintage*

Barboursville; Barboursville Used Auto Parts, *see Late Vintage*

Blacksville; Chissy's Auto Wreckers, *see Late Vintage*

Bluefield; Lambert's Used Auto Parts, *see Late Vintage*

Buckhannon; Central Salvage, *see Late Vintage*

Bunker Hill; Shane's Auto & Truck Salvage, *see Late Vintage*

Charleston; Smitty's Used Auto Parts, *see Late Vintage*

Chester; Wade's Towing, Snow Hill Rd, 26034; 304-387-3132, FAX 304-387-1722; Sa, Sp, UR; 500+; **D, F, PU, 4x4; B**3, **AMC, Jp, VW**

Clarksburg; Chip's Auto Parts, *see Late Vintage*

Posey's Auto Wrecking Inc, *see Late Vintage*

State Auto Wrecking Svc, RR 3 Box 65C, 26301; 304-622-5161, 800-839-5553; CC, Sa, Sp, PL; 3000; **D, F, PU, 4x4; B**3, **Jp, VW**

Core; Ben's Auto Wrecking, *see Vintage*

Elkins; G & G Slvg, Rt 3 Box 209-1, Ward Rd, 26241; 304-636-7502, FAX 304-636-3917, 800-339-0327; Sa, Sp; 100+; **D, F; B**3

Fairmont; Knoll's Auto Wrecking & Paint, *see Vintage*
 Morris Auto Wrecking, *see Vintage*

Glen Easton; Bungard Used Auto Parts, *see Vintage*

Hedgesville; Bowers Salvage Yard, , 25427; 304-754-3548; Sa; 10+; **D**

Huntington; Cooper's Used Auto Parts, *see Late Vintage*

Jane Lew; B & G Salvage, *see Late Vintage*

Kearneysville; Cody's Salvage, *see Late Vintage*

Leon; Schoonover Auto Salvage, *see Vintage*

Martinsburg; Ernie's Salvage Yard, *see Late Vintage*

Mathias; Strawderman's Salvage, *see Vintage*

Maysville; Miller's Used Auto Parts, *see Late Vintage*

Moorefield; C & K Salvage Yard, *see Late Vintage*

Morgantown; Burnside's Auto Salvage, IH 79, 26502; 304-292-8192; Sa, Br; 800; **D, F; B**3; **"a workingman's salvage yard"**
 Buster's Auto Salvage & Sales, 26505; 304-292-8759, 800-969-9225; CC, Sa, Sp; **D, F, PU, 4x4; B**3

Parkersburg; Eddie's Auto Parts Co, *see Late Vintage*

Princeton; Fred & Jack's Auto Salvage, *see Late Vintage*

Ranson; Alger's Auto Recycling, 211 E Park Av, 25438; 304-725-7066, 800-828-4229; CC, Sa, Sp; 200; **D, F, PU; B**3

Ridgeley; Jump's Recycled Auto Parts, *see Vintage*
 Peer's Used Auto Parts, Route 28, 26753; 304-738-2007, FAX 304-738-3702, 877-633-3869, www.globaljunkyard.com; CC, Sa, Sp; 1200+; **D, F, PU, 4x4; B**3**, Jp, VW**
 Shanholtz Used Auto Parts, *see Late Vintage*

Roceverte; Bill's Repair Shop & Salvage, *see Vintage*

Triadelphia; Crow's Auto Salvage, RR 40 Box 148, 26059; 304-547-0436; Sp; 3000; **D, F, PU, 4x4; B**3
 Orum's Salvage, *see Vintage*

Wellsburg; Wellsburg Auto Sales & Salvage, *see Late Vintage*

West Columbia; J & D's Auto Parts & Salvage, *see Vintage*

You may be a car nut if

You borrow your son's little red wagon to go to the car parts swap meet

WISCONSIN

VINTAGE

Arkdale; Roller's Auto Slvg, 2059 Chicago Dr, 54613; 608-564-7717; CC, Sp, UR; 4000+;
30+; D, F, PU, 4x4, Trk, Fm; Be, AMC, Jp, IH, Hd, Ns, St, Pk, Ks, Fr, Cr, Wy, VW

Beloit; Schoonover Auto Salvage, 2175 Thomas Rd, 53511; 608-362-1427; UR; 1ac; **40-80;
D, PU, 4x4; B3**

Boscobel; Golden Sands Salvage, 501 Airport Rd, 53805; 608-375-5353; Sa, Sp, Br; 400+;
30-79; D, PU, Trk, Fm, In, Cn; B3, AMC, Jp, IH, Hd, Ns, St, Pk; School Buses

Cadott; Glenz Auto Salvage, 2060 County Rd XX, 54727; 715-877-3371; Sp, Sa, UR; 6ac,
700; 3**5-85, few earlier; D, F, PU, 4x4, Trk; B3, AMC, Jp, IH, Hd, Ns, St, Pk, VW**

Camp Douglas; C L Chase Used Auto & Truck Parts, Rt 1 Box 291, 54618; 608-427-6734,
800-250-8557; Sa, UR; 6000+; 1**0+; D, F, PU, 4x4, Trk, Fm, Mil; B3, AMC, Jp, IH, Hd,
Ns, St, Pk, Ks, Fr, Cr, Wy, VW**

Edgar; Bee Line Auto Parts, W3961 Hwy 97, 54426; 715-687-2451; Sa, Sp, Br; 12ac; **50+;
D, few F, PU, 4x4, Trk; B3, De Soto**

Edgerton; Newville Auto Salvage, 279 E State Rd 59, 53534; 608-884-3114; CC, UR; 2000;
30+; D, F; B3, AMC, Wy; Spc: Buick, Chevy

314

Eland; Hwy 45 Auto, N7816 US Hwy 45, 54427; 715-253-2425; 2000; **52-88; D, F; B3, Pk, Ks**

Fond du Lac; American Auto Iron & Metal Inc, W6811 County Rd 000, 54937; 920-923-6602, FAX 920-923-4779; Sa, Sp; 400+; **50+; D, PU, 4x4; B3**

Fredonia; Auto Parts & Recycling Inc, W4726 County Rd A, 53021; 262-692-2447; CC, Sa, UR; 14ac; **40-90; D, F, PU, 4x4, Trk; B3, AMC, Jp, St, Ks**

Green Bay; Smitty's Salvage & Supply, 2325 Main St, 54311; 920-468-7715, FAX 920-468-9208, 800-236-6892; Sp, PL; 800+; **40+; D, F, PU, 4x4, Trk, few Cn; B3; Spc: 60-70s headers**

Hayward; Simons Enterprises Inc, , 54843; 715-634-4594, 888-414-7611; CC, Sa, UR; 2400; **35+; D, F, PU, 4x4; B3, Ns, St, Pk, Ks, Wy**

Hortonville; Don Bennett Sport Cars, 415 E Main St, 54944; 920-779-6922, FAX 920-779-0748, 800-543-3667; CC, Sa, Sp; 10ac; **50+; D, F; B3**

Kenosha; Schneider's Auto Sales & Parts, 8521 Sheridan Rd, 53143; 262-694-4330, 888-608-5865; CC, Sa, Sp; 800+; **40-90; D, F; B3, Ns**

La Crosse; Shiftar Auto Salvage, N3568 Shiftar Rd, 54603; 608-781-1990; Sa, Sp, UR; 1500; **47+; D, F, PU, 4x4, Trk, Fm; B3**

Lake Geneva; Como Auto Salvage, N3364 County Rd H, 53147; 262-248-1920, FAX 262-248-6270, 800-424-8490; CC, Sa, Sp; 1000+; **50-90; D, F; B3**

Marinette; Erdman's Auto Sales & Salvage, N1944 Dahl Rd, 54143; 715-732-0541, 800-472-0281; CC, Sa, Sp; 2800+; **60+; D, F, PU, 4x4; B3**

Marshfield; Shaw's Wrecking Yard, 9193 Mill Creek Dr, 54449; 715-676-3621, FAX 715-765-2453; Sa; 40ac; **60+; D, F, PU, 4x4, Trk, Fm; B3**

Mason; Rich's Auto Slvg, 54856; 715-746-2966; CC, Sa, Sp, UR; 300+; **60-92; D, F, PU, 4x4; B3**

Milton; Seward Auto Salvage, 2506 E Vincent Rd, 53563; 608-752-5166; Sa, Sp, UR; 2400+; **37-93; D, F, PU, 4x4; B3, Hd, Ns, St, Pk, Ks, Fr, VW**

Milwaukee; Auto Paradise Inc, 6102 S 13th St, 53221; 414-762-2650, FAX 414-768-4854, 800-232-0685; CC, Sa, Sp, UR; 40ac; **65+; D, F; B3**

B S Wisniewski, 1801-11 S 2nd St, 53204; 414-645-5454, FAX 414-645-5457, 800-328-6554, www.wizzis.com; CC, Sp, Wr; **20-75; D, PU; B3, Hd, Ns, St, Pk, Ks, Fr, Cr**

Neenah; Gibson's Auto Wrecking Inc, 139 S Fieldcrest Dr, 54956; 920-722-6721; Sa, UR; 6000; **70+, few 60s; D, F, PU; B3**

Oakfield; Kedinger Auto Salvage, W9484 County Rd TC, 53065; 920-923-3920; Sa, Sp, UR; 7ac, 800; **60-70s, few 80s; D, PU; B3**

Pulaski; Karcz Auto Salvage, 8702 Jaworski Rd, 54162; 920-822-5508, 800-335-5508; Sa, Sp, UR; 10ac, 1500; **50+; D, F, PU, 4x4; B3, AMC, Jp, IH, St**

Sheboygan; Ehrenreich's Corvair Service, 1728 Manor Pkwy, 53083; 920-458-1170; 60-68; D; Corvair only; Call for appointment

Sheboygan Falls; Lima Auto Enterprises Inc, W2254 Ourtown Rd, 53085; 920-467-3411; CC, Sp, UR; 6ac, 300+; **75-95, few 50-60s; D, F, PU, 4x4; B3; Spc: Chevy Pickup**

Siren; Marlow Auto Salvage, 24695 Lind Rd, 54872; 715-349-5560; Sa, Br; 500; **35-90; D, PU, 4x4; B3; Spc: Toronado 67-70**

Somerset; Somerset Auto Salvage, 1920 Hwy 35N, 54025; 715-247-5136, FAX 715-247-4311, 888-247-5753; CC, Sa, Sp, Br; 2500; **60+; D, F, PU, 4x4, Trk; B3, AMC, Jp, IH, VW; Spc: 4x4**

Stanley; Stanley Truck Sales, 1000 N Dahl St, 54768; 715-644-5548, FAX 715-644-5858, 800-844-7400; CC, Sa, Sp; 500; **50+PU, 70+cars; D, F, PU, 4x4, Trk, Fm, Mil; B3, AMC, Jp, IH, St**

Stevens Point; McDill Auto Wrecking Inc, 2200 Post Rd, 54481; 715-344-4491, FAX 715-344-1070, 800-332-4491; CC, Sa, Sp, Wr; 2ac, 300; **70+; D, F, PU, 4x4, Trk; B3, AMC, Jp, IH; Pre-70 parts on shelf**

Sturgeon Bay; C & W Auto Sales & Salvage, 5505 Jorns Ln, 54235; 920-743-3385, FAX 920-743-4981, 800-472-9111; CC, Sa, Sp; 60ac, 6000; **40+; D, F, PU, 4x4; B3, IH, Hd, Ns, St, Pk, Ks, Fr**

Wisconsin - Vintage

Tigerton; Zeb's Salvage, N 3181 Bernitt Rd, 54486; 715-754-5885; Sa, Sp, UR; 1000; **25-90; D, PU, 4x4; B**3**, Jp, St, Pk, Ks, Wy**

Trempealeau; Ray's Salvage & Repair, 11862 King St, 54661; 608-534-6477; Sa; 10ac, 2500+; **50-89; D, PU; B**3

Two Rivers; Avery's Auto Salvage, 12930 Avery Rd, 54241; 920-755-2848; Sa, Sp, UR; 40ac, 3100+; 36-**95; D, F, PU, 4x4, few Trk, In, Cn; B**3**, St**

Washburn; Ray's Automotive, 605 W Bayfield, 54891; 715-373-2669, 888-404-2669; CC, Sa, Sp, Br, PL; 700+; **60+; D, F, PU, 4x4, Trk; B**3

Watertown; Jack's Auto Ranch, N 6848 Islandview Rd, 53094; 920-699-2521, FAX 920-699-2985, jasksautoranch@gdinet.com; CC, Sa, Sp, Wr; 35ac, 3500; 36-**93; D; B**3**; Spc: Buick**

Westfield; Stevens Auto Wrecking, 460 Duck Creek Av, 53964; 608-339-6002; Sa, UR; 300; **40+; D, PU, 4x4; B**3**, AMC, IH, Hd, St, Pk, Ks, Fr, Wy**

Whitewater; Prisk Auto Salvage, N260 US Hwy 12, 53190; 262-473-5539; Sa, Sp; 1500; **50-89; D, PU; B**3**, IH**

LATE VINTAGE

Albany; Pence Slvg, N7072 McDermott Rd, 53502; 608-882-5575; Sa, UR; 700; **78+; F**

Antigo; Cousineau Auto Inc, N2267 US Hwy 45 S, 54409; 715-623-2371, FAX 715-623-2156, 800-472-1631; CC, Sa, Sp, UR; 400; **80-89; D, PU, 4x4; B**3**, AMC; Home office for this group.**

Appleton; Appleton Auto Recyclers, W4982 Country Road O, 54915; 920-730-1055, 800-352-1055, 242-8309; Sa, Sp, UR; 16ac; **70+; D, F, PU, 4x4; B**3

Arkdale; Roller's Auto Salvage, *see Vintage*

Beloit; Schoonover Auto Salvage, *see Vintage*

Boscobel; Golden Sands Salvage, *see Vintage*

Brodhead; Auto Transformer Salvage, 1817 N Knutson Rd, 53520; 608-882-5462, 800-479-9395; Sp, UR; 500; **70-80; D, F, PU; B**3**, Jp, IH**

Cadott; Cadott Auto Recyclers & Sales, 21089 County Hwy X, 54727; 715-723-1193, FAX 715-723-4536, 800-472-3112; CC, Sa, Sp; 2000; **80+; D, F, PU, 4x4; B**3**, AMC, Jp**

Glenz Auto Salvage, *see Vintage*

Camp Douglas; C L Chase Used Auto & Truck Parts, *see Vintage*

Downing; Kandinger Auto Salvage, 9919 130th St, 54734; 715-643-4211, 800-503-8895; CC, Sa, Sp; 40ac; **69+; D, PU, 4x4, Trk; B**3**, AMC**

East Troy; East Troy Auto Recyclers Inc, 2566 Energy Dr, 53120; 262-642-7233, 800-632-9780; 10ac; **76-94; D, F, 4x4; B**3**, AMC, Jp**

Eau Claire; A to Z Towing & Salvage, 204 E Madison St, 54703; 715-835-6653; Sa, Sp, UR; 24ac; **70+; D, F, PU, 4x4, few Trk, few Mil; B**3

B J Auto Salvage, 5501 Winget Dr, 54703; 715-832-5851, 800-548-0874; CC, Sa, Sp; 9ac; **80+; D, F; B**3**, AMC**

Nick's Auto Salvage & Repair, 3281 Early Dr, 54703; 715-723-1581, 800-381-2233; Sa, Sp; 4ac; **80-93; D, F, PU, 4x4, Trk; B**3**, AMC**

Edgar; Bee Line Auto Parts, *see Vintage*

Edgerton; Newville Auto Salvage, *see Vintage*

Eland; Highway 45 Auto, *see Vintage*

Eleva; Lund Truck & Auto Sales, S10744 State Rd 93, 54738; 715-878-4311, 800-657-6763; CC, Sa, UR; 1500+; **70+; D, F, PU, 4x4; B**3

Fond du Lac; American Auto Iron & Metal Inc, *see Vintage*

Franklin; Al's Auto in Franklin, 10942 S 124th St, 53132; 414-425-1890; CC, Sa, UR; 1000+; **70+; D, F, PU, 4x4; B**3**, AMC**

Durham's Auto Salvage & Sales, 10568 S 124th St, 53132; 414-425-2514; Sa, Br; 800; **75+; D, F, PU, 4x4, Trk; B**3**, AMC**

Fishers Auto Parts & Salvage, 10386 S 124th St, 53132; 414-529-2300; CC, Sa, UR; 800; **70+; D, F, PU, few 4x4; B**3**, AMC**

Fredonia; Auto Parts & Recyc
ling Inc, *see Vintage*

316

Germantown; Rocky's Meeker Hill Automotive, W215N1125 Appleton Av, 53022; 262-628-4142; UR; 900+; **70-90; D, F, PU; B**3, **AMC**

Green Bay; Kozloski Towing Svc, 531 Maywood Av, 54303; 920-434-0789; 50; **70+; D, PU, 4x4; B**3

Smitty's Salvage & Supply, *see Vintage*

Hayward; Simons Enterprises Inc, *see Vintage*

Hortonville; Don Bennett Sport Cars, *see Vintage*

J & C Auto Salvage, W 10801 Shakey Lake Rd, 54944; 920-779-4944; Sa, Sp; 5ac; **70+; D, PU, 4x4; B**3

Kenosha; Jantz Auto Sales & Svc, 3405 Washington Rd, 53144; 262-654-0238, 800-554-4770; CC, Sa; 12ac; **80-90; D, F; B**3, **AMC**

Schneider's Auto Sales & Parts, *see Vintage*

La Crosse; Shiftar Auto Salvage, *see Vintage*

Lake Geneva; Cocroft Auto Parts & Sales, 6988 Buckby Rd, 53147; 262-248-2833, FAX 262-248-6527; Sp; 500+; **78+; D, F, PU, 4x4, Fm; B**3

Como Auto Salvage, *see Vintage*

Lena; Iron Yard Auto Salvage, 5968 Younger Rd, 54139; 920-846-8153; Sa, UR; 2ac; **70-92; D, F, PU, 4x4; B**3

Madison; Chief Auto Parts Inc, 1208 E Broadway, 53716; 608-222-2626, FAX 608-222-0846; Sa; 1000+; **76-79; D, F, PU, 4x4; B**3

Marinette; Chet's Auto Wrecking Co, W1311 State Hwy 64, 54143; 715-735-5052, 800-564-0868; Sa, Sp; 500+; **80+; D, F, PU, 4x4; B**3

Erdman's Auto Sales & Salvage, *see Vintage*

Marshfield; Shaw's Wrecking Yard, *see Vintage*

Mason; Rich's Auto Salvage, *see Vintage*

Milton; Seward Auto Salvage, *see Vintage*

Milwaukee; A & D Truck & Auto Parts, 450 S 11th St, 53204; 414-643-1189; CC, Sa; 400+; **80+; D, F, PU, 4x4; B**3

A B Rauth Auto Parts & Salvage, 9802 W Schlinger Av, 53214; 414-476-9850; 600+; **80+; D, F; B**3

Acme Auto Slvg, 934 S Barclay St, 53204; 414-384-0600; Sa; 2ac; **70-92; D, F; B**3

Advance Auto Slvg, 2375 S 43rd St, 53219; 414-384-6404; Sa, Sp; 250+; **78-88; D, F; B**3

Affordable Auto Salvage Inc, 4485 N Green Bay Av, 53209; 414-562-5440; Sa; 1000+; **78+; D; B**3, **AMC**

Al's Auto Sales & Salvage Inc, 5290 N 124th St, 53225; 414-438-1660; CC, Sa, UR; 800+; **70+; D, F, PU, 4x4; B**3

Auto Paradise Imports Inc, 4903 W Burnham St, 53219; 414-384-8120, FAX 414-384-5153; CC, Sa, Sp; 500+; **80+; F**

Auto Paradise Inc, *see Vintage*

B S Wisniewski, *see Vintage*

Brand Auto Parts, 1144 W Bruce St, 53204; 414-643-9484, FAX 414-643-9495; Sa, Sp; 300; **80+; D, F, PU, 4x4; B**3, **AMC, Jp, VW**

Burnham Auto Slvg, 4901 W Burnham St, 53219; 414-384-9854; Sa; 200+; **80+; D, F; B**3

C & C Weddle Auto Co, 4030 W Douglas Av, 53209; 414-466-3550, FAX 414-461-4241; Sa, Sp; 100+; **80-90; D; B**3

Ed's Auto Salvage, 8611 W Kaul Av, 53225; 414-353-8186; Sa, Sp, UR; 1ac; **80-89; D, F, PU, 4x4; B**3

Hampton Auto Slvg, 11840 W Hampton Av, 53225; 414-463-4740; Sa; 500; **81-93; D; B**3

J & J Auto Salvage Co, 6780 N Industrial Rd, 53223; 414-358-0125; 2ac; **70+; D, F: B**3

Lee's Auto Parts, 5150 N 124th St, 53225; 414-466-8433; Sa; 4ac; **80+; D, F, PU; B**3

Northwest Truck Parts Inc, 8550 N Granville Rd, 53224; 414-354-8300, FAX 414-354-8357; Sp; 300+; **70+; D, PU, 4x4; B**3, **IH; PU only**

Roz Auto Salvage, 5848 S 13th St, 53221; 414-282-9862, 800-281-2479, www.rozauto.com; Sa, Sp; 13ac; 3000; **80+; D, F, PU, 4x4; B**3

South Side Auto Salvage Inc, 2108 W Holt Av, 53215; 414-671-5800; Sa, Sp; 1000; **80+; D, F, PU, 4x4; B**3

Wisconsin – Late Vintage

Neenah; Gibson's Auto Wrecking Inc, *see Vintage*

New Franken; Heim Auto & Recycling, 5523 Luxemburg Rd, 54229; 920-866-2688; Sa, Sp; 5ac, 450+; **80-90; D, PU; B3**

Oakfield; Kedinger Auto Salvage, *see Vintage*

Oshkosh; Barney's Towing, 2110 Jackson St, 54901; 920-235-4600; CC; **65+; F; VW only**

Fox Valley Iron Metal & Auto, 3446 Witzel Av, 54904; 920-231-8187, FAX 920-231-3888; Sa, UR; 400; **80-92; D, F PU; B3**

Holmes Automotive Recycling, 4578 County Rd N, 54904; 920-235-7553, 800-235-7560; CC, Sp; 12ac, 700; **80+; D, F, PU; B3**

Wally's Auto Inc, 4266 State Rd 21, 54904; 920-235-8070, 800-242-8282; Sa, Sp; 60ac, 650+; **80+; D, PU, 4x4; B3**

Poynette; Rocky's Auto Parts Inc, N5329 US Hwy 51, 53955; 608-635-4765, FAX 608-635-8452; CC, Sa, Sp, UR; 1500; **70+; D, F, PU, 4x4; B3, AMC, Jp, IH, VW**

Pulaski; Karcz Auto Salvage, *see Vintage*

Racine; Chuck Sheridan Auto Inc, 3037 Capitol Av, 53403; 262-637-6551, FAX 262-637-7501, www.chucks.com; Sa, Sp; **70+; D, F, PU, 4x4; B3; 4 locations**

Floyd & Sons Inc, 1525 Durand Av, 53403; 262-637-6589, FAX 262-637-7808, 800-304-0010 WI only; CC, Sa; 3ac, 250+; **70+; D, F, PU; B3**

Mason's Service, 3121 S Memorial Dr, 53403; 262-634-1030; Sa, Br; 6ac, 250+; **70-89, few 50-60s; D; B3, AMC, IH**

Town & Country Auto & Truck Co, 1900 Three Mile Rd, 53404; 262-639-4717, FAX 262-639-5499; CC, Sa, UR; 3ac, 200; **80-89; D, F, PU; B3, AMC**

Rhinelander; Bob's Auto Salvage, 4208 Oak Leaf Rd, 54501; 715-369-2228; **85-89; D, F**

Rhinelander Auto Salvage, 4161 Fox Farm Ln, 54501; 715-362-5639, FAX 715-362-1231, 800-236-5639, www.rhinlanderautosalvage.com; CC, Sp, PL; 750+; **80+; D, F, PU, 4x4; B3**

Rice Lake; Bob's Auto Salvage, 1996 25th St, 54868; 715-234-3120; Sa, UR; 160ac, 1200; **80-90; D, F, PU, 4x4, Mil; B3, AMC**

Richland Center; Terry's Exhaust, Rt 4 Hwy Y & Hwy 80 S, 53581; 608-647-3252, 647-3490; Sa, Sp; 3500+; **72-93; D, F, PU, 4x4, Fm; B3, AMC, IH, VW**

Rio; All Auto Acres Inc, W3862 State Rd 16, 53960; 920-992-5362, FAX 920-992-3432, 800-637-4661 WI only; CC, Sa, Sp, UR; 18ac, 1800+; **80+; D, F, PU, 4x4; B3**

Salem; Ace Auto Wrecking & Salvage, 27520 75th St, 53168; 262-843-3100, FAX 262-843-1933; Sa, Sp; 10ac, 800; **83-93; D, PU, 4x4; Spc: PU**

Saukville; Lakeland Metal Processing Inc, 3909 Lakeland Rd #B, 53080; 262-675-2922; Sa; 250+; **70+; D, F, PU, 4x4, Trk; B3**

Sheboygan Falls; Lima Auto Enterprises Inc, *see Vintage*

Siren; Marlow Auto Salvage, *see Vintage*

Somerset; Somerset Auto Salvage, *see Vintage*

Stanley; Stanley Truck Sales, *see Vintage*

Stevens Point; McDill Auto Wrecking Inc, *see Vintage*

Sturgeon Bay; C & W Auto Sales & Salvage, *see Vintage*

Discount Auto, 7542 Hwy 57, 54235; 920-743-6559, FAX 920-743-0175, 800-982-6400, discountauto@ipol.com; Sa, Sp; 450; **80+; D, PU, 4x4, Trk; B3, AMC, Jp**

Sturtevant; Sturtevant Auto Salvage, 2145 NE Frontage Rd, 53177; 262-835-2914, FAX 262-835-1691, 888-835-2914; CC, Sa, Sp, UR; 4ac, 200+; **70+; D, F, PU, 4x4; B3**

Theresa; Weise Auto Recycling Inc, Rt 1 Box 32, 1421 Hwy TW, 53091; 920-488-3030, FAX 920-488-6505, 800-236-3306; Br; 900; **80+; D, F, PU, 4x4; B3, AMC, Jp**

Tigerton; Zeb's Salvage, *see Vintage*

Tomahawk; Nokomis Auto Salvage, 2838 US Hwy 51, 54487; 715-453-8544; CC, Sa, UR; 350+; **77+; D, F, PU, 4x4; B3**

Trempealeau; Ray's Salvage & Repair, *see Vintage*

Two Rivers; Avery's Auto Salvage, *see Vintage*

Viroqua; Sheldon's Auto Wrecking Co, Rt 3, 54665; 608-637-2230; Sa, Wr; 10ac, 1000; **77+; D, F, PU, 4x4; B3**

Washburn; Ray's Automotive, *see Vintage*

Watertown; Jack's Auto Ranch, *see Vintage*

318

Sellnows Used Car Parts, W6516 Rhine Rd, 53098; 920-261-4830; 7ac; **72-90; D, PU, 4x4; B**3

Waupun; Derksen Auto Wrecking, N11496 County Rd M, 53963; 920-324-5848; Sa, UR; **80s, few 90s; D, F, PU, 4x4, vans, Trk; B**3

Wausau; Hilltop Auto Wrecking, 6806 N 33rd St, 54403; 715-675-3258; Sa; 40ac, 2500; **75-93; D, F, PU, 4x4; B**3**, AMC, Jp, VW**

Westfield; Stevens Auto Wrecking, *see Vintage*

Whitewater; Prisk Auto Salvage, *see Vintage*

Wisconsin Dells; Auto Care Ctr, E8522 County Rd P, 53965; 608-254-2787, FAX 608-524-1021; CC, Sa, UR; 175+; **70+; D, F, PU, 4x4; B**3

Craddock & Sons Salvage Yard, 3196 State Rd 13, 53965; 608-254-7971; Sa, UR; 10ac, 1500; **77-87; D, F, PU; B**3**, AMC**

Wisconsin Rapids; Badger Motors, 11701 Hwy 54 E, 54494; 715-341-4394, FAX 715-421-2280; Sa, Sp; 4500+; **70+; D, F, PU, 4x4; B**3**; Spc: early 70s Chevy**

Dahlke Auto Inc, 9230 State Hwy 54 E, 54494; 715-423-8988, 800-229-6452; Sa, Sp; 10ac, 1500; **70+; D, F, PU, 4x4; B**3**, AMC, Jp, VW**

LATE MODEL

Albany; Pence Salvage Co, *see Late Vintage*

Altoona; ATI, 2153 S Hastings Way, 54720; 715-834-7278; 1ac; **D, F, PU, 4x4; B**3**, AMC**

Appleton; Appleton Auto Recyclers, *see Late Vintage*

Cousineau Auto, 2225 W Nordale Dr, 54914; 920-734-3700, FAX 920-734-3611, 800-642-2550, 472-1631, 521-1443, www.cousineau.com; CC, Sa, Sp; 5500+; **D, F, PU, 4x4; B**3

Valley Auto Parts Inc, 1820 W Northland Av, 54914; 920-733-5776, 800-242-3558; CC, Sp; 5ac, 300; **D, PU, 4x4; B**3**, AMC**

Arkdale; Roller's Auto Salvage, *see Vintage*

Barron; Kadingers II, 1631 131/2 Av, 54812; 715-537-3157, 800-552-2995; CC, Sa, Sp, UR; 500; **D, F; B**3**, Jp, IH, VW**

Belleville; James Watkins Auto Slvg, W2898 Pernot Ln, 53508; 608-424-3581, FAX 608-623-2156, 800-472-1631; CC, Sa, Sp; 1750+; **D, F, PU, 4x4, Trk; B**3**, Jp, IH**

Black Creek; Northside Imports, State Hwy 47, 54106; 920-738-6888; **F; Jpa**

Cadott; Cadott Auto Recyclers & Sales, *see Late Vintage*

Camp Douglas; C L Chase Used Auto & Truck Parts, *see Vintage*

Cedarburg; Kirchhayn Auto Salvage Inc, 1199 Western Rd, 53012; 262-677-3123, FAX 262-377-3967, 800-257-2576; CC, Sp, UR; 10ac; **D, F, PU, 4x4, Trk; B**3**, AMC, Jp, IH**

Cleveland; Cleveland Auto Sales & Salvage, 7726 North Av, 53015; 920-693-8115, FAX 920-693-3682, 800-278-2178; CC, Sa, Sp; 23ac; **D, few PU, 4x4; B**3

Downing; Kandinger Auto Salvage, *see Late Vintage*

East Troy; East Troy Auto Recyclers Inc, *see Late Vintage*

Eau Claire; A to Z Towing & Salvage, *see Late Vintage*

B J Auto Salvage, *see Late Vintage*

Connell's Auto Salvage, 8040 Connell Rd, 54703; 715-835-5534, 800-345-5373; Sp; 15ac; **D, F, PU, 4x4; B**3**, AMC, Jp, IH**

Import Auto Recyclers, 38 Maple St, 54703; 715-832-8184, FAX 715-832-1614, 800-489-8184; Sp; 2ac; **F**

Nick's Auto Salvage & Repair, *see Late Vintage*

Remington Auto Salvage, 4004 Curvue Rd, 54703; 715-834-2560, FAX 715-834-7088, 800-871-2560; CC, Sp; 15ac, 3000; **D, PU, 4x4, Trk, Fm; B**3**, AMC, Jp, IH**

Edgar; Bee Line Auto Parts, *see Vintage*

Edgerton; Morrison Auto Salvage, 6307 W State Rd 59, 53534; 608-884-4436, FAX 608-884-8215; CC, Sp, UR; 750+; **D, F, PU; B**3

Newville Auto Salvage, *see Vintage*

Eleva; Lund Truck & Auto Sales, *see Late Vintage*

Fond du Lac; American Auto Iron & Metal Inc, *see Vintage*

Fort Atkinson; Dependable Auto Parts, N1814 US Hwy 12, 53538; 920-563-7363, FAX 920-563-7958, 800-262-1033; CC, Sa, Sp; 10ac; **D, F, PU, 4x4; B**3

319

Franklin; Al's Auto in Franklin, *see Late Vintage*
  Durham's Auto Salvage & Sales, *see Late Vintage*
  Fishers Auto Parts & Salvage, *see Late Vintage*
Green Bay; Bay Auto Parts, 1750 Velp Av, 54303; 920-494-8100, FAX 920-494-2675, 800-BAY AUTO; CC, Sa, Sp; 24ac; **D, F, PU, 4x4; B**3
  Kozloski Towing Svc, *see Late Vintage*
  Smitty's Salvage & Supply, *see Vintage*
Hayward; Simons Enterprises Inc, *see Vintage*
Hortonville; Don Bennett Sport Cars, *see Vintage*
  J & C Auto Salvage, *see Late Vintage*
Kenosha; Courtesy Auto Parts Inc, 5020 52nd St, 53144; 262-652-1391; CC, Sa; 800+; **D, F, PU, 4x4; B**3, **AMC; engine exchange**
Kewaskum; Star Auto Inc, N205 County Rd V, 53040; 414-626-2929 or 920-528-8032, FAX 414-533-4620; CC, Sa, Sp, UR; 2000+; **D, F, PU, 4x4, Trk; B**3
La Crosse; Shiftar Auto Salvage, *see Vintage*
Lake Geneva; Cocroft Auto Parts & Sales, *see Late Vintage*
Lena; Iron Yard Auto Salvage, *see Late Vintage*
Madison; A-Z Auto Dismantling, 1034 Walsh Rd, 53714; 608-244-8400; 500+; **D, F; B**3
Marinette; Chet's Auto Wrecking Co, *see Late Vintage*
  Erdman's Auto Sales & Salvage, *see Vintage*
Marshfield; Shaw's Wrecking Yard, *see Late Vintage*
Mason; Rich's Auto Salvage, *see Vintage*
Menasha; Jahnke Auto Parts, 1047 Valley Rd, 54952; 920-739-3181, 800-236-3181; Sp, Wr; 4ac; **D, few F, PU, 4x4**
Milton; Seward Auto Salvage, *see Vintage*
Milwaukee; A Auto, 5140 N 124th St, 53225; 414-466-9050; CC, Sp; 500+; **D, F, PU, 4x4**
  A & D Truck & Auto Parts, *see Late Vintage*
  A B Rauth Auto Parts & Salvage, *see Late Vintage*
  A-Able Trans, 138 E Becher St, 53207; 414-483-0302; CC, Sa, Sp, UR; 2ac; **D, F; B**3
  A-Action Salvage & Sales, 641 S 29th St, 53215; 414-384-5148; CC, UR; 2ac; **D, F; B**3
  AAA Auto Truck Salvage Co, 2007 W National Av, 53204; 414-643-9005, FAX 414-643-0669; CC, Sa, Sp; 500+; **D, F, PU; B**3
  Ace Auto Salvage, 2393 S 43rd St, 53219; 414-645-1790; CC, Sa, Sp; 600+; **D, F; B**3
  Acme Auto Salvage Inc, *see Late Vintage*
  Affordable Auto Salvage Inc, *see Late Vintage*
  Al's Auto Sales & Salvage Inc, *see Late Vintage*
  American Auto Salvage, 3015 W Center St, 53210; 414-444-3838, FAX 414-444-3837; Sa; 100; **D, PU, 4x4; B**3
  Auto Ambulance, 2485 S 13th St, 53215; 414-645-5007, FAX 414-645-5026; Sa, UR; 40; **D, PU, 4x4; B**3, **AMC**
  Auto Paradise Imports Inc, *see Late Vintage*
  Auto Paradise Inc, *see Vintage*
  Brand Auto Parts, *see Late Vintage*
  Burnham Auto Salvage, *see Late Vintage*
  Calumet Auto Parts Inc, 8501 W Calumet Rd, 53224; 414-355-2222, FAX 414-355-2466, 800-215-6500; CC, Sp, UR; 300+; **D, F; B**3
  Hampton Auto Salvage Inc, *see Late Vintage*
  J & J Auto Salvage Co, *see Late Vintage*
  K K Auto Slvg, 3626 W Mill Rd, 53209; 414-358-1211; CC, Sa, Sp, UR; 800+; **D, F; B**3
  K K Auto Salvage Inc, 2003 S Kinnickinnic Av, 53207; 414-483-7000; CC, Sa, Sp, UR; 750+; **D, F, PU; B**3
  Lee's Auto Parts & Sales Inc, *see Late Vintage*
  Northwest Truck Parts Inc, *see Late Vintage*
  Roz Auto Salvage, *see Late Vintage*
  South Side Auto Salvage Inc, *see Late Vintage*
Neenah; Gibson's Auto Wrecking Inc, *see Vintage*

Oshkosh; Barney's Towing Svc, *see Late Vintage*
  Fox Valley Iron Metal & Auto, *see Late Vintage*
  Holmes Automotive Recycling, *see Late Vintage*
  Wally's Auto Inc, *see Late Vintage*
Packwaukee; Packwaukee Auto Sales, W6216 County D, 53953; 608-589-5260, FAX 608-589-5080, 800-686-3036, packauto@mhus.net; Sa, Sp; 400; **D, F; B3**
Pardeeville; Wyocena Auto Sales Inc, N5599 State Rd 22, 53954; 608-429-2161, FAX 608-429-2162; CC, Sp; 15ac, 1500; **D, F, PU, 4x4; B3**
Poynette; Rocky's Auto Parts Inc, *see Late Vintage*
Pulaski; Karcz Auto Salvage, *see Vintage*
Racine; Chuck Sheridan Auto Inc, *see Late Vintage*
  Floyd & Sons Inc, *see Late Vintage*
Rhinelander; Rhinelander Auto Salvage, *see Late Vintage*
Richland Center; Terry's Exhaust, *see Late Vintage*
Rio; All Auto Acres Inc, *see Late Vintage*
River Falls; Jerry's Salvage Yard, W9880 710th Av, 54022; 715-425-6993, FAX 715-425-2780; CC, Sp, Br; 800; **D, F, PU, 4x4, Trk; B3; Tractor Trailer repair service**
Saint Francis; St Francis Auto Wreckers Inc, 4043 S Pennsylvania Av, 53235; 414-481-4540, FAX 414-481-4943, 800-905-8580; CC, Sa, Sp; 250+; **D, F, PU, 4x4; B3**
Salem; Ace Auto Wrecking & Salvage, *see Late Vintage*
Saukville; Lakeland Metal Processing Inc, *see Late Vintage*
Schofield; Cousineau Auto Inc, 6702 Ryan St, 54476; 715-359-9419, 800-521-1443, www.cousineau.com; CC, Sa, Sp, UR; 2500; **D, F, PU, 4x4; B3**
Sheboygan Falls; Akright Auto Parts, 106 N Bluebird Ln, 53085; 920-467-4201, FAX 920-467-1450, 800-400-4201; CC, Sp; 450+; **D, PU, 4x4; B3**
  Lima Auto Enterprises Inc, *see Vintage*
Somerset; Somerset Auto Salvage, *see Vintage*
South Range; Country Boy Sales, 7566 E County Rd E, 54874; 715-398-6235, FAX 715-398-6434, 888-263-0592; CC, Sa, Sp, Br; 1500; **D, F, PU, 4x4, Trk; B3, AMC, Jp, VW; Spc: GM**
Stanley; Stanley Truck Sales, *see Vintage*
Stevens Point; McDill Auto Wrecking Inc, *see Vintage*
Sturgeon Bay; C & W Auto Sales & Salvage, *see Vintage*
  Discount Auto, *see Late Vintage*
Sturtevant; Sturtevant Auto Salvage, *see Late Vintage*
Superior; Twin Ports Auto Salvage Inc, 1015 Elm Av, 54880; 715-392-4729, FAX 715-392-8829, 800-649-2868; Sa, Sp; 3ac, 350; **D, F, PU, 4x4; B3; Open Sa only in winter**
Theresa; Weise Auto Recycling Inc, *see Late Vintage*
Tomahawk; Nokomis Auto Salvage, *see Late Vintage*
Two Rivers; Avery's Auto Salvage, *see Vintage*
Viroqua; Sheldon's Auto Wrecking Co, *see Late Vintage*
Washburn; Ray's Automotive, *see Vintage*
Watertown; Jack's Auto Ranch, *see Vintage*
Waukesha; B & M Auto Sales & Parts Inc, W227S2698 Racine Av, 53186; 262-542-2255, FAX 262-542-0263, 800-236-2301; Sp, UR; 13ac, 500; **D, F, PU, 4x4; B3**
Waunakee; Schmidt's Auto Inc, 6918 Meffert Rd, 53597; 608-255-1311, FAX 608-831-2795, www.schmidtsauto.com; Sa, Sp, UR; 7000+; **D, F, PU, 4x4, Trk; B3**
Waupun; Derksen Auto Wrecking, *see Late Vintage*
Wausau; Hilltop Auto Wrecking, *see Late Vintage*
West Bend; Bradley Auto Inc, 2026 Hwy A, 53095; 262-334-4653; Sa; 900+; **D, PU, 4x4; B3**
Westfield; Stevens Auto Wrecking, *see Vintage*
Whitewater; Kienbaum Iron & Metal Inc, 564 N Jefferson St, 53190; 262-473-4533, FAX 262-473-1975; Sa, UR; 2ac, 50; **D, PU, 4x4; B3**
Wisconsin Dells; Auto Care Ctr, *see Late Vintage*
Wisconsin Rapids; Badger Motors, *see Late Vintage*
  Dahlke Auto Inc, *see Late Vintage*

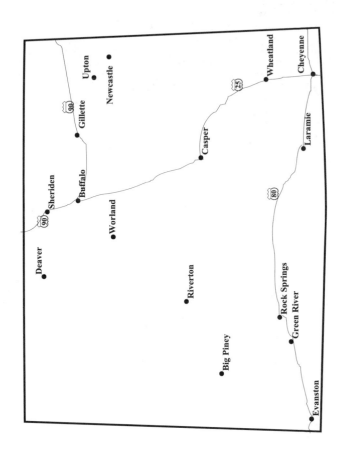

Wyoming

Please mention you saw'em in Ray's wReckingyard Roster when contacting these yards

WYOMING

VINTAGE

Buffalo; Mr. R's Auto Salvage, 321 TW Rd, 82834; 307-684-2288, FAX 307-684-0963, 800-834-8307; CC, Sp, UR; 20ac; **30+; D, F, PU, 4x4; B**3**, AMC, Jp, IH, St, Pk; Spc: Pickup**

Casper; Clark's Auto Recycling, 5635 Hanly St, 82604; 307-265-0020; Sa, Sp, UR; **50+; D, F, PU, 4x4, Trk, Fm, In, Cn; B**3**, Jp, VW, Jpa, Eur; Triumphs**

Ed's Auto Wrecking, 5660 Hanly St, 82604; 307-472-3558, 800-880-3558; CC, Sa, Sp, UR; 10ac, 800+; **60+; D, F, PU, 4x4; B**3**, AMC, Jp, IH, VW, Jpa**

Terry's Salvage, 2061 Bryan Evansville Rd, 82609; 307-577-1193, 800-303-1193; Sa; 1500+; **47+; D, F, PU, 4x4; B**3**, AMC, Jp; Spc: Mustang**

Cheyenne; Action Automotive, 1701 S Greeley Hwy, 82007; 307-634-3377, 800-442-2399; CC, Sp, Br; 18ac, 2200; **50+; D, F, PU, 4x4; B**3**, AMC, Jp, IH, St, VW; some VW bugs**

Balcaen's Auto Parts, 3001 S Greeley Hwy, 82001; 307-634-5859, FAX 307-634-4413, 800-288-5859; CC, Sp, Br, PL; 20ac, 3300; **30+; D, F, PU 4x4, Trk; B**3**, AMC, Jp, IH, Hd, Ns, St, Pk, Ks, Fr, Wy VW, Hr; Jpa, few Eur; Spc: 4x4**

Bud's Wrck, 7508 Tate Rd, 82001; 307-632-0309; Sa, UR; 800; **40-88; D, F, PU, 4x4**

CRH Salvage, 5001 S Greeley Hwy, 82003; 307-635-6593; UR; 2.75ac; **60-89; D; B**3**, Hr**

Curly's Auto Salvage, 2711 S Greeley Hwy, 82007; 307-634-5088; Sa, UR; 2.5ac; **70-89, few 50s & 60s; D, F, PU, 4x4; B**3

Lincoln Valley Auto Salvage, 2607 Whitney Rd, 82001; 307-638-0076; UR; 1000+; **40+; D, F, PU, 4x4, Trk, Fm, Cn, Mil; B**3**, Jpa**

Rhodes Towing & Auto Salvage, 4600 S Greeley Hwy, 82007; 307-632-6028, FAX 307-632-1586, 800-303-6028, rhodes@sisna.com; CC, Sa, Sp, Br; 7.5ac, 700; **50-89, few 40s; D, F, PU, 4x4, Trk, Fm, In, Cn; B**3**, AMC, Jp, IH, Hd, Ns, St, Pk, Wy, VW, Ks; few VW Bugs**

Deaver; Woody's Auto Salvage, 245 Lane 4 W, 82421; 307-664-2348; Sa, Sp, UR; 3000; **56+; D, F, PU, 4x4; B**3

Douglas; Blackburn Equipment, 7 Inez Rd, 82633; 307-358-3563; Sa, Sp, Br; 10ac; **30+ D, Fm, Cn, Mil; Spc: Farm & Construction equipment**

Gillette; Nanneman Bros, 1810 Gold Rd, 82716; 307-682-9082, FAX 307-682-0346, 800-462-5673, nanneman@vcn.com; CC, Sp, Br; 7ac; **24-95; D, F, PU, 4x4, B**3**, AMC, Jp, IH, St, Pk**

Wolf Pup Enterprises, 12-14 Patrick Henry Rd, 82716; 307-687-2821; Sp, Br; 4ac; **67+; D, F, PU, 4x4, Trk; B**3**; Spc: Rear Ends & Transmissions**

Green River; Green River Wrecking, 508 Jefferson Way, 82935; 307-875-2870; Sa, Sp, UR; 200; **60+; D, F, PU, 4x4; B**3

Newcastle; Black Hills Antique Auto, PO Box 713, 82701; 605-749-2242; CC, Sp; 150ac, 350; **30-69; D, F; B**3**, Hd, St, Ns, Wy, VW**

Outback Salvage, 3451 W Main St, 82701; 307-746-2966; Sa, Sp, UR; 6ac, 700+; **20+; D, F, PU, 4x4, Trk, Mil; B**3**, AMC, Jp, IH, VW; Jpa, few Eur; Ramblers**

Riverton; Federal Auto Recycling, 605 S Federal Blvd, 82501; 307-857-1603, FAX 307-856-1603; 4000+; **40+; D, F, PU, 4x4, Trk; B**3 **Mescil older parts-prefer to sell whole cars**

Rock Springs; Auto Recyclers, 654180 Service Rd, 82901; 307-382-9710, FAX 307-382-6366, 800-498-9710; CC, Sp, PL; 2600; **60+; D, F, PU, 4x4; B**3**, VW**

Sheriden; Sheriden Auto Salvage & Sales, 5311 Cofteen Ave, 82801; 307-672-3880; CC, Sa, Sp, UR; 5ac; **40-91; D, F, PPU, 4x4, Trk; Fm, In; B**3

Upton; Mellor Rpr Wrckng & Weld, 1120 2nd St, 82730; 307-468-2615; Sa, Sp, UR; 1200+; **40-89; D, F, PU, 4x4, Trk, In, Fm, Cn; B**3**, AMC, Jp, IH, VW, Jpa; Spc: 60s Chevy**

LATE VINTAGE

Big Piney; Garry Eiden Auto Salvage, 242 W 2nd St, 83113; 307-276-3413; CC, UR; 40ac; **70-89; D, F, PU, 4x4; B**3**, AMC, Jpa**

Buffalo; Mr. R's Auto Salvage, *see Vintage*

Casper; Clark's Auto Recycling, *see Vintage*

Ed's Auto Wrecking, *see Vintage*

J & B Auto Salvage & Repair, 6810 W Yellowstone Hwy, 82604; 307-473-8162, FAX 307-237-4816, 888-534-8398; CC, Sa, Sp, UR, PL; 350; 90+ cars, **70+ PU; D, F, PU, 4x4; B**3**, AMC, Jp, IH, VW & Jpa**

Terry's Salvage, *see Vintage*
Cheyenne; A-1 Auto Salvage, 2813 S Greeley Hwy, 82007; 307-638-8883; Sa, UR; 5ac; **70-80s; D, F, PU, 4x4; B**3
   Action Automotive, *see Vintage*
   Balcaen's Auto Parts, *see Vintage*
   Bud's Wrecking, *see Vintage*
   CRH Used Auto Parts, *see Vintage*
   Curly's Auto Salvage, *see Vintage*
   Lincoln Valley Auto Salvage, *see Vintage*
   Rhodes Towing & Auto Salvage, *see Vintage*
Deaver; Woody's Auto Salvage, *see Vintage*
Douglas; Blackburn Equipment, *see Vintage*
Evanston; P O P Salvage, 402 Duncomb Hollow Dr, 82930; 307-789-6666, FAX 307-789-2634, 800-289-7778; CC, Sa, Sp, Br, PL; 5ac, 200; **80+; D, F, PU, 4x4, Trk; B**3
Gillette; Nanneman Bros, *see Vintage*
   Wolf Pup Enterprises, *see Vintage*
Green River; Green River Wrecking, *see Vintage*
Laramie; Rinkers Auto Salvage, 203 E Baker St, 82070; 307-745-8951, 800-228-9427; Sp; 3ac; **80+; D, F, PU, 4x4; B**3, **AMC, Jp, IH, VW; Jpa & Eur**
Newcastle; Outback Salvage, *see Vintage*
Riverton; Federal Auto Recycling, *see Vintage*
   Pro Parts, 1100 E Monroe Ave, 82501; 307-856-3305, FAX 307-857-2043, 800-726-7082, skaggs@trib.com; CC, Sp; 10ac; **80+; D, F, PU, 4x4; B**3; **Spc: Pickup**
Rock Springs; Auto Recyclers, *see Vintage*
Sheriden; Sheriden Auto Salvage & Sales, *see Vintage*
Worland; Washakie Garage & Auto Salvage, 1054 Hwy 20 N, 82401; 307-347-4156; CC, Sp, Br; 900; **75+; D, F, PU, 4x4; B**3
Upton; Mellor Repair Wrecking & Weld, *see Vintage*
Wheatland; B & M Salvage & Towing, 12 Sawmill Rd, 82201; 307-322-2420, 800-732-7922; CC, Sa, Sp, Br; 300; **80+; D, PU, 4x4; B**3; **Spc: Pickup**

LATE MODEL
Buffalo; Mr. R's Auto Salvage, *see Vintage*
Casper; Clark's Auto Recycling, *see Vintage*
   Ed's Auto Wrecking, *see Vintage*
   J & B Auto Salvage & Repair, *see Late Vintage*
   Nick's Auto Salvage, 1688 Bryon Stock Trail, 82602; 307-265-5833, FAX 307-265-0924, 800-367-0376; CC, Sa, Sp; 5ac; **D, F, PU, 4x4**
   Terry's Salvage, *see Vintage*
Cheyenne; Action Automotive, *see Vintage*
   Balcaen's Auto Parts, *see Vintage*
   Lincoln Valley Auto Salvage, *see Vintage*
Deaver; Woody's Auto Salvage, *see Vintage*
Douglas; Blackburn Equipment, *see Vintage*
Evanston; P O P Salvage, *see Late Vintage*
Gillette; Nanneman Bros, *see Vintage*
   Wolf Pup Enterprises, *see Vintage*
Green River; Green River Wrecking, *see Vintage*
Laramie; Rinkers Auto Salvage, *see Late Vintage*
Newcastle; Outback Salvage, *see Vintage*
Riverton; Federal Auto Recycling, *see Vintage*
   Pro Parts, *see Late Vintage*
Rock Springs; Auto Recyclers, *see Vintage*
Sheriden; Sheriden Auto Salvage & Sales, *see Vintage*
Worland; Washakie Garage & Auto Salvage, *see Late Vintage*
Wheatland; B & M Salvage & Towing, *see Late Vintage*

Cross-Reference by Make

A number of yards took the time to tell us what they had, but others may also have these Marquees but will not be listed because we were not given the information. It is our hope that this cross-reference will make it easier for you to find the parts you are looking for.

Camaro

Alabama; *Albertville*; Billy's Used Parts
    Calera; Graham's Camaro & Firebird
    Mobile; Camaro Heaven
Arizona; *Glendale*; AAA United Auto Parts
    Phoenix; All Mustang All Camaro
          Precision Auto Parts
California; *Lamont*; Weedpatch Auto Dismantling
    Placentia; Dave's Placentia Auto Wrecking
    Rancho Cordova; Rancho Chevy Recycling
    Rio Linda; Capital Auto Parts & Towing
    Rohnert Park; Camaroland
    Sacramento; Payless Auto Dismantlers
    San Jose; GM Sports Salvage
Colorado; *Denver*; American Graffiti
    Englewood; Fair Auto & Truck Wrecking
Delaware; *New Castle*; Breitenbach Towing & Auto Salvage
Florida; *Clearwater*; Doc & Bill's Auto Salvage
    Ft Lauderdale; Bailey's Camaros & Firebirds
    Mims; Mims East Coast Auto Salvage
    Rockledge; Lucky's Auto Salvage
Iowa; *Colfax*; Batt's Camaro
Kansas; *Lawrence*; Mid-America Auto Recycling
Kentucky; *Upton*; Wheeler's Auto Salvage & Svc
Louisiana; *Basile*; Roger's Classic Restoration
Mississippi; *Booneville*; Lambert Auto Sales & Salvage
New Hampshire; *Rochester*; Camaro Heaven
New Jersey; *Paterson*; CFS Auto Wreckers
Oklahoma; *Oklahoma City*; American Camaro & Firebird
Oregon; *Portland*; Chevy Store
          Crystal Lane Auto Salvage Inc
          Division Street Auto Wrecking
Pennsylvania; *Shamokin*; Winnick's Auto Sales & Parts
    York; Christine's Auto Recycling
South Carolina; *Lexington*; Brock's Camaro & Firebird Prts
Tennessee; *Fayetteville*; Bradford's Auto Salvage
Virginia; *Ashland*; Old Dominion Mustang
Washington; *Vancouver*; All American Classics Inc

Corvette

Alabama; *Mobile*; Camaro Heaven
Arizona; *Glendale*; AAA United Auto Parts
    Phoenix; 20th St Auto Parts
          A-AA 20th St Auto Parts Inc
Arkansas; *Fort Smith*; Mayberry Auto Salvage
    Springdale; Horn's Auto Salvage
California; *Campbell*; Corvette Heaven
    Placentia; Dave's Placentia Auto Wrecking
    Rancho Cordova; Rancho Chevy Recycling
    San Jose; GM Sports Salvage
    Santa Clara; Carol's Automotive & Corvette
    Yuba City; B & B Auto Parts Inc
Connecticut; *New Haven*; A & A Used Auto Parts
Florida; *Dade City*; Sunshine Corvettes
Georgia; *Griffin*; A & B Auto Salvage
    Thomaston; Stallings Used Auto Parts
Kentucky; *Corbin*; Davis Salvage
Maryland; *Marlow Heights*; Chuck's Used Auto Parts
Michigan; *Riga*; Michigan Corvette Recyclers
Minnesota; *Jordan*; Cedar Auto Parts
Missouri; *St Charles*; Just Corvettes
New York; *Brewster*; Simon Auto Wreckers
    Monticello; Fast Eddie's Auto Wreckers
    Webster; Elmer's Auto Parts

Corvette

North Carolina; *Moyock*; Robert Cannon's Corvette Parts
Oregon; *Portland*; Chevy Store
GM Toys
South Dakota; *Sioux Falls*; Howard's Corvettes

Crosley

Arizona; *Casa Grande*; Wisemans Auto Salvage
Holbrook; Kachina Auto Salvage
Huachuca City; Fort Auto Parts & Wrecker Service
Maricopa; Hidden Valley Auto Parts
California; *Modesto*; Holt Auto Wrecking
Colorado; *Englewood*; Svigel's Auto Parts
Windsor; Martin Supply & Salvage Yard
Connecticut; *Barkhansted*; Stewart's Used Auto Parts
Kansas; *Junction City*; Easy Jack & Sons Antique Auto
Louisiana; *Ponchatoula*; Fannaly's Auto Exchange
Minnesota; *New London*; Windy Hill Auto Parts
Missouri; *Goodman*; J & M Vintage Auto
Montana; *Helena*; Al & Buzz Rose Wrecking Yard
New Hampshire; *Louden*; Lane's Garage & Auto Body
New Jersey; *Berlin*; Albion Auto Parts
New Egypt; Price's Auto Recyclers
New Mexico; *Alamogordo*; Wild Bills Auto Wrecking
New York; *Bellmore*; Used Auto Glass
Buffalo; Carpenters Auto Parts Inc
Cold Spring; Cold Spring Auto Parts
Ohio; *Columbus*; All City Auto Wrecking
Oklahoma; *Sand Springs*; Grigsby's Auto Salvage
South Dakota; *Rapid City*; A & A Auto Salvage
Texas; *Wellington*; South Side Salvage
Washington; *Centralia*; Grasser Auto Wrecking
Spokane; Antique Auto Items
Antique Auto Ranch
Woodinville; Vintage Auto Parts
Wisconsin; *Arkdale*; Roller's Auto Salvage
Camp Douglas; C L Chase Used Auto & Truck Parts
Milwaukee; B S Wisniewski
West Virginia; *Core*; Ben's Auto Wrecking

DeSoto

Alaska; *Palmer*; Boot Hill Auto Salvage
Arkansas; *Bentonville*; Gillis Used Cars & Auto Salvage
Berryville; Berryville Auto Salvage
Bradford; Vintage Auto Salvage
California; *Arroyo Grande*; R & R Auto Wrecking
Iowa; *Fayette*; Lau Auto Repair & Salvage
Illinois; *Jerseyville*; Ehlers Auto Salvage & Towing
Kansas; *Waverly*; Terry's Auto Sales & Salvage
Louisiana; *Ponchatoula*; Fannaly's Auto Exchange
Michigan; *Fenton*; Fenton Auto Salvage
Minnesota; *Pierz*; Okroi's Auto Salvage Inc
Missouri; *Bourbon*; I-44 Auto Salvage
Oregon; *Coos Bay*; Greenacres Auto Wrecking
Utah; *Nephi*; Nephi Auto Wrecking & Towing
Wisconsin; *Edgar*; Bee Line Auto Parts

Edsel

Connecticut; *Wallingford*; Chick's Used Auto Parts
Idaho; *Indian Valley*; Morris Antique & Classic Cars & Parts
Illinois; *Mendota*; Sprowls Body Shop & Auto
Kansas; *Carbondale*; Weekleys Auto Salvage
Junction City; McDonald Auto Sales & Salvage
Valley Center; Watkins Auto Salvage Inc
Michigan; *Lapeer*; Lapeer Auto & Truck Salvage
Minnesota; *Newport*; Bill's Auto Parts
New Hampshire; *Canaan*; Parts of the Past
New Jersey; *New Egypt*; Price's Auto Recyclers
North Dakota; *Beulah*; Walker's Garage
Texas; *San Angelo*; Clark Auto Wrecking
Utah; *Ogden*; B & R Old Car Parts
Virginia; *Lanexa*; Philbates Auto Wrecking Inc

English/British

Arizona; *Maricopa*; Hidden Valley Auto Parts
 Phoenix; All European Models
    Angel Auto
    J & R Auto Salvage
    Phoenix; K & D Auto Wrecking
Arkansas; *Fort Smith*; Branson & Sons Salvage
California; *Antelope*; Antelope Foreign Dismantlers
 Campbell; British Motorsports
 Carson; Jags Services
 Chula Vista; American & Foreign Auto Wrecking
    Fords Forever
 Fontana; M & M #1 Parts Center
 Hayward; Alfa Parts Exchange
 Lincoln; Euro Sport
 Riverside; Riverside All Foreign Parts
 San Diego; British Foreign Auto Salvage
 Shafter; Dan's Auto Sales & Wrecking
 Stockton; Jaguar Heaven
    Stockton Auto Dismantlers
 Sun Valley; Galaxy Used Auto Parts
    Pacoima Auto Recyclers
Colorado; *Englewood*; Eur-Asian Foreign Auto Parts
 Erie; Blake's Small Car Salvage
Florida; *Baker*; C & J Auto Salvage
 Homosassa; A & J Auto Salvage
Georgia; *Thomaston*; W & W Used Auto Parts
Louisiana; *Lafayette*; A Lafayette Auto Salvage
New York; *Macedon*; British Auto
    Staten Island; Edkins Foreign Auto Parts
North Carolina; *Clayton*; Johnston County Auto Salvage
Oklahoma; *S Coffeyville*; Collins Auto Salvage
 Shady Cove; European Auto-Winch-Em Towing
Oregon; *Troutdale*; Burns Marsh Twin Lakes Jag
Rhode Island; *Middletown*; Gold Auto Wrecking
Virginia; *Vinton*; Auto Salvage & Sales Inc

European

Alabama; *Mobile*; American & Import Auto Salvage
Arizona; *Maricopa*; Alley Towing & Recycling
Arizona; *Phoenix*; All European Models
    All Models Foreign
 Phoenix; All Models Ltd
    Angel Auto
    Arizona Auto Imports
    Blair & Sons Auto Parts
    J & L Auto Wreckers
    Salvage City
Arkansas; *Jonesboro*; Sharp Industries
California; *Berkeley*; European Auto Salvage
 Chula Vista; American & Foreign Auto Wrecking
    West Auto Wreckers
 Emeryville; European Auto Salvage Yard
 Fontana; Bill's Auto Wrecking
 Fremont; A C European
 Gardena; Schulberg Auto Wreckers
 Hayward; Alfa Parts Exchange
 Los Angeles; T & J Foreign Auto Salvage
 Pacoima; M G M
 Rancho Cordova; All Foreign Auto Dismantlers
 Reseda; Fiat Auto Svc
 San Diego; San Diego Foreign Auto
 San Jose; European Specialty Auto Dismantling
 San Ysidro; Uruapan Auto Wreckage
 Santa Ana; Wrecks West
 Santa Clara; A & A Foreign Auto Wreckers
    European Wholesale Parts
 Stockton; Stockton Auto Dismantlers
 Sun Valley; Daytona Auto Wrecking
 Watsonville; Gerry's Foreign Auto Wreckers
Colorado; *Durango*; Mac's Foreign Auto Parts
 Englewood; Eur-Asian Foreign Auto Parts
Florida; *Apopka*; Cheap Dave's Auto Salvage
Georgia; *Atlanta*; Eagle Auto Parts & Salvage
 Marietta; Fiat Lancia World

European

Kansas; *Kansas City*; Bud's Auto Wrecking
Louisiana; *Lafayette*; A Lafayette Auto Salvage
Maryland; *Westminster*; Jones Auto & Salvage
Montana; *Arlee*; Kelly's Auto Salvage
Nebraska; *Chadron*; Ed's Auto Salvage & Rebuilders
    Lincoln; Olston's Import Auto Salvage
New Jersey; *Berlin*; Albion Auto Parts
New Mexico; *Albuquerque*; Complete Auto & Truck Parts
North Carolina; *Clayton*; Johnston County Auto Salvage
North Dakota; *Minot*; Action Auto
Ohio; *Toledo*; Cherry Auto Parts
Oklahoma; *Chandler*; Country Auto
   Tulsa; East West Auto Parts
Oregon; *Albany*; Loops Auto Wrecking & Salvage
   Shady Cove; European Auto-Winch-Em Towing
Rhode Island; *Providence*; International Auto Salvage
South Carolina; *Belton*; Anderson Auto Salvage
   Greer; A-1 Import Salvage Inc
South Dakota; *Rapid City*; B & B Auto Salvage
Utah; *Orem*; European Only
   Salt Lake City; A-1 National Foreign Auto
       Foreign Car Parts
Virginia; *Spout Spring*; Smith's Foreign Used Auto Parts
Washington; *Seattle*; Northern European Auto Recyclers
   Woodinville; Gerry's Foreign Auto Parts Ltd
Wyoming; *Casper*; Clark's Auto Recycling
   Cheyenne; Balcaen's Auto Parts
   Laramie; Rinkers Auto Salvage
   Newcastle; Outback Salvage

Farm Equipment

Alabama; *Attalla*; Gibbs Junk Yard
Arizona; *Chinle*; Arrowhead Auto Salvage
   Holbrook; Kachina Auto Salvage
Arkansas; *El Dorado*; Fallin's Wrecking Yard & Used Parts
   Fordyce; Big Bens Used Cars & Salvage
   Harrison; Poor Boy's Auto Salvage
   Little Rock; Caples Auto Repair & Wrecking
   Pine Bluff; Steve's Auto Salvage & Scrap
Arkansas; *Van Buren*; Shibley's Salvage
California; *Chula Vista*; South Bay Auto Wreckers
   Gerber; Jim & Jerri's Auto Wreckers
   Oakley; Two Friends Auto Dismantlers
   Rancho Cordova; German Auto Recycling
Colorado; *Longmont*; Auto Truck Salvage
   Windsor; Martin Supply & Salvage Yard
Connecticut; *Barkhansted*; Stewart's Used Auto Parts
Florida; *Bunnell*; A-1 Auto Parts & Salvage
   Okeechobee; Action Auto Salvage
   Panama City; Budget Auto Salvage
Georgia; *Broxton*; Kenny's Auto & Truck Salvage
   Calhoun; South Forty-One Auto Salvage
   Jefferson; Jones Autoparts & Recycling
   Milledgeville; Baldwin Auto Salvage
   Montezuma; Martin's Auto Salvage
Idaho; *Kamiah*; Jackson's Wrecking
   Potlatch; Potlatch Auto Sales
   Preston; Idaho Salvage & Metals
   Weiser; Myers Auto Salvage
Illinois; *Chebanse*; Thompson Auto Wreckers
   Joliet; Low Cost Auto Parts
   Melrose Park; West Melrose Auto Wreckers
   Mendota; Sprowls Body Shop & Auto
   Plainfield; Speicher & Gaylord Wrckrs
   Sycamore; B-O Used Auto Parts
   Tonica; Ace Auto Salvage
Indiana; *Noblesville*; Bill Shank Auto Parts
Iowa; *Aurelia*; County Line Auto Salvage
   Decorah; Borsheim & Son Auto Salvage
   Des Moines; Don's Auto & Truck Salvage
   Fort Dodge; Ron's Auto Parts
   Keokuk; E & E Auto & Truck Salvage
   Kimballton; D & L Salvage
   Nashua; Wilken Auto Wrecking

328

Iowa; *Pleasantville*; Mid State Truck & Auto Salvage
    Spencer; Hurst Salvage
    Stanley; Berry's Salvage Yard
    Urbana; Mid-State Salvage
Kansas; *Danville*; Bob Lent Motor Shop
    Liberal; Friesen Salvage One
    Salina; Charlie Heath West 40 Salvage
Kentucky; *Benton*; Universal Auto Recycling
    Clay City; Richardson's Used Auto Parts
Louisiana; *Mansfield*; 175 Salvage
Maryland; *Hurlock*; Era's Auto Salvage
    Mount Airy; Mt Airy Auto Wrecking Inc
    Smithsburg; Elwood's Auto Exchange
Michigan; *Cass City*; Bartnik Sales & Service
    Clifford; La Blanc Auto Salvage
    Crystal; Crystal Mike's Salvage Yard
    North Pine River; Pine River Salvage
    Smiths Creek; Dave's Auto & Truck Salvage
Minnesota; *Glenville*; Bridley Auto Salvage
    Litchfield; Mies Auto Salvage
    New London; Windy Hill Auto Parts
    Sanborn; Hilltop Auto & Truck Salvage
    Silver Lake; R & R Auto & Truck Salvage
Mississippi; *Bruce*; Patterson's Garage & Salvage
    Hickory; Harrison Auto Salvage & Garage
    Magnolia; Sandifer Auto Salvage
    Pascagoula; Delmas Salvage
        Pascagoula Auto Salvage Inc
Missouri; *Doniphan*; Bargain Auto Salvage
Montana; *Havre*; M & M Auto Parts Salvage
    Kalispell; R & J Wrecking
    Opportunity; S & S Salvage
Nebraska; *Rulo*; Koelzer Salvage
    South Sioux City; Garvin Used Auto Sales & Salvage
New Hampshire; *Charlestown*; Morway's Auto Salvage
    Concord; Little's Auto Parts
    Greenville; Fitchburg Rd Sales & Salvage
    Meredith; Royea's Auto Wrecking
New Jersey; *Browns Mills*; Buster's Garage
New Mexico; *Estancia*; Hooker Salvage
New York; *Freedom*; Previty's Auto Wrecking
    Frewsburg; Twin Auto Sales
    Niagra Falls; Airport Auto Wrecking
    Sanborn; A Able Auto Wrecking
    Westbury; Nassau Suffolk Recycling Corp
North Carolina; *Fayetteville*; R C Auto Salvage
North Dakota; *Bismark*; Don's Auto Salvage
    Thompson; J & S Auto Wrecking
    Williston; Pete's Truck & Salvage
    Wishek; Martell's Salvage
Ohio; *Andover*; A Ds Auto Wrecking
    Byesville; Bartholow Auto Wrecking
    Cleveland; Fulton Auto Wrecking
    Clyde; B & K Auto Svc
    Columbus; Woody's Auto Salvage
    Kinsman; Countryside Salvage
    Lima; Hartman's Wrecker Svc
    Mansfield; Bowman Auto Recycling
    Miamisburg; Stark Wrecking
    New Philadelphia; Howenstine Auto Salvage
    Newark; Crispin Auto Wrecking
    Perry; Great Lakes Auto
    Toledo; Ray's Wrecking Auto & Truck
    Wooster; Wayco Automotive
Oklahoma; *Blanchard*; JpCounty Line Salvage
    Lawton; C & W Auto Salvage Inc
    Madill; Buddy's Crushed Cars
    Stilwell; Collins Salvage
Oregon; *Albany*; Linn Auto Salvage
    Bend; Bend Salvage & Auto Wrecking
    Oregon City; Dales Auto Wrecking
Pennsylvania; *Big Cove Tannery*; Shives Auto Salvage
    Bloomsburg; Swartz Salvage Inc
    Cochranton; Peterson Brothers Salvage
    Enon Valley; Feezle Auto Wrecking

Farm Equipment

Pennsylvania; *Mineral Point*; Gillins Auto & Truck Salvage
    Scenery Hill; Ritenour & Sons Wreckers
    Scranton; Anthracite Auto Wreckers
South Carolina; *Cottageville*; April's Used Auto Parts
South Dakota; *Box Elder*; Lefler Auto Salvage
    Milbank; Berkner Auto Repair & Salvage
Tennessee; *South Gibsen*; Privitt Garage
Texas; *Corpus Christi*; Ace Auto Parts
    Denton; Denton County Auto Salvage
    Ector; James Cobb Wrecking Yard
    Mineral Wells; Jack's Auto Salvage
Utah; *Ogden*; B & R Old Car Parts
    Salt Lake City; Special Editions
    Sigurd; Dwights Auto Wrecking
    Springville; Anderson's Auto Wrecking
Virginia; *Lanexa*; Philbates Auto Wrecking Inc
    Staunton; Byrd's Wrecking Yard
Washington; *Burlington*; Larry's Auto & Truck Parts
    Olympia; John's Radiator & Towing
    Pasco; Pasco Auto Wrecking
    Snohomish; Mid-City Towing & Wrecking
    Spokane; Art Santa Rosa's Auto & Truck
        C & T Truck Parts Inc
        Triangle Truck Parts
    Sunnyside; Bill's Towing Inc
    Tenino; Columbia Industries Auto Repair
    Wapato; Douglas Wrecking & Scrapping
    Yakima; Central Salvage & Auto Wrecking
        Poor Boys Auto Wrecking
West Virginia; *Mathias*; Strawderman's Salvage
Wisconsin; *Arkdale*; Roller's Auto Salvage
    Boscobel; Golden Sands Salvage
    Camp Douglas; C L Chase Used Auto & Truck Parts
    Eau Claire; Remington Auto Salvage
    La Crosse; Shiftar Auto Salvage
    Lake Geneva; Cocroft Auto Parts & Sales
    Marshfield; Shaw's Wrecking Yard
    Richland Center; Terry's Exhaust
    Stanley; Stanley Truck Sales
Wyoming; *Casper*; Clark's Auto Recycling
    Cheyenne; Lincoln Valley Auto Salvage
        Rhodes Towing & Auto Salvage
    Douglas; Blackburn Equipment
    Sheriden; Sheriden Auto Salvage & Sales
    Upton; Mellor Repair Wrecking & Weld

Ford: Models A & T

Arizona; *Phoenix*; Broadway Auto Wreckers
California; *Needles*; Needles Auto Wrecking
    Orange Cove; Donaldson's Auto Dismantling
    Shafter; Dan;s Auto Sales & Wrecking
Colorado; *Windsor*; Martin Supply & Salvage Yard
Idaho; *Kuma*; Mustang Idaho
Iowa; *Estherville*; Dean's Auto Salvage & Repair
Kansas; *Baxter Springs*; CRS Garage & Wrecker Svc
    Junction City; Easy Jack & Sons Antique Auto
Missouri; *Chillicothe*; Nick Anderson Auto Salvage
Nebraska; *Alliance*; Taylor's Auto Repair & Salvage
Nevada; *Las Vegas*; Fords Only
New Hampshire; *Concord*; Little's Auto Parts
    Sullivan; Northeast Ford & Mustang Parts
New Jersey; *New Egypt*; Price's Auto Recyclers
North Dekota; *Park River*; Porter Auto Repair & Salvage
Washington; *Spokane*; Antique Auto Ranch

Frasier

Arizona; *Casa Grande*; Wisemans Auto Salvage
    Huachuca City; Fort Auto Parts & Wrecker Service
    Maricopa; Hidden Valley Auto Parts
    Phoenix; Desert Valley Auto Parts
    Thatcher; Valley Auto Wrecking, Inc
    Wilcox; Wilcox Wrecking Yard
Arkansas; *Bradford*; Vintage Auto Salvage
California; *Porterville*; Cemo Motor Sales & Auto Wrecking

Frasier

California; *Redding*; Gustafson's Auto Wrecking
 Rosamond; Hi Desert Auto & Truck Salvage
Colorado; *Dacono*; Elliotts Auto Parts
 Englewood; Svigel's Auto Parts
 Pueblo; Bonnie's Car Crushers
Idaho; *Caldwell*; Hopkins Antique Autos & Parts
 Indian Valley; Morris Antique & Classic Cars & Parts
Indiana; *North Salem*; Joe Goode Excavating
Iowa; *Allison*; Ron's Auto Salvage
 Fort Dodge; Frank's Auto & Truck Salvage
Kansas; *Dodge City*; Stapleton Salvage
Louisiana; *Ponchatoula*; Fannaly's Auto Exchange
Maryland; *Finksburg*; Vogt Parts Barn
 Mount Airy; Mt Airy Auto Wrecking Inc
Massachusetts; *Sturbridge*; Curboy's Used Auto Parts
 Wrentham; Tosy's Ford Mustang Farm
Minnesota; *Glenville*; Bridley Auto Salvage
 New London; Windy Hill Auto Parts
Missouri; *Goodman*; J & M Vintage Auto
Montana; *Glendive*; Glendive Auto Parts
Nevada; *Las Vegas*; Larry's Auto Wrecking
New Hampshire; *Canaan*; Parts of the Past
 Louden; Lane's Garage & Auto Body
New Jersey; *Washington*; Studebaker Sanctuary
New Mexico; *Alamogordo*; North Fifty-Four Salvage
New York; *Albany*; Jim Meisner Auto Parts
 Bellmore; Used Auto Glass
 Buffalo; Carpenters Auto Parts Inc
 Cold Spring; Cold Spring Auto Parts
North Dakota; *Park River*; Porter Auto Repair & Salvage
 Wishek; Martell's Salvage
Ohio; *Frazeysburg*; Minnich Auto Wrecking
Oklahoma; *Aline*; Bud's Salvage
 Stillwater; Hauf Auto Supply
Pennsylvania; *Glenville*; Ed Lucke's Auto Parts
 West Sunbury; Renicks Used Auto Parts
South Dakota; *Gettysburg*; A G Sales & salvage
 Rapid City; A & A Auto Salvage
   Moore's Auto Salvage
 Sturgis; Westside Dismantlers
 Winner; Wayne's Auto Salvage
Texas; *Kaufman*; Henderson Auto Parts
 Wellington; South Side Salvage
Virginia; *Lanexa*; Philbates Auto Wrecking Inc
Washington; *Centralia*; Grasser Auto Wrecking
 Spokane; Antique Auto Items
  Antique Auto Ranch
  C & T Truck Parts Inc
  Triangle Truck Parts
 Woodinville; Vintage Auto Parts
Wisconsin; *Arkdale*; Roller's Auto Salvage
 Camp Douglas; C L Chase Used Auto & Truck Parts
 Milton; Seward Auto Salvage
 Milwaukee; B S Wisniewski
 Sturgeon Bay; C & W Auto Sales & Salvage
 Westfield; Stevens Auto Wrecking
Wyoming; *Cheyenne*; Balcaen's Auto Parts

German

Alabama; *Mobile*; American & Import Auto Salvage
 New Market; North Alabama Used Auto Parts
Arizona; *Phoenix*; 20th St Auto Parts
  A-AA 20th St Auto Parts Inc
  All European Models
  All Mercedes Benz Parts
  Angel Auto
  Benrich Auto Wrecking
  Eagle Auto & Truck
  German Auto Salvage
  Ray & Bobs Truck Salvage
  Sports Car Recycling
 Tempe; Mercedes Pete
  Tri Star Pete
 Tucson; Big Southwest Import Salvage

German

California; *Anaheim*; A-Professional Benz & Beemer
AASE Bros Porsche Car
Berkeley; Bay Motor Wrecking
European Auto Salvage
Wolfsport
Chula Vista; Onager Corp
True Way Wrecking
Costa Mesa; Mesa West German Auto
Duarte; Russ Recycling
Emeryville; Easy Auto Salvage Yard
European Auto Salvage Yard
Fontana; Bill's Auto Wrecking
Liberty Auto
M & M #1 Parts Center
Fremont; A C European
Gardena; Aaron Auto Parts
Geyserville; A-Auto Dismantlers
Hayward; Parts Heaven
Hesperia; Chris Volkswagen Parts
Lincoln; Euro Sport
Oakland; All Mercedes Dismantlers Inc
Dyno Automotives Inc
Mercedes Depot
Rancho Cordova; Bavarian BMW Auto Recycling
Dad's Auto Dismantling
German Auto Recycling
German Parts Warehouse
Silver Star Mercedes Benz & Porsche
Redwood City; High Performance House
Riverside; K C Auto Dismantler
Riverside All Foreign Parts
Roseville; B W Auto Dismantlers
San Diego; F & D Foreign
San Jose; A-German Auto Parts & Svc
American Import Auto Dismantlers
Bay City Auto Wreckers
European Specialty Auto Dismantling
Santa Clara; European Wholesale Parts
South El Monte; Southern California Import
Stanton; Best Deal
Stockton; Ben's Auto Dismantlers
Stockton Auto Dismantlers
Sun Valley; 2002 AD
Bells Auto Recycling
Best Auto Parts & Salvage
M-Mercedes Dismantlers
Statewide Auto Wrecking
Vista; Interstate VW Auto
Colorado; *Castle Rock*; Audi Salvage
Denver; Foreign Used Auto Parts
Rocky Mountain Imports
Tams #1 Imports
Englewood; Accurate Import Parts
Adams Imports & Wrecking
Ft. Collins; Aragon Iron & Metal Inc
Florida; *Baker*; C & J Auto Salvage
Boca Raton; Programma Tools
Homosassa; A & J Auto Salvage
Pensacola; Expert Auto Parts & Salvage
Georgia; *Alpharetta*; Grimes Auto Salvage
Atlanta; Best & Reliable Used Auto Parts
Eagle Auto Parts & Salvage
Jefferson; Jones Autoparts & Recycling
Marietta; Marietta Foreign Auto Parts
Smyrna; Embee Parts, Inc.
Thomaston; W & W Used Auto Parts
Indiana; *Noblesville*; Bill Shank Auto Parts
Kansas; *Great Bend*; Nobody's Auto Recycling
Maryland; *Baltimore*; The Mercedes Connection
Clinton; B & M Used Foreign & American
Frederick; Potomac German Auto
Michigan; *Lapeer*; Lapeer Auto & Truck Salvage
Southfield; Midwestern Motors & Dismantlers
Minnesota; *Bemidji*; Aassee's Auto Salvage Inc
Nebraska; *Blair*; Nebraska Porsche Recyclers

German

Nevada; *Sparks*; D & D Foreign Dismantlers
New Jersey; *Toms River*; Toms River Auto Recyclers
New Mexico; *Albuquerque*; Discount Auto Parts
New York; *Glen Cove*; Glen Cove Auto Salvage Inc
 New Hyde Park; F & S Auto Parts Inc
 Staten Island; Brothers Foreign Car Specs
  Edkins Foreign Auto Parts
Oklahoma; *Chandler*; Country Auto
Oregon; *Boring*; German Auto Salvage
 Portland; Import Auto Salvage & Repair
  Michael's Auto Parts
Pennsylvania; *Milroy*; Aumiller's Auto Wreckers Inc
South Carolina; *Belton*; Anderson Auto Salvage
Texas; *Atascosa*; All Bimmers & Benzes
Virginia; *Castlewood*; B & B Auto Salvage
 King George; Accurate Foreign Car Parts Inc
Washington; *Adna*; Audi Volkswagon Specialist
 Arlington; Campbell Nelson Auto Wrecking
 Edmonds; Campbell Nelson Volkswagen
 Seattle; Bry's Auto Wrecking
West Virginia; *Clarksburg*; Chip's Auto Parts

Hudson

Alabama; *Dothan City;* Used Parts Co
Arizona; *Casa Grande*; Wisemans Auto Salvage
 Huachuca City; Fort Auto Parts & Wrecker Service
 Maricopa; Al's Hudson Cars & Parts
 Phoenix; All Auto & Truck
  Desert Valley Auto Parts
Arkansas; *Bradford*; Vintage Auto Salvage
 Centerton; 102 Towing & Salvage
California; *Fontana*; Vintage Coach - Twin H Ranch
 Fresno; Globe Antique Auto Parts
  Romo Auto Wrecking & Towing
 Hesperia; Cox Auto Salvage
 Pomona; A-Car Auto Wrecking
 Porterville; Cemo Motor Sales & Auto Wrecking
 Shafter; Santa Fe Dismantling
 Sun Valley; Memory Lane Collector Car Dismantlers
Colorado; *Craig*; Ikes Automatic Transmission
 Dacono; Elliotts Auto Parts
 Erie; Speedway Auto Wrecking
 Grand Junction; American Auto Salvage
 Pueblo; West 29th Auto Inc
 Salida; South Side Salvage
Connecticut; *Barkhansted*; Stewart's Used Auto Parts
 Plymouth; Mt Tobe Auto Parts
Florida; *Avon Park*; Mac's Auto Salvage
 Lake City; Sunrise Auto Sales & Salvage
Georgia; *Auburn*; Collins Auto Salvage
 White; Old Car City USA
Idaho; *Hayden*; Pegasus Auto Wrecking
 Idaho Falls; Charlie's Auto Recycling
 Indian Valley; Morris Antique & Classic Cars & Parts
 Preston; Idaho Salvage & Metals
 Weiser; Myers Auto Salvage
 Wendell; L & L Classic Auto
Illinois; *Lockport*; Southwest Auto Salvage
Indiana; *New Waverly*; Canfield Motors
Iowa; *Burlington*; Plank Road Salvage
 Estherville; Dean's Auto Salvage & Repair
 Fort Dodge; Frank's Auto & Truck Salvage
  Netlands Auto-Truck Salvage
 Pleasantville; Mid State Truck & Auto Salvage
Kansas; *Coffeyville*; Purkey's Auto Salvage
 Columbus; Larison's Classics
 Dodge City; Stapleton Salvage
 Enterprise; Enterprise Auto Salvage
 Junction City; Easy Jack & Sons Antique Auto
 Valley Center; Watkins Auto Salvage Inc
Kentucky; *Union*; Boone Country Auto & Truck Slvg
Maine; *Caribou*; Beaulieu's Auto Salvage
 Monmouth; Phil's Garage & Salvage Yard
Maryland; *Finksburg*; Vogt Parts Barn

Maryland; *Mount Airy*; Mt Airy Auto Wrecking Inc
    Smithsburg; Elwood's Auto Exchange
Massachusetts; *Bellin;gham*; John's Used Auto Parts
    Deerfield; East Deerfield Auto Wrecking
    Sturbridge; Curboy's Used Auto Parts
    Wrentham; Tosy's Ford Mustang Farm
Michigan; *Fostoria*; Bob's Auto Parts
Minnesota; *Austin*; Crews Auto Salvage
    Glenville; Bridley Auto Salvage
Missouri; *Goodman*; J & M Vintage Auto
    Kansas City; Little Wills Auto Salvage
Montana; *Butte*; Zimp's Enterprises
    Glendive; Glendive Auto Parts
    Great Falls; S & C Repair-Wrecker Svc
    Helena; Al & Buzz Rose Wrecking Yard
    Kalispel; l R & J Wrecking
    Sidney; Sidney Auto Wrecking
Nebraska; *Alliance*; Taylor's Auto Repair & Salvage
    Blue Springs; Antique Cars, Trucks & Parts
    Elmwood; Eastern Nebraska Auto Sales
    Fairbury; Paneitz Salvage
    Scottsbluff; Goodro Auto Salvage
New Hampshire; *Canaan*; Parts of the Past
    Concord; Little's Auto Parts
    Louden; Lane's Garage & Auto Body
New Jersey; *Avenel*; Riverside Auto Parts
    Berlin; Albion Auto Parts
    New Egypt; Price's Auto Recyclers
    Toms River; Tice Brothers
    Washington; Studebaker Sanctuary
New Mexico; *Alamogordo*; North Fifty-Four Salvage
    Wild Bills Auto Wrecking
    Roswell; Diamond Auto
    Tucumcari; Quay Valley Salvage
New York; *Albany*; Jim Meisner Auto Parts
    Bellmore; Used Auto Glass
    Buffalo; Carpenters Auto Parts Inc
    Center Moriches; Moriches Used Auto Parts
    Mohawk; Reardon Enterprises
    Speonk; Outpost Automotive Inc
    Weedsport; Nash Auto Parts
North Carolina; *Sophia*; Hooker's Auto Sales
North Dakota; *Cavalier*; I & H Auto Repair & Salvage
    Park River; Porter Auto Repair & Salvage
    Wishek; Martell's Salvage
Ohio; *Columbus*; All City Auto Wrecking
    Conneaut; Ed Matt Auto Wreckers
    Crestling; Moyer's Auto Wrecking
    Frazeysburg; Minnich Auto Wrecking
    Lima; Hartman's Wrecker Svc
    Youngstown; Schulte Auto Wrecking
Oklahoma; *Aline*; Bud's Salvage
    Grove; Ten & Fifty Nine Salvage
    Sand Springs; Grigsby's Auto Salvage
    Tecumseh; Rath's Auto Salvage
Oregon; *Albany*; Loops Auto Wrecking & Salvage
    Aurora; Aurora Wreckers & Recyclers
    Bend; Bend Salvage & Auto Wrecking
Pennsylvania; *Fayetteville*; Beechers Auto Salvage Inc
    Glenville; Ed Lucke's Auto Parts
    West Sunbury; Renicks Used Auto Parts
South Dakota; *Rapid City*; A & A Auto Salvage
    Rapid City; Moore's Auto Salvage
    Sturgis; Jim's Auto Salvage
    Westside Dismantlers
    Winner; Wayne's Auto Salvage
Texas; *Bertram*; David's Auto Parts
    Kaufman; Henderson Auto Parts
    Wellington; South Side Salvage
Utah; *Salt Lake City*; King Size Auto & Truck
    Special Editions
    W W Auto Wrecking & Sales
Virginia; *Lanexa*; Philbates Auto Wrecking Inc
    Mount Crawford; Harold Ludholtz's
Washington; *Belfair*; Belfair Truck & Auto Wrecking

334

Hudson

Washington; *Centralia*; Grasser Auto Wrecking
Outlook; Tee Pee Auto Wreckers
Pasco; Tommy's Steel & Salvage
Spokane; Antique Auto Items
Antique Auto Ranch
Woodinville; Vintage Auto Parts
West Virginia; *Fairmont*; Knoll's Auto Wrecking & Paint
Fairmont; Morris Auto Wrecking
Wisconsin; *Arkdale*; Roller's Auto Salvage
Boscobal; Golden Sands Salvage
Cadott; Glenz Auto Salvage
Camp Douglas; C L Chase Used Auto & Truck Parts
Milton; Seward Auto Salvage
Milwaukee; B S Wisniewski
Sturgeon Bay; C & W Auto Sales & Salvage
Westfield; Stevens Auto Wrecking
Wyoming; *Cheyenne*; Balcaen's Auto Parts
Rhodes Towing & Auto Salvage
Newcastle; Black Hills Antique Auto

Industrial/Construction Equipment

Arizona; *Kingman*; Freds Auto & Truck Salvage
Arkansas; *Pine Bluff*; Steve's Auto Salvge & Scrap
California; *Chula Vista*; South Bay Auto Wreckers
Nipomo; Almond Automotive
Oakley; Two Friends Auto Dismantlers
Shafter; Santa Fe Dismantling
Colorado; *Erie*; Erie Auto Wreckers
Connecticut; *Barkhansted*; Stewart's Used Auto Parts
Florida; *Bunnell*; A-1 Auto Parts & Salvage
Panama City; Budget Auto Salvage
Summerfield; Highway 42 Salvage
Idaho; *Potlatch*; Potlatch Auto Sales
Preston; Idaho Salvage & Metals
Weiser; Myers Auto Salvage
Illinois; *Lemont*; Cal-Sag Auto Parts
Melrose Park; West Melrose Auto Wreckers
Mendota; Sprowls Body Shop & Auto
Sycamore; B-O Used Auto Parts
Indiana; *Noblesville*; Bill Shank Auto Parts
Iowa; *Aurelia*; County Line Auto Salvage
Des Moines; Don's Auto & Truck Salvage
Dubuque; Roger's Auto Sales & Salvage
Lacona; Jacob's Boneyard
Kentucky; *Brandenburg*; Watt's Auto Salvage
Clay City; Richardson's Used Auto Parts
Louisiana; *Mansfield*; 175 Salvage
Maryland; *Hurlock*; Era's Auto Salvage
Smithsburg; Elwood's Auto Exchange
Massachusetts; *Norfolk*; Call & Wait Auto Svc
Michigan; *Dundee*; Bonnie & Clyde's Auto Salvage
Lapeer; Lapeer Auto & Truck Salvage
Ypsilanti; Michigan Avenue Auto Salvage
Minnesota; *Litchfield*; Mies Auto Salvage
New London; Windy Hill Auto Parts
St Charles; Timm's Auto Salvage
Mississippi; *Magnolia*; Sandifer Auto Salvage
Montana; *Havre*; M & M Auto Parts Salvage
Nebraska; *Fairbury*; Paneitz Salvage
Nevada; *Carson City*; Buena Vista Auto Recyclers
Little John Auto Wrecking
Reno; North Valley Wreckers
New Hampshire; *Grafton*; V H McDow & Sons Salvage
Littleton; Red's Auto Wrecking
Louden; Lane's Garage & Auto Body
Meredith; Royea's Auto Wrecking
New Jersey; *Avenel*; Frank's Auto Wrecking
Browns Mills; Buster's Garage
Freehold; A & A Truck Parts
Union; Union Auto Wreckers
New Mexico; *Artesia*; Clark Auto
Estancia; Hooker Salvage
Ohio; *Andover*; A Ds Auto Wrecking
Byesville; Bartholow Auto Wrecking

Industrial/Construction Equipment

Ohio; *Clyde*; B & K Auto Svc
Coldwater; Graveyard II Auto Parts
Columbus; Buckeye Auto Parts
Woody's Auto Salvage
Delaware; Colonial Automotive Recycling
Garrettsville; Kohler Auto Wrecking
Kinsman; Countryside Salvage
Lima; Hartman's Wrecker Svc
Massillon; Massillon Auto Salvage
Miamisburg; Stark Wrecking
New Philadelphia; Howenstine Auto Salvage
New Richmond; Mahaffey Auto Salvage
Perry; Great Lakes Auto
Toledo; Ray's Wrecking Auto & Truck
Washington Court House; Cartwright Salvage
Wooster; Wayco Automotive
Youngstown; Al's Auto Salvage
Center Street Auto
Zanesville; Ron's Auto Parts
Oklahoma; *Wyandotte*; State Line Salvage
Oregon; *Bend*; Bend Salvage & Auto Wrecking
Newport; Kings Towing
Oregon City; Dales Auto Wrecking
Redmond; Brad's Auto & Truck Parts
Saint Helens; Ralph's Auto & Truck Wrecking
Pennsylvania; *Bloomsburg*; Swartz Salvage Inc
Scranton; Anthracite Auto Wreckers
South Dakota; *Sioux Falls*; Barneys Auto Salvage
Texas; *Dallas*; Nabors Auto Wrecking
Mineral Wells; Jack's Auto Salvage
San Angelo; Chatham Salvage Co
Utah; *Ogden*; B & R Old Car Parts
Washington; *Burlington*; Larry's Auto & Truck Parts
Ellensburg; A & A Auto Wrecking & Towing
Mount Vernon; Farrells Auto Wrecking
Olympia; John's Radiator & Towing
Pasco; Pasco Auto Wrecking
Port Orchard; Airport Auto Wrecking Too
Snohomish; Mid-City Towing & Wrecking
Spokane; Art Santa Rosa's Auto & Truck
Tenino; Columbia Industries Auto Repair
Wisconsin; *Boscobel*; Golden Sands Salvage
Green Bay; Smitty's Salvage & Supply
Two Rivers; Avery's Auto Salvage
Wyoming; *Casper*; Clark's Auto Recycling
Cheyenne; Lincoln Valley Auto Salvage
Rhodes Towing & Auto Salvage
Douglas; Blackburn Equipment
Sheriden; Sheriden Auto Salvage & Sales
Upton; Mellor Repair Wrecking & Weld

Kaiser

Alabama; *Daleville*; Baird's Auto & Truck Salvage
Alaska; *Palmer*; Boot Hill Auto Salvage
Arizona; *Casa Grande*; Wisemans Auto Salvage
Huachuca City; Fort Auto Parts & Wrecker Service
Phoenix; Desert Valley Auto Parts
Thatcher; Valley Auto Wrecking, Inc
Wilcox; Wilcox Wrecking Yard
Arkansas; *Centerton*; 102 Towing & Salvage
California; *Bishop*; Mingo's Automotive
Hesperia; Cox Auto Salvage
Porterville; Cemo Motor Sales & Auto Wrecking
Redding; Gustafson's Auto Wrecking
Richmond; Carlos Auto Wreckers
Sun Valley; Memory Lane Collector Car Dismantlers
Yermo; D & M Auto Truck & RV Repair
Colorado; *Dacono*; Elliotts Auto Parts
Englewood; Svigel's Auto Parts
Erie; Erie Auto Wreckers
Pueblo; Bonnie's Car Crushers
Windsor; Martin Supply & Salvage Yard
Connecticut; *Barkhansted*; Stewart's Used Auto Parts
Georgia; *Jonesboro*; Jonesboro Salvage & Recycle

Kaiser

Georgia; *White*; Old Car City USA
Idaho; *Caldwell*; Hopkins Antique Autos & Parts
    Indian Valley; Morris Antique & Classic Cars & Parts
    Wendell; L & L Classic Auto
Indiana; *New Waverly*; Canfield Motors
Iowa; *Allison*; Ron's Auto Salvage
    Fort Dodge; Frank's Auto & Truck Salvage
    North Salem; Joe Goode Excavating
Kansas; *Dodge City*; Stapleton Salvage
    Junction City; Easy Jack & Sons Antique Auto
    Liberal; Friesen Salvage One
Kentucky; *Oak Grove*; Oak Grove Auto Salvage
Louisiana; *Ponchatoula*; Fannaly's Auto Exchange
Maryland; *Finksburg*; Vogt Parts Barn
    Mount Airy; Mt Airy Auto Wrecking Inc
Massachusetts; *Sturbridge*; Curboy's Used Auto Parts
    Wrentham; Tosy's Ford Mustang Farm
Missouri; *Goodman*; J & M Vintage Auto
Montana; *Cut Bank*; Jim's Auto
    Glendive; Glendive Auto Parts
    Helena; Al & Buzz Rose Wrecking Yard
Nebraska; *Holdrege*; Richardson & Son Auto Wrecking
    Scottsbluff; Goodro Auto Salvage
Nevada; *Las Vegas*; Larry's Auto Wrecking
New Hampshire; *Andover*; Andover Auto Wrecking
    Canaan; Parts of the Past
New Mexico; *Alamogordo*; North Fifty-Four Salvage
New York; *Albany*; Jim Meisner Auto Parts
    Bellmore; Used Auto Glass
    Buffalo; Carpenters Auto Parts Inc
    Cold Spring; Cold Spring Auto Parts
    Ithaca; Danby Motors
    Mohawk; Reardon Enterprises
    Yorkshire; Tidds Auto Parts
North Dakota; *Park River*; Porter Auto Repair & Salvage
    Wishek; Martell's Salvage
Ohio; *Columbus*; All City Auto Wrecking
    Frazeysburg; Minnich Auto Wrecking
    Lima; T & T Auto Parts
Oklahoma; *Aline*; Bud's Salvage
    Grove; Ten & Fifty Nine Salvage
    Sand Springs; Grigsby's Auto Salvage
    Stillwater; Hauf Auto Supply
Oregon; *Coos Bay*; Greenacres Auto Wrecking
Pennsylvania; *Erie*; Carl's Auto Parts
    West Sunbury; Renicks Used Auto Parts
South Dakota; *Gettysburg*; A G Sales & salvage
    Rapid City; A & A Auto Salvage
        Moore's Auto Salvage
    Sturgis; Jim's Auto Salvage
        Westside Dismantlers
    Winner; Wayne's Auto Salvage
Texas; *Kaufman*; Henderson Auto Parts
    Wellington; South Side Salvage
Virginia; *Lanexa*; Philbates Auto Wrecking Inc
    Mount Crawford; Harold Ludholtz's
Washington; *Centralia*; Grasser Auto Wrecking
    Shelton; Mason County Salvage
    Spokane; Antique Auto Items
        Antique Auto Ranch
        C & T Truck Parts Inc
        Triangle Truck Parts
    Tacoma; A-1 Auto Wrecking
    Vancouver; All American Classics Inc
    Woodinville; Vintage Auto Parts
West Virginia; *Fairmont*; Morris Auto Wrecking
Wisconsin; *Arkdale*; Roller's Auto Salvage
    Camp Douglas; C L Chase Used Auto & Truck Parts
    Eland; Highway 45 Auto
    Fredonia; Auto Parts & Recycling Inc
    Hayward; Simons Enterprises Inc
    Milton; Seward Auto Salvage
    Milwaukee; B S Wisniewski
    Sturgeon Bay; C & W Auto Sales & Salvage
    Tigerton; Zeb's Salvage

Kaiser

Wisconsin; *Westfield*; Stevens Auto Wrecking
Wyoming; *Cheyenne*; Balcaen's Auto Parts

Mazda

California; *Oakley*; Foreign Auto Dismantlers
    Rancho Cordova; Mazda Auto Dismantlers
        Mazda Auto Recycling
    San Jose; Honda Heaven
    Sun Valley; Arts Auto Salvage
    Sunnyvale; A & H Auto Dismantling
Colorado; *Denver*; Mr. Mazda Inc
Florida; *Sanford*; Marc's Import Auto Salvage
Massachusetts; *West Springfield*; Auto Salvage-West Springfield
Minnesota; *Roseville*; RX7 Heaven
Washington; *Spanaway*; Roy Y Auto Wrecking

Military

Alaska; *Anchorage*; Engine & Core Supply
Arizona; *Phoenix*; Just Truck & Van
    Thatcher; Valley Auto Wrecking, Inc
California; *Oakley*; Two Friends Auto Dismantlers
    Visalia; Allied Auto Dismantling
Colorado; *Grand Junction*; American Auto Salvage
Connecticut; *North Haven*; Camerota Truck Parts
Georgia; *Dublin*; Ben Maddox Used Parts
Idaho; *Preston*; Idaho Salvage & Metals
Illinois; *Mendota*; Sprowls Body Shop & Auto
    Plainfield; Speicher & Gaylord Auto Wrckrs
    Tonica; Ace Auto Salvage
Kansas; *Enterprise*; Enterprise Auto Salvage
    Salina; Charlie Heath West 40 Salvage
Louisiana; *Mansfield*; 175 Salvage
Maryland; *North East*; King Salvage
Minnesota; *Glenville*; Bridley Auto Salvage
    Melrose; Skunk's Auto Salvage & Part
    New London; Windy Hill Auto Parts
Mississippi; *Leland*; Rodgers Salvage Inc
    Pascagoula; Pascagoula Auto Salvage Inc
Missouri; *Doniphan*; Bargain Auto Salvage
Nevada; *Carson City*; Buena Vista Auto Recyclers
New Hampshire; *Meredith*; Royea's Auto Wrecking
New Jersey; *Freehold*; A & A Truck Parts
New Jersey; *South Plainfield*; Auto Salvage
    Whiting; J & S Auto Wreckers
New York; *Queensbury*; Ray's Salvage
Ohio; *Andover*; A Ds Auto Wrecking
    Byesville; Bartholow Auto Wrecking
    Clyde; B & K Auto Svc
    Coshocton; Nelson's Auto Wrecking
    Delaware; Colonial Automotive Recycling
    Lima; Hartman's Wrecker Svc
    Maple Heights; Deneman's Automotive
Oregon; *Cave Junction*; Phillips Auto Wrecking
    Madras; Ira's Sales & Svc
    Portland; Truck Wrecking Yard Inc
Washington; *Mount Vernon*; Farrells Auto Wrecking
    Port Angeles; K B Auto Wrecking & Towing
    Port Orchard; Airport Auto Wrecking Too
    Sedro Woolley; Art's Auto Wrecking
    Snohomish; Mid-City Towing & Wrecking
    Spokane; Art Santa Rosa's Auto & Truck
        C & T Truck Parts Inc
Wisconsin; *Camp Douglas*; C L Chase Used Auto & Truck Parts
    Eau Claire; A to Z Towing & Salvage
    Rice Lake; Bob's Auto Salvage
    Stanley; Stanley Truck Sales
Wyoming; *Cheyenne*; Lincoln Valley Auto Salvage
    Newcastle; Outback Salvage

Muscle Cars including GTO & Firebird

Alabama; *Calera*; Graham's Camaro & Firebird
    Mobile; Camaro Heaven
Arizona; *Phoenix*; All Mustang All Camaro

Muscle Cars including GTO & Firebird

Arizona; *Phoenix*; Big Daddy's Auto Salvage
    Precision Auto Parts
    Reeves Auto Wrecking
Arkansas; *Springdale*; Horn's Auto Salvage
California; *Bakersfield*; A & A Auto Wrecking
    Delano; Millikin & Sons Auto Wrecking
    Los Angeles; GTO Auto Glass
    Placentia; Dave's Placentia Auto Wrecking
    Rancho Cordova; Chevy Sports Recycling
    Rancho Chevy Recycling
    San Jose; GM Sports Salvage
    San Leandro; Phelp's Auto Wreckers
    Stockton; Red Wagon Recycling
    Sun Valley; Memory Lane Collector Car Dismantlers
    Turlock; Turlock Auto Wreckers
Colorado; *Englewood*; Fair Auto & Truck Wrecking
    Lamar; Woller Auto Parts
Delaware; *New Castle*; Breitenbach Towing & Auto Salvage
Florida; *Clearwater*; Doc & Bill's Auto Salvage
    Ft Lauderdale; Bailey's Camaros & Firebirds
    Hollywood; Pre 73 Pontiac Sales
    Rockledge; Lucky's Auto Salvage
Maryland; *Frederick*; Potomac Classic Pontiac
Massachusetts; *East Bridgewater*; A Regal Used Auto Parts
Nevada; *Sparks*; D & S Auto & Truck Dismantlers
New Hampshire; *Rochester*; Camaro Heaven
New York; *Jamaica*; Liberty Auto Wrecking
    Lindenhurst; Albin Auto Salvage
    J & C Auto Salvage
    Tri-State Auto
    Webster; Elmer's Auto Parts
North Carolina; *Fayetteville*; Diffin's Auto Salvage
Ohio; *Bedford*; Berger Scrap Metal Auto Parts
    Elyria; Universal Joint Auto Wrecking
Oklahoma; *Oklahoma City*; American Camaro & Firebird
Pennsylvania *Gettysburg*; Road Rangers Towing
South Carolina; *Lexington*; Brock's Camaro & Firebird Prts
Virginia; *Louisa*; Dave's Ferncliff Auto Parts
    Staunton; Byrd's Wrecking Yard
    Tabb; Bottom Line Salvage
Washington; *Bothell*; American & Japanese Cascade
    Tacoma; Ikan Auto
    Vancouver; All American Classics Inc
West Virginia; *Leon*; Schoonover Auto Salvage

Mustang

Alabama; *Mobile*; Camaro Heaven
    Moulton; Larry's Mustang Supply
Arizona; *Glendale*; AAA United Auto Parts
    Phoenix; AAA Broadway Auto Parts
    All Mustang All Camaro
    Arizona Mustang Mart
    Tucson; Sanford & Sons Auto & Truck
Arkansas; *Bentonville*; Gillis Used Cars & Auto Salvage
    Conway; Potter Salvage
    Rose Bud; Matthews Mustang Parts & Svc
California; *Bakersfield*; A & A Auto Wrecking
    Corning; All-Star Auto Wrecking
    El Cajon; Mustang Auto & Classic Cars
    Fontana; Mustang Village
    Fresno; Levan Auto Body Parts
    Miro Loma; Crossroads Classic Mustang
    Modesto; Benson's Auto Dismantling
    Oakland; Cypress Salvage
    Orange; Mustang Salvage & Auto Parts
    Paramount; Mustang Country
    Placentia; Dave's Placentia Auto Wrecking
    Rancho Cordova; American Mustang Parts
    Santa Clara; Mustang Fever
    Stockton; Mustangs Plus
Colorado; *Aurora*; Colorado Mustang Specialists
    Lamar; Woller Auto Parts
Florida; *Palm City*; Florida Mustang
Georgia; *Byron*; Mustang Central

Mustang

Georgia; *Clarkston*; Prestige Mustangs
  Cussetta; Cusseta Auto Salvage
  Thomaston; Stallings Used Auto Parts
Idaho; *Kuma*; Mustang Idaho
Indiana; *Greenfield*; Jack & Son's Auto Salvage
  Valpraiso; Metro Auto Parts
Kansas; *Lawrence*; Mid-America Auto Recycling
Louisiana; *Chalmette*; L & L Auto Salvage
Maine; *Oxford*; Lashin's Auto Sales & Salvage
Maryland; *Westminster*; Jones Auto & Salvage
Massachusetts; *Wrentham*; Tosy's Ford Mustang Farm
New Hampshire; *Sullivan*; Northeast Ford & Mustang Parts
New Jersey; *Pennsauken*; Certi-Fit Body Parts
New York; *Monticello*; Fast Eddie's Auto Wreckers
North Carolina; *Kenansville*; Rackley Auto Salvage
Ohio; *Dayton*; Mr Mustang
Oklahoma; *Choctaw*; Dollar & Salvage
  Okay; McDaniel Salvage & Wrecking
Oregon; *Albany*; R & S Mustang Supply
  Portland; Bob's Ford Parts
    Division Street Auto Wrecking
    Mustang Specialties
    Rose City Mustang Ltd
Pennsylvania; *Shamokin*; Winnick's Auto Sales & Parts
Rhode Island; *Ashaway*; Ocean State Ford Mustang
Texas; *San Antonio*; All Foreign Auto Parts Inc
  Temple; Action Auto Recyclers
Vermont; *Bennington*; Le Blanc's Auto Salvage
Virginia; *Ashland*; Old Dominion Mustang
  Chesapeake; Johnson's Mustang & Truck Parts
Washington; *Eatonville*; Mustang Ranch
  Tacoma; Mustang Empire
  Woodinville; Wild West Mustang Ranch
Wyoming; *Casper*; Terry's Salvage

Nash

Alabama; *Andalusia*; Morris Auto Salvage
Arizona; *Casa Grande*; Wisemans Auto Salvage
  Huachuca City; Fort Auto Parts & Wrecker Service
  Phoenix; Askren Auto Parts
    Desert Valley Auto Parts
  Thatcher; Valley Auto Wrecking, Inc
  Wilcox; Wilcox Wrecking Yard
California; *Fresno*; Globe Antique Auto Parts
    Romo Auto Wrecking & Towing
  Hesperia; Cox Auto Salvage
  Mariposa; Pearson's Auto Dismantling
  Placentia; Atwood Auto Wrecking
  Porterville; Cemo Motor Sales & Auto Wrecking
  Redding; Gustafson's Auto Wrecking
  Sun Valley; Memory Lane Collector Car Dismantlers
Colorado; *Capulin*; Ernest's Auto Wrecking
  Craig; Ikes Automatic Transmission
  Dacono; Elliotts Auto Parts
  Erie; Speedway Auto Wrecking
  Fountain; Santa Fe Automotive
  Pueblo; West 29th Auto Inc
Connecticut; *Barkhansted*; Stewart's Used Auto Parts
  Plymouth; Mt Tobe Auto Parts
Florida; *Sarasota*; Collector's Choice Antique Auto
Georgia; *White*; Old Car City USA
Idaho; *Caldwell*; Hopkins Antique Autos & Parts
  Grangeville; Dale Resuce Towing
  Indian Valley; Morris Antique & Classic Cars & Parts
  Wendell; L & L Classic Auto
Illinois; *Lockport*; Southwest Auto Salvage
Indiana; *New Waverly*; Canfield Motors
Iowa; *Allison*; Ron's Auto Salvage
  Burlington; Plank Road Salvage
  Fort Dodge; Frank's Auto & Truck Salvage
    Netlands Auto-Truck Salvage
Kansas; *Coffeyville*; Purkey's Auto Salvage
  Columbus; Larison's Classics
  Dodge City; Stapleton Salvage

Nash

Kansas; *Junction City*; Easy Jack & Sons Antique Auto
    Peru; Peru Auto Wrecking
    Valley Center; Watkins Auto Salvage Inc
Kentucky; *Union*; Boone Country Auto & Truck Slvg
Maryland; *Finksburg*; Vogt Parts Barn
    Frederick; Schroyers Recycling Center
    Mount Airy; Mt Airy Auto Wrecking Inc
    Smithsburg; Elwood's Auto Exchange
Massachusetts; *Sturbridge*; Curboy's Used Auto Parts
Minnesota; *Austin*; Crews Auto Salvage
    Glenville; Bridley Auto Salvage
    Newport; Bill's Auto Parts
Missouri; *Goodman*; J & M Vintage Auto
Montana; *Arlee*; Kelly's Auto Salvage
    Butte; Zimp's Enterprises
    Cut Bank; Jim's Auto
    Glendive; Glendive Auto Parts
    Great Falls; S & C Repair-Wrecker Svc
Montana; *Helena*; Al & Buzz Rose Wrecking Yard
    Libby; Jim's Auto Wrecking
Nebraska; *Blue Springs*; Antique Cars, Trucks & Parts
    Elmwood; Eastern Nebraska Auto Sales
New Hampshire; *Canaan*; Parts of the Past
    Louden; Lane's Garage & Auto Body
New Jersey; *Avenel*; Riverside Auto Parts
    Berlin; Albion Auto Parts
    Toms River; Tice Brothers
    Washington; Studebaker Sanctuary
New Mexico; *Alamogordo*; North Fifty-Four Salvage
    Wild Bills Auto Wrecking
    Albuquerque; Chavez Auto Parts
    Roswell; Diamond Auto
    Tucumcari; Quay Valley Salvage
New York; *Albany*; Jim Meisner Auto Parts
    Bellmore; Used Auto Glass
    Buffalo; Carpenters Auto Parts Inc
    Speonk; Outpost Automotive Inc
    Weedsport; Nash Auto Parts
    Yorkshire; Tidds Auto Parts
North Carolina; *Trinity*; Prospect Auto Parts
North Dakota; *Park River*; Porter Auto Repair & Salvage
    Wishek; Martell's Salvage
Ohio; *Columbus*; All City Auto Wrecking
    Crestling; Moyer's Auto Wrecking
    Washington Court House; Cartwright Salvage
    Youngstown; Schulte Auto Wrecking
Oklahoma; *Aline*; Bud's Salvage
    Earlsboro; Willie's Salvage
    Grove; Ten & Fifty Nine Salvage
    Stillwater; Hauf Auto Supply
Oregon; *Albany*; Loops Auto Wrecking & Salvage
    Aurora; Aurora Wreckers & Recyclers
Pennsylvania; *Glenville*; Ed Lucke's Auto Parts
    Pine Grove; Klinger's Used Auto Sales
South Carolina; *Waterloo*; Burdette Auto Salvage Svc
South Dakota; *Rapid City*; A & A Auto Salvage
    Moore's Auto Salvage
    Sturgis; Westside Dismantlers
    Winner; Wayne's Auto Salvage
    Yankton; Merrigan's Auto Salvage
Texas; *Bertram*; David's Auto Parts
    Wellington; South Side Salvage
Utah; *Ogden*; B & R Old Car Parts
    Salt Lake City; S & B Foreign Car Parts
    W W Auto Wrecking & Sales
    Tooele; Moore Auto Shop
Virginia; *Lanexa*; Philbates Auto Wrecking Inc
    Mount Crawford; Harold Ludholtz's
Washington; *Belfair*; Belfair Truck & Auto Wrecking
    Centralia; Grasser Auto Wrecking
    Pasco; Tommy's Steel & Salvage
    Spokane; Antique Auto Items
    Antique Auto Ranch
    Woodinville; Vintage Auto Parts
Wisconsin; *Arkdale*; Roller's Auto Salvage

341

Nash

Wisconsin; *Boscobel*; Golden Sands Salvage
  Cadott; Glenz Auto Salvage
  Camp Douglas; C L Chase Used Auto & Truck Parts
  Hayward; Simons Enterprises Inc
  Kenosha; Schneider's Auto Sales & Parts
  Milton; Seward Auto Salvage
  Milwaukee; B S Wisniewski
  Sturgeon Bay; C & W Auto Sales & Salvage
Wyoming; *Cheyenne*; Balcaen's Auto Parts
    Rhodes Towing & Auto Salvage
  Newcastle; Black Hills Antique Auto

Packard

Alabama; *Fultondale*; Best Auto Parts & Salvage
Arizona; *Casa Grande*; Wisemans Auto Salvage
  Dudleyville; Desert Air Salvage
  Golden Valley; Dans Auto Salvage
  Holbrook; Kachina Auto Salvage
  Huachuca City; Fort Auto Parts & Wrecker Service
  Maricopa; Hidden Valley Auto Parts
  Phoenix; Desert Valley Auto Parts
  Show Low; Show Low Auto Sales & Wrecking
Arkansas; *Bradford*; Vintage Auto Salvage
  Springdale; Horn's Auto Salvage
California; *Elk Grove*; Elk Grove Auto Dismantlers
  Fresno; Globe Antique Auto Parts
    Romo Auto Wrecking & Towing
  Hesperia; Cox Auto Salvage
  Modesto; Farriester Auto Wreckers
  Paso Robles; Paso Robles Auto Wrecking
  Placentia; Atwood Auto Wrecking
  Pomona; A-Car Auto Wrecking
  Redding; Gustafson's Auto Wrecking
  Sun Valley; Memory Lane Collector Car Dismantlers
    Miller's Auto Dismantling
Colorado; *Alamosa*; L & M Auto
  Craig; Ikes Automatic Transmission
  Dacono; Elliotts Auto Parts
  Englewood; Svigel's Auto Parts
  Erie; Erie Auto Wreckers
    Speedway Auto Wrecking
  Grand Junction; American Auto Salvage
  Pueblo; Bonnie's Car Crushers
  Rifle; Spangler's Auto Salvage
  Salida; South Side Salvage
  Windsor; Martin Supply & Salvage Yard
Connecticut; *Plymouth*; Mt Tobe Auto Parts
Florida; *Lake City*; Sunrise Auto Sales & Salvage
  Sarasota; Collector's Choice Antique Auto
Georgia; *White*; Old Car City USA
Idaho; *Caldwell*; Hopkins Antique Autos & Parts
  Hayden; Pegasus Auto Wrecking
  Hayden Lake; Classic Auto Parts
  Lewiston; Central Crade Auto Parts
  Wendell; L & L Classic Auto
Illinois; *Braidwood*; Hilemans Motor Mart
  Lockport; Southwest Auto Salvage
Indiana; *New Waverly*; Canfield Motors
  Peru; Wright's Auto & Truck Salvage
  Richmond; Junction Auto
Iowa; *Allison*; Ron's Auto Salvage
  Des Moines; Yaw's Auto Salvage
  Fayette; Lau Auto Repair & Salvage
  Fort Dodge; Frank's Auto & Truck Salvage
    Netlands Auto-Truck Salvage
  Keokuk; E & E Auto & Truck Salvage
  Palo; Hayes Salvage
Kansas; *Coffeyville*; Purkey's Auto Salvage
  Dodge City; Stapleton Salvage
  Junction City; Easy Jack & Sons Antique Auto
  Kansas City; Muncie Auto Salvage Inc
Kentucky; *Union*; Boone Country Auto & Truck Slvg
Louisiana; *Ponchatoula*; Fannaly's Auto Exchange
Maine; *Caribou*; Beaulieu's Auto Salvage

342

Packard

Maine; *Monmouth*; Phil's Garage & Salvage Yard
Maryland; *Finksburg*; Vogt Parts Barn
    Hampstead; Smith Brother's Auto Parts
    Mount Airy; Mt Airy Auto Wrecking Inc
    Smithsburg; Elwood's Auto Exchange
Massachusetts; *Deerfield*; East Deerfield Auto Wrecking
    Sturbridge; Curboy's Used Auto Parts
    Wrentham; Tosy's Ford Mustang Farm
Michigan; *Clifford*; La Blanc Auto Salvage
    Fostoria; Bob's Auto Parts
Minnesota; *Glenville*; Bridley Auto Salvage
    New London; Windy Hill Auto Parts
    Silver Lake; R & R Auto & Truck Salvage
Mississippi; *Magnolia*; Sandifer Auto Salvage
Missouri; *Goodman*; J & M Vintage Auto
    Kansas City; Little Wills Auto Salvage
Montana; *Arlee*; Kelly's Auto Salvage
    Cut Bank; Jim's Auto
    Glendive; Glendive Auto Parts
    Great Falls; S & C Repair-Wrecker Svc
    Helena; Al & Buzz Rose Wrecking Yard
Nebraska; *Alliance*; Taylor's Auto Repair & Salvage
Nevada; *Las Vegas*; Larry's Auto Wrecking
New Hampshire; *Canaan*; Parts of the Past
    Louden; Lane's Garage & Auto Body
New Jersey; *Berlin*; Albion Auto Parts
    New Egypt; Price's Auto Recyclers
    Washington; Studebaker Sanctuary
New Mexico; *Alamogordo*; North Fifty-Four Salvage
          Southside Salvage & Used Cars
          Wild Bills Auto Wrecking
New York; *Albany*; Jim Meisner Auto Parts
    Bellmore; Used Auto Glass
    Buffalo; Carpenters Auto Parts Inc
    Cold Spring; Cold Spring Auto Parts
    Ithaca; Danby Motors
    Mohawk; Reardon Enterprises
    Speonk; Outpost Automotive Inc
    Waverly; Williams Auto Salvage
    Weedsport; Nash Auto Parts
    Yorkshire; Tidds Auto Parts
North Dakota; *Park River*; Porter Auto Repair & Salvage
    West Fargo; Hazer's Auto & Truck Salvage
Ohio; *Columbus*; All City Auto Wrecking
    Crestling; Moyer's Auto Wrecking
    Frazeysburg; Minnich Auto Wrecking
    Lima; T & T Auto Parts
    Windham; A-1 Auto Wrecking & Sales
    Youngstown; Schulte Auto Wrecking
Oklahoma; *Aline*; Bud's Salvage
    Chandler; Country Auto
    Earlsboro; Willie's Salvage
    Grove; Ten & Fifty Nine Salvage
    Sand Springs; Grigsby's Auto Salvage
    Shawnee; S & S Auto
    Stillwater; Hauf Auto Supply
Oregon; *Albany*; Loops Auto Wrecking & Salvage
    Aurora; Aurora Wreckers & Recyclers
Pennsylvania; *Butler*; James Winters Auto Wrecking
    Carlisle; Failors Salvage Yard
    Fayetteville; Beechers Auto Salvage Inc
    Glenville; Ed Lucke's Auto Parts
    Johnstown; Auto Wreckers
South Carolina; *Easley*; Bruce O'Shields Used Auto Parts
South Dakota; *Box Elder*; Lefler Auto Salvage
    Rapid City; A & A Auto Salvage
          Moore's Auto Salvage
    Winner; Wayne's Auto Salvage
Texas; *Bertram*; David's Auto Parts
    Kaufman; Henderson Auto Parts
    Wellington; South Side Salvage
Utah; *Salt Lake City*; King Size Auto & Truck
          Special Editions
          W W Auto Wrecking & Sales
Virginia; *Lanexa*; Philbates Auto Wrecking Inc

343

Packard

Virginia; *Mount Crawford*; Harold Ludholtz's
Washington; *Belfair*; Belfair Truck & Auto Wrecking
    Centralia; Grasser Auto Wrecking
    Spokane; Antique Auto Items
             Antique Auto Ranch
    Tenino; Columbia Industries Auto Repair
    Vancouver; All American Classics Inc
    Woodinville; Vintage Auto Parts
    Yelm; Yelm Auto Wrecking & Repair
West Virginia; *Core*; Ben's Auto Wrecking
    Elkview; Antique Auto Parts
Wisconsin; *Arkdale*; Roller's Auto Salvage
    Boscobel; Golden Sands Salvage
    Cadott; Glenz Auto Salvage
    Camp Douglas; C L Chase Used Auto & Truck Parts
    Eland; Highway 45 Auto
Wisconsin; *Hayward*; Simons Enterprises Inc
    Milton; Seward Auto Salvage
    Milwaukee; B S Wisniewski
    Sturgeon Bay; C & W Auto Sales & Salvage
    Tigerton; Zeb's Salvage
    Westfield; Stevens Auto Wrecking
Wyoming; *Buffalo*; Mr. Rs Auto Salvage`
    Cheyenne; Balcaen's Auto Parts
             Rhodes Towing & Auto Salvage
Gillette; Nanneman Bros

Saab - Volvo

Alabama; *New Market*; North Alabama Used Auto Parts
    Thomasville; Larrimore's Salvage
Arizona; *Glendale*; JBS Imports
    Phoenix; All European Models
             Benrich Auto Wrecking
             Hirsch Industries Inc
             Ray & Bobs Truck Salvage
             Sports Car Recycling
    Tucson; Revolvstore Volvo Parts
Arkansas; *Vilonia*; Volvos Only
California; *Chula Vista*; RC Import Auto Recycling
    El Cajon; Autotech
    Gardena; Aaron Auto Parts
             Thomas Auto Salvage
    Hayward; East Bay Auto Dismantling
    Highland; Volvo Express Tom's Enterprises
    Irvine; Volvo Express
    Rancho Cordova; Dad's Auto Dismantling
             Volvo & Saab Auto Dismantlers
    Redding; Gustafson's Auto Wrecking
    Riverside; Honda & Foreign Parts
    Sacramento; Sweden Auto Warehouse
California; *San Jose*; A-German Auto Parts & Svc
             American Import Auto Dismantlers
             Bay City Auto Wreckers
             European Specialty Auto Dismantling
             Saab & Volvo Auto Wreckers
    Santa Ana; Certified Auto Salvage
    Santa Clara; A & A Foreign Auto Wreckers
             Volpar Inc
    Santa Cruz; Specialized Auto Parts
    Santa Rosa; Faraudos Auto Dismantlers
    Stockton; Ben's Auto Dismantlers
    Sun Valley; Statewide Auto Wrecking
Colorado; *Denver*; Mile Hi Body Shop Inc
             Tams #1 Imports
             Volvoparts Inc
Florida; *Boca Raton*; Programma Tools
    Reddick; Chuck's Used Parts
Kansas; *Kansas City*; Griffith Foreign Car Salvage
Maine; *Gorham*; Gorham Used Auto Parts Co
New Jersey; *Toms River*; Toms River Auto Recyclers
    Washington; Kober's Used Truck Parts
North Carolina; *Clayton*; Johnston County Auto Salvage
Ohio; *Windham*; A-1 Auto Wrecking & Sales
Oregon; *Shady Cove*; European Auto-Winch-Em Towing

Saab - Volvo

South Carolina; *Greer*; A-1 Import Salvage Inc
Texas; *Houston*; Volvo Parts Independent
Utah; *Ogden*; D & B Foreign
Virginia; *Chesapeake*; Edmonds Corner Salvage Yard
    King George; Accurate Foreign Car Parts Inc
Washington; *Arlington*; Campbell Nelson Auto Wrecking
    Edmonds; Campbell Nelson Volkswagen
    Everett; Shop Nine - TJ Martin Saab Repair
    Seattle; Northern European Auto Recyclers

Studebaker

Alabama; *Attalla*; Gibbs Junk Yard
    Daleville; Rodgers Used Parts
    Fultondale; Best Auto Parts & Salvage
Alaska; *Palmer*; Boot Hill Auto Salvage
Arizona; *Apache Junction*; Franks Auto & Truck Salvage
    Casa Grande; Wisemans Auto Salvage
    Glendale; J & J Salvage CO
    Golden Valley; A 1 Auto & Wrecking
    Holbrook; Kachina Auto Salvage
    Huachuca City; Fort Auto Parts & Wrecker Service
    Maricopa; Hidden Valley Auto Parts
    Parker; Debs Garage
    Phoenix; All Auto & Truck
        Askren Auto Parts
        Boatwrights Wrecking Yard
        Desert Valley Auto Parts
    Wilcox; Wilcox Wrecking Yard
Arkansas; *Bradford*; Vintage Auto Salvage
    Centerton; 102 Towing & Salvage
    Fordyce; Big Bens Used Cars & Salvage
    Mc Neil; B & J Used Car & Truck Parts
    Springdale; Horn's Auto Salvage
California; *Bishop*; Mingo's Automotive
    California City; Whites Auto Dismantling
    Fontana; Inland Auto Wreckers
        J B Autowrecking
    Fresno; Dan's Auto Parts & Wrecking
        Globe Antique Auto Parts
        Romo Auto Wrecking & Towing
    Grass Valley; Kilroy's Auto Dismantling
    Hesperia; Cox Auto Salvage
    Mariposa; Pearson's Auto Dismantling
    Modesto; Holt Auto Wrecking
        Holt Auto Wrecking
    Paso Robles; Paso Robles Auto Wrecking
    Placentia; Atwood Auto Wrecking
    Pomona; A-Car Auto Wrecking
    Porterville; Cemo Motor Sales & Auto Wrecking
    Redding; Gustafson's Auto Wrecking
    San Bernardino; Downtown Auto Wrecking
        U & I Auto Wrecking
    Shafter; Santa Fe Dismantling
    Stockton; Mathis Auto Wreckers & Parts
    Sun Valley; Memory Lane Collector Car Dismantlers
        Miller's Auto Dismantling
    Tulare; Tulare Auto Wrecking
    Yermo; D & M Auto Truck & RV Repair
Colorado; *Alamosa*; L & M Auto
    Capulin; Ernest's Auto Wrecking
    Craig; Ikes Automatic Transmission
    Dacono; Elliotts Auto Parts
    Durango; Lon's Automotive Inc
    Englewood; Svigel's Auto Parts
    Erie; Speedway Auto Wrecking
    Fountain; Santa Fe Automotive
    Grand Junction; American Auto Salvage
    Greeley; A & S Salvage & Towing
        A to Z Auto Salvage
    Pueblo; Bonnie's Car Crushers
        West 29th Auto Inc
    Rifle; Spangler's Auto Salvage
    Salida; South Side Salvage
    Windsor; Martin Supply & Salvage Yard

Studebaker

Connecticut; *Barkhansted*; Stewart's Used Auto Parts
    Plymouth; Mt Tobe Auto Parts
Florida; *Lake City*; Sunrise Auto Sales & Salvage
    Sarasota; Collector's Choice Antique Auto
    Umatilla; Umatilla Auto Salvage
Georgia; *Auburn*; Collins Auto Salvage
    Monroe; Hodges Salvage Yard & Wrecker
    Montezuma; Martin's Auto Salvage
    White; Old Car City USA
Idaho; *Caldwell*; B & T Auto Salvage
    Hopkins Antique Autos & Parts
    Grangeville; Dale Resuce Towing
    Hayden; Pegasus Auto Wrecking
    Heyburn; Kelley Truck & Auto Salvage
    Idaho Falls; Charlie's Auto Recycling
    Indian Valley; Morris Antique & Classic Cars & Parts
    Kuma; Mustang Idaho
    Montpelier; Hennings Auto Salvage
    Nampa; All Hours Auto Salvage
    Weiser; Myers Auto Salvage
    Wendell; L & L Classic Auto
Illinois; *Braidwood*; Hilemans Motor Mart
    Chebanse; Thompson Auto Wreckers
    Lockport; Southwest Auto Salvage
Indiana; *New Waverly*; Canfield Motors
    Peru; Wright's Auto & Truck Salvage
    Richmond; Junction Auto
Iowa; *Des Moines*; Yaw's Auto Salvage
    Fort Dodge; Frank's Auto & Truck Salvage
    Netlands Auto-Truck Salvage
    Garber; Sear's Auto Salvage
    Iowa City; Boot Hill Auto Recycling
    Russell; Pollard Salvage
    Spirit Lake; Hawn's Salvage Co
Kansas; *Chase*; Patterson's Auto Salvage
    Coffeyville; Purkey's Auto Salvage
    Danville; Bob Lent Motor Shop
    Dodge City; Stapleton Salvage
    Inman; Jim's Auto Sales
    Junction City; Easy Jack & Sons Antique Auto
    Liberal; Friesen Salvage One
Kentucky; *Campbellsville*; Nolley auto Sales
    Union; Boone Country Auto & Truck Slvg
Louisiana; *Ponchatoula*; Fannaly's Auto Exchange
Maine; *Caribou*; Beaulieu's Auto Salvage
Maryland; *Finksburg*; Vogt Parts Barn
    Hampstead; Smith Brother's Auto Parts
    Mount Airy; Mt Airy Auto Wrecking Inc
    Smithsburg; Elwood's Auto Exchange
Massachusetts; *Bellingham*; John's Used Auto Parts
    Deerfield; East Deerfield Auto Wrecking
    Sturbridge; Curboy's Used Auto Parts
    West Bridgewater; Perry's Auto Sales & Parts
    Wrentham; Tosy's Ford Mustang Farm
Michigan; *Clifford*; La Blanc Auto Salvage
    Fostoria; Bob's Auto Parts
    Smiths Creek; Dave's Auto & Truck Salvage
Minnesota; *Austin*; Crews Auto Salvage
    Crookston; Crookston Auto Salvage
    Glenville; Bridley Auto Salvage
    Milaca; Freyholtz Auto Salvage
    New London; Windy Hill Auto Parts
    Newport; Bill's Auto Parts
    Sleepy Eye; Sleepy Eye Salvage Co
    Winona; Papenfuss Salvage
Mississippi; *Magnolia*; Sandifer Auto Salvage
Missouri; *Chillicothe*; Nick Anderson Auto Salvage
    Goodman; J & M Vintage Auto
    Kansas City; Little Wills Auto Salvage
Montana; *Arlee*; Kelly's Auto Salvage
    Columbia Falls; American Auto Towing & Salvage
    Cut Bank; Jim's Auto
    Glendive; Glendive Auto Parts
    Great Falls; S & C Repair-Wrecker Svc
    Helena; Al & Buzz Rose Wrecking Yard

Studebaker

Montana; *Libby*; Jim's Auto Wrecking
    Missoula; Missoula Auto Salvage
    Opportunity; S & S Salvage
    Somers; Flathead Salvage & Storage
Nebraska; *Alliance*; Taylor's Auto Repair & Salvage
    Blue Springs; Antique Cars, Trucks & Parts
    Elmwood; Eastern Nebraska Auto Sales
    Fairbury; Paneitz Salvage
    Holdrege; Richardson & Son Auto Wrecking
    Malcolm; Walkies Auto Salvage
    Scottsbluff; Goodro Auto Salvage
New Hampshire; *Canaan*; Parts of the Past
    Louden; Lane's Garage & Auto Body
New Jersey; *Berlin*; Albion Auto Parts
    Toms River; Tice Brothers
    Washington; Studebaker Sanctuary
    Westfield; John Bosco Enterprises
New Mexico; *Alamogordo*; North Fifty-Four Salvage
    Southside Salvage & Used Cars
    Wild Bills Auto Wrecking
    Albuquerque; Chavez Auto Parts
    Clovis; Wholesale Wrecking
    Kirtland; Gilmores Truck & Auto Salvage
    Tijeras; Route 66 Reutillization
    Tucumcari; Quay Valley Salvage
New York; *Albany*; Jim Meisner Auto Parts
    Bellmore; Used Auto Glass
    Buffalo; Carpenters Auto Parts Inc
    Center Moriches; Moriches Used Auto Parts
    Cold Spring; Cold Spring Auto Parts
    Ithaca; Danby Motors
    Newfane; Newfane Auto Parts
    Patchogue; Wards Used Auto Parts
    Sanborn; A Able Auto Wrecking
    Speonk; Outpost Automotive Inc
    Weedsport; Nash Auto Parts
    Yorkshire; Tidds Auto Parts
North Carolina; *Elm City*; Cox Auto Salvage
    Robersonville; Jim's Auto & Salvage
    West Jefferson; Barkers Automotive & Salvage
North Dakota; *New Town*; LA Wrecking/Salvage
    Park River; Porter Auto Repair & Salvage
    West Fargo; Hazer's Auto & Truck Salvage
    Wishek; Martell's Salvage
Ohio; *Columbus*; All City Auto Wrecking
    Crestling; Moyer's Auto Wrecking
    Lima; Hartman's Wrecker Svc
    Salem; Hilltop Auto Wrecking
    Youngstown; Schulte Auto Wrecking
Oklahoma; *Aline*; Bud's Salvage
    Chandler; Country Auto
    Earlsboro; Willie's Salvage
    Grove; Ten & Fifty Nine Salvage
    Kiowa; Larry's Auto & Truck Salvage
    Sand Springs; Grigsby's Auto Salvage
    Shawnee; S & S Auto
    Stillwater; Hauf Auto Supply
    Tecumseh; Rath's Auto Salvage
Oregon; *Albany*; Loops Auto Wrecking & Salvage
    Aurora; Aurora Wreckers & Recyclers
    Bend; Bend Salvage & Auto Wrecking
    Tired-Iron
    Canby; South Canby Auto Wreckers
    Springfield; Springfield Auto Recyclers Inc
Pennsylvania; *Butler*; Soose Auto Wrecking
    Columbia; Earl & Jack's Auto Parts
    Enon Valley; Feezle Auto Wrecking
    Erie; Carl's Auto Parts
    Glenville; Ed Lucke's Auto Parts
    Johnstown; Auto Wreckers
    Pine Grove; Klinger's Used Auto Sales
    West Sunbury; Renicks Used Auto Parts
South Carolina; *Easley*; Bruce O'Shields Used Auto Parts
    Waterloo; Burdette Auto Salvage Svc
South Dakota; *Armour*; Dakota Studebaker Parts

347

Studebaker

South Dakota; *Box Elder*; Lefler Auto Salvage
　　Gettysburg; A G Sales & salvage
　　Mitchell; Dakota Salvage
　　Rapid City; A & A Auto Salvage
　　　　　　Moore's Auto Salvage
　　Sturgis; Jim's Auto Salvage
　　Winner; Wayne's Auto Salvage
Texas; *Bertram*; David's Auto Parts
　　Elm Mott; Elm Mott Auto Salvage
　　Gainesville; Wayne Gilbert Auto Salvage
　　Kaufman; Henderson Auto Parts
　　Wellington; South Side Salvage
Utah; *Nephi*; Nephi Auto Wrecking & Towing
　　Ogden; B & R Old Car Parts
　　Salt Lake City; Hansen Auto Wrecking
　　　　　　King Size Auto & Truck
　　　　　　Sommers Auto Wrecking
　　Sigurd; Dwights Auto Wrecking
　　Springville; Anderson's Auto Wrecking
　　Tooele; Moore Auto Shop
　　Tremonton; Hathaways Towing-Auto Salvage
Virginia; *Fredricksburg*; Fredricksburg Auto Salvage
　　Lanexa; Philbates Auto Wrecking Inc
　　Martinsville; A & B Used Auto & Truck Parts
　　Mount Crawford; Harold Ludholtz's
　　Norfolk; Antique Auto Parts
　　Ruckersville; Carr Svc Ctr
　　Staunton; Byrd's Wrecking Yard
　　Vinton; Auto Salvage & Sales Inc
Washington; *Belfair*; Belfair Truck & Auto Wrecking
　　Centralia; Grasser Auto Wrecking
　　Colville; A-Z Auto Parts
　　Everett; Ray's Auto Wrecking
　　Outlook; Tee Pee Auto Wreckers
　　Shelton; Mason County Salvage
　　Spokane; Antique Auto Items
　　　　　　Antique Auto Ranch
　　　　　　Art Santa Rosa's Auto & Truck
　　Sunnyside; Boyd's Auto Sales
　　Tacoma; A-1 Auto Wrecking
　　Tenino; Columbia Industries Auto Repair
　　Vancouver; All American Classics Inc
　　Woodinville; Vintage Auto Parts
　　Yelm; Yelm Auto Wrecking & Repair
Wisconsin; *Arkdale*; Roller's Auto Salvage
　　Boscobel; Golden Sands Salvage
　　Cadott; Glenz Auto Salvage
　　Camp Douglas; C L Chase Used Auto & Truck Parts
　　Fredonia; Auto Parts & Recycling Inc
　　Hayward; Simons Enterprises Inc
　　Milton; Seward Auto Salvage
　　Milwaukee; B S Wisniewski
　　Pulaski; Karcz Auto Salvage
　　Stanley; Stanley Truck Sales
　　Sturgeon Bay; C & W Auto Sales & Salvage
　　Tigerton; Zeb's Salvage
　　Two Rivers; Avery's Auto Salvage
　　Westfield; Stevens Auto Wrecking
West Virginia; *Elkview*; Antique Auto Parts
　　Fairmont; Morris Auto Wrecking
　　Kearneysville; A & D Auto Parts Inc
　　Leon; Schoonover Auto Salvage
Wyoming; *Buffalo*; Mr. Rs Auto Salvage`
　　Cheyenne; Action Automotive
　　　　　　Balcaen's Auto Parts
　　　　　　Rhodes Towing & Auto Salvage
　　Gillette; Nanneman Bros
　　Newcastle; Black Hills Antique Auto

Willys

Alabama; *Fultondale*; Best Auto Parts & Salvage
Alaska; *Fairbanks*; Miller Salvage Inc
　　Wasilla; Durgeloh's Truck Salvage
　　Wasilla; Knik Towing & Wrecking

Willys

Arizona; *Casa Grande*; Wisemans Auto Salvage
    Huachuca City; Fort Auto Parts & Wrecker Service
    Phoenix; Desert Valley Auto Parts
Arkansas; *Springdale*; Horn's Auto Salvage
California; *Coachella*; Desert Truck & Auto Parts
    Sun Valley; Memory Lane Collector Car Dismantlers
Colorado; *Denver*; AA Auto Parts Inc
    Durango; Lon's Automotive Inc
    Englewood; Svigel's Auto Parts
    Fountain; Santa Fe Automotive
    Grand Junction; American Auto Salvage
    Rifle; Spangler's Auto Salvage
Connecticut; *Barkhansted*; Stewart's Used Auto Parts
    Plymouth; Mt Tobe Auto Parts
Idaho; *Caldwell*; B & T Auto Salvage
    Indian Valley; Morris Antique & Classic Cars & Parts
    Lewiston; Central Crade Auto Parts
    Pinehurst; Pine Creek Wrecking & Repair
Iowa; *Allison*; Ron's Auto Salvage
Kansas; *Salina*; Central Kansas Salvage
Massachusetts; *Sturbridge*; Curboy's Used Auto Parts
    Wrentham; Tosy's Ford Mustang Farm
Michigan; *Crystal*; Crystal Mike's Salvage Yard
    Lapeer; Lapeer Auto & Truck Salvage
    North Pine River; Pine River Salvage
Minnesota; *Winona*; Papenfuss Salvage
Missouri; *Goodman*; J & M Vintage Auto
Montana; *Helena*; Al & Buzz Rose Wrecking Yard
    Libby; Jim's Auto Wrecking
    Missoula; Missoula Auto Salvage
    Opportunity; S & S Salvage
    Somers; Flathead Salvage & Storage
New Hampshire; *Canaan*; Parts of the Past
New Jersey; *Berlin*; Albion Auto Parts
New Mexico; *Roswell*; Diamond Auto
New York; *Albany*; Jim Meisner Auto Parts
    Bellmore; Used Auto Glass
    Buffalo; Carpenters Auto Parts Inc
    Center Moriches; Moriches Used Auto Parts
    Cold Spring; Cold Spring Auto Parts
    Yorkshire; Tidds Auto Parts
North Dakota; *West Fargo*; Hazer's Auto & Truck Salvage
    Wishek; Martell's Salvage
Ohio; *Columbus*; All City Auto Wrecking
    Sidney; B & B Truck & Auto Parts
    Washington Court House; Cartwright Salvage
Oklahoma; *Aline*; Bud's Salvage
    Oklahoma City; Steve's Classic Chevy & Ford
    Sand Springs; Grigsby's Auto Salvage
    Shawnee; S & S Auto
Oregon; *Aurora*; Aurora Wreckers & Recyclers
    Corvallis; Corvallis Auto Wrecking & Sls
    Norway; Norway Auto Recycling
Pennsylvania; *Columbia*; Earl & Jack's Auto Parts
    Glenville; Ed Lucke's Auto Parts
    Philadelphia; Chuck's Used Auto Parts
    Plymouth; J-L Used Auto Parts Inc
South Carolina; *Waterloo*; Burdette Auto Salvage Svc
South Dakota; *Mitchell*; Dakota Salvage
    Rapid City; A & A Auto Salvage
        Moore's Auto Salvage
    Winner; Wayne's Auto Salvage
    Yankton; Merrigan's Auto Salvage
Texas; *Kaufman*; Henderson Auto Parts
Utah; *Nephi*; Nephi Auto Wrecking & Towing
    Ogden; AAA Auto Salvage & Auto Body
    Sigurd; Dwights Auto Wrecking
Virginia; *Lanexa*; Philbates Auto Wrecking Inc
    Martinsville; A & B Used Auto & Truck Parts
    Staunton; Byrd's Wrecking Yard
Washington; *Outlook*; Tee Pee Auto Wreckers
    Snohomish; Olympic 4x4 Supply
    Spokane; Antique Auto Items
        Antique Auto Ranch
        Art Santa Rosa's Auto & Truck

Willys

Washington; *Spokane*; C & T Truck Parts Inc
Triangle Truck Parts
Woodinville; Vintage Auto Parts
Wisconsin; *Edgerton*; Newville Auto Salvage
Hayward; Simons Enterprises Inc
Tigerton; Zeb's Salvage
Westfield; Stevens Auto Wrecking
Wyoming; *Cheyenne*; Balcaen's Auto Parts
Rhodes Towing & Auto Salvage
Newcastle; Black Hills Antique Auto

Nash Healey, Richard Belveal,
Scottsdale, AZ

You may be a car nut if

You've added to
your garage 6
times and are
planning the 7th

350

1963 Mercedes Station Wagon on 1959 Chasis, Actually built in 1964
Robert Gunthrop, Mgr Onager Corp
Chula Vista, CA

NOTES

Ray's wReckingyard Roster makes a perfect gift for the car enthusiast on your shopping list. It's a must for any vehicle library or remember a second one for the glove box. We have included order forms to make it easy to order extra Ray's wReckingyard Rosters for yourself or as gifts. We will include a note with your gift acknowledging your thoughtfulness. Call for shipping costs outside US & Canada.

30s & 40s Cars
Martin Supply & Salvage Yard
Windsor, CO

For Additional Books. . . .

Please send _____ copies of *Ray's wReckingyard Roster*
If paying by Credit Card, please use exact name & address on the Card.
Indicate if a different shipping address is applicable on reverse of order form.
To:

Name Mr/Mrs/Ms_____

Address_____

City_____

State_____ Zip_____

I enclose $14.95 plus $4.95 shipping (US & Canada) for the 1st book.
For each additional book, $14.95 plus $3.95 shipping per book.
Call for shipping costs to other destinations.

Method of payment: ☐ Check or money order
        Payable to Impact Information Services
☐ MasterCard ☐ VISA ☐ Discover
Card # _ _ _ _ _ _ _ _ _ _ _ _ _ _ _ _
    Cardholder's Signature_____
        Expiration Date _____ / _____
                Month   Year

Thank you for your order. Orders are shipped
Book Rate. Please allow 10-20 working days for delivery.
For gift orders, please give mailing address on reverse side.
A gift acknowledgement will accompany the book.

Please send _____ copies of *Ray's wReckingyard Roster*
If paying by Credit Card, please use exact name & address on the Card.
Indicate if a different shipping address is applicable on reverse of order form
To:

Name Mr/Mrs/Ms_____

Address_____

City_____

State_____ Zip_____

I enclose $14.95 plus $4.95 shipping (US & Canada) for the 1st book.
For each additional book, $14.95 plus $3.95 shipping per book.
Call for shipping costs to other destinations.

Method of payment: ☐ Check or money order
        Payable to Impact Information Services
☐ MasterCard ☐ VISA ☐ Discover
Card # _ _ _ _ _ _ _ _ _ _ _ _ _ _ _ _
    Cardholder's Signature_____
        Expiration Date _____ / _____
                Month   Year

Thank you for your order. Orders are shipped
Book Rate. Please allow 10-20 working days for delivery.
For gift orders, please give mailing address on reverse side.
A gift acknowledgement will accompany the book.

Name_____

Address_____

State_____ **Zip**_____

Name_____

Address_____

State_____ **Zip**_____

Name_____

Address_____

State_____ **Zip**_____

Name_____

Address_____

State_____ **Zip**_____

Name_____

Address_____

State_____ **Zip**_____

Name_____

Address_____

State_____ **Zip**_____

Name_____

Address_____

State_____ **Zip**_____

Name_____

Address_____

State_____ **Zip**_____

Hauf's Antique & Classic Salvage
Stillwater, OK

Do you know of a yard we missed? Since we plan periodic revisions, please use these cards to add a yard to our data base. Because changes can occur, yards could be sold and policies altered since the time we contacted a yard, we ask that you, our valued readers, help by sending corrections on the postcard on the opposite page.

Additional rosters are planned for Canada and Europe. We would like to do another roster of specialty parts suppliers with new, reproduction and NOS parts as well as restoration services. If you have information related to yards outside the US or suppliers of specialty parts or services, please use these cards to send data for these businesses as well.

Please use these cards to add or correct information contained in this or future projects. Thanks for your help!

Ray's wReckingyard Roster
1042 Stallion Dr
Cheyenne, WY 82009

You may be a car nut if

The only thing your wife sees of you when you're home is feet sticking out from under your '57 Chevy

Submitted By

____

____

____

NO POSTAGE
NECESSARY
IF MAILED
IN THE
UNITED STATES

BUSINESS REPLY MAIL

FIRST-CLASS MAIL PERMIT NO. 826 CHEYENNE, WY

POSTAGE WILL BE PAID BY ADDRESSEE

RAY'S WRECKINGYARD ROSTER
IMPACT INFORMATION SERVICES, LLC
1042 STALLION DR
CHEYENNE WY 82010-0138

Submitted By

____

____

____

NO POSTAGE
NECESSARY
IF MAILED
IN THE
UNITED STATES

BUSINESS REPLY MAIL

FIRST-CLASS MAIL PERMIT NO. 826 CHEYENNE, WY

POSTAGE WILL BE PAID BY ADDRESSEE

RAY'S WRECKINGYARD ROSTER
IMPACT INFORMATION SERVICES, LLC
1042 STALLION DR
CHEYENNE WY 82010-0138

Mail In Info Card:

Correction _____   Addition _____

Wrecking Yard Name _____

Address _____

City, State Zip _____

Phone # _____ Fax _____

800 _____ e-mail/web _____

Does the yard: Take Credit Cards _____ Ship Parts _____ Parts Locator Service _____

Let Cust. Remove Parts _____ Let Cust. Browse _____ Warehouse Parts _____

Staff Remove Parts _____ Have Shop _____

Size of Yard _____ acres, or _____ number of vehicles: Open: Sat. or Sun.

Is this a Late Model ('90+) _____ Late Vintage ('70-89) _____ Vintage (Pre '70) _____

Domestic ___ Foreign ___ Pickups ___ 4x4 ___ Truck (over 1 ton) ___ Const./Indust. _____

Farm _____ Military _____ Bus _____ Motorhome _____ Motorcycle _____ Boat _____

Years covered: Oldest _____ Newest _____ Have Inventory List _____

Makes in Yard: B3 ___ AMC ___ Jp ___ IH ___ Hd ___ St ___ Pk ___ Ns ___ Wy ___ Ks
___

Fr ___ Cr ___ VW ___ Euro/British ___ Japan/Asian ___ Other_____

Pre-War _____ Other Makes _____

Contact Person _____ Specialty/ Comments _____

_____

_____

_____

✂ ⸻⸻⸻⸻⸻⸻⸻⸻⸻⸻⸻⸻⸻⸻⸻⸻⸻⸻⸻⸻⸻⸻⸻⸻⸻⸻ ✂

Mail In Info Card:

Correction _____   Addition _____

Wrecking Yard Name _____

Address _____

City, State Zip _____

Phone # _____ Fax _____

800 _____ e-mail/web _____

Does the yard: Take Credit Cards _____ Ship Parts _____ Parts Locator Service _____

Let Cust. Remove Parts _____ Let Cust. Browse _____ Warehouse Parts _____

Staff Remove Parts _____ Have Shop _____

Size of Yard _____ acres, or _____ number of vehicles: Open: Sat. or Sun.

Is this a Late Model ('90+) _____ Late Vintage ('70-89) _____ Vintage (Pre '70) _____

Domestic ___ Foreign ___ Pickups ___ 4x4 ___ Truck (over 1 ton) ___ Const./Indust. _____

Farm _____ Military _____ Bus _____ Motorhome _____ Motorcycle _____ Boat _____

Years covered: Oldest _____ Newest _____ Have Inventory List _____

Makes in Yard: B3 ___ AMC ___ Jp ___ IH ___ Hd ___ St ___ Pk ___ Ns ___ Wy ___ Ks
___

Fr ___ Cr ___ VW ___ Euro/British ___ Japan/Asian ___ Other_____

Pre-War _____ Other Makes _____

Contact Person _____ Specialty/ Comments _____

_____

_____

_____